God
and the
World

CHRISTIAN TEXTS IN PERSPECTIVE

The Orbis series *Christian Texts in Perspective* provides readers with a selection of foundational texts upon which the Christian tradition has been built, as well as texts that move the tradition in new directions. The texts and their introductions, along with biographical sketches and a timeline, will aid students and other readers to understand central Christian doctrines in the context of both church and general western history.

The series — edited by William Madges and Gillian T. W. Ahlgren of Xavier University, Cincinnati — focuses on specific doctrines and traces their development from the origins of the church to the present. Each volume introduces major periods with a substantive interpretative essay, and the editors' selections aim to widen the canon by including texts by significant female authors. The timeline places in context events in Christian history, theological authors, and major political, social, intellectual, and cultural achievements in western civilization from the first to the twentieth century.

In addition to the present volume, the series includes the following:

- *The Human Person and the Church,* edited by Gillian T. W. Ahlgren (published simultaneously with this volume)

- *Spirituality,* edited by Gillian T. W. Ahlgren (forthcoming)

- *Christ and Salvation,* edited by William Madges (forthcoming)

- *Sacraments of the Christian Life,* edited by Gillian T. W. Ahlgren and William Madges (forthcoming)

God
and the
World

Christian Texts in Perspective

William Madges

ORBIS  BOOKS

Maryknoll, New York 10545

The Catholic Foreign Mission Society of America (Maryknoll) recruits and trains people for overseas missionary service. Through Orbis Books, Maryknoll aims to foster the international dialogue that is essential to mission. The books published, however, reflect the opinions of their authors and are not meant to represent the official position of the society.

Library of Congress Cataloging-in-Publication Data

God and the world / [edited by] William Madges.
     p.   cm. – (Christian texts in perspective)
   Includes bibliographical references.
   ISBN 1-57075-212-5 (pbk.)
   1. God I. Madges, William, 1952- . II. Series.
BT102.G593 1998
231–dc21   98-42940

For Mike

*Brother, lover of wisdom,
good friend*

Contents

Part Two
GOD'S ACTIVITIES
IN RELATION TO THE WORLD

Part Three
BIOGRAPHICAL AND TEXTUAL
INFORMATION

Part Four
TIMELINE
Chronological Relationships among Political and Social Events,
Intellectual and Cultural Developments, Christian History,
Major Christian Writers / 395

Preface

Christian Texts in Perspective is a series that offers readers an understanding of the development of central Christian doctrines within the context of western church history. This series not only provides the reader with important theological texts from all periods of church history. It also puts those texts within their historical contexts so that the new directions taken in the doctrine's development become intelligible and meaningful. Although there are other collections of primary sources on the market, the Christian Texts in Perspective series is designed to meet a need unmet by most of the other currently available collections.

First, each volume in the series focuses on a specific doctrine and traces its development from the origins of the church to the present. This volume, which is divided into two major parts, examines the doctrine of God. Each part of *God and the World* is further divided into three historical periods: early church (up to 600), medieval and Reformation church (600–1600), and modern church (1600 to present). Part One deals with the questions: "who" or "what" is God? It traces the development of the Christian idea of trinity in the early church. It then identifies the various paths for knowing and naming God in the medieval and Reformation periods. Part One concludes with an exploration of the different ways in which the nature of God and the divine attributes are being reinterpreted and reformulated in the modern period. Part Two deals with the question: what does God do in relation to the world and humanity? It examines the ways in which God's activities, such as creation, providence, and predestination, are handled in the three different periods of the western church's history.

Second, each volume in this series includes a wider range of theological authors than what can usually be found in standard "readers" in Christian thought or theology. That is, each volume includes not only the classic authors who have given definitive shape to the doctrine in question. Each volume also includes other authors who have challenged the received understanding of the doctrine or who have pointed its interpretation in new directions. Consequently, you will find in these volumes the writings of authors such as Hildegard of Bingen, James Cone, Dorothee Soelle, Leonardo Boff, and Elizabeth Johnson, as well as writings from Irenaeus of Lyons, Augustine, Aquinas, Luther, and Calvin. In the selection of authors, we have sought to give a fuller picture of the richness of theological reflection upon the church's doctrines by including significant female authors, often excluded from standard histories of doctrine. For example, the writings of authors such as Hadewijch of Brabant, Catherine of Siena, Julian of Norwich, and Teresa of Avila have been included. In addition, texts that might traditionally be regarded as more "spiritual" than "theological" have been included in the series when the texts offer a significant or illuminating perspective from which the doctrine in question can be understood.[1]

---

1. The authors of this series are in substantial agreement with Joan Nuth, who writes: "Present

Third, the series offers more than a collection of texts. It offers appropriate tools for helping the reader to understand the texts in context and to identify the continuities or divergences between them. The principal tool that assists this process of understanding is the interpretative essay that precedes each set of texts from the three different periods of the church's history (early, medieval and Reformation, and modern periods). In this volume you will find three interpretative essays in each of the book's two main parts. These essays introduce the texts, describe the main lines of doctrinal development in each period, and situate the texts within their historical context. In addition to the essays, each volume in the series contains a biography and bibliography for each of the authors whose writings are included. These biographical and textual introductions are often more extensive than what can be found in other available readers in Christian theology.

Fourth, each volume in the series contains a detailed timeline, in which church events and theological authors are set into relation with the major political, social, intellectual, and cultural achievements in western civilization from the first to the twentieth century. By consulting the timeline, the reader can not only learn the dates of important events in the church and western civilization, but also see connections between the cultural temperament or social development of a period and the theological creativity of authors who lived during that period. Use of the timeline can help the reader avoid thinking of theological reflection upon Christian doctrines as disconnected from the sweep of other historical events.

This series was developed according to certain guidelines. Because we wanted to provide a broad portrait of theological thinking about central Christian doctrines, we did not write the series as a history of official dogmatic statements. Although they refer substantively to the official (that is, ecclesiastically approved) development of doctrine, the books in the series do not restrict themselves to official statements, but include other theological analyses of the doctrines in question. Our intent thereby is to help the reader not only to understand the foundations of the classic understanding of the doctrine, but also to appreciate the theological creativity and to assess the theological adequacy of the new directions that understanding of the doctrine has taken over time.

Moreover, the series does not purport to provide a complete picture of how specific doctrines developed in both the eastern and western traditions of the church. Such an undertaking would exceed the competence of the authors and stretch the length of these volumes beyond acceptable levels. In general, we have selected authors who stand within the western Christian tradition or whose thoughts have contributed in a significant way to doctrinal development in the West. This choice does not mean to suggest that the eastern Christian tradition has no significant contributions to make to understanding central Christian doctrines. Rather, the exclusion of the East was a pragmatic decision, not an evaluative judgment. In general, philosophers have also been excluded from the series. An occasional exception is made if the author's writing is judged to be sufficiently

parameters for what designates legitimate theology need to be stretched to include the more experientially oriented mystical and devotional writings, many of which were produced by women. Careful investigation might reveal in such writings valuable doctrinal insights to add to our record of how the Christian faith has been experienced and understood in history, thereby enriching our own experience and understanding" (*Wisdom's Daughter: The Theology of Julian of Norwich* [New York: Crossroad, 1991], 1–2).

"theological" in character and sufficiently influential upon the thinking of theologians in the West. Of course, a case could be made to include authors, both theological and philosophical, who have been excluded from this series. Although our selection of texts will not please everyone, we believe that we have put together a judicious collection that includes both foundational texts and texts that move in new directions.

The texts and the interpretative essays are arranged in chronological order. If you wish to acquire a more comprehensive sense of the development of theological thinking upon a specific doctrine, you should begin at the beginning of the book and read the subsequent material in order. If you are primarily interested in understanding developments within a particular historical period, you should go directly to that portion of the book. Each historical period is indicated in the table of contents. Before reading the selections from each historical period, you are encouraged to read the biographical and textual introduction for the respective authors. The biographical introductions, listed in alphabetical order, are located in Part Three of the book. If you are already very familiar with the life and work of the author in question, you might choose to read the text without consulting the biographical introduction. The bibliography for each author, however, might still be useful. You will find these bibliographies at the end of each biographical introduction.

The translations included in this and other volumes in the Christian Texts in Perspective series are the best English versions we could find. In some cases, they were the only English translations available. Unfortunately, most translations of classic texts are not sensitive to the use of gender-inclusive language, which the editors would have preferred, even though the originals in Latin or Greek would not have what we would today call a grammatically "sexist" bias. As a consequence and for a variety of reasons, including copyright laws, the editors of the series have not changed the texts to reflect our own preference.

For the most part, only the actual texts are reprinted in this volume. Footnotes that appear in the original have generally not been reprinted. We have given exact bibliographic references to the texts proper, so the reader can consult them easily.

We have attempted to make the Christian Texts in Perspective series useful to a range of readers, from the adult nonspecialist to graduate theology and seminary students. Whatever your situation or need, we hope that you will find this book an aid in understanding the development of Christian thinking about the doctrine of God from the first century to the beginning of the third millennium.

Acknowledgments

I would like to express my thanks to a number of people who have helped me to bring this book to completion. First, I would like to acknowledge Gillian Ahlgren, my colleague in the Theology Department at Xavier University. Together we developed the concept of a series entitled Christian Texts in Perspective. As a result of many hours of discussion and collaboration, we were able to refine the nature and scope of the project. In addition, we collaborated with each other in making decisions about authors to include and in evaluating each other's interpretative approach. We supported each other in the long process of creating the first volumes in this Orbis series. Second, I would like to express my gratitude to Bradford Hinze of Marquette University and Zachary Hayes of Catholic Theological Union, who read portions of the manuscript and offered helpful comments. Third, I want to acknowledge Xavier colleagues who provided good critique and constructive suggestions for improving the timeline and other portions of the manuscript. In particular, I express my gratitude to Walker Gollar, Joseph Wessling, and John LaRocca. In addition, I would like to thank Darleen Frickman for secretarial services, especially for her typing the timeline and correcting formatting problems; Brennan Hill, chairperson of my department, and Max Keck, dean of my college, for their support of the project; and William Burrows, managing editor at Orbis Books, for his enthusiastic endorsement of the project and his patience at the pace of its completion. Finally, I wish to express publicly my gratitude to my wife, Marsha Erickson, and to my daughters, Katie and Sarah, for their understanding support. Oftentimes they found me still working on the manuscript when they had hoped I would finally be free to join in "family fun." Their long-standing patience and their love have been a great blessing throughout this project.

Acknowledgments

God
and the
World

Part One

GOD

Nature and Attributes

– 1 –

The Early Period

INTRODUCTION

Theological reflection in the first four centuries was driven by three major forces: the need to defend the faith and the community from outside critique or attack, the need to articulate an acceptable understanding of "being Christian" against distortions from within the Christian community, and the desire to think through more fully the implications of Christian faith. Maurice Wiles has referred to these three motives epigrammatically as the church's "self-understanding in relation to those outside, in relation to those half outside and half inside her borders, and finally in relation to herself."[1] To the outside world, Christians had to defend their beliefs as intelligible and their manner of living as morally and politically acceptable. Until the fourth century, Christianity was not legally recognized within the Roman Empire. Rather, it was regarded by many as intellectually indefensible, morally objectionable, and politically subversive. The Christian apologists of the second and third centuries, such as Justin Martyr, Athenagoras, and Tertullian, wrote defenses of Christianity against their pagan and Jewish critics.

Christian thinkers in the early centuries, however, also needed to address the plurality of viewpoints within the Christian community. As they struggled to articulate their beliefs in a detailed and systematic way, Christians embarked upon many different paths. They drew upon different resources (e.g., cultural values, philosophical schools, personal experiences) to formulate different understandings of what it meant to be Christian. Some interpretations were regarded by the majority of the community, or the community's leaders, as destructive of the "authentic" beliefs and practices of the church. Other interpretations were regarded as dangerous or misleading. Sometimes these "heterodox" (i.e., "different") opinions were judged to be "heretical" (i.e., opinions that were so different and so tenaciously held that they separated those who held them from the church). Christian leaders had to contend with many different "heresies" in the early centuries, including docetism, Gnosticism, and Montanism. Dealing with heterodox or heretical points of view, however, contributed constructively to the development of Christian doctrine. The interaction with different viewpoints compelled Christians to put their beliefs into precise words. Of course, they were attempting sometimes to express in words what transcends the capaci-

---

1. Maurice Wiles, *The Making of Christian Doctrine: A Study in the Principles of Early Doctrinal Development* (New York: Cambridge University Press, 1967), 19.

ties of human language and thought. As Hilary of Poitiers (ca. 315–67) observed (*On the Trinity*, 2.2), the error of others compels us to err in daring to embody in human terms truths which ought to be hidden in the silent veneration of the heart.

Christians also wanted to think through as fully and as deeply as they could the meaning and implications of Christian discipleship. They did not need attacks from the outside or dissension from within the community to move them to reflection. Faith naturally seeks understanding. To understand the faith in the early church meant to situate it in relation to the scriptures, but also in relation to Judaism, Roman religion, and Greek and Roman philosophy. In the early church, all three factors — defense against outside attack, response to internal dissension, and natural desire for understanding — played important roles in the development of the doctrine of God.

The early centuries in the life of the Christian church were foundational for the development of the doctrine of God. During the first four centuries, the Christian community worked out both the basic conceptuality and the approved language for describing its distinctive understanding of God. In continuity with their Jewish roots, Christians affirmed the oneness of God. In fidelity to their experience of the saving activity of God in Jesus and to their experience of the continuing presence of the divine spirit in their midst, they affirmed "multiplicity" in the Godhead. By the end of the fourth century, they had come to declare that God is one in being, essence, or substance, yet three in persons. According to this conception of the deity, the divine persons, though really distinct from one another, are not separate beings. The essence of God is neither divided nor parceled out in portions to the three persons. God is indivisibly one, early Christians declared, yet unalterably and eternally "three."

The path that led to this conclusion was neither straight nor smooth. The Christian community came to this conclusion of "triunity" only after several centuries of reflection concerning the revelation of God in scripture and in their experience, heated denunciations of fellow Christians as heretics, and the convocation of several local synods and two ecumenical ("worldwide") councils (Nicea I and Constantinople I). By 381 (Council of Constantinople I), Christians had not penetrated definitively the mystery of the divine nature, but they had come to agree upon conceptuality and language that expressed basic tenets of their faith. This trinitarian conception of God established the normative parameters of acceptable Christian talk about God from the fourth century to the present day.

Although the trinitarian conception of the one God clearly distinguishes Christianity from the monotheism of the other great Abrahamic religions (Judaism and Islam), the Christian conception initially maintained continuity, in a significant way, with the Jewish understanding of God. The Jewish understanding of God, expressed in the Hebrew scriptures, holds together divine transcendence and divine immanence in dialectical tension. On the one hand, God transcends the created order. God is not only distinct from and superior to the elements of nature. The God of the Hebrews is also superior to the gods of other ancient peoples. On the other hand, God is passionately concerned about and powerfully involved in the history of the Hebrew people. As Exodus 3:7–8 declares:

Then the LORD said, "I have observed the misery of my people who are in Egypt; I have heard their cry on account of their taskmasters. Indeed, I know their sufferings, and I have come down to deliver them from the Egyptians, and to bring them up out of that land to a good and broad land, a land flowing with milk and honey...."

As infinite and holy, God transcends the finite world. As loving, faithful, and righteous, God is present in the establishment, direction, and preservation of the people with whom God has made a covenant.

The followers of Jesus acknowledged a similar tension between transcendence and immanence in their understanding of God. The one God, whom Jesus addressed as Abba ("Dad"; see Mark 14:36) is in "heaven" (see Matt. 6:9, 14; Luke 11:13). This God is different from the created order in both essence and activity. God cannot be seen (see John 1:18; 5:37; 6:46). And God's way of dealing with others is utterly different from the behavior of other ancient gods and also from the behavior of human beings (see Matt. 5:44–48). And yet this same God, Jesus affirms, is concerned about the well-being of the least of creatures (see Matt. 6:26; Luke 12:24) and has counted every hair of our heads (Luke 12:6–7).

Especially after the powerful events of Jesus' death and resurrection, his followers came to acknowledge him as the definitive presence of God in the world. Through him God's reign has entered into the world (see Mark 1:14–15; Matt. 12:28; Luke 11:20). And through him one comes to God (Luke 10:22; Matt. 11:25–27). The connection between Jesus and God is so intimate that Jesus can say in John's gospel: "The Father and I are one" (John 10:30). How then were his followers to understand Jesus' oneness with the Father? If Jesus the Christ were God's Son, then were they two Gods? How are Son and Spirit related to the one God? Questions such as these stimulated Christian reflection during the centuries immediately following the death and resurrection of Jesus.

Prior to the decisions of the ecumenical councils of the fourth century, Christians gave different answers to these questions. There was considerable fluidity in understanding the relationship of the Son and the Spirit to God the Father. Christians in the second and third centuries spoke of the Son and the Spirit, but they usually did not articulate with precision their relationship to God the Father. Irenaeus of Lyons, for example, speaks of the Son and the Spirit as the "hands" with which God made all things (*Against Heresies,* Book 4, ch. 20:1; see selection below). This metaphor suggests that the Son and the Spirit are subordinate to the Father, while still affirming that they are a "part" of God (*Against Heresies,* Book 4, ch. 20:3; see selection below).

Up through the early part of the fourth century, the principal focus of Christian reflection about God was the Son. The Son held such a prominent position because divine revelation and human salvation were believed to have taken place decisively through the Son's incarnation in Jesus and through Jesus' life and death. Both points, divine revelation and human salvation, were important. Both are expressed succinctly in the Letter to the Colossians:

He [i.e., God] has rescued us from the power of darkness and transferred us into the kingdom of his beloved Son, in whom we have redemption, the forgiveness of sins. He [i.e., the Son] is the image of the invisible God, the firstborn of all creation; for in him all things in heaven and on earth were created, things visible and invisible, whether thrones or dominions or rulers or powers — all things have been created through him and for him.

(Col. 1:13–16)

In these early centuries, Christians found the metaphor of speech particularly fruitful for describing this close relationship between the Father and his image, the incarnate Son. The Christ, they said, was the word God chose to speak to the world. In this word God's very self is revealed, and this life-giving word is given for the salvation of the world. Just as in human speech we first think the words we wish to say before we utter them, so too God possessed internally the word that God eventually spoke externally. The immanent word, the Son, became the expressed word in Jesus the Christ.

In Greek, which was the language of the New Testament and the language of the eastern church, *Logos* was the term for "word." The very same word, however, also expresses the idea of "reason." Christians in the early centuries of the church's life found both denotations useful in describing the Son's nature and his relation to the Father. On the one hand, this Logos theology had clear roots both in the Wisdom theology of the Hebrew scriptures and in the Gospel of John. In Proverbs 8:22–31, Wisdom is presented as the divine instrument of creation. In John's gospel the Wisdom of God is identified as God's Word. In both cases, the Wisdom, or Word, was present in the beginning and active in the creation of the world:

In the beginning was the Word, and the Word was with God, and the Word was God. He was in the beginning with God. All things came into being through him, and without him not one thing came into being. What has come into being in him was life, and the life was the light of all people.

(John 1:1–4)

Early Christian thinkers laid the foundation for the development of a "Word theology" that profoundly influenced the subsequent Christian tradition.

On the other hand, Logos theology had resonance with some currents of Greek philosophy. The Stoics, for example, held that the world is directed by a cosmic intelligence and that human beings have reason only insofar as they share in this cosmic intelligence. The word they used to refer to this universal intelligence was *Logos*. In philosophical systems such as this, early Christians found rich soil for planting their ideas about the Son as God's Logos.[2] The Greek idea of the Logos was useful in two ways. First, it provided Christians with a means for correlating Christian revelation with the elements of truth found in classical philosophers. Justin the Martyr, the second-century apologist, declared, for example, that "Christians" are those who have been definitively enlightened by

---

2. Jaroslav Pelikan cautions, however, that the doctrine of the Logos was not primarily determined by Greek cosmological speculation, even though Greek speculation did prove useful to Christian apologists. One indication of the presence of a Logos doctrine not primarily determined by Greek cosmological speculation was the translation of the term as *sermo* ("word") in some of the earliest Latin versions of the New Testament. Similarly, Tertullian and Cyprian of Carthage used *sermo* as the term for Logos in their writings. See Jaroslav Pelikan, *The Christian Tradition: A History of the Development of Doctrine*, vol. 1: *The Emergence of the Catholic Tradition (100–600)* (Chicago: University of Chicago Press, 1971), 186–87.

the Logos. Insofar as they were enlightened with the truth, even those who lived before the time of Jesus, such as Socrates and the Hebrew prophets, could be regarded as "Christians." They had been enlightened by divine "Reason himself," who at a later time "took form and became man and was called Jesus Christ."[3] Second, the Logos idea provided a means of correlating the transcendence and immanence of God. Insofar as God is transcendent, God requires an agent through whom both creation and redemption could be accomplished. As the Logos of God, the Son was precisely such an agent.

Affirming the Son as the Logos of God, however, raised questions and difficulties. If the Logos is God, what happens to God's oneness? If the Son is God and therefore, according to the dominant conceptions of deity, eternal and unchangeable, how could he enter human history, which is contingent and changing? Perhaps the Logos is like God, but not God? In the second and third centuries, a number of attempts were made to formulate an understanding of the Son's relationship to the Father that would, on the one hand, preserve the unity of God and, on the other, establish the distinction of the Son from the Father without making the Incarnate Son, Jesus the Christ, identical in nature to all other human beings.

One theory that was proposed came to be known as dynamic monarchianism. The term "monarchianism" underlines the intent of its proponents to maintain the unity of God. The Greek words that make up the term "monarchy" literally mean "rule by one." The point these Christians wished to emphasize is that there is one and only one God who rules the world. The term "dynamic" distinguishes this form of monarchianism from modalist monarchianism, which was also committed to the absolute unity of God, but attempted to preserve it by obliterating any real distinctions between Father, Son, and Spirit. Whereas modalist monarchianism, or modalism, denies real distinctions between Father, Son, and Spirit, dynamic monarchianism emphasizes the distinctions.

"Dynamic" comes from the Greek word for "power" (*dynamis*). According to the perspective of dynamic monarchianism, the human being Jesus received the divine power of Christ at some point in life, such as his baptism or his resurrection. From this perspective, there is only one God, and this one God imparted divine power to the human being Jesus so that he could accomplish the salvific mission which God had assigned him. Theodotus, the earliest known person to have held this point of view,[4] propounded this theory toward the end of the second century. The theory could appeal for support to the biblical account of Jesus' baptism. The evangelist in Luke's gospel declares:

> Now when all the people were baptized, and when Jesus also had been baptized and was praying, the heaven was opened, and the Holy Spirit descended upon him in bodily form like a dove. And a voice came from

---

3. *The First Apology of Justin, the Martyr,* par. 5, in *Early Christian Fathers,* ed. Cyril C. Richardson (New York: Macmillan, 1970), 245. See also par. 46, p. 272: "We have been taught that Christ is the First-begotten of God, and have previously testified that he is the Reason of which every race of man partakes. Those who lived in accordance with Reason are Christians, even though they were called godless, such as, among the Greeks, Socrates and Heraclitus and others like them; among the barbarians, Abraham . . . and Elijah, and many others . . . those who lived by Reason, and those who so live now, are Christians, fearless and unperturbed."

4. See Justo L. González, *A History of Christian Thought,* vol. 1: *From the Beginnings to the Council of Chalcedon* (Nashville: Abingdon Press, 1970), 147.

heaven, "You are my Son, the Beloved; with you I am well pleased." (Luke 3:21–22; cf. Matt. 3:13–17; Mark 1:9–11; John 1:29–34)[5]

Based on this passage, one might draw the conclusion that Jesus *became* the Son of God at this moment.[6] Although condemned by the Christian community in Rome since 195 C.E., Theodotus's position found a more articulate proponent in Paul of Samosata, who became bishop of Antioch around 260 C.E.

Although it is not clear whether he held that the Son already existed from the moment of Jesus' conception or only from the moment of Jesus' baptism, it is relatively clear that Paul of Samosata did not understand the sonship of Christ to be ontological or essential.[7] From Paul's perspective, God did not become flesh in Jesus the Christ. Rather, God's power and wisdom came to *dwell* in him. Since God's presence in Jesus was similar to God's presence in the Hebrew prophets, albeit to a greater degree, Paul could uphold the uniqueness of Jesus vis-à-vis other human beings, while protecting the ontological oneness of God. In the context of explaining his view, Paul declared that the Word present in Christ was "of the same substance" (*homoousios*) as the Father. By this declaration, he apparently meant to affirm that the Word had no subsistence of its own, distinct from that of God the Father. The Word that dwelled in Christ derived from the substance of God, but it was not united with Christ's humanity in an essential or ontological way. The implication of Paul's teaching was that Christ was ontologically or essentially a human being. This explains why he forbade in his church the singing of psalms or hymns to Christ. His teaching scandalized many, and it was condemned at several regional synods held in Antioch. As historians of doctrine have observed, the second council of Antioch, in the late third century, is important for the history of the doctrine of God. It condemned the view that the Word is consubstantial (*homoousios*) with the Father because it wanted to reject Paul of Samosata's understanding of the relationship between God and Jesus the Christ. When the Council of Nicea in 325 used the same term to oppose Arianism, some Christians feared that Nicea was returning to the condemned doctrine of Paul, even though Paul had meant *homoousios* in a different sense.

Although dynamic monarchianism (also sometimes referred to as adoptionism) maintained God's unity, it did not make Christ God in the full sense of the term. Yet Christians had been praying directly to Christ, and not solely *to* the Father *through* the Son, since at least the beginning of the second century. Is it not idolatrous to pray to someone who is not God? Moreover, how could anyone but God bring about the redemption of humanity? Certainly a human being, even one

---

5. "A widespread tradition of the text [i.e., Luke 3:22] of the New Testament, supported by evidence from manuscripts, versions, and early citations from orthodox fathers, rendered the word from the cloud at the baptism of Jesus as the decree of Psalm 2:7: 'You are my Son, today I have begotten you'; the Ebionites likewise read the text that way, in support of their teaching that Jesus was a man endowed with special powers of the Spirit" (Pelikan, *The Christian Tradition*, 1:176).

6. This "divine power theory" could also make use of the many references in the gospels to Jesus' power of healing. That a human being possessed such power made some people suspect that Jesus' power came from a demonic source. In the gospels, Jesus replies to such critics: "If I cast out demons by Beelzebul, by whom do your own exorcists cast them out? Therefore they will be your judges. But if it is by the Spirit of God that I cast out demons, then the kingdom of God has come to you" (Matt. 12:22–28; cf. Mark 3:22–27; Luke 11:14–20).

7. Whereas Pelikan suggests that Jesus' baptism was the decisive event of divine sonship for Paul, González argues that Jesus' conception was the decisive moment. See Pelikan, *The Christian Tradition*, 1:176; cf. González, *A History of Christian Thought*, 1:254–58.

who possessed some of God's power, could not do that. Dynamic monarchianism did not adequately explain the fact of redemption or protect Christian practice from the charge of idolatry. Dynamic monarchianism failed to give an adequate explanation of popular piety and the church's worship of Christ.[8]

A different solution to the problem of explicating the relationship of Father to Son was proposed by modalist monarchianism. This theory is so named because it held that there is no real distinction of "persons" or "realities" in God, but that the one God is active in the world in three distinct operations or modalities. God was active in the history of the Israelites as Father. God was then active as Son in the new dispensation of God's salvific will. And God continues to be active in the world in the form of the divine Spirit. These are not different persons in the Godhead, but different modes according to which God operates. Ideas such as these were promoted by Praxeas in the late second century and by Sabellius in the third century. Modalist monarchianism is sometimes called Sabellianism because of its association with this third-century Roman Christian.

Modalism did not encounter the same problems as dynamic monarchianism in justifying worship of the Son or in explaining how the Son incarnate in Jesus could effect human redemption. In fact, modalist monarchianism may be defined as "an effort to provide a theology for the language of devotion."[9] By simply identifying the Father and the Son, modalism could account for the appropriateness of regarding Christ as God. Did not the Letter to the Romans after all declare Christ to be "God who is over all" (Rom. 9:5)?

Modalist monarchianism, however, did encounter a different set of questions. If, according to this theory, the Son is really and substantially God, how could the incarnate Son pray at Gethsemane, "My Father, if it is possible, let this cup pass from me; yet not what I want but what you want"? (Matt. 26:39; see also Mark 14:36; Luke 22:42). How could there be, even for a moment, a difference in will between Father and Son if both are the same reality? How were Christians to explain the many passages in scripture where Jesus declares the distinction between Father and Son, if not also the inferiority of Son to Father? What about the scriptural references to apparent distinctions between Father, Son, and Spirit, such as we find in John 14:25–28?

> I have said these things to you while I am still with you. But the Advocate, the Holy Spirit, whom the Father will send in my name, will teach you everything, and remind you of all that I have said to you.... Do not let your hearts be troubled, and do not let them be afraid.... If you loved me, you would rejoice that I am going to the Father, because the Father is greater than I.

Moreover, if the modalists were right, then God the Father also died on the cross of Christ. For this reason, the modalist position was sometimes referred to as "patripassianism" (the theory that "the Father suffers"). It was difficult enough to ascribe suffering and death to God's Son. It was sheer blasphemy to ascribe them to the Godhead in an undifferentiated way.

---

8. See Maurice Wiles, *The Making of Christian Doctrine*, 65–70.
9. Pelikan, *The Christian Tradition*, 1:178.

Whereas modalism preserved the unity of God by rejecting distinctions in the Godhead, dynamic monarchianism preserved the unity of God by undermining the full divinity of the Son. Was it possible to formulate the divinity of the Son and maintain distinctions in the Godhead without making the Christian understanding of God "ditheistic" or "tritheistic," that is, belief in two or three Gods?

Tertullian formulated his understanding of God within this context of debate and counterproposal. The first excerpt from Tertullian included in this volume is directed against Praxeas, one of the proponents of modalism. Here Tertullian attempts to establish both the unity of God and distinctions within the Godhead; or, in his own words from chapter 2, he wants to show how God is "susceptible of number without division." Tertullian is very important in the development of the doctrine of God in the West because he introduces the terminology that later will be endorsed as appropriate for describing an orthodox Christian understanding of God. Tertullian speaks of "substance" (*substantia*), "person" (*persona*), and "trinity" (*trinitas*). He says that God is one in substance or essence, but that this divine unity is distributed into a trinity of persons. To explain how Father, Son, and Spirit are distinct from one another, yet not separable, Tertullian appeals to illustrations from nature. Just as the root and the tree, the fountain and the river, or the sun and its ray are distinct yet indivisible, Tertullian says (see *Against Praxeas*, ch. 8 below), so too are Father and Son two, yet indivisible. And the Spirit is the fruit of the tree, the stream of the river, and the apex of the ray.

Like all analogies for God drawn from human experience, Tertullian's analogies or illustrations are not fully adequate. Each of his nature metaphors allows a certain primacy to the first of the three elements. The root gives rise to the tree and its fruit; the tree and its fruit depend on the root for their existence in a way that the root is not dependent on them. This subordination of elements within the trinity is quite commonplace in the thinking of third-century Christians. It should come as no surprise that we find it in Tertullian. Thus, in setting out (*Against Praxeas*, ch. 3) his explanation of how the governing of the world by one God does not preclude the monarchy from being administered by God's agents (the Son and the Spirit), Tertullian makes the Son and the Spirit subordinate to the Father. Although they are "so closely joined with the Father in His substance," they have been assigned "the second and third places" in the administration of the one divine empire. The theme of subordination is more pronounced in chapter 9, where Tertullian confesses that "the Father is the entire substance, but the Son is a derivation and portion of the whole." And again: "Thus the Father is distinct from the Son, being greater than the Son, inasmuch as He who begets is one, and He who is begotten is another...." In opposition to Praxeas, Tertullian insists that the Father, Son, and Spirit are distinct from one another. But, he declares, this distinction does not mean either separation or that the three persons are of a different substance. Distinction of person (without separation) and unity of substance, two characteristics that Tertullian upholds, will be hallmarks of the orthodox description of God after the fourth century. The subordination of the second and third persons to the first person of the trinity, which Tertullian also expresses, will be "corrected" in the conciliar pronouncements of the fourth century.

The first ecumenical (or worldwide) council was convoked at Nicea in the early fourth century to deal with the statements of another North African, Arius. Arius was a presbyter in Alexandria, where the church was overseen by Bishop Alexander. Like others before him, Arius was determined not to allow the oneness of God to be compromised. As his "Letter to Alexander" makes clear, Arius rejected the idea that the Son was of the very same substance as the Father because he feared that such a formulation made the Son an "emanation" of the Father. If the Son is of the same substance as the Father, reasoned Arius, then the one divine substance is divided into two parts, the substance that is in the Father and the substance that is in the Son. Arius's solution was to declare that the Son is a creature, created by the Father out of nothing "before eternal times, through whom he made the ages and everything." By insisting that the Son was created out of nothing, Arius believed he preserved the oneness and uncompounded nature of the divine substance. By declaring that the Son was the instrument through whom God created the entire world, Arius believed he was preserving the dignity of the Son as radically different from other creatures. In Arius's scheme of things, the Son was the preeminent of God's creatures and, as God's instrument of creation, could be regarded as "divine" in a loose sense. Unlike the Paulianists, who followed Paul of Samosata, the Arians did not cease to worship the Son or to address prayers and hymns to Christ. Their critics promptly noted this inconsistency between Arian dogmatic principles and liturgical practice.

Arius's interpretation of the Son-Father relationship was unacceptable to his bishop. Alexander moved to have Arius's teaching declared heretical and to have him removed from his position of leadership in the Alexandrian church. At a regional council at Antioch early in 325, Arius's teaching was condemned, even though Arius was not mentioned by name. Arius, for his part, appealed to support from other leaders of the church, including other bishops, who found his position not seriously objectionable or, in some cases, actually preferable to Alexander's. The first letter from Arius included in the selection below is addressed to one of his supporters from the East, Eusebius of Nicomedia. Whereas the western portion of the church generally emphasized the oneness of God, the eastern portion tended to emphasize distinctions between the divine persons. And, as the "Letter to Eusebius" makes clear, Arius regarded himself and some of his supporters as faithful students of Lucian of Antioch, who had vigorously insisted upon the distinctions between Father and Son.

We have no conclusive, extensive knowledge of Lucian's life. It seems that Lucian had founded in Antioch a school that opposed the allegorical interpretation of scripture that had become commonplace in Alexandria. Instead, he championed a historical and grammatical method of exegesis. In his understanding of God, he seems to have followed the direction laid out by Origen, who had spoken of the Son as both the "image" of the Father and a "creature." Although Origen had also spoken of the eternal generation of the Son from the Father and had declared that Sonship was by nature and not merely by adoption, Lucian emphasized the distinction that Origen had identified between Son and Father.[10]

---

10. In opposition to modalism, Origen insisted that the Son was distinct from the Father. In opposition to dynamic monarchianism, Origen insisted that the Son existed prior to the birth of Jesus. Drawing upon Proverbs 8:22–31 as a lens through which to read those passages in scripture that seemed to define

Lucian's disciples, in turn, developed this distinction to its logical consequence, so that it was no longer clear that the Son was authentically divine in the same way that the Father was divine. At any rate, when the Arian controversy erupted some years after Lucian's death, all of the prominent leaders of Arianism were former pupils of Lucian. The fact that Lucian had died as a martyr for the faith, however, made his doctrine difficult to attack.

Because the theological issue at stake was crucial and because bishops were lined up on different sides of the issue, the unity of the church was sorely tested by the Arian controversy. So much so that when the emperor Constantine became emperor of the eastern portion of the empire in 324, in addition to being emperor of the western portion, he felt compelled to convene a council to resolve the dispute. The Council of Nicea convened in late spring of 325. Most of the two hundred to three hundred bishops in attendance were from the East; fewer than ten had come from the West. Emperor Constantine himself apparently presided over the assembly. At the beginning of the council, the bishops fell roughly into three groups. One group, headed by Eusebius of Nicomedia, were supporters of Arius or "Collucianists" (followers of Lucian of Antioch). A second group, led by Alexander of Alexandria, were committed to the denunciation of Arius's position as heretical. The third group, by far the largest of the three, consisted of bishops who were either uncommitted to either of the two other parties or who were reluctant to condemn absolutely even extreme forms of subordinationism out of fear of modalism.[11]

What we know of the council's actions derives from unofficial and often later reports. Apparently Eusebius of Nicomedia, expecting considerable support, committed a tactical error by reading an exposition of the Arian position in its most extreme form. Many of the bishops who were previously uncommitted reacted in horror. The majority who now opposed the Arian position sought to formulate a statement that clearly opposed the Arian point of view on the basis of the testimony of scripture. Some hoped that it would be sufficient to declare with scripture that the Son was "from God." But when Arius's supporters pointed out that "from God" could be interpreted to mean simply that something had been "created by God," Arius's opponents had to devise a different plan of attack. Apparently it was this stalemate between competing interpretations of scripture that caused the emperor himself to intervene. Either he or his ecclesiastical adviser at the council, Bishop Hosius (or Ossius) of Cordova (Spain), suggested that the term *homoousios* (Greek for "of the same substance or essence") be used to designate the nature of the Son in relation to the Father. Although not a scriptural term, it had the clear advantage of simultaneously ruling out Arius's dual claims, namely, that the Son was created out of nothing and that the Son was a creature. *Homoousios* suggested, by contrast, that the Son was generated not out of nothing, but out of the divine substance and that the Son, possessing the divine nature, was not a creature, but was truly God. With this understanding in mind, a group

---

the relationship between Son and Father as one of derivation, Origen concluded (*On First Principles*, Book 4, ch. 4, sect. 1) that the Son is "'the firstborn of all creation,' a thing *created,...* and ... as he is a likeness of the Father *there is no time when he did not exist*" (emphasis added; Origen, *On First Principles*, trans. G. W. Butterworth [Gloucester, Mass.: Peter Smith, 1973], 314–15).

11. See González, *A History of Christian Thought*, 1:272–74.

of bishops at the council were commissioned to draft a creed, incorporating this word and its meaning into the exposition of faith.

The creed we refer to today as the Nicene Creed is not identical with the creed that was produced at the council in 325. That creed, as you can see from the text below, focused primarily on the nature of the Son, giving virtually no attention to the Spirit. In addition, it attached to the basic creedal statement a series of anathemas, which were intended to declare as heretical the Arian viewpoint. The creed we refer to today as the Nicene Creed is the result of the work at Nicea in 325 and the work of the second ecumenical council at Constantinople in 381. If we wished to be more precise, we would have to refer to the creed we say today as the Niceno-Constantinopolitan Creed.

The core of the creed adopted at Nicea was not first created at the council. Scholars today generally believe that the creed was the revision of an already existing baptismal creed, probably originating in Syria or in Palestine. The creeds had their first use in the context of baptism, identifying for the catechumens the faith and commitment they were about to confess as they entered into the church community through the ritual of baptism. A comparison of the Apostles', the Nicene, and the Constantinopolitan creeds (see below) reveals both those articles that were regarded as basic as well as those which needed special emphasis in order to combat what were perceived to be erroneous alternative views. Thus the description of the nature of God's Son receives considerable elaboration in the creed of Nicea beyond what is contained in the Apostles' Creed.

In the time between the two councils, Nicea and Constantinople, tremendous efforts were expended to maintain or regain support for the formulas of Nicea, to develop language that would further clarify the relationship of the three divine persons, and to incorporate the Spirit into the formal doctrine of the church as a divine person, equal in substance and inseparable from the other persons of the trinity. Such efforts were necessary because many Christians, including bishops, were dissatisfied with the theological formulas of Nicea. Some were in fact able to persuade the emperor to support them instead of the defenders of Nicea. Emperor Constantine himself had established the dubious precedent of using imperial force to achieve theological ends when he banished Arius from the empire.

Eusebius of Nicomedia was particularly successful in exerting influence over Constantine. He was able to persuade the emperor to allow Arius to return from exile in 330 C.E. And he raised suspicions in the emperor's mind about Nicene defenders, such as Eustathius of Antioch and Athanasius of Alexandria. When Emperor Constantine died in 337, he was succeeded by his three sons, who took responsibility for the different portions of the empire. Whereas the sons responsible for the western portions tended to support Nicea, Constantius, the son who ruled over the eastern portion, lent his support to the defenders of Arianism. Like his father, Constantius wanted theological harmony in the empire so that his political rule would remain stable. Moreover, Constantius was anxious to uphold the importance of the bishop of his capital (Constantinople) over that of other bishoprics, such as Antioch, Alexandria, and Rome. The bishop of Constantinople was now Eusebius of Nicomedia, who had been Arius's most ardent defender at the Council of Nicea. The strength of Arian opposition to Nicea increased when Constantius became sole ruler of the western and eastern portions of the empire in 353.

Personal rivalry and political motivation were not the only forces behind opposition to Nicea. The opponents of Nicea believed they had good theological reasons for opposing its declarations about the Son of God. Theological opposition focused on the term *homoousios*.[12] From the perspective of its opponents, not only was the term philosophical rather than scriptural, it also seemed to blur the distinctions between Father, Son, and Spirit. The word could be understood in a Sabellian sense, implying that Father, Son, and Spirit were actually the same. Although many of the eastern bishops who had concerns about the Nicene formula did not support Arius's claim that the Son was a creature, made out of nothing, who at one time did not exist, they did not feel that the supporters of Nicea stated the distinctions between Father, Son, and Spirit clearly enough. For their part, the Nicene party felt that their opponents did not state the deity of Christ clearly enough.

In addition to differences of theological emphasis, there were linguistic problems. Latin was the language of Christians in the western portion of the Roman Empire. From the time of Tertullian on, it had become customary in the West to use the Latin term *substantia* ("substance") to refer to the common divinity of Father, Son, and Spirit. *Persona* ("person"), on the other hand, was used to designate the distinctions within the trinity. Whereas "substance" denoted the unity of God, "person" denoted the differentiation within the Godhead. When Greek-speaking eastern Christians wished to understand what these terms meant in their language, they usually translated *persona* as *prosopon*. The Greek word *prosopon* can refer to the idea of a "person," but it can also be understood to mean a face or mask. In ancient Greek drama, the same actor would switch masks (*prosopa* in the plural) as he took on the role of different characters in the play. The phrase "three persons," when understood in the sense of "three masks or faces," created problems for some eastern Christians who thought they saw in the western formula an unacceptable inclination toward modalist monarchianism.

The typical eastern formula, conversely, created some difficulties for Latin-speaking Christians in the West. Up to the time of the Council of Nicea, Greek-speaking Christians used two different terms, sometimes interchangeably, to refer to the divine nature or essence. These two terms were *ousia* and *hypostasis*. Gradually *hypostasis* came to be the preferred term for referring to the individual subsistence of the "persons" of the Godhead. Latin-speaking Christians did not have an exact equivalent in their language for *hypostasis*. Consequently, they simply transliterated the word from Greek into Latin, with the result that *hypo-stasis* was rendered *sub-stantia*. The eastern formula that there are "three hypostases" in the trinity, when understood in the sense of "three substances," created problems for some western Christians who thought they saw in the eastern formula an unacceptable tritheism.

With the support of Emperor Constantius, opponents of the formula of Nicea

---

12. "The variety of its meanings [i.e., of *homoousios*] and its previous association with Gnosticism — and, as Arius had pointed out, with Manicheism — made it suspect to the orthodox; its identification with the condemned ideas of Paul of Samosata was to be a source of embarrassment to its defenders long after Nicea" (Pelikan, *The Christian Tradition,* 1:202).

held several regional synods in the 350s that produced alternative creeds. One such synod, the Synod of Sirmium, declared that there ought to be no mention of unscriptural terms such as *ousia* and *homoousios*. Sirmium's own description of the relation of Father to Son, appealing to scripture for support, was clearly subordinationist. It stated:

> And to none can it be a question that the Father is greater: for no one can doubt that the Father is greater in honor and dignity and Godhead, and in the very name of Father, the Son Himself testifying, "The Father that sent Me is greater than I" (John 10:29). And no one is ignorant, that it is Catholic doctrine, that there are two Persons of Father and Son, and that the Father is greater, and the Son subordinated to the Father together with all things which the Father has subordinated to Him, and that the Father has no beginning, and is invisible, and immortal, and impassible; but that the Son has been generated from the Father, God from God, Light from Light, and that his origin . . . no one knows, but the Father only.[13]

Some of the opponents of Nicea suggested that the church should confess that the Son is "like" the Father; others preferred to say that the Son is "unlike" the Father. Others still, such as Basil of Ancyra, thought it best to declare the Son to be "of a similar substance" (*homoiousios*) rather than to say that he is "of the same substance" (*homoousios*) as the Father.[14]

Athanasius, Bishop Alexander's successor in Alexandria, deserves much of the credit for finding a way to win back a sufficient number of the critics of Nicea so as to be able to decisively uphold the Nicene formula as the orthodox proclamation of the church. Although he was known as the black dwarf because of his diminutive size, he proved to be anything but a dwarf when it came to integrity in defending what he regarded as the truth. He endured five separate exiles, totaling seventeen years, for his continued defense of the Council of Nicea after imperial politics no longer supported it. Most of his works were dedicated to the struggle against Arianism. Best known of these works, and also his longest treatise, is the *Orations against the Arians,* from which we have an excerpt below.

For Athanasius, the dispute about the nature of the Son was not simply a matter of philosophical ideology or ecclesiastical politics. The question whether Jesus Christ, incarnate Son of the Father, was truly divine was at the heart of the Christian faith. If Christ were not fully God, argued Athanasius, then Christ did not have the power to save. Just as only God could create the world, so too only God could effect the re-creation of the divine image in humanity, which Adam and Eve's sin deformed.

---

13. Athanasius, *De synodis,* sect. 28 in *A Select Library of Nicene and Post-Nicene Fathers,* ed. Philip Schaff and Henry Wace, 2d series, vol. 4: *St. Athanasius* (Grand Rapids: Eerdmans Publishing Co., 1978), 466.

14. The heated dispute between whether *homoousios* or *homoiousios* was the better term to describe the Son's nature led Edward Gibbon to remark in the nineteenth century that "the profane of every age have derided the furious contests which the difference of a single diphthong excited" between them (Gibbon, *The History of the Decline and Fall of the Roman Empire,* 7 vols. [London: J. B. Bury, 1974], 2:352). The dispute, however, was not mere quibbling about a single letter. It had to do with fundamental questions about the status of the Son and an adequate explanation of the power of the Son to redeem humanity.

At a synod he convened in 362 in Alexandria, he was able to get the so-called Homoiousians (those who said the Son is "of a similar substance" as the Father) to side with him in opposing those extreme supporters of Arius who declared that the Son was unlike the Father. In addition, he helped to forge an agreement that both his own understanding of God (that God was "one hypostasis") and the understanding of some of Nicea's opponents (that God is "three hypostases") were orthodox. When the former formula is not construed in a modalist or Sabellian fashion and the latter not construed in a tritheistic fashion, then both formulas could be understood to uphold the triunity of God.

In the excerpt we have below from *Orations against the Arians,* we see that Athanasius had to refute the use his opponents made of scripture. The devil, he declares, uses the language of scripture to lead Christians into heretical conceptions of the deity (Book I, sect. 8). Consequently, Athanasius engages in a two-pronged tactic of response. On the one hand, he appeals to scripture to defend the nonscriptural term *homoousios* used at Nicea, arguing that it is an accurate expression of what the scriptures wish to say about the Son (sect. 9). On the other hand, he shows how the Arian interpretation of some scripture passages is erroneous. For example, in section 64 of Book I (see below) he argues that the scriptural statements about the Word becoming flesh do not mean to say that the Word first came into *being* at a particular time, but rather that the Word first came to exercise its "ministry and economy" at a particular time, that is, when the Word became a human being. In addition to his appeal to scripture, Athanasius also adduces reasoned arguments to refute the assertions of the Arians.

All of this theological debate did not receive a formal and official resolution until the Council of Constantinople in 381. Emperor Theodosius, a staunch defender of Nicea, convened the meeting. After discussion of differing points of view, the council condemned as heretical three theological opinions: Arianism, Macedonianism, and Apollinarianism. Confirming the teaching of Nicea about the Son of God, Constantinople condemned Arianism. But it went beyond Nicea by also affirming the full divinity of the Holy Spirit against the Macedonians (also known as the Pneumatomachians), who believed the Spirit to be a creature.[15] Although it vigorously reaffirmed the full divinity of Christ, the council did not want to undermine in the process his full humanity. Consequently, it also condemned the position of Apollinaris, who undermined the full humanity of Christ by denying that he had a human spirit. How it was possible for Christ to be both fully God and fully human was left to the Council of Ephesus (431) and the Council of Chalcedon (451) to work out.

Among the most important theologians who paved the way for the success of the Nicene position and the official affirmation of the full deity of the Holy Spirit are the fourth-century Cappadocian Fathers. The Cappadocian Fathers were three theologians and bishops who came from the Roman province of Cappadocia in modern-day Turkey: Basil of Caesarea (also known as Basil the Great), his younger brother Gregory of Nyssa, and their friend Gregory of Nazianzus. The

---

15. In the first two centuries, it was not uncommon for the term "Spirit" to be used to refer to the divine in Christ. Clement of Alexandria, for example, speaks in *The Tutor* (1:6.43.3) of Jesus as "the Word of God, the Spirit incarnate." For this reason, some historians speak of ancient "binitarianism," according to which only two forms of the divine were distinguished: the Father and the Son-Spirit.

Cappadocians articulated an explanation of how Father, Son, and Spirit could simultaneously be one substance (the Nicene position) and yet three distinct *hypostases*. In the course of this explanation, the Cappadocians had to differentiate the meaning of *ousia* (substance or essence) and *hypostasis,* which terms previously had often been used interchangeably. Basil the Great said that the difference between substance and hypostasis was the difference between the universal and the particular (see his Letter 214:4). Just as each human individual is comprised of the substance of "humanity" common to all people (the universal element) together with their own distinguishing individual features (the particular element), so too each of the three hypostases of God is the common substance of deity together with each's own distinctive features. Although such an explanation underlined the deity of Father, Son, and Spirit while keeping each distinct from the other, it seemed to fall into tritheism.

Gregory of Nyssa, the most speculative and philosophically oriented of the Cappadocian Fathers, addressed this problem in his treatise that argued that there are "Not Three Gods." In this work he points out the inadequacies of colloquial speech and of analogies drawn from human experience for understanding the mystery of God. He attempts to establish the point that the basis of difference within the Godhead is neither nature nor activity, but "cause." If the basis of difference were nature or substance, then one or more of the persons of the trinity would not be divine. If the basis of difference were activity or operation, then the unity of the Godhead would be destroyed. The basis of difference, Gregory insists, is "cause," that is, the difference in the manner of existence of each of the persons of the trinity. Only the Father is Uncaused or Ungenerated, even though the Son and the Spirit are also eternal with the Father and equally God.

Both Gregory of Nyssa and Gregory Nazianzus were present at the Council of Constantinople. The latter played a leading role. They were able to win support for the Cappadocian understanding of God, which was then encapsulated in the creed. Although this Niceno-Constantinopolitan Creed, the most ecumenical of the Christian creeds, is widely used in both Christian churches of the East and the West, there is one important difference. In the East, it is believed that the Holy Spirit proceeds from the Father (as the ancient creedal text states). In the West, the belief developed that the Spirit proceeds from the Father *and* the Son. It therefore became customary in the West to add the words "and the Son" to the text of Constantinople. This unilateral decision to alter the creed approved by an ecumenical council became one of the reasons for the eventual break between the churches of the East and the West in the middle of the eleventh century. The Council of Florence came close to resolving this difference, but the planned reunification of East and West did not finally take place.

If the Cappadocian Fathers represent the high point in trinitarian reflection in the East, then Augustine represents the high point in trinitarian reflection in the West during the early history of the church. Like the Cappadocians, Augustine was concerned to explain how God can be one, yet three. He confesses that the human person cannot adequately grasp the nature of God. On the other hand, he asserts that we can know something of God's nature from the things God has made, in particular, human beings themselves. Insofar as human beings are made in God's image, we can expect to see something of God reflected in them. The trinity Augustine discovers in the human person are memory, understanding, and will. Alternatively, Augustine speaks of the mind, the knowledge whereby it knows itself, and the love whereby it loves itself (see *The Trinity*, Book XV, sect. 10 below). Although these three powers of the one person provide an analogy for thinking about God, the analogy itself is flawed.

In sections 11, 12, and 43 of Book XV of *The Trinity*, Augustine identifies some of the deficiencies of his original analogy. For example, knowledge, understanding, and will are powers or capacities *in* the human person, but they are not by themselves the entire human person. Moreover, the human person who possesses these capacities is one person, not three. The detrimental effects of original sin make God, who is already beyond the mind's grasp, even more difficult to understand. But, concludes Augustine, even if humanity did not exist in its current state of infirmity, it would not be able to comprehend God for there "can be no equality between creature and Creator" (sect. 43). Although we are thrown back upon faith for what we affirm about God, Augustine's psychological analogy, as well as his analogy of the lover, the beloved, and love, provided Christians in the West with useful ways of making some sense of the mystery of God.

This recognition of the mystery of God is most forcefully emphasized by Pseudo-Dionysius, who modern scholars believe was a sixth-century Syrian monk. In *The Mystical Theology*, Pseudo-Dionysius uses the language of paradox to make the point that God is "beyond all being and knowledge" (see selection below). If God is beyond knowledge, yet Christians are said to grow spiritually insofar as their knowledge and love of God increase, how is one to develop or enhance their relationship with God? Not through the powers of intellectual speculation, says Pseudo-Dionysius, but through personal union with God. Although our desire to know and to understand compels us to speak of the God whom we experience, we must recognize that every affirmation we make about God must also be denied in some sense. Every statement about God needs to be qualified. Every statement we make falls short of the divine reality. As we come closer to God, language falters until we finally fall silent.

The early period of the church's history is foundational for the development of its doctrine of God. In this period, we see how consideration of the "economic" trinity (the historical activity of God in Christ and in the church through the Holy Spirit) moved Christians to speculate about the "immanent" trinity (the inner nature of God and the interrelationship of the divine persons). We see how the church struggled to find language that would define the parameters of appropriate God-talk. We see how opposition to heresy as well as the inner drive of faith to seek understanding moved doctrinal reflection forward. We also see dialectical tension between the articulation of the divine nature in human terms and the surrender of the intellect before an experience of the "brilliant darkness" of God.

The medieval period will build upon this legacy. It will build upon the doctrinal conclusions of the early church. It will experience the same dialectic between the need to speak of God and the acknowledgment of God's ineffability. But we will also see new categories and new concerns. Some will attempt to define God with tools drawn from philosophy, and not simply from the scriptures. They will extol the path of *scientia* (intellectual understanding of God) over the path of *sapientia* (experiential wisdom concerning God). Yet others will extol visions and mystical experiences, rather than intellectual comprehension, as the medium of true knowledge of God. But all of these new formulations will be worked out within the basic framework constructed by Christians in the early centuries of the church.

TEXTS

Irenaeus of Lyons (ca. 130–202)

Against Heresies (ca. 185), Book 4, Chapter 20, Sections 1–3*

Chapter XX: That One God Formed All Things in the World, by Means of the Word and the Holy Spirit: And That Although He Is to Us in This Life Invisible and Incomprehensible, Nevertheless He Is Not Unknown; Inasmuch As His Works Do Declare Him, and His Word Has Shown That in Many Modes He May Be Seen and Known.

1. As regards His greatness, therefore, it is not possible to know God, for it is impossible that the Father can be measured; but as regards His love (for this it is which leads us to God by His Word), when we obey Him, we do always learn that there is so great a God, and that it is He who by Himself has established, and selected, and adorned, and contains all things; and among the all things, both ourselves and this our world. We also then were made, along with those things which are contained by Him. And this is He of whom the Scripture says, "And God formed man, taking clay of the earth, and breathed into his face the breath of life" [Gen. 2:7]. It was not angels, therefore, who made us, nor who formed us, neither had angels power to make an image of God, nor anyone else, except the Word of the Lord, nor any Power remotely distant from the Father of all things. For God did not stand in need of these [beings], in order to the accomplishing of what He had Himself determined with Himself beforehand should be done, as if He did not possess His own hands. For with Him were always present the Word and Wisdom, the Son and the Spirit, by whom and in whom, freely and spontaneously, He made all things, to whom also He speaks, saying, "Let Us make man after Our image and likeness [Gen. 1:26]"; He taking from Himself the substance of the creatures [formed], and the pattern of things made, and the type of all the adornments in the world.

2. Truly, then, the Scripture declared, which says, "First of all believe that there is one God, who has established all things, and completed them, and having caused that from what had not being, all things should come into existence."[1] He who contains all things and is Himself contained by no one. Rightly also has Malachi said among the prophets: "Is it not one God who hath established us? Have we not all one Father? [Mal. 2:10]" In accordance with this, too, does the apostle say, "There is one God, the Father, who is above all, and in us all [Eph. 4:6]...."

---

*From *Ante-Nicene Fathers*, ed. Alexander Roberts and James Donaldson, vol. 1: *The Apostolic Fathers: Justin Martyr–Irenaeus* (Grand Rapids: Eerdmans, 1979), 487–88.

1. Note that this quotation is taken from the Shepherd of Hermas, book 2. sim. 1.

3. I have also largely demonstrated that the Word, namely, the Son, was always with the Father; and that Wisdom also, which is the Spirit, was present with Him, anterior to all creation, He declares by Solomon: "God by Wisdom founded the earth, and by understanding hath He established the heaven. By His knowledge the depths burst forth, and the clouds dropped down the dew [Prov. 3:19, 20]." And again: "The Lord created me the beginning of His ways in His work: He set me up from everlasting, in the beginning, before He made the earth, before He established the depths, and before the fountains of waters gushed forth; before the mountains were made strong, and before all the hills, He brought me forth [Prov. 8:22–25]." And again: "When He prepared the heaven, I was with Him, and when He established the fountains of the deep; when He made the foundations of the earth strong, I was with Him preparing [them]. I was He in whom He rejoiced, and throughout all time I was daily glad before His face, when He rejoiced at the completion of the world, and was delighted in the sons of men [Prov. 8:27–31]."

Irenaeus of Lyons, "Proof of the Apostolic Preaching" (ca. 185), Sections 6 and 7*

The Three Articles of the Faith

6. And this is the drawing up of our faith, the foundation of the building, and the consolidation of a way of life. God, the Father, uncreated, beyond grasp, invisible, one God the maker of all; this is the first and foremost article of our faith. But the second article is the Word of God, the Son of God, Christ Jesus our Lord, who was shown forth by the prophets according to the design of their prophecy and according to the manner in which the Father disposed; and through Him were made all things whatsoever. He also, *in the end of times,* for the recapitulation of all things, is become a man among men, visible and tangible, in order to abolish death and bring to light life, and bring about the communion of God and man. And the third article is the Holy Spirit, through whom the prophets prophesied and the patriarchs were taught about God and the just were led in the path of justice, and who *in the end of times* has been poured forth in a new manner upon humanity over all the earth, renewing man to God.

The Trinity and Our Rebirth

7. Therefore the baptism of our rebirth comes through these three articles, granting us rebirth unto God the Father, through His Son, by the Holy Spirit. For those who are bearers of the Spirit of God are led to the Word, that is, to the Son; but the Son takes them and presents them to the Father; and the Father confers incorruptibility. So without the Spirit there is no seeing the Word of God, and without the Son there is no approaching the Father; for the Son is knowledge of the Father, and knowledge of the Son is through the Holy Spirit. But the Son,

*Reprinted from *St. Irenaeus: Proof of the Apostolic Preaching,* ed. Johannes Quasten, S.T.D., and Joseph C. Plumpe, Ph.D., trans. Joseph P. Smith, S.J., © 1952 by The Missionary Society of St. Paul the Apostle in the State of New York. Used by permission of Paulist Press. Pp. 51–52.

according to the Father's good-pleasure, administers the Spirit charismatically as the Father will, to those to whom He will.

Tertullian (ca. 160–225)

Against Praxeas (213), Chapters 2, 3, 8, and 9*

Chapter 2: The Catholic Doctrine of the Trinity and Unity. Sometimes Called the Divine Economy, or Dispensation of the Personal Relations of the Godhead.

In the course of time, then, the Father forsooth was born, and the Father suffered — God Himself, the Lord Almighty, whom in their preaching they declare to be Jesus Christ. We, however, as we indeed always have done (and more especially since we have been better instructed by the Paraclete, who leads men indeed into all truth), believe that there is one only God, but under the following dispensation, or *oikonomia,* as it is called, that this one only God has also a Son, His Word, who proceeded[1] from Himself, by whom all things were made, and without whom nothing was made. Him *we believe* to have been sent by the Father into the Virgin, and to have been born of her — being both Man and God, the Son of Man and the Son of God, and to have been called by the name of Jesus Christ; *we believe* Him to have suffered, died, and been buried, according to the Scriptures, and, after He had been raised again by the Father and taken back to heaven, to be sitting at the right hand of the Father, *and* that He will come to judge the quick and the dead; who sent also from heaven from the Father, according to His own promise, the Holy Ghost, the Paraclete [the Comforter], the sanctifier of the faith of those who believe in the Father, and in the Son, and in the Holy Ghost. That this rule of faith has come down to us from the beginning of the gospel, even before any of the older heretics, much more before Praxeas, *a pretender* of yesterday, will be apparent both from the lateness of date which marks all heresies, and also from the absolutely novel character of our new-fangled Praxeas. In this principle also we must henceforth find a presumption of equal force against all heresies whatsoever — that whatever is first is true, whereas that is spurious which is later in date. But keeping this prescriptive rule inviolate, still some opportunity must be given for reviewing (the statements of heretics), with a view to the instruction and protection of divers persons; . . . especially in the case of this heresy, which supposes itself to possess the pure truth; in thinking that one cannot believe in one only God in any other way than by saying that the Father, the Son, and the Holy Ghost are the very selfsame Person. As if in this way also one were not All, in that All are of One, by unity (that is) of substance; while the mystery of the dispensation [*oikonomia*] is still guarded, which distributes the Unity into a Trinity, placing in their order [*Dirigens*] the three *Persons* — the Father, the

---

*From *The Ante-Nicene Fathers: Translations of the Writings of the Fathers down to A.D. 325,* ed. Alexander Roberts and James Donaldson, vol. 3: *Latin Christianity: Its Founder, Tertullian* (Grand Rapids: Eerdmans, 1978), 598–99, 602–4.

1. The Church after Nicea applied this term exclusively to the Holy Spirit, making the distinction between the generation of the Son and the procession of the Spirit.

Son, and the Holy Ghost: three, however, not in condition [*statu*], but in degree; not in substance, but in form; not in power, but in aspect [*specie*]; yet of one substance, and of one condition, and of one power, inasmuch as He is one God, from whom these degrees and forms and aspects are reckoned, under the name of the Father, and of the Son, and of the Holy Ghost. How they are susceptible of number without division, will be shown as our treatise proceeds.

Chapter 3: Sundry Popular Fears and Prejudices. The Doctrine of the Trinity in Unity Rescued from These Misapprehensions.

The simple, indeed (I will not call them unwise and unlearned), who always constitute the majority of believers, are startled at the dispensation [*oikonomia*] (of the Three in One), on the ground that their very rule of faith withdraws them from the world's plurality of gods to the one only true God; not understanding that, although He is the one only God, He must yet be believed in with His own *oikonomia*. The numerical order and distribution of the Trinity they assume to be a division of the Unity; whereas the Unity which derives the Trinity out of its own self is so far from being destroyed, that it is actually supported by it. They are constantly throwing out against us that we are preachers of two gods and three gods, while they take to themselves preeminently the credit of being worshippers of the One God; just as if the Unity itself with irrational deductions did not produce heresy, and the Trinity rationally considered constitute the truth. We, say they, maintain the *Monarchy* (or, *sole government* of God). And so, as far as the sound goes, do even Latins (and ignorant ones too) pronounce the word in such a way that you would suppose their understanding of the *monarxia* (or *Monarchy*) was as complete as their pronunciation of the term. Well, then Latins take pains to pronounce the *monarxia* (or *Monarchy*), while Greeks actually refuse to understand the *oikonomia,* or *Dispensation* (*of the Three in One*). As for myself, however, if I have gleaned any knowledge of either language, I am sure that *monarxia* (or *Monarchy*) has no other meaning than single and individual [*Unicum*] rule; but for all that, this monarchy does not, because it is the government of one, preclude him whose government it is, either from having a son, or from having made himself actually a son to himself, or from ministering his own monarchy by whatever agents he will. Nay more, I contend that no dominion so belongs to one only, as his own, or is in such a sense singular, or is in such a sense a monarchy, as not also to be administered through other persons most closely connected with it, and whom it has itself provided as officials to itself. If, moreover, there be a son belonging to him whose monarchy it is, it does not forthwith become divided and cease to be a monarchy, if the son also be taken as a sharer in it; but it is as to its origin equally his, by whom it is communicated to the son; and being his, it is quite as much a monarchy (or *sole empire*), since it is held together by two who are so inseparable [*Tam unicis*]. Therefore, inasmuch as the Divine Monarchy also is administered by so many legions and hosts of angels, according as it is written "Thousand thousands ministered unto Him, and ten thousand times ten thousand stood before Him" [Dan. 7:10]; and since it has not from this circumstance ceased to be the rule of one (so as no longer to be a monarchy), because it is administered by so many thousands of powers; how comes it to pass that God should be thought to suffer division and severance in the Son and in the Holy Ghost, who have the second and third places assigned to them, and who are so closely joined with the Father in His substance, when He suffers no such (division and severance) in the multitude of so many angels? Do you really suppose that Those, who are naturally members of the Father's own substance, pledges of His love, instruments of His might, nay, His power itself and the entire system of His monarchy, are the overthrow and destruction thereof? You are not right in so thinking. I prefer your exercising yourself on the meaning of the thing rather than on the sound of the word. Now you must understand the overthrow of a monarchy to be *this*, when another dominion, which has a framework and a state peculiar to itself (and is therefore a rival), is brought in over and above it: when, e.g., some other god is introduced in opposition to the Creator, as in the opinions of Marcion, or when many gods are introduced, according to your Valentinuses and your Prodiscuses. Then it amounts to an overthrow of the Monarchy, since it involves the destruction of the Creator.

Chapter 8: Though the Son or Word of God Emanates from the Father, He Is Not, Like the Emanations of Valentinus, Separable from the Father. Nor Is the Holy Ghost Separable from Either. Illustrations from Nature.

If any man from this shall think that I am introducing some *probole* — that is to say, some prolation[2] of one thing out of another, as Valentinus does when he sets forth Aeon from Aeon, one after another — then this is my first reply to you: Truth must not therefore refrain from the use of such a term, and its reality and meaning, because heresy also employs it. The fact is, heresy has rather taken it from Truth, in order to mold it into its own counterfeit. Was the Word of God put forth or not? Here take your stand with me, and flinch not. If He was put forth, then acknowledge that the true doctrine has a prolation; and never mind heresy, when in any point it mimics the truth. The question now is, in what sense each side uses a given thing and the word which expresses it. Valentinus divides and separates his prolations from their Author, and places them at so great a distance from Him, that the Aeon does not know the Father: he longs, indeed, to know Him, but cannot; nay, he is almost swallowed up and dissolved into the rest of matter [see *Adv. Valentin.* 100:14, 15]. With us, however, the Son alone knows the Father [Matt. 11:27], and has Himself unfolded "the Father's bosom" [John 1:18]. . . . But the Word was formed by the Spirit, and (if I may so express myself) the Spirit is the body of the Word. The Word, therefore, is both always in the Father, as He says, "I am in the Father" [John 14:11]; and is always with God, according to what is written, "And the Word was with God" [John 1:1]; and never separate from the Father, or other than the Father, since "I and the Father are one" [John 10:30]. This will be the prolation, taught by the truth, the guardian of the Unity, wherein we declare that the Son is a prolation from the Father, without being separated from Him. For God sent forth the Word, as the Paraclete also declares, just as the root puts forth the tree, and the fountain the river, and the

---

2. The word *probole* refers to anything which proceeds or is sent forth from the substance of another, as the fruit of a tree or the rays of the sun. In Latin it is translated by *prolatio*. Tertullian apologizes here for using the term because it was also used by Valentinus, a heretical Gnostic.

sun the ray. For these are *probolai,* or *emanations,* of the substances from which they proceed. I should not hesitate, indeed, to call the tree the son or offspring of the root, and the river of the fountain, and the ray of the sun; because every original source is a parent, and everything which issues from the origin is an offspring. Much more is (this true of) the Word of God, who has actually received as His own peculiar designation the name of *Son.* But still the tree is not severed from the root, nor the river from the fountain, nor the ray from the sun; nor, indeed, is the Word separated from God. Following, therefore, the form of these analogies, I confess that I call God and His Word — the Father and His Son — *two.* For the root and the tree are distinctly two things, but correlatively joined; the fountain and the river are also two forms, but indivisible; so likewise the sun and the ray are two forms, but coherent ones. Everything which proceeds from something else must needs be second to that from which it proceeds, without being on that account separated. Where, however, there is a second, there must be two; and where there is a third, there must be three. Now the Spirit indeed is third from God and the Son; just as the fruit of the tree is third from the root, or as the stream out of the river is third from the fountain, or as the apex of the ray is third from the sun. Nothing, however, is alien from that original source when it derives its own properties. In like manner the Trinity, flowing down from the Father through intertwined and connected steps, does not at all disturb the *Monarchy* [Or oneness of the divine empire], whilst it at the same time guards the state of the *Economy* [or dispensation of the divine tripersonality].

Chapter 9: The Catholic Rule of Faith Expounded in Some of Its Points. Especially in the Unconfused Distinction of the Several Persons of the Blessed Trinity.

Bear always in mind that this is the rule of faith which I profess; by it I testify that the Father, and the Son, and the Spirit are inseparable from each other, and so will you know in what sense this is said. Now, observe my assertion is that the Father is one, and the Son one, and the Spirit one, and that They are distinct from Each Other. This statement is taken in a wrong sense by every uneducated as well as every perversely disposed person, as if it predicated a diversity, in such a sense as to imply a separation among the Father, and the Son, and the Spirit. I am, moreover, obliged to say this, when (extolling the *Monarchy* at the expense of the *Economy*) they contend for the identity of the Father and Son and Spirit, that it is not by way of diversity that the Son differs from the Father, but by distribution: it is not by division that He is different, but by distinction; because the Father is not the same as the Son, since they differ one from the other in the mode of their being. For the Father is the entire substance, but the Son is a derivation and portion of the whole, as He Himself acknowledges: "My Father is greater than I" [John 14:28]. In the Psalm His inferiority is described as being "a little lower than the angels" [Ps. 8:5]. Thus the Father is distinct from the Son, being greater than the Son, inasmuch as He who begets is one, and He who is begotten is another; He, too, who sends is one, and He who is sent is another; and He, again, who makes is one, and He through whom the thing is made is another. Happily the Lord Himself employs this expression of the person of the

Paraclete, so as to signify not a division or severance, but a disposition (of mutual relations in the Godhead); for He says, "I will pray the Father, and He shall send you another Comforter.... even the Spirit of truth" [John 14:16], thus making the Paraclete distinct from Himself, even as we say that the Son is also distinct from the Father; so that He showed a third degree in the Paraclete, as we believe the second degree is in the Son, by reason of the order observed in the *Economy*. Besides, does not the very fact that they have the distinct names of *Father* and *Son* amount to a declaration that they are distinct in personality [*Aliud ab alio*]? For, of course, all things will be what their names represent them to be; and what they are and ever will be, that will they be called; and the distinction indicated by the names does not at all admit of any confusion, because there is none in the things which they designate. "Yes is yes, and no is no; for what is more than these, cometh of evil" [Matt. 5:37].

Arius (ca. 250–336)

"Letter to Eusebius of Nicomedia" (ca. 319)*

1. To a most longed-for lord, a faithful man of God, orthodox Eusebius; Arius, who is unjustly persecuted by Pope Alexander on account of the all-prevailing truth which you also protect, sends greetings in the Lord.

2. Since my father Ammonius was coming into Nicomedia, it appeared to me reasonable and fitting to address you through him and in like manner to remind your innate love and disposition, which you have toward the brothers because of God and his Christ, that the bishop greatly pillages us and persecutes us, and invoking all things moves against us, so that he might drive us as godless men from the city. All this because we do not agree with him when he states in public, "Always God always Son," "At the same time Father, at the same time Son," "The Son ingenerably co-exists with God," "Ever-begotten, ungenerated-created, neither in thought nor in some moment of time does God proceed [sic] the Son," "Always God always Son," "The Son is from God himself."

3. And since Eusebius, your brother in Caesarea, and Theodotus, Paulinus, Athanasius, Gregory, Aetius, and all the bishops throughout the East, say that God without beginning exists before the Son, an anathema was pronounced against them — except Philogonius, Hellanicus, and Macareius — heretical and ignorant men, who speak about the Son. Some of them say that he is a belching, others an emanation, and still others alike-ingenerate.

4. If the heretics should threaten us with myriads of deaths, we are not able even to hear these impieties.

But what do we say and think? What have we taught and what do we teach? That the Son is not unbegotten or a portion of the unbegotten in any manner or from any substratum, but that by the will and counsel of the Father he subsisted before times and ages, full of grace and truth, God, only-begotten, unchangeable.

*Reprinted from *The Trinitarian Controversy* by William Rusch, copyright © Fortress Press. Used by permission of Augsburg Fortress. Pp. 29–30.

5. And before he was begotten or created or defined or established, he was not. For he was not unbegotten. But we are persecuted because we say, "The Son has a beginning, but God is without beginning." Because of this we are persecuted because we say, "The Son has a beginning, but God is without beginning." We are persecuted because we say, "He is from nothing." But we speak thus inasmuch as he is neither part of God or from any substratum. On account of this we are persecuted. You know the rest. I pray that you are strong in the Lord, recalling our afflictions, fellow pupil of Lucian, truly "Eusebius."

Arius, "Letter to Alexander of Alexandria" (320)*

(1) The presbyters and deacons send greetings in the Lord to our blessed pope and bishop, Alexander.

(2) Our faith, from our ancestors, which we have learned also from you, is this. We know one God — alone unbegotten, alone everlasting, alone without beginning, alone true, alone possessing immortality, alone wise, alone good, alone master, judge of all, manager, director, immutable and unchangeable, just and good, God of Law, Prophets, and New Testament — who begot an only begotten Son before eternal times, through whom he made the ages and everything. But he begot him not in appearance but in truth, having submitted him to his own will, an immutable and unchangeable perfect creature of God, (3) but not as one of the creatures — an offspring, but not as one of those born — nor as Valentinus decreed that the offspring of the Father is an emanation, nor as Manes propounded that the offspring of the Father is part of the same substance, nor as Sabellius, who divides the monad, says "Father-and-Son," nor as Hieracas believes a light from a light as a lamp divided into two; nor is he the one who was before, later begotten or created into a Son as you yourself also, Blessed Pope, very often have forbidden throughout the midst of the church and in council those who teach these things. But, as we say, he was created by the will of God before times and ages, and he received life, being, and glories from the Father as the Father has shared them with him. (4) For the Father, having given to him the inheritance of all, did not deprive himself of those things which he has in himself without generation, for he is the source of all. Thus there are three *hypostases*. God being the cause of all is without beginning, most alone; but the Son, begotten by the Father, created and founded before the ages, was not before he was begotten. Rather, the Son begotten timelessly before everything, alone was caused to subsist by the Father. For he is not everlasting or co-everlasting or unbegotten with the Father. Nor does he have being with the Father, as certain individuals mention things relatively and bring into the discussion two unbegotten causes. But God is thus before all as a monad and cause. Therefore he is also before the Son, as we have learned from you when you preached throughout the midst of the church.

(5) Therefore, insofar as he has from God being, glories, and life, and all things have been handed over to him, thus God is his cause. For he, as his God and being before him, rules him. But if "from him" [Rom. 11:36] and "from the womb"

---

*Reprinted from *The Trinitarian Controversy* by William Rusch, copyright © Fortress Press. Used by permission of Augsburg Fortress. Pp. 31–32.

[Ps. 110:3] and "I came from the Father and I come" [John 16:28] are thought by some to signify that he is a part of him and an emanation, the Father will be according to them compounded, divided, mutable and a body, and, as far as they are concerned, the incorporeal God suffers things suitable to the body.

> I pray that you are well in the Lord, Blessed Pope.
> Arius, Aeithales, Achillas, Carpones, Sarmates, and Arius—presbyters.
> Euzoius, Lucius, Julius, Menas, Helladius, Gaius—deacons.
> Bishops Secundus of Pentapolis, Theonas of Libya, and Pistus.

The Early Creeds

Christian creeds first developed for use in baptismal rites and catechetical instruction. They were generally divided into three sections, dealing with God the Father, Jesus Christ, and the Holy Spirit. The Nicene and Constantinopolitan Creeds, however, became more than a simple baptismal confession. Because they were formulated in the context of opposition to heretical teaching, they have become a binding standard of orthodox Christian belief.

The Apostles' Creed

This creed is a basic statement of faith used in the Roman Catholic, Anglican, and many Protestant churches. Because it is not officially recognized in the Eastern Orthodox churches, it does not have the same status as the present Nicene Creed. The name of the creed derives from the belief that it was written by the twelve apostles, with each responsible for one of its clauses. Although it is first mentioned by the name Apostles' Creed in the fourth century, its present wording is not found in texts prior to the eighth century. The apostolic authorship of the creed began to be questioned in the fifteenth and sixteenth centuries. This creed, like many of the earliest creeds in the church, developed in the context of preparing catechumens for baptism and entry into the church. Catechumens (those receiving instructions in preparation for baptism) would be asked a series of questions, such as "Do you believe in God the Father Almighty?" and so forth through the major Christian beliefs. Stated affirmatively, the required answers to these questions became a creed.

The present text of the Apostles' Creed is similar to the baptismal creed used in the church of Rome in the third and fourth centuries. The sources behind the creed may go back to the second century. As is true of other creeds, clauses were added at different times either to oppose heretical alternatives or to affirm a belief that was in dispute. For example, the creed emphasizes, in contrast to the Gnostics, that God, not an evil demiurge, is the creator of the world. Against those who denied the real humanity of Jesus (docetists, for example, said Jesus only "appeared" human), the creed stresses that he was born of Mary and actually suffered, died, and was buried. Belief in the "communion of the saints" was probably added to defend the growing cult of the saints (i.e., veneration of saints and their relics). The Apostles' Creed reached its final form in southwestern

France in the late sixth or early seventh century. Between the ninth and the twelfth centuries, the Apostles' Creed gradually replaced other baptismal creeds. By the beginning of the thirteenth century it was acknowledged as the official statement of faith for the entire western church.

The Nicene Creed

For a long time scholars believed that the basis of the creed formulated at Nicea was the baptismal creed used in Eusebius of Caesarea's own church. Modern research, however, has pointed out that the creed used as a starting point at Nicea was probably a local baptismal creed, deriving from Syria or Palestine. To this creed were added statements that clearly presented the desired alternative to the claims of Arius as well as a series of anathemas. Two of the prominent features in the creed for combatting Arianism are the declaration that Christ is the "only begotten" Son of God and the declaration that this Son is of "one substance" or "of the same substance" (*homoousios*) with the Father. The first declaration was intended by the defenders of Nicea to make clear that the Son, and only the Son, comes directly from God, whereas all creatures come from God in the sense that they were created by God with the Son. The second declaration was intended to make clear that the Son was begotten out of the very essence of the Father, whereas creatures were created out of nothing. In order to emphasize the point that the Son was not a creature, contrary to the Arian assertion, the creed insisted that the Son was "begotten, not made." Underlying this distinction between "begotten" and "created" was a dispute about how to interpret and use Proverbs 8:22–31. This Hebrew text describes the role of Wisdom in the creation of the world. Christians had come to associate the Son with Wisdom described in the text. The problem, however, was that the text states: "The Lord *created* me [i.e., Wisdom] at the beginning of his work, the first of his acts of long ago" (Prov. 8:22; emphasis added). As Jaroslav Pelikan has observed, the Arian controversy apparently broke out over the exegesis of this text.[1]

Constantinopolitan Creed

The Council of Constantinople met in 381 to deal with the continuing Arian controversy and several other doctrinal and ecclesiastical matters. After decades of support for Arianism or semi-Arianism[2] from some bishops and other emperors, Emperor Theodosius, a supporter of the decrees of Nicea, was eager to deal with Arianism once and for all. He called the council. Two of the Cappadocian Fathers, Gregory of Nyssa and especially Gregory of Nazianzus, played an important role at the council. As a comparison of the Constantinopolitan and Nicene Creeds makes clear, the Council of Constantinople reaffirmed the basic anti-Arian declarations of Nicea. The council retained the nonscriptural term *homoousios*, the appropriateness of which to describe the Son's divinity and relationship to the

---

1. Jaroslav Pelikan, *Christian Tradition: A History of the Development of Doctrine,* vol. 1: *The Emergence of the Catholic Tradition (100–600)* (Chicago: University of Chicago Press, 1971), 193–96.
2. The semi-Arian position holds that the Son is "like" (*homoiousios*) the Father in nature, but not of the *same* nature or substance (*homoousios*) with him.

Father had been hotly disputed in the years following the Council of Nicea. Having affirmed that the Son is fully God, the only-begotten of the Father, and of one substance with the Father, the bishops at Constantinople removed the series of Arian anathemas that had been appended to the creed of Nicea.

The Constantinopolitan Creed also expanded upon the creed of Nicea by making a fuller statement about the Holy Spirit. The council tried unsuccessfully to win over Macedonians, who believed in the deity of the Son, but held that the Holy Spirit was a creature. The creed refrains from explicitly calling the Holy Spirit God, but implies the Spirit's deity by affirming that the Spirit is worshiped and glorified with Father and Son. From the time of Constantinople the deity of the Spirit has been a standard part of orthodox Christian belief. The eastern and western church, however, eventually disagreed about how to describe the Spirit's relationship to Father and Son. In the East the belief was and is that the Spirit proceeds from the Father *through* the Son. In the West, by contrast, the belief developed that the Spirit proceeds from the Father *and* the Son. This verbal difference reflects a theological difference in understanding the trinity. Whereas the East tended to emphasize more the distinctions within the Godhead, the West tended to emphasize more the unity of the divine substance. In keeping with this different orientation, the Father is understood in the East as the source and principle of the Godhead. Consequently, the Spirit is said to proceed from the Father. All of the approximately 150 bishops at Constantinople were from the East. Pope Damasus I (366–84) in Rome appears to have accepted the creed, thus showing western support for regarding the creed as ecumenical. After the council, however, Arianism continued to be a problem in certain portions of the western church, especially Spain. In order to strengthen the equality of the Son with the Father, Spanish councils, beginning in the fifth century, began to state that the Spirit proceeds from the Father and the Son (in Latin, "and the Son" is *filioque*). King Recaredo moved the Council of Toledo III (589) to insert the filioque clause into the Nicene Creed. This practice gradually spread to all western churches. It was one of the theological issues that contributed to the Great Schism of 1054, when the eastern and western churches decisively separated. Eastern Christians claimed that by unilaterally inserting the filioque clause into the text of an "ecumenical" creed, the West had performed a schismatic act. The Council of Ephesus (431), after all, had pronounced an anathema on anyone who professed a faith different from that of the previous councils.[3] Although eastern Christians continue to reject this addition of the filioque clause, they do not now generally regard it as heretical, especially if it is understood in the sense of "through the Son."

The creed regularly referred to today as the "Nicene" Creed is more accurately the Niceno-Constantinopolitan Creed because it resulted from the combined work of both councils. For the sake of convenience, the Niceno-Constantinopolitan Creed is simply called today the Nicene Creed. It is the most fully ecumenical of Christian creeds, accepted in East and West alike, including the major Protestant churches. In eastern churches, it is regularly used in the context of both

---

3. See Leonardo Boff, *Trinity and Society,* trans. Paul Burns (Maryknoll, N.Y.: Orbis Books, 1988), 70–71.

Apostles' Creed; Received Text	Nicene Creed of 325	Constantinopolitan Creed of 381
(The clauses in brackets are the later additions.)	(The clauses in brackets are omitted in the received text.)	(The later additions are italicized.)
I believe in God the Father Almighty.	We believe in one God, the Father Almighty,	We believe in one God, the Father Almighty,
[Maker of heaven and earth.]	Maker of all things visible and invisible.	Maker of *heaven and earth, and of* all things visible and invisible.
And in Jesus Christ, his only Son, our Lord;	And in one Lord Jesus Christ, the Son of God, begotten of the Father [the only-begotten; that is, of the essence of the Father, God of God], Light of Light, very God of very God, begotten, not made, being of one substance (*homoousion*) with the Father; by whom all things were made [both in heaven and on earth]; who for us men, and for our salvation, came down and was incarnate and was made man;	And in one Lord Jesus Christ, the *only-begotten* Son of God, begotten of the Father *before all worlds* (aeons), Light of Light, very God of very God, begotten, not made, being of one substance with the Father; by whom all things were made; who for us men, and for our salvation, came down *from heaven* and was incarnate *by the Holy Ghost of the Virgin Mary,* and was made man;
Who was [conceived] by the Holy Ghost, born of the Virgin Mary;		
[Suffered] under Pontius Pilate, was crucified [dead], and buried;	he suffered,	he *was crucified for us under Pontius Pilate, and* suffered, *and was buried,*
[He descended into Hades];		
The third day he rose again from the dead; He ascended into heaven, and sitteth on the right hand of [God] the Father [Almighty];	and the third day he rose again, ascended into heaven;	and the third day he rose again, *according to the Scriptures,* and ascended into heaven; *and sitteth on the right hand of the Father;*
From thence he shall come to judge the quick and the dead.	from thence he shall come to judge the quick and the dead.	from thence he shall come *again, with glory,* to judge the quick and the dead; *whose kingdom shall have no end.* And
And [I believe] in the Holy Ghost;	And in the Holy Ghost.	in the Holy Ghost, *the Lord and Giver of life, who proceedeth from the Father, who with the Father and the Son together is worshiped and glorified, who spake by the prophets.*
	[But those who say: "There was a time when he was not"; and "He was not before he was made"; and "He was made out of nothing," or "He is of another substance" or "essence," or "The Son of God is created," or "changeable" or "alterable" — they are condemned by the holy catholic and apostolic Church.]	
the holy [catholic] Church;		*In one holy catholic and apostolic Church;*
[the communion of saints]; the forgiveness of sins;		*we acknowledge one baptism for the remission of sins;*
the resurrection of the flesh [body];		*we look for the resurrection of the dead,*
[and the life everlasting].		*and the life of the world to come. Amen.* *

*Reprinted from *The Creeds of Christendom*, vol. I: *The History of Creeds* by Philip Schaff (New York: Harper & Brothers, 1877), 27–29.

baptism and eucharistic worship. In the West, it is regularly used in the Eucharist, and chiefly by Roman Catholics, Anglicans, and Lutherans.

Athanasius (ca. 296–373)

Orations against the Arians (356), Book I, Sections 8, 9, 11, 14, 17, 19–21, 26, 29, and 64*

(8) If then they [i.e., Christians who accept Arius's position] think that because certain scriptural phrases are written in the *Thalia* this makes blasphemies words of praise, then they, seeing how the Jews of the present day know accurately the Law and the Prophets, should deny Christ with the Jews. Perhaps they, hearing the Manichees reading certain sections of the Gospels, will also deny with them the Law and the Prophets. If they do not know that they are troubled and babble such things, let them understand from the Scriptures that the devil, that designer of heresy, on account of the peculiar ill smell of evil, borrows the language of Scripture so that with Scripture as a veil, sowing his own poison, he might outwit the guileless. He outwitted Eve; he shaped other heresies. Even now he persuaded Arius to speak and demean himself against other heresies, so that without notice he might introduce his own.... How could he [Arius] speak the truth about the Father, denying the Son who reveals him? How could he think correctly about the Spirit when he slanders the Word who equips the Spirit? Who will believe him when he speaks about the resurrection when he denies the statement "From the dead, Christ became for us the firstborn" [Col. 1:18]? And since he is ignorant about the legitimate and true begetting of the Son from the Father, will he not err about his incarnate presence?...

(9) Behold, we speak freely about the religious faith on the basis of the divine Scriptures; we place it as a light on the lampstand saying, "He is by nature true Son and legitimate from the Father, peculiar to his substance, the only-begotten Wisdom and true and only Word of God. He is neither a creature nor a work, but an offspring peculiar to the Father's substance. Therefore he is true God, *homoousios* with the true Father.... He is the image of the Father's *hypostasis* [Heb. 1:3] and light from light, power and true image of the Father's substance. The Lord also said, "He who has seen me has seen the Father" [John 14:9]. He always was and is, and never was he not. Because the Father is everlasting, his Word and Wisdom would be everlasting. But what do they present to us from the universally censured *Thalia*? Let them first read it, copying the manner of the author, so that when they are mocked by others they might learn in what sort of disaster they are placed. Then let them explain. On its basis, what might they say except, "God was not always Father but became Father later; the Son was not always, for not was he before he was begotten. He is not from the Father, but even he himself subsisted from nothing. He is not peculiar to the substance of the Father, for he is a creature and a work. Christ is not true God, but he was made

---

*Reprinted from *The Trinitarian Controversy* by William Rusch, copyright © Fortress Press. Used by permission of Augsburg Fortress. Pp. 69–71, 73, 76–77, 80, 82–84, 89, 92–93, and 129.

God by participation. The Son does not accurately know the Father; the Word does not see the Father perfectly. Neither does the Word understand or know the Father. He is not the true and only Word of the Father, but he is called in name only Word and Wisdom and is called by grace Son and Power." . . . If anyone who carefully examined the claims of both sides would be asked to choose the faith of one, or whose words he would judge appropriate to God — let these flatterers of impiety rather state, for him who is asked to answer, what is appropriate concerning God (for the Word was God). From this one request the entire issue will be known, what it is appropriate to say: he was or he was not, always or before coming into existence, everlasting or from where and when, true or by adoption, from participation and according to design, he is one of the originated or he is united with the Father, he is unlike the substance of the Father or he is like and peculiar to the Father, or he is a creature or through him creatures came into existence, he is the Father's Word or there is another Word beside him, and by this other word he came into existence, and by another wisdom, only by name he has been called Wisdom and Word, and has become a partaker of that Wisdom and second to it. . . .

(11) Because the devil suggested it to you, you have said and think that there was once when the Son was not. It is necessary to strip off this first layer of your thinking. Tell them, O evil and impious ones, what was once when the Son was not. If you say the Father, your blasphemy is greater. It is impious to say that once he was or to signify him by the term "once." For he is always and is now, and as the Son is, he is, and he himself is the one who is and the Father of the Son. . . . Your former declaration, "The Son was not before he was begotten," is the same thing as the statement "There was once when he was not," for it signifies that there was that time and it was before the Word. What is the source of your discovery of these things? "Why did you, as the nations, snort and practice empty phrases against the Lord and against his Anointed?" [Ps. 2:1]. Nowhere have the Holy Scriptures said such things about the Savior; rather, they have used such words as "always," "everlasting," and "always coexisting with the Father." "For in the beginning was the Word and the Word was with God and the Word was God" [John 1:1]. And in the Apocalypse he says, "The one who is and who was and who comes" [Rev. 1:8]. Who would take away the eternal from "who is" and "who was"? . . .

(14) After these things were shown, they [the Arians] behave even more impudently, saying, "If there was not once when he was not, but the Son is everlasting and coexists with the Father, you say no longer that he is the Father's Son but that he is the Father's brother." Foolish and obstinate persons! If we only said that he exists everlastingly, and is not the Son, their assumed caution would be somewhat plausible. But if when we say that he is eternal we confess that he is the Son from the Father, how is he who was begotten able to be called a brother of him who has begotten? If our faith is in the Father and Son, what sort of brother is there between them? How is the Word able to be called the brother of him whose Word he is? . . . The Father and Son were not begotten from some preexisted first cause so that they might be called brothers. The Father is the origin of the Son and begat him, and the Father is Father and did not become anyone's son. The Son is Son and not a brother. If he is called the everlasting offspring of

the Father, he is called so correctly.... Since he is the peculiar Son of God who always is, he exists everlastingly. It is distinctive of men to reproduce in time because of the imperfection of their nature. God's offspring is everlasting because of the continual perfection of his nature. Therefore if he is not a Son but a work that came into existence from nothing, let them prove it! Then as they are being imaginative about a work, let them call out, "There was once when he was not." Originated things, not always existing, come into existence. But if he is Son — for the Father declares this and the Scriptures shout it, and "Son" is nothing other than that begotten from the Father, and that which is begotten from the Father is his Word and Wisdom and reflection — then what is it necessary to say about those who state that "there was once when the Son was not," except that they are robbers who deprive God of his Word and they openly cry out against him that he was once without his peculiar Word and Wisdom, and the light "was once" without any gleam, and the fountain was barren and dry? Pretending to fear the term "time," because there are those who reproach them, they would say that he is "before time," but nevertheless they grant certain intervals, in which they imagine that he was not. This is nothing less than to act with extreme profanity, to declare the times and charge God with a lack of reason.

(17)... If the Word is not everlastingly with the Father, the Triad is not everlasting, but a monad was first, and later by addition it became a Triad, and according to them [Arians], as time went on, the knowledge of the teaching about God increased and was solidified. If the Son is not the peculiar offspring of the Father's substance but came into existence from nothing, the Triad is composed from nothing, and once there was not a Triad but a monad, and a Triad sometimes defective, sometimes completely defective, before the Son came into existence, but complete when he came into existence. Thus, thereafter, a thing originated is counted with the creator, and that which once was not is worshiped and glorified with him who always is. Of greater concern, the Triad is discovered to be unlike itself, composed of strange and foreign natures and substances. But this is nothing other than to say that the composition of the Triad is originated. Therefore, what sort of worship of God is this which is not even like itself but is completed by the addition of time — sometimes it is not thus, sometimes it is? Probably it will again receive an addition, and this process could be without limit, since once, and at the beginning, its composition was characterized by additions. Thus it is possible that it will decrease. Obviously, things added can be taken away....

(19) If God exists and is called the fountain of wisdom and life — as by Jeremiah [Jer. 2:13; 17:13]... and in Baruch [Bar. 3:12]... it would follow that life and wisdom are not foreign to the substance of the fountain but peculiar to it, and that they were not once nonexistent but always were. The Son is these things, who says, "I am the life" [John 14:6] and "I Wisdom have encamped with prudence" [Prov. 8:12]. Therefore, is not the individual impious who says, "There was once when the Son was not"? For this is the same thing as saying, "There was once when the fountain was dry, without life and wisdom." ... And although God is called, and is, a fountain of wisdom, these ones dare to slander him as destitute without his own wisdom. And if the fountain is everlasting, wisdom must be everlasting, for in it all things came into existence, as David sings in the Psalter, "In Wisdom you made all things" [Ps. 104:24]. Solomon says, "God

by Wisdom founded the earth, and he prepared the heavens in thoughtfulness" [Prov. 3:19]. And this Wisdom is the Word, and "through him" as John says, "all things came into existence" [John 1:3]. This Word is Christ, "for there is one God the Father, from whom are all things; we are for him, and one Lord Jesus Christ, through whom are all things, and we are through him" [1 Cor. 8:6]. If all things are through him, he himself should not be counted with the all things. He who dares to say that he, through whom are all things, is one of all the things will have the same opinion about God, from whom are all things. If anyone flees from this as absurd and distinguishes God as different from all things, it would follow that even the only-begotten Son, since he is peculiar to the Father's substance, is different from all things.

(20) When was God without that which is peculiar to him? Or how is anyone able to conclude about something peculiar that it is strange and foreign? The other things such as are originated have no resemblance according to substance with their maker. They are external to him, having come into existence by his grace and will, by his Word, so that they have the potential of ceasing to be, if their maker would wish it, for this is the nature of originated things. Concerning that which is peculiar to the Father's substance (this has already been confessed to be the Son), is it not audacious and impious to say "from nothing" and that "he was not before he was begotten" but that he came into existence subsequently and is able not to be at some time? But let the thoughtful person note how the perfection and fullness of the Father's substance is deprived. Anyone would see more clearly the heresy's absurdity if he would consider that the Son is the "image" and "reflection of the Father," and "characteristic mark" and "truth." If when there is light, there is its image, its reflection; and when there exists a *hypostasis,* there is a complete characteristic mark of it; and when the Father exists, there is truth (the Son). Let them who measure the image and form of the deity by time ascertain how great a pit of impiety they are falling into. If the Son was not before he was begotten, truth was not always in God. But it is not right to say this. Since the Father exists, there is always in him truth, which is the Son who says, "I am the truth" [John 14:6]....

(21) Come, then. Let us look at the characteristics of the Father, that we may decide if the image is his. The Father is everlasting, immortal, powerful, Light, King, almighty God, Lord, Creator, and Maker. These characteristics are necessarily in the image, so that truly "he who has seen the Son saw the Father" [John 14:9]. And if the Son is not thus — but as the Arians think, originated and not the everlasting Son — this is not a true image of the Father, unless afterward ceasing to blush they would say that to call the Son an image is to denote not a similar substance but only his name. But, O enemies of Christ, this is not an image or a characteristic mark, for what sort of resemblance is there between things which are from nothing and the one who rendered the things which are from nothing into being? ... The Arians, wishing him to be of such a kind, designed for themselves conclusions such as "If the Son is the Father's offspring and image and is like the Father in all things, then just as he is begotten, the Son necessarily ought to beget, and he becomes father of a son" ... Inventors of evils, truly enemies of God, in order that they do not confess the Son as the image of the Father think corporeal and earthly things about the Father himself, accusing him of segments,

emanations, and influxes. Therefore, if God is as a man let him become a parent as a man, so that the Son should become a father of another, and thus in succession one from another they should come into existence, so that the succession, in their opinion, might increase into a multitude of gods. But if God is not as man (for he is not), it is not necessary to attribute to him the characteristics of man....

(26)... You [Arians] said that he prepared for himself as an instrument the Son out of nothing, in order that through him he might make all things. Therefore, what is better — that which needs or that which fills a need? Or do both supply those things which are lacking in the other? With such statements you show the weakness of the preparer, if he alone did not have the power to fashion all things but externally contrives for himself an instrument, just as a carpenter or shipbuilder who is unable to produce anything without an ax and saw. What is more impious than this? Why is it necessary to spend time on things so fearful, when what was said before is sufficient to show that their opinions are only an apparition?

(29)... A work is external to the one who makes it, as has been said, but the Son is the peculiar offspring of the substance. Thus it is not necessary that a work always exist, for when the fashioner wishes, he works; the offspring is not subject to a wish but is a peculiar nature of substance. A person might be a maker, and may be so called, even if the works do not yet exist, but he would not be called father, nor would he be a father, if a son does not exist.... Although he was able to send his Word from the beginning in the time of Adam, Noah, or Moses, he did not send him until the consummation of the ages — he saw that this was an advantage to every creature — and thus he made originated things, when he wished and when it was advantageous for them. But the Son, being not a work but peculiar to the Father's substance, always is. Since the Father always is, it is necessary that what is peculiar to his substance always is, and this is his Word and Wisdom. The fact that creatures are not yet in existence does not detract from the maker, for he has the power to fashion them when he wishes. But if the offspring would not always be with the Father, this is a depreciation of the perfection of his substance. Wherefore the works were fashioned through his Word when he wished, but the Son is always the peculiar offspring of the Father's substance....

(64) [The First Book ends with a discussion of what it means to say that God or the Word "becomes."]... That whatever, and how often, would be said such expressions as "he has become" and "become," these should preserve the same meaning, so that the statements "having become better than the angels" and "he has become" should not lead to the conclusion there was some beginning of the becoming of the Word, or to the fantasy that he is originated, but Paul's expression should be understood in regard to his ministry and economy, when he became man. When "the Word became flesh and dwelled among us" [John 1:14], he came "that he might minister and might give salvation to all" [Matt. 20:28]; then he became deliverance for us and he became life and propitiation. Then his economy on our behalf "became better than the angels," and he became a way and resurrection. And just as "Be to me a God, a protector" does not signify the beginning of the substance of God himself but, as has been said, the love of humankind, thus the expressions "Having become better than the angels," "He has become," and "So much more has Jesus become a better surety" do signify

not that the substance of the Word is originated (Heaven forbid!) but the kindness which happened to us from his incarnation, although heretics might be ungrateful and contentious in regard to their impiety.

Gregory of Nyssa (ca. 330–94)

"On 'Not Three Gods': To Ablabius" (ca. 390)*

In truth, the question you propound to us is no small one, nor such that but small harm will follow if it meets with insufficient treatment. For by the force of the question, we are at first sight compelled to accept one or other of two erroneous opinions, and either to say "there are three Gods," which is unlawful, or not to acknowledge the Godhead of the Son and the Holy Spirit, which is impious and absurd.

The argument which you state is something like this: Peter, James, and John, being in one human nature, are called three men: and there is no absurdity in describing those who are united in nature, if they are more than one, by the plural number of the name derived from their nature. If, then, in the above case, custom admits this, and no one forbids us to speak of those who are two as two, or those who are more than two as three, how is it that in the case of our statements of the mysteries of the Faith, though confessing the Three Persons, and acknowledging no difference of nature between them, we are in some sense at variance with our confession, when we say that the Godhead of the Father and of the Son and of the Holy Ghost is one, and yet forbid men to say "there are three Gods"? The question is, as I said, very difficult to deal with: yet, if we should be able to find anything that may give support to the uncertainty of our mind, so that it may no longer totter and waver in this monstrous dilemma, it would be well: on the other hand, even if our reasoning be found unequal to the problem, we must keep forever, firm and unmoved, the tradition which we received by succession from the fathers, and seek from the Lord the reason which is the advocate of our faith. . . .

We say, then, to begin with, that the practice of calling those who are not divided in nature by the very name of their common nature in the plural, and saying they are "many men," is a customary abuse of language, and that it would be much the same thing to say they are "many human natures." And the truth of this we may see from the following instance. When we address anyone, we do not call him by the name of his nature, in order that no confusion may result from the community of the name, as would happen if every one of those who hear it were to think that he himself was the person addressed, because the call is made not by the proper appellation but by the common name of their nature: but we separate him from the multitude by using that name which belongs to him as his own; — that, I mean, which signifies the particular subject. Thus there are many who have shared in the nature — many disciples, say, or apostles, or martyrs — but the man in them all is one; since, as has been said, the term "man" does not belong to the nature of the individual as such, but to that which is common. For

*From A Select Library of Nicene and Post-Nicene Fathers of the Christian Church, 2d series, vol. 5: Gregory of Nyssa (Grand Rapids: Eerdmans, 1979), 331–36.

Luke is a man, or Stephen is a man; but it does not follow that if anyone is a man he is therefore Luke or Stephen: but the idea of the persons admits of that separation which is made by the peculiar attributes considered in each severally, and when they are combined is presented to us by means of number; yet their nature is one, at union in itself, and an absolutely indivisible unit, not capable of increase by addition or of diminution by subtraction, but in its essence being and continually remaining one, inseparable even though it appear in plurality, continuous, complete, and not divided with the individuals who participate in it. And as we speak of a people, or a mob, or an army, or an assembly in the singular in every case, while each of these is conceived as being in plurality, so according to the more accurate expression, "man" would be said to be one, even though those who are exhibited to us in the same nature make up a plurality. Thus it would be much better to correct our erroneous habit, so as no longer to extend to a plurality the name of the nature, than by our bondage to habit to transfer to our statements concerning God the error which exists in the above case. But since the correction of the habit is impracticable (for how could you persuade anyone not to speak of those who are exhibited in the same nature as "many men"? — indeed, in every case habit is a thing hard to change), we are not so far wrong in not going contrary to the prevailing habit in the case of the lower nature, since no harm results from the mistaken use of the name: but in the case of the statement concerning the Divine nature the various use of terms is no longer so free from danger: for that which is of small account is in these subjects no longer a small matter. Therefore we must confess one God, according to the testimony of Scripture, "Hear, O Israel, the Lord thy God is one Lord," even though the name of Godhead extends through the Holy Trinity. This I say according to the account we have given in the case of human nature, in which we have learnt that it is improper to extend the name of the nature by the mark of plurality....

As we have to a certain extent shown by our statement that the word "Godhead" is not significant of nature but of operation, perhaps one might reasonably allege as a cause why, in the case of men, those who share with one another in the same pursuits are enumerated and spoken of in the plural, while on the other hand the Deity is spoken of in the singular as one God and one Godhead, even though the Three Persons are not separated from the significance expressed by the term "Godhead" — one might allege, I say, the fact that men, even if several are engaged in the same form of action, work separately each by himself at the task he has undertaken, having no participation in his individual action with others who are engaged in the same occupation.... But in the case of the Divine nature we do not similarly learn that the Father does anything by Himself in which the Son does not work conjointly, or again that the Son has any special operation apart from the Holy Spirit; but every operation which extends from God to the Creation, and is named according to our variable conceptions of it, has its origin from the Father, and proceeds through the Son, and is perfected in the Holy Spirit. For this reason the name derived from the operation is not divided with regard to the number of those who fulfil it, because the action of each concerning anything is not separate and peculiar, but whatever comes to pass, in reference either to the acts of His providence for us, or to the government and constitution of the universe, comes to pass by the action of the Three, yet what does come to pass is not three things....

But if it pleases our adversaries to say that the significance of the term [i.e., Godhead] is not operation, but nature, we shall fall back upon our original argument, that custom applies the name of a nature to denote multitude erroneously: since according to true reasoning neither diminution nor increase attaches to any nature, when it is contemplated in a larger or smaller number.... For we say that gold, even though it be cut into many figures, is one, and is so spoken of, but we speak of many coins or many staters, without finding any multiplication of the nature of gold by the number of staters; and for this reason we speak of gold, when it is contemplated in greater bulk, either in plate or in coin, as "much," but we do not speak of it as "many golds" on account of the multitude of the material — except when one says there are "many gold pieces" (Darics, for instance, or staters), in which case it is not the material, but the pieces of money to which the significance of number applies: indeed, properly, we should not call them "gold" but "golden."

As, then, the golden staters are many, but the gold is one, so too those who are exhibited to us severally in the nature of man, as Peter, James, and John, are many, yet the man in them is one. And although Scripture extends the word according to the plural significance, where it says "men swear by the greater" [Heb. 6:16], and "sons of men," and in other phrases of the like sort, we must recognize that in using the custom of the prevailing form of speech, it does not lay down a law as to the propriety of using the words in one way or another.... For this reason Scripture admits the naming of "men" in the plural, because no one is by such a figure of speech led astray in his conceptions to imagine a multitude of humanities, or supposes that many human natures are indicated by the fact that the name expressive of that nature is used in the plural. But the word "God" it employs studiously in the singular form only, guarding against introducing the idea of different natures in the Divine essence by the plural signification of "Gods." This is the cause why it says, "the Lord our God is one Lord" [Deut. 6:4], and also proclaims the Only-begotten God by the name of Godhead, without dividing the Unity into a dual signification, so as to call the Father and the Son two Gods, although each is proclaimed by the holy writers as God. The Father is God: the Son is God: and yet by the same proclamation God is One, because no difference either of nature or of operation is contemplated in the Godhead....

If, however, anyone cavils at our argument, on the ground that by not admitting the difference of nature it leads to a mixture and confusion of the Persons, we shall make to such a charge this answer; — that while we confess the invariable character of the nature, we do not deny the difference in respect of cause, and that which is caused, by which alone we apprehend that one Person is distinguished from another; — by our belief, that is, that one is the Cause, and another is of the Cause; and again in that which is of the Cause we recognize another distinction. For one is directly from the first Cause, and another by that which is directly from the first Cause; so that the attribute of being Only-begotten abides without doubt in the Son, and the interposition of the Son, while it guards His attribute of being Only-begotten, does not shut out the Spirit from His relation by way of nature to the Father.

But in speaking of "cause," and "of the cause," we do not by these words denote nature (for no one would give the same definition of "cause" and of "nature"), but we indicate the difference in manner of existence. For when we say that one is "caused," and that the other is "without cause," we do not divide the nature by the word "cause," but only indicate the fact that the Son does not exist without generation, nor the Father by generation: but we must needs in the first place believe that something exists, and then scrutinize the manner of existence of the object of our belief: thus the question of existence is one, and that of the mode of existence is another. To say that anything exists without generation sets forth the mode of its existence, but what exists is not indicated by this phrase. If one were to ask a husbandman about a tree, whether it were planted or had grown of itself, and he were to answer either that the tree had not been planted or that it was the result of planting, would he by that answer declare the nature of the tree? Surely not; but while saying how it exists he would leave the question of its nature obscure and unexplained. So, in the other case, when we learn that He is unbegotten, we are taught in what mode He exists, and how it is fit that, we should conceive Him as existing, but *what* He is we do not hear in that phrase. When, therefore, we acknowledge such a distinction in the case of the Holy Trinity, as to believe that one Person is the Cause, and another is of the Cause, we can no longer be accused of confounding the definition of the Persons by the community of nature.

Thus, since on the one hand the idea of cause differentiates the Persons of the Holy Trinity, declaring that one exists without a Cause, and another is of the Cause; and since on the one hand the Divine nature is apprehended by every conception as unchangeable and undivided, for these reasons we properly declare the Godhead to be one, and God to be one, and employ in the singular all other names which express Divine attributes.

Augustine (354–430)

The Trinity (399–419), Book 15, Sections 10–12, 43, 49–51*

10. We may recall that it was in the eighth Book that the manifestation of the Trinity to our understanding began. There we essayed to lift up, so far as might be, the effort of our mind to the understanding of that most excellent and changeless being which is other than our mind. In contemplation we were aware of it as not far from us and yet above us — not spatially but by its own most reverend and wonderful excellence, so that we found it present in us in virtue of its own pervading light. But so far we had no glimpse of the Trinity, because we could not in that dazzling brightness direct our mind's eye steadily to look for it [Book VIII, 3 (ii)]. All that we could with some clearness distinguish was that it was no measurable mass in which the quantity of two or three must be believed greater than that of the two. Only when we came to consider charity, which in Holy Scripture is called God, the light began to break upon a Trinity, consisting

*From *Augustine: Later Works,* ed. John Burnaby, Library of Christian Classics. Used by permission of Westminster John Knox Press. Pp. 136–38, 170–71, 177–79.

in lover, the beloved, and love. But from that ineffable light our gaze flinched away: we had to confess that our mind in its weakness was not yet strong enough to be conformed to it. And therefore, in order to recruit our laboring efforts, we paused in the pursuit of our undertaking and turned back to the more familiar consideration of that same mind of ours, in which man has been made after the image of God; and from the ninth to the fourteenth Book we occupied ourselves with our own creaturely nature, in order that we might be able to apprehend and perceive the invisible things of God through the things that are made.

And now the time has come, when after this exercise of our understanding in a lower sphere for so long as need required (and maybe for longer), we would lift ourselves up to perceive the supreme Trinity which is God. Yet our strength fails us. Many trinities we can see most surely. . . . There are trinities when things arising in the mind apart from the bodily senses are distinguished by clear reasoning and comprehended in knowledge, such as our faith, and those virtues which are ways of living. There are trinities when the mind itself, by which we know all that we truthfully claim to know, is known to itself or thinks of itself, or when it perceives an eternal and unchanging object other than itself. In all these processes we see trinities with assurance, since they occur or exist in us as we remember, regard, and will. But can we perceive therein by an act of understanding a Speaker and his Word, the Father and the Son, and proceeding thence the Charity common to both which is the Holy Spirit? It may be urged that while trinities belonging to the sphere of sense or mind are for us objects of sight rather than belief, the fact that God is Trinity must be believed rather than seen. If that be so, it must follow, either that the invisible things of him are nowhere apprehended and perceived by us through the things that are made; or, that in none of them which we perceive can we perceive the Trinity — that there is something in that sphere which we may perceive, but something also which we are obliged to believe though unperceived. Yet the eighth Book showed that we do perceive a changeless good, other than ourselves; and the same was indicated in the fourteenth Book when we spoke of the wisdom which comes to man from God. Why then can we not recognize there the Trinity? It is impossible to maintain that this wisdom which is called God neither understands nor loves itself; and it is patent that where there is no knowledge there cannot possibly be wisdom. That the wisdom which is God knows or loves other things but neither knows nor loves itself, cannot be asserted or believed without foolishness and impiety; and if so, here surely is Trinity: wisdom, its knowledge of itself, and its love of itself. That was how we discovered a trinity in man: the mind, the knowledge whereby it knows itself, and the love whereby it loves itself.

11 (vii). But these three are *in* man, without, by themselves, constituting man; for if we follow the definition of the ancients, man is a rational and mortal animal. The three things named are then man's highest part, but not by themselves man. Moreover, the one person which is the individual man possesses those three in his mind. Even if we adopt a different definition of man, to the effect that he is a rational substance composed of soul and body, it remains indubitable that man possesses a soul which is not body and a body which is not soul. And then our triad is not equivalent to man but belongs to man or is in man. . . . But we cannot say that the Trinity is in God in this manner — a part of God but not itself God.

The individual man, who is called the image of God not in respect of all that belongs to his nature but in respect of his mind alone, is a personal unity, having the image of the Trinity in his mind. But the Trinity of whom he is image is as a whole nothing but God, is as a whole nothing but Trinity. Nothing belongs to God's nature that does not belong to this Trinity. The three Persons are of one essence, not like the individual man one person.

12. In another respect also there is a wide difference to be noted. In man, whether we speak of mind, its knowledge and its love, or of memory, understanding, and will, nothing in the mind is remembered but through memory, or understood but through understanding, or loved but through will. In the divine Trinity, reverence forbids us to say that the Father understands neither himself nor his Son nor the Holy Spirit, save through the Son, nor loves save through the Holy Spirit; or that through himself he does no more than remember either himself or the Son or the Holy Spirit. . . .

43 (xxiii). Thus there is a difference between the reality of the Trinity and its image in another subject, the image in virtue of which the mind embracing our three elements is itself called an image; just as the word "image" is applied both to the panel and to the painting on it, the panel being named an image because of the picture it supports. The absolute transcendence of the supreme Trinity defies comparison. A trinity of men cannot be called one man; but such is the inseparable unity of the divine Trinity, that in it both for our naming and in reality there is one God and the Trinity is not *in* one God but is itself one God. Again, the image, the man in whom our triad is contained, is a single person; the Trinity is three Persons, Father in relation to Son, Son in relation to Father, Spirit in relation to Father and Son. In our image of the Trinity, the human memory, especially as distinguished from that of beasts by containing ideas not conveyed to it through the bodily senses, offers in its own measure a likeness, however inadequate, of the Father. The human understanding which receives form therefrom in the effort of thought, when the thing known is spoken as an inward word belonging to no language, offers in all its disparity a certain likeness of the Son. The human love, which proceeds from knowledge and is link between memory and understanding, as being common to parent and offspring — so that it cannot be identified with either — offers in that image a likeness, even if an inadequate likeness, of the Holy Spirit. But whereas in the image the three do not compose one man but belong to him, in the supreme Trinity whose image it is the three do not "belong" to one God but *are* one God, and the Persons are not one but three. And what is marvelously inexpressible, or inexpressibly marvelous, though the image of the Trinity is one person and the divine Trinity itself is three, yet the Trinity of three Persons is more inseparable than the imaged trinity of one. For the divine Trinity by the nature of its divinity — or Godhead if the term be preferred — is what it is, changelessly and always equal to itself. At no time was it not, or was different: at no time will it not be or be different. But the three elements contained in the inferior image, though not spatially separate (not being corporeal), yet in this present life are quantitatively variable. The fact that material mass is wanting does not prevent us seeing in one man more memory than understanding, in another the reverse; while in a third these two may be exceeded by love, whether they are equal to one another or not. Thus we may find a superiority of any one

severally to the other two, of two together to any one severally, of any several one to any other, of the greater to the less. Even when they shall be made whole from all infirmity and equal to one another, the being that owes its constancy to grace will not attain equality to the being which is essentially changeless. There can be no equality between creature and Creator; and the making whole from all infirmity will itself be a change....

49. Unbelievers indeed may lack the power to contemplate God's image in them, and to see the reality of the three elements in their own mind, which are three not as three persons but as all pertaining to the one person of a man. Then they had best believe what the holy Books contain concerning the supreme Trinity that is God, instead of demanding for themselves a perfectly clear and rational account such as weak and sluggish human minds can take in. By all means, once they have an unshakable belief in the truth of Holy Scripture's witness, let them go on by prayer and enquiry and right living to the pursuit of understanding — which means the seeing with the mind (so far as seeing is possible) of what is firmly held by faith. Who should forbid them? Who indeed would not encourage them to do so? But if they suppose that the reality must be denied because their minds are too blind to perceive it, then the blind from birth may with equal right deny the existence of the sun. The light shineth in the darkness: if the darkness comprehend it not [John 1:5], let those who are darkness first become enlightened by the gift of God into believing, and so begin in comparison with the unbelieving world to be light. Upon that foundation they may be built up to see what they believe, and in due course gain the power of sight.... As for such discernment as is possible for the understanding of the supreme, ineffable, immaterial and changeless being of God: there is no field wherein the human mind can better train its insight, under the guidance of the rule of faith, than in that possession of human nature which is better than anything in the beasts, and better than any other part of the human soul, namely, the mind itself. To it has been granted a certain vision of things invisible; it is the authority, raised upon the seat of honor in its inner chamber, for whose judgment the bodily senses deliver all their messages; above it there is none to whose ruling it is subject, save God.

50. In all this long discourse, I dare not claim to have said anything worthy of the unspeakable greatness of the supreme Trinity.... Yet thou [i.e., my soul] hast seen many truths, not with the eyes that see the hues of bodily things, but with those for which the Psalmist made his prayer: "Let mine eyes look upon equity" [Ps. 17:2]. Thou has seen many truths indeed, and not confused them with that Light that enabled thee to see them. Lift thine eyes to the Light itself and fix them upon it, if thou canst. Then only shalt thou see the difference of the begetting of God's Word from the procession of God's Gift: wherefore the only-begotten Son has said that the Holy Spirit proceeds from the Father, and is not begotten of him so as to be his brother. Being a certain consubstantial communion between Father and Son, the Spirit is called the Spirit of both, never the son of Both. But to perceive this plainly and clearly, thou are not able to keep thine eye fixed firmly: I know thou art not able. I speak truth to myself, I know what exceeds my power. Yet the light itself displays to thee those three elements in thyself, wherein thou mayest recognize the image of the supreme Trinity, whom thou hast not yet the strength to contemplate with unwavering eyes. The light

itself shows thee that a true word is in thee, when it is begotten of thy knowledge, that is, when we say what we know; though it be with no people's tongue that we utter or think a sound with meaning, but our thought receives a form from the object of our knowledge. In the view of the thinker arises an image nearly alike to that knowledge which memory contained, while the will or love unites the two to one another, as parent and offspring. That will proceeds from knowledge, for no one wills a thing of whose being or nature he is altogether ignorant; yet it is not an image of knowledge. And thus there is a suggestion in this mental reality of the difference between begetting and proceeding, inasmuch as to view in thought is not the same as to pursue or to enjoy with the will. So much is to be perceived and discerned by him who is able. And thou too hast been able to perceive it, although thou couldst not and canst not set forth in adequate expression that truth which through the mists of material similitudes, that never cease to invade men's thinking, thou didst hardly see. Yet the light which is not thyself shows thee also that the immaterial likenesses of material things are wholly other than the reality which our understanding contemplates when they are rejected. This and the like certainties are manifested by that light to thine inward eye. Is there any reasons why thou canst not behold the light itself with a gaze unwavering, but thine own infirmity? And what has made thee infirm but thine own iniquity? [cf. Book VIII, 3 (ii)]. Therefore there is none that can heal all thy sicknesses, but he that has mercy upon all thine iniquities. So were it better to bring this Book at last to an end, not with argument but with prayer.

51 (xxviii). O Lord our God, we believe in thee, Father, Son, and Holy Spirit. If thou wert not Trinity, the Truth would not have said: "Go ye, baptize all nations in the name of the Father and of the Son and of the Holy Spirit...."

Pseudo-Dionysius (ca. 500)

The Mystical Theology (ca. 500), Chapters 1, 3–5*

Chapter One: What Is the Divine Darkness?

> 1. Trinity!! Higher than any being,
>   any divinity, any goodness!
> Guide of Christians
>   in the wisdom of heaven!
> Lead us up beyond unknowing and light,
>   up to the farthest, highest peak
>   of mystic scripture,
> where the mysteries of God's Word
>   lie simple, absolute and unchangeable
>   in the brilliant darkness of a hidden silence.
> Amid the deepest shadow
>   they pour overwhelming light on what is most manifest.

---

*Reprinted from *Pseudo-Dionysius* by Colm Luibheid © 1987 by Colm Luibheid. Used by permission of Paulist Press. Pp. 135–41.

> Amid the wholly unsensed and unseen
>   they completely fill our sightless minds
>   with treasures beyond all beauty.

For this I pray; and, Timothy, my friend, my advice to you as you look for a sight of the mysterious things, is to leave behind you everything perceived and understood, everything perceptible and understandable, all that is not and all that is, and, with your understanding laid aside, to strive upward as much as you can toward union with him who is beyond all being and knowledge. By an undivided and absolute abandonment of yourself and everything, shedding all and freed from all, you will be uplifted to the ray of the divine shadow which is above everything that is.

2. But see to it that none of this comes to the hearing of the uninformed, that is to say, to those caught up with the things of the world, who imagine that there is nothing beyond instances of individual being and who think that by their own intellectual resources they can have a direct knowledge of him who has made the shadows his hiding place. And if initiation into the divine is beyond such people, what is to be said of those others, still more uninformed, who describe the transcendent Cause of all things in terms derived from the lowest orders of being, and who claim that it is in no way superior to the godless, multiformed shapes they themselves have made? What has actually to be said about the Cause of everything is this. Since it is the Cause of all beings, we should posit and ascribe to it all the affirmations we make in regard to beings, and, more appropriately, we should negate all these affirmations, since it surpasses all being. Now we should not conclude that the negations are simply the opposites of the affirmations, but rather that the cause of all is considerably prior to this, beyond privations, beyond every denial, beyond every assertion.

3. This, at least, is what was taught by the blessed Bartholomew. He says that the Word of God is vast and minuscule, that the Gospel is wide-ranging and yet restricted. To me it seems that in this he is extraordinarily shrewd, for he has grasped that the good cause of all is both eloquent and taciturn, indeed wordless. It has neither word nor act of understanding, since it is on a plane above all this, and it is made manifest only to those who travel through foul and fair, who pass beyond the summit of every holy ascent, who leave behind them every divine light, every voice, every word from heaven, and who plunge into the darkness where, as scripture proclaims, there dwells the One who is beyond all things. It is not for nothing that the blessed Moses is commanded to submit first to purification and then to depart from those who have not undergone this. When every purification is complete, he hears the many-voiced trumpets. He sees the many lights, pure and with rays streaming abundantly. Then, standing apart from the crowds and accompanied by chosen priests, he pushes ahead to the summit of the divine ascents. And yet he does not meet God himself, but contemplates, not him who is invisible, but rather where he dwells. This means, I presume, that the holiest and highest of the things perceived with the eye of the body or the mind are but the rationale which presupposes all that lies below the Transcendent One. Through them, however, his unimaginable presence is shown, walking the heights of those holy places to which the mind at least can rise. But then he [Moses] breaks free

of them, away from what sees and is seen, and he plunges into the truly mysterious darkness of unknowing. Here, renouncing all that the mind may conceive, wrapped entirely in the intangible and the invisible, he belongs completely to him who is beyond everything. Here, being neither oneself nor someone else, one is supremely united by a completely unknowing inactivity of all knowledge, and knows beyond the mind by knowing nothing....

Chapter Three: What Are the Affirmative Theologies and What Are the Negative?

In my *Theological Representations*,[1] I have praised the notions which are most appropriate to affirmative theology. I have shown the sense in which the divine and good nature is said to be one and then triune, how Fatherhood and Sonship are predicated of it, the meaning of the theology of the Spirit.... In *The Divine Names* I have shown the sense in which God is described as good, existent, life, wisdom, power, and whatever other things pertain to the conceptual names for God. In my *Symbolic Theology*, I have discussed analogies of God drawn from what we perceive.... I have spoken of his anger, grief, and rage, of how he is said to be drunk and hungover, of his oaths and curses, of his sleeping and waking, and indeed of all those images we have of him, images shaped by the workings of the symbolic representations of God. And I feel sure that you have noticed how these latter come much more abundantly than what went before, since *The Theological Representations* and a discussion of the names appropriate to God are inevitably briefer than what can be said in *The Symbolic Theology*. The fact is that the more we take flight upward, the more our words are confined to the ideas we are capable of forming; so that now as we plunge into that darkness which is beyond intellect, we shall find ourselves not simply running short of words but actually speechless and unknowing. In the earlier books my argument traveled downward from the most exalted to the humblest categories, taking in on this downward path an ever-increasing number of ideas which multiplied with every stage of the descent. But my argument now rises from what is below up to the transcendent, and the more it climbs, the more language falters, and when it has passed up and beyond the ascent, it will turn silent completely, since it will finally be at one with him who is indescribable.

Now you may wonder why it is that, after starting out from the highest category when our method involved assertions, we begin now from the lowest category when it involves a denial. The reason is this. When we assert what is beyond every assertion, we must then proceed from what is most akin to it, and as we do so we make the affirmation on which everything else depends. But when we deny that which is beyond every denial, we have to start by denying those qualities which differ most from the goal we hope to attain. Is it not closer to reality to say that God is life and goodness rather than that he is air or stone? Is it not more accurate to deny that drunkenness and rage can be attributed to him than to deny that we can apply to him the terms of speech and thought?

---

1. A lost or fictitious treatise.

Chapter Four: That the Supreme Cause of Every Perceptible Thing Is Not Itself Perceptible...

Chapter Five: That the Supreme Cause of Every Conceptual Thing Is Not Itself Conceptual

Again, as we climb higher we say this. It is not soul or mind, nor does it possess imagination, conviction, speech, or understanding. Nor is it speech per se, understanding per se. It cannot be spoken of and it cannot be grasped by understanding. It is not number or order, greatness or smallness, equality or inequality, similarity or dissimilarity. It is not immovable, moving, or at rest. It has no power, it is not power, nor is it light. It does not live nor is it life. It is not a substance, nor is it eternity or time. It cannot be grasped by the understanding since it is neither knowledge nor truth. It is not kingship. It is not wisdom. It is neither one nor oneness, divinity nor goodness. Nor is it a spirit, in the sense in which we understand that term. It is not sonship or fatherhood and it is nothing known to us or to any other being. It falls neither within the predicate of nonbeing nor of being. Existing beings do not know it as it actually is and it does not know them as they are. There is no speaking of it, nor name nor knowledge of it. Darkness and light, error and truth — it is none of these. It is beyond assertion and denial. We make assertions and denials of what is next to it, but never of it, for it is both beyond every assertion, being the perfect and unique cause of all things, and, by virtue of its preeminently simple and absolute nature, free of every limitation, beyond every limitation; it is also beyond every denial.

– 2 –

The Medieval and Reformation Period

INTRODUCTION

The period from roughly 600 to 1600 was a time of major social and political upheaval. Rival "barbarian" groups fought for control of the former Roman Empire in the West from the end of the fifth century to the eighth century. Later in the period the eastern Roman Empire was first threatened by Muslim expansion and then fell to Muslim invaders (1453). The rise of nation states, beginning with France and England in the thirteenth century, led to the eclipse of papal political power and the eventual collapse of "Christendom." The creation of universities, the Renaissance, the invention of the printing press, the Protestant Reformation, and Copernican theory all left discernible and significant marks on western civilization.

Christian reflection upon the doctrine of God in this period built upon the classical trinitarian foundation established in the previous period at the Councils of Nicea I and Constantinople I. Distinctions between the eastern and the western approaches to the doctrine, however, remained evident. Whereas eastern reflections about the trinity continued to start from the distinction of persons in the unity of the Godhead, western reflections continued to begin with the unity of the Godhead in the distinction of persons. Or viewed from a different perspective, the East located the source of the trinity's unity in the person of the Father, while the West located it in the divine essence. With the trinitarian nature of God secure, attention in this period could be devoted to other aspects of the doctrine of God or to new questions occasioned by changing contexts. With the introduction of "dialectic" into cathedral schools and universities, for example, critical questions arose about the existence of God and the rational "necessity" of divine actions such as the incarnation. In the context of monasteries and convents, Christian writers developed more personal reflections about God. Oftentimes these reflections arose out of profound spiritual or mystical experiences. With the Protestant Reformation, the scholastic ways of thinking and talking about God, which had developed in the universities, were challenged. Biblical images and metaphors replaced more philosophical interpretations of God. Straightforward biblical exegesis sought to displace the subtle rational distinctions of theological treatises.

Epistemological and linguistic issues provide important threads with which the doctrine of God is woven in this period. The epistemological issue has to do with how we know God. Here different avenues were taken. Some said we know God through faith and reason; others appealed primarily to personal experience; still others appealed to the testimony of the sacred scriptures and to nothing else. And

49

what we can know about God, regardless of the approach, was described differently. The linguistic issue has to do with what we can say about God. Once again different approaches and different emphases are evident in this period. Some, in the tradition of Pseudo-Dionysius, emphasized the apophatic tradition (i.e, what we must say God is not), while others emphasized the cataphatic tradition (i.e., what we can say about God based upon observations of the created order). Others insisted that our talk about God must always be analogical. That is, the meaning of words drawn from our experience, when applied to God, is both similar to and different from the meaning of the words when applied to creatures. Still others eschewed the university-based distinctions in the attribution of terms and drew primarily on the language of the Bible. And all of these theological discussions developed within specific social and political situations. Let us begin then with the transition from the so-called patristic age to the medieval age.

With the collapse of the Roman Empire in the West at the end of the fifth century, western Europe was plunged into a chaotic period of invasion and warfare. Waves of so-called Vandals, Huns, and Franks were succeeded by migrations of Goths (Visigoths to the western reaches of the former empire; Ostrogoths in the eastern portion) and Lombards. With the relocation of the emperor to the eastern capital of Constantinople, the bishop of Rome could assume the dual role of central religious and political leader in the West. Leo the Great in the fifth century and Gregory the Great in the late sixth century assumed such a position. Under the leadership of popes such as these, and the leadership of local bishops, the church came to provide many of the social and cultural functions once taken care of by the empire. Although this period (the end of the fifth century to the beginning of the eleventh century) has often been referred to as the Dark Age, Christian monks exercised energy and care so that the intellectual light of Europe was not wholly extinguished. Some monks made it part of their work to copy and to illustrate the learned texts of the ancient classical world as well as to copy and to illustrate scriptural and theological texts.

Despite several tumultuous migrations (sometimes called "barbarian" invasions) into the territory, there were periods of stability in western and central Europe from the fifth to the eleventh centuries. Such periods occurred commonly when one ethnic group was able to cement its control over a significant portion of territory under the leadership of strong kings. One such period was the Carolingian period, so named because of the line of rulers named Charles (Carolus). This empire came to prominence in the eighth century, due to the military and political skills of Pepin III and especially Charles the Great (Charlemagne), who ruled the Franks from 768 to 814.

The Carolingian kings or emperors changed the form of western politics in the eighth and ninth centuries. Since the collapse of the Roman Empire, western rulers tended to be tribal war-leaders whose main aim was to gain glory for themselves and their followers. Germanic kings by the late eighth century, however, had come to think of themselves as much more.[1] The most significant force in this transformation was Charlemagne, who thought of himself as a "new David."

---

1. Henry Mayr-Harting, "The West: The Age of Conversion (700–1050)" in *The Oxford History of Christianity*, ed. John McManners (New York: Oxford University Press, 1993), 110–11.

That is, Charlemagne conceived of himself as both the military-political leader and the religious leader of his tribe. With the Carolingians, the rite of anointing kings became important. The Carolingian Empire, with its seat in Aachen (Aix-la-Chapelle), extended over much of modern-day France, Germany, Holland, and western Austria. The culmination of Charlemagne's power was symbolized in his coronation as "Emperor of the Romans" by Pope Leo III on Christmas in the year 800.[2]

Under the leadership of Charlemagne, there was a rebirth of learning and art in western Europe. Regarding himself as both a protector and a leader of the church, Charlemagne raised the educational level of the clergy, standardized the liturgy in his territories, and intervened in doctrinal disputes. With regard to the doctrine of God, Charlemagne insisted that the creed declare that the Holy Spirit proceeds from the Father and the Son.[3] Western precedent for this emendation of the Niceno-Constantinopolitan Creed could be found already at the beginning of the fifth century. The Latin church saw this affirmation of the role of the Son in the "procession" of the Spirit as yet another way to combat the subordinationism and Arianism that still lingered, for example in Spain, after the councils of the fourth century.[4] Alcuin, who became Charlemagne's adviser in religious and educational matters, established libraries in the capital and in Tours. Under Charlemagne's successors, clergy often advised the emperors how to rule. Insofar as bishops felt themselves responsible for the souls of kings, they gradually began to assert more influence in political and social matters. The stage was thus set for later conflict between bishops, including the pope (bishop of Rome), and kings or emperors. But in the eighth and ninth centuries, the Carolingians did not see the clergy as a challenge to their authority. After all, church and society were not seen as separate entities.

One of the greatest intellectuals of this time was the theologian John Scotus Erigena (ca. 810–77), who was head of the palace school at Paris under the emperor Charles the Bald, the grandson of Charlemagne. Erigena was one of the few westerners of his day who knew Greek. He put his linguistic skills to work in translating the works of Pseudo-Dionysius into Latin. This translation exercised considerable influence upon later theologians, including Thomas Aquinas. But Erigena was a creative thinker and not just a translator (see the essay on the medieval church in Part Two). His work illustrates in vivid fashion the tension between faith and reason. On the one hand, he asserts that the authority

---

2. Although the title "Holy Roman Empire" was not used until at least the twelfth century to designate the territory now controlled by the Franks, Charlemagne's title "Emperor of the Romans" shows that the Carolingian Franks regarded their empire as a continuation of the Roman Empire. The adjective "holy" indicates that the Carolingian emperors believed that they held the reins of authority by the will of God and that they regularly envisioned their rule to be theocratic.

3. This understanding of the procession of the Holy Spirit provoked controversy with the eastern church, which held that the Holy Spirit proceeds from the Father (through the Son). The controversy is called the "filioque" controversy because the Latin word that characterizes the western position means "and from the Son." Several centuries earlier, Augustine had declared that the Holy Spirit proceeds principally from the Father, but also from the Son. Concerning the issues at stake and the reasons for difference between western and eastern conceptions of the trinity, see Leonardo Boff, *Trinity and Society* (Maryknoll, N.Y.: Orbis Books, 1988), 200–207.

4. The first Council of Toledo in 400 declared that the Spirit proceeds from the Father and the Son. See Heinrich Denzinger, *Enchiridion Symbolorum, definitionum et declarationum de rebus fidei et morum* (1854), 188.

of scripture must be followed in all things (*Division of Nature*, 1:64).[5] On the other, he states that every authority which is not confirmed by reason seems to be weak, whereas reason does not need to be supported by any authority (*Division of Nature*, 1:69).[6] Like the scholastics who will come after him in subsequent centuries, Erigena may have found both statements compatible insofar as both faith and reason derive from the same source, divine wisdom. When seen from this perspective, Erigena can be seen as standing in a line of continuity between Augustine, who preceded him, and Anselm of Canterbury, who followed him. All of these Christian thinkers attempted to move from faith to understanding by means of reason.

With the collapse of the Carolingian Empire upon the death of Charles the Fat in 888, western European society once again experienced fragmentation under the force of new invasions. Normans or "Norsemen" (i.e., Danes, Swedes, and Norwegians) raided and pillaged the northern French coast. Saracens (Syrian-Arabian Muslims) made raids from the south, taking Sicily and southern Italy by the mid-ninth century. And Magyars (Hungarians) made incursions from the East. With trade routes blocked or subject to frequent attack by bandits, commerce declined. Local rulers, rather than emperors, became the locus of power. They used land to reward their friends. To capture new land or to retain the land already in their possession, they needed a cavalry. Thus the feudal system came to be. In the context of feudalism, bishops were often subsumed under the control of secular rulers, who had come to realize that the easiest way to retain control of their fiefs was to grant them to men who would have no legitimate sons.

Although this arrangement had obvious benefits for the secular lords, it created serious problems for the church. Those who were appointed to bishoprics in payment of a political debt tended to be young noble men, far more interested in warfare and hunting than in their pastoral duties. The arrangement also tempted secular rulers to keep episcopal sees vacant for long stretches of time, so that they could directly collect the revenue attached to bishoprics and episcopal fiefs. The customary payment of "relief," a payment made to a feudal lord for the privilege of succeeding to a feudal estate, appeared tantamount to simony when made by bishops. This entire complex of problems was epitomized in the investiture of bishops, the act of giving them the physical symbols of their authority (crosier and ring), by secular rulers.

Although there was friction in the eleventh and twelfth centuries between popes and kings or emperors because of the investiture controversy, it was also a time of vitality and growth. By this time virtually all of western Europe was Christian, except for Jews in ghettoes and Muslims in portions of Spain. There was a sense of cohesive Christian identity. If Christians in the fourth and fifth centuries had accepted many of the conventions of pagan society, now the situation was

---

5. John the Scot, *Periphyseon: On the Division of Nature*, trans. Myra L. Uhlfelder (Indianapolis: Bobbs-Merrill Co., 1976), 86: "Of course, the authority of sacred Scripture must be followed in all matters since truth resides in it as in its secret dwelling place."

6. John the Scot, *Periphyseon*, 91: "All authority not approved by true reason seems weak. Since true reason, however, holds an impregnable position as valid and unchangeable by its own powers, it does not have to be strengthened by the assent of any authority. True authority seems to me simply the truth discovered by the power of reason and entrusted to writing by the holy fathers for the edification of posterity."

different. The leaders of the Christian church consciously used their positions and influence to bring humanity under the law of Christ, whether through programs of evangelization, education, or holy war. In the eleventh and twelfth centuries, Europeans expressed an increasing sense of common identity, often summed up in the word "Christendom."[7]

At the same time, commerce increased and cities grew. Under these conditions, there arose a renewed interest in education. By the early twelfth century, a *studium generale* was in place in Bologna and in Paris. A *studium generale* connotes a place of studies whose facilities were open to all students. By the latter portion of the twelfth century, such "general" facilities for study came to include at least one of the three higher faculties, that is, theology, law, or medicine. With this development, one of the crucial factors contributing to the full flowering of medieval theology was in place, namely, the universities. The most important of the early universities in the field of theology was the University of Paris. In addition to the establishment of universities, the rediscovery of Aristotle (as well as Jewish and Arabic commentaries on Aristotle) and the creation of the mendicant orders of Franciscans and Dominicans promoted the development of medieval theology.

At the time that universities were developing, an evolution in the understanding of theology and theological method was also taking place. Among the individuals from the eleventh through the thirteenth centuries who contributed to this evolution, special mention must be made of several. First, we must consider the Italian Anselm, born in Aosta in 1033, who was prior and then abbot in the Benedictine monastery of Bec (in Normandy) before becoming archbishop of Canterbury (1093–1109). Anselm has been called "the highest achievement of . . . the medieval Augustinian use of dialectic, the summit of the early scholastic genius and the ripest fruit of the monastic schools."[8] Much of his significance resides in the way he used reason in the explication of faith. Temporarily bracketing arguments drawn from scripture and tradition, Anselm attempted to use arguments drawn solely from reason to demonstrate the truth of what people of faith believe. Although from our contemporary perspective, these arguments do not appear to be as free from Christian presuppositions as Anselm may have declared, his application of reason to questions of faith brought a new spirit to theological inquiry in the Middle Ages. Thus, says González, with Anselm "a new era began in the history of Christian thought."[9]

It is important, however, not to exaggerate Anselm's uniqueness. Anselm's *Proslogion*, an excerpt from which is included below, contains points of continuity with the work of other theologians. The *Proslogion* looks backward to Augustine in that Anselm understands theology as faith seeking understanding.

---

7. "Europeans expressed an increasing sense of common identity, which seems to have been forged particularly by the First Crusade. Its chroniclers use a terminology which, although it was not completely new, had been rare in the past; for the first time people were regularly describing themselves as 'westerners' or 'Christians' or as fellow members of *Christianitas*, a word which means both Christianity and Christendom and which came into common use at this time" (Colin Morris, "Christian Civilization (1050–1400)," in *The Oxford History of Christianity*, ed. John McManners [New York: Oxford University Press, 1993], 215).

8. David Knowles, *The Evolution of Medieval Thought* (New York: Vintage Books, 1962), 98.

9. Justo L. González, *A History of Christian Thought*, vol. 2: *From Augustine to the Eve of the Reformation* (Nashville: Abingdon Press, 1971), 166.

Echoing Augustine he declares that "I do not seek to understand in order to believe, but I believe in order to understand" (ch. 1). Similarly, his theological reflections are situated within the context of prayer. He begins his treatise by thanking God for creating the divine image in human beings, by which we are able to know God. But the *Proslogion* also looks forward to the high scholasticism of Aquinas and others in that it utilizes reason to make subtle distinctions. Thus, for example, in chapter 4 Anselm explains how it is possible for someone to think that there is no God by distinguishing two senses in which we can mean "think." Making this kind of distinction becomes commonplace in the scholastic period.

The *Proslogion* is significant not only because of its method, but also because of its content. Here Anselm attempts to work out a rational demonstration of the reality of God. The *Proslogion* (*An Address*) was written about a year after the *Monologion* (1076/77), in which Anselm developed three arguments to demonstrate the existence of God. The *Monologion* was written at the request of his students, who apparently wanted to know how faith in God could be rationally supported. Using the Platonic assumption that the "universal" (the Idea of something) is more real than the "particular" (the concrete manifestations of the Idea) and accepting the Platonic theory of participation, Anselm argued that, insofar as there are good things in the world, there must be some being, supremely good, in which the being of particular good things participates. In the Platonic scheme this supreme good is the Idea of the Good. Expressed in Christian terms, this supreme good is God. In the *Proslogion,* Anselm attempts to reduce the various arguments for the existence of God to one that is sufficient by itself. In the excerpt below, we see this one argument, which has come to be known as the ontological argument. Insofar as Anselm's argument involves the analytical unpacking of his definition of God, it would be better to speak of his argument or "proof" of God's existence as an analytical argument. At any rate, Anselm offers two forms of his analytic argument. In chapter 2 he argues from his definition of God to the conclusion that God must exist not only as a thought in our heads, but also as a real being outside of our thoughts. In chapter 3, he suggests that we intuitively know that God is a necessary being that cannot be thought of as not existing.

Anselm's demonstrations for the existence of God were not universally received. In his own day, Gaunilo, a Benedictine monk, published a rebuttal entitled *In Defense of the Fool,* referring to the fool mentioned in the Psalms who said in his heart that there is no God. Gaunilo's point was that it is improper to conclude that what one can imagine in the mind must exist in reality if it is perfect. Just because I can imagine, says Gaunilo, an island more fertile than any other that can be conceived does not mean that such a perfect island actually exists. Anselm, however, had a reply. God, he said, is simply a unique case. There is a difference between claiming that the perfect member of any class of finite things must exist in reality and claiming that the Perfect Being, who transcends all classes of things, must exist in reality. God is something greater than the most perfect island that can be thought. If one accepts the definition of God as "that than which nothing greater can be thought," then God cannot be thought of as not existing.[10]

---

10. In later centuries, his rebuttals notwithstanding, Anselm continued to have his critics. In the

Another important figure in the development of medieval theology is Peter Abelard (1079–1141). Although his work is not included in this volume, Abelard is important for understanding both the style and the structure of medieval scholastic theology. From the early days of the church, theology had consisted primarily of the interpretation of scripture. Even up until the time of Anselm and later, the term *sacra pagina* ("sacred page") was used to describe what theologians did, namely, provide reasoned commentary on the pages of sacred scripture. Of course, as anyone who reads scripture carefully knows, the meaning of some scriptural passages is obscure, while some portions of the Bible actually seem to contradict others. In order to resolve these difficulties, Christian thinkers had appealed to the biblical interpretations offered by their predecessors for guidance in their own attempt to uncover the Bible's meaning. In the Middle Ages, Christian thinkers could refer to the interpretation of the so-called "fathers of the church," important Christian thinkers of the first five centuries, such as Irenaeus, Tertullian, and Augustine. But what if these "patristic" sages did not resolve the scriptural difficulties? Or what if they disagreed among themselves concerning the meaning of scripture or tradition?

The problem of reconciling conflicting interpretations was highlighted in a text Peter Abelard wrote in 1122, *Sic et Non* (*Yes and No*). In this work, Abelard juxtaposed apparently conflicting passages from the Bible, the church fathers, and other authorities, without effecting a resolution of the conflicts. Whereas some believed that his aim was to discredit these traditional authorities, others, especially today, point out that his intent was to compel Christian thinkers to use dialectical reasoning and logic to resolve difficulties in the accepted sources of truth. Abelard's contemporary, Gratian, used logic to reconcile contradictions in patristic texts, conciliar decrees, and papal pronouncements concerning church law (canon law). His *Concordantia Discordantium Canonum* (*Concord of Discordant Canons;* often referred to simply as Gratian's *Decretum*) became a standard textbook for canon law, being incorporated into the *Corpus Iuris Canonici,* the chief collection of canon law in the western church. Abelard applied a similar method to theology.

Whereas Anselm of Canterbury's approach to theology may be characterized as faith seeking understanding through the assistance of reason, Abelard's may be characterized as questioning seeking the truth of faith. The difference between Anselm and Abelard, exemplified in the questions Abelard raised about the theological adequacy of Augustine's and Anselm's explanation of redemption, should not be exaggerated. Each used reason to uncover the inner coherence of Christian doctrine. Nonetheless, Abelard opened up a larger place for doubt and critical questioning within the very activity of theology. As he observed in the preface to *Yes and No,* by doubting we come to inquire and by inquiring we reach the truth.

Peter Lombard (ca. 1100–1160), one of Abelard's students, utilized this method of questioning in his four-volume *Sentences,* which took the development of medieval theology to another stage. Lombard organized the kinds of questions

---

thirteenth century, Aquinas did not find Anselm's argument compelling. In the eighteenth century, the German philosopher Immanuel Kant attempted to rationally refute it. Anselm, however, has also had his defenders. Among the most significant of recent defenders is the twentieth-century philosopher of religion Charles Hartshorne.

people might reasonably have about Christian teaching into four books: the trinity; creation and sin; incarnation and the virtues; the sacraments and "the last things." In the thirteenth century, Lombard's *Sentences* became the standard textbook of theology, upon which theologians wrote commentaries. It was copied and commented upon more than any other book, except the Bible, between the twelfth and the sixteenth centuries for several reasons. The *Sentences* were written at a time (in the middle of the twelfth century) when people felt a need for a detailed summary of the teaching of the church that could be used in the developing system of formal education. Moreover, the work was produced before rival theological "schools" (e.g., Scotists vs. Thomists) had formed. Consequently, Lombard's work was not regarded as partisan and could be used by all parties.[11]

Hildegard of Bingen's (1098–1179) *Scivias* (*Know the Ways of the Lord*) falls within the time period between Abelard's *Yes and No* and Lombard's *Sentences*. Unlike Abelard's and Lombard's works, Hildegard's engages in the interpretation of inspired visions rather than in the posing of questions and the resolving of conflicting answers to them. But like Lombard's *Sentences,* the *Scivias* also offers a compendium of Christian doctrine, though in a quite different form. Perhaps the closest parallel to Hildegard's *Scivias* is Hugh of St. Victor's *On the Sacraments of the Christian Faith* (written in the 1130s). The topics Hildegard treats in her *Scivias* overlap considerably with those treated by Hugh. For this reason, Barbara Newman has said that if "Hildegard had been a male theologian, her *Scivias* would undoubtedly have been considered one of the most important early medieval summas."[12]

The excerpt from Hildegard included below is the second of seven visions reported in Book Two of the *Scivias.* Although it seems illogical to have the vision of the trinity follow that of the redeemer (the first vision), Hildegard could well have chosen this order because the trinity was first revealed through the incarnation of God in Christ. Hildegard's vision of the trinity emphasizes the unity and the interconnectedness of the divine persons. This emphasis is, of course, not original. The inseparability of the trinitarian persons had long been a standard part of orthodox teaching about God. Even the analogies of the flame and the word were by this time traditional. What is original in Hildegard is the analogy of the stone as well as her explication of the three analogies. It is interesting to note that the three analogies for the trinity that Hildegard draws from nature are not gender-specific. In addition, Hildegard comments that the trinity has been revealed to humanity not for the sake of satisfying our curiosity about the nature of God, but rather for the sake of communicating divine love to us and eliciting our love in return. In contrast to Anselm of Canterbury, who, in *Why God Became Human* (*Cur Deus Homo*), identified God's justice and mercy as the factors that required the incarnation, Hildegard emphasizes divine love. For example, in section 4 of Vision Two (see below), she speaks of the gentleness by which Christ brought back to life those who had fallen into sin. God moves us to penitence when our spiritual life becomes ill. God's love gives us life. Thus she writes: "That through

---

11. See David Knowles, *The Evolution of Medieval Thought,* 182.
12. Barbara J. Newman, "Introduction" to *Hildegard of Bingen: Scivias,* trans. Mother Columba Hart and Jane Bishop (New York: Paulist Press, 1990), 23.

this fountain of life came the embrace of God's maternal love, which has nourished us unto life and is our help in perils, and is the deepest and sweetest charity and prepares us for penitence."

Hadewijch, a contemporary of Aquinas, continues this theme of love. Although there is a clear contrast in tone and genre between Hadewijch's poems, letters, and visions, on the one hand, and Aquinas's theological compendia and scholastic questions, on the other, we should not infer sharp differences in the content of what they have to say about God. Hadewijch names many of the traditional attributes of God: greatness, power, wisdom, and goodness; she affirms the distinctness of persons and the unity of nature in God; and she attributes specific traditional qualities to the three persons, e.g., power to the Father (Creator); knowledge or wisdom to the Son (the idea of Logos), etc.

In Letter 28 of Hadewijch we do hear, however, a different way of speaking about God. Here speech about God is not the language of highly structured, rational exposition, but rather the language of mystical experience. Whereas Aquinas makes careful distinctions concerning what we can know and say about God, Hadewijch offers a series of assertions about God that flow out of her blissful experience of enjoying "tender friendship" with God. In this way, Hadewijch expresses an experiential knowledge of God (*sapientia*) that contrasts with, but does not eliminate, an intellectual knowledge of God (*scientia*). The contrasts we discover between Hildegard, Hadewijch, and Julian of Norwich, on the one hand, and Anselm and Thomas, on the other, are not necessarily contrasts that automatically result from the differences between female and male approaches to God. These contrasts perhaps reflect the differences of context just as much as they illustrate the differences of gender. To work in the context of a nunnery, beguine community, or hermitage is different from working in the context of a monastic school or university. Not only the locus of work but also the needs of one's colleagues or audience in such situations is quite different.

Until quite recently, it had been customary to think of the Middle Ages in terms of an Anselm of Canterbury or Thomas Aquinas or Bonaventure, rather than in terms of a Hildegard or Hadewijch or Julian. Due in large part to the scholarship of female historians and theologians, that situation has begun to change. Over the past thirty years, the contributions of women to the development of the Christian tradition have been recovered and recognized. We now can see greater richness and diversity in the ways in which the church has understood and defined its doctrines. Female writers and theologians of the past are taking their rightful place alongside men, such as Aquinas, who have already established their place in the story of the church's life.

By the thirteenth century, we can speak of the achievement of a grand medieval synthesis, that is, the harmonious integration of different significant elements of western European culture. This synthesis was both social-political and theological. Socially and politically, Europe had become, generally speaking, one Christian society. In this society political rulers and ecclesial leaders were expected to work together to maintain or promote a Christian way of life. As was noted earlier, this cohesion of beliefs, practices, and goals is sometimes designated by the term "Christendom." Social cohesion, however, did not always entail political harmony. During the lay investiture controversy of the eleventh and twelfth centuries,

German bishops often sided with German emperors, while German princes supported popes, in the struggle for political power between emperors and popes. And in the thirteenth century, the popes were in regular conflict with the Hohenstaufen family concerning political power in Sicily and Italy. Nonetheless, political and ecclesial leaders were generally interested in upholding the truth of Christian faith and in overseeing the Christian character of European society. And their Christian faith — not just their social class or geographical location — was one of the primary constituents of the people's self-identification.

Theologically, the synthesis was expressed in the distinct yet complementary roles assigned to faith and reason, grace and nature. For Anselm of Canterbury in the eleventh century, faith was the starting point for theological understanding. Reason could be used, but its role in theological understanding was ancillary to that of revelation and faith. By the time of Aquinas, the works of Aristotle on physics and metaphysics had been reintroduced into the West, together with commentaries by Arabic scholars such as Averroës (Ibn Rushd). As some of these commentaries made clear, the conclusions of reason (e.g., the eternity of matter) seemed to contradict the convictions of faith (e.g., the creation of matter by God). Some Christian followers of Averroës even adopted the principle that what was true in philosophy was not necessarily true in theology. In reaction, Thomas Aquinas articulated a finely wrought affirmation of the medieval synthesis. Faith and reason each has a proper role to play in human life. Each can provide access to truth. But truth discovered in one domain cannot contradict truth discovered in the other domain, since the source of all truth is God. Consequently, reason is directed toward faith for its perfection.

An example can illustrate the distinct yet complementary roles of reason and faith in Thomas's system. The reality of God, he declared, can be established by rational reflection. In fact, Thomas offered five rational arguments in support of God's reality (see below). That God is trinity, however, can be revealed only in faith. For this reason, Aquinas declared that the existence of God and other like truths about God, which can be known by natural reason, "are not articles of faith, but are preambles to the articles; for faith presupposes natural knowledge, even as grace presupposes nature, and perfection supposes something that can be perfected" (*Summa*, Pt. I, ques. 2, art. 2, reply to obj. 1; see below).

Insofar as he represents one of the richest medieval fruits to develop from the roots prepared by Anselm, Abelard, and other predecessors, Thomas Aquinas deserves the attention he is usually accorded in histories of theology. Aquinas's *Summa Theologiae* eventually displaced Lombard's *Sentences* as the fundamental textbook of theology. Although scholastic theology, including Thomas's own work, was severely challenged by the biblical theology of the Protestant Reformers and its descendants, Thomistic theology continued to have its strong defenders into the twentieth century. Pope Leo XIII's 1879 endorsement of Thomas's theology as *the* model for Catholic theologians provided additional support for the preeminence of the Thomistic approach in Roman Catholic theology.

The *Summa* is a compendium of Christian beliefs and an encyclopedia of theology. Organized into three major parts (with the second part subdivided into two sections), it exemplifies the classic "scholastic" way of doing theology. First a question is posed. For example, Is there a God? (Part I, ques. 2; see below). The question is divided into "articles"; each article addresses a significant aspect of the question. Each article begins with two or more answers to the specific question under consideration (answers with which Thomas does not agree or which he wishes to qualify). Then comes an opposing point of view, generally drawn from scripture or another theological authority. This is followed by Thomas's reply, which makes up the bulk of each article. The article concludes with a response to the answers or "objections" with which the article had begun. This approach to theology includes the activities of questioning, summarizing the relevant statements of scripture and other theologians on the issue, formulating one's own answer to the question, and responding to the possible objections of those who offer a different answer. Faith and reason, belief and questioning are integrated into a tightly structured, logical format.

In the first question of Part One of the *Summa,* Aquinas deals with the question: what is theology? He explains that it is *sacra doctrina,* that is, sacred teaching. The ultimate teacher in theology is God, and therefore the certitude of theology's teaching ("doctrine") is greater than the certitude of any other academic discipline. Nonetheless, theology is like other "sciences" (in Latin *scientiae,* forms of knowledge) in that it examines the things revealed by God with critical rigor and draws logical conclusions from what has been revealed. After explaining what theology is, Aquinas immediately turns to a consideration of God and God's activity. The bulk of Part One deals with God, beginning with a consideration of the divine essence, followed by an exploration of God's providence and the distinction of persons in the trinity, and concluding with an exposition of God's creative and directive activities in the world.

The first aspect of the question about the divine essence that Aquinas addresses is whether or not God exists. In the first article of question 2, Aquinas asks whether God's existence is self-evident. Two things may be noted here about his reply. First, typical of the scholastic approach to theology, he makes a distinction between something that is self-evident of itself and something that is self-evident to us. Although self-evident of itself, the proposition "God exists" is not self-evident to us, but needs to be demonstrated. Second, without mentioning him by name, Aquinas declares that Anselm's analytic argument does not render God's existence self-evident. In contrast to Anselm, Aquinas attempts to demonstrate the reality of God, not by analyzing the definition of God we have in our mind, but by analyzing the evidence of God's effects in the world. In this regard, we see the influence of Aristotle's epistemology upon Aquinas. Unlike the Platonic tradition, which asserts that we arrive at knowledge by means of intellectual intuition, the Aristotelian tradition holds that we arrive at knowledge by attending to the data of the senses and then abstracting from those to form concepts and to formulate conclusions. Insofar as all human beings can attend to the data of their senses, all people, not just Christians, can come rationally to know that God exists. Christians, however, differ from other people who know that God exists in that they also know that God exists as three persons in one God. Here we see how faith perfects the knowledge of God that is possible on the basis of reason.

Having declared that God's existence can be demonstrated from effects, Aquinas proceeds in article 3 to lay out five ways in which God's existence can be demonstrated. The first two ways disclose Aquinas's indebtedness to Aristotle.

Aquinas utilizes Aristotle's explanation of potentiality and actuality as well as his categorization of causes to develop what is sometimes called the cosmological argument. The cosmological argument seeks to demonstrate that the cosmos or universe of phenomena must have a primary cause and that cause is God. The argument is based on the Aristotelian principle that whatever is in the process of moving from the state of potentiality (possibility) to actuality (real existence) has to be put into such motion by something else. Because the chain of cause and effect ("mover" and "what is moved") cannot go on in an infinite series, we must conclude that there is a First Mover, put into motion by no other. This First Mover, says Aquinas, is God.

The fifth demonstration Aquinas offers is sometimes referred to as the teleological argument. It is so called because it is based on the observation that things without the power of self-direction appear to move toward a specific *telos* (goal or end). For example, we discover regular patterns in the natural world such as the change of seasons or the motion of the planets. Insofar as whatever lacks intelligence cannot move toward an end, unless it be directed by some being endowed with knowledge and intelligence, Aquinas concludes that some intelligent being exists by whom all natural things are directed to their end. This being, Aquinas says, is God.

In the wake of the philosophical Enlightenment of the eighteenth century and the scientific developments of the eighteenth to the twentieth centuries, Aquinas's five demonstrations (in Latin *viae*, "ways") do not carry the probative force they once did. What Aquinas regarded as a certain presupposition (e.g., that the maximum in any genus is the cause of all in that genus, as in way no. 4) or as an incontestable observation (e.g., that things which lack intelligence, such as natural bodies, act always, or nearly always, in the same way, so as to obtain the best result, as in way no. 5) has been called into question. Nonetheless, his arguments in support of the reality of God have had a lasting influence on the western Christian tradition.

Aquinas also defined a classic position with regard to what we can know and say about God. In typical fashion, he differentiated knowledge and comprehension of God. It must be possible to know God, he argues, because human happiness consists in the use of humanity's highest function, which is the operation of the intellect. If we suppose that the created intellect could never know God (which Aquinas describes in terms of an intellectual vision), it would either never attain to happiness (beatitude) or its happiness would consist in something other than God, an idea which is opposed to faith (see ques. 12, art. 1; see also ques. 2, art. 1, reply to obj. no. 1 below). Human beings, therefore, must be able to know God.

On the other hand, human beings know God in proportion to their capacities as finite creatures. Because God is infinite, God exceeds the grasp of finite knowledge. Abstractly considered within Thomas's Aristotelian framework, God is supremely knowable because everything is knowable according to its actuality. Insofar as God is pure being without limitation, God is supremely actual or real. The human mind, however, is limited and cannot completely comprehend something that is without limit (the Infinite). Concretely considered, therefore, human beings can know God, but not as perfectly as God is capable of being known (see ques. 12, art. 7). Aquinas ultimately holds a median position between those who maintain that God is beyond all knowing and those who maintain that God can be comprehended by those who have received grace and illumination. For Aquinas, our knowledge of God is real, yet limited.

In a similar way, Aquinas defines a median position with regard to what we can say about God. When we say that God is good or wise or loving, these words do refer legitimately to God's nature, yet they do not fully express God's nature. Just as we come to know God through the things God has created, so what we say about God is drawn from the good qualities we see represented in creatures. Creatures, however, image God imperfectly. Consequently, when we take words drawn from our experience of creatures and apply them to God, we must take care to note that these words, although really saying something true about God, have a meaning that exceeds their meaning when applied to creatures. "So when we say, *God is good*," Thomas writes, "the meaning is not, *God is the cause of goodness*, or, *God is not evil*; but the meaning is, *Whatever good we attribute to creatures, pre-exists in God*, and in a more excellent and higher way" (ques. 13, art. 2 below).

In the fifth article of question 13, Aquinas further refines his median position. There he asserts that the names we apply to both God and creatures are used neither univocally (in the exact same sense) nor equivocally (in a completely different sense). Rather, they are used in an analogical sense, that is, in a similar sense. This analogical language about God is the natural consequence of Aquinas's firm principle that we know God from the creatures God has made. Because there is a relation between creatures (the effect of God's activity) and God (the cause of creatures' existence), there is also a relation between what we say about creatures and what we say about God. This analogical principle became a hallmark of Catholic talk about God. In a sense, we could refer to this kind of talk about God as language "from below." From what we know of the perfections of creatures, we rise up to what we can know and say about God. The Protestant tradition, by contrast, tends to engage in God talk "from above," from revelation as witnessed to in the Bible.

In Aquinas's reflections we see a contrast between the Dominican approach to theology, which Thomas represented, and the Franciscan, which his contemporary Bonaventure represented.[13] Whereas the Dominican approach emphasized the intellect as the most important aspect of human activity, the Franciscan emphasized the will. Correlatively, the Dominican approach tended to give greater weight to the theoretical aspect of theology (that is, theology's capacity for authentic knowl-

---

13. George Boas contrasts Bonaventure's and Aquinas's approaches to establishing the reality of God as empirical and rational respectively. Bonaventure says that we can actually see the traces of God around us. "It means that one does not have to be a great rationalist, an erudite theologian, a *doctor*, to know religious truths. One has only to look about one and observe that certain laws obtain; that there is order; that all things are 'disposed in weight, number, and measure.' This can be seen; and when it is seen, one has a reflection of the divine mind in one's sensory experience. One has only to contrast this with the method of St. Thomas Aquinas in the *Summa Theologica*, in which God's existence is proved by a series of rational arguments — where objections are analyzed, authorities are consulted and weighed, multiple distinctions are made, and the whole emphasis is upon reason rather than observation. St. Bonaventura seems to have as his purpose a demonstration of God's existence and of His traits which is not irrational but nonrational. That is, he would be far from saying that his conclusions would not stand up under rational criticism, but would insist that his method, to use modern language, is empirical rather than rational" ("Introduction," *The Mind's Road to God* [Indianapolis: Bobbs-Merrill, 1953], xvi).

edge of God) whereas the Franciscan approach tended to give greater weight to the practical aspect (that is, theology's capacity to render a deeper experience and love for God). Without separating these two aspects, Aquinas insisted that theology is primarily *scientia* (an intellectual knowledge of God) and secondarily *sapientia* (wisdom that comes from an experience of God in love).

In the excerpt we have from Bonaventure's *The Mind's Road to God,* we see not only the Franciscan orientation toward an experiential knowledge of God, but also the Augustinian orientation toward a trinitarian interpretation of reality. Bonaventure's treatise is constructed about the seraph with six wings, representing six stages of illumination by which the soul can ascend to a mystical encounter with God. The human person makes this journey by employing the three principal human faculties of sensual perception, spirit, and mind. Each faculty provides a particular kind of sight. At the lowest level it is the sight of sensory observation; at the highest level it is the sight of mystical vision. In all cases, this sight involves direct experience of God and God's traces in the world, and not merely knowledge about God and God's traces. By doubling each of the three aspects of the human person, one arrives at the six gradations in the soul's ascent to God.[14] At the seventh level, the mind comes to rest in a mystical experience of God.

Meister Eckhart (ca. 1260–1327), however, reminds us not to turn a difference in emphasis between Dominican and Franciscan into a radical disjunction. In his work, Eckhart, a Dominican, often united the speculative interests of "scientific" theology and the experiential knowledge of mystical theology. On the one hand, he declares that the understanding is nobler than the will, and that seeing God "bare" is better than perceiving God's goodness (see German Sermon no. 9 below). He affirms that God is of an intellectual nature and that God is revealed in creatures. Here we see parallels with Aquinas. On the other hand, Eckhart declares that God is not a being, not even pure being. Here we see contrasts with Aquinas. Whereas Aquinas held that our speaking about God can be substantial and analogical, Eckhart emphasized the inadequacy of our speech. Whereas Aquinas held that the distinction of divine attributes has a real foundation in the richness of God's nature, Eckhart so emphasized God's unity that he affirms that "no distinction can exist or be understood in God himself."[15] Yet Eckhart followed Aquinas in holding that affirmative statements about God are inappropriate with regard to the manner of signifying, but are not inappropriate with regard to the perfections signified. For this reason, more recent studies of Aquinas's and Eckhart's thought have attempted to avoid simple contrasts between the two thinkers on this issue.[16] By stressing the ineffability of God and by advocat-

---

14. Ray Petry describes the result of this doubling: "Thus in the range of sense perception one sees God mirrored in the external world, not only *per speculum*, i.e., as the cause of this world, but, also, *in speculo*, or as present in this outer world. Similarly, man, in gauging his interior depths, contemplates therein not only the image of the God who is his Creator and Sustainer but also the image of that One who is his intimately experienced Re-Creator and Re-Former. Finally, the soul is able to contemplate the Transcendent Being beyond him who is recognized both as the God who is the 'Esse' of metaphysics and the gracious, beneficent, Trinitarian God of Christian revelation" (*Late Medieval Mysticism* [Philadelphia: Westminster Press, 1957], 128).

15. Meister Eckhart, *Commentary on Exodus,* par. 60 in *Meister Eckhart: Teacher and Preacher,* ed. Bernard McGinn (New York: Paulist Press, 1986), 64. See also p. 19. This statement became article 23 in the papal bull of 1329 that condemned propositions taken from Eckhart's works.

16. "On the problem of speaking about God, the positions of all three [Maimonides, Aquinas, and Eckhart] might be best described as subtle combinations of the *via negationis* and the *via eminentiae*.

ing that we become an "adverb" to God's "word," Eckhart invokes both the *via negationis* of scholastic theology (i.e., the terms we use of things must be denied of God) and the desire for union with God, characteristic of the mystical tradition.

Although they often underlined the human incapacity to fully comprehend God, medieval Christian thinkers also thought they could say something true about God. Sometimes they used striking metaphors to describe God's nature. One such metaphor they used is mother. Although many Christians today might regard language about God the Mother to be novel, it is not. Referring to God, especially Christ, as Mother is not unique to Julian of Norwich in the fourteenth century, nor to female Christian thinkers generally. The image of Jesus as Mother appears in the patristic period and flowers in the twelfth century in the works of Cistercians, such as Bernard of Clairvaux (1090–1153) and Guerric of Igny (died ca. 1157), and in the devotional writing of Anselm of Canterbury. Devotion to Jesus the Mother was part of certain kinds of medieval piety.[17]

Why was God — particularly, the second person of the trinity — called Mother? The mother image was chosen to emphasize the life-giving and loving qualities of Christ. As a mother gives birth to her children and nourishes them with her milk, so too Christ gives birth to the soul, previously dead in sin, and nourishes it to grow and develop. It is interesting to note that, at least in the works of male authors, the female imagery generally corresponded to a stereotyped understanding of the father as ruling and disciplining and the mother as nurturing and compassionate.[18] Maternal imagery was used in the twelfth century to describe not only Jesus, but also leaders in the church who were charged with responsibility for instructing and providing pastoral care to others. We find such use of maternal imagery in Bernard of Clairvaux, who often used it in describing the duties of abbots, including himself.

Although maternal metaphors are occasionally used in the early church and can be found later (e.g., in the creed of the Council of Toledo in 675 c.e.), their use in the twelfth through the fourteenth centuries reflects new trends. Caroline Walker Bynum has called these trends the rise of affective spirituality and the feminization of religious language. She points out that seeing God or Christ as female is part of a later medieval devotional tradition that is characterized, among other things, by increasing preference for analogies drawn from human relationships and a growing sense of God as loving and accessible. "The affective piety of the high Middle Ages is based on an increasing sense of, first, humankind's creation 'in the image and likeness' of God and, second, the humanity of Christ as

---

Maimonides and Eckhart lay greater stress on the former, Thomas on the latter" (Bernard McGinn, "Introduction" to *Meister Eckhart: Teacher and Preacher* [New York: Paulist Press, 1986], 25).

17. For a detailed description of this phenomenon, see Caroline Walker Bynum, *Jesus as Mother: Studies in the Spirituality of the High Middle Ages* (Berkeley: University of California Press, 1982), esp. 110–69. See also Jean Leclercq's Preface to Julian of Norwich, *Showings,* trans. Edmund Colledge and James Walsh (New York: Paulist Press, 1978), 8–11.

18. "Both of you [Paul and Jesus] are therefore mothers.... For you accomplished, one through the other, and one through himself, that we, born to die, may be reborn to life. Fathers you are then by result, mothers by affection; fathers by authority, mothers by kindness; fathers by protection, mothers by compassion. You [Lord] are a mother and you [Paul] are also. Unequal by extent of love, you do not differ in quality of love.... You have given birth to me when you made me a Christian, ... You [Lord] by the teaching coming from you and you [Paul] by the teaching he inspires in you" (Anselm of Canterbury, prayer 10 to St. Paul, *Opera omnia,* ed. Franciscus S. Schmitt, 6 vols. [Edinburgh: T. Nelson, 1940–61], 3:39–41).

guarantee that what we are is inextricably joined with divinity."[19] Moreover, this emphasis upon the goodness of creation and the union of humanity and divinity in Christ countered some of the heresies, such as that of the Cathars, operative at the time.

Bynum discerns three basic characterizations of motherhood in a number of spiritual writers from Anselm of Canterbury to Julian of Norwich. First, the mother is generative and sacrificial (i.e., suffers birth pangs) in giving birth. Second, the mother is loving and tender. Third, the mother nurtures her offspring with her own bodily fluid. Such imagery could easily bring an affective response. It is imagery that stresses God's creative power and love. The male Cistercians who used maternal imagery for God or for their male superiors generally were expressing a need to achieve intimate dependence on God and a sense (not without ambivalence) of a need to nurture other men.[20]

The feminization of religious language that occurs in the period from the twelfth to the fourteenth centuries stands in contrast to the continuing negative image of women in theological and medical treatises of the time. Women were generally regarded as inferior to men, both physically and spiritually.[21] Women such as Hildegard of Bingen and Julian of Norwich exercised their creativity and made their theological contributions despite the negative female stereotype. During this same time period, devotion to Mary and female saints increased as well as the use of female sexual experience to describe the soul's ecstatic union with Christ.

Different theories have been put forth to explain this general feminization of religious language. Some think that it is imagery developed especially for use by women; others think that it is simply the reflection of larger numbers of women in religious life. Because the maternal image of God appears in male authors such as Anselm, the Cistercians mentioned earlier, Bonaventure, and Aquinas, it is not accurate to claim that the motherhood of God is an exclusively female insight. Hildegard of Bingen, for example, was not attracted to the idea of Christ as mother, but she did speak of God's charity and wisdom as feminine. In this regard, Christian thinkers could draw on the testimony of the Bible, especially Proverbs 8 and Wisdom of Solomon 7:22–30, where God's Wisdom ("Sophia" in Greek) is female and is described as "a pure emanation of the glory of the Almighty" (Wisd. 7: 25).

In general, the theme of God's motherhood is a minor one in all writers of the high Middle Ages except Julian of Norwich. By the late fourteenth century, devotional use of the theme of Mother Jesus is different in some ways from twelfth-century male usage. The later medieval writing stresses suckling with blood and is more frankly eucharistic. More emphasis is placed on Christ's suf-

---

19. Bynum, *Jesus as Mother*, 130.

20. See ibid., 168.

21. In his *Summa Theologiae*, Aquinas echoed the sentiments of Augustine that women are necessary to help in the work of procreation, but that a male is to be preferred as a help in every other kind of undertaking. Building upon Aristotle's conception of things, Aquinas further declared that the procreation of a female human being is the result of some defect in the normal process of procreation. See *Summa* I, ques. 92, art. 1, especially ad 1. The *Malleus Maleficarum*, published in 1486 by the inquisitors Heinrich Kraemer and Jacob Sprenger, declared that woman was inferior to man by nature in both body and spirit. This handbook insisted that woman by nature is always a deceiver and is more likely than man to fall away from the faith.

fering. Considerable attention is devoted to sin, but sin is seen more as separation from God rather than as rebellion against God. In this context, what the love of Mother God expresses most frequently to these later writers is less the ecstasy of union than the impossibility of ever being really lost or alone.

Of all the medieval Christian writers, Julian of Norwich made the most sophisticated use of the divine motherhood theme in her trinitarian theology. In *Showings,* she also emphasized strongly, as did Hadewijch, the theme of God's love, which creates a virtually unbreakable bond between God and humanity. Although there are these threads of continuity with predecessors, Julian exhibits a different understanding of these themes and a different development of them. Julian gives a fuller development and exposition of the motherhood theme than did her male predecessors. And unlike some of her female predecessors, such as Hadewijch, Julian emphasizes the love of God without explicating it in terms of courtly love poetry or in terms of ecstatic or erotic rapture. Julian, moreover, does not stay at the level of devotional contemplation, but moves to a doctrinal explication of her visions of Christ and God.[22]

Julian's articulation of the divine motherhood is complex. On the one hand, she asserts that there are three properties in the trinity, fatherhood, motherhood, and lordship, to which correspond might, wisdom, and love (see *Showings,* chapter 58 below). On the other, she declares that there are three ways of contemplating motherhood in God, namely, the motherhood of creation, the motherhood of grace, and the motherhood at work (chapter 59). In short, it seems that Julian wishes to affirm that motherhood can appropriately be attributed not only to the second person of the trinity, but also to all three divine persons. The previous tradition had associated specific activities or operations of God with specific persons of the trinity, even though — strictly speaking — all divine activities are performed by all three trinitarian persons. Thus, the Father creates, the Son redeems, and the Spirit sanctifies. Following this pattern, Julian speaks of the Father as giving us our being, the Son as providing for our "increasing" or our "restoring," and the Spirit as bringing about our fulfillment (chapter 58). She also declares that the Father wills, the Mother (or Son) works, and the Lord (the Spirit) confirms (chapter 59 below). But just as the Nicene theology of the early church did not want to divide the Godhead according to functions, so too Julian avoids division by insisting that we have the substance of who we are from Father, Son, and Spirit. Correlatively, all three persons of the trinity exemplify motherhood in their actions toward us. And the cumulative activity of God is aptly named love.

At the time of Julian's death, the church had just gone through a century of turmoil. The fourteenth century had begun with political conflict between the pope, Boniface VIII, and the king of France, Philip the Fair. With a growing sense of nationalism the king had challenged some of the traditional social and economic privileges of the clergy in France. The pope responded by reminding the king that, in Christian society, the pope held a higher position than the monarch. But Boniface VIII claimed more than that. Obedience to the pope, he declared in *Unam Sanctam* (1302), was necessary to salvation. Undeterred by such papal utterances,

22. Joan M. Nuth, *Wisdom's Daughter: The Theology of Julian of Norwich* (New York: Crossroad, 1991), 14.

the French king took political and military action against the pope. Boniface VIII was humiliated. After the pope's death, the French monarchy exercised considerable influence over the papacy. Boniface's successor, Pope Clement V, relocated the papal headquarters from Rome to Avignon, just outside of French territory. Thus began the period in church history known as the Avignon Papacy (1309–78). During this time, a lavish papal palace was begun in Avignon. It provided a stark contrast to the apostolic poverty lived by the mendicant orders and advocated so strongly by Franciscans, in particular. During the same time, the Avignon popes, such as Clement VI (1342–52), appeared to be morally corrupt and politically partisan. For this reason, the Avignon papacy is sometimes referred to as the Babylonian Captivity of the Church.

Pope Gregory XI (1370–78) eventually became convinced that the papacy needed to return to Rome. Absent from Rome, the pope could not exercise effective control over the papal states. Moreover, Rome was the appropriate place from which to work for reunion with the eastern church and from which to launch a crusade. Confirmed in his resolve by the prodding of Catherine of Siena (1347–80), Gregory XI returned to Italy in 1376 and took up residence again in the Vatican in January 1377. Approximately a year later he died. As the conclave of cardinals met to elect his successor in the spring of 1378, the people of Rome were fearful that the cardinals, most of whom were French, would elect a Frenchman and return the papacy to Avignon. The streets were noisy with citizens shouting for an Italian pope. Fifteen of the sixteen cardinals in conclave cast their vote for Bartolomeo Prignano, the archbishop of Bari, who took the name Urban VI. The cardinals, however, were not prepared to accept Urban's plan for reform of the curia nor were they ready to accept his violent temper and obstinacy. Within months of the original election, they decided to have Urban deposed. In September of 1378, they elected Cardinal Robert of Geneva as pope. He took the name Clement VII (following the tradition of French popes at Avignon). Thus began the Great Schism (1378–1417). It initially saw two men (Urban VI and Clement VII) claiming to be the legally elected pope. Eventually the number was increased to three, after the Council of Pisa (1409) failed to heal the papal schism. Only with the Council of Constance (1414–18), and its declaration of the superiority of a general council over the pope, did the Great Schism come to an end. In the intervening years, simony (the selling of church offices) greatly increased, as the rival popes sought funds to support their respective military and diplomatic campaigns. The general image of the papacy was badly tarnished in the process.

If the prestige of the papal office was diminished by the dubious character of some of the policies of the Avignon papacy and by the Great Schism, the king's prestige in society was on the increase. Beginning with England and France, the king was coming to be seen as the embodiment of the whole national community. Correlatively, the claims of Rome with regard to benefices and judicial decisions in lands outside Italy were checked by the legislation of national communities. The unity of European society under the headship of the pope was shaken.

Parallel to the dissolution of the hegemony of the papacy and the fracture of the idea of Christendom occurred the dissolution of the theological medieval synthesis. Aquinas, a chief architect of this synthesis, had attempted to show that revelation builds upon reason and that grace perfects nature. The truths of faith and the truths of reason, he said, cannot contradict each other for both have their source in God. This harmonious synthesis began to crumble in the wake of his death.

Figures like John Duns Scotus (ca. 1265–1308) questioned Aquinas's theory of analogy and sought a different basis for demonstrating the reality of God. In keeping with the Augustinian tradition maintained by many medieval Franciscans, Scotus asserted the primacy of God's will and love over divine reason and knowledge. Aquinas held that the will follows what reason presents to it as the highest good. From this perspective, God's will can be explained by the use of reason. Scotus, however, maintained that reason shows the will what is possible and the will is free to choose whichever course of action it wills. Scotus's emphasis upon the primacy of divine will and freedom did not mean that he believed that God acted arbitrarily, but it did suggest that God's actions are not required to operate within human notions of rationality. God brought about the redemption of humanity through the death of Christ, for example, not because it was rationally necessary to do so, but because God chose to do it that way. Human reasoning, Scotus argued, was not able to demonstrate all the traditional beliefs about God and God's actions in the world. Many of these beliefs had to be simply accepted on faith. In the words of Étienne Gilson, Scotus "considerably increased the list of those revealed truths which a Christian should believe, but cannot prove."[23]

In the fourteenth century some thinkers, continuing Scotus's emphasis upon God's freedom, distinguished between God's absolute power (*potentia Dei absoluta*) and God's "ordered" power (*potentia Dei ordinata*).[24] Although this distinction was used differently, some of the more radical "nominalists" used the distinction to imply that God, using absolute power, could change the basic difference between good and evil, so that what is now evil would then be good. The ultimate consequence of this stress upon God's power was the destruction of the synthesis of faith and reason, upon which the great scholastic systems of the thirteenth century had been built. In some cases, there no longer seemed to be any sense in trying to argue for the prior rationality of God's actions. For example: If, as William of Ockham (ca. 1285–1347) suggested, God can forgive an unrepentant sinner, then the sacrament of penance can be defended, not on the basis of a probative argument from reason, but only on the basis of the revealed fact that God has freely decided to connect forgiveness with repentance and the sacrament of penance.

Ockham's "razor" (the principle which holds that the simplest explanation is best) led to his critique of the standard understanding of "universals" (i.e., general concepts applicable to all the members of a class or genus) and to his emphasis upon the individual. "Humanity," for example, is a useful, "universal" mental category or "name." From Ockham's perspective, it has no reality outside of the mind thinking this concept. Individual human beings, however, do exist outside the mind. The individual is real in a way that the universal is not. This "nominalist" position (i.e., the position that holds that universals are names, not real entities) had important repercussions.

---

23. Étienne Gilson, *Reason and Revelation in the Middle Ages* (New York: Scribner's, 1938), 85.

24. See Heiko Oberman, *The Harvest of Medieval Theology: Gabriel Biel and Late Medieval Nominalism* (Cambridge: Harvard University Press, 1963), 30–47.

One area in which the repercussions were felt was science. Although the relation of the nominalist position to scientific method is complicated, nominalism's focus on the concrete individual and Ockham's principle of simplicity delineate characteristics of modern science. Another area in which the repercussions were felt was Christian teaching concerning original sin and redemption. According to the traditional understanding, all human beings were born in a state of original sin because our common humanity had been tainted by the sinful disobedience of Adam and Eve. If, however, there is no "humanity" in which we all participate, but only particular human beings, a different basis would have to be found to explain the inevitability of original sin. Similarly, a different basis would have to be found to explain how Christ's death benefitted all humanity. Whether or not Ockham only leaned toward nominalism or was in fact one of its best proponents, his criticism raised questions about the limits of reason.

Ockham's critique and nominalism also had important social consequences. Medieval "realists" tended to believe that the social order, with its institutions and hierarchies, corresponds to an eternal and true order intended by God. But if, as the nominalists suggested, things are called what they are, not because they somehow participate in an eternal universal concept, but because we have decided to give them the name that they have, then maybe the same is true of the social order. Perhaps the pope is pope and the emperor is emperor, not because this accords with an eternal, external order, but simply because we have so decided. The politically revolutionary nature of such ideas is revealed in the work of one of Ockham's contemporaries, Marsiglio of Padua. In his 1324 treatise, *Defensor Pacis* (*Defender of the Peace*), Marsiglio (Marsilius in Latin) argued that the state, not the church, is the unifying power of society. The political ruler's authority, however, derives from the people, who have the right to censure and depose their rulers. In ecclesiastical matters, a general council representing all Christians has greater authority than the pope. William Placher has summarized the effects of these ideas this way:

> Just as God has not given us an eternally ordered world but left us to order it for ourselves, so God has not given us a perfect church to be obeyed, but left the task of shaping the church to us.... Thus in different ways principles of both modern science (stick close to observed data) and modern democracy (the people decide how things should be ordered) began with nominalism and the belief in the absolute power of God.[25]

When we recall that the fourteenth and early fifteenth centuries were the age of the Avignon papacy and the Great Schism, it should not surprise us that the idea that church and society should be ordered differently found a receptive audience among some people. John Wycliffe (ca. 1330–84) in England, for example, was not a nominalist, but the deficiencies of the institutional church, especially evident after the beginning of the Great Schism in 1378, demanded his attention. He declared that only God has a legitimate lordship over others. Human beings have dominion over other creatures only to the extent that God grants them a small

25. William C. Placher, *A History of Christian Theology: An Introduction* (Philadelphia: Westminster Press, 1983), 167.

part of divine lordship for the sake of implementing God's will. Leaders of church and state lose their lordship when they cease to use it justly. In such situations, the people no longer owe allegiance to their leaders.

Because the papacy did not appear to be leading a life of piety in conformity with God's will, Wycliffe concluded that the pope had lost the rightful claim to dominion over the faithful. One year after the Great Schism (that is, the schism due to rival claimants to the papacy) began, Wycliffe published his *The Power of the Pope* (1379), in which he declared that the papacy is an office of human, not divine creation. If the corrupt leaders of the church no longer had rightful lordship over the members of the church, the faithful should no longer regard them as Christian authorities. True authority, Wycliffe declared, resides in the Bible. The church, its leaders, and its traditions were to be judged according to scriptural norms. Because the Bible was for Wycliffe *the* authority in the church, all believers, not just the clergy, should read it. Hence the need for translating it into English.

Although a number of his teachings were condemned by English bishops, Wycliffe's ideas did not die out, though they were not widely accepted at the time. His ideas were kept alive in England by the Lollards, who, some say, prepared a fertile ground for the rise of the English Reformation. The Lollards traveled in poverty around England, carrying the English translation of the Bible to the ordinary people. Wycliffe's ideas also passed over to the European mainland, where they influenced the work of John Hus (ca. 1372–1415) and his followers in Bohemia. Hus too adopted a twofold program of church reform. On the one hand, criticism of the moral corruption of the church. As preacher in the Prague chapel of the Holy Innocents of Bethlehem, Hus denounced wealthy and sinful clergy. On the other hand, appeal to the authority of scripture. Appealing to the Bible, Hus and his followers defended the practice of popular preaching and demanded that the people receive both the wine and the bread in the Eucharist. The leaders of the church responded at the Council of Constance (1414–18) by burning Hus at the stake and ordering Wycliffe's remains to be removed from the consecrated ground where he had been buried.[26]

All of these factors — corruption of the institutional church, emphasis upon the individual, the enlargement of the role of the laity in society — help to explain the resurgence of mysticism in the fourteenth and fifteenth centuries. If the hierarchy of the church was corrupt, then perhaps one could find access to God outside of the sacramental system over which the hierarchy exercised control. If women could not administer the sacraments or attain a place in the ecclesiastical hierarchy, then perhaps they could achieve implicit authority in the church through their direct, personal encounters with God in mystical experience. If the community of individuals was the source of both the state's and the church's power, then perhaps lay men and women had the right to form communities of prayer and service, without requiring the approval of ecclesiastical authorities. Personal holiness and fidelity to Christ and the example of the apostolic church, not the

---

26. Tony Lane, *The Lion Concise Book of Christian Thought* (Tring, England: Lion Publishing, 1984), 104–5. González, *A History of Christian Thought*, 2:325–31.

holding of ecclesiastical office, became for some Christians the hallmark of the true Christian.

As more recent scholarship has made clear, late medieval religion was a diverse, not a uniform reality. Although it is easy to identify any number of corruptions in the late medieval church, it is not clear that the church was any more corrupt then than in earlier generations. The church's educated critics, however, perceived the church to be more corrupt in the fifteenth and early sixteenth centuries. Some have recently argued that late medieval Europe, especially its rural areas, was a Christian society in only a superficial sense. According to this perspective, it was waiting "not so much for a change of religious orientation as for its primary conversion to an informed, disciplined religion worthy of the name of Christianity."[27] There were Christian movements, such as the Brethren of the Common Life, which had indeed experienced conversion to a disciplined form of Christianity. But as minority movements in late medieval Christianity, their importance should not be overemphasized. As scholarship continues to sort out the various factors and their relative weight in explaining the Reformation and Counter-Reformation, the fact remains that the late medieval period was a time of social, political, and ecclesial turmoil.

Academic scholarship in the fifteenth century contributed to the turmoil. Lorenzo Valla (1405–57), for example, demonstrated that the text upon which some of the arguments in support of papal power had been built, the so-called Donation of Constantine, was a forgery. He also advocated a scholarly investigation of the different translations of the Bible.[28] At the same time, Christian humanists, such as John Colet (ca. 1466–1519) and Sir Thomas More (1478–1535) in England and Erasmus of Rotterdam (1469–1536) on the European mainland, criticized scholastic theology. They called for a theology that was simpler and more biblical. Erasmus, in particular, enjoyed skewering the scholastic theologians.[29] By returning to the "sources" of Christianity (the Bible and the early "fathers" of the church), Christian living and the church's institutional life, they argued, could be corrected and enriched. To aid in the study of scripture, Erasmus published a text of the Greek New Testament with his own Latin translation in 1516. Thanks to the invention of the printing press in the middle of the fifteenth century, Erasmus's text was the first printed edition of the New Testament in Greek. At about the same time, Francisco Jiménez de Cisneros

---

27. See Patrick Collinson, "The Late Medieval Church and Its Reformation, 1400–1600," in *The Oxford History of Christianity,* 259.

28. Philip McNair, in "Seeds of Renewal," observes that Valla deserves to be regarded as the father of modern biblical criticism. McNair writes: "In 1444 he [Valla] published a daring comparison between the Latin *Vulgate* translation and the Greek original in his *Annotations on the New Testament.* For Valla everything was subjected to the same scholarly investigation. Jerome's *Vulgate* Bible was a text to be examined on the same principles of criticism as the *Annals* of Tacitus.... By meticulous scholarship and comparison of text with text he undermined the medieval tradition which was based on authority. In many ways he foreshadowed Erasmus. His writings deeply influenced the German Reformers of the next century, and were especially prized by Luther" (*Eerdmans' Handbook to the History of Christianity,* ed. Tim Dowley et al. [Grand Rapids: Eerdmans, 1977], 350–51).

29. Erasmus "once described a contemporary as 'a scab of a fellow, theology incarnate.' He condemned them as pedants, logic-choppers, manipulators of meaningless notions, constructors of syllogisms, warriors over terms. 'A man might sooner find his way out of a labyrinth than the intellectual mazes of the Realists, Nominalists, Thomists, Albertists, Occamists, Scotists.' This public scorn of the school-theologians weakened the bastions of traditional doctrine" (Owen Chadwick, *The Reformation* [Middlesex, England: Penguin Books, 1964], 33).

(1436–1517), archbishop of Toledo (Spain), assembled a group of scholars at the University of Alcalá to produce a polyglot edition of the whole Bible.

It is in this context of dissatisfaction with the institutional church, the rise of nationalism, social turmoil, and academic appeals to "return to the sources" that the Protestant Reformation was born. Although the Council of Constance had endorsed a plan for the gradual reform of the church "in head and members," reformation was still needed at the beginning of the sixteenth century. Lateran Council V (1512–17) criticized papal absorption in politics as well as the poor training of priests, but its reform program was resisted. Simony, pluralism (holding multiple church benefices), absenteeism (priests and bishops being absent from the churches to which they had been assigned), and sexual impropriety among the clergy were problems that still plagued the church. Albrecht of Brandenburg exemplifies these problems. At the age of twenty-three, already in charge of the church in Magdeburg and Halberstadt, Albrecht wished to become bishop of Mainz. Holding episcopal office in such an important city would not only increase his income, but also make him one of the electors of the Holy Roman Emperor. In order to beat out his rivals, he bribed the papal curia and paid a large sum of money to arrange for dispensation from the law restricting the number of bishoprics one person could hold. In order to pay back the money he had borrowed from the Fugger banking establishment to win over the curia, Albrecht had the St. Peter indulgence sold in his territories. It was the sale of this indulgence that Martin Luther protested in the fall of 1517.

Luther was a professor of Bible at the University of Wittenberg. Through his study of scripture, he came to an insight about the righteousness or justice of God that resolved for him a personal crisis and propelled him into the position of an outspoken reformer. Luther had been taught theology by those steeped in the "modern way" of Ockham and his successors (in distinction from the "old way" of Aquinas and Duns Scotus). The modern way, you will recall, emphasized the power of God and questioned the ability of the human mind to comprehend God's ways. But insistence upon the absolute power and freedom of God did not mean that God changes the mode of divine operation from one moment to the next. As Ockham himself admitted, "God can do many things that he will not do."[30] His point was that, although in principle God could do whatever God wanted, in fact God chooses to follow certain rules. One rule that God chooses to follow is that grace, which is necessary for salvation, will be given to those who do their best (quod in se est, according to the medieval Latin). Although this understanding of the relation between human effort and divine grace was rejected by Thomas Bradwardine and others as Pelagian or semi-Pelagian heresy, it became the conventional wisdom of the modern way of doing theology. This modern approach is exemplified by Gabriel Biel (ca. 1420–95), who clearly stated in his Commentary on the Sentences (Book II, ch. 27:1) that God accepts the act of a person who does his very best as a basis for bestowing the first grace. Luther was taught theology by Biel's students.

This teaching contributed to Luther's serious spiritual turmoil as a young Au-

---

30. William of Ockham, Quodlibetal question 6:1, quoted in Gordon Leff, The Dissolution of the Medieval Outlook (Albany: New York University Press, 1976), 63.

gustinian monk. No matter how hard he tried to "do his best," Luther always felt that there was more that he could have done. If only he had prayed more fervently or fasted more assiduously, then he could say that he had done his best. Because he had been taught that God's justice means that God would give grace only to those who did their very best and who loved God above all else, Luther was on the verge of despair. How could he bring himself to love this God who carefully weighed human merits and demerits in a divine scale? But if he didn't love this God above all else, God would not accept him and grant him the grace he needed for salvation. By his own admission, Luther came to hate God until one day he came to discover a different meaning in the phrase, the justice or righteousness of God. God's "righteousness" is not the justice by which God *measures* people and declares them to be sinners, but the righteousness that God *gives* to people *freely*. This insight, which he derived from study of the Bible (e.g., Paul's Letter to the Romans, 1:17), became the key to all of Luther's theology. To know that the basis of his justification was not his own holiness but God's mercy and grace transformed Luther's despair about attaining salvation into peace and assurance.

Although the teaching of scripture in the matter of righteousness or justification seemed to conflict with the modern theology of Biel and others, "modern" theology's suspicion of speculative flights beyond what had been divinely revealed was a principle that Luther could endorse. This principle is evident in the excerpt below from the Heidelberg Disputation of 1518. Here we find both an emphasis upon revelation and a critique of human works. On the one hand, Luther criticizes theology for speculating about the invisible nature of God, when God has been visibly revealed in the person of the suffering Christ. On the other, he criticizes the notion that human works bring us glory. True wisdom, Luther declares, consists in recognizing God "in the humility and shame of the cross" and acknowledging that Christ's suffering love on our behalf, not our own works, is the authentic basis of our glory or justification. In this text we find an intimation of one of the central Reformation principles, namely, justification by faith.[31]

Germany, although the site of the initial spark of the Protestant Reformation, was not the only place where significant change in the structure, doctrine, and practice of the church was undertaken by critics of the Roman Church. In the Swiss cantons reform and revolt were underway. Ulrich (Huldreich) Zwingli (1484–1531), a contemporary of Luther and a former Catholic priest, led the reform of Zurich. Through his humanistic studies and intensive study of the Bible, Zwingli came to the conclusion that certain practices of the church had no sanction in the Bible and had dubious pastoral utility. By the early 1520s he had come to criticize publicly the practice of Lenten fasting and the invocation of the saints as well as the Roman Church's teaching concerning purgatory and clerical celibacy. Zwingli's reform movement, largely independent of Luther's, was more radical than the Lutheran reform underway in Germany. Whereas Luther

---

31. The central Reformation principles, articulated in Luther's major treatises of 1520, are (1) justification by grace through faith (*sola fide*), (2) scripture alone as the true authority in the church (*sola scriptura*), and (3) priesthood of all believers. In the excerpt we have from the Heidelberg Disputation, we do not see a clear articulation of the idea of justification by faith alone, but we do see an explicit critique of human works as worthless. "Faith alone" was for Luther the alternative to "human works" as the basis of a right relationship with God.

was willing to tolerate church practices and customs that did not clearly contradict the testimony of scripture, Zwingli only allowed those practices and customs that could find explicit support in the Bible. Employing this stricter biblical criterion, Zwingli removed statues and images from the Grossmünster Church in Zurich and forbade the use of organ music in worship services. The city council supported Zwingli, but some of the surrounding cantons sought to regain Zurich by force for Catholicism. Zwingli strapped on a helmet and fought. He was killed in the Battle of Kappel in 1531.

John Calvin arrived in Geneva, to the southwest of Zurich, about five years after the death of Zwingli. Hostility from King Francis I toward reform-minded humanism made it dangerous to remain in Paris. After brief trips to Basel, Italy, and a return to Paris, Calvin intended to go to Strasbourg to meet with the reformers of that city and to visit other French refugees there. The military situation, however, forced him to make a long detour to the south through Geneva. Although he did not intend to stay, William Farel convinced him to remain and to assist him in bringing Geneva over to the side of the Protestant Reformation.

At the time of Calvin's arrival, Geneva had just gained its independence of Catholic Savoy and had aligned itself with Bern and the other Protestant cantons. Native Genevans, however, were not eager to replace the lordship of Savoy with the lordship of foreign French ministers, such as Calvin. The antagonism between Calvin and the city council, especially over the right of excommunication, led to Calvin's expulsion from the city in 1538. When the city council of Geneva invited him back in the fall of 1541, Calvin's first concern was to organize the church of Geneva according to the Word of God and the example of the early church. Calvin drew up his ideas about church structure in the *Ecclesiastical Ordinances,* which the council accepted. According to these ordinances, a consistory was formed. Made up of pastors and twelve lay elders, the consistory sought to bring every aspect of Genevan life under God's law. The inclusion of elders (from the Greek word "presbyters") in the governance of the church was one aspect of Calvin's legacy.

In the 1550s Calvin established two additional elements of his legacy, the final version of his *Institutes of the Christian Religion* (1559) and the Genevan Academy. The *Institutes,* whose first edition had appeared more than two decades earlier, was the first detailed and comprehensive expression of a Protestant understanding of Christian faith. The Academy was a college designed to prepare students for ministry and civic leadership. Through these two institutions, Calvin's influence was able to spread far beyond the confines of Geneva. By the early seventeenth century, Calvinism was prominent in Scotland, Holland, and North America and it had significant minority status in France and Germany.

In the excerpt below from Calvin's *Institutes of the Christian Religion,* we see a second Reformation principle, namely, the authority of scripture. Calvin began his *Institutes* with an idea that resonates well with the position of Luther. Calvin declares that authentic knowledge of God entails authentic knowledge of ourselves. As with Luther, so too here we find a sharp contrast between the glory and majesty of God and the lowliness of humankind. Calvin elevates God's glory and grace, while he deflates human pride and works.

Calvin, like Luther, also emphasized the centrality of revelation in contrast to the speculation of human reason concerning God. For this reason, the first book of the *Institutes* is entitled "The Knowledge of God the Creator." Instead of discussing the metaphysical nature of God (e.g., as pure being), Calvin describes God's work as revealed in creation and redemption. Whereas some of the scholastic theologians of the Middle Ages give the impression that they were principally interested in theoretical or abstract knowledge about God, Calvin makes clear that he is interested in a "practical" knowledge of God. That is, Calvin focuses his attention, on the one hand, upon what the reality of God means for human living. On the other, he insists that we come to a real knowledge of God only if we possess piety, that is, the reverence for God and love of God that arises from awareness of the many benefits God has bestowed upon humankind (see Book I, ch. 2, 1 below).

Like medieval thinkers before him, Calvin holds that God's presence is evident in creation. God is indeed evident in God's effects. Vision of God's presence in creation, to say nothing of knowledge of God as Father or Redeemer, however, has been blurred because of original sin. For this reason, God has given us God's own word, contained in scripture, so that we can see God more clearly. "Just as old or bleary-eyed men and those with weak vision, if you thrust before them a most beautiful volume, even if they recognize it to be some sort of writing, yet can scarcely construe two words, but with the aid of spectacles will begin to read distinctly; so Scripture, gathering up the otherwise confused knowledge of God in our minds...clearly shows us the true God" (see Book I, ch. 6, 1 below).

In Teresa of Avila (1515–82) we also find an interest in a "practical" knowledge of God. But this knowledge comes primarily not through reading scripture and reflection upon it, but through the life of prayer. It was obvious to most people in the sixteenth century that the church and the forms of Christian life needed to be reformed and renewed. Teresa entered the Carmelite monastery at Avila in 1535, eighteen years after the Protestant Reformation began and ten years before the commencement of the Council of Trent. After about twenty years in this religious order, Teresa had a profound spiritual experience that changed the course of her life. Similar turning points had occurred in the lives of some of her contemporaries, such as Ignatius of Loyola and Martin Luther. In this experience Teresa became aware of how ungrateful she had been up to this point in her life to Christ, who had suffered so grievously on behalf of humanity. She was moved by the powerful love of God for her. In the wake of this experience, she developed an intense life of prayer.

The excerpt below is taken from *The Interior Castle,* a work Teresa wrote in 1577. The castle is a metaphor for the human soul, in which there are seven dwelling places. The purpose of prayer, according to Teresa, is to progress through these dwelling places to God, who resides in the seventh, innermost dwelling place. We can gain access to the first three dwelling places by our own efforts if they are assisted by God's grace. But entry into the final four dwelling places is a gift of God. The final four dwelling places represent infused recollection, prayer of union with God, spiritual betrothal to God, and finally spiritual marriage.

In the mystical union that occurs in this seventh dwelling place, Teresa speaks about being allowed to see the trinity. This intellectual vision of God brings understanding of who God is and communication with the three persons of the trinity. This clear vision of God is not a human achievement, but a gift of God's mercy. Nonetheless, even in this vision, God's presence is felt only partially: "For if the presence were felt so clearly, the soul would find it impossible to be engaged in anything else or even to live among people" (see Book 7, ch. 1, par. 9 below). As it is, this experience moves its recipient to become even more fully engaged in service to God.

It is interesting to note that Teresa, like Calvin, emphasizes at the very beginning of her work (Book I, ch. 2, par. 9) the link between knowledge of God and self-knowledge. There she wrote:

> While we are on this earth nothing is more important to us than humility. So I repeat that it is good, indeed very good, to try to enter first into the room where self-knowledge is dealt with rather than fly off to other rooms. This is the right road, and if we can journey along a safe and level path, why should we want wings to fly? Rather, let's strive to make more progress in self-knowledge, for in my opinion we shall never completely know ourselves if we don't strive to know God. By gazing at His grandeur, we get in touch with our own lowliness; by looking at His purity, we shall see our own filth; by pondering His humility, we shall see how far we are from being humble.[32]

Like Calvin, she emphasized the greatness of God and the lowliness of humankind. Unlike Calvin, however, she also emphasized the possibility of union with God. Through prayer and the development of the spiritual life, one can be prepared for a spiritual marriage with God. The lowly human being can experience the ecstasy of mystical union with the deity. This mystical element and the concomitant life of contemplative prayer distinguish the Catholic Teresa from the Protestant Calvin. Although they shared a similar assessment of the human condition, they sought to reform and enrich it in different ways. Whereas a strict biblical faith was for Calvin the means to reform, contemplative spirituality was Teresa's preferred path.

Throughout the medieval and Reformation period, we see a recurring exploration of how we can come to know God and how we should speak about God. Analytic reasoning, visions, deductions from observations of creation, turning inward, reflection upon revelation contained in scripture, and mystical union are some of the paths taken in the pursuit of knowledge of God. In addition to the diversity of paths, we have also seen diversity in the kinds of knowledge achieved. Intellectual and theoretical knowledge of God as well as experiential and practical knowledge of God are explored in this period. We see careful attempts to define what reason can affirm about God and to explain how these affirmations, though true, are incomplete without revelation. We see attempts to demonstrate rationally the reality of God, while acknowledging — in continuity with the previous period — the ultimate incomprehensibility of God. The medieval and Reformation period also offers more detailed and sometimes competing explanations of how we ought to speak about God. The subtle language of analogy, the intense

---

32. Teresa of Avila, *The Interior Castle*, trans. Kieran Kavanaugh and Otilio Rodriguez (New York: Paulist Press, 1979), 43.

language of vision and mystical experience, and the concrete language of the Bible are all advocated in this period. In the next period, this very ability to speak credibly about God will be challenged.

TEXTS

Anselm of Canterbury (ca. 1033–1109)

Proslogion (1078), Chapters 1–5*

I acknowledge, O Lord, with thanksgiving, that thou hast created this thy image in me, so that, remembering thee, I may think of thee, may love thee. But this image is so effaced and worn away by my faults, it is so obscured by the smoke of my sins, that it cannot do what it was made to do, unless thou renew and reform it. I am not trying, O Lord, to penetrate thy loftiness, for I cannot begin to match my understanding with it, but I desire in some measure to understand thy truth, which my heart believes and loves. For I do not seek to understand in order to believe, but I believe in order to understand. For this too I believe, that "unless I believe, I shall not understand."

Chapter II: God Truly Is

And so, O Lord, since thou givest understanding to faith, give me to understand — as far as thou knowest it to be good for me — that thou dost exist, as we believe, and that thou art what we believe thee to be. Now we believe that thou art a being than which none greater can be thought. Or can it be that there is no such being, since "the fool hath said in his heart, 'There is no God'"? [Ps. 14:1; 53:1]. But when this same fool hears what I am saying — "A being than which none greater can be thought" — he understands what he hears, and what he understands is in his understanding, even if he does not understand that it exists. For it is one thing for an object to be in the understanding, and another thing to understand that it exists. When a painter considers beforehand what he is going to paint, he has it in his understanding, but he does not suppose that what he has not yet painted already exists. But when he has painted it, he both has it in his understanding and understands that what he has now produced exists. Even the fool, then, must be convinced that a being than which none greater can be thought exists at least in his understanding, since when he hears this he understands it, and whatever is understood is in the understanding. But clearly that than which a greater cannot be thought cannot exist in the understanding alone. For if it is actually in the understanding alone, it can be thought of as existing also in reality, and this is greater. Therefore, if that than which a greater cannot be thought is in the understanding alone, this same thing than which a greater

---

*Reprinted from *A Scholastic Miscellany: Anselm to Ockham,* ed. and trans. Eugene R. Fairweather, Library of Christian Classics. All rights reserved. Used by permission of Westminster John Knox Press. Pp. 73–76.

cannot be thought is that than which a greater can be thought. But obviously this is impossible. Without doubt, therefore, there exists, both in the understanding and in reality, something than which a greater cannot be thought.

Chapter III: God Cannot Be Thought of As Nonexistent

And certainly it exists so truly that it cannot be thought of as nonexistent. For something can be thought of as existing, which cannot be thought of as not existing, and this is greater than that which *can* be thought of as not existing. Thus, if that than which a greater cannot be thought can be thought of as not existing, this very thing than which a greater cannot be thought is *not* that than which a greater cannot be thought. But this is contradictory. So, then, there truly is a being than which a greater cannot be thought — so truly that it cannot even be thought of as not existing.

And *thou* art this being, O Lord our God. Thou so truly art, then, O Lord my God, that thou canst not even be thought of as not existing. And this is right. For if some mind could think of something better than thou, the creature would rise above the Creator and judge its Creator; but this is altogether absurd. And indeed, whatever is, except thyself alone, can be thought of as not existing. Thou alone, therefore, of all being, hast being in the truest and highest sense, since no other being so truly exists, and thus every other being has less being. Why, then, has "the fool said in his heart, 'There is no God,' " when it is so obvious to the rational mind that, of all beings, thou dost exist supremely? Why indeed, unless it is that he is a stupid fool?

Chapter IV: How the Fool Has Said in His Heart What Cannot Be Thought

But how did he manage to say in his heart what he could not think? Or how is it that he was unable to think what he said in his heart? After all, to say in one's heart and to think are the same thing. Now if it is true — or, rather, since it is true — that he thought it, because he said it in his heart, but did not say it in his heart, since he could not think it, it is clear that something can be said in one's heart or thought in more than one way. For we think of a thing, in one sense, when we think of the word that signifies it, and in another sense, when we understand the very thing itself. Thus, in the first sense God can be thought of as nonexistent, but in the second sense this is quite impossible. For no one who understands what God is can think that God does not exist, even though he says these words in his heart — perhaps without any meaning, perhaps with some quite extraneous meaning. For God is that than which a greater cannot be thought, and whoever understands this rightly must understand that he exists in such a way that he cannot be nonexistent even in thought. He, therefore, who understands that God thus exists cannot think of him as nonexistent.

Thanks be to thee, good Lord, thanks be to thee, because I now understand by thy light what I formerly believed by thy gift, so that even if I were to refuse to believe in thy existence, I could not fail to understand its truth.

Chapter V: God Is Whatever It Is Better to Be Than Not to Be, and He, the Only Self-Existent Being, Makes All Other Things from Nothing

What, therefore, art thou, O Lord God, than whom nothing greater can be thought? What are thou, save the highest of all beings, alone self-existent, who has made all other things from nothing? For whatever is not this highest being is less than can be thought. But we cannot think this of thee. What good, then, is lacking to the highest good, through which every good exists? Therefore thou art just, truthful, blessed, and whatever it is better to be than not to be. For it is better to be just than not just, blessed than not blessed.

Hildegard of Bingen (1098–1179)

Scivias (1141–51), Book 2, Vision 2: The Trinity*

Then I saw a bright light, and in this light the figure of a man the color of a sapphire, which was all blazing with a gentle glowing fire. And that bright light bathed the whole of the glowing fire, and the glowing fire bathed the bright light; and the bright light and the glowing fire poured over the whole human figure, so that the three were one light in one power of potential. And again I heard the living Light, saying to me: . . .

2. On the Three Persons

Therefore you see *a bright light,* which without any flaw of illusion, deficiency or deception designates the Father; *and in this light the figure of a man the color of a sapphire,* which without any flaw of obstinacy, envy or iniquity designates the Son, Who was begotten of the Father in Divinity before time began, and then within time was incarnate in the world in Humanity; *which is all blazing with a gentle glowing fire,* which fire without any flaw of aridity, mortality, or darkness designates the Holy Spirit, by Whom the Only-Begotten of God was conceived in the flesh and born of the Virgin within time and poured the true light into the world. *And that bright light bathes the whole of the glowing fire, and the glowing fire bathes the bright light; and the bright light and the glowing fire pour over the whole human figure, so that the three are one light in one power of potential.* And this means that the Father, Who is Justice, is not without the Son or the Holy Spirit; and the Holy Spirit, Who kindles the hearts of the faithful, is not without the Father or the Son; and the Son, Who is the plenitude of fruition, is not without the Father or the Holy Spirit. They are inseparable in Divine Majesty, for the Father is not without the Son, nor the Son without the Father, nor the Father and the Son without the Holy Spirit, nor the Holy Spirit without Them. Thus these three Persons are one God in the one and perfect divinity of majesty, and

---

*Reprinted from *Hildegard of Bingen* by Mother Columba Hart and Jane Bishop, © 1990 by the Abbey of Regina Laudis: Benedictine Congregation Regina of the Strict Observance Inc. Used by permission of Paulist Press. Pp. 161–64.

the unity of Their divinity is unbreakable; the Divinity cannot be rent asunder, for it remains inviolable without change. But the Father is declared through the Son, the Son through Creation, and the Holy Spirit through the Son incarnate. How? It is the Father Who begot the Son before the ages; the Son through Whom all things were made by the Father when creatures were created; and the Holy Spirit Who, in the likeness of a dove, appeared at the baptism of the Son of God before the end of time.

3. People Must Not Forget to Invoke the One God in Three Persons

Hence let no person ever forget to invoke Me, the sole God, in these Three Persons, because for this reason I have made Them known to Man, that he may burn more ardently in My love; since it was for love of him that I sent My Son into the world, as My beloved John testifies, saying:

4. John on the Charity of God

"By this the charity of God has appeared toward us: that God has sent His Only-Begotten Son into the world, that we may live by Him. In this is charity, not that we have loved God, but that He has loved us, and sent His Son to be a propitiation for our sins" [1 John 4:9–10]. What does this mean? That because God loved us, another salvation arose than that we had had in the beginning, when we were heirs of innocence and holiness; for the Supernal Father showed His charity in our dangers, though we deserved punishment, in sending by supernal power His Holy Word alone into the darkness of the world for the people's sake. There the Word perfected all good things, and by His gentleness brought back to life those who had been cast out because of their unclean sins and could not return to their lost holiness. What does this mean?

That through this fountain of life came the embrace of God's maternal love, which has nourished us unto life and is our help in perils, and is the deepest and sweetest charity and prepares us for penitence. How?

God has mercifully remembered His great work and His precious pearl, Man, whom He formed from the mud of the earth and into whom He breathed the breath of life. How? By devising the life of penitence, which will never fail in efficacy. For through his proud suasion the cunning serpent deceived Man, but God cast him into penitence, which calls for the humility the Devil did not know and could not practice; for he knew not how to rise up to the right way.

Hence this salvation of charity did not spring from us, and we were ignorant and incapable of loving God for our salvation; but He Himself, the Creator and Lord of all, so loved His people that for their salvation He sent His Son, the Prince and Savior of the faithful, Who washed and dried our wounds. And He exuded the sweetest balm, from which flow all good things for salvation. Therefore, O human, you must understand that no misfortune or change can touch God. For the Father is the Father, the Son is the Son, and the Holy Spirit is the Holy Spirit, and these Three Persons are indivisible in the Unity of the Divinity. How?

5. On the Three Qualities of a Stone

There are three qualities in a stone and three in a flame and three in a word. How? In the stone is cool dampness and solidity to the touch and sparkling fire. It has cool dampness that it may not be dissolved or broken; solidity to the touch that it may make up habitations and defenses; and sparkling fire that it may be heated and consolidated into hardness. Now this cool dampness signifies the Father, Who never withers and Whose power never ends; and this solidity of touch designates the Son, Who was born of the Virgin and could be touched and known; and the sparkling fire signifies the Holy Spirit, Who enkindles and enlightens the hearts of the faithful. What does this mean?

As a person who in the body often touches the cool dampness of stone falls sick and grows weak, so one who in his unsteady thoughts rashly tries to contemplate the Father loses his faith. And as people build their dwellings and defend themselves against their enemies by handling the solidity of stone, so too the Son of God, Who is the true cornerstone, is the dwelling of the faithful people and their protector from evil spirits. And as sparkling fire gives light to dark places by burning what it touches, so also the Holy Spirit drives out unbelief and consumes the blight of iniquity.

And as these three qualities are in one stone, so the true Trinity is in the true Unity.

6. On the Three Qualities in a Flame

Again, as the flame of a fire has three qualities, so there is one God in three Persons. How? A flame is made up of brilliant light and red power and fiery heat. It has brilliant light that it may shine, and red power that it may endure, and fiery heat that it may burn. Therefore, by the brilliant light understand the Father, Who with paternal love opens His brightness to His faithful; and by the red power, which is in the flame that it may be strong, understand the Son, Who took on a body born from a Virgin, in which His divine wonders were shown; and by the fiery heat understand the Holy Spirit, Who burns ardently in the minds of the faithful. But there is no flame seen where there is neither brilliant light nor red power nor fiery heat; and thus also where neither the Father nor the Son nor the Holy Spirit is known God is not properly worshipped.

Therefore as these three qualities are found in one flame, so Three Persons must be understood in the Unity of the Divinity.

7. On the Three Causes of Human Words

And as three causes for the production of words are seen, so the Trinity in the Unity of the Divinity is to be inferred. How? In a word there is sound, force, and breath. It has sound that it may be heard, meaning that it may be understood, and breath that it may be pronounced. In the sound, then, observe the Father, Who manifests all things with ineffable power; in the meaning, the Son, Who was miraculously begotten of the Father; and in the breath, the Holy Spirit, Who sweetly burns in Them. But where no sound is heard, no meaning is used and no breath is lifted, there no word will be understood; so also the Father, Son, and Holy Spirit are not divided from one another, but do Their works together.

So as there are these three causes for one word, the celestial Trinity is likewise in the celestial Unity. So as in a stone there exists and there operates no cool dampness without solidity to the touch and sparkling fire, or solidity to the touch without cool dampness and sparkling fire, or sparkling fire without cool dampness and solidity to the touch; and as in a flame there exists and there operates no brilliant light without red power and fiery heat, or red power without brilliant light and fiery heat, or fiery heat without brilliant light and red power; and as in a word there exists and there operates no sound without meaning and breath, or meaning without sound and breath, or breath without sound and meaning, but all keep indivisibly together to operate; so also these Three Persons of the true Trinity live inseparably in the majesty of the Divinity and are not divided from each other.

Thus, O human, understand the One God in Three Persons. In the foolishness of your mind you think that God is so powerless that He cannot truly live in three Persons, but only exist weakly in one. What does this mean? God is, in three Persons, the true God, the First and the Last.

Bonaventure (ca. 1221–74)

The Mind's Road to God (1259), Chapters 1 and 7*

Chapter One: Of the Stages in the Ascent to God and of His Reflection in His Traces in the Universe

1. Blessed is the man whose help is from Thee. In his heart he hath disposed to ascend by steps, in the vale of tears, in the place which he hath set [Ps. 83:6, Vg; Ps. 84:5, NRSV]. Since beatitude is nothing else than the fruition of the highest good, and the highest good is above us, none can be made blessed unless he ascend above himself, not by the ascent of his body but by that of his heart. But we cannot be raised above ourselves except by a higher power raising us up. For howsoever the interior steps are disposed, nothing is accomplished unless it is accompanied by divine aid. Divine help, however, comes to those who seek it from their hearts humbly and devoutly; and this means to sigh for it in this vale of tears, aided only by fervent prayer. Thus prayer is the mother and source of ascent (*sursum-actionis*) in God. Therefore Dionysius, in his book *Mystical Theology* [ch. 1, 1], wishing to instruct us in mental elevation, prefaces his work by prayer. Therefore let us pray and say to the Lord our God, "Conduct me, O Lord, in Thy way, and I will walk in Thy truth; let my heart rejoice that it may fear Thy name" [Ps. 85:11, Vg; Ps. 86:11, NRSV].

2. By praying thus one is enlightened about the knowledge of the stages in the ascension to God. For since, relative to our life on earth, the world is itself a ladder for ascending to God, we find here certain traces [of His hand], certain images, some corporeal, some spiritual, some temporal, some aeviternal; consequently some outside us, some inside. That we may arrive at an understanding

The Mind's Road to God, Saint Bonaventura, trans., with an Introduction by George Boas, © 1953. Reprinted by permission of Prentice-Hall, Inc. Upper Saddle River, N.J. Pp. 7–13, 43–46.

of the First Principle, which is most spiritual and eternal and above us, we ought to proceed through the traces which are corporeal and temporal and outside us; and this is to be led into the way of God. We ought next to enter into our minds, which are the eternal image of God, spiritual and internal; and this is to walk in the truth of God. We ought finally to pass over into that which is eternal, most spiritual, and above us, looking to the First Principle; and this is to rejoice in the knowledge of God and in the reverence of His majesty.

3. Now this is the three day's journey into the wilderness [Exod. 3:18]; this is the triple illumination of one day, first as the evening, second as the morning, third as noon; this signifies the threefold existence of things, as in matter, in [creative] intelligence, and in eternal art, wherefore it is said, *Be it made, He made it,* and *It was so done* [Gen. 1]; and this also means the triple substance in Christ, Who is our ladder, namely, the corporeal, the spiritual, and the divine.

4. Following this threefold progress, our mind has three principal aspects. One refers to the external body, wherefore it is called animality or sensuality; the second looks inward and into itself, wherefore it is called spirit; the third looks above itself, wherefore it is called mind. From all of which considerations it ought to be so disposed for ascending as a whole into God that it may love Him with all its mind, with all its heart, and with all its soul [Mark 12:30]. And in this consists both the perfect observance of the Law and Christian wisdom.

5. Since, however, all of the aforesaid modes are twofold — as when we consider God as the alpha and omega, or insofar as we happen to see God in one of the aforesaid modes as *through* a mirror and *in* a mirror, or as one of those considerations can be mixed with the other conjoined to it or may be considered alone in its purity — hence it is necessary that these three principal stages become sixfold, so that as God made the world in six days and rested on the seventh, so the microcosm by six successive stages of illumination is led in the most orderly fashion to the repose of contemplation. As a symbol of this we have the six steps to the throne of Solomon [3 Kings 10:19, Vg; 1 Kings 10:19, NRSV]; the Seraphim whom Isaiah saw have six wings; after six days the Lord called Moses out of the midst of the cloud [Exod. 24:16]; and Christ after six days, as is said in Matthew [17:1], brought His disciples up into a mountain and was transfigured before them.

6. Therefore, according to the six stages of ascension into God, there are six stages of the soul's powers by which we mount from the depths to the heights, from the external to the internal, from the temporal to the eternal — to wit, sense, imagination, reason, intellect, intelligence, and the apex of the mind, the illumination of conscience (*Synteresis*). These stages are implanted in us by nature, deformed by sin, reformed by grace, to be purged by justice, exercised by knowledge, perfected by wisdom.

7. Now at the Creation, man was made fit for the repose of contemplation, and therefore God placed him in a paradise of delight [Gen. 2:15]. But turning himself away from the true light to mutable goods, he was bent over by his own sin, and the whole human race by original sin, which doubly infected human nature, ignorance infecting man's mind and concupiscence his flesh. Hence man, blinded and bent, sits in the shadows and does not see the light of heaven unless grace with justice succor him from concupiscence, and knowledge with wisdom

against ignorance. All of which is done through Jesus Christ, Who of God is made unto us wisdom and justice and sanctification and redemption [1 Cor. 1:30]. He is the virtue and wisdom of God, the Word incarnate, the author of grace and truth — that is, He has infused the grace of charity, which, since it is from a pure heart and good conscience and unfeigned faith, rectifies the whole soul in the threefold way mentioned above. He has taught the knowledge of the truth according to the triple mode of theology — that is the symbolic, the literal, and the mystical — so that by the symbolic we may make proper use of sensible things, by the literal we may properly use the intelligible, and by the mystical we may be carried aloft to supermental levels.

8. Therefore he who wishes to ascend to God must, avoiding sin, which deforms nature, exercise the above-mentioned natural powers for regenerating grace, and do this through prayer. He must strive toward purifying justice, and this in intercourse [i.e., social intercourse and life]; toward the illumination of knowledge, and this in meditation; toward the perfection of wisdom, and this in contemplation. Now just as no one comes to wisdom save through grace, justice, and knowledge, so none comes to contemplation save through penetrating meditation, holy conversation, and devout prayer. Just as grace is the foundation of the will's rectitude and of the enlightenment of clear and penetrating reason, so, first, we must pray; secondly, we must live holily; thirdly, we must strive toward the reflection of truth and, by our striving, mount step by step until we come to the high mountain where we shall see the God of gods in Sion [Ps. 84:7].

9. Since, then, we must mount Jacob's ladder before descending it, let us place the first rung of the ascension in the depths, putting the whole sensible world before us as a mirror, by which ladder we shall mount up to God, the Supreme Creator, that we may be true Hebrews crossing from Egypt to the land promised to our fathers; let us be Christians crossing with Christ from this world over to the Father [John 13:1]; let us also be lovers of wisdom, which calls to us and says, "Come over to me, all ye that desire me, and be filled with my fruits" [Ecclus. 24:19]. For by the greatness of the beauty and of the creature, the Creator of them may be seen [Wisd. 13:5].

10. There shine forth, however, the Creator's supreme power and wisdom and benevolence in created things, as the carnal sense reports trebly to the inner sense. For the carnal sense serves him who either understands rationally or believes faithfully or contemplates intellectually. Contemplating, it considers the actual existence of things; believing, it considers the habitual course of things; reasoning, it considers the potential excellence of things.

11. In the first mode, the aspect of one contemplating, considering things in themselves, sees in them weight, number, and measure [Wisd. 11:20] — weight, which directs things to a certain location; number, by which they are distinguished from one another; and measure, by which they are limited. And so one sees in them mode, species, and order; and also substance, power, and operation. From these one can rise as from the traces to understanding the power, wisdom, and immense goodness of the Creator.

12. In the second mode, the aspect of a believer considering this world, one reaches its origin, course, and terminus. For by faith we believe that the ages are fashioned by the Word of Life [Heb. 11:3]; by faith we believe that the ages of the

three laws — that is, the ages of the law of Nature, of Scripture, and of Grace — succeed each other and occur in most orderly fashion; by faith we believe that the world will be ended at the last judgment — taking heed of the power in the first, of the providence in the second, of the justice of the most high principle in the third.

13. In the third mode, the aspect of one inquiring rationally, one sees that some things merely are; others, however, are and live; others, finally, are, live, and discern. And the first are lesser things, the second midway, and the third the best. Again, one sees that some are only corporeal, others partly corporeal and partly spiritual, from which it follows that some are entirely spiritual and are better and more worthy than either of the others. One sees, nonetheless, that some are mutable and corruptible, as earthly things; others mutable and incorruptible, as celestial things, from which it follows that some are immutable and incorruptible, as the supercelestial things.

From these visible things, therefore, one mounts to considering the power and wisdom and goodness of God as being, living, and understanding; purely spiritual and incorruptible and immutable.

14. This consideration, however, is extended according to the sevenfold condition of creatures, which is a sevenfold testimony to the divine power, wisdom, and goodness, as one considers the origin, magnitude, multitude, beauty, plenitude, operation, and order of all things. For the *origin* of things, according to their creation, distinction, and beauty, in the work of the six days indicates the divine power producing all things from nothing, wisdom distinguishing all things clearly, and goodness adorning all things generously. *Magnitude* of things, either according to the measure of their length, width, and depth, or according to the excellence of power spreading itself in length, breadth, and depth, as appears in the diffusion of light, or again according to the efficacy of its inner, continuous, and diffused operation, as appears in the operation of fire — magnitude, I say, indicates manifestly the immensity of the power, wisdom, and goodness of the triune God, Who exists unlimited in all things through His power, presence, and essence. *Multitude* of things, according to the diversity of genus, species, and individuality, in substance, form, or figure, and efficacy beyond all human estimation, clearly indicates and shows the immensity of the aforesaid traits in God. *Beauty* of things, according to the variety of light, figure, and color in bodies simple and mixed and even composite, as in the celestial bodies, minerals, stones and metals, plants and animals, obviously proclaims the three mentioned traits. *Plenitude* of things — according to which matter is full of forms because of the seminal reasons; form is full of power because of its activity; power is full of effects because of its efficiency — declares the same manifestly. *Operation,* multiplex inasmuch as it is natural, artificial, and moral, by its very variety shows the immensity of that power, art, and goodness which indeed are in all things the cause of their being, the principle of their intelligibility, and the order of their living. *Order,* by reason of duration, situation, and influence, as prior and posterior, upper and lower, nobler and less noble, indicates clearly in the book of creation the primacy, sublimity, and dignity of the First Principle in relation to its infinite power. The order of the divine laws, precepts, and judgments in the Book of Scripture indicates the immensity of His wisdom. The order of the divine sacraments, rewards, and punishments in the body of the Church indicates the immensity of His goodness.

Hence order leads us most obviously into the first and highest, most powerful, wisest, and best.

15. He, therefore, who is not illumined by such great splendor of created things is blind; he who is not awakened by such great clamor is deaf; he who does not praise God because of all these effects is dumb; he who does not note the First Principle from such great signs is foolish. Open your eyes therefore, prick up your spiritual ears, open your lips, and apply your heart, that you may see your God in all creatures, may hear Him, praise Him, love and adore Him, magnify and honor Him, lest the whole world rise against you. For on this account the whole world will fight against the unwise [Prov. 5:21]; but to the wise will there be matter for pride, who with the Prophet can say, "Thou has given me, O Lord, a delight in Thy doings; and in the works of Thy hands I shall rejoice [Ps. 91:5, Vg; Ps. 92:4, NRSV].... How great are Thy works, O Lord; Thou hast made all things in wisdom; the earth is filled with Thy riches" [Ps. 103:24, Vg; Ps. 104:24, NRSV]....

Chapter Seven: Of Mental and Mystical Elevation, in Which Repose Is Given to the Intellect When the Affections Pass Entirely into God through Elevation

1. Now that these six considerations have been studied as the six steps of the true throne of Solomon by which one ascends to peace, where the truly peaceful man reposes in peace of mind as if in the inner Jerusalem; as if, again, on the six wings of the Cherub by which the mind of the truly contemplative man grows strong to rise again, filled with the illumination of supreme wisdom; as if, once again, during the first six days in which the mind has to be exercised that it may finally arrive at the Sabbath of rest after it has beheld God outside itself through His traces and in His traces, within itself by His image and in His image, above itself by the likeness of the divine light shining down upon us and in that light, insofar as possible in this life and the exercise of our mind — when, finally, on the sixth level we have come to the point of beholding in the first and highest principle and the Mediator of God and men, Jesus Christ, those things of which the likeness cannot in any wise be found in creatures and which exceed all the insight of the human intellect, there remains that by looking upon these things it [the mind] rise on high and pass beyond not only this sensible world but itself also. In this passage Christ is the way and the door, Christ is the stairway and the vehicle, like the propitiatory over the ark of God and the mystery which has been hidden from eternity [Eph. 3:9]....

4. In this passage [i.e., passage over into God via contemplation], if it is perfect, all intellectual operations should be abandoned, and the whole height of our affection should be transferred and transformed into God. This, however, is mystical and most secret, which no man knoweth but he that hath received it [Rev. 2:17], nor does he receive it unless he desire it; nor does he desire it unless the fire of the Holy Spirit, Whom Christ sent to earth, has inflamed his marrow. And therefore the Apostle says that this mystic wisdom is revealed through the Holy Spirit.

5. Since, therefore, nature is powerless in this matter and industry but slightly

able, little should be given to inquiry but much to unction, little to the tongue but much to inner joy, little to the word and to the writings and all to the gift of God, that is, to the Holy Spirit, little or nothing to creation and all to the creative essence, Father, Son, and Holy Spirit.…

6. If you should ask how these things come about, question grace, not instruction; desire, not intellect; the cry of prayer, not pursuit of study; the spouse, not the teacher; God, not man; darkness, not clarity; not light, but the wholly flaming fire which will bear you aloft to God with fullest unction and burning affection. This fire is God, and the furnace of this fire leadeth to Jerusalem; and Christ the man kindles it in the fervor of His burning Passion, which he alone truly perceives who says, "My soul rather chooseth hanging and my bones death" [Job 7:15]. He who chooses this death can see God because this is indubitably true: "Man shall not see me and live" [Exod. 33:20]. Let us then die and pass over into darkness; let us impose silence on cares, concupiscence, and phantasms; let us pass over with the crucified Christ from this world to the Father [John 13:1], so that when the Father is shown to us we may say with Philip, "It is enough for us" [John 14:8]; let us hear with Paul, "My grace is sufficient for thee" [2 Cor. 12:9]; let us exult with David, saying, "For Thee my flesh and my heart hath fainted away; Thou art the God of my heart, and the God that is my portion forever [Ps. 72:26, Vg; Ps. 73:26, NRSV].… Blessed be the Lord God of Israel from everlasting to everlasting; and let all the people say: So be it, so be it" [Ps. 105:48, Vg; Ps. 106:48, NRSV]. Amen.

Thomas Aquinas (1224/25–1274)

Summa Theologiae (1266–73), Part One, Questions 2, 12, and 13*

Question 2: The Existence of God

First Article: Whether the Existence of God is Self-Evident?

We proceed thus to the First Article:

Objection 1. It seems that the existence of God is self-evident. Now those things are said to be self-evident to us the knowledge of which is naturally implanted in us, as we can see in regard to first principles. But as Damascene says (*De Fid. Orth.* i, 1, 3), *the knowledge of God is naturally implanted in all.* Therefore the existence of God is self-evident.

Obj. 2. Further, those things are said to be self-evident which are known as soon as the terms are known, which the Philosopher (1 *Poster.* iii) says is true of the first principles of demonstration. Thus, when the nature of a whole and of a part is known, it is at once recognized that every whole is greater than its part. But as soon as the signification of the word "God" is understood, it is at once seen that God exists. For by this word is signified that thing than which nothing

---

*Reprinted from St. Thomas Aquinas, *Summa Theologica*, trans. Fathers of the English Dominican Province, 5 vols., originally published in 1911, reprinted 1981 by Christian Classics, 200 E. Bethany Drive, Allen, TX 75002. Copyright © 1948 by Benziger Brothers, Inc. Used by permission of Benziger Brothers and Christian Classics. Vol. 1, pp. 11–14, 49, 54–55, 60–64, 70–71.

greater can be conceived. But that which exists actually and mentally is greater than that which exists only mentally. Therefore, since as soon as the word "God" is understood it exists mentally, it also follows that it exists actually. Therefore the proposition "God exists" is self-evident.

Obj. 3. Further, the existence of truth is self-evident. For whoever denies the existence of truth grants that truth does not exist; and, if truth does not exist, then the proposition "Truth does not exist" is true: and if there is anything true, there must be truth. But God is truth itself: *I am the way, the truth, and the life* (John 14:6). Therefore "God exists" is self-evident.

On the contrary, No one can mentally admit the opposite of what is self-evident; as the Philosopher (*Metaph.* iv., lect. vi) states concerning the first principles of demonstration. But the opposite of the proposition "God is" can be mentally admitted: *The fool said in his heart, There is no God* (Ps. 52:1, Vg; Ps. 53:1, NRSV). Therefore, that God exists is not self-evident.

I answer that, A thing can be self-evident in either of two ways; on the one hand, self-evident in itself, though not to us; on the other, self-evident in itself, and to us. A proposition is self-evident because the predicate is included in the essence of the subject, as "Man is an animal," for animal is contained in the essence of man. If, therefore, the essence of the predicate and subject be known to all, the proposition will be self-evident to all; as is clear with regard to the first principles of demonstration, the terms of which are common things that no one is ignorant of, such as being and nonbeing, whole and part, and such like. If, however, there are some to whom the essence of the predicate and subject is unknown, the proposition will be self-evident in itself, but not to those who do not know the meaning of the predicate and subject of the proposition. Therefore, it happens, as Boethius says (*Hebdom.,* the title of which is: "Whether all that is, is good"), "that there are some mental concepts self-evident only to the learned, as that incorporeal substances are not in space." Therefore I say that this proposition, "God exists," of itself is self-evident, for the predicate is the same as the subject; because God is His own existence as will be hereafter shown (q. 3, a. 4). Now because we do not know the essence of God, the proposition is not self-evident to us; but needs to be demonstrated by things that are more known to us, though less known in their nature — namely, by effects.

Reply Obj. 1. To know that God exists in a general and confused way is implanted in us by nature, inasmuch as God is man's beatitude. For man naturally desires happiness, and what is naturally desired by man must be naturally known to him. This, however, is not to know absolutely that God exists; just as to know that someone is approaching is not the same as to know that Peter is approaching, even though it is Peter who is approaching; for many there are who imagine that man's perfect good which is happiness, consists in riches, and others in pleasures, and others in something else.

Reply Obj. 2. Perhaps not everyone who hears this word "God" understands it to signify something than which nothing greater can be thought, seeing that some have believed God to be a body. Yet, granted that everyone understands that by this word "God" is signified something than which nothing greater can be thought, nevertheless, it does not therefore follow that he understands that what the word signifies exists actually, but only that it exists mentally. Nor can it be argued that it actually exists, unless it be admitted that there actually exists something than which nothing greater can be thought; and this precisely is not admitted by those who hold that God does not exist.

Reply Obj. 3. The existence of truth in general is self-evident but the existence of a Primal Truth is not self-evident to us.

Second Article: Whether It Can Be Demonstrated That God Exists?

We proceed thus to the Second Article:

Objection 1. It seems that the existence of God cannot be demonstrated. For it is an article of faith that God exists. But what is of faith cannot be demonstrated, because demonstration produces scientific knowledge; whereas faith is of the unseen (Heb. 11:1). Therefore it cannot be demonstrated that God exists....

Obj. 3. Further, if the existence of God were demonstrated, this could only be from His effects. But His effects are not proportionate to Him, since He is infinite and His effects are finite; and between the finite and infinite there is no proportion. Therefore, since a cause cannot be demonstrated by an effect not proportionate to it, it seems that the existence of God cannot be demonstrated.

On the contrary, The Apostle says: *The invisible things of Him are clearly seen, being understood by the things that are made* (Rom. 1:20). But this would not be unless the existence of God could be demonstrated through the things that are made....

I answer that.... When an effect is better known to us than its cause, from the effect we proceed to the knowledge of the cause. And from every effect the existence of its proper cause can be demonstrated, so long as its effects are better known to us; because since every effect depends upon its cause, if the effect exists, the cause must pre-exist. Hence the existence of God, insofar as it is not self-evident to us, can be demonstrated from those of His effects which are known to us.

Reply Obj. 1. The existence of God and other like truths about God, which can be known by natural reason, are not articles of faith, but are preambles to the articles; for faith presupposes natural knowledge, even as grace presupposes nature, and perfection supposes something that can be perfected. Nevertheless, there is nothing to prevent a man, who cannot grasp a proof, from accepting, as a matter of faith, something which in itself is capable of being scientifically known and demonstrated.

...Reply Obj. 3. From effects not proportionate to the cause no perfect knowledge of that cause can be obtained. Yet from every effect the existence of the cause can be clearly demonstrated, and so we can demonstrate the existence of God from His effects; though from them we cannot perfectly know God as He is in His essence.

Third Article: Whether God Exists?

We proceed thus to the Third Article:

Objection 1. It seems that God does not exist; because if one of two contraries be infinite, the other would be altogether destroyed. But the word "God" means that He is infinite goodness. If, therefore, God existed, there would be no evil discoverable; but there is evil in the world. Therefore God does not exist....

On the contrary, it is said in the person of God: *I am Who am* (Exod. 3:14).

I answer that, The existence of God can be proved in five ways.

The first and more manifest way is the argument from motion. It is certain, and evident to our senses, that in the world some things are in motion. Now whatever is in motion is put in motion by another, for nothing can be in motion except it is in potentiality to that towards which it is in motion; whereas a thing moves inasmuch as it is in act. For motion is nothing else than the reduction of something from potentiality to actuality. But nothing can be reduced from potentiality to actuality, except by something in a state of actuality. Thus that which is actually hot, as fire, makes wood, which is potentially hot, to be actually hot, and thereby moves and changes it. Now it is not possible that the same thing should be at once in actuality and potentiality in the same respect, but only in different respects. For what is actually hot cannot simultaneously be potentially hot; but it is simultaneously potentially cold. It is therefore impossible that in the same respect and in the same way a thing should be both mover and moved, i.e., that it should move itself. Therefore, whatever is in motion must be put in motion by another. If that by which it is put in motion be itself put in motion, then this also must needs be put in motion by another, and that by another again. But this cannot go on to infinity, because then there would be no first mover, and, consequently, no other mover; seeing that subsequent movers move only inasmuch as they are put in motion by the first mover, as the staff moves only because it is put in motion by the hand. Therefore it is necessary to arrive at a first mover, put in motion by no other; and this everyone understands to be God.

The second way is from the nature of the efficient cause. In the world of sense we find there is an order of efficient causes. There is no case known (neither is it, indeed, possible) in which a thing is found to be the efficient cause of itself; for so it would be prior to itself, which is impossible. Now in efficient causes it is not possible to go on to infinity, because in all efficient causes following in order, the first is the cause of the intermediate cause, and the intermediate is the cause of the ultimate cause, whether the intermediate cause be several, or one only....Therefore it is necessary to admit a first efficient cause, to which everyone gives the name of God.

The third way is taken from possibility and necessity, and runs thus. We find in nature things that are possible to be and not to be, since they are found to be generated, and to corrupt, and consequently, they are possible to be and not to be. But it is impossible for these always to exist, for that which is possible not to be at some time is not. Therefore, if everything is possible not to be, then at one time there could have been nothing in existence. Now if this were true, even now there would be nothing in existence, because that which does not exist only begins to exist by something already existing. Therefore, if at one time nothing was in existence, it would have been impossible for anything to have begun to exist; and thus even now nothing would be in existence — which is absurd.... Therefore we cannot but postulate the existence of some being having of itself its own necessity, and not receiving it from another, but rather causing in others their necessity. This all men speak of as God.

The fourth way is taken from the gradation to be found in things. Among beings there are some more and some less good, true, noble, and the like. But "more" and "less" are predicated of different things, according as they resemble in their different ways something which is the maximum, as a thing is said to be hotter according as it more nearly resembles that which is hottest; so that there is something which is truest, something best, something noblest, and, consequently, something which is uttermost being; . . . Now the maximum in any genus is the cause of all in that genus; as fire, which is the maximum of heat, is the cause of all hot things. Therefore there must also be something which is to all beings the cause of their being, goodness, and every other perfection; and this we call God.

The fifth way is taken from the governance of the world. We see that things which lack intelligence, such as natural bodies, act for an end, and this is evident from their acting always, or nearly always, in the same way, so as to obtain the best result. Hence it is plain that not fortuitously, but designedly, do they achieve their end. Now whatever lacks intelligence cannot move towards an end, unless it be directed by some being endowed with knowledge and intelligence; as the arrow is shot to its mark by the archer. Therefore some intelligent being exists by whom all natural things are directed to their end; and this being we call God.

Reply Obj. 1. As Augustine says (*Enchir.* xi): *Since God is the highest good, He would not allow any evil to exist in His works, unless His omnipotence and goodness were such as to bring good even out of evil.* This is part of the infinite goodness of God, that He should allow evil to exist, and out of it produce good.

Question 12: How God Is Known by Us

First Article: Whether Any Created Intellect Can See the Essence of God?

We proceed thus to the First Article:

Objection 1. It seems that no created intellect can see the essence of God. For Chrysostom (*Hom. xiv. In Joann.*) commenting on John 1:18, *No man hath seen God at any time,* says: *Not prophets only, but neither angels nor archangels have seen God.* For how can a creature see what is increatable? Dionysius also says (*Div. Nom.* i), speaking of God: *Neither is there sense, nor image, nor opinion, nor reason, nor knowledge of Him.*

. . . *Obj.* 4. Further, there must be some proportion between the knower and the known, since the known is the perfection of the knower. But no proportion exists between the created intellect and God; for there is an infinite distance between them. Therefore the created intellect cannot see the essence of God.

On the contrary, It is written: *We shall see Him as He is* (1 John 3:2).

I answer that, Since everything is knowable according as it is actual, God, Who is pure act without any admixture of potentiality, is in Himself supremely knowable. But what is supremely knowable in itself may not be knowable to a particular intellect, on account of the excess of the intelligible object above the intellect; as, for example, the sun, which is supremely visible, cannot be seen by the bat by reason of its excess of light.

Therefore some who considered this held that no created intellect can see the essence of God. This opinion, however, is not tenable. For as the ultimate beatitude of man consists in the use of his highest function, which is the operation of the intellect; if we suppose that the created intellect could never see God, it would either never attain to beatitude, or its beatitude would consist in something else beside God; which is opposed to faith. For the ultimate perfection of the rational creature is to be found in that which is the principle of its being; since a thing is perfect so far as it attains to its principle. Further the same opinion is also against reason. For there resides in every man a natural desire to know the cause of any effect which he sees; and thence arises wonder in men. But if the intellect of the rational creature could not reach so far as to the first cause of things, the natural desire would remain void.

Hence it must be absolutely granted that the blessed see the essence of God.

Reply Obj. 1. Both of these authorities speak of the vision of comprehension. Hence Dionysius premises immediately before the words cited, *He is universally to all incomprehensible*, etc. Chrysostom, likewise after the words quoted, says: *He says this of the most certain vision of the Father, which is such a perfect consideration and comprehension as the Father has of the Son.*

...*Reply Obj.* 4. Proportion is twofold. In one sense it means a certain relation of one quantity to another, according as double, treble, and equal are species of proportion. In another sense every relation of one thing to another is called proportion. And in this sense there can be a proportion of the creature to God, inasmuch as it is related to Him as the effect to its cause, and as potentiality to its act; and in this way the created intellect can be proportioned to know God....

Question 13: The Names of God

Second Article: Whether Any Name Can be Applied to God Substantially?

We proceed thus to the Second Article:

Objection 1. It seems that no name can be applied to God substantially. For Damascene says (*De Fid. Orth.* i.9): *Everything said of God signifies not His substance, but rather shows forth what He is not; or expresses some relation, or something following from His nature or operation....*

Obj. 3. Further, a thing is named by us according as we understand it. But God is not understood by us in this life in His substance. Therefore neither is any name we can use applied substantially to God.

On the contrary, Augustine says (*De Trin.* vi): *The being of God is the being strong, or the being wise, or whatever else we may say of that simplicity whereby His substance is signified.*

Therefore all names of this kind signify the divine substance.

I answer that, Negative names applied to God or signifying His relation to creatures manifestly do not at all signify His substance, but rather express the distance of the creature from Him, or His relation to something else, or rather, the relation of creatures to Himself.

But as regards absolute and affirmative names of God, as good, wise, and the like, various and many opinions have been given. For some have said that all such names, although they are applied to God affirmatively, nevertheless have been brought into use more to express some remotion from God, rather than to express anything that exists positively in Him. Hence they assert that when we say that God lives, we mean that God is not like an inanimate thing; and the same in like manner applies to other names; and this was taught by Rabbi Moses.[1] Others say that these names applied to God signify His relationship towards creatures: thus in the words, *God is good,* we mean, God is the cause of goodness in things; and the same rule applies to other names.

Both of these opinions, however, seem to be untrue for three reasons. First because in neither of them can a reason be assigned why some names more than others are applied to God. For He is assuredly the cause of bodies in the same way as He is the cause of good things; therefore if the words *God is good,* signified no more than, *God is the cause of good things,* it might in like manner be said that God is a body, inasmuch as He is the cause of bodies. So also to say that He is a body implies that He is not a mere potentiality, as is primary matter. Secondly, because it would follow that all names applied to God would be said of Him by way of being taken in a secondary sense, as healthy is secondarily said of medicine, forasmuch as it signifies only the cause of health in the animal which primarily is called healthy. Thirdly, because this is against the intention of those who speak of God. For in saying that God lives, they assuredly mean more than to say that He is the cause of our life, or that He differs from inanimate bodies.

Therefore we must hold a different doctrine — viz., that these names signify the divine substance, and are predicated substantially of God, although they fall short of a full representation of Him. Which is proved thus. For these names express God, so far as our intellects know Him. Now since our intellect knows God from creatures, it knows Him as far as creatures represent Him. Now it was shown above (q. 4, a. 2) that God prepossesses in Himself all the perfections of creatures, being Himself simply and universally perfect. Hence every creature represents Him, and is like Him so far as it possesses some perfection: yet it represents Him not as something of the same species or genus, but as the excelling principle of whose form the effects fall short, although they derive some kind of likeness thereto, even as the forms of inferior bodies represent the power of the sun. This was explained above (q. 4, a. 3), in treating of the divine perfection. Therefore the aforesaid names signify the divine substance, but in an imperfect manner, even as creatures represent it imperfectly. So when we say, *God is good,* the meaning is not, *God is the cause of goodness,* or, *God is not evil;* but the meaning is, *Whatever good we attribute to creatures, pre-exists in God,* and in a more excellent and higher way. Hence it does not follow that God is good, because He causes goodness; but rather, on the contrary, He causes goodness in things because He is good; according to what Augustine says (*De Doctr. Christ.* I. 32), *Because He is good, we are.*

Reply Obj. 1. Damascene says that these names do not signify what God is, forasmuch as by none of these names is perfectly expressed what He is; but each one signifies Him in an imperfect manner, even as creatures represent Him imperfectly.

Reply Obj. 3. We cannot know the essence of God in this life, as He really is in

---

1. Aquinas is referring here to Moses Maimonides, the great Jewish medieval thinker.

Himself; but we know Him accordingly as He is represented in the perfections of creatures; and thus the names imposed by us signify Him in that manner only. . . .

Fifth Article: Whether What Is Said of God and of Creatures Is Univocally Predicated of Them?

We proceed thus to the Fifth Article:

. . . *Obj.* 2. Further, there is no similitude among equivocal things. Therefore as creatures have a certain likeness to God, according to the word of Genesis (1:26), *Let us make man to our image and likeness,* it seems that something can be said of God and creatures univocally.

Obj. 3. Further, measure is homogeneous with the thing measured. But God is the first measure of all beings. Therefore God is homogeneous with creatures; and thus a word may be applied univocally to God and to creatures.

. . . *I answer that,* Univocal predication is impossible between God and creatures. The reason of this is that every effect which is not an adequate result of the power of the efficient cause receives the similitude of the agent not in its full degree, but in a measure that falls short, so that what is divided and multiplied in the effects resides in the agent simply, and in the same manner. . . . In the same way, as said in the preceding article, all perfections existing in creatures divided and multiplied pre-exist in God unitedly. Thus, when any term expressing perfection is applied to a creature, it signifies that perfection distinct in idea from other perfections; as, for instance, by this term *wise* applied to a man, we signify some perfection distinct from a man's essence, and distinct from his power and existence, and from all similar things; whereas when we apply it to God, we do not mean to signify anything distinct from His essence, or power, or existence. Thus also this term *wise* applied to man in some degree circumscribes and comprehends the thing signified; whereas this is not the case when it is applied to God; but it leaves the thing signified as incomprehended, and as exceeding the signification of the name. Hence it is evident that this term *wise* is not applied in the same way to God and to man. The same rule applies to other terms. Hence no name is predicated univocally of God and of creatures.

Neither, on the other hand, are names applied to God and creatures in a purely equivocal sense, as some have said. Because if that were so, it follows that from creatures nothing could be known or demonstrated about God at all; for the reasoning would always be exposed to the fallacy of equivocation. Such a view is against the philosophers, who proved many things about God, and also against what the Apostle says: *The invisible things of God are clearly seen being understood by the things that are made* (Rom. 1:20). Therefore it must be said that these names are said of God and creatures in an analogous sense, that is, according to proportion.

Now names are thus used in two ways: either according as many things are proportionate to one, thus for example *healthy* is predicated of medicine and urine in relation and in proportion to health of a body, of which the latter is the sign and the former the cause: or according as one thing is proportionate to another, thus *healthy* is said of medicine and animal, since medicine is the cause of health in the animal body. And in this way some things are said of God and creatures analogically, and not in a purely equivocal nor in a purely univocal sense. For we can name God only from creatures (a. 1). Thus, whatever is said of God and creatures, is said according to the relation of a creature to God as its principle and cause, wherein all perfections of things pre-exist excellently. Now this mode of community of idea is a mean between pure equivocation and simple univocation. For in analogies the idea is not, as it is in univocals, one and the same, yet it is not totally diverse as in equivocals; but a term which is thus used in a multiple sense signifies various proportions to some one thing; thus healthy applied to urine signifies the sign of animal health, and applied to medicine signifies the cause of the same health....

Reply Obj. 2. The likeness of the creature to God is imperfect, for it does not represent one and the same generic thing (q. 4, a. 3).

Reply Obj. 3. God is not the measure proportioned to things measured; hence it is not necessary that God and creatures should be in the same genus.

The arguments adduced in the contrary sense prove indeed that these names are not predicated univocally of God and creatures; yet they do not prove that they are predicated equivocally....

Eleventh Article: Whether This Name, HE WHO IS, Is the Most Proper Name of God?

We proceed thus to the Eleventh Article:

Objection 1. It seems that this name HE WHO IS is not the most proper name of God. For this name *God* is an incommunicable name. But this name HE WHO IS is not an incommunicable name. Therefore this name HE WHO IS is not the most proper name of God.

...I answer that, This name HE WHO IS is most properly applied to God, for three reasons:

First, because of its signification. For it does not signify form, but simply existence itself. Hence since the existence of God is His essence itself, which can be said of no other (q. 3, a. 4), it is clear that among other names this one specially denominates God, for everything is denominated by its form.

Secondly, on account of its universality. For all other names are either less universal, or, if convertible with it, add something above it at least in idea;... Now our intellect cannot know the essence of God itself in this life, as it is in itself, but whatever mode it applies in determining what it understands about God, it falls short of the mode of what God is in Himself. Therefore the less determinate the names are, and the more universal and absolute they are, the more properly they apply to God....

Thirdly, from its consignification, for it signifies present existence; and this above all properly applies to God, whose existence knows not past or future, as Augustine says (*De. Trin.* v).

Reply Obj. 1. This name HE WHO IS is the name of God more properly than this name *God,* as regards its source, namely, existence; and as regards the mode of signification and consignification, as said above. But as regards the object intended by the name, this name *God* is more proper, as it is imposed to signify the divine nature; and still more proper is the Tetragrammaton, imposed to signify the substance of God itself, incommunicable and, if one may so speak, singular.

Hadewijch of Brabant (mid-thirteenth century)

Letter 28, "Trinitarian Contemplation Caught in Words" (mid-1200s)*

1. In the riches of the clarity of the Holy Spirit, the blissful soul celebrates wonderful feasts. These feasts are holy words exchanged in holy rapture with the holiness of our Lord. These words give every soul who hears them and understands them essentially four things in full holiness: They give her pleasure, and sweetness, and joy, and bliss, and all in veritable spiritualness.

10. So whenever God gives the blissful soul this clarity, which enables it to contemplate him in his Godhead, it contemplates him in his Eternity, and in his Greatness, and in his Wisdom, and in his Nobility — and in his Presence, and in his Effusion, and in his Totality. It sees how God is in his Eternity: God through his own Divinity. It sees how God is in his Greatness: powerful in his own power. It sees how God is in his Wisdom: blissful in his own bliss. It sees how God is in his Nobility: glorious in his own glory. It sees how God is in his Presence: sweet with his own sweetness. It sees how God is in his Effusion: rich with his own riches. It sees how God is in his Totality: happy in his own happiness....

48. And this soul itself says further: "The soul who walks *with God* (Gen. 5:22) in his Presence gladly speaks of his pleasure, and of his sweetness, and of his greatness. The soul who walks yet farther with God in his Effusion speaks gladly of his love, and of his bliss, and of his nobility. The soul who walks yet farther with God in his Totality speaks gladly of heavenly riches, and heavenly joy, and heavenly happiness. This blissful soul who walks in God (cf. Col. 2:6) with all these, and walks *with God* (Gen. 5:22) in all these knows every kind of grace; and it is master and blissful with the same bliss in divine riches as God, who is one eternal Lord, and who is all good, and who is God, and who created all things.

65. "God is greatness, and power, and wisdom. God is goodness, and presence, and sweetness. God is subtlety, and nobility, and happiness. God is eminent in his greatness, and perfect in his power, and blissful in his wisdom. God is wonderful in his goodness, and total in his presence, and joy in his sweetness. God is true in his subtlety, and blessed in his nobility, and wholly overflowing in his happiness. Thus is God in Three Persons with himself in the manifoldness of the divine riches. God is one blessed Beatitude, and he subsists with the fullness of his omnipotence in wonderful exalted riches."

80. These are words that come surging up in the soul with bliss from God's excellence. And what is God's excellence? It is the Being of the Godhead in the Unity, and the Unity in the totality, and the totality in the manifestation, the man-

---

*Reprinted from *Hadewijch* by Mother Columba Hart, O.S.B. © 1980 by The Missionary Society of St. Paul the Apostle in the State of New York. Used by permission of Paulist Press. Pp. 109–11.

ifestation in glory, and glory in fruition, and fruition in eternity. God's graces are all excellent. But he who understands this — how this is in God, and in the throne of thrones, and in the riches of heaven — possesses the excellence of all kinds of graces. He who wishes to say more about this must speak with his soul.

93. God abides in bliss and is present in the midst of his glory. And therein he is, within himself, ineffable in his goodness, riches, and wondrousness. God by himself pronounces himself within himself in full beatitude; and the beatitude of his creatures consists in what he is. This is why heaven and earth are full of God; anyone spiritual enough to know God by experience can understand this.

101. A blessed soul saw with God according to God; and it saw God enclosed and yet overflowing. And it saw God overflowing in totality, and total in over-flowingness. And this soul spoke with its totality and exclaimed: "God is a great and unique Lord in eternity, and he has in his Godhead the Being of Three Persons: He is Father in his power; he is Son in his knowableness; he is Holy Spirit in his glory. God gives, in the Father; and he reveals, in the Son; and he enables us to taste, in the Holy Spirit. God works with the Father in power; with the Son in knowableness; and with the Holy Spirit in subtlety. Thus God works with Three Persons as one Lord; and with one Lord as Three Persons; and with Three Persons in a manifoldness of the divine riches; and with the manifoldness of the divine riches in the souls he has blessed, whom he has led into the mystery of his Father, and all of whom he has made blissful."

121. Between God and the blissful soul that has become God with God, there reigns a spiritual charity. So whenever God reveals this spiritual charity to the soul, there rises within it a tender friendship (cf. Rom. 8:28). That is, it feels within it how God is its friend before all pain, in all pain, and above all pain, yes, beyond all pain, in fidelity toward his Father. And this tender friendship gives rise to a sublime confidence. In this sublime confidence there rises a genuine sweet-ness. In this genuine sweetness rises a veritable joy. In this veritable joy rises a divine clarity. Then the soul sees, and it sees nothing. It sees a truth — Subsistent, Effusive, Total — which is God himself in eternity. The soul waits; God gives, and it receives. And what it then receives in verity, and spiritualness, and pleasure, and wonder can be communicated to no one. And it must remain in silence, in the liberty of this bliss. What God then says to it of sublime spiritual wonders, no one knows but God who gives it, and the soul who, conformed to God's spiritual Nature, is like God above all spiritualness.

146. Thus spoke one person in God [This is a reference to Hadewijch herself.]: "My soul is completely torn by the power of eternity, and melted by the friend-ship of Paternity; and it is streamed through by God's greatness. This greatness is without measure. And the Heart of my heart is that rich wealth which my God and Lord is in his eternity."

153. Thus spoke one person in God's friendship: "I have heard the voice of bliss (Bar. 2:23); I have seen the land of clarity; and I have tasted the fruit of joys. Since this has happened, all the senses of my soul await lofty spiritual wonders, and all my prayers in the presence are continually filled with a sweet confidence that is God himself in veritable truth. Because this is so, I am immeasurably enriched with the same bliss as God is in his Godhead...."

Meister Eckhart (ca. 1260–1328)

German Sermon No. 9 (ca. 1320s)*

Quasi stella matutina in medio nebulae et quasi luna plena in diebus suis lucet et quasi sol refulgens, sic iste refulsit in templo dei. (Sir. 50:6–7)

As the morning star through the mist and as the full moon in its days and as the resplendent sun, so did this man shine in the temple of God.

First I shall take the last phrase: "temple of God." What is "God" and what is "temple of God"?

Twenty-four philosophers came together and wanted to discuss what God is. They came at the appointed time and each of them gave his definition. I shall now take up two or three of them. One said: "God is something compared to which all changeable and transitory things are nothing, and everything that has being is insignificant in his presence." The second said: "God is something that is of necessity above being; that in himself needs no one and that all things need." The third said: "God is intellect living in the knowledge of himself alone."

I shall leave aside the first and the last definition and speak about the second, that God is something that of necessity must be above being. Whatever has being, time, or place does not touch God. He is above it. God is in all creatures, insofar as they have being, and yet he is above them. That same thing that he is in all creatures is exactly what he is above them. Whatever is one in many things must of necessity be above them.... If I take a segment of time, it is neither today nor yesterday.[1] But if I take "now," that contains within itself all time. The "now" in which God made the world is as near to this time as the "now" in which I am presently speaking, and the last day is as near to this "now" as the day that was yesterday.

One authority says: "God is something that works in eternity undivided in himself; that needs no one's help or instrumentality, and remains in himself; that needs nothing and that all things need, and toward which all things strive as to their final end." This end has no limited manner of being. It grows out beyond manner and spreads out into the distance....

Everything works in being; nothing works above its being. Fire cannot work except in wood. God works above being in vastness, where he can roam. He works in nonbeing. Before being was, God worked, He worked being when there was no being. Unsophisticated teachers say that God is pure being. He is as high above being as the highest angel is above a gnat. I would be speaking as incorrectly in calling God a being as if I called the sun pale or black. God is neither this nor that. A master says: "Whoever imagines that he has understood God, if he knows anything, it is not God that he knows." However, in saying that God is not a being and is above being, I have not denied being to God; rather, I have

*Reprinted from *Meister Eckhart: Teacher and Preacher* by Bernard McGinn, © 1986 by Bernard McGinn. Used by permission of Paulist Press. Pp. 255–60.

1. This sentence would seem to be more intelligible if it read: "If I take a segment of time, it is *either* today *or* yesterday." However, there is no backing for this in the manuscripts.

elevated it in him. If I take copper [mixed] with gold, it is still present and is present in a higher manner than it is in itself. St. Augustine says: God is wise without wisdom, good without goodness, powerful without power [Augustine, *The Trinity*, Book 5.1.2].

Young masters say in the schools that all being is divided into ten modes of being and they deny them completely of God. None of these modes touches God, but neither does he lack any of them. The first mode, which has the most of being and in which all things receive being, is substance; and the last mode, which contains the least of being, is called relation, and in God this is the same as the greatest of all which has the most of being. They have equal images in God. In God the images of all things are alike, but they are images of unlike things. The highest angel and the soul and a gnat have like image in God. God is neither being nor goodness. Goodness adheres to being and is not more extensive. If there were no being, neither would there be goodness. Yet being is purer than goodness. God is neither good nor better nor best of all. Whoever would say that God is good would be treating him as unjustly as though he were calling the sun black.

And yet God says: No one is good but God alone. What is good? Good is that which shares itself. We call a person good who shares with others and is useful. Because of this a pagan master says: A hermit is neither good nor evil in a sense because he does not share and is not useful. God shares most of all. Nothing [else] shares itself out of what is its own, for all creatures are nothing in themselves. Whatever they share they have from another. Nor is it themselves that they give. The sun gives its radiance yet remains where it is; fire gives its heat but remains fire. God, however, shares what is his because what he is, he is from himself. And in all the gifts he gives he always gives himself first of all. He gives himself as God, as he is in all his gifts, to the extent that the person who can receive him is capable. St. James says: "All good gifts flow down from above from the Father of lights" (James 1:17).

When we grasp God in being, we grasp him in his antechamber, for being is the antechamber in which he dwells. Where is he then in his temple, in which he shines as holy? Intellect is the temple of God. Nowhere does God dwell more properly than in his temple, in intellect, as the second philosopher said: "God is intellect, living in the knowledge of himself alone," remaining in himself alone where nothing ever touches him; for he alone is there in his stillness. God in the knowledge of himself knows himself in himself....

I said in a lecture that the intellect is nobler than the will, and yet they both belong in this light. A professor in another school [the Franciscan Gonsalvo of Spain, with whom Eckhart debated] said that the will was nobler than the intellect because the will grasps things as they are in themselves, while the intellect grasps things as they are in it. This is true. An eye is nobler in itself than an eye that is painted on a wall. Nevertheless, I say that the understanding is nobler than the will. The will perceives God in the garment of goodness. The understanding perceives God bare, as he is stripped of goodness and being. Goodness is a garment by which God is hidden, and the will perceives God in this garment of goodness. If there were no goodness in God, my will would want nothing of him. If someone wanted to clothe a king on the day when he was to be made king, and if one clothed him in gray attire, such a one would not have clothed him well. I am not happy because God is good. I shall never beg that God make me happy with his goodness because he could not do it. I am happy for this reason alone — because God is of an intellectual nature and because I know this. . . .

"As the morning star through the mist." I would now like to focus on the little word *quasi* which means "as." Children in school call this an adverb. This is what I focus on in all my sermons. What one can most properly say about God is that he is word and truth. God called himself a word. St. John said: "In the beginning was the Word" (John 1:1). He means that one should be an ad-verb to the Word. The planet Venus, after which Friday is named, has many names. When it precedes and rises before the sun, it is called the morning star; when it so follows that the sun sets first, it is called an evening star. Sometimes its path is above the sun, sometimes below the sun. In contrast to all the other stars it is always equally near the sun. It never departs farther from, nor approaches nearer to, the sun. It stands for a man who wants always to be near to and present to God in such a way that nothing can separate him from God, neither happiness nor unhappiness, nor any creature.

The sage also says: "as the full moon in its days" (Sir. 50:6). The moon rules over all moist nature. The moon is never so near the sun as when it is full and is receiving its light directly from the sun. . . . It is never so powerful as when it is farthest from the earth, because then it causes the ocean to rise the most. The more it wanes, the less it causes it to rise. The more the soul is raised above earthly things, the more powerful it is. Whoever knew but one creature would not need to ponder any sermon, for every creature is full of God and is a book. The person who wants to achieve what we have just spoken about — and this is the whole point of the sermon — should be like the morning star: always present to God, always with him and equally near him, and raised above all earthly things. He should be an ad-verb to the Word.

There is one kind of word which is brought forth, like an angel and a human being and all creatures. There is a second kind of word, thought out and not brought forth, as happens when I form a thought. There is yet another kind of word that is not brought forth and not thought out, that never comes forth. Rather, it remains eternally in him who speaks it. It is continually being conceived in the Father who speaks it, and it remains within. The understanding always works internally. The more refined and immaterial a thing is, the more powerfully it works internally. And the more powerful and refined the understanding is, the more that which it knows is united with it and is more one with it. This is not the case with material things — the more powerful they are, the more they work outside themselves. God's happiness depends on his understanding's working internally, where the Word remains within. There the soul should be an ad-verb and work one work with God in order to receive its happiness in the same inwardly hovering knowledge where God is happy.

That we may be forever an ad-verb to this Word, for this may we receive the help of the Father and the same Word and the Holy Spirit. Amen.

Julian of Norwich (ca. 1342–1416)

Showings (ca. 1393, Long Text), Chapters 58 and 59*

The Fifty-Eighth Chapter

God the blessed Trinity, who is everlasting being, just as he is eternal from without beginning, just so was it in his eternal purpose to create human nature, which fair nature was first prepared for his own Son, the second person; and when he wished, by full agreement of the whole Trinity he created us all once. And in our creating he joined and united us to himself, and through this union we are kept as pure and as noble as we were created. By the power of that same precious union we love our Creator and delight in him, praise him and thank him and endlessly rejoice in him. And this is the work which is constantly performed in every soul which will be saved, and this is the godly will mentioned before.

And so in our making, God almighty is our loving Father, and God all wisdom is our loving Mother, with the love and the goodness of the Holy Spirit, which is all one God, one Lord. And in the joining and the union he is our very true spouse and we his beloved wife and his fair maiden, with which wife he was never displeased; for he says: I love you and you love me, and our love will never divide in two.

I contemplated the work of all the blessed Trinity, in which contemplation I saw and understood these three properties: the property of the fatherhood, and the property of the motherhood, and the property of the lordship in one God. In our almighty Father we have our protection and our bliss, as regards our natural substance, which is ours by our creation from without beginning; and in the second person, in knowledge and wisdom we have our perfection, as regards our sensuality, our restoration, and our salvation, for he is our Mother, brother, and savior; and in our good Lord the Holy Spirit we have our reward and our gift for our living and our labor, endlessly surpassing all that we desire in his marvelous courtesy, out of his great plentiful grace. For all our life consists of three: In the first we have our being, and in the second we have our increasing, and in the third we have our fulfillment. The first is nature, the second is mercy, the third is grace.

As to the first, I saw and understood that the high might of the Trinity is our Father, and the deep wisdom of the Trinity is our Mother, and the great love of the Trinity is our Lord; and all these we have in nature and in our substantial creation. And furthermore I saw that the second person, who is our Mother, substantially the same beloved person, has now become our mother sensually, because we are double by God's creating, that is to say, substantial and sensual. Our substance is the higher part, which we have in our Father, God almighty; and the second person of the Trinity is our Mother in nature in our substantial creation, in whom we are founded and rooted, and he is our Mother of mercy in taking our sensuality. And so our Mother is working on us in various ways, in whom our parts are kept undivided; for in our Mother Christ we profit and increase, and in mercy he reforms and restores us, and by the power of his Passion, his

*Reprinted from *Julian of Norwich* by James Walsh, S.J., © 1978 by The Missionary Society of St. Paul the Apostle in State of New York. Used by permission of Paulist Press. Pp. 293–97.

death and his Resurrection he unites us to our substance. So our Mother works in mercy on all his beloved children who are docile and obedient to him, and grace works with mercy, and especially in two properties, as it was shown, which working belongs to the third person, the Holy Spirit. He works, rewarding and giving. Rewarding is a gift for our confidence which the Lord makes to those who have labored; and giving is a courteous act which he does freely, by grace, fulfilling and surpassing all that creatures deserve.

Thus in our Father, God almighty, we have our being, and in our Mother of mercy we have our reforming and our restoring, in whom our parts are united and all made perfect man, and through the rewards and the gifts of grace of the Holy Spirit we are fulfilled. And our substance is in our Father, God almighty, and our substance is in our Mother, God all wisdom, and our substance is in our Lord God, the Holy Spirit, all goodness, for our substance is whole in each person of the Trinity, who is one God. And our sensuality is only in the second person, Christ Jesus, in whom is the Father and the Holy Spirit; and in him and by him we are powerfully taken out of hell and out of the wretchedness on earth, and gloriously brought up into heaven, and blessedly united to our substance, increased in riches and nobility by all the power of Christ and by the grace and operation of the Holy Spirit.

The Fifty-Ninth Chapter

And we have all this bliss by mercy and grace, and this kind of bliss we never could have had and known, unless that property of goodness which is in God had been opposed, through which we have this bliss. For wickedness has been suffered to rise in opposition to that goodness; and the goodness of mercy and grace opposed that wickedness, and turned everything to goodness and honor for all who will be saved. For this is that property in God which opposes good to evil. So Jesus Christ, who opposes good to evil, is our true Mother. We have our being from him, where the foundation of motherhood begins, with all the sweet protection of love which endlessly follows.

As truly as God is our Father, so truly is God our Mother, and he revealed that in everything, and especially in these sweet words where he says: I am he; that is to say: I am he, the power and goodness of fatherhood; I am he, the wisdom and the lovingness of motherhood; I am he, the light and the grace which is all blessed love; I am he, the Trinity; I am he, the unity; I am he, the great supreme goodness of every kind of thing; I am he who makes you to love; I am he who makes you to long; I am he, the endless fulfilling of all true desires. For where the soul is highest, noblest, most honorable, still it is lowest, meekest, and mildest.

And from this foundation in substance we have all the powers of our sensuality by the gift of nature, and by the help and the furthering of mercy and grace, without which we cannot profit. Our great Father, almighty God, who is being, knows us and loved us before time began. Out of this knowledge, in his most wonderful deep love, by the prescient eternal counsel of all the blessed Trinity, he wanted the second person to become our Mother, our brother, and our savior. From this it follows that as truly as God is our Father, so truly is God our Mother. Our Father wills, our Mother works, our good Lord the Holy Spirit confirms. And therefore it is our part to love our God in whom we have our being, reverently thanking and praising him for our creation, mightily praying to our Mother for mercy and pity, and to our Lord the Holy Spirit for help and grace. For in these three is all our life: nature, mercy, and grace, of which we have mildness, patience, and pity, and hatred of sin and wickedness; for the virtues must of themselves hate sin and wickedness.

And so Jesus is our true Mother in nature by our first creation, and he is our true Mother in grace by his taking our created nature. All the lovely works and all the sweet loving offices of beloved motherhood are appropriated to the second person, for in him we have this godly will, whole and safe forever, both in nature and in grace, from his own goodness proper to him.

I understand three ways of contemplating motherhood in God. The first is the foundation of our nature's creation; the second is his taking of our nature, where the motherhood of grace begins; the third is the motherhood at work. And in that, by the same grace, everything is penetrated, in length and in breadth, in height and in depth without end; and it is all one love.

Martin Luther (1483–1546)

Heidelberg Disputation (1518), Theses 20 and 21*

> Thesis 20: *He deserves to be called a theologian, however, who comprehends the visible and manifest things of God seen through suffering and the cross.*

The "back" and visible things of God are placed in opposition to the invisible, namely, his human nature, weakness, foolishness. The Apostle in 1 Cor. 1 [:25] calls them the weakness and folly of God. Because men misused the knowledge of God through works, God wished again to be recognized in suffering, and to condemn wisdom concerning invisible things by means of wisdom concerning visible things, so that those who did not honor God as manifested in his works should honor him as he is hidden in his suffering. As the Apostle says in 1 Cor. 1 [:21], "For since, in the wisdom of God, the world did not know God through wisdom, it pleased God through the folly of what we preach to save those who believe." Now it is not sufficient for anyone, and it does him no good to recognize God in his glory and majesty, unless he recognizes him in the humility and shame of the cross. Thus God destroys the wisdom of the wise, as Isa. [45:15] says, "Truly, thou art a God who hidest thyself."

So, also, in John 14 [:8], where Philip spoke according to the theology of glory: "Show us the Father." Christ forthwith set aside his flighty thought about seeking God elsewhere and led him to himself, saying, "Philip, he who has seen me has seen the Father" [John 14:9]. For this reason true theology and recognition of God are in the crucified Christ, as it is also stated in John 14 [John 14:6]: "No one comes to the Father, but by me." "I am the door" [John 10:9], and so forth.

---

*Reprinted from *Luther's Works*, vol. 31, ed. Harold Grimm, copyright © 1957 Fortress Press. Used by permission of Augsburg Fortress. Pp. 52–53.

Thesis 21: *A theologian of glory calls evil good and good evil. A theologian of the cross calls the thing what it actually is.*

This is clear: He who does not know Christ does not know God hidden in suffering. Therefore he prefers works to suffering, glory to the cross, strength to weakness, wisdom to folly, and, in general, good to evil. These are the people whom the apostle calls "enemies of the cross of Christ" [Phil. 3:18], for they hate the cross and suffering and love works and the glory of works. Thus they call the good of the cross evil and the evil of a deed good. God can be found only in suffering and the cross, as has already been said. Therefore the friends of the cross say that the cross is good and works are evil, for through the cross works are destroyed and the old Adam, who is especially edified by works, is crucified. It is impossible for a person not to be puffed up by his good works unless he has first been deflated and destroyed by suffering and evil until he knows that he is worthless and that his works are not his but God's.

John Calvin (1509–64)

Institutes of the Christian Religion (1559), Book 1, Chapter 1, Par. 1; Chapter 2, Par. 1; Chapter 5, Par. 9; Chapter 6, Par. 1*

Chapter 1: The Knowledge of God and That of Ourselves Are Connected. How They Are Interrelated.

1. Without Knowledge of Self There Is No Knowledge of God

Nearly all the wisdom we possess, that is to say, true and sound wisdom, consists of two parts: the knowledge of God and of ourselves. But, while joined by many bonds, which one precedes and brings forth the other is not easy to discern. In the first place, no one can look upon himself without immediately turning his thoughts to the contemplation of God, in whom he "lives and moves" [Acts 17:28]. For, quite clearly, the mighty gifts with which we are endowed are hardly from ourselves; indeed, our very being is nothing but subsistence in the one God. Then, by these benefits shed like dew from heaven upon us, we are led as by rivulets to the spring itself. Indeed, our very poverty better discloses the infinitude of benefits reposing in God. The miserable ruin, into which the rebellion of the first man cast us, especially compels us to look upward. Thus, not only will we, in fasting and hungering, seek thence what we lack; but, in being aroused by fear, we shall learn humility. For, as a veritable world of miseries is to be found in mankind, and we are thereby despoiled of divine raiment, our shameful nakedness exposes a teeming horde of infamies. Each of us must, then, be so stung by the consciousness of his own unhappiness as to attain at least some knowledge of God. Thus, from the feeling of our own ignorance, vanity, poverty, infirmity, and — what is more — depravity and corruption, we recognize that the true light of wisdom, sound virtue, full abundance of every good, and purity of righteousness rest in the Lord alone. To this extent we are prompted by our own ills to

*Reprinted from *Calvin: Institutes of the Christian Religion,* Library of Christian Classics, ed. John T. McNeill. Used by permission of Westminster John Knox Press. Pp. 35–37, 39–41, 61–62, 69–70.

contemplate the good things of God; and we cannot seriously aspire to him before we begin to become displeased with ourselves. For what man in all the world would not gladly remain as he is — what man does not remain as he is — so long as he does not know himself, that is, while content with his own gifts, and either ignorant or unmindful of his own misery? Accordingly, the knowledge of ourselves not only arouses us to seek God, but also, as it were, leads us by the hand to find him....

Chapter 2: What It Is to Know God, and to What Purpose the Knowledge of Him Tends

1. Piety Is Requisite for the Knowledge of God

Now, the knowledge of God, as I understand it, is that by which we not only conceive that there is a God but also grasp what befits us and is proper to his glory, in fine, what is to our advantage to know of him. Indeed, we shall not say that, properly speaking, God is known where there is no religion or piety. Here I do not yet touch upon the sort of knowledge with which men, in themselves lost and accursed, apprehend God the Redeemer in Christ the Mediator; but I speak only of the primal and simple knowledge to which the very order of nature would have led us if Adam had remained upright. In this ruin of mankind no one now experiences God either as Father or as Author of salvation, or favorable in any way, until Christ the Mediator comes forward to reconcile him to us. Nevertheless, it is one thing to feel that God as our Maker supports us by his power, governs us by his providence, nourishes us by his goodness, and attends us with all sorts of blessings — and another thing to embrace the grace of reconciliation offered to us in Christ. First, as much in the fashioning of the universe as in the general teaching of Scripture the Lord shows himself to be simply the Creator. Then in the face of Christ [cf. 2 Cor. 4:6] he shows himself the Redeemer. Of the resulting twofold knowledge of God we shall now discuss the first aspect; the second will be dealt with in its proper place.[1]

Moreover, although our mind cannot apprehend God without rendering some honor to him, it will not suffice simply to hold that there is One whom all ought to honor and adore, unless we are also persuaded that he is the fountain of every good, and that we must seek nothing elsewhere than in him. This I take to mean that not only does he sustain this universe (as he once founded it) by his boundless might, regulate it by his wisdom, preserve it by his goodness, and especially rule mankind by his righteousness and judgment, bear with it in his mercy, watch over it by his protection; but also that no drop will be found either of wisdom and light, or of righteousness or power or rectitude, or of genuine truth, which does not flow from him, and of which he is not the cause. Thus we may learn to await and seek all these things from him, and thankfully to ascribe them, once received, to him. For this sense of the powers of God is for us a fit teacher of piety, from which religion is born. I call "piety" that reverence joined with love of God which the knowledge of his benefits induces. For until men recognize that they owe everything to God, that they are nourished by his fatherly care, that he

---

1. I.e., Books 2–4, especially beginning with Book 2, ch. 6.

is the Author of their every good, that they should seek nothing beyond him — they will never yield him willing service. Nay, unless they establish their complete happiness in him, they will never give themselves truly and sincerely to him....

Chapter 5: The Knowledge of God Shines Forth in the Fashioning of the Universe and the Continuing Government of It

...9. We Ought Not to Rack Our Brains about God; but Rather, We Should Contemplate Him in His Works

We see that no long or toilsome proof is needed to elicit evidences that serve to illuminate and affirm the divine majesty; since from the few we have sampled at random, whithersoever you turn, it is clear that they are so very manifest and obvious that they can easily be observed with the eyes and pointed out with the finger. And here again we ought to observe that we are called to a knowledge of God: not that knowledge which, content with empty speculation, merely flits in the brain, but that which will be sound and fruitful if we duly perceive it, and if it takes root in the heart. For the Lord manifests himself by his powers, the force of which we feel within ourselves and the benefits of which we enjoy. We must therefore be much more profoundly affected by this knowledge than if we were to imagine a God of whom no perception came through to us. Consequently, we know the most perfect way of seeking God, and the most suitable order, is not for us to attempt with bold curiosity to penetrate to the investigation of his essence, which we ought more to adore than meticulously to search out, but for us to contemplate him in his works whereby he renders himself near and familiar to us, and in some manner communicates himself. The apostle was referring to this when he said that we need not seek him far away, seeing that he dwells by his very present power in each of us [Acts 17:27–28]. For this reason, David, having first confessed his unspeakable greatness [Ps. 145:3], afterward proceeds to mention his works and professes that he will declare his greatness [Ps. 145:5–6; cf. Ps. 40:5]. It is also fitting, therefore, for us to pursue this particular search for God, which may so hold our mental powers suspended in wonderment as at the same time to stir us deeply. And as Augustine teaches elsewhere, because, disheartened by his greatness, we cannot grasp him, we ought to gaze upon his works, that we may be restored by his goodness....

Chapter 6: Scripture Is Needed as Guide and Teacher for Anyone Who Would Come to God the Creator

1. God Bestows the Actual Knowledge of Himself upon Us Only in the Scriptures

That brightness which is borne in upon the eyes of all men both in heaven and on earth is more than enough to withdraw all support from men's ingratitude — just as God, to involve the human race in the same guilt, sets forth to all without exception his presence portrayed in his creatures. Despite this, it is needful that another and better help be added to direct us aright to the very Creator of the universe. It was not in vain, then, that he added the light of his Word by which to become known unto salvation; and he regarded as worthy of this privilege those whom he pleased to gather more closely and intimately to himself. For because he saw the minds of all men tossed and agitated, after he chose the Jews as his very own flock, he fenced them about that they might not sink into oblivion as others had. With good reason he holds us by the same means in the pure knowledge of himself, since otherwise even those who seem to stand firm before all others would soon melt away. Just as old or bleary-eyed men and those with weak vision, if you thrust before them a most beautiful volume, even if they recognize it to be some sort of writing, yet can scarcely construe two words, but with the aid of spectacles will begin to read distinctly; so Scripture, gathering up the otherwise confused knowledge of God in our minds, having dispersed our dullness, clearly shows us the true God. This, therefore, is a special gift, where God, to instruct the church, not merely uses mute teachers but also opens his own most hallowed lips. Not only does he teach the elect to look upon a god, but also shows himself as the God upon whom they are to look. He has from the beginning maintained this plan for his church, so that besides these common proofs he also put forth his Word, which is a more direct and more certain mark whereby he is to be recognized.

Teresa of Avila (1515–82)

The Interior Castle (1577), Book 7, Chapter 1, Sections 3, 6–9*

3. When our Lord is pleased to have pity on this soul that He has already taken spiritually as His Spouse because of what it suffers and has suffered through its desires, He brings it, before the spiritual marriage is consummated, into His dwelling place, which is this seventh. For just as in heaven so in the soul His Majesty must have a room where He dwells alone. Let us call it another heaven....

6. In this seventh dwelling place the union comes about in a different way: Our good God now desires to remove the scales from the soul's eyes and let it see and understand, although in a strange way, something of the favor He grants it. When the soul is brought into that dwelling place, the Most Blessed Trinity, all three Persons, through an intellectual vision, is revealed to it through a certain representation of the truth. First there comes an enkindling in the spirit in the manner of a cloud of magnificent splendor; and these Persons are distinct, and through an admirable knowledge the soul understands as a most profound truth that all three Persons are one substance and one power and one knowledge and one God alone. It knows in such a way that what we hold by faith, it understands, we can say, through sight — although the sight is not with the bodily eyes nor with the eyes of the soul, because we are not dealing with an imaginative vision. Here all three Persons communicate themselves to it, speak to it, and explain those words of the

*Reprinted from *Teresa of Avila* by Kieran Kavanaugh, O.C.D., and Otilio Rodriguez, O.C.D. © 1979 by the Washington Province of Discalced Carmelites, Inc. Used by permission of Paulist Press. Pp. 173, 175–76.

Lord in the Gospel: that He and the Father and the Holy Spirit will come to dwell with the soul that loves Him and keeps His commandments [John 14:23].

7. O God help me! How different is hearing and believing these words from understanding their truth in this way! Each day this soul becomes more amazed, for these Persons never seem to leave it any more, but it clearly beholds, in the way that was mentioned [i.e., through an intellectual vision], that they are within it. In the extreme interior, in some place very deep within itself, the nature of which it doesn't know how to explain, because of a lack of learning, it perceives this divine company.

8. You may think that as a result the soul will be outside itself and so absorbed that it will be unable to be occupied with anything else. On the contrary, the soul is much more occupied than before with everything pertaining to the service of God, and once its duties are over it remains with that enjoyable company. If the soul does not fail God, He will never fail, in my opinion, to make His presence clearly known to it. It has strong confidence that since God has granted this favor He will not allow it to lose the favor. Though the soul thinks this, it goes about with greater care than ever not to displease Him in anything.

9. It should be understood that this presence is not felt so fully, I mean so clearly, as when revealed the first time or at other times when God grants the soul this gift. For if the presence were felt so clearly, the soul would find it impossible to be engaged in anything else or even to live among people. But even though the presence is not perceived with this very clear light the soul finds itself in this company every time it takes notice. Let's say that the experience resembles that of a person who after being in a bright room with others finds himself, once the shutters are closed, in darkness. The light by which he could see them is taken away. Until it returns he doesn't see them, but not for that reason does he stop knowing they are present. It might be asked whether the soul can see them when it so desires and the light returns. To see them does not lie in its power, but depends on when our Lord desires that the window of the intellect be opened. Great is the mercy He shows in never departing from the soul and in desiring that it perceive Him so manifestly.

– 3 –

The Modern Period

INTRODUCTION

Like the medieval and Reformation period, the period from 1600 to the present has been a time of social and political upheaval. It has also been a time of dramatic scientific and technological developments, developments that could scarcely be imagined in the preceding centuries. These scientific developments, together with new directions in philosophy, profoundly transformed western culture. In the process the God question took on new contours. In fact, the very reality of God was questioned in a way that it had not been in previous periods of western civilization. During the modern period, the locus of authority shifted from church and state to the individual. The primacy of faith in making affirmations about God was challenged by appeals to reason, logic, and empirical verification. More recently, the "objectivity" of the truth claims of both the Christian tradition and its modern critics has been scrutinized and "deconstructed" by our "postmodern" contemporaries.

Socially and politically, the modern period begins with warfare occasioned by the split of the western church into Roman and Protestant camps. With the excommunication of Martin Luther from the Roman Church and his subsequent sentencing as an outlaw of the Holy Roman Empire at the Diet of Worms (1521), German Christians took sides. Some noblemen, such as Frederick the Wise and Phillip of Hesse, sided with Luther against Rome. Others remained loyal to the papacy. The people in these territories generally followed the direction of their leaders. Thus, areas of northern and eastern Germany moved into the Lutheran camp, while areas of southern Germany, such as Bavaria, remained Catholic. The emperor Charles V (emperor from 1519 to 1556) was in a difficult position. Although personally Roman Catholic, he had to attend to the political reality of presiding over a divided empire and being the pope's rival with regard to some portions of Italy. Initially, Charles V permitted the princes of the empire to determine how they would enforce the Edict of Worms, which had declared Luther, and by extension his followers, to be outlaws. His political supporters could claim that Luther's case would not be definitively decided until a general council, which Luther called for in 1518, had passed final judgment on whether his theological views were evangelical or heretical. Such a council (Trent) was not convened until 1545. By 1529 the spread of Lutheran support, however, so alarmed the Catholic imperial princes that, at the Diet of Speier (Speyer) II, they demanded that all the members of the empire enforce the Edict of Worms. Luther's imperial supporters lodged a formal legal appeal and protest. From this protest in 1529 the name "Protestant" was born.

In order to protect themselves, the Protestant princes of the empire formed a military alliance called the Schmalkald League. The Catholic princes responded by forming the Nuremberg League. Religious skirmishes ensued, punctuated by periodic truces and compromises. Finally in 1555 a political settlement between Lutherans and Catholics was reached. By the terms of this settlement, the Peace of Augsburg, the ruler of each imperial territory would determine the religion of the land. Those who wished to publicly practice a different form of Christianity could emigrate. Although it was not used in 1555, the Latin phrase — *cuius regio, eius religio* (Whose region, his religion) — succinctly summarizes this political settlement. It is important to note, however, that only one of two choices could be legally adopted: either Roman (Catholic) or Lutheran. No legal accommodation was made at this time for Calvinism or the communities of the Radical Reformation (e.g., the Mennonites, the Hutterites).

That situation changed as a result of the Thirty Years War, which actually was a series of wars that were fought in central Europe between 1618 and 1648. The causes of the war were religious and political; the destruction it caused was vast; and the conclusion of the war brought with it important political and religious changes.

The Thirty Years War was ignited by a local controversy in Bohemia. In 1617 Ferdinand of Styria (1578–1637) became king of Bohemia. A staunch Counter-Reformation Catholic, he began to close the Protestant chapels that were being constructed in the towns of Broumov and Hrob. This action, however, violated the guarantees of religious liberty that had been laid down by Emperor Rudolf II in 1609. When the Protestant leaders who had come to the royal palace to air their grievances did not receive a sympathetic hearing from the king's advisers, they threw the royal advisers out of the window of the Prague Castle on May 23, 1618. This act, known as the "defenestration" of Prague, inflicted no serious injury on those ejected, but highlighted the religious animosity that initiated the first phase of the Thirty Years War.

The dispute quickly escalated into more than a local controversy. In 1619, the largely Protestant diet of Bohemia deposed Ferdinand and elected Frederick V, the imperial elector of the Palatinate and relative of King James I of England, as their king. Later in the same year, King Ferdinand of Bohemia became Emperor Ferdinand II, head of the Holy Roman Empire. The principal battle lines were thus drawn. On the one side stood the Holy Roman Empire, which was Roman Catholic and Hapsburg. On the other stood a network of Protestant towns and principalities that relied primarily on the anti-Catholic powers of Scandinavia and the Netherlands. With support from Spain, Poland, and various German princes, especially Maximilian I, duke of Bavaria, Ferdinand was able to militarily defeat the Protestant rebels. By the end of the 1620s, Ferdinand had confiscated the estates of the rebel noblemen, reduced the Bohemian Diet to impotence, and forced Protestants in Bohemia and Austria to convert to Roman Catholicism.[1] In

---

1. Owen Chadwick writes: "In 1620–27 Bohemia, for so long Hussite and Protestant, was made forcibly Catholic by Austrian armies, the Protestants were deprived of civil rights, the university of Prague was given to the Jesuits, and some 30,000 Protestant families were expelled. This was the most signal and permanent triumph of the Counter-Reformation, and was accompanied by similar measures elsewhere in the imperial lands, especially in Austria. In 1628 it looked as though the forcible conversion

return for Maximilian's support, Ferdinand transferred to him the electoral office previously held by Frederick V.

Throughout this first phase of the war, fighting occurred mainly in Germany. There the devastation was extensive. In some regions the population was reduced by a third or more. And towns were plundered and farms ravaged by the many mercenaries who resorted to pillaging when they could not collect their pay.

The Thirty Years War, however, was not simply a religious war. It was also a political conflict. Emperor Ferdinand's ability to force Protestants to return to the Roman Catholic Church all property seized in his territory since 1552 raised profound fears among his neighbors of imperial absolutism. In the same year (1630) the young Swedish king, Gustavus Adolphus, who was a Lutheran, entered the war. Adolphus saw that he could help his fellow Protestants and his country by entering the war. If Sweden could conquer Germany's Baltic coast, it could control shipping in the Baltic. The political nature of the war in this phase was especially highlighted by the financial support the Protestant king of Sweden received from the Catholic Cardinal Richelieu, chief adviser to the French king. King Louis XIII, king of France from 1610 to 1643, saw the war as a way simultaneously to diminish the power of the Hapsburg family and to increase the power of the French monarchy. Despite some political compromises in the mid-1630s, and even the death of Ferdinand in 1637, the war continued. Finally the Peace of Westphalia brought the war to an end in 1648.

The Peace of Westphalia acknowledged a change in the balance of power in Europe. Sweden obtained northern German territory which gave it control of the Baltic Sea and the estuaries of the Oder, Elbe, and Weser rivers. France gained sovereignty over Alsace; its possession of Metz and Verdun, which it had seized a century before, was confirmed. France thus gained a solid frontier west of the Rhine River. In addition, Sweden and France, as guarantors of the peace, acquired the right of interference in the affairs of the German Empire. The independence of Holland and the Swiss Confederation was recognized, thus formally confirming a status which these two states had actually held for several decades. The approximately three hundred member states of the Holy Roman Empire were granted almost full sovereignty, thus delaying by two centuries German national unification. In short, the emperor's authority in the Holy Roman or German Empire was greatly reduced and the influence of France in European affairs was greatly increased.

The peace treaty also made important decisions regarding religious matters. The Peace of Westphalia confirmed the Peace of Augsburg (1555), which had granted Lutherans religious tolerance in the empire and which had been rescinded by Emperor Ferdinand II in his Edict of Restitution (1629). In addition, the peace treaty extended Augsburg's provisions for religious toleration to Calvinists. Moreover, Catholics, Lutherans, and Calvinists were not forced to emigrate if their choice of Christian denomination differed from that of their ruler; instead their freedom of conscience and freedom of private worship were upheld. Non-Catholics in the hereditary lands of the house of Hapsburg, however, were not

---

of Protestant Germany would proceed much further" (*The Reformation* [New York: Penguin Books, 1964], 317–18).

granted similar toleration. Church land, buildings, or other property seized during the war were to be returned to the religious confessions that held them in 1624. By the important provision that a prince should forfeit his lands if he changed his religion, an obstacle was thereby placed in the way of a further spread both of the Reformation and the Counter-Reformation. The Thirty Years War destroyed the medieval notion of a Roman Catholic empire of Europe, headed spiritually by a pope and temporally by an emperor. Instead, it sanctioned the essential structure of modern Europe as a community of sovereign, secular states. The decisions at Westphalia established the basic religious map of modern Europe.

The Thirty Years War was a significant event in the history of western civilization not only because it was the last major religious war occasioned by the Reformation and Counter-Reformation, but also because it coincided with — if not occasioned — a shift in attitude toward the role of religion in European society. Roman Catholics, Lutherans, and Calvinists all claimed to possess the one true faith. Each group regarded the others not simply as mistaken, but as heretical and evil. If truth were to triumph, the other groups, who had deviated from the one truth, would have to be destroyed. The natural consequence of this kind of thinking was religious warfare. To a number of European intellectuals, not only the destruction caused by religious war, but also the rigid religious sentiments that gave rise to such war were repellent.

In this context, the development of a "rational" and "universal" in contrast to a "dogmatic" and "particular" approach to Christianity is comprehensible. If Christianity now existed in diverse forms, how could one decide which form was true? If appeals to scripture and tradition could not decisively answer this question, what criterion could determine the truth of diverse Christian claims? Human reason was the answer offered by a number of intellectuals in the seventeenth century. Christianity, they argued, should take a form that Christian believers, whether Protestant or Catholic, could endorse on the basis of commonsense reflection. Such a form of Christianity would be a dramatically pared down version of Christianity in comparison to the orthodox systems constructed by Catholics, Lutherans, and Calvinists in the sixteenth and seventeenth centuries. One of the first intellectuals to propose such a streamlined, rational core of Christian faith was Lord Edward Herbert of Cherbury in England (1583–1648). In his treatise on truth, he identified these "common notions" of religion:

> There is a Supreme God. This Sovereign Deity ought to be worshiped. The connection of virtue and piety ... is and always has been held to be, the most important part of religious practice. The minds of men have always been filled with horror for their wickedness. Their vices and sins have always been obvious to them. They must be expiated by repentance. There is reward or punishment after this life.[2]

All other doctrines, including the insistence on the necessity of Christ's incarnation, were not regarded as essential to Christianity. Although some scholars find it misleading to classify Herbert as a deist, his ideas were influential on and similar

---

2. Lord Edward Herbert of Cherbury, *De veritate*, cited in *Deism*, ed. Peter Gay (Princeton: Van Nostrand Co., 1968), 32–38.

to ideas of the deists in the late seventeenth and eighteenth centuries.[3] Deists attacked the supernatural and historical foundations of Christian revelation, while elevating the "natural religion" of reason as true religion. Although they were clearly not atheists, the deists were also clearly not orthodox believers for they denied the necessity of divine revelation. Matthew Tindal's *Christianity as Old as the Creation* (1730), sometimes referred to as "the Deist's Bible," is a paradigmatic illustration of deistic thought. As the full title of his book makes clear, Tindal saw Christianity, properly understood, and natural religion as identical. Jesus' gospel does not bring decisively new knowledge into the world. Rather it merely "republishes" the claims of natural religion. The essence of those claims is belief in God and moral living.

The motivation behind the endorsement of natural religion was both practical and moral. Natural religion was a practical and reasonable way to overcome the animosity often generated by religious diversity. It was also a moral response to the insistence of orthodox Christians upon the necessity of Christian faith. If Christian faith is necessary for salvation, as orthodox Christians maintained, then God has apparently abandoned a large segment of the human population to damnation. Such a view raises disturbing questions about the goodness or benevolence of God.[4] Concerns such as these moved Voltaire (1694–1778) to write that every sensible and decent person should regard "the Christian sect" in horror.[5]

Deism's rejection of supernatural religion became part of the legacy of the Enlightenment. This legacy affected modern Christian theology by giving a strong impetus to the critical study of the Bible, especially the biblical reports of miracles.

> It also raised in the clearest form the issues surrounding religious diversity and divine justice which still preoccupy theology and the philosophy of religion. Above all, its questions and solutions remain alive in all those versions of liberal Christianity and theism, popular and academic, in which the morality of religion is placed higher than doctrine and history, and a lowest common denominator of religion is sought in some form of natural law.[6]

It is one thing to make claims about what "reason" or "common sense" knows, but it is quite another thing to explain why what reason knows should be regarded as true. Here we enter the realm of epistemology (theory of knowledge). Important developments took place in epistemology during the seventeenth century that left a lasting impression on modern western culture, in general, and on Christian theology, in particular. Two of the most important figures in these developments are René Descartes (1596–1650) and John Locke (1632–1704).

---

3. Although Lord Herbert of Cherbury is mentioned in accounts of deism by Placher and González, Byrne says that Herbert exhibits certain idiosyncrasies that distinguish him from typical deists. See William C. Placher, *A History of Christian Theology: An Introduction* (Philadelphia: Westminster Press, 1983), 242–43; Justo González, *The Story of Christianity*, vol. 2: *The Reformation to the Present Day* (San Francisco: Harper & Row, 1984), 190; Peter Byrne, *Natural Religion and the Nature of Religion* (London: Routledge, 1989), 26–32.

4. This issue is explored in detail in Part Two of this volume.

5. Voltaire [François Marie Arouet], "Examen Important de Milord Bolingbroke," in *Oeuvres complètes*, vol. 26 (Paris: Garnier Frères, 1879), 298.

6. Peter Byrne, "Deism," in *The Blackwell Encyclopedia of Modern Christian Thought*, ed. Alister E. McGrath (Cambridge, Mass.: Basil Blackwell, 1993), 105.

In the very same year in which Emperor Ferdinand II died (1637) during the Thirty Years War, the mathematician and philosopher René Descartes published his *Discourse on Method*. In order to arrive at certain truth, Descartes proposed four rules for thinking. The first of these rules advocated methodical doubt.[7] The first indubitable idea at which Descartes arrived by this method was the reality of the thinking or questioning self. "Cogito, ergo sum," Descartes declared. ("I think, therefore I am.") Even if I can doubt the reality of everything that my senses allegedly perceive, I cannot doubt, Descartes argued, the reality of a consciousness or self which is doing the doubting.[8] From this self-evident fact, Descartes sought to deduce other rational conclusions. The significance of his methodological proposal is that it sanctioned the value of doubt and raised up the thinking self as the arbiter of truth. For this reason, Descartes has conventionally been regarded as a father, if not *the* father, of modern philosophy. For those among whom Descartes's ideas took root, it was no longer possible to assert with certitude that they knew the truth because the Bible, or the pope, or the state told them so. Something was true only if it was deemed true by the intellect of the inquiring individual.

John Locke represents a different facet of the so-called Age of Reason that began to dawn in the seventeenth century. Although he read the philosophy of Descartes, Locke was influenced more by experimental science. He collaborated with Robert Boyle, one of the founders of modern chemistry, and he was a friend of Sir Isaac Newton (1642–1727). Unlike Descartes, who was suspicious of the testimony of the senses, Locke held that knowledge of the world began in sense perception. He argued that knowledge was not innate, but acquired. It did not begin with general principles, nor did it proceed by syllogistic reasoning from such principles. On the contrary, knowledge was inductive from the testimony of experience, rather than deductive from the principles of reason. As he expressed it in Book II of his *Essay Concerning Human Understanding* (1690), sense experience and reflection provide the mind with the material of knowledge. From this perspective, we judge something to be true on the relative strength of the evidence provided by sense experience and reflection.

Because the necessary evidential grounds for many Christian doctrines were lacking, Locke believed that it was wrong to persecute someone for failing to adhere to these doctrines. Each person, as a moral being, is responsible before God. Responsibility presupposes freedom. Consequently, Locke was a strong supporter of the freedom of thought, speech, and worship. As a latitudinarian Anglican, he disliked the rigidity and "fanaticism" of some English Puritans and strict Calvinists. Yet he also disapproved of radical deism. Like free-thinking deists, Locke

---

7. René Descartes, *Discourse on Method*, Pt. II in *Discourse on Method and Meditations*, trans. Laurence J. Lafleur (Indianapolis: Bobbs-Merrill Co., 1960), 15: "The first rule was never to accept anything as true unless I recognized it to be certainly and evidently such: that is, carefully to avoid all precipitation and prejudgment, and to include nothing in my conclusions unless it presented itself so clearly and distinctly to my mind that there was no reason or occasion to doubt it."

8. Descartes, *Discourse on Method*, Pt. IV, 24: "Thus as our senses deceive us at times, I was ready to suppose that nothing was at all the way our senses represented them to be....But I soon noticed that while I thus wished to think everything false, it was necessarily true that I who thought so was something. Since this truth, *I think, therefore I am, or exist,* was so firm and assured that all the most extravagant suppositions of the sceptics were unable to shake it, I judged that I could safely accept it as the first principle of the philosophy I was seeking."

affirmed the reasonableness of Christianity. Unlike them, however, he affirmed the need for revelation and redemption through Christ. As his book *The Reasonableness of Christianity* (1695) makes clear, Locke held that being Christian meant accepting Christ as the messiah and living in accordance with his moral teaching. Because no one can fulfill Christ's moral law perfectly, faith in him as the messiah "is allowed to supply the defect of full obedience; and so the believers are admitted to life and immortality as if they were righteous."[9] Faith in Christ and doing our moral best constitute the essence of Christianity. From Locke's perspective, it was not necessary for a Christian to hold any additional doctrines promulgated by the different Christian churches. Locke's social and political liberalism, as well as his empiricist epistemology, exerted considerable influence in western society in subsequent centuries.

The dramatic consequences of adopting an empiricist epistemology had already become evident in the work of Galileo Galilei (1564–1642). Galileo made use of the telescope to amass evidence in support of the Copernican theory of heliocentrism. The Polish astronomer Nicolaus Copernicus (1473–1543) in 1543 had challenged the dominant understanding of the operation of the solar system, which held that the earth was at rest at the center of our solar system and that the planets and sun revolved around the earth. Such an understanding had the philosophical support of Aristotle, the astronomical support of Ptolemy, and — at least implicitly — the religious support of the Bible. Moreover, this understanding of the solar system seemed to be the necessary conclusion of the observation of the senses. It certainly appears to be the case that the sun moves through the heavens from east to west. And in their daily lives people have little direct experience of the rapid rotation of the earth on its axis. Copernicus's theory defied conventional wisdom and simple observation.

It is important to note that Copernicus espoused his mathematical theory in the midst of the Reformation. Just as the Protestant Reformation challenged the traditional authority of the pope, so the Copernican revolution challenged the traditional authority of ancient and conventional wisdom. If Copernicus's theory was correct, the earth was no longer the center of the universe and earth's most important inhabitants, human beings, were no longer the focus of cosmic history.

About sixty-five years after Copernicus's death, Galileo learned of the recent invention of the telescope. By improving its magnifying power, he was able to make a number of astronomical discoveries that confirmed Copernicus's theory.[10]

Galileo's ideas precipitated resistance from defenders of the Aristotelian and Ptolemaic systems. Some accused Galileo of contradicting the testimony of the Bible. In response, Galileo reminded his readers that it was standard practice in the church to interpret the scriptures allegorically whenever they came into con-

---

9. John Locke, *The Reasonableness of Christianity*, ed. I. T. Ramsey (Stanford: Stanford University Press, 1958), 30.

10. Among the more important discoveries was his observation of moons around Jupiter. This discovery answered one of the objections against the Copernican theory. Critics had argued that the Copernican theory was inconsistent in that it made all the planets circle around the sun, except for the one peculiar instance of the moon circling the earth. Galileo's discovery of some of Jupiter's moons showed that our moon was no longer a unique case. It also demonstrated that the moon's orbit around the earth could not be used as evidence in support of the Ptolemaic theory of the earth's centrality. See Jeffery Hopper, *Understanding Modern Theology*, vol. 1: *Cultural Revolutions and New Worlds* (Philadelphia: Fortress Press, 1987), 15.

flict with scientific truth. As his letter to the Grand Duchess Christina of Tuscany (1615) makes clear, Galileo saw the Bible and science as dealing with two distinct realms of reality. The former deals with spiritual reality, the latter with physical. The primary purpose of the biblical writings, Galileo asserted, is "the service of God and the salvation of souls." Because the heliocentric theory has nothing to do with the salvation of souls, it could be held or rejected without any harm being done to Christian faith. The Bible and science are both true in their respective spheres.[11]

Although some ecclesiastical experts were sympathetic to Galileo, Cardinal Robert Bellarmine, the Roman Church's chief theologian, had Copernicanism declared "false and erroneous" in 1616. In the 1620s, Galileo went to Rome, hoping to obtain a revocation of the decree of 1616. Although he did not gain the revocation, Pope Urban VIII, who had been a personal friend of Galileo before his pontificate, granted Galileo permission to write about the system of the world as long as he discussed it noncommittally and admitted that humanity cannot presume to know fully how the world is really made. Galileo spent the next several years working on his great book, *Dialogue Concerning the Two Principal Systems of the World*. When it was published in the early 1630s, the book received praise from some literary and philosophical circles and condemnation from advisers to the pope. In 1633 Galileo was put on trial for violating the injunction of 1616. He was found guilty of having held and taught the Copernican theory and was ordered to recant. Galileo recited a formula in which he abjured his "past errors," and Pope Urban VIII commuted Galileo's sentence of imprisonment into house arrest on his estate near Florence. The sentence of house arrest remained in effect throughout the last eight years of his life.

Although he himself confessed that the Bible could not speak untruth, Galileo's work raised serious questions about the Bible's validity. By raising the question about how the Bible's statements about the world should be interpreted, Galileo also implicitly raised the question about who should interpret the Bible. Does the theologian, the pope, or the scientist decide when evidence is sufficient to require the surrendering of a long-accepted interpretation? The question about authority was not entirely new. Luther and the Protestant Reformers had questioned the authority of the pope. They did so on the basis of an appeal to scripture. As

---

11. "Especially in view of the fact that these things [what the Bible says about the earth, sun, etc.] in no way concern the primary purpose of the sacred writings, which is the service of God and the salvation of souls — matters infinitely beyond the comprehension of the common people.

"This being granted, I think that in discussions of physical problems we ought to begin not from the authority of scriptural passages, but from sense experiences and necessary demonstrations; for the holy Bible and the phenomena of nature proceed alike from the divine Word, the former as the dictate of the Holy Ghost and the latter as the observant executrix of God's commands" ("Galileo's Letter to Grand Duchess Christina of Tuscany on the Use of Biblical Quotations in Matters of Science" (1615), reprinted in *Readings in Church History,* ed. Colman J. Barry, rev. ed., 3 vols. in one [Westminster, Md.: Christian Classics, 1985], 768).

And then Galileo's conclusion: "From these things it follows as a necessary consequence that, since the Holy Ghost did not intend to teach us whether heaven moves or stands still, ... whether the earth is located at its center or off to one side, then so much the less was it intended to settle for us any other conclusions of the same kind. . . . Now if the Holy Spirit has purposely neglected to teach us propositions of this sort as irrelevant to the highest goal (that is, to our salvation), how can anyone affirm that it is obligatory to take sides on them, and that one belief is required by faith, while the other side is erroneous? Can an opinion be heretical and yet have no concern with the salvation of souls? ... I would say here something that was heard from an ecclesiastic of the most eminent degree: 'The intention of the Holy Ghost is to teach us how one goes to heaven, not how heaven goes' " (pp. 769–70).

the Marburg Colloquy in 1529 between Luther and Zwingli demonstrated, however, Christians convinced of the veracity and sufficiency of the Bible could cite different passages in support of different conclusions.

These previous disputes about the meaning of the Bible, however, were fought largely on biblical grounds or in an ecclesiastical context. With Galileo and his successors, science — not theology — was raising questions about the meaning of the holy book. And science was raising such questions precisely at the time when Protestantism was unfolding a doctrine of the literal inerrancy of the Bible, inerrancy in theological, moral, historical, and "scientific" matters. Assertions of the total inerrancy of the Bible notwithstanding, theological authority in physical matters has been in retreat ever since the seventeenth century. Moreover, by jealously clinging to untenable claims of biblical and church authority in matters of science, some believers increased general doubt about the authority of the Bible and the church in other matters as well.

By the eighteenth century, advances in science and philosophical developments had made it difficult for educated Europeans to accept the medieval understanding of God's activity in the world. In fact, these advances raised for some people the question of God's reality. If God is the kind of being that believers claim God to be, how can divine reality and divine activity in the world be asserted in a way compatible with the mechanistic understanding of the world proposed by some seventeenth- and eighteenth-century scientists and philosophers? Some people drew the conclusion of atheism.

> Within what is now called the modern period, a new conclusion appeared. ...The conclusion was that there were men who judged themselves to be atheists, who called themselves atheists. In the ancient world, and even more in the medieval world, this was unheard of. "Atheist" had been vituperative and polemic; now it became a signature and a boast....Paris boasted what medieval Oxford and ancient Athens did not command: a band of thinkers who celebrated their denial of anything which one could call "god."[12]

Theologians, of course, did not simply recapitulate to the critics of traditional belief in God. Some tried to accommodate the newer, scientific understanding of physical reality with belief in God. For Anglican William Paley (1743–1805), for example, the "immutable laws" of nature propounded by Newton and his successors, although they made sense of the physical operation of the world, did not mean there was no longer a place for God. In his *View of the Evidences of Christianity* (1794) and *Natural Theology* (1802), Paley made a clear case for God upon the evidence of the orderly operation of the world and the adaptation of the different parts of creation to allegedly evident purposes. One of his most popular analogies was that of the watch (the world) and the watchmaker (God). Each of the gears of the watch has a specific function in the operation of the whole; and the watch as a whole operates according to regular cycles. The world seems to be the same way. Each part of creation has a specific purpose or function in the operation of the whole; and the whole of creation operates according to regular

---

12. Michael J. Buckley, *At the Origins of Modern Atheism* (New Haven: Yale University Press, 1987), 14–17; the quotation is from p. 27.

cycles (e.g., the "laws of nature," the seasons). Just as the existence of the watch implies the existence of a watchmaker, so too the existence of an orderly world implies the existence of a Creator.

The critical spirit of philosophy and the experimental method of science, however, could erode the cogency of this type of thinking. In the realm of philosophy, the Scottish empiricist David Hume and the German philosopher Immanuel Kant advanced arguments in the eighteenth century that challenged the argument from design offered by Paley and others. In the realm of science, the English naturalist Charles Darwin presented an explanation of the origin of species in the nineteenth century that undermined, in a similar way, the idea that the natural operation of the world and the development of its life forms were the result of God's providential care.

The radically empiricist approach to knowledge of David Hume (1711–76) raised doubts about both traditional, orthodox claims for the superiority of Christianity and deistic claims for the reasonableness of natural religion. Experience, Hume said, gives us all of our knowledge in the form of isolated impressions. The connections we make between these impressions, such as the notion of cause and effect, are habits of the mind. They are not realities that we actually perceive.[13] Similarly, we do not have direct experience of "substances." We perceive the outward characteristics of things, but not their inward substance. In fact, we have no empirical evidence of the "I" who is believed to underlie my experiences and give them unity. Hume clearly showed that if we take the empiricist perspective in its strictest form, we must be skeptical of the allegedly commonsense claims of the deists and the religious claims of orthodox Christians. If cause and effect are ruled out, then arguments for God's existence that are based upon them are invalid. If the category of substance is ruled out, then arguments for individual immortality are philosophically groundless.

Hume applied the skepticism entailed by his epistemology to the question of God and to orthodox claims for the superiority of Christianity. On the first point, he claimed that the argument from design yields at best a conjecture about the reality of a divine creator. Because it is dependent upon our experience of finite realities, the argument makes a questionable leap when it makes assertions about an infinite cause. In the *Dialogues Concerning Natural Religion*, published after Hume's death, Philo reminds his interlocutors that we experience flaws in the created order. If, as orthodox believers assert, causes are proportionate to their effects, then perhaps we should conclude that the defects of nature derive from a defective God. On the second point, Hume criticized one of the major warrants long used by orthodox Christians to support the superiority of Christ over other religious leaders, namely, miracles. Insofar as Jesus fulfilled the prophecies of the Hebrew scriptures and performed miracles that far exceed the amazing deeds of other religious leaders, he deserves to be regarded as a unique and unsurpassable

---

13. Hume admitted that much of everyday life, including his own, depended upon the habit of inference by which we believe that where fire is found, so also will heat be present. But he distinguished between what we do in practice from what we can assert in theory: "My practice, you say, refutes my doubts. But you mistake the purport of my question. As an agent, I am quite satisfied in the point; but as a philosopher who has some share of curiosity, I will not say skepticism, I want to learn the foundation of this inference" (David Hume, *An Inquiry Concerning Human Understanding*, ed. Charles W. Hendel [New York: Liberal Arts Press, 1955], 52).

manifestation of God's power on earth. In Section X of his *Inquiry Concerning Human Understanding* (1758), Hume argued that, because experience attests to the uniformity of nature much more firmly than to the infallibility of human testimony, the probability that error or deception has led to the report of a miracle is much greater than that the uniform course of nature has been truly interrupted.

Hume's contemporaries paid attention to him, and his influence on subsequent generations was quite significant. He was one of the influences that led Auguste Comte, the nineteenth-century French mathematician and sociologist, to positivism. In Britain he contributed to the development of utilitarian moral theory in Jeremy Bentham and John Stuart Mill. And in Germany, he awakened Immanuel Kant, as Kant himself put it, from his dogmatic slumbers.

Immanuel Kant (1724–1804) is one of the most important western philosophers of the modern period. It is often said that the revolution that he effected in modern philosophy is analogous to the revolution Copernicus had caused in astronomy two centuries earlier. Kant brought together the rationalist strain of thought, which went back to Descartes and was dominant in eighteenth-century Germany, and the empirical strain of thought, which went back to Locke and was dominant in Britain. Reading Hume caused Kant to have doubts about the metaphysics of Leibniz (1646–1716) and Christian Wolff (1679–1754), who held that the human mind can arrive, by pure thought, at truths about entities such as God, human freedom, and immortality. In the first of his major "critiques," *The Critique of Pure Reason* (1781), Kant argued that the mind has no such power. Like Hume, he believed that knowledge of the world must have a basis in sense experience. But, unlike Hume, he denied that all our ideas are derived from simple sense impressions. The mind has certain categories by which it classifies experience. Unless the sense impressions are conformed to the mind's forms of intuition (space and time) and classified according to the mind's categories of understanding (quantity, quality, relation, and modality), knowledge does not take place. In short, knowledge, according to Kant, is the product of perception from without, to which form is given by the laws of the mind. The knowledge that results from these two elements, however, is not knowledge of things as they truly are in themselves (what Kant referred to as *noumena*). Rather, what results is knowledge of things as they appear to the human mind (what Kant referred to as *phenomena*). Although we use the ideas of self, world, and God to synthesize our experiences into a unity, we cannot claim to have knowledge of them because they transcend direct empirical experience. The implications for theology of Kant's critique is clear. Knowledge of God is not possible. Not surprisingly, Kant was accused of atheism. In response, he argued that it was impermissible to apply principles of knowledge, which extend only to objects of possible experience, to what cannot be an object of experience (such as God and immortality). The rejection of knowledge, however, did not mean the rejection of belief. In the preface to the second edition of his critique, Kant wrote: "I have therefore found it necessary to deny knowledge, in order to make room for faith."[14]

Moral responsibility, however, was even more important to Kant than religious

---

14. Immanuel Kant, *Critique of Pure Reason*, trans. Norman Kemp Smith (New York: Macmillan, 1929), 29.

faith. In his second critique, *The Critique of Practical Reason* (1788), Kant established the validity of some of the very ideas about which he declared in his first critique we could have no knowledge. How could this be? Viewed from the perspective of pure reason, God and the immortality of the soul cannot be objects of knowledge. This is so because God and immortality transcend experience. Viewed, however, from the perspective of practical reason, God and the immortality of the soul are "regulative ideas" or "postulates" that practical reason commands us to hold. Kant came to this conclusion from his analysis of the "categorical imperative" that human beings encounter within themselves. The categorical imperative is the command to do our moral duty unconditionally. Although in the realm of rational theory, we cannot claim to know that we are free, that our souls are immortal, and that there is a God, in the realm of rational practice, we must act as if freedom, immortality, and God are real. Our experience of the categorical imperative makes sense only if there is a God who will ultimately provide happiness for the morally good. We experience the imperative to do our moral duty. If we ought to do our duty, then we must have freedom. By leading virtuous lives — doing our duty — we deserve to be happy. Experience, however, shows that morally good people sometimes suffer and morally bad people sometimes prosper. It is reasonable to postulate that there is a time (namely, the afterlife) when virtue will result in happiness; it is reasonable to postulate that there is a power (namely, God) who can bring together for us virtue and happiness. This line of reasoning does not constitute "proof" of the existence of God or the immortality of the soul. It does suggest, however, that, if our moral experience is not irrational, such ideas are valid postulates. Simply stated, although we cannot *know* that there is a God and that we possess freedom and immortality, we act in conformity with practical reason when we live *as if* there is a God and *as if* we are free and immortal.[15]

These ideas elicited lively discussion and sharp critique. Many found them to be revolutionary. Revolution in philosophy, however, was not isolated from political and social revolution in the late eighteenth century. This century ended with the American and French Revolutions, which in different forms and ways gave powerful voice to democratic and liberal ideals, including the right to representation in government and the freedom of speech and press. The warrants for these ideals were articulated in the works of eighteenth-century Enlightenment philosophers, such as Charles-Louis de Secondat, better known as Montesquieu (1689–1755). In his monumental work *The Spirit of Laws* (1750), Montesquieu argued that a republic, based on virtue, is a better form of government than a monarchy, based on honor, or despotism, based on fear. In addition, he declared that the legislative, executive, and judicial powers must be assigned to different individuals or bodies, acting independently, in any state concerned about effectively promoting liberty. Montesquieu's ideas gave inspiration to the Declaration of the Rights of Man in France and to the Constitution of the United States. By arguing that the locus of power should be relocated from the privileged few to the many of society, these Enlightenment ideas stirred up many in support of the rights of the

---

15. Immanuel Kant, *Critique of Practical Reason and Other Works on the Theory of Ethics*, trans. Thomas Kingsmill Abbott (London: Longmans, Green & Co., 1909), 220–23.

individual. In *A Vindication of the Rights of Woman* (1792), Mary Wollstonecraft challenged the idea that women exist only to please men and laid out arguments to give women the same opportunities as men in education, work, and politics.

Changes occurred not only in political theory, but also in political and social practice. As serfdom was suppressed in Europe, ordinary people were able to come and go as they pleased, without fear of legal reprisal. As a greater degree of personal freedom was guaranteed by law, parents could no longer dictate the religious choices of their children or impose marriage partners on them. Economic modernization and the emergence of a marketplace mentality gave many in the lower and working classes autonomy and a revitalized sense of self. This development was particularly significant for women, who began to transfer the notions of self-interest and autonomy in economic matters to their personal lives. Because paid employment meant that women brought a quantifiable and distinct contribution to the family's resources, women came to feel entitled to a greater voice in the disposal of those resources. The balance of power in the family began to shift.[16]

In the United States, the struggle on behalf of individual rights was dynamically expressed in the abolitionist movement and the woman suffrage movement. In the course of campaigning against slavery, women such as Lucretia Mott (1793–1880), Elizabeth Cady Stanton (1815–1902), and Sarah Grimké (1792–1873) came to see that not only the rights of black slaves, but also the rights of women needed redress. Just as Enlightenment philosophers exercised a "hermeneutics of suspicion" (a theory of interpretation that critically examines the power structures and motives behind actions and texts) with regard to notions of the "divine right of kings," so too women in the late eighteenth and nineteenth centuries exercised a hermeneutics of suspicion with regard to the traditional claims of male superiority. Some female writers of the period critically exposed the connection between an uncritical reading of scripture and tradition and the subordination of women to men.[17] As Elizabeth Cady Stanton observed in the nineteenth century, the first step in the elevation of women to a position of equality is "the cultivation of the religious sentiment in regard to her dignity and equality" and the recognition of the motherhood (in addition to the fatherhood) of God (see excerpt below). In

---

16. The economic, social, and political changes at the end of the eighteenth century affected not only the general self-identity of "the masses," but also their social and sexual behavior. See William Madges, "Sex, Celibacy, and the Modern Self in Nineteenth-Century Germany," in *Broken and Whole: Essays on Religion and the Body*, ed. Maureen A. Tilly and Susan A. Ross (Lanham, Md.: University Press of America, 1995), 71–95.

17. In defending her right to speak out publicly against slavery, Sarah Grimké, for example, found that she had to criticize the interpretations of the New Testament offered by men. In 1837 Grimké wrote: "The New Testament has been referred to, and I am willing to abide by its decisions, but must enter my protest against the false translation of some passages by the MEN who did that work, and against the perverted interpretation by the MEN who undertook to write commentaries thereon. . . . The Lord Jesus defines the duties of his followers in his Sermon on the Mount. He lays down grand principles by which they should be governed, without any reference to sex or condition. — 'Ye are the light of the world. . . . Let your light so shine before men, that they may see your good works, and glorify your Father which is in Heaven' (Matt. 5:14–16). I follow him through all his precepts, and find him giving the same directions to women as to men, never even referring to the distinction now so strenuously insisted upon between masculine and feminine virtues: this is one of the anti-christian 'traditions of men' which are taught instead of the 'commandments of God.' Men and women were CREATED EQUAL; they are both moral and accountable beings, and whatever is *right* for man to do, is *right* for woman" (*Letters on the Equality of the Sexes and the Condition of Woman*, ed. with an intro. Elizabeth A. Bartlett [New Haven: Yale University Press, 1988], 38).

July 1848 Stanton and Mott led the first women's rights convention in the United States, at Seneca Falls, New York.

What was theology to say and how should theology be done in this new context of critique of tradition and affirmation of the individual? If Christianity were to remain relevant to critically minded people, theology would have to find a way to accommodate Christian faith to changes in society. Taking seriously the philosophical assaults upon many of the church's traditional beliefs and the effects of historically critical interpretations of the Bible, Christian thinkers sought to show that it was possible to be quite modern in outlook and still a believer. Some, like Kant,[18] did this by reducing Christianity to its moral core. From this perspective, one could remain a Christian in an age of Enlightenment by endorsing the moral teaching of Jesus without having to adhere to the doctrines of supernatural revelation. By the beginning of the nineteenth century, supernatural religion and dogmatic Christianity were ignored or despised by many educated people.

To these "cultured despisers" of religion, Friedrich Schleiermacher (1768–1834) addressed his *Speeches on Religion* (1799). Schleiermacher told religion's critics that they misunderstood the essential nature of religion if they thought it consisted primarily in the intellectual acceptance of religious dogmas or in the practical performance of moral duty. On the contrary, the essence, or "kernel," of religion is the immediate feeling of the Infinite and the Eternal. Religion essentially consists, Schleiermacher declared, in neither knowing nor doing, but in feeling. By "feeling" Schleiermacher did not mean the ecstatic conversion experiences extolled by Pietists in the eighteenth century or the emotionalism of nineteenth-century revivals. Rather, he meant to refer to our immediate consciousness or awareness of self.[19] In our consciousness of ourselves, we are also aware of the Infinite which permeates all finite things and upon which we are dependent. Drawing upon the resources of Romanticism, Schleiermacher described the essence of religion this way in his Second Speech:

> It is true that religion is essentially contemplative.... But this contemplation is not turned, as your knowledge of nature is, to the existence of a finite thing.... It has not even, like your knowledge of God — if for once I might use an old expression — to do with the nature of the first cause, in itself and in its relation to every other cause and operation. The contemplation of the pious is the immediate consciousness of the universal existence of all finite things, in and through the Infinite, and of all temporal things in and through the Eternal. Religion is to seek this and find it in all that lives and moves, in all growth and change, in all doing and suffering. It is to have life and to know life in immediate feeling, only as such an existence in the Infinite and Eternal.... Wherefore it is a life in the infinite nature of the Whole, in the One and in the All, in God, having and possessing all things in God, and God in all. Yet religion is not knowledge and science, either of the world or of God. Without being knowledge, it recognizes knowledge and science. In

---

18. See his 1793 text, *Religion within the Limits of Reason Alone,* trans. Theodore M. Green and Hoyt H. Hudson (New York: Harper & Row, 1960), esp. 94–100.

19. See, for example, Colin Brown, *Jesus in European Protestant Thought, 1778–1860* (Durham, N.C.: Labyrinth Press, 1985), 116.

itself it is an affection, a revelation of the Infinite in the finite, God being
seen in it and it in God.[20]

As the above quotation makes clear, by distinguishing religious feeling from
knowing and doing, Schleiermacher did not intend to separate feeling from these
activities. Theological knowledge and moral activity are normal signs of religious
feeling. In fact, "to wish to have true science or true practice without religion . . . is
obstinate, arrogant delusion, and culpable error."[21] His point was that the core
of religion is feeling and that all human activity — whether artistic, scientific, or
moral — was incomplete without such religious feeling.

In *The Christian Faith* (1821/22, 1830) Schleiermacher developed his ideas
about religion into a specific Christian exposition of faith. In this work, he defined the Christian as the person who is possessed by the feeling of his or her
dependence upon God as manifested in Jesus Christ. These two elements are inseparable in the life of the Christian: a general awareness of God and a special
relation to Christ. The general awareness of God is, according to Schleiermacher,
an "original revelation." But as the excerpt below discloses (§4, 3), this awareness
of God is not the same as knowledge of God as an object. In our consciousness
of ourselves, we are also conscious of God in the sense that we are aware of being absolutely or utterly dependent. Schleiermacher seeks to avoid the problem of
asserting that we have knowledge of God, which Kantian epistemology declared
impossible, by making the experience of dependence, not the concept of God, the
fundamental datum of Christian consciousness. God is connected with this datum
of experience as its "whence." Thus Schleiermacher concludes (see §4, 4 below):
"in the first instance God signifies for us simply that which is the co-determinant
in this feeling and to which we trace our being in such a state; and any further
content of the idea [i.e., of God] must be evolved out of this fundamental import
assigned to it."

Schleiermacher is a landmark figure in the history of Christian thought because he reformulated the nature and task of theology or "dogmatics." Theology's
principal task is not to explicate and defend the doctrines of the church, but to
identify and describe the experiences of the Christian church that give rise to such
doctrines. Since the time of Schleiermacher, it has become customary for human
experience, and not merely the testimony of scripture and tradition, to be included
as theological resources.

By starting with Christian experience, Schleiermacher intended to make proofs
for the existence of God unnecessary. When Christians attend to their self-
consciousness, they are immediately aware of their utter dependence, which is
the same thing as being in relation with God. The "reality" of God, therefore,
can be confirmed at every moment in the consciousness of the believer. Consequently, proofs for the existence of God are not a constitutive element in a system
of Christian doctrine because "a system of doctrine," rightly understood, seeks to
describe the consciousness of Christians, in which "the inner certainty of God" is
already present (see §33, 3 below).

---

20. Friedrich Schleiermacher, *On Religion: Speeches to Its Cultured Despisers*, trans. John Oman from
the 3d ed. (1821) (New York: Harper & Brothers, 1958), 36.
    21. Ibid., 39.

Another consequence of Schleiermacher's making experience the starting point of theology was his reinterpretation of the doctrine of the trinity. Rather than including a discussion of the trinity in the primary section of a systematic exposition of Christian faith, Schleiermacher relegated it to the conclusion. Theology had previously traced the union of God with Christ and the union of God with the church back to an alleged distinction posited independently and eternally in God (namely, the distinction of Son and Spirit from the Father). But, Schleiermacher claims, "the assumption of an eternal distinction in the Supreme Being is not an utterance concerning the religious consciousness, for there it never could emerge" (see §170, 2 below). From Schleiermacher's perspective, the orthodox doctrine of the trinity is the result of speculative construction from the experience of the divine in Christ and in the Christian community. What is essential is the experience of the divine, present in Christ and in the Christian community. Therefore, the conventional doctrine of the trinity, which is one (speculative) expression of this experience, need not be regarded as a formula adequate for all time.[22] Schleiermacher was interested in reformulating the doctrine of the trinity in such a way that it would be possible to affirm the experiential root of the doctrine — faith in the divine, present in Christ and in the church — without having to subscribe to the traditional doctrine of the immanent trinity.

Whereas Schleiermacher made the trinitarian God an afterword in his system, Georg Wilhelm Friedrich Hegel (1770–1831) made the trinitarian God a key to his articulation of reality. Whereas Schleiermacher refused to make religion a simple matter of reason or morality, Hegel affirmed the rationality of religion. Like Kant, Hegel held that the mind stamps its seal on all knowledge. Unlike Kant, he did not see this fact as proving the limits of reason. For Hegel, reason is reality. As the foremost proponent of speculative idealism, Hegel held that the rational is the real and the real is the rational. Things thought are completely present in thinking; and in thinking, thought is completely present in the things thought. Objective truth for Hegel, then, is the conformity of objects to their concept.

Knowledge, however, is more than conceptual. It is also dynamic. Knowledge is a process that moves toward the identity of object and concept. The process is dialectical, just as reality itself is dialectical. By "dialectical" Hegel meant the opposition of thesis to antithesis and their reconciliation in a synthesis, wherein the contrasts are overcome while the differences are preserved. In short, Hegel saw conflict and its resolution at the heart of reality. Reality is not static, but a dynamic process. The dynamic development Hegel had in mind was not the or-

---

22. Schleiermacher stated: "If we take the original tendency of the doctrine, namely, to make clear that it is no hyperbolical expression of our consciousness of Christ and of the common Spirit of the Church to assert that God is in both, the first task of the doctrine is clearly this — to define this peculiar being of God in that which is other, in its relation both to the being of God in Himself and to the being of God in relation to the world in general. And obviously there is no prospect of ever so accomplishing this task that a formula adequate for all time could be constructed, and every departure therefrom repudiated as unchristian. We have only to do with the God-consciousness given in our self-consciousness along with our consciousness of the world; hence we have no formula for the being of God in Himself as distinct from the being of God in the world, and should have to borrow any such formula from speculation, and so prove ourselves disloyal to the character of the discipline at which we are working" (*The Christian Faith*, trans. of the 2d German edition, ed. H. R. Mackintosh and J. S. Stewart [Philadelphia: Fortress Press, 1976], §172, 1; pp. 747–48.

ganic, untroubled unfolding that some Romantics meant by development. Rather, it was development by means of tension and struggle. This understanding of reality had a profound influence upon nineteenth-century historiography as well as upon Karl Marx's philosophy.

Because he understood himself to be both a philosopher and a Christian, Hegel was interested in resolving the apparent conflict between reason and revealed religion. Like Schleiermacher and others, he wished to find a way beyond both Enlightenment and stale orthodoxy. The intention of his lectures on the philosophy of religion, for example, was "to reconcile reason and religion, and to show how we know the latter to be in all its manifold forms necessary, and to rediscover in revealed religion the truth and the Idea."[23] Hegel conceived of God as the Infinite Spirit which manifests itself in the finite forms of the natural world and in the human spirit. God, Hegel believed, becomes truly self-conscious in the activity of human consciousness. In fact, incarnation is the essential idea of religion. Insofar as Christianity made this idea explicit, whereas the idea was only implicitly understood in other religions, Christianity deserved to be regarded as the "absolute" religion.[24]

As Claude Welch has observed, the despised doctrine of the immanent trinity was the place where Hegel found "above all the center of Christianity and the expression of the true nature of Spirit."[25] The immanent trinity is a dynamic process of self-generation and differentiation.[26] What transpires immanently in the trinity is also replicated in the world. God is not a static substance, totally external to the finite world. Rather, God is the dialectical process of self-differentiation and return, whereby creation is taken up into God, and God is expressed in the development of history. Although there is ambiguity on this point, Hegel seems to affirm that it is improper to separate the movement of the Idea in itself (immanent trinity) from the dialectical process of differentiation and reconciliation of the Idea in the form of finitude (creation).[27] Hegel's formulation of the God-world relation elicited from orthodox Christians the charge of pantheism. He, however, did not simply assert that the world is God. "Rather, like Schleiermacher, Hegel was attempting to formulate a panentheistic conception of God

23. G. W. F. Hegel, *Lectures on the Philosophy of Religion*, 3 vols., trans. E. B. Speirs and J. B. Sanderson (New York: Humanities Press, 1962), 3:151.

24. In the Christian proclamation of Jesus as the Son of God, the form and content of human religious consciousness adequately mirrors for the first time the form and content of God's consciousness of self as living Spirit. See Hegel, *The Philosophy of History*, trans. J. Sibree (New York: Dover Publications, 1956), 319. Cf. James Yerkes, *The Christology of Hegel* (Albany: State University of New York Press, 1983), 119.

25. Claude Welch, *Protestant Thought in the Nineteenth Century*, vol. 1: 1799–1870 (New Haven: Yale University Press, 1972), 100.

26. "God simply as Father is not yet the True. . . . He is rather beginning and end, he is his presupposition, constitutes himself his presupposition (this is simply another form of the differentiation), he is the eternal process. . . . God in his eternal universality is the differentiating of himself, determining himself, positing another to himself and at the same time abolishing and taking up the distinction, thereby being with himself, and he is Spirit only by being so brought forth" (Hegel, *Lectures on the Philosophy of Religion*, 3:22).

27. "A distinction has to be made, yet the two are said to be intrinsically the same, hence the sameness must be defined exactly so as not to imply the false idea that the eternal Son of the Father is simply identical with the world. Yet it is of course also true that for Hegel God has his self-consciousness in man's consciousness of him, that Spirit thus comes to self-consciousness. God, one may say, is true though not real apart from his manifestation in the world" (Welch, *Protestant Thought in the Nineteenth Century*, 101–2).

and the world, to give a new shape to the concepts both of creation and of the personality of God, a new shape demanded by post-Enlightenment thought, especially since Fichte and the atheism controversy."[28] This panentheistic conception of God (everything is in God and God is in everything), together with his dialectical description of God in process, is an important legacy that Hegel left to nineteenth- and twentieth-century theology.

In the wake of the philosophical and scientific critiques of traditional Christianity, some Christians in the nineteenth century reformulated Christianity to better correlate with modernity. "Protestant liberals," for example, endorsed an evolutionary understanding of cultural development, stressed the moral teaching of the historical Jesus, and held an optimistic assessment of the human person. Among such liberals, the idea of a supernatural God intervening in the events of the world from the outside was suspect. Correlatively, belief in divine miracles, understood as interruptions of the causal nexus of nature, was also widely rejected. Adolf Harnack gave classic expression to the Protestant liberal understanding of Christian faith in *What Is Christianity?* (1900). There he summed up Jesus' teaching and Christian faith under three headings: the kingdom of God, God the Father and the infinite value of the human soul, and the commandment of love. Here there was emphasis upon the inner dimension of the religious life and upon the ethical dimension of the gospel. For many Protestant liberals, Jesus was primarily a profound moral teacher who taught that God is our Father and we are all brothers (no reference yet to "sisters" in this context).

The Roman Catholic corollary to liberal Protestantism is Modernism. "Modernism" is a term that was used by Pope Pius X in the early twentieth century to identify those Catholic theologians who made use of the historical-critical method in the study of the Bible and were critical of some of the traditional dogmas of their church. The Modernists, although not constituting a well-defined school of thought, were those Catholics who sought to coordinate Christian faith with the spirit of the modern Enlightenment. Among their number were Alfred Loisy (1857–1940), a French biblical scholar, and George Tyrrell (1861–1900), a British Jesuit.

Also characteristic of nineteenth-century theological liberalism, in both its Protestant and Catholic forms, was a belief in the continuing progress of society, if allowed to be guided by the modern spirit and modern science. It is easy to understand how many people could adopt such an up-beat assessment of the future. The discovery of a host of inventions in the nineteenth century, including steam-powered transportation, electricity, the telegraph, the telephone, and the use of general anesthesia in surgery, made life easier, transportation faster, and industry more productive. The modern human being seemed capable of everything. If the outdated customs and superstitions of the past could be left behind, society would continue to move forward into a bright future. Science and technology seemed to give humanity clear mastery over nature and control of human destiny. Within such a context, it is no wonder that, for many Christians, the reality of human weakness and sinfulness was obscured or rejected.

Of course, liberal or modernist Christians were not the only kind of Christians

---

28. Ibid., 104.

in the nineteenth and early twentieth centuries. The liberal programs provoked a strong reaction. Despite the progressive theological work of Catholic theologians such as Johann Sebastian Drey (1777–1853), Johann Adam Möhler (1796–1838), Johannes von Kuhn (1806–87), J. J. Ignaz von Döllinger (1799–1890), and others, the official Roman Catholic response to the emergence of modern western culture was largely negative. In his *Syllabus of Errors* (1864), Pope Pius IX (1846–78) rejected ideas such as freedom of conscience in religious matters, freedom of the press, and the separation of church and state. His list of modern errors concluded with the (mistaken) idea that the pope "can or should reconcile himself to, or agree with, progress, liberalism, and modern civilization." Pius X (1903–14) called modernism a "synthesis of all heresies." He condemned "modernism" in his encyclical *Pascendi* (1907) and imposed on all Catholic clergy an oath against it.

In Protestant circles, the reaction against liberalism in the nineteenth and early twentieth centuries was most pronounced in approaches to the Bible. Whereas liberals generally adopted a historically critical interpretation, conservatives used a literal interpretation of the Bible. The critical analysis of the Bible raised questions about its divine inspiration and its authority. Charles Hodge (1797–1878), American Presbyterian theologian, defended the doctrine of plenary (full) inspiration against the erosion of the Bible's authority. A much more vigorous rejection of liberalism took shape in fundamentalism. The term "fundamentalism" originated in the United States in the early twentieth century to refer to evangelical Protestants who fiercely defended the "fundamentals" of Christianity against their erosion by modern thought. The Niagara Bible Conference of 1895 identified five Christian fundamentals: the total inerrancy of the Bible, the deity of Christ, the virgin birth, Christ's substitutionary atonement for sin, and his physical resurrection and future return. Because the Bible was the central authority for Protestant Christians, anything that threatened its authority needed careful attention. Thus when Charles Darwin's *Origin of Species* was published in 1859, conservative Protestants felt compelled to criticize Darwin and to reject his theory of evolution.

The theory of evolution seemed to challenge not only the Bible's authority, but also traditional Christian beliefs about God and humanity. On the one hand, the idea that species, including the human species, had evolved from earlier and different life forms stood in contradiction to a literal reading of the story of creation in the book of Genesis. In addition, the principal mechanism of evolution, natural selection, implied that random, natural forces — not the providential will of God — directed the course of biological history. And if human beings were not directly created by God but had evolved from and were quite closely related to other forms of primate life, then the idea of being "made in God's image" and being uniquely different from all other animals was challenged. For these reasons, Darwin's theory of evolution quickly became the symbol of all that fundamentalism rejected in the modern worldview.

One did not need to be a fundamentalist, however, to be critical of theological liberalism. Early in the twentieth century, a new current in Protestant theology developed that was roundly critical of the liberalism exhibited by Schleiermacher, Harnack, and others. This new current was called "dialectical" or "crisis" theology because it named the crisis of Christianity that occurred after World War I.

The liberals of the nineteenth century were convinced that human society would continue to improve insofar as it was guided by confidence in the human spirit and in modern science. The use of human science and ingenuity to devise newer and more lethal weapons and the tremendous destruction that resulted from their use in World War I raised serious questions about the notion of progress. Foremost among the leaders of the movement were Karl Barth (1886–1968) and Emil Brunner (1889–1966) in Europe and Reinhold Niebuhr (1892–1971) in the United States. They and their supporters were regarded as "neo-orthodox" theologians because they spoke the traditional language of the Christian Church as found in the Bible, the creeds, and the main line of orthodox Protestant theology. But this was not simply a reincarnation of the orthodoxy of Luther or Calvin. The so-called neo-orthodox theologians, accepting modern methods of biblical interpretation, rejected the literalism of traditional orthodoxy. But like Luther and Calvin, they spoke of God as the Sovereign who speaks a divine Word to humanity and obligates humanity to respond. The neo-orthodox theologians believed that liberal theologians had domesticated God and inappropriately elevated humanity. In contrast, they emphasized the difference between God and humanity. Analogous to the ways in which Luther had contrasted an authentic theology of the cross with the mistaken theology of glory and in which Calvin had contrasted the sovereign, self-disclosive God of the scriptures with the God of the philosophers, neo-orthodox theologians emphasized how the God of revelation is other than what humans may want to know or can say about God.

Unlike liberal theologians, neo-orthodox theologians highlighted once again the sinfulness of human nature. Unless people know themselves as limited and sinful, they know neither themselves nor God. Whereas Protestant liberalism emphasized the harmonious integration of Christian faith and human culture, neo-orthodoxy emphasized the difference between Christianity and culture. Such a countercultural stance made it possible for neo-orthodox theologians to voice strong opposition to Nazi totalitarianism in the 1930s. The Barmen Declaration (1934), whose principal author was Barth, repudiated the false teaching that the church can recognize other powers or truths as divine revelation alongside the one Word of God. In addition, it repudiated the false teaching that there are areas of life "in which we belong not to Jesus Christ but another lord."[29]

The implications of neo-orthodoxy for the doctrine of God are decisively disclosed in the excerpt below from Karl Barth. From the outset he makes it clear that an authentic doctrine of God must be derived from revelation. In clear repudiation of the Enlightenment, Barth declares that revelation, not reason, is the final court from which there can be no appeal. "Revelation," he declares," is not made real and true by anything else, whether in itself or for us. Both in itself and for us it is real and true through itself . . . " (see below). Not only by his appeal to revelation, but also by placing the doctrine of the trinity at the beginning of the doctrine of God, Barth diverged from much previous modern theology. Rather than commencing with demonstrations of God's existence or discussions of God's essence, Barth began his exposition of the doctrine of God with the trinity. We

---

29. "The Barmen Declaration," in Franklin Littell, ed., *The German Phoenix: Men and Movements in the Church in Germany* (Garden City, N.Y.: Doubleday & Co., 1960), 186–87.

must deal first with *who* God is, not *that* God is or *what* God is (see excerpt below). In response to the question of who God is, Barth answered that God is the Lord who reveals Godself through Godself.

Although neo-orthodoxy was a potent current in theology from the 1930s to the 1960s, there were other approaches to theology and the doctrine of God. In contrast to Barth, some Christian thinkers and theologians still found it legitimate to begin with the human person or to begin with experience, rather than revelation, in the formulation of a contemporary understanding of God.

Charles Hartshorne (b. 1897), for example, drew upon the ideas of Alfred North Whitehead, a distinguished British mathematician and philosopher, to develop an understanding of God that contrasts sharply with the orthodox understanding of God as absolute, unchanging, and eternal. In his book *Process and Reality* (1929), Whitehead (1861–1947) theorized that the universe consists entirely of becomings, each of them a process of appropriating and integrating the infinity of items provided by the antecedent universe and by God. Hartshorne developed these ideas as they pertain to God in his book *The Divine Relativity* (1948). From the "process" perspective of Whitehead and Hartshorne, all of reality is in flux and in relationship with everything else. Consequently, the universe is characterized by creativity and dynamic change. If the reality we perceive is dynamic and relational, then this must also be true of ultimate reality, God.

In Hartshorne's process perspective, God is relational and social. Whereas the previous tradition described God as a changeless being, unaffected by the world yet affecting or causing everything that happens, Hartshorne describes God as a reality who both affects and is affected by everything else. Such a reconception of God obviously raises questions about whether, and to what extent, God is supreme, absolute, or perfect. Is Hartshorne's God still God and worthy of human worship? In response, Hartshorne distinguishes "absolute" from "supreme," redefines the idea of perfection, and reformulates the idea of divine absoluteness in conjunction with the idea of divine relativity. To say that God is "relative" in some respect is not to say God is absolute in no respect. Revising Anselm's definition of God, Hartshorne speaks of God as the perfect being "than which no other individual being could conceivably be greater, but which itself, in another 'state,' could become greater (perhaps by the creation within itself of new constituents)" (see below). Each entity is potentially enriched by its interaction with other entities. Because God's capacity for relationship and interaction with entities is infinitely greater than any other reality, God is "superior" to all other realities and, in this respect, God's capacity for enrichment is "absolute."

Karl Rahner (1904–84), one of the most influential Roman Catholic theologians of the twentieth century, also made experience a central category in his theology. But unlike process theologians who analyzed the nature of reality and experience in general, Rahner focused on the experience of the person as a thinking and inquiring being. Viewed from one perspective, Rahner's theology could be labeled Catholic neo-*orthodox* because the philosophical underpinnings of his theological approach drew explicitly upon Thomas Aquinas, whom Pope Pius V (1567) had named "Universal Doctor of the Church" and whose thought Pope Leo XIII declared (1879) to be the touchstone of Roman Catholic theology. It also could be designated *neo*-orthodox because Rahner interpreted Aquinas in light of subsequent modern transcendental philosophy. Viewed from another perspective, his theology could be called liberal. He was interested in reconciling modern scientific and philosophical thought with the Catholic theological tradition, and he made human experience a central category in his theological reflections. Yet he did not deny the necessity or the relevance of historical revelation. Nor did he deny the inability of humanity to grasp God directly and immediately. For Rahner God is "Other" and "Holy Mystery." Throughout his theological career, Rahner sought to demonstrate the meaningfulness of the Catholic doctrinal tradition in terms of a "transcendental" analysis of the human condition.

Rahner sought answers to the question of the possibility of a revelation from God in the transcendental, or given, structures of the human subject. For this reason, his theological method is often termed both "transcendental" and "anthropological." That is, Rahner's theology does not begin with God, scripture, or official church teachings, but with the person who is presupposed by Christianity as the hearer of the gospel. This attention to the meaning of the human person, this "anthropological" focus, is distinctive. For Rahner the fundamental experience in which we become conscious of ourselves as selves is that of questioning. In opening ourselves to the unlimited horizon of questioning, we have already transcended ourselves and have moved beyond the limits of any particular explanation. In short, we discover that we are oriented to the Infinite. This orientation, which Rahner called the "supernatural existential," marks the person as a potential hearer of God's word. The radical experience of this unlimited horizon of knowing, this experience of "transcendence," can be ignored or remain unnoticed. Nonetheless, the basis of all our conscious thinking and activity, Rahner insists, lies in this deeper, prereflective consciousness of infinite reality, toward which we are directed by the very structures of our being as free and knowing subjects.

Although their methods and categories are different, the Catholic Rahner and the Protestant Schleiermacher both assert that the awareness of God accompanies, if only in an implicit or unthematic way, every human activity. Both affirm that knowledge of self and knowledge of God are inextricably bound together. And both affirm that the experience of God is primary, whereas human reflection about God is secondary. Whereas Schleiermacher develops his ideas within the context of Romanticism and with the central category of feeling, Rahner develops his ideas within the context of transcendental Thomistic philosophy and with the central category of knowing.

From Rahner's perspective, human life and Christian existence presuppose each other. Human life opens out toward the fulfillment of which the gospel speaks. And Christian existence not only presupposes certain human structures, but is their ultimate source: the natural structures of human life as we know them are created by God. In the context of his theological anthropology, Rahner can speak of the "anonymous Christianity" of those who are not members of the Christian church. The universal human orientation to God (supernatural existential) is already a share in God's grace or divine self-communication. God communicates God's own being definitively through the Word, who enters into human history, and through the Spirit, who transforms human subjectivity so that it may receive and rejoice in the Word. Insofar as prereflective consciousness of infinite reality is the basis of all our conscious thinking and acting, even the atheist "knows" God, albeit not consciously as an object of thought, but prereflectively ("transcendentally") as the source of his or her freedom and the goal of his or her ever striving to know more and to act morally. Rahner's distinction between the transcendental and the categorial dimensions of human thought as well as his articulation of the interconnection of theology and anthropology made it possible for Christianity to enter into dialogue with moral, yet nonreligious atheists. And for many Christians, Rahner's approach to theology made Christian doctrines intelligible and meaningful in an age of scientific and critical inquiry.

For most of the second half of the twentieth century, most Roman Catholic and mainline Protestant theologians continued to make human experience a fundamental theological resource. What is new in recent years, however, is the specific experience reflected upon theologically. Beginning in the late 1960s, "political" theologians in Europe and "liberation" theologians in Latin America made the point that it was insufficient to talk about human experience in general philosophical terms. Rather, they argued, we must talk about concrete human experience — the concrete experience of the poor and the marginalized — and use those specific human experiences as resources in the construction of new theological systems. The various forms of contemporary liberation theology — socio-economic, black, Latino/a, feminist — all attempt to bring the rich and diverse experiences of human beings into correlation with the Christian gospel. Liberation theologians, against old-style liberal and conservative Christians alike, have argued the point that one's "social location" has a profound effect upon his or her interpretation of Christian faith. One's race, gender, and class make a difference in understanding one's self, the world, and God.

There are many factors that contributed to the development of this new perspective on theology. Only a few can be mentioned here. First, the renewed Christian concern for the social implications of the gospel goes back to the tremendous social transformation taking place in the nineteenth century. Industrialization and economic modernization bore bitter as well as sweet fruit. The apparent exploitation of workers in the newly developed capitalist systems called out for attention. At the mid-point of the nineteenth century, Karl Marx and Friedrich Engels had issued their call for the workers of the world to unite in a struggle to create a classless society, in which all would have what they needed for a humane existence (*Communist Manifesto*, 1848). Marx was critical of Christianity because it offered illusory happiness (the afterlife) instead of seeking to establish real happiness in this life. Marx's criticism of religion, including his oft-quoted assertion that religion is the "opium of the people," appears in an article critical of Hegel.[30] Although he accepted Hegel's dialectical interpretation of his-

---

30. "*Religious* suffering is at the same time an *expression* of real suffering and a *protest* against real suffering. Religion is the sigh of the oppressed creature, the sentiment of a heartless world, and the soul of soulless conditions. It is the *opium* of the people.

"The abolition of religion as the *illusory* happiness of men, is a demand for their *real* happiness. The call to abandon their illusions about their condition is a *call to abandon a condition which requires illusions*. The criticism of religion is, therefore, *the embryonic criticism of this vale of tears* of which religion is the *halo*" (Karl Marx, "Contribution to the Critique of Hegel's Philosophy of Right," in *Karl Marx: Early Writings*, ed. and trans. T. B. Bottomore [New York: McGraw-Hill, 1964], 43–44).

tory, he replaced the idealistic orientation of Hegelianism (concern with thought and ideas) with his own materialistic orientation (concern for economic and social conditions). Marx's point was that it is insufficient to interpret the world; one has to transform it. Many contemporary liberation theologians have adopted Marx's economic analysis of society, while rejecting his critique of religion and advocacy of class warfare. Their concern to have Christian faith transform the social and political structures of the world for the better echoes Marx's critique of Hegel.

Second, Christian initiatives developed in the late nineteenth and early twentieth centuries to bring out the social implications of the gospel. Some Christian socialist parties came into being in the nineteenth century in response to the social misery of the lower classes. The Christian Socialist movement, for example, began in England in the mid-nineteenth century. Christians with this kind of social sensitivity were critical of competitive individualism and unrestrained laissez-faire economic policies. In the United States, the Social Gospel movement developed among liberal Protestants from about 1870 to 1920. One of the leaders of the movement, Walter Rauschenbusch, argued that the Bible is dominated by social concern. In his last major work, *A Theology for the Social Gospel* (1917), Rauschenbusch used the social gospel to formulate a doctrine of the Kingdom of God appropriate to modern society. He declared that the Kingdom of God implies a progressive reign of love in human affairs, including redemption of social life from "all forms of slavery in which human beings are treated as mere means to serve the ends of others," from "political autocracies and economic oligarchies," and from "private property in the natural resources of the earth, and from any condition in industry which makes monopoly profits possible."[31]

The Roman Catholic Church officially addressed the new social conditions created by industrial capitalism in a series of papal encyclicals. Pope Leo XIII's *Rerum Novarum* (1891) defended the right of workers to form unions, while upholding private property and rejecting class warfare as a means to improving social conditions. This encyclical was followed by a long line of encyclicals, concerned with social, economic, and political issues, down to Pope John Paul II's *Centesimus Annus* (1991), which commemorated the centenary of Leo XIII's *Rerum Novarum*. In addition to the social teaching of the Catholic encyclicals, the Second Vatican Council (1962–65) gave a powerful impetus to overcoming the dualism between this world and the world to come. The bishops gathered for the council declared that the transformation of the world into something better was an important part of human salvation. Expectation of the afterlife ought not to weaken, but "rather stimulate our concern for cultivating this one [i.e., our earthly world]."[32] This orientation was taken up by the General Conference of Latin American Bishops (CELAM), which, in its 1968 meeting in Medellín, Colombia, and its 1979 meeting in Puebla, Mexico, acknowledged the need for social change and agrarian reform. The bishops at these conferences affirmed liberation as an important dimension of the church's mission.

---

31. Walter Rauschenbusch, *A Theology for the Social Gospel* (New York: Macmillan Co., 1917), 142–45.
32. "Pastoral Constitution on the Church in the Modern World," par. 39, in *The Documents of Vatican II*, ed. Walter M. Abbott (New York: Guild Press, 1966), 237.

Why are reform and liberation necessary? Because, say liberation theologians, the conditions under which too many people live are too miserable. According to a World Bank Report released in summer of 1996, more than one-fifth of the world's population lives on less than one dollar a day. In Latin America, two-thirds of the population is severely undernourished. About 5 percent of the population in Latin America holds 80 percent of the wealth, while two-thirds of the usable land is in the hands of a few Latin Americans and foreign multinational corporations. The issue of social justice in poorer nations is not unrelated to the political and economic position of the powerful, industrialized nations. Only 18 percent of the world's population lives in North America, northern Europe, and Japan, yet the people in these regions pull in 82 percent of the world's income, and they have a per capita income twenty-six times greater than the rest of the world. The United States constitutes approximately 6 percent of the world's population, but uses more than 30 percent of the world's resources.[33]

Liberation theology, especially in its socio-economic forms, has been criticized, however, by conservative Protestants and Catholics as a politicization and corruption of the gospel. In 1984 and again in 1986, the Vatican's Congregation for the Doctrine of the Faith issued "instructions" that criticized the use of Marxist concepts in liberation theology and warned about the danger of using violence to change society. Nonetheless, the same documents affirmed liberation, rightly understood, as a central commitment of the church.

Other forms of liberation theology — for example, the various forms of feminist theology, African and Asian liberationist theology — have also been charged with subverting the Christian tradition by their partisan "subjective" interpretations of Christian faith. In reply, many liberationists have appealed to the claims of postmodernist philosophers and literary theorists, who argue that, insofar as every person and every interpretation is shaped by "social location" (one's race, gender, class, etc.), there is no such thing as an "objective" or "value free" position. Every interpretation of Christian faith, even the orthodox, traditional one, represents a particular point of view. As feminists and other liberationists have pointed out, the dominant point of view has been largely European or American, male, and white. Liberationist theologians feel perfectly justified, therefore, in drawing upon their own particular experiences for elucidating a contemporary theology, for this is what theologians have always done.

James Cone's black theology of liberation developed within the context of the civil rights movement in the United States during the 1960s. At that time Martin Luther King, Jr. (1929–68) had challenged the idea that Christian responsibility consisted simply in preaching the good news and saving souls. He claimed that Christians had to get involved in issues of social justice because God is a God of justice, who is present in human striving for justice. Malcolm X and black nationalists were critical of King, however, for his adoption of nonviolence as the means to effect social change. Whereas King believed that black people were called to bear Jesus' cross and to experience a "season of suffering" in order to achieve a just society, Malcolm X advocated using whatever means necessary to promote

33. For some of the important information concerning the global social and economic situation, see *World Social Situation in the 1990s* (New York: United Nations Publications, 1994).

black power and independence and to defend blacks against white violence. King spoke of love for all humanity, redemptive suffering, and an integrated society. Malcolm X, on the other hand, spoke of self-love, self-defense, and black independence. The critique of King's strategies by black nationalists and Malcolm X's indictment of white Christianity led a number of African-American Christians to proclaim God and Christ as black.

Although it has roots in the religion of black slaves, the idea of a black God or Christ has been explicitly articulated only in the past century. As early as 1898 Henry McNeale Turner, bishop in the African Methodist Episcopal Church, declared that "God is a Negro." Cone developed this idea in the context of the struggles of the 1960s and 1970s. In laying out his approach to theology, Cone explicitly distinguishes his approach from that of Barth. In his reading of the Bible, Cone discovers God not merely as Lord, but as Liberator. In common with Latin American liberation theologians, Cone disassociates himself from other forms of radical theological reflection in the 1960s, such as the death-of-God movement, associated with Thomas J. J. Altizer, Paul Van Buren, and William Hamilton. This movement claimed that life in modern, scientific society made talk about God nonsense. Unless the traditional God "dies," humanity cannot assume full responsibility for itself and the world. Cone found this concern with questions about human meaning after the death of God irrelevant to the black struggle for survival. As he wrote in *A Black Theology of Liberation* (see excerpt below): "Whites may wonder how to find purpose in their lives, but our purpose is forced upon us. We do not want to know how we can get along without God, but how we can survive in a world permeated with white racism." The central question in the doctrine of God is, for Cone, not the intellectual intelligibility of the doctrine but the implications of a reformulated doctrine of God (trinity) for black survival and self-determination.

Like Cone, Gustavo Gutiérrez (b. 1928) draws upon scripture to support his claim that knowledge of God occurs where there is justice and righteousness. Unlike Cone, he focuses upon the reality of economic poverty rather than racism as the particular form of oppression to be overcome. The theme of liberation from oppression also runs through the work of feminist theologians. Feminism refers generally to the movement demanding for women political, social, economic, and religious equality with men. Although there are wide differences among feminists concerning what female well-being means and how it is to be achieved, feminists are generally united in opposing sexism (discrimination because of sex) and patriarchy (social organization in which dominant males rule and women are expected to be submissive to them) and in promoting the full flourishing of women.

Major differences among feminists who have dealt with Christian theology result from different perceptions of the depth and pervasiveness of sexism and patriarchy within Christianity. Some feminists, such as Mary Daly, claim that the fundamental symbols and beliefs of Christianity are so patriarchal that they must be abandoned. Other feminists, such as Rosemary Radford Ruether and Elizabeth Johnson (see excerpts below), argue that women do not need to abandon Christianity, but rather need to radically transform its patriarchal dimensions. Carol Christ and Judith Plaskow contrast these different perspectives as "revolutionary" (or "radical") and "reformist" feminism.[34] More recently, some have referred to these differences as "post-Christian" and "Christian" feminism respectively. Despite their differences, both groups generally agree that many Christians throughout the ages have concluded that society should be male-dominated because God, who rules the world, is conceived of as a male. If God's qualities are the stereotypical masculine ones (power, strength, reason, etc.), then those who possess these qualities are most like God and, therefore, the ones most entitled to rule on this earth. In the words of Mary Daly, if God is male, then the male is God.

Christian feminists have adopted several different paths for combatting the sexist and patriarchal dimensions of the Christian tradition. One path has been to disclose the origin and subsequent history of male conceptions of God. Rosemary Radford Ruether, in *Sexism and God-Talk* (1983), theorizes about the origin of male monotheism in nomadic herding society (see excerpt below). By uncovering the social and cultural contexts in which specific conceptions of God emerged, feminists wish to relativize the notion that the now dominant male conception of God is divinely sanctioned and must be normative in theology. Another path has been to identify the negative psychological, social, and ecological implications of male conceptions of God as father, king, and lord. Such conceptions, feminists argue, can promote "spiritual infantilism" and a failure to take responsibility for one's life. They can corrupt the possibilities for human relationship on the basis of equality and mutuality. They are also irrelevant or unhelpful in addressing current crises, such as ecological destruction.

One solution proposed by Christian feminists is to think of and speak about God in new ways. Ruether suggests that the divine should be conceived of and spoken about as "God/ess." Sallie McFague, in her influential book *Models of God: Theology for an Ecological, Nuclear Age* (1987), reconceives the trinity as Mother, Lover, and Friend. Elizabeth Johnson speaks of God as Spirit and Wisdom. Feminists, such as McFague and Johnson, make it clear that "feminizing" God is insufficient. The full dignity of women is not established, they point out, by ascribing stereotypical "feminine" traits (e.g., nurture and compassion) to a primarily "male" God. Instead, they call for female metaphors and images of God. Appealing both to the testimony of scripture and to tradition of analogical speech about God, Christian feminists emphasize the metaphorical character of all our language about God and the theological conviction that God transcends human understanding. Consequently, no one image or concept of God is fully adequate. There is a need for a plurality of images.

In response to those who would trivialize the issue of God-language, Dorothee Soelle points out that the God-language we use either enables or prevents us from identifying some basic everyday experiences as experiences of God (see excerpt below). Language about God and knowledge of God are connected. The issue in feminist theology, Soelle argues, is not about exchanging female pronouns for male pronouns. Rather, it is about another way of thinking of God's transcendence and immanence. "Transcendence," she writes, "is no longer to be

---

34. Carol P. Christ and Judith Plaskow, eds., *Womanspirit Rising* (San Francisco: Harper and Row, 1979), 1–16.

understood as being independent of everything and ruling over everything else, but rather as being bound up in the web of life" (see excerpt below).

As Christianity moves into its third millennium, there is little doubt that there will continue to be a rich and wide discussion of ways to understand and speak about God. New ways of understanding God and speaking about God have been made all the more necessary by the growth of atheism and irreligion over the past two centuries. What was once the persuasion of a very few has now become the conviction of many. By the latter portion of the twentieth century, there were over two hundred million atheists in the world and more than eight hundred million people who identified themselves as "nonreligious." If we combine both groups, then we can say that more than 20 percent of the world's population professes unbelief or disbelief in some form.[35]

Not only the criticism leveled against traditional concepts of God from philosophical, scientific, social-critical, and feminist perspectives, but also the burgeoning dialogue between Christianity and other religions will lead to new theological articulations of the doctrine of God. Dialogue with Buddhism has led some Christians to probe the potential of Buddhist concepts of emptiness and nothingness as an antidote to the reifying (to turn into a "thing") tendencies of western thought about God. Out of such dialogues, some Christians have come to rediscover that God is "no-thing," but a transpersonal reality. Others have come to speak about God as "divine matrix" or as "serendipitous creativity," ways of conceiving God consonant with Hindu and Buddhist interpretations of reality and the modern, scientific story of cosmic evolution.[36] Others, of course, have vigorously resisted these new interpretations, and have called for a return to classical God-talk. The debate will no doubt continue in the years ahead.

TEXTS

Friedrich Schleiermacher (1768–1834)

The Christian Faith (1830–31), §4, Pars. 1–4; §33, Pars. 2–3; §170, Pars. 1–3*

§4. *The common element in all howsoever diverse expressions of piety, by which these are conjointly distinguished from all other feelings, or, in other words, the self-identical essence of piety, is this: the consciousness of be-*

---

35. See David B. Barrett, *World Christian Encyclopedia: A Comparative Study of Churches and Religions in the Modern World, AD 1900–2000* (Nairobi: Oxford University Press, 1982), 6.

36. See, for example, Joseph Bracken, *The Divine Matrix: Creativity as Link between East and West* (Maryknoll, N.Y.: Orbis Books, 1995), and Gordon D. Kaufman, *God, Mystery, and Diversity: Christian Theology in a Pluralistic World* (Minneapolis: Fortress Press, 1996).

ing absolutely dependent, or, which is the same thing, of being in relation with God.

1. In any actual state of consciousness, no matter whether it merely accompanies a thought or action or occupies a moment for itself, we are never simply conscious of our Selves in their unchanging identity, but are always at the same time conscious of a changing determination of them....Thus in every self-consciousness there are two elements, which we might call respectively a self-caused element [*ein Sichselbstsetzen*] and a non-self-caused element [*ein Sichselbstnichtsogesetzthaben*]; or a Being and a Having-by-some-means-come-to-be [*ein Sein und ein Irgendwiegewordensein*]. The latter of these presupposes for every self-consciousness another factor besides the Ego, a factor which is the source of the particular determination, and without which the self-consciousness would not be precisely what it is. But this Other is not objectively presented in the immediate self-consciousness with which alone we are here concerned. For though, of course, the double constitution of self-consciousness causes us always to look objectively for an Other to which we can trace the origin of our particular state, yet this search is a separate act with which we are not at present concerned. In self-consciousness there are only two elements: the one expresses the existence of the subject for itself, the other its co-existence with an Other.

Now to these two elements, as they exist together in the temporal self-consciousness, correspond in the subject its *Receptivity* and its (spontaneous) *Activity*....But as we never do exist except along with an Other, so even in every outward-tending self-consciousness the element of receptivity, in some way or other affected, is the primary one; and even the self-consciousness which accompanies an action (acts of knowing included), while it predominantly expresses spontaneous movement and activity, is always related (though the relation is often a quite indefinite one) to a prior moment of affective receptivity, through which the original "agility" received its direction. To these propositions assent can be unconditionally demanded; and no one will deny them who is capable of a little introspection and can find interest in the real subject of our present inquiries.

2. The common element in all those determinations of self-consciousness which predominantly express a receptivity affected from some outside quarter is the *feeling of Dependence*. On the other hand, the common element in all those determinations which predominantly express spontaneous movement and activity is the *feeling of Freedom*....

3. ...But if...the feeling of freedom expresses only an inward movement of activity, not only is every such individual movement bound up with the state of our stimulated receptivity at the moment, but, further, the totality of our free inward movements, considered as a unity, cannot be represented as a feeling of absolute freedom, because our whole existence does not present itself to our consciousness as having proceeded from our own spontaneous activity. Therefore in any temporal existence a feeling of absolute freedom can have no place. As regards the feeling of absolute dependence which, on the other hand, our proposition does postulate: for just the same reason, this feeling cannot in any wise arise from the influence of an object which has in some way to be *given* to us; for upon such an object there would always be a counter-influence, and even a voluntary

renunciation of this would always involve a feeling of freedom. Hence a feeling of absolute dependence, strictly speaking, cannot exist in a single moment as such, because such a moment is always determined, as regards its total content, by what is *given,* and thus by objects towards which we have a feeling of freedom. But the self-consciousness which accompanies all our activity, and therefore, since that is never zero, accompanies our whole existence, and negatives absolute freedom, is itself precisely a consciousness of absolute dependence; for it is the consciousness that the whole of our spontaneous activity comes from a source outside of us in just the same sense in which anything towards which we should have a feeling of absolute freedom must have proceeded entirely from ourselves. But without any feeling of freedom a feeling of absolute dependence would not be possible.

4. As regards the identification of absolute dependence with "relation to God" in our proposition: this is to be understood in the sense that the *Whence* of our receptive and active existence, as implied in this self-consciousness, is to be designated by the word "God," and that this is for us the really original signification of that word. In this connection we have first of all to remind ourselves that . . . this "Whence" is not the world, in the sense of the totality of temporal existence, and still less is it any single part of the world. For we have a feeling of freedom (though, indeed, a limited one) in relation to the world, since we are complementary parts of it, and also since we are continually exercising an influence on its individual parts; and, moreover, there is the possibility of our exercising influence on all its parts; and while this does permit a limited feeling of dependence, it excludes the absolute feeling. In the next place, we have to note that our proposition is intended to oppose the view that this feeling of dependence is itself conditioned by some previous knowledge of God. And this may indeed be the more necessary since many people claim to be in the sure possession of a concept of God, altogether a matter of conception and original, i.e., independent of any feeling; and in the strength of this higher self-consciousness, which indeed may come pretty near to being a feeling of absolute freedom, they put far from them, as something almost infra-human, that very feeling which for us is the basic type of all piety. Now our proposition is in no wise intended to dispute the existence of such an original knowledge, but simply to set it aside as something with which, in a system of Christian doctrine, we could never have any concern, because plainly enough it has itself nothing to do directly with piety. If, however, word and idea are always originally one, and the term "God" therefore presupposes an idea, then we shall simply say that this idea, which is nothing more than the expression of the feeling of absolute dependence, is the most direct reflection upon it and the most original idea with which we are here concerned, and is quite independent of that original knowledge (properly so called), and conditioned only by our feeling of absolute dependence. So that in the first instance God signifies for us simply that which is the co-determinant in this feeling and to which we trace our being in such a state; and any further content of the idea must be evolved out of this fundamental import assigned to it. Now this is just what is principally meant by the formula which says that to feel oneself absolutely dependent and to be conscious of being in relation with God are one and the same thing; and the reason is that absolute dependence is the fundamental relation which must include all others in itself. This last expression includes the God-consciousness in the self-

consciousness in such a way that, quite in accordance with the above analysis, the two cannot be separated from each other. The feeling of absolute dependence becomes a clear self-consciousness only as this idea comes simultaneously into being. In this sense it can indeed be said that God is given to us in feeling in an original way; and if we speak of an original revelation of God to man or in man, the meaning will always be just this, that, along with the absolute dependence which characterizes not only man but all temporal existence, there is given to man also the immediate self-consciousness of it, which becomes a consciousness of God. In whatever measure this actually takes place during the course of a personality through time, in just that measure do we ascribe piety to the individual. On the other hand, any possibility of God being in any way *given* is entirely excluded, because anything that is outwardly given must be given as an object exposed to our counter-influence, however slight this may be. The transference of the idea of God to any perceptible object, unless one is all the time conscious that it is a piece of purely arbitrary symbolism, is always a corruption, whether it be a temporary transference, i.e., a theophany, or a constitutive transference, in which God is represented as permanently a particular perceptible existence.

> §33. *This feeling of absolute dependence, in which our self-consciousness in general represents the finitude of our being, is therefore not an accidental element, or a thing which varies from person to person, but is a universal element of life; and the recognition of this fact entirely takes the place, for the system of doctrine, of all the so-called proofs of the existence of God.*

...Finally, the third type of godlessness is the so-called definite denial of God—atheism, which is propounded as a speculative theory in the midst of a Christian society, in a condition of full development and even in the highest stage of culture. This again is twofold. In part it is a wicked fear of the sternness of the God-consciousness, and hence, though moments of enlightenment intervene, clearly a product of licentiousness and thus a sickness of the soul usually accompanied by contempt of everything intellectual; and of this (godlessness) it can be said that it is naught, because it entirely lacks inner truth. And in part it is simply a reasoned opposition to the current and more or less inadequate representations of the religious consciousness. Moreover, the atheism of the eighteenth century was, for the most part, a struggle against the petrified, anthropomorphic presentations of doctrine, a struggle provoked by the tyranny of the Church. But when, over and above the defects of representation, the inner facts of self-consciousness themselves are thus wholly misconstrued, this serious misunderstanding is none the less merely a disease of the understanding which may revive sporadically and from time to time, but never produces anything that is historically permanent. This fact cannot therefore be pled against our assertion that the feeling of absolute dependence, as here expounded, and the God-consciousness contained in it are a fundamental moment of human life.

3. But even supposing its universality could be disputed, still no obligation would arise for the system of doctrine to prove the existence of God; that would be an entirely superfluous task. For since in the Christian Church the God-consciousness should be developed in youth, proofs, even if youth were capable of understanding them, could only produce an objective consciousness, which

is not the aim here, nor would it in any way generate piety. We are not concerned here with the question whether there are such proofs, and whether, if we have no immediate certitude of God, then that of which we do have immediate certitude, and by which God could be proved, must not itself be God. Our point simply is that these proofs can never be a component part of the system of doctrine; for that is only for those who have the inner certainty of God, as we have already described it, and of that they can be directly conscious at every moment.... Dogmatics must therefore presuppose intuitive certainty of faith; and thus, as far as the God-consciousness in general is concerned, what it has to do is not to effect its recognition but to explicate its content....

§170. *All that is essential in this Second Aspect of the Second Part of our exposition is also posited in what is essential in the doctrine of the Trinity; but this doctrine itself, as ecclesiastically framed, is not an immediate utterance concerning the Christian self-consciousness, but only a combination of several such utterances.*

...1. An essential element of our exposition in this Part has been the doctrine of the union of the Divine Essence with human nature, both in the personality of Christ and in the common Spirit of the Church; therewith the whole view of Christianity set forth in our Church teaching stands and falls. For unless the being of God in Christ is assumed, the idea of redemption could not be thus concentrated in His Person. And unless there were such a union also in the common Spirit of the Church, the Church could not thus be the Bearer and Perpetuator of the redemption through Christ. Now these exactly are the essential elements in the doctrine of the Trinity, which, it is clear, only established itself in defense of the position that in Christ there was present nothing less than the Divine Essence, which also indwells the Christian Church as its common Spirit, and that we take these expressions in no reduced or sheerly artificial sense, and know nothing of any special higher essences, subordinate deities (as it were) present in Christ and the Holy Spirit. The doctrine of the Trinity has no origin but this; and at first it had no other aim than to equate as definitely as possible the Divine Essence considered as thus united to human nature with the Divine Essence itself....

2. But at this point we would call a halt; we cannot attach the same value to the further elaboration of the dogma, which alone justifies the ordinary term. For the term "Trinity" is really based on the fact that each of the two abovementioned unions is traced back to a separate distinction posited independently of such union, and eternally, in the Supreme Being as such; further, after the member of this plurality destined to union with Jesus had been designated by the name "Son," it was felt necessary to posit the Father in accordance therewith as a special distinction. The result was the familiar dualism — unity of Essence and trinity of Persons. But the assumption of an eternal distinction in the Supreme Being is not an utterance concerning the religious consciousness, for there it never could emerge. Who would venture to say that the impression made by the divine in Christ obliges us to conceive such an eternal distinction as its basis?...

3. Hence the second part of our paragraph must not be understood as meaning that the orthodox doctrine of the Trinity is to be regarded as an immediate or even a necessary combination of utterances concerning the Christian

self-consciousness. On the contrary, the intermediate step has been taken of eternalizing, in separation, the being of God in itself, and the being of God which makes union with human nature possible. Now if this arose so definitely out of the utterances of Christ Himself and of the Apostles concerning Him that we had to accept it on their testimony, the doctrine of the Trinity in that case would be a fully elaborated doctrine of this type, and we should accept it as a combination of testimonies regarding a supersensible fact; but it would no more be a "doctrine of faith" in the really original and proper sense of that phrase than the doctrines of the resurrection and ascension of Christ; and it would resemble these last also in this respect that our faith in Christ and our living fellowship with Him would be the same although we had no knowledge of any such transcendent fact, or although the fact itself were different. But the exegesis meant to establish the position just mentioned has never been able to entrench itself so strongly as to escape constant attacks upon it. Hence it is important to make the point that the main pivots of the ecclesiastical doctrine — the being of God in Christ and in the Christian Church — are independent of the doctrine of the Trinity.

Let it be supposed that we further elaborate our knowledge of this supersensible fact and — to avoid the idea that the said distinction within the Supreme Being led to nothing up to the beginning of the union — teach besides that both the Second and the Third Person in the Trinity were implicated even in the creation of the world, while the Second Person was also the subject thereafter of all the Old Testament theophanies, and it was from the Third Person that the whole prophetic movement of the Old Testament received its impulse. Then these statements are still further removed from being utterances about our Christian consciousness. And we can wait all the more calmly to see whether the exegetical results on which these expansions of the doctrine rest are any more fully confirmed by the latest work on the subject than has hitherto been the case.

Elizabeth Cady Stanton (1815–1902)

The Woman's Bible (1895), *Comments on Genesis**

The Book of Genesis, Chapter 1:26–28

> And God said, Let us make man in our image, after our likeness: and let them have dominion over the fish of the sea, and over the fowl of the air, and over the cattle, and over all the earth, and over every creeping thing that creepeth upon the earth. So God created man in his own image, in the image of God created he him; male and female created he them. And God blessed them, and God said unto them, Be fruitful, and multiply, and replenish the earth, and subdue it; and have dominion over the fish of the sea, and over the fowl of the air, and over every living thing that moveth upon the earth.

*Reprinted from *The Woman's Bible*, Part 1 (New York: European Publishing Co., 1895). Pp. 14–16.

Here is the sacred historian's first account of the advent of the woman; a simultaneous creation of both sexes, in the image of God. It is evident from the language that there was consultation in the Godhead, and that the masculine and feminine elements were equally represented. Scott in his commentaries says, "This consultation of the Gods is the origin of the doctrine of the trinity." But instead of three male personages, as generally represented, a Heavenly Father, Mother, and Son would seem more rational.

The first step in the elevation of woman to her true position, as an equal factor in human progress, is the cultivation of the religious sentiment in regard to her dignity and equality, the recognition by the rising generation of an ideal Heavenly Mother, to whom their prayers should be addressed, as well as to a Father.

If language has any meaning, we have in these texts a plain declaration of the existence of the feminine element in the Godhead, equal in power and glory with the masculine. The Heavenly Mother and Father! "God created man in his *own image, male and female.*" Thus Scripture, as well as science and philosophy, declares the eternity and equality of sex — the philosophical fact, without which there could have been no perpetuation of creation, no growth or development in the animal, vegetable, or mineral kingdoms, no awakening nor progressing in the world of thought. The masculine and feminine elements, exactly equal and balancing each other, are as essential to the maintenance of the equilibrium of the universe as positive and negative electricity, the centripetal and centrifugal forces, the laws of attraction which bind together all we know of this planet whereon we dwell and of the system in which we revolve.

In the great work of creation the crowning glory was realized, when man and woman were evolved on the sixth day, the masculine and feminine forces in the image of God, that must have existed eternally, in all forms of matter and mind. All the persons in the Godhead are represented in the Elohim, the divine plurality taking counsel in regard to this last and highest form of life. Who were the members of this high council, and whether a duality or a trinity? Verse 27 declares the image of God male and female. How then is it possible to make woman an afterthought? We find in verses 5–16 the pronoun "he" used. Should it not in harmony with verse 26 be "they," a dual pronoun? We may attribute this to the same cause as the use of "his" in verse 11 instead of "it." The fruit tree yielding fruit after "his" kind instead of after "its" kind. The paucity of a language may give rise to many misunderstandings....

Thus, the Old Testament, "in the beginning," proclaims the simultaneous creation of man and woman, the eternity and equality of sex; and the New Testament echoes back through the centuries the individual sovereignty of woman growing out of this natural fact. Paul, in speaking of equality as the very soul and essence of Christianity, said, "There is neither Jew nor Greek, there is neither bond nor free, there is neither male nor female; for ye are all one in Christ Jesus." With this recognition of the feminine element in the Godhead in the Old Testament, and this declaration of the equality of the sexes in the New, we may well wonder at the contemptible status woman occupies in the Christian Church of today.

Karl Barth (1886–1968)

Church Dogmatics (1932), Volume 1: *The Doctrine of the Word of God,* Part I*

Chapter II: The Revelation of God

Part I: The Triune God

§8. God in His Revelation: God's Word is God Himself in His revelation. For God reveals Himself as the Lord and according to Scripture this signifies for the concept of revelation that God Himself in unimpaired unity yet also in unimpaired distinction is Revealer, Revelation, and Revealedness.

I. The Place of the Doctrine of the Trinity in Dogmatics

If in order to clarify how Church proclamation is to be measured by Holy Scripture we first enquire into the prior concept of revelation, already in this enquiry itself we must keep to Holy Scripture as the witness of revelation. Perhaps more important than anything dogmatics can say with reference to the pre-eminent place of Scripture in the Church and over against the Church is the example which dogmatics itself must give in its own fundamental statements. It must try to do what is undoubtedly required of the Church in general, namely, to pay heed to Scripture, not to allow itself to take its problems from anything else but Scripture. The basic problem with which Scripture faces us in respect of revelation is that the revelation attested in it refuses to be understood as any sort of revelation alongside which there are or may be others. It insists absolutely on being understood in its uniqueness. But this means that it insists absolutely on being understood in terms of its object, God. It is the revelation of Him who is called Yahweh in the Old Testament and *theos* or, concretely, *kyrios* in the New Testament. The question of the self-revealing God which thus forces itself upon us as the first question cannot, if we follow the witness of Scripture, be separated in any way from the second question: How does it come about, how is it actual, that this God reveals Himself? Nor can it be separated from the third question: What is the result? What does this event do to the man to whom it happens? Conversely the second and third questions cannot possibly be separated from the first.... *God* reveals Himself. He reveals Himself *through Himself.* He reveals *Himself.* If we really want to understand revelation in terms of its subject, i.e., God, then the first thing we have to realize is that this subject, God, the Revealer, is identical with His act in revelation and also identical with its effect. It is from this fact, which in the first instance we are merely indicating, that we learn we must begin the doctrine of revelation with the doctrine of the triune God....

In putting the doctrine of the Trinity at the head of all dogmatics we are adopting a very isolated position from the standpoint of dogmatic history.

Yet not wholly isolated, for in the Middle Ages Peter Lombard in his *Sentences* and Bonaventura in his *Breviloquium* took the same position.

---

*Reprinted from *Church Dogmatics,* vol. 1: *The Doctrine of the Word of God,* Part One, by Karl Barth. Authorized English translation © 1957 T. & T. Clark Ltd. Used by permission of T. & T. Clark Ltd., Edinburgh. Pp. 295–96, 300–301, 304–11.

Otherwise it neither has been nor is the custom to give this place to the doctrine of the Trinity. The reason for this strange circumstance can be sought only in the fact that with overwhelming unanimity it has obviously been thought that a certain formally very natural and illuminating scheme of questioning should be followed in which one can and should speak first of Holy Scripture (or in Roman Catholic dogmatics the authority of the teaching office, or in Modernist dogmatics the reality and truth of religion) as the *principium cognoscendi* (apart from the actual content of faith), and then that even in the doctrine of God itself one can and should deal first with God's existence, nature, and attributes (again apart from the concrete givenness of what Christians call "God").

Even Melanchthon and Calvin, and after them Protestant orthodoxy in both confessions, followed this pattern in a way that was strangely uncritical, and similarly none of the later movements in Roman Catholic and Protestant theology has led to the taking of a different path at this point.

The reason why we diverge from this custom is this. It is hard to see how in relation to Holy Scripture we can say what is distinctive for the holiness of this Scripture if first we do not make it clear (naturally from Holy Scripture itself) who the God is whose revelation makes Scripture holy. It is also hard to see how what is distinctive for this God can be made clear if, as has constantly happened in Roman Catholic and Protestant dogmatics both old and new, the question who God is, which it is the business of the doctrine of the Trinity to answer, is held in reserve, and the first question to be treated is that of the That and the What of God, as though these could be defined otherwise than on the presupposition of the Who....

There is in fact a serious risk, in the doctrine of Scripture as well as the doctrine of God, that we may lose ourselves in considerations and be driven to conclusions which have nothing whatever to do with the supposed concrete theme of the two doctrines, if we begin by discarding the concreteness as it is manifest in the trinitarian form of the Christian doctrine of God. And the doctrine of the Trinity itself is threatened by the same danger, the danger of irrelevant speculation, if we state it only at a later stage and do not give it the first word as that which gives us information on the concrete and decisive question: Who is God?...

The Root of the Doctrine of the Trinity. ...According to Scripture God's revelation is God's own direct speech which is not to be distinguished from the act of speaking and therefore is not to be distinguished from God Himself, from the divine I which confronts man in this act in which it says Thou to him. Revelation is *Dei loquentis persona*.

From the standpoint of the comprehensive concept of God's Word it must be said that here in God's revelation God's Word is identical with God Himself. Among the three forms of the Word of God this can be said unconditionally and with strictest propriety only of revelation. It can be said of Holy Scripture and Church proclamation as well, but not so unconditionally and directly. For if the same can and must be said of them too, we must certainly add that their identity with God is an indirect one. Without wanting to deny or even limit their character as God's Word we must bear in mind that the Word of God is mediated here, first through the human persons of the prophets and apostles who receive it and pass it on, and then through the human persons of its expositors and preachers, so that Holy Scripture and proclamation must always become God's Word in order to be it....

According to Holy Scripture God's revelation is a ground which has no higher or deeper ground above or below it but is an absolute ground in itself, and therefore for man a court from which there can be no possible appeal to a higher court. ... Only if one denies it can one ascribe to it another higher or deeper ground or try to understand and accept or reject it from the standpoint of this higher or deeper ground. Obviously even the acceptance of revelation from the standpoint of this different and supposedly higher ground, e.g., an acceptance of revelation in which man first sets his own conscience over it as judge, can only entail the denial of revelation. Revelation is not made real and true by anything else, whether in itself or for us. Both in itself and for us it is real and true through itself....

We may sum all this up in the statement that God reveals Himself as the Lord. This statement is to be regarded as an analytical judgment. The distinction between form and content cannot be applied to the biblical concept of revelation. When revelation is an event according to the Bible, there is no second question as to what its content might be. Nor could its content be equally well manifested in another event than this. Although, in keeping with God's riches, revelation is never the same but always new, nevertheless as such it is always in all circumstances the promulgation of the *basileia tou theou,* of the lordship of God.... To be Lord means being what God is in His revelation to man. To act as Lord means to act as God in His revelation acts on man.... All else we know as lordship can only be a copy, and is in reality a sad caricature of this lordship. Without revelation man does not know that there is a Lord, that he, man, has a Lord, and that God is this Lord. Through revelation he does know it.... That God reveals Himself as the Lord means that He reveals what only He can reveal, Himself. And so, as Himself, He has and exercises His freedom and lordship, He is God, He is the ground without grounds, with whose word and will man can only begin without asking Why, so that in and with this he may receive everything that deserves to be called true and good. It becomes and is true and good through the fact that we receive it from Him, that God, as Himself, is with us, with us as a man who says I and addresses us as Thou is with others, but with us as the One He is, as the Lord, as He who is free. According to the Bible God's being with us is the event of revelation.

The statement, understood thus, that God reveals Himself as the Lord, or what this statement is meant to describe, and therefore revelation itself as attested by Scripture, we call the root of the doctrine of the Trinity.

Generally and provisionally we mean by the doctrine of the Trinity the proposition that He whom the Christian Church calls God and proclaims as God, the God who has revealed Himself according to the witness of Scripture, is the same in unimpaired unity and yet also the same thrice in different ways in unimpaired distinction. Or, in the phraseology of the Church's dogma of the Trinity, the Father, the Son, and the Holy Spirit in the biblical witness to revelation are the one God in the unity of their essence, and the one God in the biblical witness to revelation is the Father, the Son, and the Holy Spirit in the distinction of His persons.

When we call the statement that God reveals Himself as Lord, or the revelation denoted by this statement and attested by Scripture, the root of the doctrine of the Trinity, this implies two things.

First, and negatively, the statement or statements about God's Trinity cannot claim to be directly identical with the statement about revelation or with revelation itself. The doctrine of the Trinity is an analysis of this statement, i.e., of what it denotes. The doctrine of the Trinity is a work of the Church, a record of its understanding of the statement or of its object, a record of its knowledge of God or of its battle against error and on behalf of the objectivity of its proclamation, a record of its theology and to that degree of its faith, and only to that extent, only indirectly, a record of revelation. The text of the doctrine of the Trinity, whether we have in view one of its dogmatic formulations by the Church, or our own or some other theologico-dogmatic explication of the Church dogma, is not, then, identical with one part of the text of the biblical witness to revelation. The text of the doctrine of the Trinity is at every point related to texts in the biblical witness to revelation. It also contains certain concepts taken from this text. But it does this in the way an interpretation does. That is to say, it translates and exegetes the text. And this means, e.g., that it makes use of other concepts besides those in the original. The result is that it does not just repeat what is there. To explain what is there it sets something new over against what is there. We have in view this difference from revelation and Scripture, which the Church and theology must be aware of in their own work, when we call our statement about revelation — and already it, too, can be regarded only as an interpretation — merely the root of the doctrine of the Trinity....

Secondly, and positively, to call revelation the root of the doctrine of the Trinity is also to say that the statement or statements about the Trinity of God purports to be indirectly, though not directly, identical with the statement about revelation. The newness or otherness with which they stand alongside the first statement (or its content) cannot mean that a first age, which we may call biblical, had faith without revelation or knowledge of the Triune God, that what it meant by the contrast and unity between Yahweh and the angel of Yahweh, between the Father, the Son, and the Spirit, was in reality an imperfectly clarified monotheism, a greatly disrupted polytheism or the like, and then there came a second age, let us say that of the early Church, which for various reasons thought it should give to the same faith a trinitarian formulation in the sense of the dogma, and that we now stand in a third age, the modern period, for which the Bible and the dogma are both records of the faith of past ages in face of which we are free to express our own faith either in the same way or not. No, we regard the dogma — with what right and in what sense has still to be shown of course — as a necessary and relevant analysis of revelation, and we thus think that revelation itself is correctly interpreted by the dogma. The Bible can no more contain the dogma of the Trinity explicitly than it can contain other dogmas explicitly....

It thus follows that we cannot prove the truth of the dogma that is not as such in the Bible merely from the fact that it is a dogma, but rather from the fact that we can and must regard it as a good interpretation of the Bible. Later we shall have to show why it is that dogmas must be approached with some prejudgment in favor of their truth, with some very real respect for their relative, though not absolute, authority. But this includes rather than excludes the fact that dogmatics has to prove dogma, i.e., to indicate its basis, its root in revelation or in the biblical witness to revelation....

In calling revelation the root of the doctrine of the Trinity we are thus indicating that we do not confuse or equate the biblical witness to God in His revelation with the doctrine of the Trinity, but we do see an authentic and well-established connection between the two. This obviously means that the doctrine of the Trinity has a wholly actual and not just a historical significance for us and for the dogmatics of our age, even though this is a very different age from that of Arius and Athanasius. In other words, it means that the criticism and correction of Church proclamation must be done today, as it was then, in the form of developing the doctrine of the Trinity. It means that the text of the doctrine of the Trinity...must become for us a commentary that we have to make use of in expounding the Bible and therefore in employing the dogmatic criterion.

But let us come to the point: The basis or root of the doctrine of the Trinity, if it has one and is thus legitimate dogma — and it does have one and is thus legitimate dogma — lies in revelation.

Charles Hartshorne (b. 1897)

The Divine Relativity (1948), Chapter 1*

Nonidentity of Supreme and Absolute

Of course one is free to mean by "absolute" whatever is supreme or most excellent. But then one is not free to use the same word, without warning, for the nonrelative, for what is independent, immutable, impassive, and the like. It is not self-evident that independence (or immutability) as such *is* excellence, and that excellence as such *is* independence. On the contrary, as I hope in this first chapter to show, excellence or value has a dimension of dependence as well as of independence, and there is no basis for the venerable doctrine that supreme independence will constitute supreme excellence of every kind. To resolve the paradoxes connected with the contrast between relative and absolute we must, I shall argue, admit that "the absolute" is not identical with the supreme being or God, but in a strict sense is infinitely less than the supreme, and in fact is a certain kind of constituent within it. If this admission seems as much a paradox as any which it is designed to remove, the reason is that sufficient attention has not been paid to the definition of "absolute" as simply "what is nonrelative." Why must the nonrelative be more than, or even as much as, the relative? Why must a mere term be more than or equal to a term which involves relations, and hence other terms as relata?

But, it will be said, by God we mean, or for religion we require, not simply a supreme or most excellent but a perfect being. And how can a perfect being change (as it must if relations to the changing world are internal to it)? This argument I counter with a dilemma.

The perfect being either does, or does not, include the totality of imperfect things. If it does, then it is inferior to a conceivable perfection whose constituents would be more perfect. (There is no meaning to the idea of a greatest possible totality of imperfect things.) If the perfect does *not* include the totality of imperfect things, then the total reality which is "the perfect *and* all existing imperfect things" is a greater reality than the perfect alone. If it be said that the perfect, though it does not include the imperfect things, does include their values, whatever is good in them, the reply is that the existence of the imperfect must then be strictly valueless, adding nothing to the sum of values, and might exactly as well not be as be. He who says this implies that God did no good thing when he created the world, and that our human existence is metaphysically useless and meaningless. The only way to escape this is to admit that the perfect-*and*-the imperfect is something superior to the perfect "alone" — or as independent of the imperfect.

Definition of Perfection

Which horn of this dilemma shall we grasp? If perfection is defined as that which in no respect could conceivably be greater, and hence is incapable of increase, then we face paradox on either hand. But suppose we define the perfect, or supremely excellent or good, as that individual being (in what sense "individual" will appear later) than which no *other individual* being could *conceivably* be greater, but which itself, in another "state," could become greater (perhaps by the creation within itself of new constituents). Otherwise expressed, let us define perfection as an excellence such that rivalry or superiority on the part of other individuals is impossible, but self-superiority is not impossible. Or again, let us say that the perfect is the "self-surpassing surpasser of all." This formula resolves the dilemma. For suppose the self-surpassing surpasser of all has the power of unfailingly enjoying as its own constituents whatever imperfect things come to exist. Then it will be bound to possess in its own unity all the values which the imperfect things severally and separately achieve, and therefore it is bound to surpass each and every one of them. Thus it is certain of superiority to any "other individual." It must, in any conceivable state of existence, be the "most excellent being."

By speaking of the perfect as "enjoying" the values of things, I mean to exclude the idea of a mere collection of all things. The surpasser of all others must be a single individual enjoying as his own all the values of all other individuals, and incapable of failing to do so. For this, it is enough to suppose that the being is bound to have adequate knowledge of events when and as they occur, and thereafter. For adequately to know values is to possess them; and to surpass the values of other beings it is enough to possess the values of every one of them from the time these values exist. There is no need to possess them in advance of the others; or to possess them eternally, unless a being which surveys all time eternally is itself a conceivable being — which this essay seeks to disprove. To surpass other conceivable beings, there is no need to surpass inconceivable beings, as they would be if they were, which they are not, conceivable. Even the least of beings surpasses mere nonsense.

I shall hope to show in this chapter that religion does not need perfection in any other sense than that called for by our formula. (If my use of the term "perfection" be objected to, I ask that the phrase "transcendent excellence" be mentally substituted. I would have used "transcendence" were it not usually contrasted to immanence, a contrast here not directly relevant. And I know of no term except "perfect" which connotes superiority to all possible others.) Meanwhile, I wish to point out that, although the self-surpassing surpasser of all must obviously be in some aspect relative, it does not follow that it is in *no* aspect absolute. For to be capable of self-increase in *some* respect does not imply capacity to increase in every respect. Indeed, it is logically self-evident that in two respects such increase is excluded by our definition. To be absolutely guaranteed superiority to absolutely every other individual that comes to exist is an absolute maximum in certainty and universality of superiority. Moreover, this certainty and universality are intelligible only in terms of such attributes as omniscience (ideal knowledge), and we shall see that as "relational types" these are absolute in the strictest sense....

God as Social

We have also to remember that if there is religious value in the absoluteness of God, as requisite for his reliability, there is equally manifest religious value in another trait which seems unequivocally to imply relativity rather than absoluteness. This is the social or personal nature of God. What is a person if not a being qualified and conditioned by social relations, relations to other persons? And what is God if not the supreme case of personality? Those who deny this have yet to succeed in distinguishing their position from atheism, as Hume pointedly noted. Either God really does love all beings, that is, is related to them by a sympathetic union surpassing any human sympathy, or religion seems a vast fraud. The common query, Can the Absolute or Perfect Being be personal or social? should really run, In what sense, if any, can a social being be absolute or perfect? For God is conceived socially before he is conceived absolutely or as perfect. God is the highest ruler, judge, benefactor; he knows, loves, and assists man; he has made the world with the design of sharing his bliss with lesser beings. The world is a vast society governed by laws instituted by the divine monarch — the supreme personal power to whom all other persons are subject. These are all, more or less clearly, social conceptions — if you like, metaphors (though aimed, as we shall see, at a literal, intuited meaning) drawn from the social life of man. They constitute the universal, popular meaning of "God," in relation to which descriptions such as "absolute," "perfect," "immutable," "impassive," "simple," and the like, are technical refinements aimed at logical precision. They seek to define the somewhat vague ideas of *highest* ruler, *supreme* power, or *author of all*, himself without author or origin. "Immutable," for example, is an attempted definition of the superiority of deity with respect to death and degeneration, and also with respect to vacillation of will due to fear, or other weakness. Earthly rulers are all brought low by death; and their promises and protection and execution of justice must always be discounted somewhat in anticipation of the effect upon them of changing circumstances and the development of their own motives, the growth of good and evil in their own hearts. God is not under sentence of death, cannot decay; and his covenant abides, nor is his wisdom ever clouded by storms of blind passion, the effects of strong drink or of disease.

The future of theology depends, I suggest, above all upon the answer to this question: can technically precise terms be found which express the supremacy of God, among social beings, without contradicting his social character? To say, on the one hand, that God is love, to continue to use popular religious terms like Lord, divine will, obedience to God, and on the other to speak of an absolute, infinite, immutable, simple, impassive deity, is either a gigantic hoax of priestcraft, or it is done with the belief that the social connotations of the popular language are ultimately in harmony with these descriptors. Merely to speak of the "mysteriousness" of God is not sufficient. If he escapes all the resources of our language and analysis, why be so insistent upon the obviously quite human concepts, absolute, infinite, perfect, immutable? These too are our conceptions, our terms, fragments of the English or Latin languages. Perhaps after all it is not correct to say God is absolute. How shall we know, if the subject is utterly mysterious and beyond our powers?...

Karl Rahner (1904–84)

Foundations of Christian Faith (1976/78), Chapter 2, Section 2*

This second chapter is a conceptual reflection upon that transcendental experience in which a person comes into the presence of the absolute mystery which we call "God," an experience which is more primary than reflection and cannot be recaptured completely by reflection. What has to be said here has already been said less explicitly in the first chapter. If man really is a subject, that is, a transcendent, responsible, and free being who as subject is both entrusted into his own hands and always in the hands of what is beyond his control, then basically this has already said that man is a being oriented towards God. His orientation towards the absolute mystery always continues to be offered to him by this mystery as the ground and content of his being. To understand man in this way, of course, does not mean that when we use the term "God" in such a statement, we know what this term means from any other source except through this orientation to mystery. At this point theology and anthropology necessarily become one. A person knows explicitly what is meant by "God" only insofar as he allows his transcendence beyond everything objectively identifiable to enter into his consciousness, accepts it, and objectifies in reflection what is already present in his transcendentality.... This real word [God] confronts us with ourselves and with reality as a whole, at least as a question. This word exists. It is in our history and makes our history. It is a word. For this reason one can fail to hear it, with ears, as scripture says, which hear and do not understand. But it does not cease to

*Reprinted from *Foundations of Christian Faith: An Introduction to the Idea of Christianity* by Karl Rahner, trans. William V. Dych. Originally published as *Grundkurs des Glaubens: Einführung in den Begriff des Christentums,* © Verlag Herder, Freiburg im Breisgau, 1976. English translation copyright © 1978 by The Crossroad Publishing Company. All rights reserved. Used with permission of The Crossroad Publishing Company, New York. Pp. 44, 51–54, 64–66.

exist because of that. In antiquity Tertullian's insight about the *anima naturaliter Christiana,* that is, the soul that is Christian from its origins, is derived from the inescapability of the word "God." It exists. It comes from those origins from which man himself comes. Its demise can be thought of only along with the death of man himself. It can still have a history whose changing forms we cannot imagine in advance precisely because it is what keeps an uncontrollable and unplanned future open. It is our opening to the incomprehensible mystery. It makes demands on us, and it might irritate us because it disturbs the peace of an existence which wants to have the peace of what is clear and distinct and planned.

...For it is itself the final word before wordless and worshipful silence in the face of the ineffable mystery....It is an almost ridiculously exhausting and demanding word. If we were not hearing it *this way,* then we would be hearing it as a word about something obvious and comprehensible in everyday life, as a word alongside other words. Then we would have heard something which has nothing in common with the true word "God" but its phonetic sound. We are familiar with the Latin expression *amor fati,* the love of one's destiny. This resolve in the face of one's destiny means literally "love for the word that has been uttered," that is, for that *fatum* which is our destiny. Only this love for what is necessary liberates our freedom. This *fatum* is ultimately the word "God."

Transcendental and A Posteriori Knowledge of God

What we are calling transcendental knowledge or experience of God is an *a posteriori* knowledge insofar as man's transcendental experience of his free subjectivity takes place only in his encounter with the world and especially with other people. To that extent the scholastic tradition is correct when it emphasizes against ontologism that man's *only* knowledge of God is an a posteriori knowledge from the world. This is still true even with verbal revelation because this too has to work with human concepts. Hence our transcendental knowledge or experience has to be called a posteriori insofar as every transcendental experience is mediated by a categorical encounter with concrete reality in our world, both the world of things and the world of persons. This is also true of the knowledge of God. To that extent we can and we must say that all knowledge of God is an a posteriori knowledge which comes from and through encountering the world, to which, of course, we ourselves also belong.

The knowledge of God is, nevertheless, a *transcendental* knowledge because man's basic and original orientation towards absolute mystery, which constitutes his fundamental experience of God, is a permanent existential of man as a spiritual subject. This means that the explicit, conceptual, and thematic knowledge, which we usually think of when we speak of the knowledge of God or of proofs for God's existence, is a reflection upon man's transcendental orientation towards mystery, and some degree of reflection is always necessary. It is not, however, the original and foundational mode of the transcendental experience of this mystery. It belongs necessarily to the very nature of human knowledge that thought is self-reflexive, that we think of a concrete object *within* the *infinite* and apparently empty horizon of thinking itself, that thinking is conscious of itself. We must get used to taking account of the fact that when we think and when we exercise freedom we are always dealing with more and always have to do with more than that which we are talking *about* in our words and concepts, and that *with which* we are occupied here and now as the concrete object of our activity....

We become conscious of ourselves and of the transcendental structures that are given with our subjectivity only in the fact that the world presents itself to us concretely and in quite definite ways, and hence in the fact that we are involved in the world both passively and actively. This is also true of the knowledge of God. In this sense it is not a knowledge which is grounded entirely in itself. But neither is it simply a mystical process within our own personal interiority, nor, in the light of this, does it have the character of a personal, divine self-revelation. But the a posteriori character of the knowledge of God would be misunderstood if we were to overlook the transcendental element in it and understand the knowledge of God after the model of an a posteriori knowledge whose object comes entirely from without and appears in a neutral faculty of knowledge. In the knowledge of God a posteriority does not mean that we look out into the world with a neutral faculty of knowledge and then think that we can discover God there directly or indirectly among the realities that present themselves to us objectively, or that we can prove his existence indirectly.

We are oriented towards God. This original experience is always present, and it should not be confused with the objectifying, although necessary, reflection upon man's transcendental orientation towards mystery. This does not destroy the a posteriori character of the knowledge of God, but neither should this a posteriority be misunderstood in the sense that God could simply be indoctrinated from without as an object of our knowledge.

This unthematic and ever-present experience, this knowledge of God which we always have even when we are thinking of and concerned with anything but God, is the permanent ground from out of which that thematical knowledge of God emerges which we have in explicitly religious activity and in philosophical reflection. It is not in these latter that we discover God just as we discover a particular object of our experience within the world. Rather, both in this explicitly religious activity directed to God in prayer and in metaphysical reflection we are only making explicit for ourselves what we already know implicitly about ourselves in the depths of our personal self-realization. Hence we know our subjective freedom, our transcendence, and the infinite openness of the spirit even where and when we do not make them thematic at all. We also know them when such a conceptual, objectifying thematization and verbal expression of this original knowledge perhaps does not succeed at all, or succeeds very imperfectly and distortedly. Indeed we even know them when we refuse to engage at all in such a process of thematization.

For this reason the meaning of all explicit knowledge of God in religion and in metaphysics is intelligible and can really be understood only when all the words we use there point to the unthematic experience of our orientation towards the ineffable mystery. And just as it is of the nature of transcendent spirit, because it is constituted in an objective world, always to offer along with this objectivity the possibility, both in theory and in practice, of running away from its own subjectivity, from taking responsibility for itself in freedom, so too a person can also hide from himself his transcendental orientation towards the absolute mystery which we call God. As scripture says (Rom. 1:18), he can in this way suppress the most real truth about himself.

The individual realities with which we are usually dealing in our lives always become clearly intelligible and comprehensible and manipulable because we can differentiate them from other things. There is no such way of knowing God. Because God is something quite different from any of the individual realities which appear within the realm of our experience or which are inferred from it, and because the knowledge of God has a quite definite and unique character and is not just an instance of knowledge in general, it is for these reasons very easy to overlook God. The concept "God" is not a grasp of God by which a person masters the mystery, but it is letting oneself be grasped by the mystery which is present and yet ever distant. This mystery remains a mystery even though it reveals itself to man and thus continually grounds the possibility of man being a subject. There can then follow from this ground, of course, the so-called concept of God, explicit language about him, words and what we mean by them and try to say to ourselves reflexively, and certainly a person ought not to avoid the effort involved in this process of reflexive conceptualization. But in order to remain true, all metaphysical ontology about God must return again and again to its source, must return to the transcendental experience of our orientation towards the absolute mystery, and to the existentiell[1] practice of accepting this orientation freely. This acceptance takes place in unconditional obedience to conscience, and in the open and trusting acceptance of the uncontrollable in one's own existence in moments of prayer and quiet silence....

It [the term of transcendence] is beyond the control of the finite subject not only physically, but also logically.... The term of transcendence admits of no control over itself because then we would be reaching beyond it and incorporating it within another, higher and broader horizon. This contradicts the very nature of this transcendence and of the real term of this transcendence. This infinite and silent term is what disposes of us. It presents itself to us in the mode of withdrawal, of silence, of distance, of being always inexpressible, so that speaking of it, if it is to make sense, always requires listening to its silence.

Since we experience the term of transcendence only in the experience of this bottomless and endless transcendence, we have avoided any kind of *ontologism* in the usual sense. For this term is not experienced in itself, but is only known unobjectively in the experience of subjective transcendence. The presence of the term of transcendence is the presence of this transcendence, which is only present as the condition of possibility for categorical knowledge, and not by itself. We can see by this statement (and it is one of the most fundamental statements about the real understanding of God and is a really correct approach to the knowledge of God) that the tendency today to talk not about God, but about one's neighbor, and to use not the term "God," but "world" and "responsibility for the world" — we can see that this tendency has an absolutely solid foundation. However, going to the extreme of banishing God and of being radically silent about him is and remains false and does violence to the true nature of Christianity.

---

1. "Existentiell" refers to one's concrete existence and particular experience as opposed to a formal analysis of human existence in general.

But what is correct about all of these statements is the plain fact that we do not know God by himself as one individual object alongside others, but only as the term of transcendence. This transcendence takes place only in a categorical encounter in freedom and in knowledge with concrete reality, which indeed appears as world only vis-à-vis God as absolutely other than world. Hence the term of this transcendence is present only in the mode of otherness and distance. It can never be approached directly, never be grasped immediately. It gives itself only insofar as it points wordlessly to something else, to something finite as the object we see directly and as the immediate object of our action. And for this reason the term of this transcendence is mystery.

The Term of Transcendence as the "Holy Mystery"

We have already and by way of anticipation called the term of transcendence the *holy* mystery. The reason why we had to call it "mystery" consisted ultimately in the fact that we experience it as that which cannot be encompassed by a pre-apprehension which reaches beyond it, and hence it cannot be defined. But why do we characterize it as the "holy" mystery?

We have already emphasized in the first chapter that when we speak of transcendence we do not mean only and exclusively the transcendence which is the condition of possibility for categorical knowledge as such. We mean also and just as much the *transcendence of freedom, of willing,* and *of love.* This transcendence, which is constitutive of the subject as a free and personal subject of action within an unlimited realm of action, is just as important, and is basically just another aspect of the transcendence of a spiritual, and therefore knowing, and precisely for this reason free subject.... But for a subject who is present to himself to affirm freely vis-à-vis another subject means ultimately to love.

Hence when we reflect here upon transcendence as will and as freedom, we must also take into account the character of the term and source of transcendence as love. It is a term which possesses absolute freedom, and this term is at work in freedom and in love as that which is nameless and which is not at our disposal, for we are completely at its disposal. It is what opens up my own transcendence as freedom and as love. But the term of transcendence is always and originally the source of the mystery which offers itself. This term itself opens our transcendence; it is not established by us and by our own power as though we were absolute subjects. Hence if transcendence moves in freedom and in love towards a term which itself opens this transcendence, then we can say that that which is nameless and which is not at our disposal, and at whose complete disposal we exist, that this very thing is present in loving freedom, and this is what we mean when we say "holy mystery."...

If we have arrived in this way at the basic and original idea of mystery and of the holy, and if it is correct to designate the term of transcendence by this name, there can be no question, of course, of giving a *definition* of the essence of this holy mystery. Mystery is as indefinable as every other transcendental "concept." They do not admit of definition because what is expressed in them is known only in transcendental experience, and transcendental experience, as always and everywhere given antecedently, has nothing outside of itself by which it and its term could be defined.

Gustavo Gutiérrez (b. 1928)

A Theology of Liberation (1971/73), Chapter 10*

The modes of God's presence determine the forms of our encounter with him. If humanity, each man, is the living temple of God, we meet God in our encounter with men; we encounter him in the commitment to the historical process of mankind.

To Know God Is to Do Justice

The Old Testament is clear regarding the close relationship which exists between God and the neighbor. This relationship is a distinguishing characteristic of the God of the Bible. To despise one's neighbor (Prov. 14:21), to exploit the humble and poor worker, and to delay the payment of wages are to offend God: "You shall not keep back the wages of a man who is poor and needy, whether a fellow-countryman or an alien living in your country in one of your settlements. Pay him his wages on the same day before sunset, for he is poor and his heart is set on them: he may appeal to the Lord against you, and you will be guilty of sin" (Deut. 24:14–15; cf. Exod. 22:21–23). This explains why "a man who sneers at the poor insults his maker" (Prov. 17:5).

Inversely, to know, that is to say, to love Yahweh is to do justice to the poor and oppressed.... Where there is justice and righteousness, there is knowledge of Yahweh; when these are lacking, it is absent: "There is no good faith or mutual trust, no knowledge of God in the land, oaths are imposed and broken, they kill and rob; there is nothing but adultery and license, one deed of blood after another" (Hos. 4:1–2; cf. Isa. 1). To know Yahweh, which in Biblical language is equivalent to saying to love Yahweh, *is* to establish just relationships among men, it *is* to recognize the rights of the poor. The God of Biblical revelation is known through interhuman justice. When justice does not exist, God is not known; he is absent.... Medellín asserts: "Where this social peace does not exist there will we find social, political, economic, and cultural inequalities, there will we find the rejection of the peace of the Lord, and a rejection of the Lord himself" ("Peace," no. 14).

On the other hand, if justice is done, if the alien, the orphan, and the widow are not oppressed, "Then I will let you live in this place, in the land which I gave long ago to your forefathers for all time" (Jer. 7:7). This presence of Yahweh is active; he it is who "deals out justice to the oppressed. The Lord feeds the hungry and sets the prisoner free. The Lord restores sight to the blind and straightens backs which are bent; the Lord loves the righteous and watches over the stranger;

---

*Reprinted from *A Theology of Liberation: History, Politics and Salvation* by Gustavo Gutiérrez, trans. and ed. Sister Caridad Inda and John Eagleson. Copyright © 1973 Orbis Books. Used by permission of Orbis Books, Maryknoll, N.Y. Pp. 194–96.

the Lord gives heart to the orphan and widow but turns the course of the wicked to their ruin." So "the Lord shall reign forever" (Ps. 146:7–10).

This encounter with God in concrete actions towards others, especially the poor, is so profound and enriching that by basing themselves on it the prophets can criticize — always validly — all purely external worship. This criticism is but another aspect of the concern for asserting the transcendence and universality of Yahweh. "Your countless sacrifices, what are they to me? Says the Lord; I am sated with whole offerings of rams.... The offer of your gifts is useless, the reek of sacrifice is abhorrent to me.... Though you offer countless prayers, I will not listen. There is blood on your hands.... Cease to do evil and learn to do right, pursue justice and champion the oppressed; give the orphan his rights, plead the widow's cause" (Isa. 1:10–17).... Only then will God be with us, only then will he hear our prayer and will we be pleasing to him (Isa. 58:9–11). God wants justice, not sacrifices. Emphasizing the bond between the knowledge of God and interhuman justice, Hosea tells us that Yahweh wishes knowledge and not holocausts: "O Ephraim, how shall I deal with you? How shall I deal with you, Judah? Your loyalty to me is like the morning mist, like dew that vanishes early. Therefore have I lashed you through the prophets and torn you to shreds with my words; loyalty is my desire, not sacrifice, not whole-offerings but the knowledge of God" (Hos. 6:4–6).

Dorothee Soelle (b. 1929)

Theology for Skeptics (1995), Chapter 3*

...I ask God my Mother... to rid me of the God of men.

The issue is more than about "feminine aspects in God," to which enlightened men today readily admit. Their talk disturbs me, as if God were intrinsically and primarily masculine and as if those feminine elements which had been kept hidden must now be brought out as a supplement. According to this scheme of thought, the feminine lies hidden in God as the child is known to lie hidden in the man. But it is not sufficient to want to discover the yet unknown feminine in the well-known masculine God; within the framework of this deconstruction, the feminist critique has not yet gone far enough. Wouldn't we with equal justification have to discover the negroid traits and the youthful elements in God in order finally to get rid of the old white man in heaven? Our inner difficulty does not lie in the more or less false pictures of God which have been handed down to us, and we cannot overcome the spiritless desolation in which we live by setting up statues of goddesses or pictures of matriarchy in the temples that have been emptied. We are not lacking in pictures but in identifiable experiences of God. Caught in a straitjacket of masculine authoritarian language, we have been rendered incapable of identifying the secret of life which we call God as something experienced.

I do not mean that people experience God less today than in earlier times. God's presence and absence are given to us, too, in jubilation and desperation and

*Reprinted by permission from *Theology for Skeptics* by Dorothee Soelle, copyright © 1995 Augsburg Fortress. Pp. 40–44, 46, 48–50.

sometimes even in the puzzling mixture of both. Life itself is so permeated with this quality that we call God that we cannot avoid feeding on it and hungering after it. Only we often don't know that because we have been rendered incapable of speaking. We do not dare connect that which in fact deserves to be called an "experience of God" with the God of the religion administered by men. The priests and theologians have talked so long that we have become mute. They have locked God up in Bible and liturgy instead of using Bible and liturgy as eyeglasses for understanding our everyday lives.

While in reality God is present and recognizable at many places in our lives, we lack the language to name God. The power of trivialization which especially harms women convinces us that what we experience is "nothing but" technological necessity, the result of causes which are beyond our control, emotional overstimulation, etc. The know-it-all attitude and insensitivity of this "nothing but" diminishes the spirit, sensibilities, and fantasies of women. We have been trained to trivialize everyday life instead of sanctifying it.... The God-from-above which religion made into a fetish has truncated our lives from their connection to God.

I am reminded of hearing a report from a young woman about the events at Greenham Common, where women regularly met in vigil against Britain's nuclear-missile deployment. While she spoke I saw in the light of the searchlights the faces of the unarmed women in front of me. But more precisely I saw the face of God, about which the Bible speaks, shining in them.... [But] the word [God] is occupied by the language of the patriarchate and its worship of power. Within the framework of this occupation the Bible and liturgy can no longer do that for which they are intended, namely, to make the mystery of God visible also for us, *pro nobis*. The dominant theology has given both of these an authoritarian unapproachability, so that people can no longer express their deepest experiences in the language of God and cannot share them with others. Without form, without language, the experiences die; they are not appropriated. Language not only depicts what is, it also restores to consciousness what has been experienced. In this sense successful God language is a steady knocking on the door of memory. It says, "Do you not know more?... Just remember.... It was like this for you too." At the same time it is an interpretation of reality that we cannot do without, an emphatic interpretation that protects us from trivialization of ourselves....

But is this presupposition really correct? Do these wonderful and painful experiences and afflictions from God exist? Do we really experience that God is nearer to me than I am to myself? I remember a feminist group in New York where we tried to speak of our own religious experiences. A woman who has been my friend ever since that day reported on the destructive and humiliating experiences of her Christian socialization. Then she paused and spoke about her sexual experience, which showed her for the first time what might be meant by the word "God" — that oceanic feeling of not being separate from anything or hindered by anything, the happiness of being one with everything living, the ecstasy in which the old "I" is abandoned and I am new and different. Goethe spoke once of the "freshness of the nights of love, which begot you as you begot." That is expressed in male language, but the experience of being born where we conceive and give birth, of not being able to separate the passive and active experiencing and enduring, of being neither the one acting nor the one being acted upon, is rooted in women's experience. The language of religion, by which I do not mean the stolen language in which a male God ordains and imperial power radiates forth, is the language of mysticism: I am completely and utterly in God, I cannot fall out of God, I am imperishable. "Who shall separate us from the love of God?" we can then ask with Paul the mystic; "neither death nor life, height nor depth, neither present nor future" (Rom. 8:35 and 38).

I would like to relate one more example, one of the many experiences of being abandoned by God. In November 1983 the German Parliament in Bonn decided to agree to the stationing of medium-range missiles. I was on the street in Bonn with many friends, both male and female. It was a slap in the face for us after years of work in persuasion and liberation, in which we had spent time, energy, and money. It was a humiliation for democracy, for the great majority of the people rejected the weapons of mass destruction. It was an assault on the truth with the argument that first-strike weapons should ostensibly serve for "defense." I was supposed to give a talk and I didn't know what to say. Many of us who were demonstrating were drenched by water cannons and driven through the streets by the police. Why have you abandoned us, God, I thought. Why do you not show your face? Why do you not prepare us a "table in the presence of our enemies" (Ps. 23) rather than inviting those who do not ask for you to a banquet? I no longer know what I said in that dark night, but one sentence was, "Truth will make us free," an oath of God that truth will not always remain buried under lies. Many regarded what I said as a prayer, even though I hardly used religious vocabulary. In any case this prayer was not directed to an authoritarian power-up-above, who might have forced a different decision with lightning, thunder, supernatural intervention, or magical appearances. The God to whom this prayer went was sad like us, small like us, without bank accounts or bombs as backing, exactly like us.

... To learn to speak to God is more important in this [i.e., in the search for an existential God-language] than to speak about God. There is a consensus that the new language does not need to be gender-exclusive. There is controversy on whether the "Goddess" or similar concepts taken mainly from matriarchal culture, like the Great Mother, are productive and liberating or whether with them, as I think, the search is broken off too quickly and we do not carry out Eckhart's leave-taking from God. Is not parental symbolism in many respects powerless, because it can indeed express protection and security, but not the Godhead who goes with us out of Egypt, not liberation. Mary Daly once called attention to the fact that a noun is not the appropriate type of word for speaking about God. "Why not a verb — the most active and dynamic of all? ... The anthropomorphic symbols for God may be intended to convey personality, but they fail to convey that God is Be-ing. Women now who are experiencing the shock of nonbeing and the surge of self-affirmation against this are inclined to perceive transcendence as the Verb in which we participate — live, move, and have our being."

The question of feminist liberation theology is not, "Does God exist?" but rather, "Does God occur also among us?" In the process of becoming conscious, on the path out of socially imposed nonbeing, the question whether we need God is excavated from the rubble of tradition. I often have the impression that the longing to transcend actual circumstances is clearest in the fear and desperation of women. It is futile to pursue theology if we do not approach this complicated Brechtian "use" of God. (Herr K. in Berthold Brecht's Keuner stories answers the question whether he believes in God with the counterquestion whether anything would change thereby.) The assurance of divinity is *used* when it rescues us and places our feet on wide open spaces. Without the God-within-us, this God-above-us hardens into a fetish who willed Auschwitz....

In feminist theology, therefore, the issue is not about exchanging pronouns but about another way of thinking of transcendence. Transcendence is no longer to be understood as being independent of everything and ruling over everything else, but rather as being bound up in the web of life. Goethe says in his aphorisms about love: "Voluntary dependence, the most beautiful state, and how would it be possible without love?" God is no less voluntarily dependent than all of us can be through love. That means that we move from God-above-us to God-within-us and overcome false transcendence hierarchically conceived. We must approach mysticism, which comes closest to overcoming the hierarchical masculine conception of God—a mysticism, to be sure, in which the thirst for real liberation does not lead to drowning in the sea of unconsciousness.

According to a sentence of Jacob Boehme, God is "the Nothing that wants to become everything." The actually experienced, powerless Nothing of the injured life with which feminist liberation theology begins, is not redeemed from the outside. For us also, "no higher Being, no God or emperor or tribunal" is present, but there is an integration into the sisterly ground of the living. The mystical certainty that nothing can separate us from the love of God grows when we ourselves become one with love by placing ourselves, freely and without guarantee of success, on the side of love.

Rosemary Radford Ruether (b. 1936)

Sexism and God-Talk: Toward a Feminist Theology (1983), Chapter 2*

Male Monotheism and the Dualizing of Gender Metaphors

Male monotheism has been so taken for granted in Judeo-Christian culture that the peculiarity of imaging God solely through one gender has not been recognized. But such an image indicates a sharp departure from all previous human consciousness. It is possible that the social origins of male monotheism lie in nomadic herding societies. These cultures lacked the female gardening role and tended to image God as the Sky-Father. Nomadic religions were characterized by exclusivism and an aggressive, hostile relationship to the agricultural people of the land and their religions.

Male monotheism reinforces the social hierarchy of patriarchal rule through its religious system in a way that was not the case with the paired images of

God and Goddess. God is modeled after the patriarchal ruling class and is seen as addressing this class of males directly, adopting them as his "sons." They are his representatives, the responsible partners of the covenant with him. Women as wives now become symbolically repressed as the dependent servant class. Wives, along with children and servants, represent those ruled over and owned by the patriarchal class. They relate to man as he relates to God. A symbolic hierarchy is set up: God-male-female. Women no longer stand in direct relation to God; they are connected to God secondarily, through the male. This hierarchical order is evident in the structure of patriarchal law in the Old Testament, in which only the male heads of families are addressed directly. Women, children, and servants are referred to indirectly through their duties and property relations to the patriarch. In the New Testament this hierarchial "order" appears as a cosmic principle:

> But I want to understand that the head of every man is Christ, the head of a woman is her husband, and the head of Christ is God.... For a man ought not to cover his head, since he is the image and glory of God, but the woman is the glory of man. (1 Cor. 11:3, 7)

Male monotheism becomes the vehicle of a psychocultural revolution of the male ruling class in its relationship to surrounding reality. Whereas ancient myth had seen the Gods and Goddesses as within the matrix of one physical-spiritual reality, male monotheism begins to split reality into a dualism of transcendent Spirit (mind, ego) and inferior and dependent physical nature. Bodiless ego or spirit is seen as primary, existing before the cosmos. The physical world is "made" as an artifact by transcendent, disembodied mind or generated through some process of devolution from spirit to matter.

Both the Hebrew Genesis story and the Platonic creation story of *Timaeus* retain reminiscences of the idea of primal matter as something already existing that is ordered or shaped by the Creator God. But this now becomes the lower pole in the hierarchy of being. Thus the hierarchy of God-male-female does not merely make woman secondary in relation to God, it also gives her a negative identity in relation to the divine. Whereas the male is seen essentially as the image of the male transcendent ego or God, woman is seen as the image of the lower, material nature. Although both are seen as "mixed natures," the male identity points "above" and the female "below." Gender becomes a primary symbol for the dualism of transcendence and immanence, spirit and matter.

The Appropriation of the Goddess in Jewish and Christian Monotheism

In Hebrew religious development, male monotheism does not, by any means, succeed in simply supplanting the older world of Gods and Goddesses or the cult of salvation through renewal of nature-society. Rather it imposes itself on this older world, assimilating, transforming, and reversing its symbol systems. Thus, for example, the ancient myth of the Sacred Marriage lives on in Yahwism, but in a reversed form that uses this story to exert the possessive and judgmental relation of the patriarchal God over the people of agricultural society....

Toward a Feminist Understanding of God/ess

The four preceding Biblical traditions[1] may not be adequate for a feminist reconstruction of God/ess, but they are suggestive. If all language for God/ess is analogy, if taking a particular human image literally is idolatry, then male language for the divine must lose its privileged place. If God/ess is not the creator and validator of the existing hierarchical social order, but rather the one who liberates us from it, who opens up a new community of equals, then language about God/ess drawn from kingship and hierarchical power must lose its privileged place. Images of God/ess must include female roles and experience. Images of God/ess must be drawn from the activities of peasants and working people, people at the bottom of society. Most of all, images of God/ess must be transformative, pointing us back to our authentic potential and forward to new redeemed possibilities. God/ess language cannot validate roles of men or women in stereotypic ways that justify male dominance and female subordination. Adding an image of God/ess as loving, nurturing mother, mediating the power of the strong, sovereign father, is insufficient.

Feminists must question the overreliance of Christianity, especially modern bourgeois Christianity, on the model of God/ess as parent. Obviously any symbol of God/ess as parent should include mother as well as father. Mary Baker Eddy's inclusive term, *Mother-Father God,* already did this one hundred years ago. Mother-Father God has the virtue of concreteness, evoking both parental images rather than moving to an abstraction (Parent), which loses effective resonance. Mother and father image God/ess as creator, as the source of our being. They point back from our own historical existence to those upon whom our existence depends. Parents are a symbol of roots, the sense of being grounded in the universe in those who have gone before, who underlie our own existence.

But the parent model for the divine has negative resonance as well. It suggests a kind of permanent parent-child relationship to God. God becomes a neurotic parent who does not want us to grow up. To become autonomous and responsible for our own lives is the gravest sin against God. Patriarchal theology uses the parent image for God to prolong spiritual infantilism as virtue and to make autonomy and assertion of free will a sin. Parenting in patriarchal society also becomes the way of enculturating us to the stereotypic male and female roles. The family becomes the nucleus and model of patriarchal relations in society. To that extent parenting language for God reinforces patriarchal power rather than liberating us from it. We need to start with language for the divine as redeemer, as liberator, as one who fosters full personhood and, in that context, speak of God/ess as creator, as source of being.

Patriarchal theologies of "hope" or liberation affirm the God of Exodus, the God who uproots us from present historical systems and puts us on the road to new possibilities. But they typically do this in negation of God/ess as Matrix, as source and ground of our being. They make the fundamental mistake of iden-

---

1. In the immediately preceding section of this chapter, Ruether referred to elements in the biblical tradition that are critical of the patriarchal understanding of God or that offer an alternative understanding of God. These elements include the prophetic tradition, the use of God-language to break the ties of bondage under human kings and fathers (image of God as Liberating Sovereign), the proscription of idolatry, and equivalent images for God as male and female.

tifying the ground of creation with the foundations of existing social systems. Being, matter, and nature become the ontocratic base for the evil system of what is. Liberation is liberation out of or against nature into spirit. The identification of matter, nature, and being with mother makes such patriarchal theology hostile to women as symbols of all that "drags us down" from freedom. The hostility of males to any symbol of God/ess as female is rooted in this identification of mother with the negation of liberated spirit. God/ess as Matrix is thought of as "static" immanence. A static, devouring, death-dealing matter is imaged, with horror, as extinguishing the free flight of transcendent consciousness. The dualism of nature and transcendence, matter and spirit as female against male is basic to male theology.

Feminist theology must fundamentally reject this dualism of nature and spirit. It must reject both sides of the dualism: both the image of mother-matter-matrix as "static immanence" and as the ontological foundation of existing, oppressive social systems and also the concept of spirit and transcendence as rootless, antinatural, originating in an "other world" beyond the cosmos, ever repudiating and fleeing from nature, body, and the visible world. Feminist theology needs to affirm the God of Exodus, of liberation and new being, but as rooted in the foundations of being rather than as its antithesis.

James Cone (b. 1938)

A Black Theology of Liberation (1970), Chapter 4*

Inasmuch as the perspective of black theology differs from that of both Barth and Tillich, there is also a difference in its approach to the doctrine of God. The point of departure of black theology is the biblical God as related to the black liberation struggle. It asks, "How do we *dare* speak of God in a suffering world, a world in which blacks are humiliated because they are black?" This question, which occupies the central place in our theological perspective, forces us to say nothing about God that does not participate in the emancipation of black humanity. God-talk is not Christian-talk unless it is *directly* related to the liberation of the oppressed. Any other talk is at best an intellectual hobby, and at worst blasphemy.

There are, then, two hermeneutical principles which are operative in the black theology analysis of the doctrine of God.

(1) The Christian understanding of God arises from the biblical view of revelation, a revelation of God that takes place in the liberation of oppressed Israel and is completed in the incarnation, in Jesus Christ. This means that whatever is said about the nature of God and God's being-in-the-world must be based on the biblical account of God's revelatory activity. We are not free to say anything we please about God. Although scripture is not the only source that helps us to

---

*Reprinted from *A Black Theology of Liberation*, Twentieth Anniversary Edition. Copyright © 1986, 1990 by James H. Cone. Published by Orbis Books. Used by permission of Orbis Books, Maryknoll, N.Y. Pp. 60–64.

recognize divine activity in the world, it cannot be ignored if we intend to speak of the Holy One of Israel.

(2) The doctrine of God in black theology must be of the God who is participating in the liberation of the oppressed of the land. This hermeneutical principle arises out of the first. Because God has been revealed in the history of oppressed Israel and decisively in the Oppressed One, Jesus Christ, it is impossible to say anything about God without seeing him as being involved in the contemporary liberation of all oppressed peoples. The God in black theology is the God of and for the oppressed, the God who comes into view in their liberation. Any other approach is a denial of biblical revelation....

When black theologians analyze the doctrine of God, seeking to relate it to the emerging black revolution in America, they must be especially careful not to put this new wine (the revelation of God as expressed in black power) into old wineskins (white folk-religion). The black theology view of God must be sharply distinguished from white distortions of God....

The God of black liberation will not be confused with a blood-thirsty white idol. Black theology must show that the black God has nothing to do with the God worshiped in white churches whose primary purpose is to sanctify the racism of whites and to daub the wounds of blacks. Putting new wine in new wineskins means that the black theology view of God has nothing in common with those who prayed for an American victory in Vietnam or who pray for a "cool" summer in the ghetto....

Black theology also rejects any identification with the "death of God" theology. The death-of-God question is a white issue which arises out of the white experience. Questions like "How do we find meaning and purpose in a world in which God is absent?" are questions of an affluent society. Whites may wonder how to find purpose in their lives, but our purpose is forced upon us. We do not want to know how we can get along without God, but how we can survive in a world permeated with white racism.

God Is Black

Because blacks have come to know themselves as *black,* and because that blackness is the cause of their own love of themselves and hatred of whiteness, the blackness of God is the key to our knowledge of God. The blackness of God, and everything implied by it in a racist society, is the heart of the black theology doctrine of God. There is no place in black theology for a colorless God in a society where human beings suffer precisely because of their color. The black theologian must reject any conception of God which stifles black self-determination by picturing God as a God of all peoples. Either God is identified with the oppressed to the point that their experience becomes God's experience, or God is a God of racism.... Because God has made the goal of blacks God's own goal, black theology believes that it is not only appropriate but necessary to begin the doctrine of God with an insistence on God's blackness.

The blackness of God means that God has made the oppressed condition God's own condition. This is the essence of the biblical revelation....

The blackness of God means that the essence of the nature of God is to be found in the concept of liberation. Taking seriously the Trinitarian view of the Godhead, black theology says that as Creator, God identified with oppressed Israel, participating in the bringing into being of this people; as Redeemer, God became the Oppressed One in order that all may be free from oppression; as Holy Spirit, God continues the work of liberation. The Holy Spirit is the Spirit of the Creator and the Redeemer at work in the forces of human liberation in our society today. In America, the Holy Spirit is black persons making decisions about their togetherness, which means making preparation for an encounter with whites.

Elizabeth A. Johnson (b. 1941)

She Who Is: The Mystery of God in Feminist Theological Discourse (1992), Chapters 3 and 12*

Why Female Symbols of God?

Normative speech about God in metaphors that are exclusively, literally, and patriarchally male is the real life context for this study. As a remedy some scholars and liturgists today take the option of always addressing God simply as "God." This has the positive result of relieving the hard androcentrism of ruling male images and pronouns for the divine. Nevertheless, this practice, if it is the only corrective engaged in, is not ultimately satisfactory. Besides employing uncritically a term long associated with the patriarchal ordering of the world, its consistent use causes the personal or transpersonal character of holy mystery to recede. It prevents the insight into holy mystery that might occur were female symbols set free to give rise to thought. Most serious of all, it papers over the problem of the implied inadequacy of women's reality to represent God....

The incomprehensibility of God makes it entirely appropriate, at times even preferable, to speak about God in nonpersonal or suprapersonal terms. Symbols such as the ground of being (Paul Tillich), matrix surrounding and sustaining all life (Rosemary Ruether), power of the future (Wolfhart Pannenberg), holy mystery (Karl Rahner), all point to divine reality that cannot be captured in concepts or images. At the same time God is not less than personal, and many of the most prized characteristics of God's relationship to the world, such as fidelity, compassion, and liberating love, belong to the human rather than the nonhuman world. Thus it is also appropriate, at times, even preferable, to speak about God in personal symbols.

Here is where the question of gender arises. Given the powerful ways the ruling male metaphor has expanded to become an entire metaphysical world view, and the way it perdures in imagination even when gender neutral God-language is used, correction of androcentric speech on the level of the concept alone is not sufficient. Since, as Marcia Falk notes, "Dead metaphors make strong idols," other images must be introduced which shatter the exclusivity of the male metaphor, subvert its dominance, and set free a greater sense of the mystery of God.

One effective way to stretch language and expand our repertoire of images is by uttering female symbols into speech about divine mystery. It is a complex exercise, not necessarily leading to emancipatory speech. An old danger that accompanies this change is that such language may be taken literally; a new danger lies in the potential for stereotyping women's reality by characterizing God simply as nurturing, caring, and so forth. The benefits, however, in my judgment, outweigh the dangers. Reorienting the imagination at a basic level, this usage challenges the idolatry of maleness in classic language about God, thereby making possible the rediscovery of divine mystery, and points to recovery of the dignity of women created in the image of God....

Equivalent Images of God Male and Female

While both the "traits" and the "dimensions" approach are inadequate for language about God inasmuch as in both an androcentric focus remains dominant, a third strategy speaks about the divine in images taken equivalently from the experience of women, men, and the world of nature. This approach shares with the other two the fundamental assumption that language about God as personal has a special appropriateness. Behaviorism notwithstanding, human persons are the most mysterious and attractive reality that we experience and the only creatures who bear self-reflective consciousness. God is not personal like anyone else we know, but the language of person points in a unique way to the mysterious depths and freedom of action long associated with the divine.

Predicating personality of God, however, immediately involves us in questions of sex and gender, for all the persons we know are either male or female. The mystery of God is properly understood as neither male nor female but transcends both in an unimaginable way. But insofar as God creates both male and female in the divine image and is the source of the perfections of both, either can equally well be used as metaphor to point to divine mystery. Both in fact are needed for less inadequate speech about God, in whose image the human race is created. This "clue" for speaking of God in the image of male and female has the advantage of making clear at the outset that women enjoy the dignity of being made in God's image and are therefore capable as women of representing God. Simultaneously, it relativizes undue emphasis on any one image, since pressing the multiplicity of imagery shows the partiality of images of one sex alone. The incomprehensible mystery of God is brought to light and deepened in our consciousness through imaging of male and female, beyond any person we know.

The mystery of God transcends all images but can be spoken about equally well and poorly in concepts taken from male or female reality. The approach advocated here proceeds with the insight that only if God is so named, only if the full reality of women as well as men enters into the symbolization of God along with symbols from the natural world, can the idolatrous fixation on one image be broken and the truth of the mystery of God, in tandem with the liberation of all human beings and the whole earth, emerge for our time....

Female Metaphors

Travail is a not inconsequential part of female life. Women's experiences of suffering the world over include the pain attending labor and childbirth, the penalty incurred for freely chosen actions for justice, the sorrow of grief over harm that comes to others, and the destruction known in personal degradation. Are women truly *imago Dei* even here, drinking the cup of sorrow? We are probing the capacity of symbols generated by experience of pain to evoke the mystery of God. Four such examples are adduced here, although the way God can be spoken about is not the same in all cases. In the first two instances women's suffering is the coin of creative advance. The pain of childbirth in a wanted, successful pregnancy is accompanied by a powerful sense of creativity and issues in the joy that a new child, one's own, is born. Likewise, in the midst of oppression women have consistently acted courageously and subversively for the betterment of their people. These acts, often unrecorded by official history and for which they have paid dearly, may issue in new fragments of justice and peace. But in the latter two situations we face the pit of darkness where there is no intelligibility at all. A loved one is disappeared; one's own self is violated. Even here women's courage to mourn and resist may lead to healing and new life, however scarred. Where it cannot, we are left with silence, narrative, remembrance, and witness.

Birth

Thanks to the shape and creative potential of their own bodies, women know the pain of bringing new life into the world.... When actively engaged and experienced ... this experience of labor and delivery offers a superb metaphor for Sophia-God's struggle to birth a new people, even a new heaven and a new earth. One biblical text makes this explicit as God says:

> For a long time I have held my peace,
> I have kept still and restrained myself;
> now I will cry out like a woman in labor
> I will gasp and pant. (Isa. 42:14)

The loud birthing cries evoke a God who is in hard labor, sweating, pushing with all her might to bring forth justice, the fruit of her love. Intense suffering as an ingredient in intense creative power marks the depth of divine involvement in the process. And it is not over yet; only eschatologically will the delivery take place. In the course of history human beings are partners with Holy Wisdom in the birthing process, sharing in the labor of liberating life for a new future....

Justice and Anger

Women suffer when they choose to act in situations great or small to bring about the betterment of human life through the pursuit of human rights, healing, justice, and peace. This experience too betrays an admixture of creative power and pain, for the action being taken faces off with the antagonistic structures of sin, which are not deconstructed without fierce struggle. There are Lilian Ngoyi, Rahima Moosa, Sophie Williams, and Helen Joseph who at risk of being banned or worse, losing their very lives, led twenty thousand South African women, nonentities under apartheid, in a defiant peaceful march on the government buildings in 1956 to protest the hated pass laws.... The price they paid went on for years, but the flame of freedom was kept alive. There is Maria, one of the national organizers of rural, indigenous Guatemalan widows, traditionally the most marginalized group in that country's society.... There is Rosa Parks, who for her people deliberately sat down on the bus knowing imprisonment would follow; her act provided the spark that lit the civil rights movement. In every case these and other such women signal the presence of many others in the same context who commit countless acts of courage to resist injustice and bring about change, and who suffer the consequences.

This splendid and striking women's witness offers yet more imagery for speaking about Sophia-God who hears the cry of the poor, being "moved to pity by their groanings because of those who afflicted and oppressed them" (Judg. 2:18). As the voice in the flaming bush acknowledges, she knows experientially what the people are suffering and creates a solidarity with and among them that ultimately brings about change (Exod. 3:7–8, reprised in Wisd. 10:15–19)....

Women ablaze with righteous anger offer an excellent image of God's indignant power of wrath kindled by injustice. Apart from fundamentalist preaching, the wrath of God is not a subject frequently heard in our day. This is no doubt in reaction to the traditional stress on divine anger within a patriarchal framework that laid heavy, continuous guilt on consciences and obscured the saving message of divine mercy. But in a feminist framework the wrath of God is a symbol of holy mystery that we can ill afford to lose. For the wrath of God in the sense of righteous anger against injustice is not an opposite of mercy but its correlative. It is a mode of caring response in the face of evil aroused by what is mean or shameful or injurious to beloved human beings and the created world itself.... True, God's anger lasts but a moment; true, it is always instrumental, aimed at change and conversion. But it stands as an antidote to sentimentality in our view of God's holy mystery as love, and as a legitimation of women's anger at the injustice of their own diminishment and the violation of those they love.

The wisdom writings of Scripture carry just such an image of divine wrath in the female figure of Sophia. At her first appearance in Proverbs she is shouting in the streets, in the markets, on the top of the walls, at the entrance of the city gates — it seems no one can escape her voice:

> How long, O simple ones, will you love being simple?
> How long will scoffers delight in their scoffing...?
> Give heed to my reproof....
> Because I have called you and you refused to listen,
> have stretched out my hand and no one has heeded,
> and you have ignored all my counsel,
> and would have none of my reproof,
> I also will laugh at your calamity;
> I will mock when panic strikes you....
> when distress and anguish come upon you.
>
> (Prov. 1:23–27)

These are angry words, and for a purpose. Sophia here is one symbol of God as a furious woman who goes public with her anger in the mode of the prophets, to bring about conversion.

The prophet Hosea ... portrays God, angered at injustice, like an angry mother bear who will go to any length to get back her cubs, even to tearing apart the predators (Hos. 13:7–8). In these and other images reflective of women's experience of anger over injustice, the female symbol of the suffering God who cares for the oppressed is strengthened by a feminist retrieval of the wrath of God.

God as a woman in the labor of childbirth; God as a woman courageously engaged on behalf of justice; God as a woman angry against what harms and destroys — these images at their best are based on freely chosen acts that have the possibility of a fruitful outcome. But there is also suffering that is not a concomitant of creative power; it comes against our will like a thief in the night and works to destroy. Created by systemic injustice, historical chaos, and new initiatives of personal wrongdoing, this kind of suffering affects women through harm done to those whom they love and through abuse to their own humanity.

Grief

Women's relational way of being in the world typically creates in them a deep vulnerability to being rendered desolate when suffering visits those whom they love and care about. This experience is so powerful that feminist theorists are using it to rewrite the definition of evil. Whereas in the history of western thought a preponderance of definitions of evil has concentrated on human disobedience to divine law and thus on "sin," some feminist ethical analysis now argues that women's experience identifies the most fundamental evil to be the phenomenological conditions of pain, separation, and helplessness. When these conditions affect people within the circle of women's affection, boundless anguish ensues. From Rachel weeping for her children to the mothers and grandmothers of the Argentinian Plaza de Mayo, we could not measure the pain of women occasioned by harm done to those they love....

Women who experience this kind of desolation provide another reference point for speaking about God who grieves over the harm done to her beloved creation, a way, moreover, consonant with biblical tradition....

Degradation

There is yet more, and it is terrible to speak of. In their own person women experience suffering that yields no discernible good but rather violates and destroys human dignity and even life itself. In Simone Weil's description such a situation is named affliction (French: *malheur*), a more or less attenuated equivalent of death, which takes possession of the soul and marks it with the brand of slavery. The occasions that bring on affliction may be physical, psychological, or social. But the effect is to squeeze out life, dry out power, introduce unwarranted guilt and self-hatred, plunge the sufferer into darkness. Women experience affliction in myriad ways as they drink the cup of personal humiliation, fear, violation, and degradation. Very precisely, sexual embodiment as a female of the race within patriarchal society sets every woman in danger from rape, beatings, and other forms of male abuse. Too much of this suffering bears the mark of affliction. There is nothing redemptive about it....

Holy Wisdom does not abhor the reality of women but identifies with the pain and violence that women experience on the cross, of whatever sort. So we may ask again Elie Wiesel's terrifying question. When a woman is raped and murdered, what does the Shekinah say? She says, my body is heavy with violation. Through the long night when the Bethlehem concubine is gang-raped and tortured, where is God? She is there, being abused and defiled. There too being burned to death by the Inquisition. There too being tortured by the male enforcers of unjust rule. Along with all abused women these women are *imago Dei, imago Christi,* daughters of Wisdom. Sophia-God enters into the pain of women whose humanity is profaned and keeps vigil with the godforsaken for whom there is no rescue. In turn, their devastation points to the depths of the suffering God. There is no solution here, no attempt at theoretical reconciliation of atrocity with divine will. Only a terrible sense of the mystery of evil and the absence of God, which nevertheless may betray divine presence, desecrated.

Part Two

GOD'S ACTIVITIES IN RELATION TO THE WORLD

– 4 –

The Early Period

INTRODUCTION

Traditionally, the principal activities of God have been described as creating, redeeming, and sanctifying. These activities, moreover, have customarily been assigned to one of the divine persons: the Father is the Creator, the Son is the Redeemer, and the Spirit is the Sanctifier. It is important to remember, however, that orthodox teaching declares that all three persons of the trinity are involved in every divine activity. The Son and the Spirit are also involved in creation; the Father and the Spirit are also involved in redemption; and the Father and the Son are also involved in sanctification. In the words of Gregory of Nyssa (see selection in Part One), "every operation which extends from God to the creation...has its origin from the Father, and proceeds through the Son, and is perfected in the Holy Spirit." Because of this unity of God in essence and operation, it would be appropriate to discuss God's creating, redeeming, and sanctifying activities in this portion of the book.

A detailed description of redemption and salvation, however, is not included in this volume. Affirmation of Christ's divinity and emphasis upon redemption through Christ have distinguished Christian monotheism from Jewish and Muslim monotheism in a decisive way. Reflection upon the person of Christ (his nature in relation to Father and Spirit) and upon the work of Christ (his redemptive or saving activity) have been very important topics of Christian reflection over the centuries. They are, therefore, the focus of another volume in this series from Orbis Books. Although God's redemptive activity is touched upon here, it is not developed extensively.

The doctrine of sanctification also is not extensively examined here because, until quite recently, it has not received in the history of western Christian thought the same kind of emphasis that has been given to God's activities of creation and redemption (or salvation). The reason for this probably rests with the apparently greater existential import of the doctrines of creation and redemption. The doctrine of creation defines the basic relationship between Creator and creature. It entails a description of the origin of cosmos and humanity as well as an explanation of the "character" of creation. What does it mean to be a creature of God? Is creation basically good or bad? These are questions whose answers have a significant import on how human beings understand their existence. They have an important impact on how people live their lives.

The doctrine of redemption explains why human beings need to be redeemed or saved and how redemption happens. If human creatures have fallen from their original state of innocence or "perfection," how can they be restored? If restoration to their original state or repair of the current "damage" is necessary for right relationship with God, then the doctrine of redemption also has significant existential weight. Of course, the gradual perfection of the redeemed human being through the process of sanctification is not unimportant. Unfortunately, the work of the Spirit has not until recently received in the West the kind of attention it has been granted in the eastern church. Nonetheless, it should not be forgotten that creation, redemption, and sanctification are all principal activities of the economic trinity.

Because the doctrine of creation is given considerable attention in this volume, a few additional preliminary remarks are in order. Consideration of God's creative activity raises additional issues beyond the narrow scope of the beginning of things. It raises a question about God's continuing activity in the world. If God is active in the world beyond the initial moment of creation, then how are we to understand the divine activity? Traditionally, God's maintenance of the world in a state of existence has been called divine preservation and God's continuing guidance of the world has been called providence. Applied to the question of the effects of God's activity upon human beings, God's special providence for humanity has been described in terms of predestination.

The relationship of predestination and human freedom is a central concern of theological anthropology (that is, a theological understanding of the human person). Because theological anthropology is a doctrine explored at length in another volume in this Orbis series, only the divine side of the relationship will be explored here. It is nonetheless important to remember that a full understanding of God's activity in relationship to creation involves consideration not only of creation and providence, but also of theological anthropology. In order to avoid unnecessary duplication with the content of other volumes in this series, attention in this book will be restricted to certain aspects of the doctrines of providence and predestination. Consequently, only some aspects of the question of evil will be handled here. Whether God is the source of evil is a question that falls under the doctrine of God and consideration of God's activity. Whether human beings are free when they do evil things is a question that falls more properly under consideration of theological anthropology in another book in this Orbis series.

The major ecumenical (worldwide) councils in the early church focused upon understanding and describing the nature of God and Christ. As we have seen in Part One of this book, much of the attention was given to defining the relationship of Jesus the Christ to God. The Councils of Nicea and Constantinople defined this relationship in terms of identity of essence, unity of operation, and diversity of person. The formulation of the distinction between substance and person (in the West) and between *ousia* and *hypostasis* (in the East) developed within the context of inquiry about the internal "composition" of God. Description of the internal "workings" of God — that is, the interrelationship of the three persons of the trinity — is commonly spoken of today as the "immanent trinity." The immanent trinity is often contrasted with the "economic trinity," the description of God's activities in relationship to the world. In the early church, confession of the economic trinity preceded confession of the immanent trinity. That this is so is quite understandable. The ministry of Christ in history, the experience of his continuing presence in the church, and the activity of God's Spirit in the community were concrete experiences. Reflection about these concrete experiences eventually led Christians to speak about the inner nature of God. Although experience of the "economic trinity" was the starting point for reflection upon the "immanent trinity," the latter became the more divisive issue.

Although the immanent trinity became the focus of doctrinal definition in the early ecumenical councils, this did not mean that the economic trinity was unimportant or beyond dispute. Clearly the economic trinity was very important for it was precisely God's creative, sustaining, redeeming, and sanctifying activities that made human well-being possible. As in the case of the immanent trinity, heterodox and heretical positions were proposed with regard to God's activities. Christian thinkers were required to think through and to describe God's central activities in relation to the world in a way that was faithful to the developing "rule of faith," the scriptures, and their own experience.

In developing their understanding of divine creation and providence, early Christian authors drew upon the testimony of the Hebrew scriptures. There God is depicted as powerful and wise, without rival in the heavens or on the earth. As creator of the universe, God depends on nothing. Even if something is there before God acts — for example, darkness or formlessness, it is insignificant.[1] God is the one who establishes order out of chaos. God is the one who creates life. God is the one who can control the powerful creatures of earth and sea. After being reminded by God of the divine power and wisdom, Job replies to God: "I know that you can do all things, and that no purpose of yours can be thwarted" (Job 42:2).

The Genesis accounts of creation (1:1–2:4a and 2:4b–25) emphasize that all forms of life come from God and everything God has created is good. Humanity is specifically described as having been created in God's image. As the crown of creation, made in God's very image, human beings are set over the rest of the created world (Gen. 1:27–28). God's creation of the garden of Eden for the first human beings is but one of the early signs of God's care and love for humanity. The rest of the Hebrew scriptures is filled with stories that exemplify God's love of humanity and God's faithfulness to them. Even when people fail to live up to the covenant made with God, God remains faithful (see Hos. 2:16–3:1). In the story of the patriarchs and the formation of the Hebrew tribes to the story of exodus from slavery in Egypt to the story of settlement in the Promised Land, flowing in milk and honey, God is portrayed as powerful, loving, faithful, and providential. God does not simply bring the created world into existence. God also continues to guide it, intervening sometimes powerfully in the events of nature and history to effect the divine plan.

The New Testament elaborates on this theme of divine love and personal concern for what God has created. Building upon the foundation of the Hebrew scriptures, the New Testament emphasizes that God is our Father and that all human beings are brothers and sisters to one another (see Matt. 6:9–15; Luke 11:2–4). God is portrayed as neither a distant nor a tyrannical parent, but rather as a loving father who wishes humanity nothing but goodness and grace. If even imperfect parents know how to give good gifts to their children, "how much more," Jesus notes, "will your Father in heaven give good things to those who

---

1. "In the beginning when God created the heavens and the earth, the earth was a formless void and darkness covered the face of the deep, while a wind from God swept over the face of the waters" (Gen. 1:1–2).

ask him!" (Matt. 7:11; see also Luke 11:13). But the God Jesus speaks about in the New Testament does not simply wait to be asked for help. God "knows what you need before you ask him" (Matt. 6:8). Providential care for human beings and for all that God has created is an essential part of the divine character. In Matt. 6:26, Jesus says: "Look at the birds of the air; they neither sow nor reap nor gather into barns, and yet your heavenly Father feeds them. Are you not of more value than they?" Later in the same gospel, Jesus declares that all the hairs of our head are counted by God. Therefore, we should not be anxious or fearful as we journey through life (Matt. 10:30–31).

Building upon the testimony of scripture, early Christians formulated their understanding of creation and providence. But these thinkers do not simply repeat the words of scripture. They develop the words with the tools of rational reflection, philosophical insight, and personal experience. Thus creation comes to be defined as creation from nothing (*creatio ex nihilo*). Rather than saying, as the Genesis account seems to suggest, that God created the universe out of a formless, already existing void, Christian thinkers insisted that before God's creative act nothing existed but God. Theophilus, bishop of Antioch in the later second century, was one of the first to declare that creation is out of nothing. From the end of the second century on, this doctrine gained ascendancy.

By insisting upon creation out of nothing, Christian thinkers could highlight the absolute distinction between God and the created world as well as the gratuity of God's decision to create. The former point is emphasized in the excerpt below from *Against Heresies* (Book IV, ch. 38, sect. 1), written toward the end of the second century. There Irenaeus of Lyons declares that the radical difference between being created and being uncreated explains why humanity is imperfect, whereas God is perfect. As a perfect being, God has no need of other beings. God's creative act, therefore, derives from God's benevolent will. God's act of creation, Irenaeus states, discloses God's power, goodness, and wisdom (*Against Heresies,* Book IV, ch. 38, sect. 3; see below).

Although the doctrine of creation from nothing became the accepted teaching of the early church, it did not gain the ascendancy without a struggle. Early Christian writers had to oppose the idea that God created out of pre-existent matter, that creation (conceived according to the model of emanation) was a necessary event rather than a free act of God, and that the material aspect of the world is evil. In the *Timaeus,* Plato developed the idea that the world is made out of pre-existent matter. A demi-urge (a kind of inferior deity) then shaped this matter into the present form of the world. Many Gnostics shared this conception of creation as well as the conviction that matter is evil. Neoplatonists, such as Plotinus (ca. 205–70), conceived of "creation" as a process of automatic emanation out of the Absolute, which he called the One.

Hermogenes, an artist and Gnostic who lived in Carthage, adopted the philosophical position that matter is eternal and the source of evil. He thought of creation as an act of construction from pre-existent matter. From this perspective, evil in the world is unavoidable because the material out of which God constructed the world was defective. Such a view clearly absolved God from responsibility for evil, but it also created its own problems. Not only did it make matter evil (despite the testimony of Genesis that everything God made is good), it also led in some cases to a sense of fatalism. People could not be held responsible for the evil they did, because, as creatures with a material body, they could not help themselves. Having matter within them, they could not overcome the deficiencies of their nature. The power of such ideas is clearly evident in the story of Augustine who, before becoming a Christian, was attracted to Manicheism in part because of its theory concerning the origin and nature of evil.

In his treatise (written in the early third century) against Hermogenes, Tertullian marshaled several arguments. First, he rejected Hermogenes' theological explanation of why matter must be regarded as eternal. Hermogenes had defended the eternity of matter by saying that God, who is eternally Lord, must be lord over something. In short, the eternity of God's lordship entails the eternity of some form of matter. Tertullian replied that God has always been God, but has not always been Lord. God, who always is, "became" Lord with the creation of the world. Tertullian appealed to the testimony of Genesis to support this assertion (see *Against Hermogenes*, ch. 3 below). He argued, in addition, that eternity implies an incapacity to be diminished or subjugated. If matter is both eternal and evil, then God's command to resist evil is in vain and the biblical claim of the eventual subjugation of evil to Christ is erroneous. It is more appropriate, Tertullian declared, to hold that the "quality" of eternity entails goodness. If that is the case, then matter, if it is evil, cannot be eternal (see *Against Hermogenes*, ch. 11 below).

Second, Tertullian pointed out that Hermogenes' theory did not succeed in absolving God of responsibility for evil in the world. In fact, Hermogenes' theory either made God evil or impotent. Accepting hypothetically the eternity of matter and Hermogenes' claim that matter is the source of evil, Tertullian argued that God, who is good, ought to have opposed the evil in matter before the creation of the world. Tertullian drew this unacceptable alternative out of Hermogenes' position: God was either able to correct the evil in matter, "but was unwilling; or else was willing, but being a weak God, was not able" (see *Against Hermogenes*, ch. 10 below). In opposition to Hermogenes, Tertullian defended God's power and goodness by rejecting Hermogenes' contention that God created the world out of pre-existent matter, which is the source of evil. God as God cannot depend on any other substance, even a good substance, for creation. Rather, creation must be out of nothing.

In the early church, there was not only discussion about the "what" of creation, but also about the "when." Some people, both inside as well as outside the church, claimed that creation was eternal in order to avoid admitting change in God. If creation were not from all eternity, it would appear that God existed alone for awhile and then, all of a sudden, had the new idea of creating the world. Such an understanding violates the notion of divine immutability, which was the accepted presupposition of the early church's thinkers. Ancient Greek philosophy supported such a presupposition. For Plato, the ideal essences of things always remain the same, whereas the particular objects of sense experience do not. To change is a sign of imperfection; not to change is a sign of perfection.[2]

---

2. Hence there was suspicion in the ancient world of "innovations." For many in the early church, the newness or novelty of a teaching was evidence of its heterodox or heretical character.

In the *City of God*, Augustine attempted to demonstrate that the creation of the world occurred with time, without creation implying a change in God's eternal decision to create. In response to those who held that God must always have been engaged in creative activity, Augustine challenged them to draw out the implications of their position. If God was eternally creative in time, then God must also have been eternally creative in space. Therefore one must conclude, Augustine suggested, that God created innumerable universes. Such an idea, however, is silly. There is no space beyond the universe itself; therefore, there can be no infinite number of spaces in which God has created an infinite number of universes. Augustine wanted to establish the point that we cannot say that there was a past time (before the creation of the world) during which God was unoccupied because "there was no such thing as time before the universe was made" (see *City of God*, Book XI, ch. 5 below).

Augustine offered two arguments in support of his conclusion. First, there could be no time before the universe was made because time is the measurement of movement and change. God, as a perfect being, does not change. Without the existence of a creature, whose movement would cause some change, there cannot be time. Augustine here adapted and modified Aristotle's understanding of time. According to Aristotle, what is eternal and immobile is not in time. Movement for Aristotle, however, is eternal and, therefore, time is eternal. Time, according to Aristotle, never began and will never end.[3] Augustine accepted the Aristotelian notion that time is the measure of movement as something that can be counted. He rejected, however, Aristotle's claim that the universe and time are eternal. Like Aquinas in the medieval period, Augustine was compelled to disagree with Aristotle on the basis of revelation. The revelation of scripture constituted Augustine's second argument against the existence of time prior to creation. The testimony of scripture — in particular, the Genesis account of creation — makes clear that the world was not made in time, but was made together with time[4] (see *City of God*, Book XI, ch. 6 below).

Christians had good reason to oppose the ideas that the world was created out of pre-existent matter and that matter is evil. If some entity besides God were held to be eternal, then the radical superiority and transcendence of God would be jeopardized. Alongside of God there can be no entity equivalent in power or "duration." The testimony of scripture and the experience of faith affirmed that there is no one and no thing like God. On the other hand, Christians could not legitimately regard matter as evil. The Genesis account of creation made clear that

---

3. See Aristotle, *Physics*, VIII, 1 (251a 9–251b 28).

4. "You are the Maker of all time. If, then, there was any time before you made heaven and earth, how can anyone say that you were idle? You must have made that time, for time could not elapse before you made it.

"But if there was no time before heaven and earth were created, how can anyone ask what you were doing 'then'? If there was no time, there was no 'then.'

"Furthermore, although you are before time, it is not in time that you precede it. If this were so, you would not be before all time. It is in eternity, which is supreme over time because it is a never-ending present, that you are at once before all past time and after all future time. For what is now the future, once it comes, will become the past, whereas *you are unchanging, your years can never fail*. Your years neither go nor come, but our years pass and others come after them, so that they all may come in their turn. Your years are completely present to you all at once, because they are at a permanent standstill" (Augustine, *Confessions*, trans. R. S. Pine-Coffin [New York: Penguin Books, 1961], Book 11, ch. 13, p. 263).

everything God made was good. The matter in creatures had to be good, because God had made all things good. As Augustine put it, everything, considered individually, is good; and all things, taken as a whole, are very good (see Augustine's *Enchiridion,* ch. 10 below). If the Gnostic theory about the evil nature of matter were allowed to stand, moreover, then the opinions of the docetists and Marcion would have to be permitted within the church.

The docetists held that Christ only seemed to be human, while in fact he was a thoroughly spiritual, nonbodily being. The label "docetist" derives from the Greek verb "to seem or appear." If matter is evil, then Christ the savior cannot really share in the material reality of having a body. But if Christ did not have a real, material human body, then he did not suffer and die on the cross. If the passion and death of Christ were not real, then how could redemption be real? Did not the scriptures declare that Christ's death was a ransom for many? These were some of the disturbing questions raised by the docetist movement in the second century.

Another consequence of drawing such a sharp line between material creation (bad) and the spiritual world (good) was rejection of the idea that the God of creation and the God of salvation are the same God. Marcion, for example, argued that the God whom Jesus spoke about was not the Creator described in the Hebrew scriptures. Jesus' God is a God of love and mercy; Jesus' God is "refined," sublime, spiritual. By contrast, the God of the Hebrew scriptures, Marcion said, is a harsh God of judgment; a God who is the creator of the flawed, material world. Marcion recommended that the church reject the authority and validity of the Hebrew scriptures. He was expelled from the church in Rome in the middle of the second century.

Against Gnostic theories and the arguments of Marcion, the early church declared that God the Creator and God the Redeemer are the same God. The creative and redemptive activities in the world stem from the same good source. This affirmation meant that Christians would have to produce an alternative explanation of the origin of evil. Christians in the early church believed that God's will, as all-powerful, cannot be subverted. If this is the world God wanted to create, then how could one account for the reality of evil? If God the Creator is perfect, then God's creation should also be perfect. From the days of the early church to the present, Christians have devised different interpretations to make sense of the simultaneous assertion of God's providence and omnipotence, on the one hand, and the reality of evil, on the other.

The conviction of faith led Christians to confess early on, in the words of Paul's Letter to the Romans (8:28), "that all things work together for good for those who love God." One of the problems that faced Christians was how to say that creatures, not the Creator, are responsible for evil, without undermining the goodness of God and the power and scope of divine agency. Augustine articulated clearly the presupposition of the early church about God: God, who has "supreme power over all things, being Himself supremely good, would never permit the existence of anything evil among His works, if He were not so omnipotent and good that He can bring good even out of evil" (see *Enchiridion,* ch. 11 below). Both divine power and divine goodness are affirmed. For Augustine, these two divine qualities formed the firm principle according to which statements about

God, evil, and salvation had to be understood. In chapter 102 of the *Enchiridion* (see below), Augustine stated this firm principle: the will of God is never defeated and it never can be evil. In the next chapter of his treatise, he applied this principle to his interpretation of the classic line from 1 Tim. 2:4, which declares that God wants all people to be saved. Using this principle, Augustine concluded that the biblical passage meant either that no one is saved apart from God's will or that people from all social ranks and circumstances will be saved. He even conceded that other interpretations are possible, provided that the principle of God's omnipotent and effective will is not violated.

If the omnipotence and providence of God forms the one side of the problem of evil, human responsibility forms the other side. The official teaching of the early church came to hold that the existence of moral evil (that is, evil caused by a rational agent) can be attributed neither to God nor to the material out of which human beings are made. With God and matter ruled out, human freedom remained a candidate for being the root of moral evil. Freedom is a requirement for moral responsibility. The fact that God gives humanity commandments to obey, according to the Bible's testimony, presupposes the human capacity to obey these commandments.

Responsibility or accountability, therefore, presupposes freedom. Human freedom (as well as angelic freedom), however, had to be limited so that God's freedom and power would not be infringed. In the early church Irenaeus gave great emphasis to the role of human freedom. He explained that God made human beings in the divine image. This meant that people are basically free and their own master (see "Proof of the Apostolic Preaching," sect. 11 below). If people are not free, Irenaeus added, then it would not be fair to praise or condemn them for their actions (see *Against Heresies,* Book IV, ch. 37, sect. 2 below).

But why should God have created human beings with the capacity to do evil? Why not create them incapable of transgression? Irenaeus's opponents asked. Irenaeus responded that without the capacity for transgression as well as obedience to God, human beings would not regard their relationship with God as something precious or see the good as something for which they should strive (see *Against Heresies,* Book IV, ch. 37, sect. 6 below). The desire for and performance of good deeds would be implanted in them by nature. People would seek after relationship with God mechanically, not freely. Such behavior, however, is not befitting the dignity of the human person.

This response, however, did not answer all the pertinent questions raised by the reality of evil. Although his response to the Gnostics explained why God made human beings free, Irenaeus also had to explain why humans would freely choose transgression over obedience, when they were free to choose good rather than evil. In response to this problem, Irenaeus replied that the poor exercise of freedom results from the fact that human beings were not created perfect. His presupposition is that only what is uncreated is naturally perfect. Everything created is imperfect (see *Against Heresies,* Book IV, ch. 38, sect. 1 below). In similar fashion, Augustine stated two centuries later that creatures, unlike the Creator, are not unchangeably good. Their inherent goodness can be increased or diminished (see *Enchiridion,* ch. 12 below). Whereas Irenaeus explained evil in terms of a lack of creaturely development, Augustine explained it in terms of the Neoplatonic notion of the privation of good. In "Proof of the Apostolic Preaching" (see sect. 12 below), Irenaeus spoke of the human person as "a little one" or as a "child," who had to grow and develop in order to attain perfection. Because the first human beings were imperfect "little ones," without a developed sense of discretion and wisdom, they were easily misled by the devil. Although, theoretically speaking, God could have made them perfect from the very beginning, human beings — as creatures in an infantile state — could not, practically speaking, receive perfection (see *Against Heresies,* Book IV, ch. 38, sect. 1 below). God has not left humanity, however, without help and guidance. God provides counsel, exhortation, and assistance to help humanity direct its will properly (see *Against Heresies,* Book IV, ch. 37, sect. 3 below). In fact, the ultimate goal toward which God directs human beings is, according to Irenaeus, their "deification." God's love spurs on human growth and development so that people will finally and perfectly reflect the image and likeness of God (see *Against Heresies,* Book IV, ch. 38, sect. 4 below).[5]

In the *Enchiridion,* Augustine declared that every being is good in some measure precisely because it exists or participates in being. Conversely, evil is the absence of good; it is not an entity or substance. In this mature work, written in 421, we can see how far Augustine has moved from the Manichean position that attracted him in his youth. Influential in this journey were the Neoplatonists whom Augustine read prior to his full conversion to Christianity. According to the Neoplatonist Plotinus, there is a great chain of being extending from the One at the top to matter at the bottom. The One, which Christians identified with God, is unknowable, absolute, and supremely good. From this One has emanated successive levels of being, with each higher level of being the cause of the level immediately lower. As one moves lower to each successive level of being, there is a gradual loss in being, until we arrive at "evil," which entirely lacks being and, therefore, goodness. The imperfection inherent in the lower levels of being can be overcome by their return toward their cause. As Henry Chadwick has observed, this theory of emanation and the chain of being was attractive to Augustine and others in the early church for at least three reasons. It seemed to solve the problem of how the transcendent One (God) and the world could be related, without undermining God's absoluteness. It suggested a form of redemption of the lower forms of being by means of conversion or return to the source of being (God). And finally it seemed to explain how evil could have entered into the continuum of things, when that was an overflow of the One's supreme goodness and power.[6] Revelation, however, opposed the notion of emanation and the denigration of material creation. The Neoplatonic scheme, therefore, needed to be revised.[7]

---

5. In a different volume in this Orbis series, *The Human Person and the Church,* the issue of theological anthropology will be explored in detail. There the contrast between Irenaeus's and Augustine's understanding of the human person and the Fall is made evident.

6. Henry Chadwick, *Augustine,* Past Masters series (New York: Oxford University Press, 1986), 17–24.

7. Revision of the Neoplatonic scheme did not necessarily mean rejection of the notion of reality as a hierarchically arranged whole. We see intimations of creation as structured hierarchically in the excerpt below from Irenaeus of Lyons. In the "Proof of the Apostolic Preaching," he declared that God has established laws so that each creature keeps to its place and "overstep not the bound laid down by God, each accomplishing the work marked out for him." The order extends even to the angelic realm, where the archangel is set up as "administrator-in-chief" over the angels. Creation is an ordered, structured reality.

If evil is the absence of being and goodness, then it must be, Augustine reasoned, a corruption of or defect in something good. Augustine identified the free will of rational creatures as the "something good" that was susceptible to corruption. Free will is a good gift from God. It is, however, capable of turning away from the source of its goodness and thus choosing evil. What makes the will turn away from the good? The will itself, Augustine replied. Pride made Adam and Eve disobey God's commandment not to eat of the tree of knowledge of good and evil. As a consequence of this fall from their originally good state, Adam, Eve, and their descendants lost the gift of grace which enabled them not to sin. Whereas before the Fall, humanity was free not to sin, after the Fall, humanity is free only to sin. Whereas before the Fall, the passions of the human body were subject to the direction of the human spirit or reason, after the Fall the body rebels against the spirit (see *City of God*, Book XIII, ch. 13). This is the condition into which all human beings after Adam and Eve are born. This topic of theological anthropology is taken up in another volume of this Orbis series. But for our consideration of the doctrine of God, it is important to note that Augustine emphasized that both God's initial creative activity and God's subsequent judgment of sinful humanity are good.

As Augustine observed in the *City of God* (Book XIII, ch. 14 below), God is the author of the nature of everything, but God is not the author of any of their defects. Because of the Fall, human beings are corrupt by choice and condemned by justice. All would go to eternal perdition if it were not for the love of God, exhibited in God's redemptive activity. God mercifully has decided to save some human beings from perdition while justly condemning the rest. Augustine interpreted the confession of the "Father Almighty" in the church's creed to mean that God can do whatever God pleases and that the will of no creature can hinder God's will. This being the case, God can change the evil will of a person, if God so chooses. When God does so choose, we speak of God's mercy. When God does not act to change the evil will, we speak of God's justice (see *Enchiridion*, ch. 108). Augustine appealed to scripture, especially Paul's Letter to the Romans, in support of his position. By emphasizing God's election and redemption as the cause of salvation for those who are saved, Augustine was able to uphold the absolute sovereignty and power of God over all creation as well as to emphasize the gratuity of God's redemptive activity (see *Enchiridion,* ch. 99 below). Both aspects of the divine activity will continue to be important in the Christian tradition that develops after Augustine. At the time of the Protestant Reformation, these themes will receive renewed emphasis.

The incarnation, as both Irenaeus and Athanasius emphasized, is the decisive means by which humanity's redemption is made possible. Irenaeus explained God's redemptive activity in terms of the idea of recapitulation. Christ recapitulates the history of humankind by becoming a human being and progressing, in a proper way, through the stages of childhood and adulthood. Whereas the personal history of Adam and Eve had brought about the corruption of God's image in humanity, Jesus' history brought about the restoration of that image.

Athanasius, in the excerpt below, connects redemption with creation. The point of creation was to give life to creatures and to establish communion with God. Both life and communion were dissolving because of the corruption of God's image due to sin. According to the Hebrew scriptures and the New Testament, death came into the world because of sin (see Gen. 2:16–17; 3:11, 19–23; Rom. 5:12–14). For Athanasius the image of God, in which humankind had been created, is the principle that sustains human beings in existence. Insofar as that image began to dissolve because of the deleterious effect of sin, humankind was sinking back into the state of nonexistence, out of which it had been created (see *Incarnation of the Word*, §6 below). This posed a serious problem. God had declared that Adam and Eve were not to eat of the tree of knowledge of good and evil. If they disobeyed God's command, God said that they would die (Gen. 2:17). Yet God had created human beings out of love, out of the desire to share the divine life with them. If God did not punish humanity with death, God would be unfaithful to the word God had spoken. If God allowed humanity to perish, then the purpose of creation would be thwarted.

In response to this dilemma, Athanasius argued that it is "fitting" for God to effect the redemption of humanity through the incarnation and ministry of Christ. To let humanity go to ruin would be "unseemly." Such behavior would reflect badly on God, Athanasius observed, for "neglect reveals weakness, and not goodness on God's part" (see *Incarnation*, §6 below). It would have been more appropriate not to have created human beings at all, rather than to have created them, and then let them go to ruin because of sin. As this excerpt makes clear, Athanasius emphasized goodness and love as God's motivation for incarnation and redemption. God's principal activities with regard to the world involve not only creating, but also re-creating (that is, redeeming humanity by restoring the image of God in them).

Although the creative and redemptive activities of God in relation to the world are emphasized in the early church, especially in the West, the activity of sanctification is not omitted. The church of both East and West relied heavily upon the work of the Cappadocian Fathers for help in articulating a full doctrine of the Holy Spirit and the Spirit's activity. It should come as no surprise that the excerpt below on the Spirit comes from Basil of Caesarea, one of the great Cappadocians. As you might recall, Basil, Gregory of Nazianzen, and Gregory of Nyssa contributed greatly to the official recognition of the full divinity of the Holy Spirit at the Council of Constantinople I (381).

According to Basil, the Holy Spirit executes a wide range of activities. The Spirit assists creatures in the process of their perfection. To become perfect, human beings need inspiration, intellectual illumination, and moral virtue. The Spirit is the source of all these gifts (see *On the Spirit*, ch. 9, sect. 22 below). The principal or overarching activity of the Spirit is sanctification, which literally means "making holy or sacred." The more human beings become filled with the Spirit, the more they become spiritual. The apex of this process of "spiritualization" is "deification." Like Irenaeus and Athanasius, Basil too believed that the ultimate goal of God's creation of humanity is to establish a fellowship between humanity and God so intimate that we can say that human beings become like God, even are "made God" (see *On the Spirit*, ch. 9, sect. 23 below).

Throughout the treatise *On the Spirit*, Basil was concerned to maintain the equality and inseparability of the Spirit with regard to the other persons of the trinity. But he also wanted to differentiate the contribution of each divine person. Therefore, he speaks of the Father as the original cause, the Son as the creative cause, and the Spirit as the perfecting cause of all things that are made (see *On the Spirit,* ch. 16, sect. 38 below). Basil is quick to add, however, that these different contributions do not imply that any of the three divine persons is somehow "incomplete" without the contribution of the other divine persons. His point is that each person is God and, as such, is complete; yet each wills to work in cooperation with the other persons of the trinity in effecting God's purposes. Basil particularly highlighted the Spirit's contribution as perfecting the natures of things. Perfection and sanctification are the special hallmarks of the Spirit's work.

As in the case of God's nature, so too in the case of God's activities in relation to the world, the early church laid a doctrinal foundation upon which the subsequent Christian tradition would build. Many of the same problems — for example, the reconciliation of divine providence and human freedom — are taken up by subsequent generations. To be sure, the resolution of these problems is worked out within new contexts and with different explanatory tools. Still, the early church sketched the parameters in which orthodox interpretations of God's activities were expected to be worked out.

TEXTS

Irenaeus of Lyons (ca. 130–202)

"Proof of the Apostolic Preaching" (ca. 185), Sections 10–12*

God Supreme Ruler

10. This God, then, is glorified by His Word, who is His Son forever, and by the Holy Spirit, who is the Wisdom of the Father of all. And their Powers (those of the Word and of Wisdom), which are called Cherubim and Seraphim, with unfailing voice glorify God, and the entire establishment of heaven gives glory to God, the Father of all. He has established with the Word the whole world, and angels too are included in the world; and to the whole world He has given laws, that each one keep to his place and overstep not the bound laid down by God, each accomplishing the work marked out for him.

Creation of Man

11. But man He fashioned with His own hands, taking of the purest and finest of earth, in measured wise mingling with the earth His own power; for He gave his frame the outline of His own form, that the visible appearance too should be godlike — for it was as an image of God that man was fashioned and set on

---

*Reprinted from *St. Irenaeus: Proof of the Apostolic Preaching,* ed. Johannes Quasten, S.T.D., and Joseph C. Plumpe, Ph.D., trans. Joseph P. Smith, S.J., © 1952 by The Missionary Society of St. Paul the Apostle in the State of New York. Used by permission of Paulist Press. Pp. 54–55.

earth — and that he might come to life, He *breathed into his face the breath of life,* so that the man became like God in inspiration as well as in frame. So he was free, and his own master, having been made by God in order to be master of everything on earth. And this world of creation, prepared by God before He fashioned man, was given to the man as his domain, with all things whatsoever in it. In the domain were also, with their tasks, the servants of that God who fashioned all, and this domain was in the keeping of the administrator-in-chief, who was set over his fellow-servants; and the servants were angels, but administrator-in-chief the archangel.

Paradise

12. So, having made the man lord of the earth and everything in it, He made him in secret lord also of the servants in it. They, however, were in their full development, while the lord, that is, the man, was a little one; for he was a child and had need to grow so as to come to his full perfection. And so that he might have nourishment and grow up in luxury, a place was prepared for him better than this world, well-favored in climate, beauty, light, things good to eat, plants, fruit, water, and all other things needful to life; and its name is the Garden. And so fair and goodly was the Garden, the Word of God was constantly walking in it; He would walk round and talk with the man, prefiguring what was to come to pass in the future, how He would become man's fellow, and talk with him, and come among mankind, teaching them justice. But the man was a little one, and his discretion still undeveloped, wherefore also he was easily misled by the deceiver.

Irenaeus of Lyons, *Against Heresies* (ca. 185), Book IV, Chapters XXXVII and XXXVIII*

Chapter XXXVII. Men Are Possessed of Free Will, and Endowed with the Faculty of Making a Choice. It Is Not True, Therefore, That Some Are by Nature Good, and Others Bad.

1. This expression [of our Lord], "How often would I have gathered thy children together, and thou wouldest not" [Matt. 23:37], sets forth the ancient law of human liberty, because God made man a free [agent] from the beginning, possessing his own power, even as he does his own soul, to obey the behests of God voluntarily, and not by compulsion of God. For there is no coercion with God, but a good will [towards us] is present with Him continually. And therefore does He give good counsel to all. And in man, as well as in angels, He has placed the power of choice (for angels are rational beings), so that those who had yielded obedience might justly possess what is good, given indeed by God, but preserved

---

*Reprinted from *The Ante-Nicene Fathers,* vol. 1: *The Apostolic Fathers Justin Martyr, Irenaeus,* ed. Alexander Roberts and James Donaldson (Grand Rapids: Wm. B. Eerdmans Publishing Co., 1979), 518–22.

by themselves. On the other hand, they who have not obeyed shall, with justice, be not found in possession of the good, and shall receive condign punishment: for God did kindly bestow on them what was good; but they themselves did not diligently keep it, nor deem it something precious, but poured contempt upon His super-eminent goodness.... God therefore has given that which is good, as the apostle tells us in this Epistle [i.e., Rom. 2], and they who work it shall receive glory and honor, because they have done that which is good when they had it in their power not to do it; but those who do it not shall receive the just judgment of God, because they did not work good when they had it in their power so to do.

2. But if some had been made by nature bad, and others good, these latter would not be deserving of praise for being good, for such were they created; nor would the former be reprehensible, for thus they were made [originally]. But since all men are of the same nature, able both to hold fast and to do what is good; and, on the other hand, having also the power to cast it from them and not to do it — some do justly receive praise even among men who are under the control of good laws (and much more from God), and obtain deserved testimony of their choice of good in general, and persevering therein; but the others are blamed, and receive a just condemnation, because of their rejection of what is fair and good. And therefore the prophets used to exhort men to what was good, to act justly, and to work righteousness, as I have so largely demonstrated, because it is in our power so to do, and because by excessive negligence we might become forgetful, and thus stand in need of that good counsel which the good God has given us to know by means of the prophets.

3. For this reason the Lord also said, "Let your light so shine before men, that they may see your good deeds, and glorify your Father who is in heaven" [Matt. 5:16]. And, "Take heed to yourselves, lest perchance your hearts be overcharged with surfeiting, and drunkenness, and worldly cares" [Luke 21:34]. And, "Let your loins be girded about, and your lamps burning, and ye like unto men that wait for their Lord, when He returns from the wedding, that when He cometh and knocketh, they may open to Him. Blessed is that servant whom his Lord, when He cometh, shall find so doing" [Luke 12:35–37].... All such passages demonstrate the independent will of man, and at the same time the counsel which God conveys to him, by which He exhorts us to submit ourselves to Him, and seeks to turn us away from [the sin of] unbelief against Him, without, however, in any way coercing us....

5. And not merely in works, but also in faith, has God preserved the will of man free and under his own control, saying, "According to thy faith be it unto thee" [Matt. 9:29]; thus showing that there is a faith specially belonging to man, since he has an opinion specially his own. And again "All things are possible to him that believeth" [Mark 9:23].... Now all such expressions demonstrate that man is in his own power with respect to faith. And for this reason, "he that believeth in Him has eternal life; while he who believeth not the Son hath not eternal life, but the wrath of God shall remain upon him" [John 3:36]....

6. Those, again, who maintain the opposite to these [conclusions], do themselves present the Lord as destitute of power, as if, forsooth, He were unable to accomplish what He willed; or, on the other hand, as being ignorant that they

were by nature "material," as these men express it, and such as cannot receive His immortality. "But He should not," say they, "have created angels of such a nature that they were capable of transgression, nor men who immediately proved ungrateful towards Him; for they were made rational beings, endowed with the power of examining and judging, and were not [formed] as things irrational or of a [merely] animal nature, which can do nothing of their own will...who are incapable of being anything else except just what they had been created." But upon this supposition, neither would what is good be grateful to them, nor communion with God be precious, nor would the good be very much to be sought after, which would present itself without their own proper endeavor, care, or study, but would be implanted of its own accord and without their concern....

7. ...The Lord has therefore endured all these things on our behalf, in order that we, having been instructed by means of them all, may be in all respects circumspect for the time to come, and that, having been rationally taught to love God, we may continue in His perfect love: for God has displayed long-suffering in the case of man's apostasy; while man has been instructed by means of it, as also the prophet says. "Thine own apostasy shall heal thee" [Jer. 2:19]; God thus determining all things beforehand for the bringing of man to perfection, for his edification, and for the revelation of His dispensations, that goodness may both be made apparent, and righteousness perfected, and that the Church may be fashioned after the image of His Son, and that man may finally be brought to maturity at some future time, becoming ripe through such privileges to see and comprehend God.

Chapter XXXVIII. Why Man Was Not Made Perfect from the Beginning

1. If, however, anyone says, "What then? Could not God have exhibited man as perfect from the beginning?" let him know that, inasmuch as God is indeed always the same and unbegotten as respects Himself, all things are possible to Him. But created things must be inferior to Him who created them, from the very fact of their later origin; for it was not possible for things recently created to have been uncreated. But inasmuch as they are not uncreated, for this very reason do they come short of the perfect. Because, as these things are of later date, so are they infantile; so are they unaccustomed to, and unexercised in, perfect discipline. For as it certainly is in the power of a mother to give strong food to her infant, [but she does not do so], as the child is not yet able to receive more substantial nourishment; so also it was possible for God Himself to have made man perfect from the first, but man could not receive this [perfection], being as yet an infant. And for this cause our Lord, in these last times, when He had summed up all things into Himself, came to us, not as He might have come, but as we were capable of beholding Him. He might easily have come to us in His immortal glory, but in that case we could never have endured the greatness of the glory; and therefore it was that He, who was the perfect bread of the Father, offered Himself to us as milk, [because we were] as infants. He did this when He appeared as a man, that we, being nourished, as it were, from the breast of His flesh, and having, by such a course of milk-nourishment, become accustomed to eat and

drink the Word of God, may be able also to contain in ourselves the Bread of immortality, which is the Spirit of the Father....

3. With God there are simultaneously exhibited power, wisdom, and goodness. His power and goodness [appear] in this, that of His own will He called into being and fashioned things having no previous existence; His wisdom [is shown] in His having made created things parts of one harmonious and consistent whole; and those things which, through His super-eminent kindness, receive growth and a long period of existence, do reflect the glory of the uncreated One, of that God who bestows what is good ungrudgingly. For from the very fact of these things having been created, [it follows] that they are not uncreated; but by their continuing in being throughout a long course of ages, they shall receive a faculty of the Uncreated, through the gratuitous bestowal of eternal existence upon them by God. And thus in all things God has the pre-eminence, who alone is uncreated, the first of all things, and the primary cause of the existence of all, while all other things remain under God's subjection. But being in subjection to God is continuance in immortality, and immortality is the glory of the uncreated One. By this arrangement, therefore, and these harmonies, and a sequence of this nature, man, a created and organized being, is rendered after the image and likeness of the uncreated God — the Father planning everything well and giving His commands, the Son carrying these into execution and performing the work of creating, and the Spirit nourishing and increasing [what is made], but man making progress day by day, and ascending towards the perfect, that is, approximating to the uncreated One. For the Uncreated is perfect, that is, God....

4. Irrational, therefore, in every respect, are they who await not the time of increase, but ascribe to God the infirmity of their nature. Such persons know neither God nor themselves, being insatiable and ungrateful, unwilling to be at the outset what they have also been created — men subject to passions; but go beyond the law of the human race, and before that they become men, they wish to be even now like God their Creator, and they who are more destitute of reason than dumb animals [insist] that there is no distinction between the uncreated God and man, a creature of today.... For we cast blame upon Him, because we have not been made gods from the beginning, but at first merely men, then at length gods; although God has adopted this course out of His pure benevolence, that no one may impute to Him invidiousness or grudgingness. He declares, "I have said, Ye are gods; and ye are all sons of the Highest" [Ps. 82:6, 7]. But since we could not sustain the power of divinity, He adds, "But ye shall die like men," setting forth both truths — the kindness of His free gift, and our weakness, and also that we were possessed of power over ourselves. For after His great kindness He graciously conferred good [upon us], and made men like to Himself, [that is] in their own power; while at the same time by His prescience He knew the infirmity of human beings, and the consequences which would flow from it; but through [His] love and [His] power, He shall overcome the substance of created nature. For it was necessary, at first, that nature should be exhibited; then, after that, that what was mortal should be conquered and swallowed up by immortality, and the corruptible by incorruptibility, and that man should be made after the image and likeness of God, having received the knowledge of good and evil.

Tertullian (ca. 160–225)

Against Hermogenes (ca. 201), Chapters II, III, X, and XI*

Chapter II: Hermogenes, after a Perverse Induction from Mere Heretical Assumptions, Concludes That God Created All Things Out of Pre-existing Matter.

Our very bad painter [i.e., Hermogenes] has colored this his primary shade absolutely without any light, with such arguments as these: He begins with laying down the premiss, that the Lord made all things either out of Himself, or out of nothing, or out of something; in order that, after he has shown that it was impossible for Him to have made them either out of Himself or out of nothing, he might thence affirm the residuary proposition that He made them out of something, and therefore that that something was Matter. He could not have made all things, he says, of Himself; because whatever things the Lord made of Himself would have been parts of Himself; but He is not dissoluble into parts, because, being the Lord, He is indivisible, and unchangeable, and always the same.... In like manner, he contends that He could not have made all things out of nothing—thus: He defines the Lord as a being who is good, nay, very good, who must will to make things as good and excellent as He is Himself; indeed it were impossible for Him either to will or to make anything which was not good, nay, very good itself. Therefore all things ought to have been made good and excellent by Him, after His own condition. Experience shows, however, that things which are even evil were made by Him: not, of course, of His own will and pleasure; because, if it had been of His own will and pleasure, He would be sure to have made nothing unfitting or unworthy of Himself. That, therefore, which He made not of His own will must be understood to have been made from the fault of something, and that is from Matter, without a doubt.

Chapter III: An Argument of Hermogenes. The Answer: While God Is a Title Eternally Applicable to the Divine Being, Lord and Father Are Only Relative Appellations, Not Eternally Applicable. An Inconsistency in the Argument of Hermogenes Pointed Out.

He adds also another point: that as God was always God, there was never a time when God was not also Lord. But it was in no way possible for Him to be regarded as always Lord, in the same manner as He had been always God, if there had not been always, in the previous eternity, a something of which He could be regarded as evermore the Lord. So he concludes that God always had Matter co-existent with Himself as the Lord thereof. Now, this tissue [conjecture] of his I shall at once hasten to pull abroad. I have been willing to set it out in form to this length, for the information of those who are unacquainted with

---

*Reprinted from *The Ante-Nicene Fathers*, vol. 3: *Latin Christianity: Its Founder, Tertullian*, ed. Alexander Roberts and James Donaldson (Grand Rapids: Wm. B. Eerdmans Publishing Co., 1978), 477–79, 482–83.

the subject, that they may know that his other arguments likewise need only be understood to be refuted. We affirm, then, that the name of *God* always existed with Himself and in Himself — but not eternally so the *Lord*. Because the condition of the one is not the same as that of the other. God is the designation of the substance itself, that is, of the Divinity; but Lord is (the name) not of the substance, but of power. *I maintain* that the substance existed always with its own name, which is God; *the title* Lord was afterwards added, as the indication indeed of something accruing. For from the moment when those things began to exist, over which the power of a Lord was to act, *God,* by the accession of that power, both became Lord and received the name thereof. . . . Do I seem to you to be weaving arguments, Hermogenes? How neatly does Scripture lend us its aid, when it applies the two titles to Him with a distinction, and reveals them each at its proper time! For (the title) *God,* indeed, which always belonged to Him, it names at the very first: "In the beginning God created the heaven and the earth" [Gen. 1:1]; and as long as He continued making, one after the other, those things of which He was to be the Lord, it merely mentions God. "And *God* said," "and *God* made," "and *God* saw"; but nowhere do we yet find the *Lord.* But when He completed the whole creation, and especially man himself, who was destined to understand His sovereignty in a way of special propriety, He then is designated Lord. Then also *the Scripture* added the name *Lord:* "And the Lord God, *Deus Dominus* took the man, whom He had formed" [Gen. 2:15]; "And the Lord God commanded Adam" [Gen. 2:16]. Thenceforth He, who was previously God only, is the *Lord,* from the time of His having something of which He might be the Lord. For to Himself He was always God, but to all things was He only then God, when He became also Lord. Therefore, in *as* far as (Hermogenes) shall suppose that Matter was eternal, on the ground that the Lord was eternal, in *so* far will it be evident that nothing existed, because it is plain that the Lord *as such* did not always exist. . . .

Chapter X: To What Straits Hermogenes Absurdly Reduces the Divine Being. He Does Nothing Short of Making Him the Author of Evil.

Even if Matter had been the perfection of good, would it not have been equally indecorous in Him to have thought of the property of another, however good (to effect His purpose by the help of it)? It was, therefore, absurd enough for Him, in the interest of His own glory, to have created the world in such a way as to betray His own obligation to a substance which belonged to another — and that even not good. Was He then, asks (Hermogenes), to make all things out of nothing, that so evil things themselves might be attributed to His will? . . . Hermogenes, therefore, ought to be told at once, although we postpone to another place our distinction concerning the mode of evil, that even he has effected no result by this device of his. For observe how God is found to be, if not the Author of, yet at any rate the conniver at, evil, inasmuch as He, with all His extreme goodness, endured evil in Matter before He created the world, although, as being good, and the enemy of evil, He ought to have corrected it. For He either was able to correct it, but was unwilling; or else was willing, but being a weak God, was not able. If He was able and yet unwilling, He was Himself evil, as having favored evil; and thus He now opens Himself to the charge of evil, because even if He did not create it, yet still, since it would not be existing if He had been against its existence, He must Himself have then caused it to exist, when He refused to will its nonexistence. And what is more shameful than this? When He willed that to be which He was Himself unwilling to create, He acted in fact against His very self, inasmuch as He was both willing that that should exist which He was unwilling to make, and unwilling to make that which He was willing should exist. As if what He willed was good, and at the same time what he refused to be the Maker of was evil. What He judged to be evil by not creating it, He also proclaimed to be good by permitting it to exist. By bearing with evil as a good instead of rather extirpating it, He proved Himself to be the promoter thereof; criminally, if through His own will — disgracefully, if through necessity. God must either be the servant of evil or the friend thereof, since He held converse with evil in Matter — nay more, effected His works out of the evil thereof.

Chapter XI: Hermogenes Makes Great Efforts to Remove Evil from God to Matter. How He Fails to Do This Consistently with His Own Argument.

But, after all, by what proofs does Hermogenes persuade us that Matter is evil? For it will be impossible for him not to call that evil to which he imputes evil. Now we lay down this principle, that what is eternal cannot possibly admit of diminution and subjection, so as to be considered inferior to another co-eternal Being. So that we now affirm that evil is not even compatible with it, since it is incapable of subjection, from the fact that it cannot in any wise be subject to any, because it is eternal. But inasmuch as, on other grounds, it is evident what is eternal as God is the highest good, whereby also He alone is good — as being eternal, and therefore good — as being God, how can evil be inherent in Matter, which (since it is eternal) must needs be believed to be the highest good? Else if that which is eternal prove to be also capable of evil, this (evil) will be able to be also believed of God to His prejudice; so that it is without adequate reason that he has been so anxious to remove evil from God; since evil must be compatible with an eternal Being, even by being made compatible with Matter, *as Hermogenes makes it*. But, as the argument now stands, since what is eternal can be deemed evil, the evil must prove to be invincible and insuperable, as being eternal; and in that case it will be in vain that we labor "to put away evil from the midst of us" [1 Cor. 5:13]; in that case, moreover, God vainly gives us such a command and precept; nay more, in vain has God appointed any judgment at all, when He means, indeed, to inflict punishment with injustice. But if, on the other hand, there is to be an end of evil, when the chief thereof, the devil, shall "go away into the fire which God hath prepared for him and his angels" [Matt. 25:41].... when the Father shall have put beneath the feet of His Son His enemies, as being the workers of evil — if in this way an *end* is compatible with evil, it must follow of necessity that a *beginning* is also compatible with it; and Matter will turn out to have a beginning, by virtue of its having also an end. For whatever things are set to the account of evil, have a compatibility with the condition of evil.

Athanasius (ca. 296–373)

Incarnation of the Word (ca. 335), §§6 and 8*

§6. The human race then was wasting, God's image was being effaced, and His work ruined. Either, then, God must forego His spoken word by which man had incurred ruin; or that which had shared in the being of the Word must sink back again into destruction, in which case God's design would be defeated. What then? Was God's goodness to suffer this? But if so, why had man been made? It would have been weakness, not goodness on God's part.

For this cause, then, death having gained upon men, and corruption abiding upon them, the race of man was perishing; the rational man made in God's image was disappearing, and the handiwork of God was in process of dissolution. 2. For death, as I said above, gained from that time forth a legal hold over us, and it was impossible to evade the law, since it had been laid down by God because of the transgression, and the result was in truth at once monstrous and unseemly. 3. For it were monstrous, firstly, that God, having spoken, should prove false — that, when once He had ordained that man, if he transgressed the commandment, should die the death, after the transgression man should not die, but God's word should be broken. For God would not be true, if, when He had said we should die, man died not. 4. Again, it were unseemly that creatures once made rational, and having partaken of the Word, would go to ruin, and turn again toward non-existence by the way of corruption. 5. For it were not worthy of God's goodness that the things He had made should waste away, because of the deceit practiced on men by the devil. 6. Especially it was unseemly to the last degree that God's handicraft among men should be done away, either because of their own careless-ness, or because of the deceitfulness of evil spirit. 7. So, as the rational creatures were wasting and such works in course of ruin, what was God in His goodness to do? Suffer corruption to prevail against them and death to hold them fast? And where were the profit of their having been made, to begin with? For better were they not made, than once made, left to neglect and ruin. 8. For neglect reveals weakness, and not goodness on God's part — if, that is, He allows His own work to be ruined when once He had made it — more so than if He had never made man at all. 9. For if He had not made them, none could impute weakness; but once He had made them, and created them out of nothing, it were most mon-strous for the work to be ruined, and that before the eyes of the Maker. 10. It was, then, out of the question to leave men to the current of corruption; because this would be unseemly, and unworthy of God's goodness....

§8. The Word, then, visited that earth in which He was yet always present; and saw all these evils. He takes a body of our Nature, and that of a spotless Virgin, in whose womb He makes it His own, wherein to reveal Himself, conquer death, and restore life.

For this purpose, then, the incorporeal and incorruptible and immaterial Word of God comes to our realm, howbeit he was not far from us before. For no part

---

*Reprinted from *A Select Library of Nicene and Post-Nicene Fathers of the Christian Church*, 2d series, vol. 4: *St. Athanasius*, ed. Philip Schaff and Henry Wace (Grand Rapids: Wm. B. Eerdmans Publishing Co., 1978), 39 and 40.

of Creation is left void of Him: He has filled all things everywhere, remaining present with His own Father. But He comes in condescension to show loving-kindness upon us, and to visit us. 2. And seeing the race of rational creatures in the way to perish, and death reigning over them by corruption; seeing, too, that the threat against transgression gave a firm hold to the corruption which was upon us, and that it was monstrous that before the law was fulfilled it should fall through: seeing, once more, the unseemliness of what was come to pass: that the things whereof He Himself was Artificer were passing away: seeing, further, the exceeding wickedness of men, and how by little and little they had increased it to an intolerable pitch against themselves: and seeing, lastly, how all men were under penalty of death: He took pity on our race, and had mercy on our infirmity, and condescended to our corruption, and, unable to bear that death should have the mastery — lest the creature should perish, and His Father's handiwork in men be spent for nought — He takes unto Himself a body, and that of no different sort from ours. 3. For He did not simply will to become embodied, or will merely to appear. For if He willed merely to appear, He was able to effect His divine appearance by some other and higher means as well. But He takes a body of our kind, and not merely so, but from a spotless and stainless virgin, knowing not a man, a body clean and in very truth pure from intercourse of men. For being Himself mighty, and Artificer of everything, He prepares the body in the Virgin as a temple unto Himself, and makes it His very own as an instrument, in it manifested, and in it dwelling. 4. And thus taking from our bodies one of like nature, because all were under penalty of the corruption of death He gave it over to death in the stead of all, and offered it to the Father — doing this, moreover, of His loving-kindness, to the end that, firstly, all being held to have died in Him, the law involving the ruin of men might be undone (inasmuch as its power was fully spent in the Lord's body, and had no longer holding-ground against men, his peers), and that, secondly, whereas men had turned toward corruption, He might turn them again toward incorruption, and quicken them from death by the appropriation of His body and by the grace of the Resurrection, banishing death from them like straw from the fire.

Basil of Caesarea (329–79)

On the Spirit (375), Chapters IX and XVI*

Chapter IX: Definitive Conceptions about the Spirit Which Conform to the Teaching of the Scriptures

22. Let us now investigate what are our common conceptions concerning the Spirit, as well those which have been gathered by us from Holy Scripture concerning It as those which we have received from the unwritten tradition of the Fathers. First of all we ask, who on hearing the titles of the Spirit is not lifted up in soul, who does not raise his conception to the supreme nature? It is called "Spirit of

*Reprinted from *A Select Library of Nicene and Post-Nicene Fathers of the Christian Church*, 2d series, vol. 3: *St. Basil*, ed. Philip Schaff and Henry Wace (Grand Rapids: Wm. B. Eerdmans Publishing Co., 1978), 15–16, 23–25.

God" [Matt. 12:28], "Spirit of truth which proceedeth from the Father" [John 15:26], "right Spirit" [Ps. 51:10], "a leading Spirit" [Ps. 51:12; LXX]. Its proper and peculiar title is "Holy Spirit"; which is a name specially appropriate to everything that is incorporeal, purely immaterial, and indivisible. So our Lord, when teaching the woman who thought God to be an object of local worship that the incorporeal is incomprehensible, said "God is a spirit" [John 4:24]. On our hearing, then, of a spirit, it is impossible to form the idea of a nature circumscribed, subject to change and variation, or at all like the creature. We are compelled to advance in our conceptions to the highest, and to think of an intelligent essence, in power infinite, in magnitude unlimited, unmeasured by times or ages, generous of Its good gifts, to whom turn all things needing sanctification, after whom reach all things that live in virtue, as being watered by Its inspiration and helped on toward their natural and proper end; perfecting all other things, but Itself in nothing lacking; living not as needing restoration, but as Supplier of life; not growing by additions, but straightway full, self-established, omnipresent, origin of sanctification, light perceptible to the mind, supplying, as it were, through Itself, illumination to every faculty in the search for truth; by nature unapproachable, apprehended by reason of goodness, filling all things with Its power [cf. Wisd. 1:7], but communicated only to the worthy; not shared in one measure, but distributing Its energy according to "the proportion of faith"; in essence simple, in powers various, wholly present in each and being wholly everywhere; impassively divided, shared without loss of ceasing to be entire, after the likeness of the sunbeam, whose kindly light falls on him who enjoys it as though it shone for him alone, yet illumines land and sea and mingles with the air. So, too, is the Spirit to every one who receives It, as though given to him alone, and yet It sends forth grace sufficient and full for all mankind, and is enjoyed by all who share It, according to the capacity, not of Its power, but of their nature.

23. . . . Through His aid hearts are lifted up, the weak are held by the hand, and they who are advancing are brought to perfection. Shining upon those that are cleansed from every spot, He makes them spiritual by fellowship with Himself. Just as when a sunbeam falls on bright and transparent bodies, they themselves become brilliant too, and shed forth a fresh brightness from themselves, so souls wherein the Spirit dwells, illuminated by the Spirit, themselves become spiritual, and send forth their grace to others. Hence comes foreknowledge of the future, understanding of mysteries, apprehension of what is hidden, distribution of good gifts, the heavenly citizenship, a place in the chorus of angels, joy without end, abiding in God, the being made like to God, and highest of all, the being made God. Such, then, to instance a few out of many, are the conceptions concerning the Holy Spirit, which we have been taught to hold concerning His greatness, His dignity, and His operations, by the oracles of the Spirit themselves. . . .

Chapter XVI: That the Holy Spirit Is in Every Conception Inseparable from the Father and the Son, Alike in the Creation of Perceptible Objects, in the Dispensation of Human Affairs, and in the Judgment to Come

38. . . . And in the creation bethink thee first, I pray thee, of the original cause of all things that are made, the Father; of the creative cause, the Son; of the per-

fecting cause, the Spirit; so that the ministering spirits subsist by the will of the Father, are brought into being by the operation of the Son, and perfected by the presence of the Spirit. Moreover, the perfection of angels is sanctification and continuance in it. And let no one imagine me either to affirm that there are three original hypostases[1] or to allege the operation of the Son to be imperfect. For the first principle of existing things is One, creating through the Son and perfecting through the Spirit. The operation of the Father who worketh all in all is not imperfect, neither is the creating work of the Son incomplete if not perfected by the Spirit. The Father, who creates by His sole will, could not stand in any need of the Son, but nevertheless He wills through the Son; nor could the Son, who works according to the likeness of the Father, need co-operation, but the Son too wills to make perfect through the Spirit. "For by the word of the Lord were the heavens made, and all the host of them by the breath [the Spirit] of His mouth" [Ps. 33:6]. The Word then is not a mere significant impression on the air, borne by the organs of speech; nor is the spirit of His mouth a vapor, emitted by the organs of respiration; but the Word is He who "was with God in the beginning" and "was God" [John 1:1], and the Spirit of the mouth of God is "the Spirit of truth which proceedeth from the Father" [John 15:26]. You are therefore to perceive three, the Lord who gives the order, the Word who creates, and the Spirit who confirms. And what other thing could confirmation be than the perfecting according to holiness? This perfecting expresses the confirmation's firmness, unchangeableness, and fixity in good. But there is no sanctification without the Spirit.... The revelation of mysteries is indeed the peculiar function of the Spirit, as it is written, "God hath revealed them unto us by His Spirit" [1 Cor. 2:10]. And how could "thrones, dominions, principalities and powers" [Col. 1:16] live their blessed life, did they not "behold the face of the Father which is in heaven" [Matt. 18:10]? But to behold it is impossible without the Spirit! Just as at night, if you withdraw the light from the house, the eyes fall blind and their faculties become inactive, and the worth of objects cannot be discerned, and gold is trodden on in ignorance as though it were iron, so in the order of the intellectual world it is impossible for the high life of Law to abide without the Spirit.... All the glorious and unspeakable harmony of the highest heavens both in the service of God, and in the mutual concord of the celestial powers, can therefore only be preserved by the direction of the Spirit. Thus with those beings who are not gradually perfected by increase and advance, but are perfect from the moment of the creation, there is in creation the presence of the Holy Spirit, who confers on them the grace that flows from Him for the completion and perfection of their essence.

39. But when we speak of the dispensations made for man by our great God and Savior Jesus Christ, who will gainsay their having been accomplished through the grace of the Spirit? Whether you wish to examine ancient evidence; — the blessings of the patriarchs, the succor given through the legislation, the types, the prophecies, the valorous feats in war, the signs wrought through just men; — or on the other hand the things done in the dispensation of the coming of our Lord in the flesh; — all is through the Spirit. In the first place He was made

---

1. Prior to the Council of Nicea, *hypostasis* and *ousia* were often used interchangeably. Basil rejects the application of *hypostases* to the persons of the trinity insofar as the term is understood as an equivalent for *ousiai*, i.e., "substances."

an unction, and being inseparably present was with the very flesh of the Lord, according to that which is written, "upon whom thou shalt see the Spirit descending and remaining on Him, the same is" [John 1:33] "my beloved Son" [Matt. 3:17]; and "Jesus of Nazareth" whom "God anointed with the Holy Ghost" [Acts 10:38]. . . . And He did not leave Him when He had risen from the dead; for when renewing man, and, by breathing on the face of the disciples, restoring the grace that came of the inbreathing of God, which man had lost, what did the Lord say? "Receive ye the Holy Ghost: whose soever sins ye remit, they are remitted unto them; and whose soever ye retain, they are retained" [John 20:22–23]. And is it not plain and incontestable that the ordering of the Church is effected through the Spirit? For He gave, it is said, "in the church, first Apostles, secondarily prophets, thirdly teachers, after that miracles, then gifts of healing, helps, governments, diversities of tongues" [1 Cor. 12:28], for this order is ordained in accordance with the division of the gifts that are of the Spirit.

Augustine (354–430)

The Enchiridion on Faith, Hope, and Love (421), Chapters X–XII, XCVI, XCVIII–CIII*

X. The Supremely Good Creator Made All Things Good

By the Trinity, thus supremely and equally and unchangeably good, all things were created; and these are not supremely and equally and unchangeably good, but yet they are good, even taken separately. Taken as a whole, however, they are very good, because their *ensemble* constitutes the universe in all its wonderful order and beauty.

XI. What Is Called Evil in the Universe Is But the Absence of Good

And in the universe, even that which is called evil, when it is regulated and put in its own place, only enhances our admiration of the good; for we enjoy and value the good more when we compare it with the evil. For the Almighty God, who, as even the heathen acknowledge, has supreme power over all things, being Himself supremely good, would never permit the existence of anything evil among His works, if He were not so omnipotent and good that He can bring good even out of evil. For what is that which we call evil but the absence of good? In the bodies of animals, disease and wounds mean nothing but the absence of health; for when a cure is effected, that does not mean that the evils which were present — namely, the diseases and wounds — go away from the body and dwell elsewhere: they altogether cease to exist; for the wound or disease is not a substance, but a defect in the fleshly substance — the flesh itself being a substance, and therefore something good, of which those evils — that is, privations of the good which we call health — are accidents. Just in the same way, what are called vices in the soul are nothing but privations of natural good. And when they are cured, they are not transferred elsewhere: when they cease to exist in the healthy soul, they cannot exist anywhere else.

XII. All Beings Were Made Good, but Not Being Made Perfectly Good, Are Liable to Corruption

All things that exist, therefore, seeing that the Creator of them all is supremely good, are themselves good. But because they are not, like their Creator, supremely and unchangeably good, their good may be diminished and increased. But for good to be diminished is an evil, although, however much it may be diminished, it is necessary, if the being is to continue, that some good should remain to constitute the being. For however small or of whatever kind the being may be, the good which makes it a being cannot be destroyed without destroying the being itself.... Every being, therefore, is a good; a great good, if it cannot be corrupted; a little good, if it can: but in any case, only the foolish or ignorant will deny that it is a good. And if it be wholly consumed by corruption, then the corruption itself must cease to exist, as there is no being left in which it can dwell....

XCVI. The Omnipotent God Does Well Even in the Permission of Evil

Nor can we doubt that God does well even in the permission of what is evil. For He permits it only in the justice of His judgment. And surely all that is just is good. Although, therefore, evil, insofar as it is evil, is not a good; yet the fact that evil as well as good exists, is a good. For if it were not a good that evil should exist, its existence would not be permitted by the omnipotent God, who without doubt can as easily refuse to permit what He does not wish, as bring about what He does wish. And if we do not believe this, the very first sentence of our creed is endangered, wherein we profess to believe in God the Father Almighty. For He is not truly called Almightly if He cannot do whatsoever He pleases, or if the power of His almighty will is hindered by the will of any creature whatsoever....

XCVIII. Predestination to Eternal Life is Wholly of God's Free Grace

And, moreover, who will be so foolish and blasphemous as to say that God cannot change the evil wills of men, whichever, whenever, and wheresoever He chooses, and direct them to what is good? But when He does this, He does it of mercy; when He does it not, it is of justice that He does it not; for "He hath mercy on whom He will have mercy, and whom He will He hardeneth" [Rom. 9:18]. And when the apostle said this, he was illustrating the grace of God, in connection with which he had just spoken of the twins in the womb of Rebecca, "who being not yet born, neither having done any good or evil, that the purpose of God according to election might stand, not of works, but of Him that calleth, it was said unto her, The elder shall serve the younger" [Rom. 9:11–12]. And in reference to this matter he quotes another prophetic testimony: "Jacob have I loved, but Esau have I hated" [Rom. 9:13; Mal. 1:2, 3]. But perceiving how what he had said might affect those who could not penetrate by their understanding the depth of this grace: "What shall we say then?" he says: "Is there unrighteousness with God? God forbid" [Rom. 9:14]. For it seems unjust that, in the absence of any merit or demerit, from good or evil works, God should love the one and hate the other. Now, if the apostle had wished us to understand that there were future good works of the one, and evil works of the other, which of course God foreknew, he would never have said, "not of works," but "of future works," and in that way would have solved the difficulty, or rather there would then have been no difficulty to solve. As it is, however, after answering, "God forbid"; that is, God forbid that there should be unrighteousness with God; he goes on to prove that there is no unrighteousness in God's doing this, and says: "For He saith to Moses, I will have mercy on whom I will have mercy, and I will have compassion on whom I will have compassion" [Rom. 9:15; Exod. 33:19].... Thus both the twins were born children of wrath, not on account of any works of their own, but because they were bound in the fetters of that original condemnation which came through Adam. But He who said, "I will have mercy on whom I will have mercy," loved Jacob of His undeserved grace, and hated Esau of His deserved judgment. And as this judgment was due to both, the former learnt from the case of the latter that the fact of the same punishment not falling upon himself gave him no room to glory in any merit of his own, but only in the riches of the divine grace; because "it is not of him that willeth, nor of him that runneth, but of God that showeth mercy." And indeed the whole face, and . . . every lineament of the countenance of Scripture conveys by a very profound analogy this wholesome warning to every one who looks carefully into it, that he who glories should glory in the Lord [cf. 1 Cor. 1:31].

XCIX. As God's Mercy Is Free, So His Judgments Are Just, and Cannot Be Gainsaid

Now after commending the mercy of God, saying, "So it is not of him that willeth, nor of him that runneth, but of God that showeth mercy," that he might commend His justice also (for the man who does not obtain mercy finds, not iniquity, but justice, there being no iniquity with God) he immediately adds: "For the scripture saith unto Pharaoh, Even for this same purpose have I raised thee up, that I might show my power in thee, and that my name might be declared throughout all the earth" [Rom. 9:17; Exod. 9:16]. And then he draws a conclusion that applies to both, that is, both to His mercy and His justice: "Therefore hath He mercy on whom He will have mercy, and whom He will He hardeneth" [Rom. 9:18]. "He hath mercy" of His great goodness, "He hardeneth" without any injustice; so that neither can he that is pardoned glory in any merit of his own, nor he that is condemned complain of anything but his own demerit. For it is grace alone that separates the redeemed from the lost, all having been involved in one common perdition through their common origin. Now if anyone, on hearing this, should say, "Why doth He yet find fault? For who hath resisted His will" [Rom. 9:19]? As if a man ought not to be blamed for being bad, because God hath mercy on whom He will have mercy, and whom He will He hardeneth, God forbid that we should be ashamed to answer as we see the apostle answered: "Nay, but, O man, who art thou that repliest against God? Shall the thing formed say to Him that formed it, Why hast Thou made me thus? Hath not the potter power over the clay, of the same lump to make one vessel unto honor, and another unto dishonor" [Rom. 9:20, 21]? Now some foolish people think that in this place the apostle had no answer to give; and for want of a reason to render, rebuked the presumption of his interrogator. But there is great weight in this saying: "Nay, but, O man, who art thou?" and in such a matter as this it suggests to a man in a single word the limits of his capacity, and at the same time does in reality convey an important reason. For if a man does not understand these matters, who is he that he should reply against God? And if he does understand them, he finds no further room for reply. For then he perceives that the whole human race was condemned in its rebellious head by a divine judgment so just, that if not a single member of the race had been redeemed, no one could justly have questioned the justice of God; and that it was right that those who are redeemed should be redeemed in such a way as to show, by the greater number who are unredeemed and left in their just condemnation, what the whole race deserved, and whither the deserved judgment of God would lead even the redeemed, did not His undeserved mercy interpose, so that every mouth might be stopped of those who wish to glory in their own merits, and that he that glorieth might glory in the Lord [Rom. 3:19; 1 Cor. 1:21].

C. The Will of God Is Never Defeated Though Much Is Done That Is Contrary to His Will

These are the great works of the Lord, sought out according to all His pleasure [Ps. 111:2 (LXX)], and so wisely sought out, that when the intelligent creation, both angelic and human, sinned, doing not His will but their own, He used the very will of the creature which was working in opposition to the Creator's will as an instrument for carrying out His will, the supremely Good thus turning to good account even what is evil, to the condemnation of those whom in His justice He has predestined to punishment, and to the salvation of those whom in His mercy He has predestined to grace. For, as far as related to their own consciousness, these creatures did what God wished not to be done: but in view of God's omnipotence, they could in no wise effect their purpose. For in the very fact that they acted in opposition to His will, His will concerning them was fulfilled. And hence it is that "the works of the Lord are great, sought out according to all His pleasure," because in a way unspeakably strange and wonderful, even what is done in opposition to His will does not defeat His will. For it would not be done did He not permit it (and of course His permission is not unwilling, but willing); nor would a Good Being permit evil to be done only that in his omnipotence He can turn evil into good.

CI. The Will of God, Which Is Always Good, Is Sometimes Fulfilled through the Evil Will of Man

Sometimes, however, a man in the goodness of his will desires something that God does not desire, even though God's will is also good, nay, much more fully and more surely good (for His will never can be evil): for example, if a good son is anxious that his father should live, when it is God's good will that he should die. Again, it is possible for a man with evil will to desire what God wills in His goodness: for example, if a bad son wishes his father to die, when this is also the will of God. It is plain that the former wishes what God does not wish, and that the latter wishes what God does wish; and yet the filial love of the former is more in harmony with the good will of God, though its desire is different from God's, than the want of filial affection of the latter, though its desire is the same as God's. So necessary is it, in determining whether a man's desire is one to be approved or disapproved, to consider what it is proper for man, and what it is proper for God, to desire, and what is in each case the real motive of the will. For God accomplishes some of His purposes, which of course are all good, through the evil desires of wicked men: for example, it was through the wicked designs of the Jews, working out the good purpose of the Father, that Christ was slain; and this event was so truly good, that when the Apostle Peter expressed his unwillingness that it should take place, he was designated Satan by Him who had come to be slain [Matt. 16:21–23]. . . .

CII. The Will of the Omnipotent God Is Never Defeated, and Is Never Evil

But however strong may be the purposes either of angels or of men, whether of good or bad, whether these purposes fall in with the will of God or run counter to it, the will of the Omnipotent is never defeated; and His will never can be evil; because even when it inflicts evil it is just, and what is just is certainly not evil. The omnipotent God, then, whether in mercy He pitieth whom He will, or in judgment hardeneth whom He will, is never unjust in what He does, never does anything except of His own free-will, and never wills anything that He does not perform.

CIII. Interpretation of the Expression in 1 Tim. 2:4: "Who Will Have All Men to Be Saved"

Accordingly, when we hear and read in Scripture that He "will have all men to be saved," although we know well that all men are not saved, we are not on that account to restrict the omnipotence of God, but are rather to understand the Scripture, "Who will have all men to be saved," as meaning that no man is saved unless God wills his salvation: not that there is no man whose salvation He does not will, but that no man is saved apart from His will; and that, therefore, we should pray Him to will our salvation, because if He will it, it must necessarily be accomplished. . . . Or, it is said, "Who will have all men to be saved"; not that there is no man whose salvation He does not will (for how, then, explain the fact that He was unwilling to work miracles in the presence of some who, He said, would have repented if He had worked them?), but that we are to understand by "all men," the human race in all its varieties of rank and circumstances — kings, subjects; noble, plebeian, high, low, learned, and unlearned; the sound in body, the feeble, the clever, the dull, . . . males, females, infants, boys, youths; young, middle-aged, and old men; of every tongue, of every fashion, of all arts, of all professions, with all the innumerable differences of will and conscience, and whatever else there is that makes a distinction among men. For which of all these classes is there out of which God does not will that men should be saved in all nations through His only-begotten Son, our Lord, and therefore does save them; for the Omnipotent cannot will in vain, whatsoever He may will?...And we may interpret it in any other way we please, so long as we are not compelled to believe that the omnipotent God has willed anything to be done which was not done: for, setting aside all ambiguities, if "He hath done all that He pleased in heaven and in earth" [Ps. 115:3], as the psalmist sings of Him, He certainly did not will to do anything that He hath not done.

Augustine, *The City of God* (413–26), Book XI, Chapters 4–6, and Book XIII, Chapters 13–14*

Chapter 4

Of all visible things, the universe is the greatest; of all invisible realities, the greatest is God. That the world exists we can see; we believe in the existence of God. But there is no one we can more safely trust than God Himself in regard to the fact that it was He who made the world. Where has He told us so? No-where more distinctly than in the Holy Scriptures where His Prophet said: "In the beginning God created the heavens and the earth" [Gen. 1:1]. Well, but was the Prophet present when God made heaven and earth? No; but the Wisdom of God by whom all things were made was there. And this Wisdom, entering into holy souls, makes of them the friends and prophets of God [cf. Wisd. 7:27] and reveals to them, silently and interiorly, what God has done....

But, why did it please the eternal God to create heaven and earth at that special time, seeing that He had not done so earlier? If the purpose of those who pose this question is to protest that the world is eternal, without beginning, and, therefore, not created by God, then they are far from the truth and are raving with the deadly disease of irreligion. For, quite apart from the voice of the Prophets, the very order, changes, and movements in the universe, the very beauty of form in all that is visible, proclaim, however silently, both that the world was created and also that its Creator could be none other than God whose greatness and beauty are both ineffable and invisible.

There are those who say that the universe was, indeed, created by God, denying a "temporal" but admitting a "creational" beginning, as though, in some hardly comprehensible way, the world was made from all eternity. Their purpose seems to be to save God from the charge of arbitrary rashness. They would not have us believe that a completely new idea of creating the world suddenly occurred to Him or that a change of mind took place in Him in whom there can be no change.

I do not see, however, how this position is consistent with their stand in other matters, especially in regard to the soul. For, if, as they must hold, the soul is co-eternal with God, they have no way to explain how a completely new misery can begin in an eternally existing soul....

*Reprinted from *St. Augustine: The City of God, Books VIII–XVI*, trans. Gerald G. Walsh and Grace Monahan. Copyright © 1952 by Fathers of the Church, Inc. Used by permission of The Catholic University of America Press. Pp. 190–96, 316–17.

Finally, if they say that the soul was created in time but will not perish in any future time, like numbers which begin with "one" but never end, and, therefore, that having experienced misery, it will be freed from it, never again to return to it, they will surely have no hesitation in admitting that this is compatible with the immutability of God's decision. This being so, they should also believe that the world could be made in time without God who made it having to change the eternal decision of His will.

Chapter 5

Before attempting to reply to those who, while agreeing with us that God is the Creator of the world, question us about the time at which it was created, we must see what response they make when we ask them about the space in which it was created. For, just as they ask why it was made then and not earlier, we may ask why it was made here and not elsewhere. Because, if they excogitate infinite periods of time before the world, in which they cannot see how God could have had nothing to do, they ought to conceive of infinite reaches of space beyond the visible universe. And, if they maintain that the Omnipotent can never be inactive, will they not logically be forced to dream with Epicurus of innumerable universes? (There will be merely this difference, that, while he asserts that these worlds originate and disintegrate by the fortuitous movements of atoms, they will hold that they are created by the work of God.) This is the conclusion if they insist on the premise that there is an interminable immensity of space stretching in all directions in which God cannot remain passive and that those imaginary worlds, like this visible one, are indestructible. . . .

Of course, they may admit that it is silly to imagine infinite space since there is no such thing as space beyond the cosmos. In that case, let this be the answer: It is silly for them to excogitate a past time during which God was unoccupied, for the simple reason that there was no such thing as time before the universe was made.

Chapter 6

The distinguishing mark between time and eternity is that the former does not exist without some movement and change, while in the latter there is no change at all. Obviously, then, there could have been no time had not a creature been made whose movement would effect some change. It is because the parts of this motion and change cannot be simultaneous, since one part must follow another, that, in these shorter or longer intervals of duration, time begins. Now, since God, in whose eternity there is absolutely no change, is the Creator and Ruler of time, I do not see how we can say that He created the world after a space of time had elapsed unless we admit, also, that previously some creature had existed whose movements would mark the course of time.

Again, sacred and infallible Scripture tells us that in the beginning God created heaven and earth in order. Now, unless this meant that nothing had been made before, it would have been stated that whatever else God had made before was created in the beginning. Undoubtedly, then, the world was made not in time but together with time. For, what is made in time is made after one period of time and before another, namely, after a past and before a future time. But, there could have been no past time, since there was nothing created by whose movements and change time could be measured.

The fact is that the world was made simultaneously with time, if, with creation, motion and change began. Now this seems evident from the order of the first six or seven days. For, the morning and evening of each of these days are counted until on the sixth day all that had been created during this time was complete. Then, on the seventh day, in a mysterious revelation, we are told that God ceased from work. As for these "days," it is difficult, perhaps impossible to think — let alone to explain in words — what they mean.

Book XIII, Chapter 13

As soon as our first parents had disobeyed God's commandment, they were immediately deprived of divine grace, and were ashamed of their nakedness. They covered themselves with fig leaves [cf. Gen. 3:7, 10], which, perhaps, were the first thing noticed by the troubled pair. The parts covered remained unchanged except that, previously, they occasioned no shame. They felt for the first time a movement of disobedience in their flesh, as though the punishment were meant to fit the crime of their own disobedience to God.

The fact is that the soul, which had taken perverse delight in its own liberty and disdained the service of God, was now deprived of its original mastery over the body; because it had deliberately deserted the Lord who was over it, it no longer bent to its will the servant below it, being unable to hold the flesh completely in subjection as would always have been the case, if only the soul had remained subject to God. From this moment, then, the flesh began to lust against the spirit [cf. Gal. 5:17]. With this rebellion we are born, just as we are doomed to die and, because of the first sin, to bear, in our members and vitiated nature, either the battle with or defeat by the flesh.

Chapter 14

God, the Author of all natures but not of their defects, created man good; but man, corrupt by choice and condemned by justice, has produced a progeny that is both corrupt and condemned. For, we all existed in that one man, since, taken together, we were the one man who fell into sin through the woman who was made out of him before sin existed. Although the specific form by which each of us was to live was not yet created and assigned, our nature was already present in the seed from which we were to spring. And because this nature has been soiled by sin and doomed to death and justly condemned, no man was to be born of man in any other condition.

Thus, from a bad use of free choice, a sequence of misfortunes conducts the whole human race, except in those redeemed by the grace of God, from the original canker in its root to the devastation of a second and endless death.

- 5 -

The Medieval and Reformation Period

INTRODUCTION

In this period the early church's teaching about God's creative, redemptive, and sanctifying activities was reaffirmed. Although it retained the basic teaching of the earlier period, medieval and Reformation theology did contribute to doctrinal development in the church. By articulating the faith in new ways and with new categories, medieval scholastics, for example, provided new lenses for interpreting the deposit of faith. Thomas Aquinas, for example, reaffirmed the early church's teaching about divine providence, but he used careful scholastic distinctions and categories of causation adapted from Aristotle to do so. Medieval theologians who worked outside the scholastic context also contributed to doctrinal development. Hildegard of Bingen, for example, reaffirmed the church's teaching about the creation of the world by God, but she used new metaphors and images to express this teaching.

Sometimes the reaffirmation of teaching formulated in the early church created new controversies. For example, the reaffirmation of Augustine's teaching on grace, free will, and predestination stirred up heated debates in the ninth, eleventh, twelfth, and sixteenth centuries. Particularly, the Augustinian understanding of divine predestination became a source of controversy in the ninth century. Although most of the prominent theologians of the ninth century, including John Scotus Erigena and Ratramnus of Corbie, got involved in the dispute, the origin of the controversy was a prolonged confrontation between Gottschalk of Orbais and Hincmar of Reims. Gottschalk (ca. 804–69), appealing to statements on predestination in Augustine's later writings, declared that after the Fall of Adam and Eve the human will was incapable of doing good. All would perish eternally if not for the fact that God has predestined some people to eternal blessedness, while predestinating the rest to eternal condemnation. Although he appears simply to reiterate a strict form of Augustinianism, the tone of Gottschalk's writing is different from that of Augustine. Whereas Augustine emphasized the joy of receiving divine grace, Gottschalk appeared to delight in the condemnation of the reprobate, among whom he numbered his chief opponent Hincmar.[1]

Hincmar (ca. 806–82), who was archbishop of Reims (France) from 845 to the 880s, by contrast, insisted upon the distinction between divine foreknowledge and predestination. God does not predestine people to sin, but God knows in advance who will sin. In *God's Predestination and Free Will*, Hincmar explained that God

---

1. See Justo L. González, *A History of Christian Thought*, vol. 2: *From Augustine to the Eve of the Reformation* (Nashville: Abingdon Press, 1971), 110–11.

cannot predestine the wicked to sin because God would then be responsible for sin. The human will must be involved in the process of salvation or God is unjust to condemn those who were not free to do anything but sin. Despite Hincmar's appeal for support from other theologians, his position itself was subjected to criticism. Nevertheless, at the synod of Quiercy (849), Gottschalk's affirmation of double predestination[2] was condemned, and Gottschalk was sentenced to imprisonment at the abbey of Hautvillers, near Reims, where he continued to write against Hincmar and others. In subsequent synods, the issue continued to be discussed until an ambiguous statement was issued and accepted at the Synod of Tuzey (860).

In the twelfth and thirteenth centuries the issue emerged again as Christian thinkers attempted to resolve tensions in church teaching in response to the need for a rational and coherent exposition of the faith. In *On the Harmony of the Foreknowledge, Predestination, and Grace of God with Free Will,* Anselm of Canterbury attempted to clarify the sense in which one could say that God predestined evil deeds. Such a statement was legitimate if it was understood to mean that God caused the deeds as deeds, but not that God caused the evil in those deeds. In the same work, Anselm attempted to resolve the paradox between human freedom and divine foreknowledge. If God's knowledge is always true and God had foreknowledge of Adam and Eve's sin, then doesn't the sin of Adam and Eve become "necessary?" In response, Anselm noted that there is neither past nor future in God, but only an eternal present. Therefore, it is illegitimate to speak as though God had known "in the past" what was going to happen "in the future." It is more appropriate to state that God did not *pre*-destine (i.e., determine *in advance*) anything because all things are present to God at once.[3]

Of course, the chief stumbling block in Augustine's understanding of grace remained his doctrine of reprobation. Already in the sixth century the Synod of Orange (529) had anathematized the notion of predestination to evil, while endorsing Augustine's emphasis upon the inability of free will to do good without the aid of grace. Augustine had defended the fact that many human beings will experience eternal damnation on the basis of divine justice and the seriousness of sin. The first sin, freely committed by Adam and Eve, rightly entailed punishment. But why a punishment so serious that all humankind stands under the judgment of condemnation, unless freed by the merciful grace of God? The first human beings enjoyed an intimate relationship with God. The greater the intimacy and the benefits of such a relationship, the greater the impiety of breaking that relationship with God, Augustine replied. Nonetheless, the justice of divine judgment is tempered by divine mercy. For if all of the descendants of Adam and Eve "had tasted of the punishments of justice, the grace and mercy of the Redeemer had had no place in any: and again, if all had been redeemed from death, there had been

---

2. Double predestination means that God has chosen both to save some people (election) and to damn others (reprobation). It is double because it holds that both election and reprobation are decrees of the divine will. The Synod of Orange in 529 had upheld single predestination (election), while rejecting the idea that God predestined some for damnation.

3. Anselm of Canterbury, *De concordia praescientiae et praedestinationis et gratiae dei cum libero arbitrio,* 2.2 in Franciscus S. Schmitt, ed., *Sancti Anselmi opera omnia,* 6 vols. (Rome and Edinburgh: T. Nelson, 1946–61), 2:261.

no object left for the manifestation of God's justice."[4] The issues surrounding this difficult doctrine were taken up again at the time of the Protestant Reformation.

Medieval theology not only reaffirmed tradition from the early church; it also confronted again heterodox and heretical movements with roots from the same period. One such movement was the Cathari (Latin for "the pure"), who considered only their way of life as authentically Christian. In Southern France during the twelfth century, they were known as the Albigensians. Their views were connected with the Bogomils of Bulgaria and, through them, with the ancient Manichees. The Cathari believed that an evil world could not be the product of a good creator. In support of their ideas, they appealed to Jesus' saying that a good tree cannot bear evil fruit (Matt. 7:18; Luke 6:43). Being unable to reconcile the idea of a good creator and the reality of evil, many of them concluded that God created all good things, while the devil made everything else. Good things, however, were only those things that are invisible to the eye. In short, the Cathari were radical dualists. They regarded everything material as evil, while only that which is spiritual is good. The corollary of their negative understanding of matter was their denial of the genuine humanity of Christ and the virtue of procreation. Against the Albigensian position concerning the origin of matter, Lateran Council IV in 1215 declared that God is the creator of both spiritual and corporeal reality, that God created both orders of creation out of nothing at the beginning of time, and that God alone has no beginning. Theologians were called upon to defend the orthodox understanding of creation against the heretical ideas of the Cathari. Hildegard of Bingen, for example, urged the clergy of Cologne to preach against the Cathars who had come to the city. Against them she proposed a more positive understanding of procreation and marriage.[5]

Another impetus to the development of doctrine in new terms was the encounter with the worldviews of Judaism and Islam. Of course, the encounter with the other great monotheistic faiths of the West was not new. But in the twelfth century, Christians encountered more compelling and systematic articulations of the Jewish and the Muslim positions than had their predecessors. These religions posed powerful alternatives to the Christian understanding of reality. In a way analogous to the military struggle between Christians and Muslims for control of the Holy Land, Christians in the eleventh through the thirteenth centuries found it necessary to engage in theological "warfare" with the alternative positions of Jewish intellectuals (such as Moses Maimonides) and Islamic intellectuals (such as Avicenna and Averroës). As Jaroslav Pelikan has observed, there was at this time not merely an internal impetus to understand the faith which the church professed. There was also the outer pressure to respond to Judaism and Islam as well as to the heretical movements now separated from the church.[6] When debating with such groups, who did not recognize either the authority of the Christian Bible or the authority of the church's leaders, the judge to which all could appeal was reason. The challenge of heresies and the alternative visions of other religions

---

4. *City of God*, Book XXI, ch. 12 in St. Augustine, *The City of God*, 2 vols., trans. John Healey and intro. by Ernest Barker (New York: Everyman's Library, 1945), 2:335.

5. Sabina Flanagan, *Hildegard of Bingen: A Visionary Life* (New York: Routledge, 1989), 65.

6. Jaroslav Pelikan, *The Christian Tradition: A History of the Development of Doctrine*, vol. 3: *The Growth of Medieval Theology (600–1300)* (Chicago: University of Chicago Press, 1978), 242–60.

made it imperative for Christians to give a reasoned account of the Christian faith. The recognition of this imperative "is perhaps the most important aspect of the intellectual changes that took place during the twelfth and thirteenth centuries."[7]

In this context Anselm of Canterbury appealed to "necessary reasons" rather than to the presuppositions of Christian faith in order to demonstrate the truth of Christian doctrines. Richard of Saint-Victor declared that faith, which is the foundation of every good, nevertheless occupies a place inferior to understanding in the ascent to God.[8] Although theologians in the early church also had cause to appeal to reason, they used it as an ally alongside of revelation in the defense of Christian faith against Jewish critique or pagan attack. In the twelfth and thirteenth centuries, reason was used to scrutinize the claims of revelation itself. The use of reason in this wider scope was only possible in a context in which the Christian view of the world was dominant. Such a situation did not exist in the early church, but it did exist in the medieval church. As Pelikan has remarked, "It was not until the Christian tradition stood virtually unchallenged that it could undertake the task of determining how much of its contents could be known without faith."[9]

As Christians soon discovered, the appeal to a more critical inquiry and reasoned argumentation could be used not only to provide warrants for faith. It could also be used to arrive at conclusions different from orthodox belief. This fact became apparent in the wake of the reintroduction of Aristotle's thought into the western Christian world. Until the early part of the twelfth century, medieval Christian thinkers had at their disposal only a fragment of Aristotle's work. Between approximately 1130 and 1170, the remainder of Aristotle's logical works, including his *Prior* and *Posterior Analytics,* were introduced to the West. By the third quarter of the thirteenth century, translations of Aristotle's entire corpus, including the *Physics, Metaphysics, Ethics,* and *On the Soul,* were available in the West. So much attention was accorded Aristotle's system that he was regularly referred to in the writings of Christian authors simply as "the Philosopher."

The reintroduction of Aristotle's thought into western culture was accompanied by influential commentaries from the Islamic philosophers ibn-Sina (980–1037), known in Latin as Avicenna, and ibn-Rushd (1126–98), known in Latin as Averroës. The Latin Averroists (i.e., Christian theologians who accepted Averroës's interpretation of Aristotle) held that faith and reason operate in separate spheres and that philosophy should be independent of theology. Siger of Brabant, the leading Latin Averroist in the thirteenth century, professed, as a Christian, belief in the creation of the universe by God. As a philosopher, however, he claimed that Aristotle had demonstrated the eternity of the world so convincingly that his arguments could not be refuted by reason.[10] The contrary

---

7. Ibid., 3:258.

8. Richard of Saint-Victor, *On the Trinity,* in *Sources chrétiennes* (Paris: Editions du Cerf, 1959), 63:64.

9. Pelikan, *The Christian Tradition,* 3:260.

10. Scholastic theologians of the Middle Ages understood the use of the term "eternal" in an analogical sense. They generally accepted Boethius's definition of eternity (*The Consolation of Philosophy,* V, 6) as the simultaneously whole and perfect possession of interminable life. According to a strict understanding of the term, eternity then could be predicated only of God, for whom there is no beginning, no end, and no succession (of phases or time). Used analogically in reference to the world, "eternity" could be understood to mean that the world had no beginning or end or both, but not that the world did not

assertion of Christian faith was not unproblematic. After all, how could one speak intelligibly of an eternal God creating a temporally limited universe?

In the controversy concerning the eternity of the world, Thomas Aquinas occupied a position different from both Siger of Brabant, a Latin Averroist, and Bonaventure, a staunch critic of Latin Averroism. Aquinas believed that faith and reason could not lead to contradictory conclusions because the source of their truth (namely, God) was the same. He held, moreover, that faith perfected or raised to a higher level what could be known on the basis of reason. In reaction against Siger, Aquinas argued that reason cannot demonstrate that the world could *not* have had a beginning. In reaction against Bonaventure, he argued that reason cannot demonstrate that the world *had* to have a beginning. From Aquinas's perspective, eternal creation implies no intrinsic contradiction and is therefore possible.

If the essential element in a doctrine of creation is the affirmation of the total dependence of creatures on God for their existence, then whether that dependence has a beginning or not is a secondary consideration. Creation for Aquinas denotes dependence in being.[11] Even if the world had no beginning, it would still be a created world dependent on God. Christians need not fear that a creature lacking a beginning would rival God in duration. God alone possesses eternity immutably. This means that God not only has no beginning and end, but also that God does not change or develop through successive stages. God is not in time; God is changeless. On the other hand, a creature, even without a beginning, would develop through successive stages of time. Creatures change and are in time. As Aquinas pointed out in his *Summa,* philosophical demonstrations are inconclusive because temporal creation depends on God's free will (see Part I, q. 46, a. 1 below), and God's free will can be investigated by human reason only with regard to things which God must will of necessity (see Part I, q. 46, a. 2 below). What God wills about creatures is not a matter of necessity. Therefore, what God wills with regard to creatures can be known only by revelation, upon which faith rests. In short, Christians know that the world had, in fact, a beginning because revelation discloses this fact.

The need to reconcile tensions in the theology of the early church, as exemplified in Abelard's *Sic et Non* and in Lombard's *Sentences,* the need to respond to the heretical ideas of the Cathari and others, and the need to respond to the challenges of Aristotelian, Jewish, and Muslim interpretations of reality all contributed to the shape and content of theology in the medieval period. But they were not the only factors that contributed to the formulation of doctrine in this period. Personal religious experiences (such as mystical encounters with the divine) and the personal integration of Christian faith with other ideas and trends also contributed to reflections about the nature of God's activities vis-à-vis the world. John Scotus Erigena in the ninth century, for example, integrated Neoplatonic philosophy into his interpretation of God's creative activity. As a consequence, Erigena's description of God's creative activity bears resemblance to

---

move through a series of successive states. See St. Thomas Aquinas, Siger of Brabant, St. Bonaventure, *On the Eternity of the World,* trans. and intro. Cyril Vollert et al. (Milwaukee: Marquette University Press, 1964), 5.

11. See Thomas Aquinas, *Summa Theologiae,* I, q. 44, a. 1.

the Neoplatonic notion of emanation and his understanding of the God-world relation has a pantheistic cast.[12]

In the twelfth century, Hildegard of Bingen recorded her visions and her interpretation of them in her complex and detailed *Scivias* (*Know the Ways of the Lord* or *Know the Ways of Light*). In this book we find personal, visionary experience addressed to the specific needs of the historical situation of the church. At the time, secular rulers regularly interfered in the administration of the church's operations and the clergy were often ill-suited for the pastoral duties to which they were assigned. Hildegard saw herself as a visionary and prophetic reformer. She placed herself squarely within the camp supporting the reform program begun by Pope Gregory VII (1073–85). In particular, she opposed clerical immorality, simony, and the subordination of the church's prelates to secular powers. The *Scivias* was addressed primarily to a clerical and monastic audience, in particular, male theologians who had failed to adequately preach and teach the mysteries of the faith. In the excerpt below, from Book II of the *Scivias*, Hildegard deals with the theme of redemption.

In this vision, the first vision recorded in Book II, Hildegard brings together God's creative and redemptive activities. Here she describes God's creative activity on the model of an act of production, not creation out of nothing. In the creation of heaven and earth, God is portrayed as a blacksmith who forges the world (see Vision One and sect. 6 below). Hildegard maintains the fire imagery in her depiction of the creation of human beings, but blends it with the Genesis account of humankind's creation out of the earth. She employs the interplay between light and darkness, such as is found in John's gospel, to describe the redemptive process by which the Redeemer brought humankind out of the darkness into which it had fallen. But Hildegard's interpretation of the Fall is different from what is portrayed in Genesis. Whereas Adam's taking of the fruit of the tree of knowledge of good and evil constitutes the sin in the Genesis account, here the refusal to take the "white flower" constitutes sin. As Barbara Newman has commented, the white flower represents the precept of obedience. Its refusal thrusts Adam (humanity) into deep darkness.[13] God's redemptive activity is then described as a gradual process. The darkness of sin is illumined by the "stars" of the patriarchs,

---

12. The following exchange is found in Erigena's *Periphyseon* (*Division of Nature*), Book I, sect. 72: "Teacher: 'Well, then, God did not have being before He made everything.' Student: 'No, because otherwise making everything would be accidental to Him. If it were, then motion and time would be understood in reference to Him. For He would have moved Himself to make what He had not already made, and He would be prior in time to His action, which was not coessential or coeternal with Himself.' Teacher: 'God's making [action, *facere*], then, is coeternal and coessential with Himself.... God's being and making, then, are not two different things, but the very same.... When we hear, then, that God makes all things, we should simply understand that God is in all things, i.e., that He subsists as their essence. He alone by Himself truly has being, and He alone is everything which is truly said to be in things endowed with being. None of those things with being really has being naturally inherent in itself. Whatever is truly understood in it, receives being by participation in Him who, by Himself, alone truly has being'" (John the Scot, *Periphyseon: On the Division of Nature*, trans. Myra L. Uhlfelder [Indianapolis: Bobbs-Merrill, 1976], 97).

13. "The forbidden fruit of Genesis is here transmogrified into a blossom that the man is *supposed* to pluck, so that his sin becomes one of omission; thus obedience is seen as a positive good and evil as a privation. This revisionist view expresses Hildegard's idea that the 'knowledge of good and evil' is God's gift to humanity rather than the devil's temptation" (Barbara J. Newman, "Introduction" to Hildegard of Bingen, *Scivias*, trans. Columba Hart and Jane Bishop [New York: Paulist Press, 1990], 30).

then by the prophets, culminating in John the Baptist and finally in Christ, who is described as the radiance of dawn.

In this vision, Hildegard lays out an understanding of creation that establishes a strong connection between human beings and the world. Human beings contain within themselves "the likeness of heaven and earth." Conversely, the structure of human beings is "wholly in every creature" (see Vision One, sect. 2 below). God's creative activity stamps creatures in similar ways. It is also important to note that Hildegard emphasizes the loveliness of creation and the hierarchical ordering of creatures (see sect. 6 below). God's love and power are exhibited in divine creativity. Like some other medieval theologians, she used a maternal image of God to stress the point that life and nourishment come from God (see sect. 7 below).

In the medieval period, the reconciliation of divine love and divine power with regard to human destiny posed a challenge for theologians, just as it did in other periods of the church's history. If God is love and if God created humanity because of the will to share divine life and love with them, how could one reasonably explain the condemnation of so many people to eternal damnation? If God is power and if nothing can hinder the fulfillment of the divine will, does this not mean that God willed the Fall and caused the reprobation of the damned? Why would God do such a thing? How could God be regarded as loving and just, if God made sinners to sin and then punished them for the sin they had to commit? These were the questions that challenged the theological imagination.

In the medieval period, Thomas Aquinas articulated a classic, scholastic response to this series of questions. In formulating his answers, Aquinas reaffirmed much of the Augustinian heritage. Dealing with the classic New Testament passage concerning the universal salvific will of God (1 Tim. 2:4), Aquinas offered three interpretations (see *Summa*, I, q. 19, a. 6 below). In the first two, he followed Augustine. In the third, he appealed to John Damascene in order to make a distinction between the antecedent and the consequent will of God. God's antecedent will has to do with what God wills human beings generally, without reference to the specific circumstances of each individual. God's consequent will has to do with what God wills specifically for each individual in his or her particular circumstances. Whereas God's antecedent will is not always fulfilled, God's consequent will is. According to God's antecedent will, we can say that God truly does will all people in general to be saved. According to God's consequent will, we can say that God wills those in a state of mortal sin to be condemned. Both the salvation of some and the condemnation of others happen according to God's plan. As the universal cause of all things, God's will always achieves its effect.

In the excerpt from the *Summa* below, we can see how Aquinas had to deal not only with the passage from 1 Tim. 2:4, but also with other scriptural passages that pose a problem for an understanding of God's activities in relation to human beings. In Part I, q. 19, a. 7, Aquinas sought to explain those passages in the Bible that seem to suggest that God's will changes in response to what human beings do. Like his predecessors, Aquinas rejected the notion of change in God's will so as to protect the understanding of God as immutable and eternal. Consequently, he distinguished between a change of will (which does not happen with God) and the will for a change in some things (which can happen with God). Aquinas points out, moreover, that the biblical passages that seem to suggest a change of will in

God are to be understood metaphorically. His basic point, however, is firm: God's will is always fulfilled, not only with regard to *what* actually happens, but also with regard to *how* it happens (see *Summa*, I, q. 19, a. 8 below).

Such a firm claim for the necessary effectiveness of God's willing leads immediately into the problem of evil. If God's will is always fulfilled and if evil is a reality in the world, then God must, in some sense, will evil. It is important to note that, in formulating his response to this problem, Aquinas criticized some of his theological predecessors, including Augustine (*Enchiridion,* chs. 10 and 96, also included in this volume; see above), for imprecision in their statements on the issue. Augustine and Pseudo-Dionysius had said that the existence of evil somehow contributes to the overall beauty and perfection of the universe. By contrast, Aquinas affirmed that the existence of evil does not directly, but only indirectly, contribute to the beauty of the universe. Thomas had to endorse this position because he assumed that rational beings can only directly will what is good — that is, what is desirable. Now sometimes rational beings will desire something evil indirectly as the consequence of something good they desire directly. On the basis of this distinction, Aquinas concluded that God (indirectly) wills human suffering (physical evil) when God (directly) wills the good to which suffering is attached. For example, in willing justice (directly) God wills penalty (indirectly). Or, willing to maintain the balance of nature, God wills that some things should follow their natural course and die (see *Summa*, I, q. 19, a. 9; see also I, q. 22, a. 2 ad 2). In keeping with this distinction between the direct and the indirect intent of God's activities, Aquinas concludes that God neither wills evil to be or not to be. God simply allows evil to happen, and this is good. For God can bring good out of evil.

Similarly, by making distinctions between a universal and a particular cause, Aquinas attempted to demonstrate the compatibility of human freedom and divine providence. All things fall under the sway of God as universal cause, who preserves creatures in existence. If any creature did not fall under God's universal causality, it would fall into nothingness. The very ability of human free will to function goes back to God as its cause. Yet God permits people, through the exercise of their wills, to be the particular cause of their particular actions (see *Summa*, I, q. 22, a. 2, ad 4). Although God immediately and directly assigns the purpose of everything in the divine mind, God executes this purpose not directly, but through the functioning or causality of intermediaries. Aquinas reminded his readers that God makes use of intermediaries not because of any impotence or deficiency in God, but because of the abundance of God's love and goodness. God imparts to creatures — for example, human beings — a particular dignity by permitting them to share in the causation of events (see *Summa*, I, q. 22, a. 3).

Aquinas took up the question of predestination in the context of considering God's providential activity. Aquinas's exposition of the doctrine of predestination follows the lines he established in the preceding questions. On the one hand, both predestination and reprobation fall under God's will, just as all things fall under the sway of divine universal causality. On the other hand, particular causes function under the umbrella of this universal causality. In this sense, the reprobate flounders in this or that sin on the basis of his or her own responsibility (see *Summa*, I, q. 23, a. 3 ad 3). In order to uphold the goodness and benevolence of God, Aquinas uses the language of "allow" and "permit," rather than the direct language of "make" and "cause" with regard to reprobation. He reminds his readers that God loves all creatures, including the reprobate, insofar as God wills some good for every creature (see *Summa,* I, q. 23, a. 3 ad 1). Although he shares Augustine's insistence upon the necessity of grace for salvation and Augustine's rejection of foreknowledge of merits as the cause of predestination, Aquinas nonetheless attempts to avoid the conclusion of double predestination. He does this by distinguishing between the causality of reprobation and the causality of predestination (see *Summa,* I, q. 23, a. 3 ad 2). Correlative to his discussion of evil and God's will, Aquinas affirms in this context that the predestination of some and the reprobation of others contribute, on the one hand, to the completeness of the universe and, on the other, to the revelation of God's glory and mercy, without compromise to justice (see *Summa,* I, q. 23, a. 5 ad 3).

The Augustinian heritage is also evident in the excerpt from Catherine of Siena's *Dialogue,* written approximately one century after the death of Aquinas. Both its continuity, as well as its discontinuity, with her theological predecessors is immediately evident. With regard to content, there is considerable continuity. Catherine, for example, incorporates into her work the Augustinian notion of the psychological trinity. That is, she reports that human beings are made in the trinitarian image: they possess memory (which represents the Father), understanding (which represents the Son), and will (which represents the Holy Spirit). Using the metaphor of a city to describe the soul, Catherine identifies the city's three main gates as memory, understanding, and will (see sect. 144). In addition, Catherine repeats the traditional conviction of faith that God's providence extends to all things (see sects. 135 and 137 below) and that divine providence is not incompatible with the reality of suffering and evil.

On the other hand, Catherine's interpretation of divine providence bears a different emphasis. She emphasizes very strongly love as the primary motive behind God's activities. God's love is described as "tender" (sect. 138 below), "unspeakable" in degree (sect. 143 below), and "immeasurable" in scope and depth (sect. 144 below). God's love is so strong and intense that Catherine replies to God: "O mad lover! And you have need of your creature? It seems so to me, for you act as if you could not live without her, in spite of the fact that you are Life itself..." (sect. 153 below).

The contrasts between Catherine's *Dialogue* and Thomas's *Summa* have to do not only with their different orientations, but also with the different genre of their works. Thomas's *Summa* was intended as an encyclopedic compendium of theology, to be used as a textbook for students beginning their study of theology. Catherine's *Dialogue* was intended to be a description of her mystical encounter with God as well as a guide to those who wanted to ascend higher in their spiritual journey to God. The structure and the orientation of the works, therefore, are different. Whereas Thomas's *Summa* has the tone of rational argumentation, Catherine's *Dialogue* has the tone of personal conversation. Whereas the *Summa* attempts to resolve different interpretations of the articles of faith, laid out in systematic fashion, the *Dialogue* attempts to describe an encounter with God and the ecstatic effects of such an encounter. It is worth noting that the genres of dialogue and vision are more common in this period among female Christian authors than among male Christian authors. And it is not uncommon to find in female authors, such as Catherine, Hildegard of Bingen, and Julian of Norwich, statements of profound "humility." These women often referred to themselves as unlearned and unworthy. Although these confessions can be interpreted as authentic expressions of personal self-assessment, they can also be understood to be rhetorical devices, by which the women hoped to appear in conformity with the expectations of women by medieval society. Insofar as women were not expected to be authoritative theologians, they had to find some manner of expressing their theological insights that would not "offend" the social stereotype of and bias against women. One effective device would be to identify their theological insights as simply the result of a vision or declaration they had received from God and to insist that they were unworthy to receive such a divine revelation. In such a way, women could conform to the conventional image of women while locating the authority of their statements in God, and not in themselves.

Catherine of Siena died during the early years of the Great Western Schism (1378–1417), which saw the western church divided in loyalty to at first two and then three claimants to the papal throne. Throughout the fourteenth century and into the fifteenth century, there were calls for the reform of the church "in head and members" (that is, from the top down). Some, such as Wycliffe in England and Hus in Bohemia, called for a church that lived more simply and regulated its beliefs and practices in greater conformity to the scriptures. With the development of humanism in the late fifteenth and early sixteenth century, there were calls to "return to the sources." In the church, this meant a return to the Bible and the witness of the early church. As a result, there was a renewed interest in the study of Greek and, after the publication of Johannes Reuchlin's Hebrew grammar in 1506, also Hebrew. Lay people were becoming increasingly literate. They wanted to know for themselves the roots of the church's beliefs and practices. The invention of the printing press in the mid-fifteenth century made possible the wide dissemination of lexicographical and grammatical handbooks as well as different versions of the Bible. Critical of scholastic theology as arid intellectualism, Christian humanists like Erasmus of Rotterdam proposed a simpler, less dogmatic understanding of Christian faith. The fundamental core of Christianity, according to most humanists, was the law of love as revealed by Jesus in the gospel.

Martin Luther and John Calvin wrote in this context of a return to the Bible and reform of the church. As a professor of scripture at the University of Wittenberg, Luther had occasion to reflect and comment upon the meaning of scripture. In the context of his exegesis of Paul's letter to the Romans, Luther laid out his understanding of the doctrine of predestination.[14] Already in these lectures, written and delivered in 1515 and 1516, we find evidence of the new understanding of the "righteousness of God" that set him free from the turmoil he had experienced as a monk. He had been taught that God would not love him unless he had done his very best. Through careful reflection upon the Bible, especially the letters of Paul, Luther came to see that God freely chose to make some people righteous.

---

14. Although they were published for the first time in 1908, Luther's lectures on the letter to the Romans are regarded today as one of Luther's most important works. Karl Holl, one of the preeminent Luther scholars of the first half of the twentieth century, regarded the lectures as an unsurpassed achievement in exegesis. Luther himself regarded the lectures as significant. See Wilhelm Pauck, "General Introduction," *Luther: Lectures on Romans* (Philadelphia: Westminster Press, 1961), xvii; Karl Holl, *Luthers Bedeutung für den Fortschritt der Auslegungskunst*, 2d ed. (Tübingen, 1923), 550.

Their righteousness or "justification" was a gift from God, not a human work. Righteousness was a free, unmerited gift of a loving God.

Although Luther touches upon the theme of divine love in the excerpt below, speaking of God's love as "immutable" and "steady," the theme's resonance there differs from that given it by Catherine of Siena. Like Catherine, Luther also explains the apparent contradiction between election and being subject to trials in terms of the gratuity of salvation. In Catherine's *Dialogue,* we read that God sometimes keeps the soul, beloved of God, in distress so that "she will trust not in herself but in me" (sect. 144 below). In similar fashion, Luther says that God has exposed the elect to "as many rapacious graspings as there are evils" because God "wants to show that he saves us not by our merits but by sheer election and his immutable will" (see below). Aquinas had also asserted that God's will, not human merits, determined who was predestined to eternal life and who was not.

What then is the difference between Aquinas's and Luther's exposition of predestination? In Aquinas we find an explanation of divine providence and predestination that uses distinctions between God's antecedent and God's consequent will, between final causality and meritorious causality, and so on. Scholastic theologians after Aquinas continued, and in some cases furthered, this tradition of subtle distinctions to resolve apparent tensions in the testimony of the Bible and the church's tradition concerning predestination. Luther, however, rejected this practice of subtle distinctions as empty talk or equivocation. Instead of scholastic argumentation, Luther appealed instead to the definite testimony of the Bible. He insisted on this straightforward approach to the issue for at least two reasons. First, the Bible is the principal authority in theology and in the church's life. This conviction will become the fundamental Protestant principle of *sola scriptura* (scripture alone is the church's authority). Second, biblical proclamation is more effective than scholastic argumentation in addressing the pastoral needs of the people.

In the second part of his exposition of Romans 8:28–39, Luther enumerates the principal objections against a strict doctrine of predestination. He begins with the objection from free will, which will be the source of public debate between himself and the humanist Erasmus ten years later (1525). Of all the objections raised, he finds the weightiest one to be the difficulty expressed in this question: Why does God harden the will of some people, so that they are incapable of following the law, when God has issued commandments for people to follow? In response, Luther appeals to Paul and Augustine, both of whom make two points. First, human beings are too limited in their understanding to comprehend the ways of God. Second, God has rights over humanity and can do as God pleases. Whatever God wills, is just (see section II below). Luther follows Augustine in his interpretation of the universal salvific will of God (alluded to in 1 Tim. 2:4) and in the distinction he draws between a "voluntary" will and a will that is authentically free.

Luther declares that the common arguments against predestination derive from "prudence of the flesh." This kind of prudence is foolishness in comparison with the prudence of the spirit. Luther's critique of human prudence anticipates the contrast he subsequently develops between a theology of glory, which imagines it can speak correctly and comprehensively about God on the basis of human reason, and a theology of the cross, which offers true and complete knowledge of God in Christ crucified. Those who have the "prudence of the spirit" know that salvation consists "in no way" of the person's action, but that "it can be found only outside itself, namely, in the election of God" (see III below). Those who have this spiritual prudence delight in the teaching concerning predestination. Luther's heavy emphasis on God's action in human salvation, without any significant contribution on the part of human beings, contrasts with the attempt by many scholastic theologians to defend some small role for free human activity, cooperating with grace in the process of justification and salvation. His divergence from these scholastic concerns did not trouble Luther:

> What others have learned from Scholastic theology is their own affair. As for me, I know and confess that I learned there nothing but ignorance of sin, righteousness, baptism, and of the whole Christian life. I certainly did not learn there what the power of God is, and the work of God, the grace of God, the righteousness of God, and what faith, hope, and love are. . . . Indeed, I lost Christ there, but now I have found him again in Paul.[15]

John Calvin concurred with Luther concerning both the formal and material foundational principles of the Protestant Reformation. That is, he too acknowledged scripture alone as the authoritative source of the church's teaching and he affirmed that justification and salvation occurred by faith alone. Consequently, Calvin held that those who are saved have been chosen by God, without any regard for their merits. In his exposition of the doctrine of predestination, Calvin emphasized the sovereignty and glory of God. In keeping with the Augustinian heritage, Calvin insisted that everything happens according to God's will, even the crimes of evildoers. In contrast to the major scholastics, however, Calvin rejected the distinction between divine will and divine permission. As we have seen, Aquinas and others had made this distinction in an attempt to exonerate God from direct involvement in the commission of evil, while maintaining God's omnipotence. Calvin, calling upon the support of biblical testimony (e.g., the story of Job), rejected this distinction. In the excerpt below, he concludes that "whatever men or Satan himself may instigate, God nevertheless holds the key, so that he turns their efforts to carry out his judgments" (see Book I, ch. 18, 1).

This clear, unqualified affirmation of God's providential and predestinating activity, of course, meant that Calvin would be constrained to explain the apparent contradiction between God's goodness and power, on the one hand, and the performance of evil deeds in history, on the other. In the tradition of Paul and Augustine, Calvin declared that the performance of seemingly evil deeds does not mean that the divine will is at war with itself nor that the divine will changes. It may appear so to us because of "our mental incapacity" to comprehend the ways of God (see Book I, ch. 18, 3 below). But God would not allow or will evil to be done unless God could bring good out of it. The performance of both good and evil give occasion to show forth God's glory (see Book I, ch. 15, 8). As was the case with Augustine, so too with Calvin: God's will, not human standards of

---

15. Weimar Edition of *Luther's Works*, vol. 12, p. 414, l. 22, cited by Pauck, "General Introduction," xxxix–xl.

justice, determines what is right: "For God's will is so much the highest rule of righteousness that whatever he wills, by the very fact that he wills it, must be considered righteous" (see Book III, ch. 23, 2 below). For Calvin, this means that God even predestined the fall into sin. Remaining thoroughly consistent in his insistence upon the omnipotence and sovereignty of God, Calvin rejects his critics' claim that at least before the Fall humanity was free to determine their own future destiny. In response, Calvin points out the inconsistency in their position. The critics accepted the predetermined consequences of original sin, yet they rejected the idea that the Fall itself was predetermined. Everything happens by God's decree, Calvin reminds them. God does not simply know what is to happen, God makes it happen: "The decree is dreadful indeed, I confess. Yet no one can deny that God foreknew what end man was to have before he created him, and consequently foreknew because he so ordained by his decree" (see Book III, ch. 23, 7 below).

Calvin's teaching concerning God's predestinating activity continued to be a source of controversy even after his death in 1564. In the early seventeenth century, it became the focus of debate at the Synod of Dort. Dutch Calvinism endorsed Calvin's strict and consistent position concerning predestination, while Arminius and Wesleyan Methodism moderated it. Moreover, the specific issue of predestination was taken up, beginning in the seventeenth century, into the larger question about the credibility of divine providence within an increasingly scientific understanding of the world. That part of the story continues in the next and final section of this book.

TEXTS

Hildegard of Bingen (1098–1179)

Scivias (1141–51), Book 2, Vision 1, Sections 1, 2, 5–7*

Vision One: The Redeemer

And I, a person not glowing with the strength of strong lions or taught by their inspiration, but a tender and fragile rib imbued with a mystical breath, saw a blazing fire, incomprehensible, inextinguishable, wholly living and wholly Life, with a flame in it the color of the sky, which burned ardently with a gentle breath, and which was as inseparable within the blazing fire as the viscera are within a human being. And I saw that the flame sparked and blazed up. And behold! The atmosphere suddenly rose up in a dark sphere of great magnitude, and that flame hovered over it and gave it one blow after another, which struck sparks from it, until that atmosphere was perfected and so Heaven and earth stood fully formed and resplendent. Then the same flame was in that fire, and that burning extended itself to a little clod of mud which lay at the bottom of the atmosphere, and warmed it so that it was made flesh and blood, and blew upon it until it rose up a living human. When this was done, the blazing fire, by means of that flame which

*Reprinted from *Hildegard of Bingen* by Mother Columba Hart and Jane Bishop, © 1990 by the Abbey of Regina Laudis: Benedictine Congregation Regina of the Strict Observance Inc. Used by permission of Paulist Press. Pp. 149–52.

burned ardently with a gentle breath, offered to the human a white flower, which hung in that flame as dew hangs on the grass. Its scent came to the human's nostrils, but he did not taste it with his mouth or touch it with his hands, and thus he turned away and fell into the thickest darkness, out of which he could not pull himself. And that darkness grew and expanded more and more in the atmosphere. But then three great stars, crowding together in their brilliance, appeared in the darkness, and then many others, both small and large, shining with great splendor, and then a gigantic star, radiant with wonderful brightness, which shot its rays toward the flame. And in the earth too appeared a radiance like the dawn, into which the flame was miraculously absorbed without being separated from the blazing fire. And thus in the radiance of that dawn the Supreme Will was enkindled.

And as I was trying to ponder this enkindling of the Will more carefully, I was stopped by a secret seal on this vision, and I heard the voice from on high saying to me, "You may not see anything further regarding this mystery unless it is granted you by a miracle of faith."

And I saw a serene Man coming forth from this radiant dawn, Who poured out His brightness into the darkness; and it drove Him back with great force, so that He poured out the redness of blood and the whiteness of pallor into it, and struck the darkness such a strong blow that the person who was lying in it was touched by Him, took on a shining appearance and walked out of it upright. And so the serene Man Who had come out of that dawn shone more brightly than human tongue can tell, and made His way into the greatest height of inestimable glory, where He radiated in the plenitude of wonderful fruitfulness and fragrance. And I heard the voice saying to me from the aforementioned living fire: "O you who are wretched earth and, as a woman, untaught in all learning of earthly teachers and unable to read literature with philosophical understanding, you are nonetheless touched by My light, which kindles in you an inner fire like a burning sun; cry out and relate and write these My mysteries that you see and hear in mystical visions. So do not be timid, but say those things you understand in the Spirit as I speak them through you; so that those who should have shown My people righteousness, but who in their perversity refuse to speak openly of the justice they know, unwilling to abstain from the evil desires that cling to them like their masters and make them fly from the face of the Lord and blush to speak the truth, may be ashamed. Therefore, O diffident mind, who are taught inwardly by mystical inspiration, though because of Eve's transgression you are trodden on by the masculine sex, speak of that fiery work this sure vision has shown you."

The Living God, then, Who created all things through His Word, by the Word's Incarnation brought back the miserable human who had sunk himself in darkness to certain salvation. What does this mean?

1. On God's Omnipotence

This blazing fire that you see symbolizes the Omnipotent and Living God, Who in His most glorious serenity was never darkened by any iniquity; *incomprehensible,* because He cannot be divided by any division or known as He is by any part of any of His creatures' knowledge; *inextinguishable,* because He is that Fullness that no limit ever touched; *wholly living,* for there is nothing that is hidden from Him or that He does not know; *and wholly Life,* for everything that lives takes its life from Him, as Job shows, inspired by Me, when he says:

2. Words of Job on This Subject

"Who is ignorant that the hand of the Lord has made all these things? In His hand is the soul of every living thing and the spirit of all human flesh" [Job 12:9–10]. What does this mean? No creature is so dull of nature as not to know what changes in the things that make it fruitful cause it to attain its full growth. The sky holds light, light air, and air the birds; the earth nourishes plants, plants fruit and fruit animals; which all testify that they were put there by a strong hand, the supreme power of the Ruler of All, Who in His strength has provided so for them all that nothing is lacking to them for their use. And in the omnipotence of the same Maker is the motion of all living things that seek the earth for earthly things like the animals and are not inspired by God with reason, as well as the awakening of those who dwell in human flesh and have reason, discernment, and wisdom. How?

The soul goes about in earthly affairs, laboring through many changes as fleshly behavior demands. But the spirit raises itself in two ways: sighing, groaning, and desiring God; and choosing among options in various matters as if by some rule, for the soul has discernment in reason. Hence Man contains in himself the likeness of heaven and earth. In what way? He has a circle, which contains his clarity, breath, and reason, as the sky has its lights, air, and birds; and he has a receptacle containing humidity, germination, and birth, as the earth contains fertility, fruition, and animals. What is this? O human, you are wholly in every creature, and you forget your Creator; you are subject to Him as was ordained, and you go against His commands? . . .

5. By the Power of the Word of God Every Creature Was Raised Up

And you see that *the flame sparks and blazes up.* This is to say that when every creature was raised through Him, the Word of God showed His power like a flash of flame; and when He became incarnate in the dawn and purity of virginity, it was as if He blazed up, so that from Him trickles every virtue of the knowledge of God, and Man lived again in the salvation of his soul.

6. God's Incomprehensible Power Made the World and the Different Species

And the atmosphere suddenly rises up in a dark sphere of great magnitude. This is the material of Creation while still formless and imperfect, not yet full of creatures; it is a sphere, for it is under the incomprehensible power of God, which is never absent from it, and by the Supernal Will it rises up in God's great power in the twinkling of an eye. *And that flame hovers over it like a workman and gives it one blow after another, which strike sparks from it, until that atmosphere is perfected and so Heaven and earth stand fully formed and resplendent.* For the Supernal Word, Who excels every creature, showed that they all

are subject to Him and draw their strength from His power, when He brought
forth from the universe the different kinds of creatures, shining in their miraculous awakening, as a smith makes forms out of bronze; until each creature was
radiant with the loveliness of perfection, beautiful in the fullness of their arrangement in higher and lower ranks, the higher made radiant by the lower and the
lower by the higher.

7. After the Other Creatures Man Was Created from the Earthly Mud

*But then the same flame that is in that fire and that burning extends itself to a
little clod of mud, which lies at the bottom of the atmosphere;* this is to say that
after the other creatures were created, the Word of God, in the strong will of the
Father and supernal love, considered the poor fragile matter from which the weak
frailty of the human race, both bad and good, was to be produced, now lying in
heavy unconsciousness and not yet roused by the breath of life; *and warms it so
that it is made flesh and blood,* that is, poured fresh warmth into it, for the earth
is the fleshly material of humans, and nourished it with moisture, as a mother
gives milk to her children; and blows upon it until it rises up a living human, for
He aroused it by supernal power and miraculously raised up a human being with
intelligence of body and mind.

Thomas Aquinas (1224/25–74)

Summa Theologiae (1266–73), Part I, Question 19, Articles 6–9; Question 22, Articles 2–3; Question 23, Articles 3–5; Question 46, Articles 1–2*

Question 19: Will in God

Article 6: Is God's Will Always Fulfilled?

THE SIXTH POINT: 1. It seems not. St. Paul says, *God wills all men to be saved
and to come to knowledge of the truth* [1 Tim. 2:4]. This purpose does not in
fact come about. So God's will is not always fulfilled....

3. Furthermore, although first cause, God's will does not rule out intermediate
causes, as has been stated [art. 3]. Now an effect of a first cause can be hindered
by the defect of a secondary cause, thus the power of walking is hindered by
paralysis in the leg. So also can an effect of God's will be held up by defects of
secondary causes. God's purpose, therefore, is not always realized.

ON THE OTHER HAND there is the Psalmist saying, *Whatsoever he wills, he
does* [Ps. 115:3].

REPLY: God's will inevitably is always fulfilled.

---

*Reprinted from St. Thomas Aquinas, *Summa Theologiae,* vol. 5: *God's Will and Providence,* trans. Thomas Gilby. Copyright © 1967 Blackfriars. Used by permission of Cambridge University Press. Pp. 25, 27, 29, 31, 33, 35, 37, 39, 41, 43, 91, 93, 95, 97, 99, 101, 115, 117, 119, 121, 123, 125, 127, 129, 131. St. Thomas Aquinas, *Summa Theologiae,* vol. 8: *Creation, Variety and Evil,* trans. Thomas Gilby. Copyright © 1967 Blackfriars. Used by permission of Cambridge University Press. Pp. 65, 67, 69, 71, 73, 75, 77, 79, 81, 83.

Here is the evidence. Since there is a matching of form between an effect and its agent, the same sort of reasoning applies to efficient causes as to formal causes. With formal causes this is the rule, that although a thing can fail to have some particular form, it cannot be altogether formless; a thing may be neither human nor alive, but it cannot not be a being. Likewise with efficient causes. Something can result which is out of order with regard to one particular efficient cause engaged, but not with regard to the universal cause, which covers all particular causes. That one particular cause is stopped from producing its effect comes from the interference of another particular cause, yet this last itself is enveloped by the universal cause. No effect can in any way escape from the sway of the universal cause....

Because it is the universal cause of all things, God's will cannot but achieve its effect. So whatever seems to depart from his will from one point of view returns to it from another. Thus a man who insofar as he can abandons the divine will by sinning nevertheless re-enters its plan when by divine justice he is punished.

Hence: 1. The quotation from St. Paul, that *God wills all men to be saved,* can be understood in three senses.

First, by restricted application to where it fits, that is to say, that God wills those to be saved who are saved. As Augustine explains that it is not because there is no man whom he does not will to be saved, but because none is saved whom he does not will to be saved [*Enchiridion* 103].

Second, by application to each class of every individual, not to each individual of every class; in other words, God wills some to be saved of every condition, men and women, Jews and Gentiles, humble and great, but not all of every condition.

Third, according to Damascene [*De Fide orthodoxa* II, 29], it refers to an antecedent, not a consequent will. This distinction concerns the things willed, not divine willing itself, where there is no before or after.

To appreciate what this means, reflect that as each and every thing is good so also is it willed by God. Now a thing may be good or bad at first sight and looked at in isolation yet turn out the reverse when conjoined in its context with another element; thus, just as the matter stands, for a man to live is good and for him to die is bad, yet if you go on to qualify him as a murderer or public danger then that he should be put away is good and that he should remain at large is bad. Accordingly we can speak of a justice that *antecedently* wishes every man to live, but *consequently* pronounces the capital sentence. So by analogy God antecedently wills all men to be saved, yet consequently wills some to be condemned as his justice requires.

Now to will antecedently is not to will downrightly, but only in a certain respect. For willing goes out to things just as they really are and standing in all their particularity, so that we downrightly will a thing surrounded by all its circumstances; this is what is meant by "consequent will." Accordingly we may speak of a just judge then and there quite simply willing a murderer to be hanged, though in a certain respect, when the criminal is considered as a human being, he wills him to live: this last should be termed more a wishing than a sheer willing.

Clearly, then, whatever God wills simply speaking comes about, though what he wills antecedently does not....

3. A first cause can be prevented from achieving its effect through failure in a

secondary cause when it is not the universally first cause which embraces within itself all causality. Such, as we have shown [in the body of the article], is the will of God, and from its plan no effect can stray in any way at all.

Article 7: Is God's Will Subject to Change?

THE SEVENTH POINT: 1. Yes apparently. For the Lord says, *I regret that I have made man* [Gen. 6:7]. Whoever regrets what he has done has a will that changes. So God's will is changeable.

2. So also, Jeremiah speaks in the person of the Lord, *Sometimes I threaten to pluck out and pull down and destroy a nation or a kingdom. But if that nation on which I have pronounced turns from its evil, I also will repent of the evil which I threatened to do* [Jer. 18:7–8]. God, then has a changeable will....

ON THE OTHER HAND there is the text in *Numbers, God is not a man that he should lie nor like a son of man that he should change* [Numb. 23:19].

REPLY: God's will is altogether unchangeable. All the same note that to change your will is one matter, and to will a change in some things is another. While remaining constant, a person can will this to happen now and the contrary to happen afterwards. His will, however, would change were he to begin to will what he had not willed before, or cease to will what he had willed before.

Such readjustment presupposes a change either in the substantial disposition or the knowledge of the person who wills. Since the will is set on good, he can begin to will something new in two ways. First, because it starts to be good for him, which means that he must accommodate himself to a fresh situation, thus when winter comes he likes to warm himself at the fire, which was not the case during the summer. Or secondly, he finds out for the first time that something is good for him. Indeed to discover what earlier we did not appreciate is why we deliberate.

We have already shown that God's nature as well as his knowledge is altogether immutable [Part I, ques. 9, art. 1; ques. 14, art. 5]. So, therefore, is his will also.

Hence: 1. These words of the Lord have a metaphorical turn according to a human figure of speech. When we regret what we have made we throw it away. Yet this does not always argue second thoughts or a change of will, for we may intend in the first place to make a thing and scrap it afterwards. By similitude with such a procedure we refer to God having regrets. For instance in the account of the Flood, when he washed off the face of the earth the men whom he had made [Gen. 6:7].

2. ... To speak of God as repenting is to use the language of metaphor. Men are said to repent when they do not carry out what they threatened to do....

Article 8: Does God's Will Impose Necessity on Things?

THE EIGHTH POINT: 1. It would seem so. Augustine says, *No one is saved except whom God has willed to be saved. We must therefore beseech him to will, for if he does our salvation is bound to come about* [*Enchiridion* 103].

2. Again, every cause that cannot be hindered produces its effect of necessity; even nature works always to the same effect unless something stops it, as Aristotle remarks [*Physics* II, 8. 199B18]. Now God's will cannot be held up; St. Paul asks,

Who hath resisted his will? [Rom. 9:19]. This, then, lays a necessity on the things that are willed....

ON THE OTHER HAND God wills into being every good that is made. Were his will to impose necessity on the things he wills the consequence would follow that everything good inevitably came about. And so away would go deliberation and free choice and the like.

REPLY: The divine will imposes necessity on some things but not on all.

Some have wanted to find the reason in the intermediate causes at work, explaining that what God produces through necessary causes are necessary, and what he produces through contingent causes are contingent.

The explanation seems inadequate, and on two grounds. First, an effect of some primary cause is held up and rendered contingent by a defect in a secondary cause, as when the sun's power is ineffective because of some flaw in a plant. Yet no defect in a secondary cause can stop God's will taking effect. Secondly, were the distinction between necessary and contingent causes to be introduced merely by the secondary causes engaged, it would be marginal to God's intending and willing, a conclusion that does not answer to the situation.

This is better described by invoking the very effectiveness of the divine will. From a fully effective cause in operation an effect issues not only as to the fact that arrives but also as to the mode of its coming and being. It is because the powers of reproduction are not fully causal that offspring are born unlike their parents in qualities proper to their animal being. Since God's will is of all causes the most effective, the consequence is that not only those things come about which God wills, but also that they come about in the manner that God wills them to.

God wills some things to become real necessarily, and others contingently, in order to furnish the full equipment of the universe. Accordingly for some he has designed necessary causes which cannot fail, from which effects result necessarily, and for others defectible and contingent causes from which effects result contingently. Hence the ultimate reason why some things happen contingently is not because their proximate causes are contingent, but because God has willed them to happen contingently, and therefore has prepared contingent causes for them.

Hence: 1. Augustine's words are to be understood of a necessity in things willed by God that is hypothetical, not absolute. The following conditional proposition is necessarily true, "If God wills a thing it is bound to be."

2. Indeed nothing resists God's will, and from this it follows not only that everything God wills comes about, but also that it comes about necessarily or contingently just as he wills....

Article 9: Does God Will Evil?

THE NINTH POINT: 1. He does, it seems. He wills every good that is realized. For evils to happen is good, for Augustine says, *Although insofar as they are bad things are not good, all the same it is good that not only good things but also evil things should exist* [*Enchiridion* 96]. Therefore God wills evil.

2. Moreover, Dionysius says, *There will be evil contributing to the perfection of the whole* universe [*Divine Names* 4]. And Augustine says, *The wonderful beauty of the universe is built up of every part, and there even what is called evil,*

in proportion and its proper place, commends good things, for they all are the more pleasing and praised the more edged they are and thrown into sharper relief [*Enchiridion* 10]. God wills everything that goes to the perfection and beauty of the universe, for this above all is what he wills in Creation. Therefore evils are divinely willed.

3. Again, for evils to be and not to be are contradictory opposites. God does not will evils not to be, otherwise, since some do arise in fact, his will would then not always be fulfilled. Hence he does will them.

...REPLY: Since, as we have said [Part I, ques. 5, art. 1], to be good and to be desirable signify the same, and since evil is the opposite of good, it is out of the question that any evil as such can be directly wanted, either by natural appetite, or by animal appetite, or by intelligent appetite, which is will.

Nevertheless an evil is desired indirectly, as resulting from a good. And this appears in every kind of appetite. For no natural agent intends privation or destruction, but a form of good, and this may be coupled with deprivation of an opposite form of good, and the coming to be of one that spells the destruction of another. Thus a lion kills a deer for the sake of food and this involves death, and a fornicator seeks pleasure and this involves the ugliness of sin. Evil has a good attached to it, but this goes with being deprived of another good. No one would desire evil, not even indirectly, unless the concomitant good were more desired than the good of which the evil is the deprivation.

Now God wills no good more than his own goodness, though with regard to particular goods, he wills one more than another. Hence moral evil, which upsets the ordering of things to divine good, he in no way wills. Physical evil or suffering, however, he does will by willing the good to which it is attached. For instance in willing justice he wills penalty, and in willing to maintain the balance of nature he wills that some things should follow their constitutional course and die away.

Hence: 1. Some [e.g., Hugh of St. Victor] have held that although God does not will evils, he wills them to come to be and exist, for though they are not good it is well if they enter or are present. The reason they allege is that things which in themselves are evil are arranged to some good; they fancy they point to this arrangement by speaking of the good that arises from the arrival and presence of evils. Their manner of expression, however, is not correct. For evil is not ordered to good directly, but indirectly. That good should follow is beside the intention of anyone doing wrong: thus it was no part of the purpose of tyrants that the patience of martyrs should be displayed from their persecutions. You do not imply a real orientation towards good by talking about the goodness of evil entering or being present on the scene. For things are judged by what goes with them directly and essentially, not indirectly and incidentally.

2. As we have said [response to 1], evil does not conspire to the achievement and beauty of the universe except indirectly. In fact when Dionysius refers to evil contributing to the perfection of the whole he winds up by showing that he is arguing from an untenable premise.

3. "Evils come into being" and "evils do not come into being" are contradictory statements, but "to will evils to come into being" and "to will evils not to come into being" are not so opposed, since each is affirmative. God neither

wills evils to be nor wills evils not to be; he wills to allow them to happen. And this is good. . . .

Question 22: God's Providence

Article 2: Is Everything Subject to Divine Providence?

THE SECOND POINT: 1. It would seem not. What is provided for is not fortuitous. Were everything provided for by God then nothing would be fortuitous, and out goes chance and luck would disappear. This is contrary to the general opinion.

2. Besides, any wise guardian wards off harm and evil from his charges as much as he can. Yet we see many evils in things. Either God cannot prevent them, and so is not almighty, or he does not really care for all. . . .

4. Then also, a person left all on his own is not under the charge of a governing authority. Now God leaves men to fend for themselves, according to the text, *When God made man in the beginning, he left him in the hands of his own counsel* [Ecclus. 15:14]. Particularly is this the case with evil men, according to the text, *I gave them up according to the hardness of their hearts' desire* [Ps. 80:13, Vg; Ps. 81:12, NRSV]. Not all things, therefore, come under divine Providence. . . .

ON THE OTHER HAND the Scriptures describe divine wisdom, *It reaches from end to end mightily, and disposes all things gently* [Wisd. 8:1].

REPLY: Some have denied Providence altogether, like Democritus and the Epicureans, who maintained that the world was fashioned by chance. Others held that only immortal things came under Providence. . . .

However, we are bound to profess that divine Providence rules all things, not only in their general natures, but also as individuals.

Let us make ourselves clear. Since every efficient cause acts for an end, the purposed ordering of effects extends as far as the causality of the first cause engaged. Now something may crop up in the event which is outside the purpose of a cause at work from the entrance of another cause with another purpose. Now the causality of God, who is the first efficient cause, covers all existing things, immortal and mortal alike, and not only their specific principles but also the source of their singularity. Hence everything that is real in any way whatsoever is bound to be directed by God to an end; as the Apostle remarks, *The things that are of God are well-ordered* [Rom. 13:1]. Since his Providence is naught else than the idea whereby all things are planned to an end, as we have said [art.1], we conclude quite strictly that all things insofar as they are real come under divine Providence.

Similarly it has been shown that God knows everything, both general and particular [Part I, ques. 14, a. 11]. And since his knowledge is related to things like that of an artist to his works of art, as we have noted [Part I, ques. 14, a. 8], it must be that all things are set under his ordering, like works of art under the art that makes them.

Hence: 1. The universal cause is one thing, a particular cause another. An effect can be haphazard with respect to the plan of the second, but not of the first. For an effect is not taken out of the scope of one particular cause save by another particular cause which prevents it, as when wood dowsed with water will not catch fire. The first cause, however, cannot have a random effect in its own order, since all particular causes are comprehended in its causality. When an effect does escape from a system of particular causality, we speak of it as fortuitous or a chance happening, but this is with reference to a particular cause; it cannot stray outside the sway of the universal cause, and with reference to this we speak of it as foreseen; thus the meeting of two servants, in their eyes unexpected because neither knew the other's errand, was foreseen by their master who intentionally sent them where their paths would cross.

2. To have a limited responsibility and a universal providence are different. The first wards off harm to a particular charge so far as possible, but the second allows some defect in the particular lest the good of the whole be hampered. Thus the defects and death are said to be against the nature of the particular nature concerned, yet in accordance with the purpose of Nature as a whole, in that loss to one yields gain to another, indeed to that of the whole universe, for in the cycle from death to birth species are preserved. Since God is the universal guardian of all that is real, a quality of his Providence is to allow defects in some particular things so that the complete good of the universe be disentangled. Were all evils to be denied entrance many good things would be lacking in the world: there would be no life for the lion were there no animals for its prey, and no patience of martyrs were there no persecution by tyrants. Thus Augustine says, *Almighty God in no way would permit any evil in his works unless he were not so good and powerful that he could bring good even out of evil* [*Enchiridion* 11]....

4. The text which speaks of God leaving men to themselves is not intended to banish them from divine Providence; it means that their active power, unlike that of physical things, is not set to follow one narrow track. Physical things are acted on in the sense that they are directed to an end by another; they do not act like self-determining agents who shape themselves to a purpose, in the manner of rational creatures who deliberate and choose by free judgment. Hence the pointed expression, of their being *in the hand of their own devices*. Yet because the very act of freewill goes back to God as its cause, we strictly infer that whatever men freely do on their own falls under God's Providence. Indeed their providing for themselves is contained under God's providing as a particular under a universal cause.

God makes higher provision for the just than for the unjust, inasmuch as he does not let anything happen that would finally prevent their salvation; *All things work together for good to them that love God* [Rom. 8:28]. We speak of him as abandoning sinners, because he does not hold them back from moral evil; but it is not that he casts them out from his care altogether; they would fall into nothingness unless his Providence kept them in being.

The difficulty we are meeting seems to have been that which impressed Cicero and led him to except human affairs, about which we take counsel, from the sway of Providence....

Article 3: Does God Immediately Provide for All Things Himself?

THE THIRD POINT: 1. It would seem that God is not immediately engaged, for he should be invested with all the attributes of grandeur. Regal dignity requires subordinates as intermediaries for the administration of subjects, and *a fortiori* is this true of God.

2. Besides, you provide for something by setting it in order to an end, which in every case is its own good and completion. The work of every cause is to conduct its effect to a good, and therefore from every efficient cause derives the effect of the providence at work. Consequently if God provided for all things by himself and without intermediaries, all secondary causes would be put out of action....

ON THE OTHER HAND there is the text in *Job, Who hath given him charge over the whole world? Or who hath disposed the whole earth?* [Job 34:13] On this Gregory comments, *The world he himself established he himself rules* [*Moralia* XXIV, 20].

REPLY: There are two sides to providence, namely, the idea or planned purpose for things provided, and its execution, which is called government.

As for the first, God provides for all things immediately and directly. His mind holds the reason for each of them, even the very least, and whatsoever the causes he appoints for effects, he it is who gives them the power to produce those effects. Consequently the whole of their design down to every detail is anticipated in his mind.

As for the second, divine Providence works through intermediaries. For God governs the lower through the higher, not from any impotence on his part, but from the abundance of his goodness imparting to creatures also the dignity of causing....

Hence: 1. The royal dignity demands ministers to execute its provisions, but to lack a ruling policy for them to carry out would be inept. Any practical science is so much the better for attending to the details of its business.

2. As we have said, God's immediate Providence over all things does not exclude secondary causes from executing its ordered policy....

Question 23: Predestination

Article 3: Is Anybody Rejected by God?

THE THIRD POINT: 1. How is it possible? No one rejects whom he loves. God loves every man, according to *Wisdom, You love all the things that are, and loathe nothing that you have made* [Wisd. 11:24]. So God rejects no man.

2. Besides, if God rejects people, then reprobation must be to a person rejected like predestination to a person predestined. Predestination is the cause of those predestined being saved, and the parallel is that reprobation is the cause of those rejected being lost. This, however, is untrue; *Hosea* says, *Israel, thou hast destroyed thyself; only in me is thine help* [Hos. 13:9]. God, therefore, does not reject anyone.

3. Again, nobody should be held responsible for what he cannot avoid. And nobody can avoid being lost if God rejects him. *Ecclesiastes* warns us, *Consider the workings of God; who can make straight what he has made crooked?* [Eccles. 7:13]. Human beings then should not be blamed if they perish. But this is false. God, therefore, does not reprobate anyone.

ON THE OTHER HAND there is what is said in *Malachy* [sic], *I loved Jacob, but hated Esau* [Mal. 1:2–3].

REPLY: Some people God rejects. We have seen already that predestination is a part of Providence [art. 1], and that its workings allow some failures in the things in its charge [Part I, ques. 22, a. 2 ad 2]. Since by divine Providence human beings are ordained to eternal life, it also belongs to divine Providence to allow some to fall short of this goal. This is called reprobation.

As predestination is that part of Providence which relates to those who are ordained to be saved, so reprobation is that part which relates to those who fall out. Hence reprobation does not denominate foreknowledge merely, but introduces also another notion, as was said about Providence [Part I, ques. 22, a. 1 ad 3]. For as predestination includes the will to confer grace and glory, so reprobation includes the will to permit someone to fall into fault and to inflict the penalty of damnation in consequence.

Hence: 1. God loves all men and all creatures as well, inasmuch as he wills some good to all: all the same he does not will every sort of good to each. In that he does not will to some the blessing of eternal life he is said to hold them in hate or to reprobate them.

2. The causality of reprobation differs from that of predestination. Predestination is the cause both of what the predestinated expect in the future life, namely, glory, and of what they receive in the present, namely, grace. Reprobation does not cause what there is in the present, namely, moral fault, though that is why we are left without God. And it is the cause why we shall meet our deserts in the future, namely, eternal punishment. The fault starts from the free decision of the one who abandons grace and is rejected, so bringing the prophecy to pass, *Your loss is from yourself, O Israel.*

3. God's reprobation does not subtract anything from the rejected one's own ability. To say that he cannot acquire grace must be understood as expressing a hypothetical, not an absolute impossibility; likewise, as we have explained [Part I, ques. 19, art. 8 ad 1), one predestined must needs be saved, namely, on a conditional necessity, which does not impair freewill. Hence although one whom God reprobates cannot gain grace, nevertheless the fact that he flounders in this or that sin happens of his own responsibility, and therefore is rightly imputed to him for blame.

Article 4: Are the Predestined God's Elect?

THE FOURTH POINT:...

3. Furthermore, choice implies a certain discrimination. Yet God wishes all men to be saved, according to *1 Timothy* [1 Tim. 2:4]. Predestination, then, which pre-ordains men to salvation, is without election.

ON THE OTHER HAND there is the text in *Ephesians, He chose us in himself before the foundation of the world* [Eph. 1:4].

REPLY: By its very meaning predestination presupposes election, and election chosen loving.[1] The reason for this is that predestination, as we have said [art. 1],

---

1. The term translated here as "chosen loving" is *dilectio*, which is distinguished from *electio*.

is part of Providence, which is like prudence, as we have noticed [Part I, ques. 22, a. 1], and is the plan existing in the mind of the one who rules things for a purpose. Things are so ordained only in virtue of a preceding intention for that end. The predestination of some to salvation means that God wills their salvation. This is where special and chosen loving come in. Special, because God wills this blessing of eternal salvation to some, for, as we have seen [Part I, ques. 20, a. 3], loving is willing a person good, chosen loving because he wills this to some and not to others, for, as we have seen [art. 3], some he rejects.

Election and dilection operate differently in us and in God. When we love things our will does not cause them to be good; it is because they are good already that we are roused to love them; therefore we choose someone to love, and our choice precedes our loving. With God the converse is true. For when he chooses to love another and thereby wills him good, his will is the cause of the other being singled out and so endowed. Clearly, then, the notion of God's special loving logically precedes that of his choosing, and that of his choosing that of his predestining. Therefore all the predestined are picked loves....

3. As we have shown already [Part I, ques. 19, a. 6], God wishes all men to be saved by his antecedent will, which is not downright willing, but willing in a qualified sense, not by his consequent will, which is committed willing.

Article 5: Is the Foreknowledge of Merits the Cause of Predestination?

THE FIFTH POINT: 1. Apparently yes. St. Paul says in *Romans, Whom he did foreknow he also did predestinate* [Rom. 8:29]. Also, on the text, *I will have pity on whom I will have pity on* [Rom. 9:15], the *Gloss* quotes Ambrose, *I will grant mercy to him I foresee will turn to me with all his heart*. It does seem, then, that the foreknowledge of merits is the cause of predestination....

3. There is a text in *Romans, Is there injustice on God's part? By no means* [Rom. 9:14]. To grant equals unequal rewards seems unjust. Now all men are equals with respect to their nature and to original sin. Inequality enters because of the merits or demerits of their own personal actions. In the matter of their predestination or reprobation, then, God does not deal with them unequally except through foreknowing their different merits.

ON THE OTHER HAND there is St. Paul, *Not by the works of justice which we have done, but according to his mercy has he saved us* [Titus 3:5]. As he saves us so does he predestine us to be saved. Consequently the foreknowledge of merits is not the motive or reason of predestination.

REPLY: . . .

Others have held that merits pre-existing in this life are the motive and cause of predestination as an effect. The Pelagians thought that the first steps in well-doing come from us, while the finishing comes from God. So, they thought, predestination as an effect is given to one and not to another, because one makes a good start and prepares himself for it, while the other does not. Yet this also is against what St. Paul teaches, *We are not sufficient of ourselves to think anything as of ourselves* [2 Cor. 3:5]. You can find no human principle earlier than thought. It is not tenable, then, that we can initiate anything in ourselves that can be the reason for predestination as an effect.

And so there were others who held that the merits resulting from predestination considered as an effect are the reason for predestination, this being the meaning, that God gives grace to a person and fore-ordains that he will do so because he knows it will be used well, rather like a king presenting a horse to a knight knowing that he will ride it to good service. Yet they seem to draw a distinction between what springs from grace and what from freewill, as if the same effect could not come from each. Now manifestly what is from grace is the effect of predestination, and therefore cannot be stated as the reason for predestination, since it is implied in predestination....

Let us proceed accordingly; predestination as an effect can be considered in two ways, as to its parts and in its entirety. When analyzed we find nothing to stop one effect of predestination from being the motive and reason of another, so that a later effect may be the cause of an earlier according to a system of final causality, and an earlier of a later according to a system of meritorious causality, which comes back to having the material properly disposed. Thus we may say that God pre-ordains that he will give glory because of merit, and also pre-ordains that he will give grace to a person in order to merit glory.

Secondly, the effect of being predestined can be considered in its whole sweep. Then the effect of predestination in its completeness cannot have any cause on our part. Whatever there is in man ordering him to salvation is entirely comprised in predestination as a total effect, even down to his very preparing himself for grace. For this is not without God's help; thus the text at the end of *Lamentations, Turn thou us to thee, O Lord, and we shall be turned* [Lam. 5:21]. In this manner predestination considered as an effect in its entirety has the divine goodness for its reason; to this the whole effect of predestination is ordered as to an end, and from this it issues as from its first moving principle.

Hence: 1. The good use of grace foreknown by God is not the reason for conferring it, except, as we have explained, according to the turn of final causality....

3. Grounds for the predestination of some and the reprobation of others may be taken on divine goodness itself. God is said to do everything so that his goodness may be represented in things.... Thus for the completeness of the universe diverse grades of beings are required, some of high degree and some of humble. In order to maintain multiformity of real values, God allows evils to happen, lest, as we have said [Part I, ques. 2, a. 3 ad 1; ques. 22, a. 2], many goods be hindered.

Let us look at the whole human race as we do the universe. God wills to manifest his goodness in men, in those whom he predestines in the manner of mercy by sparing them, in those whom he reprobates in the manner of justice by punishing them. This provides a key to the problem why God chooses some and rejects others; it is offered by St. Paul, *What if God, desiring to show his wrath,* that is the vindication of his justice, *and to make known his power has endured,* that is, has permitted, *with much patience the vessels of wrath fit for destruction, in order to make known the riches of his glory for the vessels of mercy, which he hath prepared beforehand for glory* [Rom. 9:22]. And again, *In a great house there are not only vessels of gold and silver, but also of wood and clay; some to honor, some to dishonor* [2 Tim. 2:20].

Why does he choose some to glory while others he rejects? His so willing is the sole ground. Augustine says, *Wherefore he draws this one and not that one, seek not to decide if you wish not to err* [*Super Joannem* 26]. . . . In very much the same way it depends on the mere will of the builder that this particular stone is selected for this part of the wall and that for another, though his very art demands that some be here and others there.

On this account we cannot complain of unfairness if God prepares unequal lots for equals. This would be repugnant to justice as such were the effect of predestination a due to be rendered, not a favor. He who grants by grace can give freely as he wills, be it more be it less, without prejudice to justice, provided he deprives no one of what is owing. In the householder's words of the parable, *Take what is thine, and go thy way. Is it not lawful for me to do what I will with my own?* [Matt. 20:14–15].

Question 46: The Beginning of the World's Duration

Article 1: Has the Universe of Creatures Always Existed?

THE FIRST POINT: 1. It seems that the universe of creatures, which we name the world, never began but always was. Whatever has had a beginning was a possible before it began, otherwise its coming to be would have been impossible. If, therefore, the world had ever begun to be antecedently it would have been a possible. Now this possible to be is matter, in potentiality alike to existence which comes through a form, and nonexistence through its absence. If the world had begun to be, then matter existed previously. Matter, however, cannot exist without form, while as for matter together with form, that is what comprises the world. Therefore you would be saying that the world was before it began, which is unthinkable. . . .

3. Further, what is ungenerated does not begin to be, Aristotle shows that matter is ungenerated, and likewise the heavens. Hence the universe had no beginning. . . .

6. Or put it like this: a thing that changes another is either a natural or a voluntary agent.[2] Yet neither starts to do this without itself undergoing change beforehand. . . . As for the will, without suffering any interior change, it can delay doing what it proposes, yet this implies some change imagined, at least in the time-series. For instance he who wills to build a house tomorrow and not today, anticipates something tomorrow that is nonexistent today, and at least he expects that today will pass and tomorrow will come. Time is the measure of change; and so change is not absent from his proposal. It remains true, therefore, that before any new change begins another change preceded it, which is the conclusion of the fifth objection, namely, that change always was. . . .

8. Besides, God is before the world by a priority either of nature only or of time.[3] In the first case, since he is from eternity then so is the world. In the second case, since a before and after in duration is what time is, then time will have been before the universe, which is impossible.

2. A natural agent acts from blind necessity; a voluntary agent, from knowledge and often with deliberation.

3. Priority of nature means that something depends on another, as an effect depends upon its cause; priority of time means something is older than another.

9. Further, posit a sufficient cause and you posit its effect: a cause from which an effect does not result is partial and requires another for success. God, however, is the sufficient cause of the world, its final cause by reason of his goodness, its exemplar cause by reason of his wisdom, its efficient cause by reason of his power: this has already been shown [Part I, ques. 44, art. 1, 3, 4]. Since he is eternal, then so, too, is the world. . . .

ON THE OTHER HAND there are the words of our Lord, *And now, Father, glorify thou me in thy own presence with the glory which I had with thee before the world was made* [John 17:5]. And in *Proverbs* it is written, *The Lord possessed me in the beginning of his work, the first of his acts of old* [Prov. 8:22].

REPLY: Nothing apart from God has been from all eternity. And this is not to assert the impossible. We have shown that God's will is the cause of things. So then the necessity of their being is that of God's willing them, for, to appeal to Aristotle, the necessity of an effect depends on that of the cause. Next it has been established [Part I, ques. 19, art. 3] that, to speak without qualification, there is no need for God to will anything but himself. Hence there is no necessity for God to will an everlasting world. Rather the world exists just so long as God wills it to, since its existence depends on his will as on its cause. Therefore its existing always is not from inner necessity, and hence cannot be demonstratively proved.

Nor do the arguments advanced by Aristotle strictly demonstrate the thesis itself; their force is limited to countering the reasons put forward by the ancients for a beginning to the world in ways veritably out of the question. . . .

Hence: 1. Before the world existed it was possible for it to be, not indeed because of the passive potentiality of matter, but because of the active power of God. And the same is true even if we leave out the reference to his might, and we regard a pure possibility just from the association of terms not mutually exclusive: that Aristotle contrasts the possible and the impossible in this sense is evident.

. . . 3. Aristotle in the *Physics* proves that matter is ungenerated from its not having a subject from which it can come about, and in the *De caelo* that the heavens are not generated from their not having a contrary from which their production can start. Hence it is clear that in both cases the only justified conclusion is that matter and the heavens do not arise through generation, and particularly the latter, as some have maintained. Whereas we have shown [Part I, ques. 45, art. 2] why we hold that both are produced in existence by creation.

. . . 6. The first cause is a voluntary agent. Yet though his is an eternal will to produce an effect nevertheless he did not produce an eternal effect. This does not imply there was a change, before and after the effect, not even in terms of imaginary time. A particular cause, which works on one thing to make another, is to be conceived of differently from the universal cause, which makes the whole. The first produces a form, but presupposes matter; accordingly the form it introduces should be proportionate to the appropriate matter. Hence quite rightly you expect the form to be induced into such and not other matter, in order to match the difference there is between them. To expect this of God, however, is not reasonable, for he produces at once both matter and form, except in this sense, that he should produce the matter that fits the form and purpose of the thing he creates.

Again, a particular cause presupposes time as well as matter. With good reason it is observed acting in time after and not in time before, according to the image of one period succeeding another. The universal cause, however, which produces both the thing and time is not to be regarded as acting now and not before by imagining a succession of periods, as though time were presupposed to its action; though it is to be considered that he dated the effect according to his good pleasure and the fitting manifestation of his power. We are led to the knowledge of divine creative power more evidently from a world that began once upon a time than from a world that never did. For having a cause is not so manifest for a thing that was always as for one that was not always.

...8. God is before the world by duration. The term "before" here means the priority of eternity, not of time. Or you might say that it betokens an everlasting imaginary time, not time as really existing, rather as when we speak of nothing being beyond the heavens, the term "beyond" betokens merely an imaginary place in a picture we can form of other dimensions stretching beyond those of the body of the heavens.

9. As an effect of a cause that acts by nature follows from it according to the mode of its form so an effect of a cause that acts through will follows from it according to a form that is preconceived and defined: earlier discussion brought this out [Part I, ques. 19, art. 4; ques. 41, art. 2]. Well then, although God from eternity was the sufficient cause of the world, this does not demand our postulating that the world made by him is any other than as it is in the predetermination of his will, namely, as having existence after nonexistence, and thus the more clearly to tell of its author.

Article 2: Is It an Article of Faith That the World Began?

THE SECOND POINT: 1. No, for it appears to be a demonstrable conclusion, not a matter of faith, that the world began. For everything that is made has a beginning to its duration. Now that God is the cause producing the world can be demonstrated; indeed the more approved philosophers draw this conclusion. Accordingly it is demonstrable that the world began.

...5. That nothing can be God's equal is certain. Yet an eternal world would be his equal in duration. Hence it is certainly not eternal.

6. Moreover, if the world had always existed an infinity of days would have preceded today. An infinity of points, however, cannot be traversed. And so we would never have arrived at today, which is patently untrue.

...ON THE OTHER HAND the article of faith cannot be demonstratively proved, for faith is about things *that appear not* [Heb. 11:1]. That God is the creator of a world that began to be is an article of faith; we profess it in the Creed....

REPLY: That the world has not always existed cannot be demonstratively proved but is held by faith alone. We make the same stand here as with regard to the mystery of the Trinity.

The reason is this: the world considered in itself offers no grounds for demonstrating that it was once all new. For the principle for demonstrating an object is its definition....

Nor is demonstration open to us through the efficient cause. Here this is a voluntary agent. God's will is unsearchable, except as regards what he cannot but will, and his willing about creatures is not necessarily bound up with that, as we have seen [Part I, ques. 19, art. 3].

His will, however, can be manifested to man through Revelation, the ground of faith. That the world had a beginning, therefore, is credible, but not scientifically demonstrable.

And it is well to take warning here, to forestall rash attempts at demonstration by arguments that are not cogent, and so provide unbelievers with the occasion for laughing at us and thinking that these are our reasons for believing the things of faith.

Hence: 1. According to St. Augustine there were two opinions among philosophers who held the world was eternal [*City of God,* Book 11, ch. 4]. To some the world's substance did not come from God, an error not to be borne and to be convincingly refuted. To others, however, it existed from all ages yet all the same was produced by God....

For the explanation: we agree that an efficient cause which works through change must precede its effect in time, for the effect enters as the term of the action whereas the agent is its start. Yet in the event of the action being instantaneous and not successive, it is not required for the maker to be prior in duration to the thing made, as appears in the case of illumination. Hence they [e.g., Averroës] point out that because God is the active cause of the world it does not necessarily follow that he is prior to it in duration, for, as we have seen [Part I, ques. 45, art. 2 ad 3] creation, whereby he produced the world, is not a successive change.

...5. Even if it were everlasting the world would not be God's equal, as Boëthius points out towards the end of his *De consolatione* [V, 6], for the divine being is existence whole and all at once without succession, while it is not so with the world's being.

6. The objection proceeds on the assumption that given two extremes there is an infinity of intermediate points between them. Now a passage is always from one term to another, and whichever day from the past we pick on, there is only a limited number between then and today, and this span can be traversed.

Catherine of Siena (1347–80)

The Dialogue (1377), Sections 135, 137, 138, 143, 144, and 153*

Divine Providence

135. *Then the high eternal Father turned the eye of his mercy toward her with ineffable kindness, as if to show her that in all things his providence for humankind never fails anyone who is willing to receive it. And he uttered a tender complaint about humankind, saying:*

*Reprinted from *Catherine of Siena* by Suzanne Noffke, O.P. © 1980 by the Society of St. Paul the Apostle in the State of New York. Used by permission of Paulist Press. Pp. 277, 282–83, 297, 299, 301–3, 325–26.

O my dearest daughter, as I have told you so often, I want to be merciful to the world and provide for my reasoning creatures' every need. But the foolish take for death what I give for life, and are thus cruel to themselves. I always provide, and I want you to know that what I have given humankind is supreme providence. It was with providence that I created you, and when I contemplated my creature in myself I fell in love with the beauty of my creation. It pleased me to create you in my image and likeness with great providence. I provided you with the gift of memory so that you might hold fast my benefits and be made a sharer in my own, the eternal Father's power. I gave you understanding so that in the wisdom of my only-begotten Son you might comprehend and know what I the eternal Father want, I who gave you graces with such burning love. I gave you a will to love, making you a sharer in the Holy Spirit's mercy, so that you might love what your understanding sees and knows....

137. In general I provided for you in the Law of Moses in the Old Testament, and in many other holy prophets. In fact, I want you to know that before the coming of the Word my only-begotten Son, the Jewish people were never without a prophet to strengthen them and give them hope in their prophecies that my Truth, Prophet of prophets, would release them from slavery and make them free, would unlock heaven for them with his blood after it had been locked for so long. But once the gentle loving Word had come, no other prophet rose up among them. Thus they were assured that the one they had been waiting for had come, and there was no further need for prophets to announce him. But they did not recognize him and still do not recognize him because of their blindness.

After the prophets I provided for you in the coming of the Word, who was your mediator with me, God eternal. And after him I sent the apostles, the martyrs, the doctors and confessors. All these things my providence has done, and so, I tell you, will I continue to provide for you right up to the end. This is the general providence granted to everyone who is willing to receive its fruit.

And in my providence I give to each of you in particular the manner of life and death I choose. Hunger, thirst, loss of worldly position, nakedness, cold, heat, insults, abuse, slander — all these things I allow people to say and do to you. Not that I am the source of the malice and ill will of those who do these evil and harmful things; I only grant them their existence and time. I did not give them existence to sin against me and their neighbors, but so that they might serve me and others with loving charity. But I permit these actions either to test the virtue of patience in the soul who is their object, or to make the sinners aware of what they are doing.

Sometimes I let the whole world be against the just, and in the end they die a death that leaves worldly people stunned in wonder. It seems to them unjust to see the just perishing now at sea, now in fire, now mangled by beasts, now physically killed when their houses collapse on top of them. How unreasonable these things seem to the eye unenlightened by most holy faith! But not so to the faithful, for through love they have found and experienced my providence in all those great things. Thus they see and grasp that I do what I do providentially, only to bring about your salvation. Therefore they hold everything in reverence. They are not scandalized in themselves nor in my works nor in their neighbors, but pass through everything with true patience. My providence is never denied to anyone; it seasons everything.

Sometimes people think that the hail and storms and lightning I rain upon their bodies are cruel. In their judgment I have no care for their well-being. I have done these things to rescue them from eternal death, but they believe the opposite.

Thus do worldly people try to distort my every work and interpret it after their own base understanding. (138) But I want you, most beloved daughter, to see how patiently I have to bear with my creatures whom I have made in my image and likeness with such tender love....

143. The soul is either living in deadly sin, or imperfectly in grace, or she is perfect. Toward all I am generous in my providence, but in different ways, very wisely, as I see people have need.

Worldly people who are dead in mortal sin I wake up with the pricking or weariness they feel within their hearts in new and different ways — so many ways your tongue could never describe them. Sometimes, because of the insistence of the pains and pricking of conscience within their souls, they abandon the guilt of deadly sin. And sometimes their heart conceives love for deadly sin or for creatures apart from my will. But I always pluck the rose from your thorns. So I deprive them of places and times for fulfilling their own wishes until they are so tired of the interior suffering their sinfulness has brought them when they cannot fulfill their perverse wishes that they return to their senses. And the pricking of their conscience and heartfelt compunction lead them to throw away their madness. It can truly be called madness because, while they thought they had set their affection on something, when they begin to see they find nothing there. True, the creature they loved with such a wretched love was and is something, but what they got from it was nothing because sin is a nothing. But from this nothingness of sin, a thorn that pierces the soul, I pluck this rose to provide for their salvation.

What constrains me to do this? Not they, for they neither seek me nor ask for my help and providence except in sin and worldly pleasures and riches and honors. It is love that constrains me, because I loved you before you came to be. Without having been loved by you, I loved you unspeakably much. This is what constrains me to do it, along with the prayers of my servants.... Thus it has been said that I do not want sinners to die but to be converted and live [Ezek. 33:11]....

144. Do you know, dearest daughter, how I raise the soul out of her imperfection? Sometimes I vex her with evil thoughts and a sterile mind. It will seem to her that I have left her completely, without any feeling whatever. She does not seem to be in the world, because she is in fact not there; nor does she seem to be in me, because she has no feeling at all other than that her will does not want to sin.

I do not allow enemies to open this gate of the will, which is free. I do let the devils and other enemies of humankind beat against other gates, but not against this, which is the main gate guarding the city of the soul. The guard that stands at this gate, free choice, I have made free to say yes or no as he pleases.

The gates of this city are many. There are three main gates — memory, understanding, and will — and the last, if it so chooses always holds firm and guards the others. But if the will gives its consent, the enemy of selfish love and all the other enemies that follow after it come in. Then understanding surrenders to the darkness that is the enemy of light, and the recollection of injury makes memory surrender to the hatred that is the enemy of loving charity for one's neighbors. The soul harbors memories of worldly pleasures and delights in as many different ways as there are different sins against the virtues. . . .

I have told you all this, dearest daughter, to give you reason to weep at the sight of the noble city of the soul come to such misery, and to let you see what great evil comes forth from its main gate, the will, which I never give the soul's enemies leave to enter. But, as I have told you, I do let these enemies beat at the other gates. Thus I let understanding be battered by spiritual darkness, and memory seem to be bereft of any thought of me. And sometimes it will seem that all the body's other senses are being besieged in different ways. Though they are seeing and touching and hearing and smelling and walking in holy things, everything will seem to be a source of inconstancy, dishonor, and corruption.

But all this is not meant to be deadly. I do not will the soul's death so long as she is not so stupid as to open the gate of her will. I let her enemies stand outside, but I do not allow them to enter. They cannot enter unless her own will chooses to let them in.

And why do I keep this soul, surrounded by so many enemies, in such pain and distress? Not for her to be captured and lose the wealth of grace, but to show her my providence, so that she will trust not in herself but in me. Then she will rise up from her carelessness and her concern will make her run for protection to me her defender, her kind Father, the provider of her salvation. I want her to be humble, to see that of herself she is nothing and to recognize that her existence and every gift beyond that comes from me, that I am her life. She will recognize this life and my providence when she is liberated through these struggles, for I do not let these things last forever. They come and go as I see necessary for her. Sometimes she will think she is in hell, and then, through no effort of her own, she will be relieved and will have a taste of eternal life. The soul is left serene. What she sees seems to cry out that God is all aflame with loving fire, as she now contemplates my providence. For she sees that she has come [safely] out of this great flood not by any effort of her own. The light came unforeseen. It was not her effort but my immeasurable charity, which wanted to provide for her in time of need when she could scarcely take any more.

Why, when she was faithful to prayer and other things, did I not relieve her with light and take away the darkness? Since she was still imperfect, I did not want her taking credit for what was not hers.

So you see how the imperfect soul comes to perfection by fighting these battles, because there she experiences my divine providence, whereas before this she only believed in it. I have now guaranteed it to her through experience, and she has conceived perfect love because she has come to know my goodness in my divine providence and has thus risen above her imperfect love.

. . . 153. *Then that soul was as if drunk with love of true holy poverty. She was filled to bursting in the supreme eternal magnificence and so transformed in the abyss of his supreme and immeasurable providence that though she was in the vessel of her body it seemed as if the fire of charity within her had taken over and rapt her outside her body. And with her mind's eye steadily fixed on the divine majesty she spoke to the high eternal Father:*

O eternal Father! O fiery abyss of charity! O eternal beauty, O eternal wisdom, O eternal goodness, O eternal mercy! O hope and refuge of sinners! O immeasurable generosity! O eternal, infinite Good! O mad lover! And you have need of your creature? It seems so to me, for you act as if you could not live without her, in spite of the fact that you are Life itself, and everything has life from you and nothing can have life without you. Why then are you so mad? Because you have fallen in love with what you have made! You are pleased and delighted over her within yourself, as if you were drunk [with desire] for her salvation. She runs away from you and you go looking for her. She strays and you draw closer to her: You clothed yourself in our humanity, and nearer than that you could not have come.

And what shall I say? I will stutter, "A-a," because there is nothing else I know how to say. Finite language cannot express the emotion of the soul who longs for you infinitely. I think I could echo Paul's words: The tongue cannot speak nor the ear hear nor the eye see nor the heart imagine [cf. 1 Cor. 2:9] what I have seen! What have you seen? "I have seen the hidden things of God!" And I—what do I say? I have nothing to add from these clumsy emotions [of mine]. I say only, my soul, that you have tasted and seen the abyss of supreme eternal providence.

I thank you now, high eternal Father, for the measureless kindness you have shown me, though I am miserably undeserving of any favor.

Martin Luther (1483–1546)

Lectures on Romans (1515–16)*

Note: Luther is commenting here on Romans 8:28–39. The text begins: "We know that all things work together for good for those who love God, who are called according to his purpose. For those whom he foreknew he also predestined to be conformed to the image of his Son, in order that he might be the firstborn within a large family. And those whom he predestined he also called; and those whom he called he also justified; and those whom he justified he also glorified."

On this text hangs the whole passage that follows to the end of the eighth chapter of the letter before us. For the apostle wants to show that to the elect who are loved by God and who love God, the Spirit makes all things, even though they are evil, work together for good. He approaches here the subject of predestination and election, indeed, he discusses it from now on. This subject is not so unfathomable as one commonly believes; we should, rather, say that it is full of sweet comfort to the elect and all who have the spirit, but bitter and hard beyond measure to the prudence of the flesh.

The only reason and cause why so many adversities and evils do not separate the saints from the love of God is that they are called, and not merely called but "called according to purpose." To them alone, therefore, and to no others "he makes everything work together for good."

*Reprinted from *Luther: Lectures on Romans*, Library of Christian Classics, ed. Wilhelm Pauck. Used by permission of Westminster John Knox Press. Pp. 247–53, 271.

If there were not the divine purpose, and our salvation rested upon our will and our works, it would be based on chance. How easily could — I shall not say: all those evils at once, but — merely a single one of them hinder or overturn this chance!

But by saying: "Who shall accuse? Who shall condemn? Who shall separate?" [Rom. 8:33–35] the apostle shows that the elect are not saved contingently but necessarily. Hence, it is obvious that neither mere chance nor wonderfully contrary resistance to so many evils can obstruct it. The reason why this is God's way of salvation and why he exposes his elect to as many rapacious graspings as there are evils — he enumerates them here, and they all try to pull the elect into damnation so that they will not be saved — the reason why God chooses this method of salvation is that he wants to show that he saves us not by our merits but by sheer election and his immutable will, and thus he renders vain the efforts of so many grasping and very fierce adversaries. For if he did not lead us through so many terrors, he would give us much leeway to think highly of our merits. But now he makes plain that we are saved by his immutable love. And he proves through all this not our freedom of decision but the inflexible and firm will of his predestination.

For how could a man possibly break through all these things in which he would despair a thousand times, unless the eternal and steady love of God led him through and the Spirit helped our infirmities by his presence and made intercession for us with unutterable groanings? . . .

Our theologians, to be sure, subtle as they are, imagine they have accomplished something, though I do not know what it could be, when they adduce in this context their notion of the "contingent." They say that the elect are necessarily saved, namely, by the necessity of the consequence but not by consequent necessity.[1] This is nothing but empty talk, especially in view of the fact that they want to understand or at least give occasion to understand the concept of "consequent contingency" to mean that salvation can or cannot come by our decision. Thus I, too, once understood the matter.

This concept of "the contingency of the consequent" is irrelevant to the theme under discussion. . . . What else does "to be contingent" mean than "to be a creature" and not God? They twist the understanding by turning the necessity of an occurrence into the necessity of the essence of a thing. This equivocation is here out of place. For no one raises the question or doubts whether a created thing is contingent in its being, i.e., whether it is mutable or whether it is God and thus immutable. But the question is about the necessity of the sequel or whether what God has predestined will necessarily happen, and they concede that it will. And yet they make this superfluous addition, after they have said all that can be said. For if you know that something will definitely happen by the necessity of the consequence, what does it matter if you know further whether, at this particular place, it is contingent or not? . . .

Simple people put the question as [sic] least in this way: Does the contingency

---

1. The "consequent necessity" (*necessitas consequentis* or *absoluta* or *simplex*) means immutability and is generally attributed to God and his attributes. The "necessity of the consequence" (*necessitas consequentiae* or *conditionis*) is the necessity that is determined by a cause that once in effect can no longer be changed, but it could have been different.

of an event constitute an impediment of the certain predestination of God? The answer must be: With God there simply is no contingency, but only with us, because not even a leaf of a tree falls to the ground without the will of the Father. Just as the essence of things, therefore, also the times are in his hands. . . .

We shall deal with this matter in three sections. First, we shall gather the proofs of immutable predestination from the words of Scripture and the works of God. Secondly, we shall critically analyze the objections and exceptions, and the arguments and reasons of those who shift guilt to God. Thirdly, in order to provide comfort to those who are frightened by all this, we shall bring out also its more pleasant aspects and thus induce them to hope.

I

In this and the following chapter of this letter [i.e., Romans 8 and 9], the apostle deals thoroughly and almost word for word with the first theme, and he begins, as I have already pointed out, with, "We know that those who love God," etc.

Accordingly, he says, first: *who are called according to purpose.* It plainly follows, therefore, that others are not called according to the purpose. "Purpose" means here God's predestination or free election or deliberation or counsel. In Book I of the *Confessions,* Blessed Augustine says about this: "Thou art wonderful, O God; thou changest thy opinion, but thou dost not change thy counsel."

Second: In the following chapter (Rom. 9:8ff.), the apostle illustrates predestination by the two stories of Isaac and Ishmael, and of Jacob and Esau. He says expressly that these differed from one another only by election.

Third: At the same place, he quotes two Scriptural passages on it; one refers to the elect: "I will have mercy on whom I have mercy" (Rom. 9:15), and the other one to the rejected: "For this very purpose did I raise you up," etc., and he concludes: "So then, he has mercy on whom he will, and whom he will, he hardens," etc. (Rom. 9:17–18). It is clear that he argues in the same way in chs. 10 and 11.

Fourth: Predestination is proved by the following quotation from John 10:29: "No one can snatch them out of the hand of my Father."

Fifth: John 13:18: "I speak not of you all; I know whom I have chosen." And John 6:44: "No one can come to me, except the Father that sent me draw him." And at the same place: "They shall all be taught of God" (John 6:45).

Sixth: Ps. 115:3: "He has done all things whatsoever he would." And 2 Tim. 2:19: "The foundation of God stands firm, having this seal: the Lord knows who are his."

A further proof are God's works: first, what, according to the following chapter, he did with Ishmael and Esau and with Pharaoh and the Egyptians.

Second: Predestination is shown by the fact that God exposes his saints to so many evils, all of which are like rapacious hands, and yet he does not let them get lost. Thereby he amply shows the firmness of his election: no creature can impede it, despite the fact that he leads the whole creature up against it, as he shows by the example of Pharaoh, who was hardened.

Third: Election is shown by the fact that he permits many to live a good life from the beginning and to do many good works and yet they are not saved; while, conversely, he lets many commit great evils who are nevertheless suddenly changed and saved. This is exemplified by Saul (1 Sam. 13:13; 15:26f.; 16:1) and Manasseh (2 Kings 21:1ff.), and likewise by Judas the Traitor (Matt. 26:14, 47ff.), and by the thief of the cross (Luke 23:33ff.), and so forth, and by many harlots and crude sinners. By way of contrast, he rejects those who think they know everything and those who try to shine with good works....

II

There are many reasons that can be advanced against predestination, but they proceed from the "prudence of the flesh." Hence, whoever does not deny himself and has not learned to submerge his questions in the will of God and to subject them to it will always ask why God wills this or does that, and he will never find an answer. And rightly so. For this foolish prudence places itself above God and passes judgment on his will as upon something inferior, while, as a matter of fact, it is about to be judged by him. The apostle, therefore, destroys all its reasons by one brief word. First, he restrains our temerity lest we sit in judgment on God's will. He says: "O man, who are you that you reply against God?" (Rom. 9:20); in other words: You are subject to the will of God; why, then, do you presume to reply to it and to argue with it? And then he advances the decisive reason: "Has not the potter a right over the clay?" (Rom. 9:21).

So then, the first objection, which is also the least weighty one, is this: Man has been given free will and thus he can earn merits or demerits. We answer to this as follows: The power of free decision insofar as it is not under the sway of grace has no ability whatsoever to realize righteousness, but it is necessarily in sins. Hence, Blessed Augustine is right, when, in his book against Julian, he calls it "the enslaved, rather than free, will." But when it has received grace, the power of decision really becomes free, at all events in respect of salvation. To be sure, it is always free according to its nature, but only with respect to that which is in its power and is inferior to it but not with respect to that which is superior to it, since it is held captive in sins and then cannot choose the good according to God.

A second objection: "God will have all men to be saved" (1 Tim. 2:4), and he gave his son for us men, and he created man for the sake of eternal life. And likewise: Everything is there for man's sake and he is there for God's sake in order that he may enjoy him, etc. But this objection and others like it can just as easily be refuted as the first one: because *all these sayings must be understood only with respect to the elect,* as the apostle says in 2 Tim. 2:10: "All for the elect." Christ did not die for absolutely all, for he says: "This is my blood which is shed for you" (Luke 22:20) and "for many" (Mark 14:24) — he did not say: for all — "to the remission of sins" (Matt. 26:28).

A third objection: God condemns none who is without sin. And a man who is necessarily in sin is wrongly condemned. To this I reply: We are all necessarily in sin and under condemnation, but nobody is a sinner by coaction and against his will. For whoever hates sin is already outside sin and belongs to the elect. But those whom God hardens, they are the ones to whom he gives the will voluntarily to be and to stay in sin and to love wickedness. Such are unavoidably in sin by the immutability of necessity but not of coaction.

A fourth objection: Why does he issue commandments and then does not want to see them fulfilled? And, what is worse, why does he harden men's will so that they want even more to act against the law? The cause, therefore, why men sin and are damned, lies in God. This is the strongest and chief objection. And the apostle replies to it mainly by saying: God wills it so and because he wills it so, it is not wicked. For everything is his as the clay is the potter's! He, therefore, gives his commandments in order that the elect fulfill them and the reprobate get entangled in them. And thus he shows his wrath as well as his mercy.

Here the prudence of the flesh speaks up and says: It is cruel and miserable of God that he seeks his glory in my wretchedness. Listen to the voice of the flesh! "My, my [wretchedness]," it says! Take away this "my" and say instead: "Glory be to thee, O Lord!" and you will be saved! Thus the prudence of the flesh seeks only its own; it fears its own misery more than a desecration of God, and, for this reason, it follows its own will rather than God's.

We must, therefore, have a mind about God different from that which we have about man. For he does not owe anyone anything....

III

This subject of predestination tastes very bitter to the prudence of the flesh. Indeed, it is so offended by it that it lets itself be carried away to the extreme of blasphemy, because here it is utterly destroyed and reduced to nothing. For it is forced to recognize that its salvation consists in no way of its own action, but that it can be found only outside itself, namely, in the election of God. But all who have the "prudence of the spirit" delight in this subject and they are filled with an ineffable happiness, as we can see here in the apostle and in Hannah, the mother of Samuel (1 Sam. 2:1ff.).... [Luther comments below on Rom. 9:16: "So then, it is not of him that wills, nor of him that runs, but of God that has mercy."]

Now it does not follow from this text that a man's running and willing amount to nothing, but what follows from it is that they do not come from his own strength. For the work of God is not nothing. And a man's willing and running is God's work. Indeed, the apostle speaks here about a willing and running according to God, i.e., about a life of love and divine righteousness. But there is a willing and running that is vain — namely, that of those who do not will and run in the way of God, though they may will great things and run strongly. For what they do is not from God and does not please him. It is of these that Isa. 41:24 says: "You are of nothing and your work of that which has no being."

Yet I want to give here this warning: No one whose mind has not yet been purged, should plunge into these speculations, lest he fall into an abyss of horror and despair. He must first purge the eyes of his heart in meditating on the wounds of Christ. Nor would I talk about this, did not the order of the lectures and necessity compel me to do so. For this is very strong wine and the most wholesome meal and solid food for the perfect, i.e., it is theology in the best sense of the word, about which the apostle says: "We speak wisdom among the perfect" (1 Cor. 2:6). I myself am still a little one in Christ that needs milk and not solid food (1 Cor. 3:1–2). Let him who is as I am do likewise. The wounds of Christ, "the clefts in the rock," are safe enough for us.

Those that are strong and perfect may discuss the first book of the Sentences, which properly should not be the first but the last book.[2] But nowadays many read this book hurriedly and heedlessly — with the result that they become strangely blinded.

John Calvin (1509–64)

Institutes of the Christian Religion (1559), Book 1, Chapter 15, Par. 8; Chapter 16, Par. 3; Chapter 17, Par. 5; Chapter 18, Pars. 1, 3; Book 3, Chapter 23, Pars. 2 and 7*

Chapter 15: Discussion of Human Nature as Created, of the Faculties of the Soul, of the Image of God, of Free Will, and of the Original Integrity of Man's Nature

8. Free Choice and Adam's Responsibility

...They [i.e., the philosophers] held this principle, that man would not be a rational animal unless he possessed free choice of good and evil; also it entered their minds that the distinction between virtues and vices would be obliterated if man did not order his life by his own planning. Well reasoned so far — if there had been no change in man. But since this was hidden from them, it is no wonder they mix up heaven and earth! They, as professed disciples of Christ, are obviously playing the fool when, by compromising between the opinions of the philosophers and heavenly doctrine, so that these touch neither heaven nor earth, in man — who is lost and sunk down into spiritual destruction — they still seek after free choice. But these matters will be better dealt with in their proper place [Book 2, ch. 2, pars. 2–4]. Now we need bear only this in mind: man was far different at the first creation from his whole posterity, who, deriving their origin from him in his corrupted state, have contracted from him a hereditary taint. For, the individual parts of his soul were formed to uprightness, the soundness of his mind stood firm, and his will was free to choose the good. If anyone objects that his will was placed in an insecure position because its power was weak, his status should have availed to remove any excuse; nor was it reasonable for God to be constrained by the necessity of making a man who either could not or would not sin at all. Such a nature would, indeed, have been more excellent. But to quarrel with God on this precise point, as if he ought to have conferred this upon man, is more than iniquitous, inasmuch as it was in his own choice to give whatever he pleased. But the reason he did not sustain man by the virtue of perseverance lies

---

2. I *Sent.* d. 35, where predestination and the problems of the divine will are discussed.

*Reprinted from *Calvin: Institutes of the Christian Religion,* Library of Christian Classics, ed. John T. McNeill. Used by permission of Westminster John Knox Press. Pp. 196, 200–201, 217, 229–30, 234–35, 949, 955.

hidden in his plan; sobriety is for us the part of wisdom. Man, indeed, received the ability provided he exercised the will; but he did not have the will to use his ability, for this exercising of the will would have been followed by perseverance. Yet he is not excusable, for he received so much that he voluntarily brought about his own destruction; indeed, no necessity was imposed upon God of giving man other than a mediocre and even transitory will, that from man's Fall he might gather occasion for his own glory.

Chapter 16: God by His Power Nourishes and Maintains the World Created by Him, and Rules Its Several Parts by His Providence

... 3. God's Providence Governs All

And truly God claims, and would have us grant him, omnipotence — not the empty, idle, and almost unconscious sort that the Sophists imagine, but a watchful, effective, active sort, engaged in ceaseless activity. Not, indeed, an omnipotence that is only a general principle of confused motion, as if he were to command a river to flow through its once-appointed channels, but one that is directed toward individual and particular motions. For he is deemed omnipotent, not because he can indeed act, yet sometimes ceases and sits in idleness, or continues by a general impulse that order of nature which he previously appointed; but because, governing heaven and earth by his providence, he so regulates all things that nothing takes place without his deliberation. For when, in the Psalms, it is said that "he does whatever he wills" [Ps. 115:3], a certain and deliberate will is meant....

But if God's governance is so extended to all his works, it is a childish cavil to enclose it within the stream of nature. Indeed, those as much defraud God of his glory as themselves of a most profitable doctrine who confine God's providence to such narrow limits as though he allowed all things by a free course to be borne along according to a universal law of nature. For nothing would be more miserable than man if he were exposed to every movement of the sky, air, earth, and waters. Besides, in this way God's particular goodness toward each one would be too unworthily reduced....

Those who ascribe just praise to God's omnipotence doubly benefit thereby. First, power ample enough to do good there is in him in whose possession are heaven and earth, and to whose beck all creatures are so attentive as to put themselves in obedience to him. Secondly, they may safely rest in the protection of him to whose will are subject all the harmful things which, whatever their source, we may fear; whose authority curbs Satan with all his furies and his whole equipage; and upon whose nod depends whatever opposes our welfare. And we cannot otherwise correct or allay these uncontrolled and superstitious fears, which we repeatedly conceive at the onset of dangers. We are superstitiously timid, I say, if whenever creatures threaten us or forcibly terrorize us we become as fearful as if they had some intrinsic power to harm us, or might wound us inadvertently and accidentally, or there were not enough help in God against their harmful acts....

Chapter 17: How We May Apply This Doctrine to Our Greatest Benefit

5. God's Providence Does Not Exculpate Our Wickedness

...Why shall a murderer be punished, who has killed one whose life the Lord had ended? If all such men are serving God's will, why shall they be punished? On the contrary, I deny that they are serving God's will. For we shall not say that one who is motivated by an evil inclination, by only obeying his own wicked desire, renders service to God at His bidding. A man, having learned of His will, obeys God in striving toward the goal to which he is called by that same will. From what source do we learn but from his Word? In such fashion we must in our deeds search out God's will which he declares through his Word. God requires of us only what he commands. If we contrive anything against his commandment, it is not obedience but obstinacy and transgression. Yet, unless he willed it, we would not do it. I agree. But do we do evil things to the end that we may serve him? Yet he by no means commands us to do them; rather we rush headlong, without thinking what he requires, but so raging in our unbridled lust that we deliberately strive against him. And in this way we serve his just ordinance by doing evil, for so great and boundless is his wisdom that he knows right well how to use evil instruments to do good. And see how absurd their argument is: they would have transgressors go unpunished, on the ground that their misdeeds are committed solely by God's dispensation.

I grant more: thieves and murderers and other evildoers are the instruments of divine providence, and the Lord himself uses these to carry out the judgments that he has determined with himself. Yet I deny that they can derive from this any excuse for their evil deeds. Why? Will they either involve God in the same iniquity with themselves, or will they cloak their own depravity with his justice? They can do neither. In their own conscience they are so convicted as to be unable to clear themselves; in themselves they so discover all evil, but in him only the lawful use of their evil intent, as to preclude laying the charge against God. Well and good, for he works through them. And whence, I ask you, comes the stench of a corpse, which is both putrefied and laid open by the heat of the sun? All men see that it is stirred up by the sun's rays; yet no one for this reason says that the rays stink. Thus, since the matter and guilt of evil repose in a wicked man, what reason is there to think that God contracts any defilement, if he uses his service for his own purpose?...

Chapter 18: God So Uses the Works of the Ungodly, and So Bends Their Minds to Carry Out His Judgments, That He Remains Pure from Every Stain

1. No Mere "Permission"

...Hence the distinction was devised between doing and permitting because to many this difficulty seemed inexplicable, that Satan and all the impious are so under God's hand and power that he directs their malice to whatever end seems good to him, and uses their wicked deeds to carry out his judgments. And perhaps the moderation of those whom the appearance of absurdity alarms would be excusable, except that they wrongly try to clear God's justice of every sinister mark by upholding a falsehood. It seems absurd to them for man, who will soon be punished for his blindness, to be blinded by God's will and command. Therefore they escape by the shift that this is done only with God's permission, not also by his will; but he, openly declaring that he is the doer, repudiates that evasion. However, that men can accomplish nothing except by God's secret command, that they cannot by deliberating accomplish anything except what he has already decreed with himself and determines by his secret direction, is proved by innumerable and clear testimonies. What we have cited before from the psalm, that God does whatever he wills [Ps. 115:3], certainly pertains to all the actions of men. If, as is here said, God is the true Arbiter of wars and of peace, and this without any exception, who, then, will dare say that men are borne headlong by blind motion unbeknown to God or with his acquiescence?

But particular examples will shed more light. From the first chapter of Job we know that Satan, no less than the angels who willingly obey, presents himself before God [Job 1:6; 2:1] to receive his commands. He does so, indeed, in a different way and with a different end; but he still cannot undertake anything unless God so wills. However, even though a bare permission to afflict the holy man seems then to be added, yet we gather that God was the author of that trial of which Satan and his wicked thieves were the ministers, because this statement is true: "The Lord gave, the Lord has taken away; as it has pleased God, so is it done" [Job 1:21, Vg.]. Satan desperately tries to drive the holy man insane; the Sabaeans cruelly and impiously pillage and make off with another's possessions. Job recognizes that he was divinely stripped of all his property, and made a poor man, because it so pleased God. Therefore, whatever men or Satan himself may instigate, God nevertheless holds the key, so that he turns their efforts to carry out his judgments....

3. God's Will Is a Unity

...And indeed, unless Christ had been crucified according to God's will, whence would we have redemption? Yet God's will is not therefore at war with itself, nor does it change, nor does it pretend not to will what he wills. But even though his will is one and simple in him, it appears manifold to us because, on account of our mental incapacity, we do not grasp how in divers [sic] ways it wills and does not will something to take place. When Paul said that the calling of the Gentiles was "a mystery hidden" [Eph. 3:9], he added shortly thereafter that in it was shown forth "God's manifold wisdom" [Eph. 3:10]. Because God's wisdom appears manifold...ought we therefore, on account of the sluggishness of our understanding, to dream that there is any variation in God himself, as if he either may change his plan or disagree with himself? Rather, when we do not grasp how God wills to take place what he forbids to be done, let us recall our mental incapacity, and at the same time consider that the light in which God dwells is not without reason called unapproachable [1 Tim. 6:16], because it is overspread with darkness. Therefore all godly and modest folk readily agree with this saying of Augustine: "Sometimes with a good will a man wills something which God does not will....For example, a good son wills that his father live, whom God wills to die. Again, it can happen that the same man wills with a bad will what God wills with a good will. For example, a bad son wills that his father die; God also wills this. That is, the former wills what God does not will; but the latter wills what God also wills. And yet the filial piety of the former, even though he wills something other than God wills, is more consonant with God's good will than the impiety of the latter, who wills the same thing as God does. There is a great difference between what is fitting for man to will and what is fitting for God, and to what end the will of each is directed, so that it be either approved or disapproved. For through the bad wills of evil men God fulfills what he righteously wills." A little before he had said that by their defection the apostate angels and all the wicked, from their point of view, had done what God did not will, but from the point of view of God's omnipotence they could in no way have done this, because while they act against God's will, his will is done in them. Whence he exclaims: "Great are God's works, sought out in all his wills" [Ps. 111:2; cf. Ps. 110:2, Vg.]; so that in a wonderful and ineffable manner nothing is done without God's will, not even that which is against his will. For it would not be done if he did not permit it; yet he does not unwillingly permit it, but willingly; nor would he, being good, allow evil to be done, unless being also almighty he could make good even out of evil.

Book 3, Chapter 23: Refutation of the False Accusations with Which This Doctrine [i.e., Reprobation] Has Always Been Unjustly Burdened

...2. God's Will Is the Rule of Righteousness

To the pious and moderate and those who are mindful that they are men, these statements should be quite sufficient. Yet because these venomous dogs spew out more than one kind of venom against God, we shall answer each individually, as the matter requires.

Foolish men contend with God in many ways, as though they held him liable to their accusations. They first ask, therefore, by what right the Lord becomes angry at his creatures who have not provoked him by any previous offense; for to devote to destruction whomever he pleases is more like the caprice of a tyrant than the lawful sentence of a judge. It therefore seems to them that men have reason to expostulate with God if they are predestined to eternal death solely by his decision, apart from their own merit. If thoughts of this sort ever occur to pious men, they will be sufficiently armed to break their force even by the one consideration that it is very wicked merely to investigate the causes of God's will. For his will is, and rightly ought to be, the cause of all things that are. For if it has any cause, something must precede it, to which it is, as it were, bound; this is unlawful to imagine. For God's will is so much the highest rule of righteousness that whatever he wills, by the very fact that he wills it, must be considered righteous. When, therefore, one asks why God has so done, we must reply: because he has willed it. But if you proceed further to ask why he so willed, you are seeking something greater and higher than God's will, which cannot be found. Let men's rashness, then, restrain itself, and not seek what does not exist, lest perhaps it fail to find what does exist. This bridle, I say, will effectively restrain anyone who wants to ponder in reverence the secrets of his God. . . .

7. God Has Also Predestined the Fall into Sin

They say it is not stated in so many words that God decreed that Adam should perish for his rebellion. As if, indeed, that very God, who, Scripture proclaims, "does whatever he pleases" [Ps. 115:3], would have created the noblest of his creatures to an uncertain end. They say that he had free choice that he might shape his own fortune, and that God ordained nothing except to treat man according to his own deserts. If such a barren invention is accepted, where will that omnipotence of God be whereby he regulates all things according to his secret plan, which depends solely upon itself? Yet predestination, whether they will or not, manifests itself in Adam's posterity. For it did not take place by reason of nature that, by the guilt of one parent, all were cut off from salvation. What prevents them from admitting concerning one man what they unwillingly concede concerning the whole human race? For why should they fritter away their effort in such evasions? Scripture proclaims that all mortals were bound over to eternal death in the person of one man [cf. Rom. 5:12ff.]. Since this cannot be ascribed to nature, it is perfectly clear that it has come forth from the wonderful plan of God. It is utterly absurd that these good defenders of God's righteousness hang perplexed upon a straw yet leap over high roofs!

Again I ask: whence does it happen that Adam's fall irremediably involved so many peoples, together with their infant offspring, in eternal death unless because it so pleased God? Here their tongues, otherwise so loquacious, must become mute. The decree is dreadful indeed, I confess. Yet no one can deny that God foreknew what end man was to have before he created him, and consequently foreknew because he so ordained by his decree.

– 6 –

The Modern Period

INTRODUCTION

In the wake of the Reformation, Christians fought to protect and to spread their understanding of Christian faith. Roman Catholics launched a two-pronged "Counter-Reformation" effort against Protestants. On the one hand, they clarified and then defended the Roman understanding of doctrine and practice against the critique of Protestants. On the other, they attacked Protestant positions, both theologically and politically. The desire was not to lose any more ground, metaphorically and literally, to Protestants, and, wherever possible, to win back Catholic territory that had been lost. Protestants also fought to protect and to spread their interpretations of Christian life. Although all Protestants were united in affirming scripture alone as the only sure source of authority in the church, they could not all agree on the supposedly clear meaning of this authority. When differences in scriptural interpretation could not be resolved, new churches were formed. Thus Luther opposed Zwingli, Zwingli opposed the Radical Reformers (specifically the Swiss Brethren), and the Radical Reformers opposed all other Protestants as well as the Catholics.

The opposition between Christians did not remain merely theological. Physical violence was used against ecclesiastical and theological opponents. The only consistent exception to this rule, at least after 1535, were Radical Reformers, such as Menno Simons (founder of the Mennonites) and Jakob Hutter (founder of the Hutterites). Although these "radicals" rejected the use of violence against their theological opponents, they were not spared the violence of other Protestants and Catholics against them. Some note that more Radical Reformers were killed by other Christians in the sixteenth and seventeenth centuries than Christians killed by "pagans" during the church's first three centuries.[1]

The division of the western Christian church into many Protestant churches and the Roman Church did not alter decisively the basic content of the doctrine of God. It did, however, bring to the fore different emphases. A perduring difference between Protestant and Catholic in this period was a difference in the methods by which Christians believed they could make valid statements about God's nature and activity. Roman Catholics continued to assert that knowledge about God could be attained both through the use of reason as well as through the reception of divine revelation. It continued to be commonplace for Catholics to distinguish between knowledge of God's existence, oneness, and goodness through the use of human reason and the fuller knowledge of God's nature (God's

---

1. Justo L. González, *The Story of Christianity*, vol. 2: *The Reformation to the Present Day* (San Francisco: Harper & Row, 1984), 56–57.

trinitarian character) and God's activities (e.g., incarnation and predestination) through their revelation in scripture and tradition. Protestants continued to assert that knowledge about God and God's activities could be attained primarily, if not exclusively, through revelation contained in the Bible. This contrast in basic method or approach has continued to differentiate Catholic and Protestant approaches to the doctrine of God, even though the sharpness of this contrast has been blurred by ecumenical efforts since the early part of the twentieth century.

Although Protestants were generally united in their appeal to the Bible as the source of knowledge about God, they, of course, highlighted different aspects of biblical revelation concerning God. Lutherans, for example, tended to highlight the fact that God is decisively revealed, as well as hidden, in the cross of Christ. This focus upon Christ's suffering rather than upon God's glory was in keeping with Luther's insistence upon a "theology of the cross," which he found classically expressed in the letters of St. Paul. Calvinists, by contrast, tended to highlight the sovereignty of God. As sovereign lord, God is totally free in creating, sustaining, and redeeming creatures. Because God is totally free in relation to us, we need to gratefully acknowledge God's activities on our behalf. Despite these different emphases, Protestants concurred in stressing the gratuity of God's actions with regard to humanity. In the seventeenth and eighteenth centuries, Protestant theologians developed their own version of scholastic systems, analogous to what Catholic theologians had constructed. Systematic presentation and rational defense of propositions concerning God came to characterize much Protestant theology in this period.

In the century following upon the outbreak of the Protestant Reformation, some Protestant churches had to resolve internal disputes concerning their understanding of God and God's activities. One dispute that was particularly heated occurred within those churches that had adopted Calvin as their theological guide. The issue was the divine action of predestination. Did God "predestine" the reprobate in the sense that God caused them to sin? Or did God "predestine" the reprobate in the sense that God decided to let those in whom grace was not received to suffer condemnation for their remaining in sin? As we saw in the preceding section, this issue had already generated considerable debate during the lifetimes of both Luther and Calvin. Both Reformers had written responses to critics of a so-called strict interpretation of predestination. In the early seventeenth century, European Calvinism was disrupted by a debate concerning predestination between Jacob Harmenszoon (1559–1609), better known by his Latin name Arminius, and Francis Gomarus (1563–1641). In 1603, after having served fifteen years as a pastor in Amsterdam, Arminius was named a professor of theology at the University of Leyden. Within a year of his arrival, he was embroiled in controversy with Gomarus, who was a strict "supralapsarian."[2]

Both Arminius and Gomarus agreed that predestination was one of God's activities. They disagreed, however, about the basis upon which God predestines.

---

2. "Supralapsarians" held that God decreed the election (or nonelection) of individuals from eternity and then permitted the Fall to happen as a means by which God's absolute decree of predestination could be carried out. By contrast, "sublapsarians" (or "infralapsarians") believed that God allowed the Fall to occur and only then decreed the election or nonelection of individuals. Calvin had provided no explicit answer to this question of the order of God's decree of predestination. His successor, Theodore Beza (1519–1605), however, taught that God eternally decreed salvation or reprobation, prior to the Fall.

Whereas Arminius placed the emphasis upon foreknowledge, Gomarus insisted that the decision of God's will determined whether one was among the elect or among the reprobate. After his death in 1609, Arminius's position was taken up by about forty ministers, who wrote a statement of their faith called the "Remonstrance." These Arminians were opposed by anti-Remonstrants. Their controversy led to the convocation of the Synod of Dort (Dordrecht today) in 1618. At this synod, in which the Remonstrants were allowed to participate only as defendants, Arminius's position was rejected. The doctrinal decisions made at Dort, which became part of the orthodox doctrine of the Dutch Reformed Church, are conveniently remembered according to the acronym "tulip." That is, Dort declared that after the Fall humankind is totally depraved ("t"); that God's election of those to be saved is not based merely on divine foreknowl- edge of the use individuals would make of the means of grace, but rather is an unconditional ("u") election by God; that the efficacy of Christ's atoning death is limited ("l") to the elect; that God's grace is irresistible ("i"); and that those whom God has chosen to be saved will persevere ("p") in this status. The Remon- strants were forbidden to preach, and some were treated harshly after their defeat at Dort. Despite their defeat within the Dutch Reformed Church, the Arminian position continued to influence the Protestant traditions through the endorsement it received from John Wesley (1703–91) and Wesleyan Methodism.[3]

Although some of the most heated debate about divine predestination occurred within the Reformed tradition, the issue was argued during this period in other churches. Within the Roman Catholic Church, the debate took place in several locations during the sixteenth and seventeenth centuries. Toward the end of the sixteenth century, the Dominican and the Jesuit religious orders engaged in sharp exchanges concerning this issue. The Council of Trent (1545–63) had declared that the justification of those to be saved began with the grace of God, but that human beings were free to assent to and cooperate with that grace. The precise range and power of freedom vis-à-vis grace was not without ambiguity.[4]

In 1588 Luis de Molina (1536–1600), a Spanish Jesuit, attempted to explain the interaction of divine grace and human free will in his treatise *On the Har- mony of Free Will with the Gifts of Grace*. In this treatise, Molina attempted to demonstrate that the Catholic teaching concerning free will and merits is not, as Protestants had charged, a Pelagian denial of the primacy of grace. Both before and after the Fall, human beings are free to choose their natural course of action, but are not free to choose by themselves those things which lead to their super- natural end. Now as before, human beings need the help of God to attain their supernatural destiny. This "general help" of God, which is offered to all people, is

---

3. See Williston Walker et al., *A History of the Christian Church*, 4th ed. (New York: Charles Scribner's Sons, 1985), 539–42.

4. Chapter 5 of the Decree Concerning Justification (1547) states: "It is furthermore declared that in adults the beginning of that justification must proceed from the predisposing grace of God through Jesus Christ, that is, from His vocation, whereby, without any merits on their part, they are called; that they who by sin had been cut off from God, may be disposed to convert themselves to their own justification by freely assenting to and cooperating with that grace; so that, while God touches the heart of man through the illumination of the Holy Ghost, man himself neither does absolutely nothing while receiving that inspiration, since he can also reject it, nor yet is he able by his own free will and without the grace of God to move himself to justice in His sight" (*Canons and Decrees of the Council of Trent*, trans. H. J. Schroeder [Rockford, Ill.: Tan Books, 1978], 31–32).

needed. Consequently, God's grace is necessary, but the difference between those who attain their supernatural end and those who do not lies in human free choice. After the Fall, justification requires the prevenient and stimulating grace of God. But this grace is not irresistible. The person's response to grace is free. The human person, even in the fallen state, has the capacity to freely assent to the workings of grace or to withhold assent. In this scheme, predestination depends upon divine foreknowledge, but "not in the sense that God has decided to withhold his divine aid from those who will reject it, but in the sense that he knows who will freely decide to make proper use of the aids that he will grant to all."[5]

Domingo Báñez (1528–1604), a Spanish Dominican, found Molina's position objectionable because it seemed to hold an inappropriately enlarged understanding of human capacities after the Fall. Báñez laid heavy accent upon God's action in the justification and sanctification of human beings. From Báñez's perspective, fallen human beings were incapable of choosing rightly without being moved by grace. Therefore, only those moved to do so by God's grace were able to freely cooperate with grace in the process of their salvation. God's predestination is not based on divine foreknowledge of the free cooperation of human beings with grace. Rather, said Báñez, it is based on God's gift of irresistible grace which transforms the fallen will, enabling and moving it to cooperate in the process of salvation. Molina complained that Báñez's position was Calvinist, not Catholic. Báñez retorted that Molina's position was Pelagian, not Catholic. The religious orders lined up behind their respective representatives.[6]

Pope Clement VIII (pope: 1592–1605) was called upon to resolve the issue. In 1598 a commission, appointed the previous year by the pope, decided that Molina's views were opposed to those of Augustine and Aquinas and that they agreed in some points with the Pelagians. With Molina's condemnation appearing imminent, a number of influential persons, including the king of Spain, asked that the matter be examined more cautiously. The pope then called for conversations between the Jesuits and the Dominicans, hoping that a compromise might be possible. No compromise, however, had been reached by the time of Clement's death in 1605. His successor, Pope Paul V (pope: 1605–21), decided that neither side taught views essentially contrary to Catholic faith. He admonished both sides to refrain from calling the other heretical.[7] In 1611 the pope ordered that all future treatises on grace and free will be submitted to the Inquisition before their publication.

The debate that had erupted in Spain between Molina and Báñez was repeated elsewhere in the seventeenth century. At the University of Louvain and also in France, a similar debate developed between Jesuits and Jansenists. The Jansenists take their name from Cornelius Jansen (1585–1638), a Dutch theolo-

---

5. Justo L. González, *A History of Christian Thought*, vol. 3: *From the Protestant Reformation to the Twentieth Century* (Nashville: Abingdon Press, 1975), 209–10.

6. The fight between Báñez and Molina in Spain had been preceded by a similar controversy between Michael Baius and Leonard Lessius at the University of Louvain (Belgium) in the 1560s–1580s. See González, *A History of Christian Thought*, 3:205–6.

7. Jean Delumeau speculates that Paul V prepared a condemnation of Molina's position, but hesitated to publish it because he feared weakening the Society of Jesus, which as a whole had gone over to Molina's point of view. See *Catholicism between Luther and Voltaire: A New View of the Counter-Reformation* (Philadelphia: Westminster Press, 1977), 101.

gian who had become the bishop of Ypres in 1638. Jansen was very concerned that the "true" Augustinian tradition be maintained, against the mistaken views of Molina, within the Roman Catholic Church. He set about writing a detailed exposition of the thought of Augustine with regard to God's actions and human nature. After his death, his three-volume work on Augustine was published. In this work, Jansen defended the positions of the later Augustine, interpreted in the most extreme way. From his perspective, grace is necessary for performing even the least good; apart from grace, the will can do nothing but evil, although it is free to choose which evil it does. The dispute between Jesuits and Jansenists concerning predestination and theological anthropology was exacerbated by disagreements concerning Jesuit pastoral practice in confession and the rights of the local church vis-à-vis Rome. Despite condemnations of the Jansenist position in 1643 and 1653, Jansenism continued to find considerable support in France. Some of the central Jansenist propositions were decisively rejected in Pope Clement XI's encyclical *Unigenitus* of 1713. A permanent schism occurred in Holland as a result of further attempts to suppress the Jansenist movement.

Internal disagreements within the different Christian churches were not the only source of discussion about the character of God's activities in relation to humanity. Critical philosophical considerations and the development of a modern scientific understanding of the world raised questions not only about God's eternal predestination, but also about God's continuing involvement in the created order. As you will recall from the essay on the modern period in Part One of this volume, Descartes's espousal of methodical doubt in the seventeenth century moved individuals to consider whether traditional convictions were certain. The critically thinking self was to determine what is true and what is not. During the same century, scientists such as Galileo Galilei promoted the critical re-examination of long-held positions concerning the operation of the solar system. By the end of the seventeenth century, Isaac Newton had formulated basic principles by which it was possible to explain the motion of physical bodies. As science improved its ability to explain the functioning of the physical world without reference to supernatural causes, traditional beliefs about God's activities with regard to the world were reconsidered.

By the early eighteenth century, a deistic understanding of God's relation to the world held sway among some European intellectuals. From the deistic perspective, God's activities with respect to the world are confined largely to the two poles of history. God was responsible for the creation of the world. God would also be responsible for executing judgment upon human beings at the end of the world. In between these two poles of history, conceived in a linear fashion, God was not intimately involved in the workings of nature and history. God had made humanity with the capacity of free self-direction. Correlatively, God had made the physical world to operate according to regular, in fact immutable, natural laws. Once God had established the laws by which the human and natural worlds could function, God no longer needed to be involved in their actual functioning.

Both areas of human intellectual endeavor, philosophy and science, continued to create challenges for traditional theological assertions during the eighteenth and nineteenth centuries. By the time of philosopher Immanuel Kant (1724–1804) at the end of the eighteenth century, it had become difficult for theology to demonstrate the reality of God and to describe God's creative, redemptive, and sanctifying activities in a way that could meet the rational standards of critical philosophy. By the time of geologist Charles Lyell (1797–1875) in the nineteenth century, it had become difficult for theology to defend cogently the traditional Christian understanding of the origin and age of the world. With the cognitive claims of theology under fire, the only safe avenue left for theology and religion appeared to many to be the path of morality. From this perspective, theology is primarily concerned with providing warrants to support moral behavior. As we saw in Part One of this volume, Friedrich Schleiermacher (1768–1834) refused to have theology forced into the primary mode of either knowledge (where it would have to defend its cognitive claims against the incisive critique of philosophy and science) or morality. Theology, Schleiermacher declared, has primarily to do with the description and explication of Christian feelings. This reinterpretation of the doctrinal task of theology provided him with a way to continue to assert some of the basic doctrines of the church, without coming into conflict with the developing claims of modern science.

What could such an approach have to say about God's relation to the world? Schleiermacher re-established Christian claims about the truth of God's creative, redemptive, and sanctifying activities on the basis of the feeling or self-consciousness of the Christian community. In particular, he used the fundamental religious feeling of absolute dependence on God to determine what is to be included in doctrinal assertions about creation. By formulating the doctrine on the basis of the present experience of absolute dependence, Schleiermacher was able to avoid conflict with scientific theories about the origin of the world. Questions about how the world began are questions of knowledge concerning physical reality. Such questions are rightly to be answered according to the methods and practices of science. Piety, however, is concerned with describing and making sense of human self-consciousness. Insofar as we are aware of our absolute dependence upon God in every given moment, we are aware of divine preservation of the world. This awareness constitutes the essence of an authentic doctrine of creation (see §39 below).

By the time of Schleiermacher's writing, science had formulated natural explanations of the basic operation of the world. In such a scientific scheme, there was no place for supernatural causes or divine interventions. Miracles, however, had been one of the principal phenomena to which Christians had traditionally pointed as evidence of God's special involvement in the world and as proof of the divine origin of Jesus' message. In the late eighteenth century, David Hume had advanced a philosophical argument against the possibility of miracles. Appealing to the uniformity of experience and highlighting the tenuousness of every historical claim, Hume concluded that reports about the occurrence of miracles in the past should be greeted with skepticism. At the same time, some theologians, in an attempt to defend the authority of scripture, in which many miracles are reported, devised natural explanations of what were initially regarded as supernatural events. H. E. G. Paulus's 1828 book, *Das Leben Jesu als Grundlage einer reinen Geschichte des Urchristentums* (*The Life of Jesus as the Basis of a Pure History of Primitive Christianity*), epitomized this approach. Paulus claimed that insufficient knowledge about the laws of nature had prevented eyewitnesses from perceiving the natural causes of Jesus' alleged miracles. Schleiermacher, writing just a few years later, had to define his own position with regard to miracles.

As the excerpt below makes clear, Schleiermacher rejected several arguments used by early modern theologians in defense of miracles. Some claimed that the notion of miracle must be maintained in order to manifest divine omnipotence. Others claimed that miracles are necessary in order for God to counteract the consequences of bad choices made by free human beings. Still others asserted that the reality of miracles is necessary in order to demonstrate that God still has contact with the world. Schleiermacher retorted that retaining miracles is not necessary to the affirmation of divine omnipotence. In fact, God's omnipotence, he argued, is better illustrated by the immutable course of nature (see §47, 1 below). To insist that divine miracles are necessary from time to time, by contrast, would be to suggest that there is some imperfection in God's work that needs to be corrected or that there is some entity or force operative in the world, not ordained by God, which is capable of frustrating the divine plan. In either event, our fundamental feeling of absolute dependence upon God would be destroyed. The feeling of absolute dependence suggests that the entire interaction of the natural world (what Schleiermacher calls "the nature-mechanism") and free human agents is the object of God's preservation. All depends on God; God is active in the world through the natural processes of life.

But what about prayer? Isn't the efficacy of prayer dramatically displayed when "miraculously" an event happens, which would not otherwise have happened? Schleiermacher replied that prayer and its fulfillment or refusal are also part of the original divine plan. Prayer does not cause God to change the plan God has already decreed. Prayer is something in which we engage not to manipulate God, but to form ourselves in patterns of recognizing our dependence upon God and for expressing gratitude for God's blessings.[8] But what about the regenerative transformation of the individual effected by the ministry of Christ? Is not this transformation supernatural? No, Schleiermacher replied, it is not something supernatural in a strict or absolute sense. Consequently, Schleiermacher concluded that "we should abandon the idea of the absolutely supernatural because no single instance of it can be known by us, and we are nowhere required to recognize it" (see §47, 3 below). Because human knowledge of the created world is continually growing, we cannot claim absolutely that anything is impossible. But we should, Schleiermacher advised, calmly trust scientific research to investigate. Schleiermacher's point is that Christian piety does not require belief in miracles as supernatural interventions; therefore, the study of so-called miraculous events can be calmly entrusted to scientific inquiry. Christian piety, however, does entail a sense of absolute dependence upon God. Such a sense constitutes the experiential essence of the doctrine of preservation and creation.

A logical corollary of Schleiermacher's insistence upon the coincidence of natural causes and divine causes in the functioning of the world is that evil must also

---

8. For Schleiermacher, the purpose of prayer is "not to bend God's will to our wishes but to bend our wishes to God's will." In God no new thought and no new decision can arise; everything God has made is good. Therefore: "To be conscious of God is not to invite divine intervention in the world but to acknowledge that the course of the world is sustained by omnipotent love and is therefore good" (B. A. Gerrish, *A Prince of the Church: Schleiermacher and the Beginnings of Modern Theology* [Philadelphia: Fortress Press, 1984], 66–67).

be, in some sense, caused by God. Progress and limitation are natural constituents of the relationship of human beings to nature. Every relation to the natural world which supports development of human life is felt by us to be good, whereas every relation which brings death nearer is felt by us to be evil. But both human progress in life and human decline are inseparable because both rely upon natural forces. Correlatively, limitation is part of the essence of being a finite creature. Consequently, it is erroneous, Schleiermacher concluded, to think that the world could exist apart from evil. He states: "The fact is rather that the very same activity or condition of a thing by which it enters on the one hand into human life as an evil, on the other hand is a cause of good, so that if we could remove the source of life's difficulties the conditions of life's progress too would disappear" (see §48, 2 below). Schleiermacher asserted that this proposition is true of both natural evil (which is not caused by a rational agent) and moral evil (which is caused by a rational agent). In short, Schleiermacher claimed that God's fundamental activity with regard to creation in general is its preservation in operation, including what we perceive to be evil as well as good.

Schleiermacher's apparently neat explanation of the reality and inevitability of evil was something that liberal Protestants could endorse. But the radical evil that erupted in the twentieth century created dissatisfaction with such an apparently facile explanation of moral evil and God's part in it. World War I saw significant advances in technology, such as airplanes, used to kill one's enemies. World War II saw the escalation in the production of new weapons and the diminishment of restraint in using everything available to destroy one's enemies, including saturation bombing and atomic weapons. Intentional genocide of Jews by the Nazis was a horrific manifestation of radical evil, as was the delayed action by the Allies to deter or to stop it. In the face of the scope and the depth of evil and suffering disclosed in the first four decades of the twentieth century, it became difficult to endorse the theological liberalism of the nineteenth century. That century's optimism about the possibility of human progress through the use of reason, science, and technology was greatly chastened.

Karl Barth became an outspoken critic of liberal Protestantism in the early twentieth century. He brought to the forefront once again the reality of human sinfulness. He resisted every attempt of human culture to co-opt the Christian message, as exemplified in the leading role he played in the writing of the Barmen Declaration. Instead of using human experience or rational argument as the foundation upon which to build his theological edifice, Barth chose biblical revelation. In doing so he followed in the steps of the sixteenth-century Protestant Reformers. Yet the context in which he embarked on this journey was quite different. The historical situation of the early twentieth century was quite different from that of the sixteenth century. And biblical interpretation in the intervening centuries had become more historically critical. In this new situation, Barth developed a *neo*-orthodox approach to theology.

Against the theological method of liberals, which began with human experience, Barth proposed beginning with God's Word. To begin anywhere else would mean that theology's subject "is not really God but a hypostatized reflection of man" (see §32, 1 below). For Barth, to begin with God's Word is to begin with Christ. Christ's voice is the source and norm of all truth. By his voice humanity is taught by Godself concerning God. What do we learn by attending to Christ's voice? We learn, Barth replied, that Christ is God in God's movement towards humanity. Christ is the decision of God in favor of relation to humanity. This relation is irrevocable. That means, once God has willed to enter into the relation and has in fact entered into it, God could not be God without it. This is indeed good news for humankind. The essence of this good news is expressed in the doctrine of the election of grace.

In the tradition of Calvin, Barth asserted that the doctrine of election is the best word we could possibly hear. This doctrine boldly declares God's love and God's grace. Election, in fact, makes a statement not only about humanity (those who are elected), but also about God, for in electing human beings God also is "predestined." Without the relation to humanity, God could not be God at all. Although God's gracious movement toward humanity is an indication of divine love, God takes this step freely. By emphasizing both points — divine love and grace, on the one side, and divine freedom and sovereignty, on the other — Barth's position reiterated strong Calvinist themes. In the process he differentiated his position from others that also emphasized God's love.[9] Like Calvin, Barth maintained that the doctrine of predestination is the good news itself, "news which uplifts and comforts and sustains" (see §32, 1 below). It can be good news because the "no" of reprobation is said for the sake of the "yes" of election. God's free and gracious election to salvation is God's principal word. God's creating, reconciling, and redeeming activities on behalf of humanity are grounded in the election of divine grace.

Karl Rahner's theological reflections provide a clear counter-point to Barth's. Whereas Barth, working within the Protestant tradition, placed renewed emphasis upon revelation as the starting point of theological reflection, Rahner, working within the Catholic tradition, emphasized the encounter with God in human experience and history. Rahner claimed that the elements of transcendence in the human person pointed in the direction of God. The transcendental dynamism toward God, according to Rahner, yields an awareness of God that is implicit and subconscious. Rahner referred to this awareness as transcendental knowledge. When human knowledge of God is explicit, conscious, and concrete, Rahner spoke of categorial or categorical knowledge. History is the effective medium through which transcendental knowledge of God can become categorial knowledge. In the events of historical revelation, knowledge of God becomes concrete and explicit.

Within this basic framework, Rahner developed his critique of those interpretations of the trinity that focused too much on the immanent trinity (that is, the internal relationships within the Godhead). As the excerpt below makes clear, Rahner called for a starting point for reflections about the trinitarian God within

---

9. For example, in Catherine of Siena, we read that God is "constrained" to be providential toward humanity because of God's immeasurable love (see *The Dialogue,* sect. 143 above). Catherine spoke of God's apparent "need" of humanity, without which God, it seems, could not live (see *The Dialogue,* sect. 153 above). To be sure, Barth too confessed that God could not be God without relation to humanity. But he emphasized that this covenant with humanity is established, maintained, and directed by God, who is the Lord of the covenant. God's loving relation with human beings and God's providential activity toward them is an act of divine freedom and an expression of divine sovereignty. Here we hear the echoes of Calvin's theology.

the historical and salvific experience of the Son and the Spirit (see "The Problem with a 'Psychological Theory of the Trinity' " below). The God experienced in our personal history and in the history of the world (the "economic" trinity) is truly Godself (the "immanent" trinity). Within this framework, Rahner developed his understanding of God's creative activity.

Creation or "being created," for Rahner, refers primarily to a present reality or experience. As in the case of his explication of other doctrines, here too Rahner begins with transcendental experience of God ("absolute being") as the real ground of every act of knowledge and of every action. Reminiscent of Schleiermacher, Rahner affirms that human beings as creatures are aware of their radical dependence upon God in every moment of their ongoing existences (see "Creatureliness as Radical Difference" below). And yet God is not, and cannot be, experienced as one object alongside other objects in the world. If this were the case, God could not be the creative ground of everything that is. As transcendent, God cannot be reduced to an object in the world. Human knowledge and human objectification of God can never capture fully who God is. God remains holy mystery.

The problem arises: How can we speak of God's activity in the world if, as the ground of everything, God transcends the world? Rahner responds to this question by drawing out the implications of the Thomistic assertion that God works through secondary causes. God causes the world, but not *in* the world. By this Rahner means to say that the chain of causality is rooted in God, but God is not one of the links in the chain of causes. From this perspective, special interventions of God into the course of history are unnecessary because God is already intrinsic to the concrete world. Rahner uses the example of getting a good idea to explicate his understanding of God's "natural" involvement in the world. Rahner concludes that "everything can be regarded as a special providence, as an intervention of God, presupposing only that I accept the concrete constellation of my life and of the world in such a way that it becomes a positive, salvific concretization of my transcendental relationship to God in freedom" (see "God's Activity in and through Secondary Causes" below).

In a similar fashion, Paul Tillich subsumes the doctrine of divine providence under the general heading of creation. For him, God is essentially creative. Although he follows the classical tradition in asserting that God's creative activity is a free act, Tillich emphasizes the point that creativity is part of the very nature of God and, therefore, creation is also God's "destiny" (see sect. 5 below). Naturally creative, God's creative activity must be expressed in the three modes of time. This scheme leads Tillich to speak of God's originating creativity (past), sustaining creativity (present), and directing creativity (future).

With regard to God's originating creativity, Tillich states that creation does not describe an event (how the world began), but rather describes what it means to be a creature. Here we find broad agreement between Tillich and Rahner. Tillich lays out his position by interpreting the classical affirmation that creation was "out of nothing" (*creatio ex nihilo*). This traditional affirmation says something both about God and about creatures. Like theologians of the classical tradition, Tillich states that creation from nothing means that God's creative work does not depend on anything else and that nothing exists that can resist God's creative work. Tillich adds, however, that the idea of creation from nothing says some-thing about creatures, namely, that they carry within themselves "the heritage of nonbeing." Created out of nothing (nonexistence), creatures are naturally subject to death (return to nonexistence) and potentially subject to the tragic. Here we see a contrast between Tillich and Rahner. Although he too was influenced by the philosophy of Martin Heidegger, Rahner developed his ideas primarily within the context of a transcendental, Thomistic philosophy. Tillich, by contrast, gave his reflections a more marked and consistent existentialist cast.

During the period of World War II and its aftermath, existentialism was a prominent movement, philosophically and theologically. With roots in the nineteenth-century philosopher Søren Kierkegaard and in the twentieth-century philosopher Martin Heidegger, existentialism focused upon the ways in which the human subject, intensely aware of its finitude and ultimate death, concretely en-counters other beings and events.[10] Conscious of one's fragility and impending death, the human person experiences anxiety. In its philosophical form, existen-tialism was often paired with atheism — as in the case of Jean-Paul Sartre. But some theologians, such as Rudolf Bultmann and Paul Tillich, attempted to use ex-istentialist categories in their interpretation of Christian faith. In his 1952 book, *The Courage to Be,* Tillich proposed God as the antidote to the threat of non-being. Insofar as the human person participates in being itself, he or she carries within the power of being, and not just the heritage of nonbeing. Insofar as they are rooted in the creative ground of being (God), human beings can choose to ex-ercise the courage to be. Through freedom persons actualize themselves, thereby avoiding a meaningless existence.

The tension between anxiety, generated by the human subject's awareness of the threat of nonbeing, and courage, generated by the subject's awareness of participation in being itself, is evident in Tillich's explication of the doc-trine of creation. Only because of its participation in the power of being itself can the creature resist nonbeing. In this context, we are led to speak about the doc-trine of preservation. In explaining God's activity of preservation, Tillich criticizes modern forms of both deism and theism that insist upon occasional divine inter-vention through miracles. Against these ideas, Tillich proposes an understanding of preservation as continuous creativity and an understanding of God as simulta-neously immanent and transcendent. Tillich points out that the historical context in which he was writing was an opportune moment for recovering a sense of God's sustaining creativity. Historical events, such as the Holocaust and World War II, had destroyed the feeling of living in an ultimately secure world. The deistic notion that the world operates independently of God, who, although ini-tially responsible for establishing its physical laws, now lives removed and aloof

---

10. Gareth Jones provides a good summary description. Existentialism, he says, "regards the individ-ual not as a biological fact, or an object, but as a subject, a discrete being which is unique in the world because it recognizes that its life is destined to end in nothingness. Thus, using the language of popu-lar psychology, existentialists speak of the individual's anguish when confronted by the reality of death, and of the pressures upon the subject's psyche which occur when the individual regards his or her life as essentially contingent and accidental. Fundamentally, existentialism ... denies individuals recourse to any form of external support. Alone, the subject must understand his or her life in terms of an inevitable journey towards death" ("Existentialism," in *The Blackwell Encyclopedia of Modern Christian Thought,* ed. Alister E. McGrath [Cambridge, Mass.: Blackwell, 1993], 200–201).

from the world, could not establish a sense of security in face of the death and meaninglessness of war. Nor could an atheistic existentialist philosophy of life. But by re-establishing a vital sense of God's sustaining creativity in every moment of temporal existence, it was possible, Tillich argued, to resist anxiety and meaninglessness.

God's sustaining activity differs from the divine originating activity in that it establishes the continuity of the structure of reality as the basis for being and acting. From this perspective, God does not create the structure of reality in the past (at the temporal origin of the world) and then let the structure operate independently throughout the rest of history. Rather, God actively creates and sustains the structure of reality in each given moment. In order to explain his understanding of divine "preservation," Tillich appeals to a nonspatial interpretation of God's immanence and transcendence, an interpretation we also find in Rahner and other twentieth-century theologians. Properly used, these terms do not answer the question whether God is in the world or above it. Rather, they express symbolically God's qualitative relationship to the world. God is immanent insofar as God is the "creative ground of the spatial structure of the world" (see sect. 5b below). God is transcendent insofar as God is not bound to the structure of the world. In this way, Tillich attempts to maintain both divine connection to the world and divine freedom.

Tillich recasts the traditional doctrine of providence in terms of God's directing creativity. He rejects as ambiguous talk about "the purpose" of creation. Instead he speaks of the goal (*telos*) and fulfillment of creatures. In light of his experience of the powerful manifestations of evil in the first half of the twentieth century and in light of contemporary psychological and philosophical analyses of the human condition, it comes as no surprise that Tillich admitted that it was difficult to believe in providence. Divine providence, properly understood, has a paradoxical character. It is not properly understood as a divine foreknowledge of what creatures will freely do, independently of God. Nor is it properly understood as a divine predestination of what creatures will do, independently of the creature's freedom. God's providence, or "directing creativity," always creates through human freedom and through the spontaneity and structural wholeness of all creatures. God directs, but does not control. God's direction is internal, not external to creatures. Thus Tillich states:

> Providence is a *quality* of every constellation of conditions, a quality which "drives" or "lures" toward fulfillment.... It is not an additional factor, a miraculous physical or mental interference in terms of supranaturalism. It is the quality of inner directedness present in every situation. The man who believes in providence does not believe that a special divine activity will alter the conditions of finitude and estrangement. He believes, and asserts with the courage of faith, that no situation whatsoever can frustrate the fulfillment of his ultimate destiny, that nothing can separate him from the love of God which is in Christ Jesus (Rom. 8). (See sect. 5c[3] below.)

In light of this understanding of God's providential activity, Tillich explicates prayer and addresses the problem of theodicy. Prayer, according to Tillich, is a condition of God's directing creativity and an expression of personal faith that transforms our experience of the situations we confront. Tillich does not treat theodicy and predestination as abstract questions about humanity in general, but as concrete questions about the existential experience of individuals. Tillich rejects the division of humanity into two classes, the elect and the reprobate. And he declares that the ultimate answer to the question of theodicy is the participation of the divine life in the negativities of creaturely life.

As the work of both Tillich and Rahner illustrate, major theologians of the twentieth century sought to articulate an understanding of God's creative and providential activity that was compatible with a scientific understanding of the world and with the presupposition of human freedom. The historical manifestations of radical evil in the twentieth century, as well as recent developments in philosophy and science, made a credible articulation more difficult. Charles Hartshorne used the categories of process, articulated in the philosophy of Alfred North Whitehead, to interpret anew a Christian understanding of God and God's activities vis-à-vis the world.

Consonant with his reinterpretation of God's nature as relational and social, Hartshorne also reinterpreted God's activities of creation and providence. Hartshorne's approach to these issues followed the path from analogy. If all of reality, according to the testimony of our senses, is relational (that is, interdependent and therefore in flux), then the nature of ultimate reality (God) must also be relational. Applied to the activity of creation, this relational principle yields the idea of creative sociality. Sociality means that each individual person, to a greater or lesser degree, makes his or her friends what they are. It is important to note that, from Hartshorne's process perspective, the fundamental category of reality is not matter, but social relations. Divine creativity therefore means that God influences and shapes, in a significant way, the web of relationships in each stage of the world. God, however, does not control those relationships. This interpretation of creation clearly diverges from the classical tradition.

Like Tillich, Hartshorne was committed to formulating an understanding of providence that releases God from full responsibility for evil while retaining God's involvement in each occasion of experience. Classical figures in the Christian tradition had dealt with this dilemma by emphasizing the fact that God permitted human freedom. Thus the responsibility for moral evil was shifted to human beings, while divine omnipotence was retained. God is still all-powerful because God has the power to "intervene" against the decisions of human free will, but God chooses not to. In this sense, the classical tradition spoke of God "permitting," but not directly "willing" evil. Calvin, as we have seen, went a step further. Because he did not want God's sovereignty and omnipotence to be eclipsed in any fashion, Calvin rejected the distinction between God's permission and God's will (see *Institutes of the Christian Religion,* Book I, ch. 18, 1 above).

In the intervening centuries between Calvin and Hartshorne, the capabilities of the human person seemed to expand greatly. Correlatively, human freedom and autonomy became increasingly valued. This increase in the value of human autonomy paralleled developments in philosophy, science, and politics. Beginning with Descartes in the seventeenth century, the arbiter of truth had shifted from authorities in church or state to the thinking self. From the time of Galileo in the same century, the natural sciences demonstrated their ability not only to explain the present physical functioning of the world, but also to predict how the world *must* behave (even in the future), according to the "laws of nature" that science had discovered. This knowledge enabled the development of new inventions, which made human work easier and more productive. In politics, French Enlightenment philosophers of the eighteenth century defended the idea that the authority of political governments rests with the people and the representatives chosen by them. Insofar as the dignity of the human person came to depend more and more upon the degree of his or her autonomy, belief in a God who controls human events became increasingly intolerable. From Schleiermacher forward, Protestant and Catholic theologians wrestled with a resolution of the tension between divine power and human freedom.

As Hartshorne himself notes, the insistence upon understanding divine providence as the ordering of all events according to a completely detailed plan has contributed to the rise of atheism in the modern world. If everything has been determined or permitted by God, including monstrous evils, then belief in God, atheists suggested, was reprehensible. Hartshorne's resolution of this dilemma involved a reinterpretation of divine omnipotence, divine perfection, and the divine will. Hartshorne suggested that power means influence or direction, but not control. Understood from this perspective, divine omnipotence means that God influences and directs everything, without controlling entities or events. But if God does not control everything, is God still God? Is such a God worthy of respect and worship? Hartshorne replied that God is still God provided that God can be relied on to do for the world all that *God* ought to do for it, leaving for the members of the world community to do for themselves all that *they* ought to be left to do. From this perspective, what happens in the world is the result of the interaction between God and the world community. No one entity, including God, controls the outcome of these interactions.

Despite the fluidity in this understanding of history, Hartshorne's reflections did not intend to leave the reader with the impression that God has no plan for the world or that the plan is constantly changing. Hartshorne held that God has a general or overall plan for the world, namely, to promote "the highest cosmic good." With regard to this goal, God's will does not change. God's specific actions, however, will change according to circumstances and the actions of other entities. This give-and-take between God and creatures is a corollary of Hartshorne's social, relational understanding of reality.

This same principle of relationality implies mutuality and reciprocity. Here too Hartshorne's interpretation of God's nature and activity diverges from the classical tradition. Whereas the classical tradition maintained that God influences everything but is influenced by nothing, Hartshorne insisted that God influences everything and is influenced by everything. Consequently, God shares in the joy and the sorrow of the world. We saw intimations of this interpretation in Tillich. The objection, however, immediately arises that such an understanding of God degradingly reduces God to the level of imperfect creatures. God's perfection, according to the classical tradition, resides in God's completeness and changelessness. Imperfect creatures are incomplete and subject to change. Hartshorne replied to this objection by redefining perfection. If perfection means being completely worthy of admiration and respect, as Hartshorne suggests it does, then a God who shares in our sorrow and our joy is a perfect being.

Elizabeth Johnson, using primarily feminist rather than process categories, makes a similar point. She points out that the traditional understanding of God's relation to the world is based on nonpersonal reality (specifically, on the notions of cause and effect or "motion"). If we understand God's relation to the world, however, on the basis of personal reality (specifically, relations), we can authentically speak of God's suffering. In the classical formulation of the early and medieval church, God's love was understood to be benevolence. That is, God "wishes well" or wants good for all of God's creatures. Understood in these terms, divine love is an intention of the divine will. Johnson criticizes this understanding of love because it is incomplete. It fails to include the reciprocity that is an essential part of mature relations between rational agents. Reciprocity means being open and vulnerable to the experiences of the beloved; it means solidarity with the well-being of the beloved. Therefore, a more appropriate understanding of love, says Johnson, includes both benevolence and compassionate solidarity.

Because divine vulnerability to the suffering of creatures is an act of freely given love, divine suffering is not an indication of imperfection in God. It is instead an act of highest excellence. Of course, one might object, sometimes we need and want someone to rescue us from a situation of terrible suffering. What good then is a suffering God who commiserates with us? Johnson responds to this objection by noting that a suffering God is not a helpless God. In fact, a God who stands in compassionate solidarity with suffering creatures provides them with at least three kinds of help: a source of comfort and energy, which does not eliminate but certainly does transform suffering; a stimulus to responsible human action in response to the suffering of others; and inspiration of a hope against hope. Whereas Hartshorne redefined divine omnipotence in light of his understanding of the relationality of all reality, Johnson redefines omnipotence in light of the experience of women. She criticizes both the classical understanding of power as "power over" and the process understanding of power as "persuasive power." Instead she says that God's power is something like "power with." That is, divine omnipotence is the "liberating power of connectedness that is effective in compassionate love" (see "Divine Power" below). God stands in compassionate solidarity with all those who suffer, enabling them from within to take up the work of resisting evil, healing, and liberating themselves and others from oppression.

The emphasis on relationship that we find in the philosophical orientation of Hartshorne and in the feminist orientation of Johnson also is evident in the social-economic-liberation orientation of Leonardo Boff. In the excerpt below from *Trinity and Society,* the Brazilian theologian uses the doctrine of the trinity to describe the kind of community human beings should create when they are inspired by God's Spirit. Boff takes the classic statement about God creating humanity in the divine image and interprets it, in the tradition of Bonaventure, in a trinitarian fashion. Thus, to be created in the image of the trinitarian God means that the person is "a permanently active web of relationships," relating "backwards" to his or her origin in God the Father, relating "outwards" to others in God the Son, and relating "inwards" to the depths of one's personality in God the Spirit.

Creation in the trinitarian image means being created for relationship. Human relationships, however, have become corrupted. The corruption or sinfulness of these relationships is exemplified in both capitalist and socialist societies. The trinitarian God is active now in the inspiration of a new kind of society, a society that respects diversity while maintaining the equality of all and the participation of all in the work of the community. God is active today, Boff says, in the process of introducing all of us to the life of the trinitarian community. In view of the evil and oppression in the world, this process of integration and inspiration is also a process of salvation. God's saving activity is a work of liberation, liberation from oppression and isolation. Here Boff draws on the etymological root of the word "salvation." He emphasizes the healing and the making whole that God's salvation essentially is.

In the work of Johnson and Boff, we find evidence of the particularity or specificity of contemporary theology. This specificity is a characteristic of theology in the second half of the twentieth century. With recognition and appreciation of the diversity of individuals and cultures, the contemporary scene witnesses a broad pluralism of theological methods and conclusions. In the tradition of Schleiermacher, Johnson and Boff make human experience a central resource in theological reflection. They, however, do not reflect upon human experience "in general." Rather, they focus on the experiences of particular human beings and bring the Christian message into conversation — or, as Tillich said, correlation — with that experience. For Johnson, the experience of women is a primary theological resource. This form of specificity perhaps has had the greatest impact on theology.[11] For Boff, the primary theological resource is the experience of poor people. In the case of James Cone, it is the experience of African and African-American Christians.[12]

Cone's *A Black Theology of Liberation* was published a few years after the emergence of the black power movement in the United States and the assassination of Martin Luther King, Jr. Writing at the end of the 1960s and the beginning of the 1970s, Cone gave eloquent expression to the frustration over and righteous anger of African Americans against the mighty obstacles on the road to civil equality. In the context of white racism and black oppression, Cone disclosed the ideological distortions in the uncritical endorsement of the traditional understanding of Christian faith. The phrases "God is love" or "God forgives all" could be understood to mean that God loves oppressors as much as the oppressed. Correlatively, the uncritical affirmation of God's providence and omnipotence could be

---

11. See Martin Marty, "Christian Theology since 1965: An Overview," in *Makers of Christian Theology in America*, ed. Mark G. Toulouse and James O. Duke (Nashville: Abingdon Press, 1997), 529: "The most far-reaching change in the theological enterprise in North America if not yet the world has been the rise of particularisms along the lines of gender, particularly through the voices of women." Marty notes that since 1965 a significant minority of theological expressions come from women in mainstream Protestantism and in Catholicism. He continues, p. 530: "After Vatican II, Catholicism gave or allowed for (still unordained) new status to the roles of women, including women as teachers of theology. Many would say, better, that women won new status, because much of the leadership yielded dominance only grudgingly and gradually. Still, whoever takes the longer view of Christian history would have to note that the changes of this third of a century have been greater than those made in the rest of the two Christian millennia."

12. Martin Marty observes: "A case can be made that the identification of theological inquiry with the expression of racial and ethnic experiences vies with the particularities of gendered understandings to make up the principal theological change of the last third of the century" ("Christian Theology since 1965," 533).

understood to suggest that the present inequality of blacks is part of God's will. Cone declares such interpretations to be serious distortions of Christian faith.

In the specific context of the black struggle for liberation, Cone insisted that God's loving activity must include wrath against white oppressors and solidarity with black liberators. In situations of injustice, God does take sides. This theme of divine "preference" can also be found in other forms of liberation theology. Cone, moreover, rejected the Protestant neo-orthodox interpretation of divine provi- dence, which suggests that everything happens within the knowledge and will of God. In view of horrendous evil, such as the genocide of Native Americans at the time of European conquest or the enslavement and lynching of blacks in America, Cone found such an interpretation wholly objectionable. Rejecting the classical distinction between God's will and God's permission, Cone insisted that black theology could not accept any understanding of God "that even *indirectly* places divine approval on human suffering" (see excerpt below).

What then might faith in divine providence and in divine omnipotence mean in the specific context of the black struggle for liberation? Drawing upon the work of Tillich, Cone asserted that providence means that God is active in every set of circumstances, including the black liberation movement, and that therefore the road to black liberation is open. Drawing upon the work of Anglican theologian John Macquarrie, Cone reinterpreted divine omnipotence. It means God's power to let something stand out from nothing, rather than God's absolute power to accomplish what God wants. In the context of the black experience in the United States during the 1960s and beyond, divine omnipotence is "the power to let blacks stand out from whiteness and to be" (see excerpt below).

Whether it focused upon the liberation of women, the poor, or people of color, liberation theology in the second half of the twentieth century regularly appealed to the biblical story of the Exodus to sanction the idea that salvation involves liberation from physical oppression, as well as liberation from sin. If one identifies with the enslaved Hebrews, then the Exodus story is good news. God has chosen the Hebrews as God's people. God hears their cries for freedom and redeems them from their captivity. But what if one identifies with other figures in the biblical narratives, such as non-Jewish slaves? Is the story of the Hebrews' election and redemption by God still good news? These are some of the questions raised by Delores Williams. From her womanist perspective, the story of Hebrew election has a different resonance.[13]

Reading the Bible critically, Williams identifies nonliberative strands in both the Hebrew scriptures and the New Testament. She concludes that slavery in the Bible is regarded as a natural institution of ancient society. Slavery is not categorically rejected in either of the testaments of the Christian Bible. Moreover, an uncritical reading of the Bible leads one to conclude that divine activity in the world some- times includes genocide, as in the Israelite conquest of Canaan. For reasons such

---

13. The label "womanist" refers to African and African-American women who are committed to the liberation of women of color. The label is used in distinction from "feminist" to signal the fact that although women of color experience many of the same forms of discrimination that white women do, their experiences and their concerns are nonetheless different from those of white feminists. Womanists generally have devoted more attention to the matters of race and economic class in the struggle for well- being. Womanists point out that women of color, in distinction from white women, often experience a triple form of oppression — oppression because of their gender, their race, and their social class.

as these, Williams criticizes James Cone and others, who assume that African-American theology today can make uncritical, paradigmatic use of the biblical account of the Hebrews' election and liberation. She does not want to remove every use of the Exodus story from African-American theology, but she does want the limitations of the story to be recognized. The story has limited use, she argues, both because of its content (e.g., questionable divine sanction for violence against others) and because of the changes in the situation of African-Americans since emancipation from slavery.

A more critical, nuanced reading of the Bible will yield a more complex understanding of God's activity in the world. Using the Hagar-Sarah story as an illustration, Williams argues that God's activity on behalf of humanity is not always liberating. Sometimes it is more appropriate to recognize God's activity as providing strategies and tools for simple survival. Survival is a good, but it is not the same thing as liberation. As we have seen in the case of other twentieth-century theologians, so too in Williams we find an attempt to balance God's role and humanity's role in the events that take place in history. God is active in the process of Hagar's liberation because God provides her with "*new vision* to see survival resources where she saw none before" (see below). Although God provides the new vision, it is Hagar, not God, who initiates the actual process of liberation. Moreover, Hagar is "liberated" into precarious circumstances. Such a reading of the Bible with regard to God's activities in the world may not yield the unambiguous conclusion some might want, but it does allow various communities of oppressed women and men "to hear and see the *doing* of the good news in a way that is meaningful for their lives" (see below).

In the last three decades of the twentieth century, increasing numbers of theologians gave considerable attention to God's liberating activities on behalf of suffering human beings. During that time, attention began to be given also to the suffering of the earth. Ecological concerns began to permeate theological reflections. Some theologians, in response to the degradation of air, water, and soil, sought ways to reinterpret the relationship between God and creation that would encourage people to adopt more ecologically appropriate ways of living. Sallie McFague has been one of the leaders in this theological movement.

Already in her *Models of God* book (1987), McFague had proposed a rethinking of the relationship between God and creation. She criticized the monarchical model of God that made God into a patriarch, demanding obedience, and the world into the political domain over which God ruled. Instead she proposed imagining God according to the models of mother, lover, and friend. In addition, she suggested imagining the world not as a kingdom external to God, but rather as God's body. In the book from which the excerpt below is taken, *The Body of God: An Ecological Theology* (1993), this theological proposal and its implications are worked out in detail.

McFague criticizes the traditional interpretations of the doctrine of creation for several reasons. They emphasize, for example, the origin of creation rather than its ongoing character; they affirm divine transcendence in such a way that divine immanence becomes difficult to affirm. These traditional interpretations, rooted in the Genesis story of creation, provide one model (namely, production) for understanding God's creative activity. A better model for our present context,

McFague argues, is an amalgam of the procreation and the emanation models. A procreation-emanationist model of creation avoids the difficulties that beset the production model. But what happens to divine transcendence if we think of the world as "bodying" forth from God? McFague notes that transcendence can be understood in different senses. If it is understood to mean "surpassing, excelling, or extraordinary," then McFague's model of creation can uphold both divine transcendence and immanence.

McFague's reinterpretation of transcendence, however, also entails a reinterpretation of God's "control" over the world. In the production model of creation, divine transcendence is equated with sovereignty or dominion over the world. In this model, God and the world are separate; God is the external lord over the world. In McFague's procreative-emanationist model, God and the world are not separate, but connected; God is the life of the body (the world). In this model, there is "no mind directing the body, but rather a body suffused with the breath and power of life" (see excerpt below). McFague argues that such an understanding is supported by the common creation story constructed by modern science, in which we see "a continuum of matter that gradually over billions of years becomes brain (mind) in varying ways and degrees."

McFague's work illustrates an important strand of contemporary theology at the dawn of the third Christian millennium. This strand of theology has become much more self-conscious of its creative and imaginative dimensions. It does not claim to provide exact pictures of reality or purely "objective" definitions of God's activity in the world. Rather it provides imaginative models or constructs for construing reality and God's activity. In such theology, symbol and metaphor are primary. This kind of theology, moreover, is more willing than many forms of theology from previous eras to acknowledge ambiguity within the Christian tradition and ambiguity within each formulation of the meaning of that tradition. There is today a growing acceptance of not only ambiguity, but also the plurality of ways in which Christian faith can be expressed. These features of theology at the end of the second and the beginning of the third Christian millennium are concisely and suggestively described in David Tracy's 1985 book, *Plurality and Ambiguity*. As we move into the third millennium, we can expect to see a continuing proliferation of particular interpretations of Christian doctrines in response to evolving needs and changing contexts. The "coherence" and "intactness" of theology that existed in the middle of the twentieth century is not likely to reappear any time soon. Similarly, the almost universally European character of theology, prevalent in the first half of the twentieth century, has waned just as European colonialism has disappeared. Today North and South American, as well as Asian and African theologians no longer look primarily to Europe for guidance or inspiration. Rather, they draw on indigenous resources for theological reflection as they address their theological interpretations to their specific contexts. While the "particularization" of theological reflections will continue, we can also expect to see theological reactions against this pluralism. Out of this interaction, the rich heritage of the western Christian tradition will be developed in diverse and dynamic ways.

T E X T S

Friedrich Schleiermacher (1768–1834)

The Christian Faith (1830–31), §39, Pars. 1–2; §47, Pars. 1 and 3; §48, Pars. 1–2*

§39. *The doctrine of Creation is to be elucidated pre-eminently with a view to the exclusion of every alien element, lest from the way in which the question of Origin is answered elsewhere anything steal into our province which stands in contradiction to the pure expression of the feeling of absolute dependence. But the doctrine of Preservation is pre-eminently to be elucidated so as to bring out this fundamental feeling itself in the fullest way.*

1. Our self-consciousness, in its universality, as both these doctrines relate to it, can only represent finite being in general so far as it is a continuous being; for we only know ourselves in this manner but have not consciousness of a beginning of being. Hence as we have seen, though not impossible, it would be extremely difficult to develop the same material principally or exclusively under the form of the doctrine of Creation. Such an attempt would be just as arbitrary as it would be inappropriate for the purpose of Dogmatics, in view of the fact that in popular religious teaching the doctrine of Preservation has a far greater importance. In general the question of the origin of all finite being is raised not in the interest of piety but in that of curiosity, hence it can only be answered by such means as curiosity offers. Piety can never show more than an indirect interest in it; i.e., it recognizes no answer to it which brings the religious man into contradiction with his fundamental feeling. And this is the position given the doctrine, both when it occurs in the New Testament and in all regular Confessions of Faith. Whereas the Old Testament basis of it lies in the beginnings of a history-book which as such chiefly satisfies the desire for knowledge.

2. In the doctrine of Creation, then, we have pre-eminently to prevent anything alien from slipping in from the field of knowledge. But the opposite danger is also certainly to be kept in view, namely, the development of our self-consciousness must not be so conceived as to set the man who desires knowledge in contradiction with the principles of research he follows in the sphere of nature or of history. But as the self-consciousness we have here to consider itself implies that we are placed in a nature-system, any doctrine of Preservation which could immediately follow from this would find no motive in the working out of this self-consciousness for wishing to overthrow that assumption. And this mistake will be the less likely to occur if the treatment of the doctrine of Creation already specified has gone before....

§47. *It can never be necessary in the interest of religion so to interpret a fact that its dependence on God absolutely excludes its being conditioned by the system of Nature.*

---

1. This proposition is so much a direct consequence of what went before that there would be no reason to make an express statement of it, but that ideas which have still a circulation in the Christian Church must be considered in their appropriate place in any Dogmatic. Now there is a general idea that the miracles which are interwoven with the beginnings of Christianity or at least in some form are reported in the Scriptures, should be regarded as events of the kind described; and yet if the idea itself is inadmissible, it cannot be applied to this or that particular fact. It is in this way that theologians from of old have generally treated the question. We have not to pass judgment here on its inherent possibility, but only on the relation of the theory to the feeling of absolute dependence. If, then, this relation is what our proposition declares it to be, we must in our field try, as far as possible, to interpret every event with reference to the interdependence of nature and without detriment to that principle.

Now some have represented miracle in this sense as essential to the perfect manifestation of the divine omnipotence. But it is difficult to conceive, on the one side, how omnipotence is shown to be greater in the suspension of the interdependence of nature than in its original immutable course which was no less divinely ordered. For, indeed, the capacity to make a change in what has been ordained is only a merit in the ordainer, if a change is necessary, which again can only be the result of some imperfection in him or in his work. If such an interference be postulated as one of the privileges of the Supreme Being, it would first have to be assumed that there is something not ordained by Him which could offer Him resistance and thus invade Him and His work; and such an idea would entirely destroy our fundamental feeling. We must remember, on the other hand, that where such a conception of miracles is commonly found, namely, in conditions where there is least knowledge of nature, there, too, the fundamental feeling appears to be weakest and most ineffectual. But where a knowledge of nature is most widely spread, and therefore this conception seldom occurs, more is found of that reverence for God which is the expression of our fundamental feeling. It follows from this that the most perfect representation of omnipotence would be a view of the world which made no use of such an idea.

Other teachers defend the conception in a more acute but scarcely more tenable way, by saying that God was partly in need of miracles that He might compensate for the effects of free causes in the course of nature, and partly that He might generally have reasons for remaining in direct contact with the world. The latter argument presupposes, for one thing, a wholly lifeless view of the divine preservation, and for another, an opposition in general between the mediate and immediate activities of God which cannot be conceived without bringing the Supreme Being within the sphere of limitation. The former sounds almost as if free causes were not themselves objects of divine preservation, and (since preservation includes in itself the idea of creation) had not come into being and been maintained in absolute dependence upon God. But if, on the contrary, they are in this condition there can be just as little necessity for God to counteract their influences as to counteract the influences which a blind natural force exercises in the domain of another natural force. But none of us understands by "the world" which is the object of the divine preservation a nature-mechanism alone, but rather the interaction of the nature-mechanism and of free agents, so that in the former the latter are taken into account just as in the latter the former is reckoned.

Moreover, the Biblical miracles, on account of which the whole theory has been devised, are much too isolated and too restricted in content for any theory to be based on them which should assign them the function of restoring in the nature-mechanism what free agents had altered. That one great miracle, the mission of Christ, has, of course, the aim of restoration, but it is the restoration of what free causes have altered in their own province, not in that of the nature-mechanism or in the course of things originally ordained by God. Nor does the interest of religion require that the free cause which performs the function of restoration in the sphere of phenomena should have a different relation to the order of nature from that of other free causes.

Two other reasons may be put forward why an absolute suspension of the interrelatedness of nature by miracles may be held to be in the interests of religion. And it cannot be denied that it is mostly for these reasons, even though they may never have been formulated as actual Church doctrine, that this conception of miracle has maintained its practical hold over many Christians. The first is that of answer to prayer; for prayer seems really to be heard only when because of it an event happens which would not otherwise have happened; thus there seems to be the suspension of an effect which, according to the interrelatedness of nature, should have followed. The other is that of regeneration, which, represented as a new creation, in part requires some such suspension and in part introduces a principle not comprised in the system of nature. Neither subject can be discussed in this place; but it may suffice to remark in relation to the first, which more concerns piety in general, that our statement places prayer, too, under divine preservation, so that prayer and its fulfillment or refusal are only part of the original divine plan, and consequently the idea that otherwise something else might have happened is wholly meaningless. With regard to the second we need only refer here to what was said above. If the revelation of God in Christ is not necessarily something absolutely supernatural, Christian piety cannot be held bound in advance to regard as absolutely supernatural anything that goes along with this revelation or flows from it. . . .

3. On the whole, therefore, as regards the miraculous, the general interests of science, more particularly of natural science, and the interests of religion seem to meet at the same point, i.e., that we should abandon the idea of the absolutely supernatural because no single instance of it can be known by us, and we are nowhere required to recognize it. Moreover, we should admit, in general, that since our knowledge of created nature is continually growing, we have not the least right to maintain that anything is impossible and also we should allow, in particular (by far the greater number of New Testament miracles being of this kind), that we can neither define the limits of the reciprocal relations of the body and mind nor assert that they are, always and everywhere, entirely the same without the possibility of extension or deviation. In this way, everything — even the most wonderful thing that happens or has happened — is a problem for scientific research; but, at the same time, when it in any way stimulates the pious feeling, whether through its purpose or in some other way, that is not in the least prejudiced by the conceivable possibility of its being understood in the future.

Moreover, we free ourselves entirely from a difficult and highly precarious task with which Dogmatics has so long labored in vain, i.e., the discovery of definite signs which shall enable us to distinguish between the false and diabolical miracle and the divine and true.

§48. *Excitations of self-consciousness expressing a repression of life are just as much to be placed in absolute dependence on God as those expressing an advancement of life.*

1. This statement deals more particularly with the contrast between the serene and the sad moments of life, but it follows so directly from our principal proposition [§46], or rather is so completely involved in it, that we should have had no reason for putting it specially forward if long experience had not taught us that imperfect piety has always found it difficult to harmonize the existence of sad and unhappy experiences with the God-consciousness, whether because it is overwhelmed by life's repressions or led astray by sceptical and unbelieving arguments. On this account almost every religious doctrine, and particularly the Christian doctrine of faith, must make it a special duty to show their compatibility. This has generally involved, however, a false complacency towards these imperfect emotions, partly by way of vindicating the Supreme Being with respect to the existence of such experiences and partly by admitting a variation in the absolute feeling of dependence in relation to them. It is sufficient here to enter a protest against both, as much against the counterfeit emotion itself as against the weak and obscure treatment of it, in order that the simple and complete apprehension of the fundamental feeling may not be endangered. Now if sad experiences only occurred separately, although frequently, and were such that we could trace no connection between them, then they would hardly have been able to produce such an effect; but it is dependent on the fact that there are conditions which bring a persistent and regularly renewed consciousness of life's obstacles. These, then, are what we usually characterize by the term *evil:* and it is to be maintained that all evil, in the full meaning of that word, is just as much wholly dependent upon God as that which is in opposition to it, i.e., good. But clearly we must reckon moral evil under the term "evil," since where it exists it always shows itself to be an inexhaustible source of life's difficulties; only here we have not to consider it as a human activity but as a state.... There is, however, a further division of evil which we need only consider in order to make clear that, just as (we maintain) evil and good are alike rooted in universal dependence on God, from this point of view there is no difference between these two types or classes of evil. To the one belong those conditions which we call natural evil, in which human existence is partially negated. To the other, which we name social evil, belong those conditions in which human activity is in conflict with another activity and is partially overcome and depressed; and here the influence of moral evil specially comes in. But clearly these two kinds of evil not only give rise to each other (since where there is diminution of being activity will more easily be depressed, and a depressed activity which is always decreasing reacts again on the whole being), but they also overlap in thought, for the being of man consists only in the totality of his activities, and *vice versa*. The difference consists then principally in this,

that the one is much more determined by the total forces of nature, and the other by the collective conditions of human activity.

2. In order to solve our problem within the prescribed limits...we have only to show that apparent oppositions come together under the universal dependence. And here two points arise with regard to both kinds of evil. First, the relation of the fluctuating and transitory to the permanent in all finite being. Individual beings belong to the transitory in the form primarily of a vital activity that takes a progressive development up to a certain climax, from thence gradually decreasing until death. Since, regarded as a whole, every relation which determines development arouses the consciousness of life as stimulated, and conversely what tends to bring death nearer is interpreted as an arrest of life, there is throughout the whole course a casual fluctuation between these two. Clearly then, on the one hand, it is the same entire relatedness of men with nature which determines both progress and arrest, so that the one cannot be apart from the other. It is just the same, again in the sphere of social life, where, for example, a later formation of community life cannot grow and expand without the earlier formation being repressed and brought to decay; and thus there are here again two modes of life, progress and limitation, each conditioning the other. The second point is the relation of what is only relatively self-existent and the corresponding and mutual limitations of the finite. That is to say, there is no absolute isolation in the finite; each is only self-existent as it conditions another, and is in turn only conditioned insofar as it is self-existent. But another thing is only conditioned by me if I can in some way cause it to progress; but then this equally implies that I can be a hindrance. The whole relation can only be presented to consciousness insofar as both terms (in both forms, that of self-existence and that of conditionedness) are presented; and consequently both obstacles and progress are equally ordained by God. This is equally valid of personal feeling and of sympathetic and social feeling. So that without a very far-reaching misunderstanding, no one can find difficulty in the fact that even what appears to him an evil (be it his own, someone else's, or one common to many) exists as a consequence of absolute dependence, and therefore is to be regarded as ordained by God. Otherwise we should in general be neither willing nor able to think of the transitory and finite as existing through God — that is, we could not think any world at all as dependent on God; and in this way our fundamental proposition would be denied.

Now this misunderstanding is due, on one side, to the fact that we look at states themselves apart from their natural conditions; and it is increased by the fact that we wrongly represent these influences which produce permanent life-repressions as if they were a separate self-contained province and thus could be isolated and eliminated — in short, that the world could exist apart from evil. The fact is rather that the very same activity or condition of a thing by which it enters on the one hand into human life as an evil, on the other hand is a cause of good, so that if we could remove the source of life's difficulties the conditions of life's progress too would disappear. This is true even of moral evil which only functions as evil insofar as it appears in external action: and it holds good not only accidentally because sin produces good effects sometimes in individuals and sometimes as a great historical lever, but as a general truth since sin only comes to be done by reason of that capacity of man to express his inner nature outwardly which is the source of all good. On the other hand, since in the same way it can be held as a general truth that in the universal system that which is the source of most of life's advancement, from some point of view has an aspect of evil, and that in virtue of the very characteristic which makes it helpful (as indeed all forces of nature and all social relations which originate in intelligence, with the single exception perhaps of intelligence itself, may be said to have this twofold aspect of good and evil), it is absolutely correct to say in another sense that evil as such is not ordained by God, because evil in isolation is never found, and the same is true of good, but each thing or event is ordained by God that it should be both.

Paul Tillich (1886–1965)

Systematic Theology (1951), Volume 1, Part II, Chapter II, Section 5*

5. God as Creating

Introduction: creation and finitude. — The divine life is creative, actualizing itself in inexhaustible abundance. The divine life and the divine creativity are not different. God is creative because he is God. Therefore, it is meaningless to ask whether creation is a necessary or a contingent act of God. Nothing is necessary for God in the sense that he is dependent on a necessity above him. His aseity implies that everything which he is he is through himself. He eternally "creates himself," a paradoxical phrase which states God's freedom. Nor is creation contingent. It does not "happen" to God, for it is identical with his life. Creation is not only God's freedom but also his destiny. But it is not a fate; it is neither a necessity nor an accident which determines him.

The doctrine of creation is not the story of an event which took place "once upon a time." It is the basic description of the relation between God and the world. It is the correlate to the analysis of man's finitude. It answers the question implied in man's finitude and in finitude generally. In giving this answer, it discovers that the meaning of finitude is creatureliness. The doctrine of creation is the answer to the question implied in the creature as creature. This question is asked continually and is always answered in man's essential nature. The question and the answer are beyond potentiality and actuality, as all things are in the process of the divine life. But actually the question is asked and is *not* answered in man's existential situation. The character of existence is that man asks the question of his finitude without receiving an answer. It follows that even if there were such a thing as natural theology, it could not reach the truth of God's creativity and man's creatureliness. The doctrine of creation does not describe an event. It points to the situation of creatureliness and to its correlate, the divine creativity.

Since the divine life is essentially creative, all three modes of time must be used in symbolizing it. God *has* created the world, he *is* creative in the present moment, and he *will* creatively fulfil his *telos*. Therefore, we must speak of originating

---

*Reprinted from *Systematic Theology*, vol. 1: *Reason and Revelation, Being and God* by Paul Tillich. Copyright 1951 by The University of Chicago. All rights reserved. Used by permission of The University of Chicago Press. Pp. 252–54, 256, 259–64, 266–67, 269–70.

creation, sustaining creation, and directing creation. This means that not only the preservation of the world but also providence is subsumed under the doctrine of the divine creativity.

(a) *God's originating creativity.* — (1) Creation and Nonbeing: The classical Christian doctrine of creation uses the phrase *creatio ex nihilo*. The first task of theology is an interpretation of these words. Their obvious meaning is a critical negation. God finds nothing "given" to him which influences him in his creativity or which resists his creative *telos*. The doctrine of *creatio ex nihilo* is Christianity's protection against any type of ultimate dualism. That which concerns man ultimately can only be that on which he ultimately depends. Two ultimates destroy the ultimacy of concern. This negative meaning of *creatio ex nihilo* is clear and decisive for every Christian experience and assertion. It is the mark of distinction between paganism, even in its most refined form, and Christianity, even in its most primitive form.

The question arises, however, whether the term *ex nihilo* points to more than the rejection of dualism. The word *ex* seems to refer to the origin of the creature. "Nothing" is what (or where) it comes from. Now "nothing" can mean two things. It can mean the absolute negation of being (*ouk on*), or it can mean the relative negation of being (*me on*). If *ex nihilo* meant the latter, it would be a restatement of the Greek doctrine of matter and form against which it is directed. If *ex nihilo* meant the absolute negation of being, it could not be the origin of the creature. Nevertheless, the term *ex nihilo* says something fundamentally important about the creature, namely, that it must take over what might be called "the heritage of nonbeing." Creatureliness implies nonbeing, but creatureliness is more than nonbeing. It carries in itself the power of being, and this power of being is its participation in being-itself, in the creative ground of being. Being a creature includes both the heritage of nonbeing (anxiety) and the heritage of being (courage). It does not include a strange heritage originating in a half-divine power which is in conflict with the power of being-itself.

The doctrine of creation out of nothing expresses two fundamental truths. The first is that the tragic character of existence is not rooted in the creative ground of being; consequently, it does not belong to the essential nature of things. In itself finitude is not tragic, that is, it is not doomed to self-destruction by its very greatness. Therefore, the tragic is not conquered by avoiding the finite as much as possible, that is, by ontological asceticism. The tragic is conquered by the presence of being-itself within the finite. The second truth expressed in this doctrine is that there is an element of nonbeing in creatureliness; this gives insight into the natural necessity of death and into the potentiality but not necessity of the tragic.

Two central theological doctrines are based on the doctrine of creation, namely, incarnation and eschatology. God can appear within finitude only if the finite as such is not in conflict with him. And history can be fulfilled in the *eschaton* only if salvation does not presuppose elevation above finitude. The formula *creatio ex nihilo* is not the title of a story. It is the classical formula which expresses the relation between God and the world....

Every theologian who is courageous enough to face the twofold truth that nothing can happen to God accidentally and that the state of existence is a fallen state must accept the point of coincidence between the end of creation and the beginning of the fall. Those theologians who are not willing to interpret the biblical creation story and the story of the fall as reports about two actual events should draw the consequence and posit the mystery where it belongs — in the unity of freedom and destiny in the ground of being. The supralapsarian Calvinists, who asserted that Adam fell by divine decree, had the courage to face this situation. But they did not have the wisdom to formulate their insight in such a way that the seemingly demonic character of this decree was avoided.

To sum up the discussion: being a creature means both to be rooted in the creative ground of the divine life and to actualize one's self through freedom. Creation is fulfilled in the creaturely self-realization which simultaneously is freedom and destiny. But it is fulfilled through separation from the creative ground through a break between existence and essence. Creaturely freedom is the point at which creation and the fall coincide.

This is the background of what is called "human creativity." If creativity means "to bring the new into being," man is creative in every direction — with respect to himself and his world, with respect to being and with respect to meaning. However, if creativity means "to bring into being that which had no being," then divine and human creativity differ sharply. Man creates new syntheses out of given material. This creation really is transformation. God creates the material out of which the new syntheses can be developed. God creates man; he gives man the power of transforming himself and his world. Man can transform only what is given to him. God is primarily and essentially creative; man is secondarily and existentially creative. And beyond this, in every act of human creativity the element of separation from the creative ground is effective. Human creation is ambiguous....

The second frequently discussed and differently answered question in Protestant theology is that of man's created goodness. The early theologians attributed to Adam as the representative of man's essential nature all perfections otherwise reserved for Christ or to man in his eschatological fulfillment. Such a description made the fall entirely unintelligible. Therefore, recent theology rightly attributes to Adam a kind of dreaming innocence, a stage of infancy before contest and decision. This interpretation of the "original state" of man makes the fall understandable and its occurrence existentially unavoidable. It has much more symbolic truth than the "praise of Adam" before the fall. The goodness of man's created nature is that he is given the possibility and necessity of actualizing himself and of becoming independent by his self-actualization, in spite of the estrangement unavoidably connected with it. Therefore, it is inadequate to ask questions concerning Adam's actual state before the fall; for example, if he was mortal or immortal, whether or not he was in communion with God, whether or not he was in a state of righteousness. The verb "was" presupposes actualization in time. But this is exactly what cannot be asserted of the state which transcends potentiality and actuality. This is true even if we use a psychological symbol and speak of the state of dreaming innocence, or if we use a theological symbol and speak of the state of being hidden in the ground of the divine life. One can speak of "was" only after the moment in which the divine command threw Adam into self-actualization through freedom and destiny....

(b) *God's sustaining creativity.* — Man actualizes his finite freedom in unity with the whole of reality. This actualization includes structural independence, the power of standing upon one's self, and the possibility of resisting the return to the ground of being. At the same time, actualized freedom remains continuously dependent on its creative ground. Only in the power of being-itself is the creature able to resist nonbeing. Creaturely existence includes a double resistance, that is, resistance against nonbeing as well as resistance against the ground of being in which it is rooted and upon which it is dependent. Traditionally the relation of God to the creature in its actualized freedom is called the preservation of the world. The symbol of preservation implies the independent existence of that which is preserved as well as the necessity of protection against threats of destruction. The doctrine of the preservation of the world is the door through which deistic concepts easily creep into the theological system. The world is conceived as an independent structure which moves according to its own laws. God certainly created the world "in the beginning" and gave it the laws of nature. But after its beginning he either does not interfere at all (consistent deism) or only occasionally through miracles and revelation (theistic deism), or he acts in a continual interrelationship (consistent theism). In these three cases, it would not be proper to speak of sustaining creation.

Since the time of Augustine, another interpretation of the preservation of the world is given. Preservation is continuous creativity, in that God out of eternity creates things and time together. Here is the only adequate understanding of preservation. It was accepted by the Reformers; it was powerfully expressed by Luther and radically worked out by Calvin, who added a warning against the deistic danger which he anticipated. This line of thought must be followed and made into a line of defense against the contemporary half-deistic, half-theistic way of conceiving God as a being alongside the world. God is essentially creative, and therefore he is creative in every moment of temporal existence, giving the power of being to everything that has being out of the creative ground of the divine life. There is, however, a decisive difference between originating and sustaining creativity. The latter refers to the given structures of reality, to that which continues within the change, to the regular and calculable in things. Without the static element, finite being would not be able to identify itself with itself or anything with anything. Without it, neither expectation, nor action for the future, nor a place to stand upon would be possible; and therefore being would not be possible. The faith in God's sustaining creativity is the faith in the continuity of the structure of reality as the basis for being and acting.

The main current of the modern world view completely excluded the awareness of God's sustaining creativity. Nature was considered a system of measurable and calculable laws resting in themselves without beginning or end. The "well-founded earth" was a safe place within a safe universe. Although no one would deny that every special thing was threatened by nonbeing, the structure of the whole seemed beyond such a threat. Consequently, one could speak of *deus sive natura,* a phrase which indicates that the name "God" does not add anything to what is already involved in the name "nature." One may call such ideas "pantheistic"; but, if one does, one must realize that they are not much different from a deism which consigns God to the fringe of reality and relegates to the world the same independence which it has in naturalistic pantheism. The symbol of God's sustaining creativity has disappeared in both cases. Today the main trend of the modern world view has been reversed. The foundations of the self-sufficient universe have been shaken. The questions of its beginning and end have become theoretically significant, pointing to the element of nonbeing in the universe as a whole. At the same time, the feeling of living in an ultimately secure world has been destroyed through the catastrophes of the twentieth century and the corresponding existentialist philosophy and literature. The symbol of God's sustaining creativity received a new significance and power.

The question whether the relation between God and the world should be expressed in terms of immanence or transcendence is usually answered by an "as well as." Such an answer, although it is correct, does not solve any problem. Immanence and transcendence are spatial symbols. God is *in* or *above* the world or both. The question is what does this mean in nonspatial terms? Certainly, God is neither in another nor in the same space as the world. He is the creative ground of the spatial structure of the world, but he is not bound to the structure, positively or negatively. The spatial symbol points to a qualitative relation: God is immanent in the world as its permanent creative ground and is transcendent to the world through freedom. Both infinite divinity and finite human freedom make the world transcendent to God and God transcendent to the world. The religious interest in the divine transcendence is not satisfied where one rightly asserts the infinite transcendence of the infinite over the finite. This transcendence does not contradict but rather confirms the coincidence of the opposites. The infinite is present in everything finite, in the stone as well as in the genius. Transcendence demanded by religious experience is the freedom-to-freedom relationship which is actual in every personal encounter. Certainly, the holy is the "quite other." But the otherness is not really conceived as otherness if it remains in the aesthetic-cognitive realm and is not experienced as the otherness of the divine "Thou," whose freedom may conflict with my freedom. The meaning of the spatial symbols for the divine transcendence is the possible conflict and possible reconciliation of infinite and finite freedom.

(c) *God's directing creativity.* — (1) Creation and Purpose: "The purpose of creation" is such an ambiguous concept that it should be avoided. Creation has no purpose beyond itself. From the point of view of the creature, the purpose of creation is the creature itself and the actualization of its potentialities. From the point of view of the creator, the purpose of creation is the exercise of his creativity, which has no purpose beyond itself because the divine life is essentially creative. If "the glory of God" is designated as the purpose of creation, as it is in Calvinist theologies, it is necessary, first of all, to understand the highly symbolic character of such a statement. No Calvinist theologian will admit that God lacks something which he must secure from the creature he has created. Such an idea is rejected as pagan. In creating the world, God is the sole cause of the glory he wishes to secure through his creation. But if he is the sole cause of his glory, he does not need the world to give him glory. He possesses it eternally in himself. In Lutheran theologies God's purpose is to have a communion of love with his creatures. God creates the world because the divine love wishes an object of love in addition to itself. Here again the implication is that God needs something he could not have without creation. Reciprocal love is interdependent love. Yet, according to Lutheran theology, there is nothing which the created world can offer God. He is the only one who gives.

The concept "the purpose of creation" should be replaced by "the *telos* of creativity" — the inner aim of fulfilling in actuality what is beyond potentiality and actuality in the divine life. One function of the divine creativity is to drive every creature toward such a fulfillment. Thus directing creativity must be added to originating and sustaining creation. It is the side of the divine creativity which is related to the future. The traditional term for directing creativity is "providence."

(2) Fate and Providence: Providence is a paradoxical concept. Faith in providence is faith "in spite of" — in spite of the darkness of fate and of the meaninglessness of existence. The term *pronoia* ("providence") appears in Plato in the context of a philosophy which has overcome the darkness of transhuman and transdivine fate by means of the idea of the good as the ultimate power of being and knowing. Faith in historical providence is the triumph of the prophetic interpretation of history — an interpretation which gives meaning to historical existence in spite of never-ending experiences of meaninglessness. In the late ancient world fate conquered providence and established a reign of terror among the masses; but Christianity emphasized the victory of Christ over the forces of fate and fear just when they seemed to have overwhelmed him at the cross. Here faith in providence was definitively established.

Within the Christian Era, however, there has been a development toward the transformation of providence into a rational principle at the expense of its paradoxical character.... The catastrophes of the twentieth century have shattered even this limited belief in rational providence. Fate overshadows the Christian world, as it overshadowed the ancient world two thousand years ago. The individual man passionately asks that he be allowed the possibility of believing in a personal fulfillment in spite of the negativity of his historical existence. And the question of historical existence again has become a struggle with the darkness of fate; it is the same struggle in which originally the Christian victory was won.

(3) The Meaning of Providence: Providence means a fore-seeing (*pro-videre*) which is a fore-ordering ("seeing to it"). This ambiguity of meaning expresses an ambiguous feeling toward providence, and it corresponds to different interpretations of the concept. If the element of foreseeing is emphasized, God becomes the omniscient spectator who knows what will happen but who does not interfere with the freedom of his creatures. If the element of foreordering is emphasized, God becomes a planner who has ordered everything that will happen "before the foundations of the world"; all natural and historical processes are nothing more than the execution of this supratemporal divine plan. In the first interpretation the creatures make their world, and God remains a spectator; in the second interpretation the creatures are cogs in a universal mechanism, and God is the only active agent. Both interpretations of providence must be rejected. Providence is a permanent activity of God. He never is a spectator; he always directs everything toward its fulfillment. Yet God's directing creativity always creates through the freedom of man and through the spontaneity and structural wholeness of all creatures. Providence works through the polar elements of being. It works through the conditions of individual, social, and universal existence, through finitude, nonbeing, and anxiety, through the interdependence of all finite things, through their re-

sistance against the divine activity and through the destructive consequences of this resistance. All existential conditions are included in God's directing creativity. They are not increased or decreased in their power, nor are they canceled. Providence is not interference; it is creation. It uses all factors, both those given by freedom and those given by destiny, in creatively directing everything toward its fulfillment. Providence is a *quality* of every constellation of conditions, a quality which "drives" or "lures" toward fulfillment. Providence is "the divine condition" which is present in every group of finite conditions and in the totality of finite conditions. It is not an additional factor, a miraculous physical or mental interference in terms of supranaturalism. It is the quality of inner directedness present in every situation. The man who believes in providence does not believe that a special divine activity will alter the conditions of finitude and estrangement. He believes, and asserts with the courage of faith, that no situation whatsoever can frustrate the fulfillment of his ultimate destiny, that nothing can separate him from the love of God which is in Christ Jesus (Rom. 8).

What is valid for the individual is valid for history as a whole. Faith in historical providence means the certainty that history in each of its moments, in eras of progress and eras of catastrophe, contributes to the ultimate fulfillment of creaturely existence, although this fulfillment does not lie in an eventual time-and-space future.

God's directing creativity is the answer to the question of the meaning of prayer, especially prayers of supplication and prayers of intercession. Neither type of prayer can mean that God is expected to acquiesce in interfering with existential conditions. Both mean that God is asked to direct the given situation toward fulfillment. The prayers are an element in this situation, a most powerful factor if they are true prayers. As an element in the situation a prayer is a condition of God's directing creativity, but the form of this creativity may be the complete rejection of the manifest content of the prayer. Nevertheless, the prayer may have been heard according to its hidden content, which is the surrender of a fragment of existence to God. This hidden content is always decisive. It is the element in the situation which is used by God's directing creativity. Every serious prayer contains power, not because of the intensity of desire expressed in it, but because of the faith the person has in God's directing activity — a faith which transforms the existential situation. . . .

(5) Theodicy: The paradoxical character of faith in providence is the answer to the question of theodicy. Faith in God's directing creativity always is challenged by man's experience of a world in which the conditions of the human situation seem to exclude many human beings from even an anticipatory and fragmentary fulfillment. Early death, destructive social conditions, feeble-mindedness and insanity, the undiminished horrors of historical existence — all these seem to verify belief in fate rather than faith in providence. How can an almighty God be justified (*theos-dike*) in view of realities in which no meaning whatsoever can be discovered?

Theodicy is not a question of physical evil, pain, death, etc., nor is it a question of moral evil, sin, self-destruction, etc. Physical evil is the natural implication of creaturely finitude. Moral evil is the tragic implication of creaturely freedom. Creation is the creation of finite freedom; it is the creation of life with its greatness and its danger. God lives, and his life is creative. If God is creative in himself, he cannot create what is opposite to himself; he cannot create the dead, the object which is merely object. He must create that which unites subjectivity and objectivity — life, that which includes freedom and with it the dangers of freedom. The creation of finite freedom is the risk which the divine creativity accepts. This is the first step in arriving at an answer to the question of theodicy.

However, this does not answer the question why it seems that some beings are excluded from any kind of fulfillment, even from free resistance against their fulfillment. Let us first inquire by whom and under what conditions this central question of theodicy can be asked. All theological statements are existential; they imply the man who makes the statement or who asks the question. The creaturely existence of which theology speaks is "my" creaturely existence, and only on this basis is the consideration of creatureliness in general meaningful. This existential correlation is abandoned if the question of theodicy is raised with respect to persons other than the questioner. The situation here is the same as that encountered when the question of predestination is applied to persons other than the questioner. This question also breaks out of the existential correlation, which makes any theological assertion on the subject questionable. A man can say with the paradoxical confidence of faith, "Nothing can separate *me* from the Love of God" (Rom. 8), but he cannot say with any degree of confidence that other persons are or are not separated from the Love of God or from ultimate fulfillment. No man can make a general or an individual judgment on this question when it falls outside the correlation of faith.

If we wish to answer the question of the fulfillment of other persons, and with it the questions of theodicy and predestination, we must seek the point at which the destiny of others becomes our own destiny. And this point is not hard to find. It is the participation of their being in our being. The principle of participation implies that every question concerning individual fulfillment must at the same time be a question concerning universal fulfillment. Neither can be separated from the other. The destiny of the individual cannot be separated from the destiny of the whole in which it participates. One might speak of a representative fulfillment and nonfulfillment, but beyond this one must refer to the creative unity of individualization and participation in the depth of the divine life. The question of theodicy finds its final answer in the mystery of the creative ground. This answer, however, involves a decision which is very definite. The division of mankind into fulfilled and unfulfilled individuals, or into objects of predestination either to salvation or to condemnation, is existentially and, therefore, theologically impossible. Such a division contradicts the ultimate unity of individualization and participation in the creative ground of the divine life.

The principle of participation drives us one step further. God himself is said to participate in the negativities of creaturely existence. This idea is supported by mystical as well as by christological thought. Nevertheless, the idea must be stated with reservations. Genuine patripassianism (the doctrine that God the Father has suffered in Christ) rightly was rejected by the early church. God as being-itself transcends nonbeing absolutely. On the other hand, God as creative life includes the finite and, with it, nonbeing, although nonbeing is eternally conquered and the finite is eternally reunited within the infinity of the divine life. Therefore, it is meaningful to speak of a participation of the divine life in the negativities of creaturely life. This is the ultimate answer to the question of theodicy. The certainty of God's directing creativity is based on the certainty of God as the ground of being and meaning. The confidence of every creature, its courage to be, is rooted in faith in God as its creative ground.

Karl Barth (1886–1968)

Church Dogmatics (1942), Volume 2: The Doctrine of God, Part 2, Chapter VII*

Chapter VII: The Election of God

§32. The Problem of a Correct Doctrine of the Election of Grace: The doctrine of election is the sum of the Gospel because of all words that can be said or heard it is the best: that God elects man; that God is for man too the One who loves in freedom. It is grounded in the knowledge of Jesus Christ because He is both the electing God and elected man in One. It is part of the doctrine of God because originally God's election of man is a predestination not merely of man but of Himself. Its function is to bear basic testimony to eternal, free, and unchanging grace as the beginning of all the ways and works of God.

1. The Orientation of the Doctrine

The time has now come to leave the doctrine of the knowledge of God and the reality of God. We have tried to learn the lofty but simple lesson that it is by God that God is known, and that He is the living God as the One who loves in freedom; living both in the unity and also in the wealth of His perfections. Our starting-point in that first part of the doctrine of God was neither an axiom of reason nor a datum of experience. In the measure that a doctrine of God draws on these sources, it betrays the fact that its subject is not really God but a hypostatized reflection of man. At more than one stage in our consideration of the earlier history of the doctrine we have had to guard steadfastly against the temptation of this type of doctrine. We took as our starting-point what God Himself said and still says concerning God, and concerning the knowledge and reality of God, by way of the self-testimony which is accessible and comprehensible because it has been given human form in Holy Scripture, the document which is the very essence and basis of the Church. As strictly as possible we have confined ourselves to the appropriation and repetition of that self-testimony as such. As strictly as possible we have let our questions be dictated by the answers which are already present in the revelation of God attested in Holy Scripture. In so doing we have listened gratefully to the voices of the church as well, both old and new. But we have continually measured those voices by the only voice which can reign in the Church. Whether we could follow them or not, we allowed ourselves to use them only

---

*Reprinted from *Church Dogmatics*, vol. 2: *The Doctrine of God*, Part 2 by Karl Barth. © 1957 by T. & T. Clark Ltd. Used by permission of T. & T. Clark. Pp. 3–14.

in order that we might learn the better to hear and understand that voice which reigns in the Church as the source and norm of all truth. It was in that way that we came to perceive the lofty but simple truth concerning the knowledge and reality of God. It was in that way that we rendered our account of what is pure and correct doctrine in this matter.

But the voice which reigns, the voice by which we were taught by God Himself concerning God, was the voice of Jesus Christ. Along all the path now behind us we could not take a single step without stumbling again and again across that name.... We stumbled across it necessarily. For as we proceeded along that path, we found that that name was the very subject, the very matter, with which we had to deal. In avoiding the different sources of error, we saw that they had one feature in common: the negligence or arbitrariness with which even in the Church the attempt was made to go past or to go beyond Jesus Christ in the consideration and conception and definition of God, and in speech about God. But when theology allows itself on any pretext to be jostled away from that name, God is inevitably crowded out by a hypostatized image of man. Theology must begin with Jesus Christ, and not with general principles, however better, or, at any rate, more relevant and illuminating, they may appear to be: as though He were a continuation of the knowledge and Word of God, and not its root and origin, not indeed the very Word of God itself.

...To be truly Christian, the doctrine of God must carry forward and complete the definition and exposition of the Subject God. It must do this in such a way that quite apart from what must be said about the knowledge and the reality of God as such, it makes the Subject known as One which in virtue of its innermost being, willing and nature does not stand outside all relationships, but stands in a definite relationship *ad extra* to another. It is not as though the object of this relationship, the other, constitutes a part of the reality of God outside of God. It is not as though it is in any other way comparable with God. It is not as though God is forced into this relationship. It is not as though He is in any way constrained or compelled by this other. As we have often enough seen and asserted, there can be no question of any such compulsion coming upon God from without. God is love. But He is also perfect freedom. Even if there were no such relationship, even if there were no other outside of Him, He would still be love. But positively, in the free decision of His love, God is God in the very fact, and in such a way, that He does stand in this relation, in a definite relationship with the other.... This relationship belongs to the Subject God, and to the doctrine of God in the narrower sense, to the extent that it rests upon a definite attitude of God which, when we speak of God, we must always and in all respects take into consideration. And that we have never so far failed to do. For how could we have said anything about the knowledge and reality of God had we not considered this positive attitude, learning from it how God gives Himself to be known, and what He is both in Himself and in all His works?...

Jesus Christ is indeed God in His movement towards man, or, more exactly, in His movement towards the people represented in the one man Jesus of Nazareth, in His covenant with this people, in His being and activity amongst and towards this people. Jesus Christ is the decision of God in favor of this attitude or relation. He is Himself the relation. It is a relation *ad extra*, undoubtedly; for both the man and the people represented in Him are creatures and not God. But it is a relation which is irrevocable, so that once God has willed to enter into it, and has in fact entered into it, He could not be God without it. It is a relation in which God is self-determined, so that the determination belongs no less to Him than all that He is in and for Himself.... That we know God and have God only in Jesus Christ means that we can know Him and have Him only with the man Jesus of Nazareth and with the people which He represents. Apart from this man and apart from this people God would be a different, an alien God. According to the Christian perception He would not be God at all. According to the Christian perception the true God is what He is only in this movement, in the movement towards this man, and in Him and through Him towards other men in their unity as His people.

That other to which God stands in relationship, in an actuality which can neither be suspended nor dissolved, is not simply and directly the created world as such. There is, too, a relationship of God to the world. There is a work of God towards it and with it. There is a history between God and the world. But this history has no independent signification. It takes place in the interests of the primal history which is played out between God and this one man and His people. It is the sphere in which this primal history is played out. It attains its goal as this primal history attains its goal. And the same is true both of man as such and also of the human race as a whole. The partner of God which cannot now be thought away is neither "man" as an idea, nor "humanity," nor indeed a large or small total of individual men. It is the one man Jesus and the people represented in Him. Only secondarily, and for His sake, is it "man," and "humanity" and the whole remaining cosmos. Even human nature and human history in general have no independent signification. They point to the primal history played out within them between God and the one man, and all other men as His people.... Everything which comes from God takes place "in Jesus Christ," i.e., in the establishment of the covenant which, in the union of His Son with Jesus of Nazareth, God has instituted and maintains and directs between Himself and His people, the people consisting of those who belong to Him, who have become His in this One. The primal history which underlies and is the goal of the whole history of His relationship *ad extra*, with the creation and man in general, is the history of this covenant. The primal history, and with it the covenant, are, then, the attitude and relation in which by virtue of the decision of His free love God wills to be and is God. And this relation cannot be separated from the Christian conception of God as such. The two must go together if this conception is to be truly Christian. For that reason, this relation must form the subject of a second part of our doctrine of God.

But as we approach this particular subject, two aspects of the one truth must be considered and two spheres of investigation are disclosed.

It is at once apparent that in the decision by which He institutes, maintains, and directs this covenant, in His decision "in Jesus Christ," God on His side does accomplish something quite definite. He executes this decision in His movement towards man, towards the man Jesus Christ and the people which He represents. And this movement is an act of divine sovereignty. To characterize it as such we must select from the fulness of His essential attributes. We must say: This act demonstrates His mercy and righteousness, His constancy and omnipotence. It is as the Lord who lives in the fulness of these perfections that God acts when He institutes and directs this covenant. He constitutes Himself the Lord of the covenant. He is, therefore, its free author. He gives it its content and determines its order. He maintains it. He directs it to its goal. He governs it in every respect. It is His decision that there is a covenant-partner. . . .

Here, again, we must deal first with grace. The fact that God makes this movement, the institution of the covenant, the primal decision "in Jesus Christ," which is the basis and goal of all His works — that is grace. Speaking generally, it is the demonstration, the overflowing of the love which is the being of God, that He who is entirely self-sufficient, who even within Himself cannot know isolation, willed even in all His divine glory to share His life with another, and to have that other as the witness of His glory. This love of God is His grace. It is love in the form of the deepest condescension. It occurs even where there is no question of claim or merit on the part of the other. It is love which is overflowing, free, unconstrained, unconditioned. And we must add at once: It is love which is merciful, making this movement, this act of condescension, in such a way that, in taking to itself this other, it identifies itself with its need, and meets its plight by making it its own concern. And we must add at once: It is love which is patient, not consuming this other, but giving it place, willing its existence for its own sake and for the sake of the goal appointed for it. . . .

The other part of the concept cannot and should not alter this fact in the least. Election should serve at once to emphasize and explain what we have already said in the word "grace." God in His love elects another to fellowship with Himself. First and foremost this means that God makes a self-election in favor of this other. He ordains that He should not be entirely self-sufficient as He might be. He determines for Himself that overflowing, that movement, that condescension. He constitutes Himself as benefit or favor. And in so doing He elects another as the object of His love. He draws it upwards to Himself, so as never again to be without it, but to be who He is in covenant with it. In this concept of election there is reflected more clearly, of course, the other element in the being of God: the freedom in which He is the One who eternally loves. The concept election means that grace is truly grace. It means that God owes His grace to no one, and that no one can deserve it. . . . He elects, i.e., He is free, and He remains free, both in what He does and in what He permits. He does what He does, but without any claim arising that He must do it, or that He must do it in this or that way. Over against Him no claim can ever arise. Nothing can precede His grace, whether in eternity or time, whether from the beginning or in the process of development. In all its manifestations, in all its activity, His grace is free grace. It is the Lord who is the Savior and Helper. His taking to Himself of that other is an act of unconditioned sovereignty. . . .

The doctrine of God's covenant-relation with the people represented in the man Jesus is the fulfillment of the doctrine of God in the narrower sense of the term. . . . Encountering man in His free love, God becomes the companion of man. That is what He determined to do "in Jesus Christ." That is the foundation-plan and sign of all His works. But in virtue of His absolute ascendancy, in virtue of the fact that in this relationship He must have both the first and the last word concerning His partner, He is of necessity the Judge. We use the expression here in its most comprehensive sense. God is for His covenant-partner both the One by whom he will be judged and also the One according to whom he must judge himself. God is for him the criterion, the standard, the question of the good or the evil, the rightness or the wrongness, of his being and activity. God ordained and created him as partner in this covenant; God elected and called him to that position; and in that position He makes him responsible. . . . Here, too, then, we have to do with the Gospel. But we have to do with the Gospel insofar as it has always the form of the Law. . . . Grace does not will only to be received and known. As it is truly received and known, as it works itself out as the favor which it is, it wills also to rule. But it rules by offering God to His covenant-partner as Lord of the covenant. That is the second basic point which we must make concerning the life of God "in Jesus Christ," in and with His people. We must be constantly aware of this point as we consider all the divine work grounded upon the grace of God and the divine election of grace. There is no grace without the lordship and claim of grace. There is no dogmatics which is not also and necessarily ethics. . . .

As we take up this theme, we enter the field of theology which is known in the history of dogma as the doctrine of predestination. Before we do anything more, it is essential that we should make emphatically the first affirmation inscribed in the synopsis at the head of this section. The truth which must now occupy us, the truth of the doctrine of predestination, is first and last and in all circumstances the sum of the Gospel, no matter how it may be understood in detail, no matter what apparently contradictory aspects or moments it may present to us. It is itself evangel: glad tidings; news which uplifts and comforts and sustains. . . . It is not a mixed message of joy and terror, salvation and damnation. Originally and finally it is not dialectical but nondialectical. It does not proclaim in the same breath both good and evil, both help and destruction, both life and death. It does, of course, throw a shadow. We cannot overlook or ignore this aspect of the matter. In itself, however, it is light and not darkness. . . . The Yes cannot be heard unless the No is also heard. But the No is said for the sake of the Yes and not for its own sake. In substance, therefore, the first and last word is Yes and not No. . . .

The election of grace is the sum of the Gospel — we must put it as pointedly as that. But more, the election of grace is the whole of the Gospel, the Gospel *in nuce*. It is the very essence of all good news. It is as such that it must be understood and evaluated in the Christian Church. God is God in His being as the One who loves in freedom. This is revealed as a benefit conferred upon us in the fact which corresponds to the truth of God's being, the fact that God elects in His grace, that He moves towards man, in his dealings within this covenant with the one man Jesus, and the people represented by Him. All the joy and the benefit of His whole work as Creator, Reconciler, and Redeemer, all the blessings which are divine and therefore real blessings, all the promise of the Gospel which has been declared: all these are grounded and determined in the fact that God is the God of the eternal election of His grace. In the light of this election the whole of the Gospel is light.

Charles Hartshorne (b. 1897)

The Divine Relativity (1948), Chapter 1*

Religious Meaning of Absolute

Why is it religiously significant that God be supposed absolute? The reason is at least suggested by the consideration that absoluteness is requisite for complete reliability. What is relative to conditions may fail us if the conditions happen to be unfavorable. Hence if there is to be anything that *cannot* fail, it must be nonrelative, absolute, in those respects to which "reliability" and "failure" have reference. But it is often not noted that this need not be every respect or aspect from which God's nature can be regarded. For there may be qualities in God whose relativity or variability would be neutral to his reliability. To say of a man that (as human affairs go) his reliability is established refers not to every quality of the man, but only to certain principles exhibited in his otherwise highly variable behavior. We do not mean that if something comes close to his eye he will not blink, or that if he is given bad-tasting food he will enjoy it as much as better fare. We mean that his fixed intention to act according to the requirements of the general welfare will not waver, and that his wisdom and skill in carrying out this aim will be constant. But in all this there is not only no implication that conditions will not have effect upon the man, but the very plain implication that they will have plenty of effect. Skill in one set of circumstances means one form of behavior, in another set another form, and the same is true of the intention to serve the general good....

A typically invalid argument in this connection is that unless God surveys at once the whole of time and thus is independent of change, he cannot be relied upon to arrange all events with due regard to their relations to all that has gone before and all that is to come after. This argument either rests on an equivocation or it destroys all religious meaning for the divine reliability. For, if it is meant in any clear sense, it implies that every event has been selected by deity as an element in the best of all possible worlds, the ideal total pattern of all time and all existence. But this ideal pattern includes all acts of sin and the most hideous suffering and catastrophe, all the tragedies of life. And what then becomes of the ideas of human responsibility and choice, and of the notion that some deeds ought not to have taken place? These are only the beginning of the absurdities into which the view thrusts us. To mitigate these absurdities theologians introduce various more or less subtle equivocations. Would they not do better to take a fresh start (as indeed many have done) and admit that we have no good religious reason for positing the notion of providence as an absolute contriving of all events according to a completely detailed plan embracing all time? The religious value of such a notion is more negative than positive. It is the mother of no end of chicanery (see the book of Job for some examples), of much deep feeling of injustice (the poor unfortunate being assured that God has deliberately contrived everything as exactly the best way events could transpire), and of philosophical quagmires of paradox and unmeaning verbiage. The properly constituted man does not want to "rely" upon God to arrange all things, including our decisions, in accordance with a plan of all events which fixes every least detail with reference to every other that ever has happened or ever "is to" happen. How many atheists must have been needlessly produced by insistence upon this arbitrary notion, which after all is invariably softened by qualifications surreptitiously introduced *ad hoc* when certain problems are stressed! We shall see later that the really usable meaning of divine reliability is quite different and is entirely compatible with a profound relativity of God to conditions and to change. For the present, I suggest that all we can assert to have obvious religious value is the faith that God is to be relied upon to do for the world all that ought to be done for it, and with as much survey of the future as there ought to be or as is ideally desirable, leaving for the members of the world community to do for themselves and each other all that they ought to be left to do. We cannot assume that what ought to be done for the world by deity is everything that ought to be done at all, leaving the creatures with nothing to do for themselves and for each other. Nor can we assume that the ideal survey of what for us at least constitutes the future is one which fully defines it in every detail, leaving no open alternatives of possibility. So far from being self-evidently of religious value, these assumptions, viewed in the light of history, seem clearly of extreme disvalue. Yet they are often either asserted, or not unequivocally denied or avoided, in the intemperate insistence upon the total absoluteness of deity....

Social Deity and Creation

It may be thought that a socially conceived God could not be the creator. Can a member of a society create that society? Here we must remember the theological principle of "eminence." God, if social, is eminently or supremely so. On the other hand, that which in the eminent form is called divine creation, in a milder or ordinary form must be exhibited by lesser beings such as man. Man certainly is social. If then ordinary sociality is ordinarily creative, eminent sociality will be eminently creative, divinely creative. And ordinary sociality is, in a humble sense, creative. A man contributes creatively to the concrete actuality of his friends and enemies, and they to his. We *make* each other what we are, in greater or less degree.

The more important members of a society contribute more largely and vitally to the actuality of other members. The supreme member of a society would contribute most vitally and largely to the actuality of all. However, we shall be told, all this is not really "creation," since it presupposes a matter and at most adds a new form. In the first place, no one has proved or can possibly prove (against Peirce, Whitehead, et al.) that there is any "matter," apart from social terms and relations. Electrons and protons are, for all that anyone knows, simply the lowest actual levels of social existence. It may well be that a human mind is not sufficiently important in the world to call an electron into being where none was before. However, we do, by our thoughts and feelings, influence the formation of nerve cells (in the first years of life), and even more, of molecules in the nerves. This is not creation in the eminent sense, but it differs from this only as we might expect the ordinary to differ from the eminent. And the influence of our thought and feeling upon nerve cells and molecules is either a blind mystery, or it is a social influence, as Peirce and Whitehead, and before them (less clearly) Leibniz, have pointed out.

That the human creator always has a given concrete actuality to work with does not of itself establish a difference between him and God, unless it be admitted as made out that there was a first moment of creation. For if not, then God, too, creates each stage of the world as successor to a preceding phase. Only a dubious interpretation of an obscure parable, the book of Genesis, stands between us and this view. What does distinguish God is that the preceding phase was itself created by God, so that he, unlike us, is never confronted by a world whose coming to be antedates his own entire existence. There is no presupposed "stuff" alien to God's creative work; but rather everything that influences God has already been influenced by him, whereas we are influenced by events of the past with which we had nothing to do. This is one of the many ways in which eminence is to be preserved, without falling into the negations of classical theology....

The Independence Which Is Admirable

Suppose a man says, I can be a good man, do my duty, only so long as a certain friend continues to live and to encourage me. Our feeling will surely be that, while it is natural and human to lean upon friends for moral assistance, still a man should do his duty whatever anyone else may do. In ethical character one should be as independent as possible of other contingent beings. Thus to depend for doing one's duty upon others is inappropriate, unadmirable dependence. God then, as object of piety, will be in highest degree, or utterly, independent of our actions and fortunes for the preservation of his holiness of will. That is, he will promote the highest cosmic good, come what may. But it does not in the least follow that what God will do to promote the cosmic good will be uninfluenced by our actions and fortunes, or that how he will think and feel about the world will in no way reflect what is going on in the world. The man who does his duty regardless of what happens will not have the same specific duties regardless of what happens. And with different duties he will perform different acts with different specific intentions, ideas, and feelings.

Suppose, on the other hand, a man says, I can be equally happy and serene and joyous regardless of how men and women suffer around me. Shall we admire this alleged independence? I think not. Why should we admire it when it is alleged of God? I have yet to learn a good answer to this question. On the other hand, if we see a person who is dragged down into helpless misery by the sight of suffering in others, we feel that this response is as inappropriate as the opposite one of gay serenity would be in the same circumstances. And there is no inconsistency in condemning both responses, for a clear logical principle can be applied to both. This is that we should respond to the total situation appropriately, not just to a part of it, or inappropriately. The suffering of the world is not the world; there is also the joy of the world. If the one should sadden us, the other should delight us. He who refuses to rejoice with the joy of others is as selfish as he who refuses to grieve with their sorrows. Indeed, as has been often remarked, it is if anything a rarer unselfishness to be really inspired by the happiness of our friends than to be saddened by their unhappiness. For the happiness of others may inspire us with envy instead of sympathetic pleasure. Such neutralization by envy of sympathetic dependence for our own happiness upon that of others is scarcely admirable!

Proportional Dependence

The notion that total emotional independence is admirable seems, then, to be without foundation in experience. There *is* an admirable independence, but it is independence in basic ethical purpose, not in specific concrete experience and happiness. There is also admirable dependence, which is appropriate response, duly proportionate to the balance of factors in the world known to us, of sympathetic rejoicing and sorrowing. Why not attribute to the divine response the ideal of such appropriateness, or proportionality, of dependence? The requirement of piety seems entirely compatible with such attribution.

To depend upon others emotionally through sympathy is to change when they change — for example, to grow in joy when they do. But if God changes, it is often argued, then he changes either for the worse or for the better. If the former, how can we admire him without stint? If the latter, then it seems he must previously have lacked something, and been incomplete and imperfect. The first horn of the dilemma need not concern us, unless it can be proved that there is ever more sorrow than joy in the world. For if there is always more satisfaction than dissatisfaction, then God should always have more reason to rejoice than to grieve over the world, and since he can retain the consciousness of past joys, there will always be a *net increment* of value accruing to God at each moment. Now if life were not more satisfying than otherwise, could it go on? Is there anything to maintain the will to live save satisfaction in living? I do not see that there is. Hence I shall confine my attention to the second horn of the dilemma, that a God who increases in value must previously have lacked some value, and therefore have been imperfect. My reply is that, as we are here using the term, perfect means completely worthy of admiration and respect, and so the question becomes, is such complete admirableness infringed by the possibility of enrichment in total value? I say it is not. We do not admire a man less because we know he would be a happier man if his son, who is wretched, became well and happy, or because we anticipate that when a child is born to him it will enrich his life with many new joys. Admiration is not directed to happiness, except so far as we feel that a person does or does not attain the happiness appropriate to the state of the world as known to him. We admire not the amount but the appropriateness of the joy. We rejoice in another's happiness, we grieve over his misfortune, but we do not praise or blame or admire on this account, unless we think the good or bad fortune is the person's own doing. So far as it is due rather to the decisions of others, which were their responsibility, not his, then it determines not our respect, but only the tone of our sympathy or participatory feeling, toward the person. Why should it be otherwise in relation to God? If God rejoices less today than he will tomorrow, but ideally appropriately at both times, our reverence for him should in no way be affected by the increase in joy. Indeed, if he were incapable of responding to a better world with greater satisfaction, this should infringe upon our respect; for it would imply a lack of proportionality in the divine awareness of things.

Gratitude is the appropriate expression of genuine indebtedness, of really hav-ing received benefit from others. Conceited men would perhaps like to avoid occasions for gratitude, so that they might boast of their independence. But no good man blessed with a beloved wife is sorry to feel that without her he could not have been so happy. To God each of us is dearer than wife to husband, for no human being knows the inner experiences of another human being so intimately as they are known to God. And to know experiences is to appreciate them; for the value of experience is just the experience itself. As we are indebted to a few per-sons for the privilege of feeling something of the quality of their experiences, so God is indebted to *all* persons for the much fuller enjoyment of the same privilege. God is not conceited or envious; therefore he has no motive for wishing to escape or deny this indebtedness. It is envious men, priests, theologians, guardians — in some cases one could almost say watchdogs — of the divine majesty, who at-tribute such an attitude, such unbridled will to independence, to God. (No doubt God's sense of indebtedness to us lacks some of the connotations of "gratitude," such as the sense of a common moral frailty, almost miraculously overcome in a certain case.)

Karl Rahner (1904–84)

Foundations of Christian Faith (1976), Chapter 4, Section 4*

4. Towards an Understanding of the Doctrine of the Trinity

The Problem of Conceptualization

With all due respect to the church's official and classical formulation of the Christian doctrine of the Trinity, and taking for granted an acceptance in faith of what is meant by these formulations, we still have to admit that the asser-tions about the Trinity in their catechetical formulations are almost unintelligible to people today, and that they almost inevitably occasion misunderstandings. When we say with the Christian catechism that in the one God there are three "persons" in the unity and unicity of one nature, in the absence of further theo-logical explanation it is almost inevitable that whoever hears this formula will understand by the word "person" the content which he associates with this word elsewhere. . . . Consequently, it is altogether possible for such a term to take on a content which carries with it at least the danger that its application to the old for-mulations, which are quite correct in themselves, puts a false and a mythological construction on these formulations which cannot be assimilated.

This situation is not surprising, for when Christian doctrine uses the terms "hy-postasis," "person," "essence" and "nature" to express the divine Trinity, it is not employing concepts which are clear and unambiguous in themselves and which

*Reprinted from *Foundations of Christian Faith: An Introduction to the Idea of Christianity* by Karl Rahner, trans. William V. Dych. Originally published as *Grundkurs des Glaubens: Einführung in den Begriff des Christentums*, © Verlag Herder, Freiburg im Breisgau 1976. English translation copyright © 1978 by The Crossroad Publishing Company. All rights reserved. Used with permission of The Crossroad Publishing Company, New York. Pp. 134–37.

are applied here in all their clarity. Rather, in order to express what was meant, these concepts were to some extent distinguished from one another in the church's language only very slowly and with great difficulty, and they were defined according to these norms of usage, although the history of the defining process shows that there would also have been other possibilities for expressing asymptotically what was meant. When in our secular use of language today we speak of one "person" as distinct from another person, we can hardly avoid the notion that in order that they be persons and be different, there is in each of these persons its own free center of conscious and free activity which disposes of itself and differentiates itself from others, and that it is precisely this which constitutes a person. But this is the very thing which is excluded by the dogmatic teaching on the single and unique essence of God. This unicity of essence implies and includes the unicity of one single consciousness and one single freedom, although of course the unicity of one self-presence in consciousness and freedom in the divine Trinity remains determined by that mysterious threeness which we profess about God when we speak haltingly of the Trinity of persons in God.

The Problem with a "Psychological Theory of the Trinity"

With regard to the imposing speculations in which, since the time of Augustine, Christian theology has tried to conceive of the inner life of God in self-consciousness and love in such a way that we acquire presumably a certain understanding of the threefold personhood of God, an understanding which portrays, as it were, an inner life of God completely unrelated to us and to our Christian existence, perhaps we can say that ultimately they are not really all that helpful. A "psychological theory of the Trinity," however ingenious the speculations from the time of Augustine down to our own time, in the end does not explain precisely what it is supposed to explain, namely, why the Father expresses himself in Word, and with the Logos breathes a Spirit which is different from him. For such an explanation must already presuppose the Father as knowing and loving himself, and cannot allow him to be constituted as knowing and loving in the first place by the expression of the Logos and the spiration of the Spirit.

Even if we prescind from these difficulties, the fact remains that such psychological speculation about the Trinity has in any case the disadvantage that in the doctrine of the Trinity it does not really give enough weight to a starting point in the history of revelation and dogma which is within the *historical and salvific* experience of the Son and of the Spirit as the reality of the divine self-communication to us, so that we can understand from this historical experience what the doctrine of the divine Trinity really means. The psychological theory of the Trinity neglects the experience of the Trinity in the economy of salvation in favor of a seemingly almost gnostic speculation about what goes on in the inner life of God. In the process it really forgets that the countenance of God which turns towards us in this self-communication is, in the trinitarian nature of this encounter, the very being of God as he is in himself, and must be if indeed the divine self-communication in grace and in glory really is the communication of God in his own self to us.

The Trinity in the History and Economy of Salvation Is the Immanent Trinity

But if conversely we make the presupposition and hold to it radically that the Trinity in the history of salvation and revelation is the "immanent" Trinity, because in God's self-communication to his creation through grace and Incarnation God really gives himself, and really appears as he is in himself, then with regard to that aspect of the Trinity in the economy of salvation which is given in the history of God's self-revelation in the Old and New Testaments we can say: in both the collective and individual history of salvation there appears in immediacy to us not some numinous powers or other which represent God, but there appears and is truly present the one God himself. In his absolute uniqueness, which ultimately nothing can take the place of or represent, he comes where we ourselves are, and where we receive him, this very God himself and as himself in the strict sense.

Insofar as he has come as the salvation which divinizes us in the innermost center of the existence of the individual person, we call him really and truly "Holy Spirit" or "Holy Ghost." Insofar as in the concrete historicity of our existence one and the same God strictly as himself is present for us in Jesus Christ, and in himself, not in a representation, we call him "Logos" or the Son in an absolute sense. Insofar as this very God, who comes to us as Spirit and as Logos, is and always remains the ineffable and holy mystery, the incomprehensible ground and origin of his coming in the Son and in the Spirit, we call him the one God, the Father. Insofar as in the Spirit, in the Logos-Son, and in the Father we are dealing with a God who gives himself in the strictest sense, and not something else, not something different from himself, we must say in the strictest sense and equally of the Spirit, of the Logos-Son and of the Father that they are one and the same God in the unlimited fullness of the one Godhead and in possession of one and the same divine essence.

Insofar as the modes of God's presence for us as Spirit, Son, and Father do not signify the same modes of presence, insofar as there really are true and real differences in the modes of presence for us, these three modes of presence for us are to be strictly distinguished. Father, Son-Logos, and Spirit are first of all not the same "for us." But insofar as these modes of presence of one and the same God for us may not nullify the real self-communication of God as the one and only and same God, the three modes of presence of one and the same God must belong to him as one and the same God, they must belong to him in himself and for himself.

Hence the assertions that one and the same God is present for us as Father, Son-Logos, and Holy Spirit, or that the Father gives himself to us in absolute self-communication through the Son in the Holy Spirit are to be understood and made in the strict sense as assertions about God *as he is in himself.* For otherwise they would basically not be assertions about God's self-communication. We may not duplicate these three modes of God's presence for us by postulating a different presupposition for them in God, and we do this by developing a psychological doctrine of the Trinity which is different from these modes of presence. In the Trinity in the economy and history of salvation and revelation we have already experienced the immanent Trinity as it is in itself. By the fact that God reveals himself for us in the modes we indicated as trinitarian, we have already experienced the immanent Trinity of the holy mystery as it is in itself, because its free and supernatural manifestation to us in grace manifests its innermost self. For the absolute identity of the Trinity with itself does not signify a lifeless and empty homogeneity. Rather, this identity includes in itself as the nature of the divine life the very thing which encounters us in the trinitarian nature of his coming to us.

We are only trying to indicate here an initial approach towards an understanding of the Christian doctrine of the Trinity. In spite of its own problems, perhaps this approach still allows us to avoid many misunderstandings about this doctrine, and to show positively that the doctrine of the Trinity is not a subtle theological and speculative game, but rather is an assertion which cannot be avoided. It is only through this doctrine that we can take with radical seriousness and maintain without qualifications the simple statement which is at once so very incomprehensible and so very self-evident, namely, that God himself as the abiding and holy mystery, as the incomprehensible ground of man's transcendent existence is not only the God of infinite distance, but also wants to be the God of absolute closeness in a true self-communication, and he is present in this way in the spiritual depths of our existence as well as in the concreteness of our corporeal history. Here lies the real meaning of the doctrine of the Trinity.

Karl Rahner, Chapter 2, Sections 4 and 5 of *Foundations of Christian Faith* (1976)*

Hence what it really means to have a created origin is experienced basically and originally in the process of transcendence. This means that in the first instance the terms "creatureliness," "being created" or "creation" do not point back to an earlier moment in time at which the creation of the creature in question once took place. They mean rather an ongoing and always actual process which for every existent is taking place now just as much as at an earlier point of time in his existence, although this ongoing creation is that of an existent extended *in time*. In the first instance, then, creation and creatureliness do not mean a momentary event, namely, the first moment of a temporal existent, but mean the establishing of this existent and his time itself, and this establishing does not enter into time, but is the ground of time.

Creatureliness as Radical Difference from and Radical Dependence on God

To understand what is meant by creatureliness as a person's fundamental relationship to God, let us begin with the transcendental experience of it. As a spiritual person, man implicitly affirms absolute being as the real ground of every act of knowledge and of every action, and affirms it as mystery. This absolute, incomprehensible reality, which is always the ontologically silent horizon of every intellectual and spiritual encounter with realities, is therefore always infinitely different from the knowing subject. It is also different from the individual, finite

*Reprinted from *Foundations of Christian Faith: An Introduction to the Idea of Christianity* by Karl Rahner, trans. William V. Dych. Originally published as *Grundkurs des Glaubens: Einführung in den Begriff des Christentums*, © Verlag Herder, Freiburg im Breisgau 1976. English translation copyright © 1978 by The Crossroad Publishing Company. All rights reserved. Used with permission of The Crossroad Publishing Company, New York. Pp. 77–82, 86–89.

things known. It is present as such in every assertion, in all knowledge, and in every action.

Proceeding from this basic starting point, we can accordingly define from two points of view the relationship between both the knower and the known as finite existents, and the absolutely infinite: as the absolute and the infinite, God must be absolutely different. Otherwise he would be an object of our knowledge and comprehension, and not the ground of such comprehension. He is and remains so even when he is named and objectified in metaphysical and conceptual reflection. For this reason, then, he cannot be in need of the finite reality called "world," because otherwise he would not really be radically different from it, but would be part of a larger whole as in the understanding of pantheism. Conversely, the world must be radically dependent on God, without making him dependent on it as a master is dependent on his servant.... This radical dependence must be ongoing, and therefore not just affect the first moment, for what is finite is related now and always to the absolute as its ground.

Christian doctrine calls this unique relationship between God and the world the createdness of the world, its creatureliness, its ongoing being-given to itself by a personal God who establishes it freely. This establishing, then, does not have some material already at hand as its presupposition, and in this sense it is "out of nothing." Basically creation "out of nothing" means to say: creation totally from God, but in such a way that the world is radically dependent on God in this creation. Nevertheless, God does not become dependent on the world, but remains free vis-à-vis the world and grounded in himself. Wherever we find a causal relationship of a categorical kind in the world, it is indeed the case that the effect is by definition dependent on its cause. But strangely enough this cause is itself also dependent on its effect, because it cannot be this cause without causing the effect. This is not the case in the relationship between God and creatures, for otherwise God would then be an element *within* our categorical realm of experience, and not the absolutely distant term of the transcendence within which an individual finite thing is known.

Radical Dependence on God and Genuine Autonomy

God establishes the creature and its difference from himself. But by the very fact that God establishes the creature and its difference from himself, the creature is a genuine reality different from God, and not a mere appearance behind which God and his own reality hide. The radical dependence and the genuine reality of the existent coming from God vary in direct and not in inverse proportion. In our human experience it is the case that the more something is dependent on us, the less it is different from us, and the less it possesses its own reality and autonomy. In the realm of the categorical, the radical dependence of the effect on the cause and the independence and autonomy of the effect vary in inverse proportion.

... Creation is the only and unique and incomparable mode which does not presuppose the other as the possibility of an effective movement outwards, but rather creates this other as other by the fact that it both retains it as its creation and sets it free in its own autonomy, and both in the same proportion.

Of course the idea of creation can ultimately be understood and assimilated only by one who has not only had the experience of his own freedom and responsibility in the depth of his existence, a freedom and responsibility which is valid before God and in our relation to God, but has also freely accepted it in an act of his freedom and in reflection.... Not until one experiences himself as a free subject responsible before God and accepts this responsibility does he understand what autonomy is, and understand that it does not decrease, but increases in the same proportion as dependence on God. On this point the only thing that concerns us is that man is at once independent and, in view of what his ground is, also dependent.

5. Finding God in the World

The Tension between a Transcendental Starting Point and Historical Religion

The question about finding God and his activity with us in our concrete, historical experience in the world creates special difficulties today. We have been considering God up to now as the creative ground of everything which can encounter us within the ultimate horizon which he himself is and which he alone forms. As he who cannot be incorporated along with what is grounded into a system which encompasses them both, we saw him as always transcendent, as the presupposition of everything which exists, and therefore as someone who cannot be thought of as one of these existents, that is, as someone comprehended or comprehensible by us. But this seems to have as its consequence the very thing which constitutes perhaps the basic difficulty which people have today with the concrete practice of religion.

As ineffable and incomprehensible presupposition, as ground and abyss, as ineffable mystery, God cannot be found in his world. He does not seem to be able to enter into the world with which we have to do because he would thereby become what he is not: an individual existent alongside of which there are others which he is not. If he wanted to appear in his world, he apparently would immediately cease to be himself: the ground of everything which appears but which itself does not appear. By definition God does not seem able to be within the world.... Every objectification of God, as localized in time and space, as definable in the here and now, seems by its very nature not to be God, but something which we have to derive as a phenomenon from other phenomena in the world which can be specified or must be postulated.

But religion as we know it, as a religion of prayer for God's intervention, as a religion of miracles, as a religion with a salvation history differentiated from other history,... as a religion with an inspired book which comes from God,... as a religion with definite prophets and bearers of revelation authorized by God,... all religion of this kind declares phenomena existing within our experience as definite and exclusive objectifications and manifestations of God. Consequently, in this way God as it were appears within the world of our categorical experience at quite definite points as distinguished from other points.

Such a religion seems incompatible with our transcendental starting point, which, on the other hand, we cannot abandon if we want to talk about God at all today. As it is practiced by people in the concrete, religion always and inevitably seems to say: "God is here and not there," or "This is in accordance with his will and not that," or "He has revealed himself here and not there." As practiced in the concrete, religion seems neither willing nor able to avoid making God a categorical object. Religion which does avoid this seems to evaporate into a mist which perhaps does exist, but in practice it cannot be the source of religious life. Conversely, our basic starting point seems to say that God is everywhere insofar as he grounds everything, and he is nowhere insofar as everything that is grounded is created, and everything which appears in this way within the world of our experience is different from God, separated by an absolute chasm between God and what is not God....

God's Activity in and through Secondary Causes

Moreover, we must repeat here what Thomas Aquinas said when he emphasized that God works through secondary causes....If it is not to be made innocuous, the statement says that God causes *the* world, but not really *in the* world. It says that the chain of causality has its basis in him, but not that by his activity he inserts himself as a link in this chain of causes as one cause among them....For the ground does not appear within what is grounded if it is really the radical and hence the divine ground, and is not a function in a network of functions. If, then, there is nevertheless to be an immediacy of God to us, if we are to find him in his own self here where we are in our categorical world of time and space, then this immediacy both in itself and in its categorical, historical objectification must be embedded in this world to begin with. Then the concrete immediacy of God to us as is presupposed by and takes place in concrete religions must be a moment in and a modality of our transcendental and at the same time historically mediated immediacy to God.

A special "intervention" of God, therefore, can only be understood as the historical concreteness of the transcendental self-communication of God which is already intrinsic to the concrete world. Such an "intervention" of God always takes place, first of all, from out of the fundamental openness of finite matter and of a biological system towards spirit and its history, and, secondly, from out of the openness of the spirit towards the history of the transcendental relationship between God and the created person in their mutual freedom. Consequently, every real intervention of God in his world, although it is free and cannot be deduced, is always only the becoming historical and becoming concrete of that "intervention" in which God as the transcendental ground of the world has from the outset embedded himself in this world as its self-communicating ground.

It is a fundamental problem for a contemporary understanding of Christianity how God can really be God and not simply an element of the world, and how, nevertheless, in our religious relationship to the world we are to understand him as not remaining outside the world. The dilemma of the "immanence" and "transcendence" of God must be overcome without sacrificing either the one or the other concern. In our considerations up to now we have already met at least twice the formal structure of this peculiar relationship between transcendental beyondness and categorical accessibility. We have understood our irreducible subjectivity as well as our freedom and responsibility as fundamental human existentials which we always experience and which of course objectify themselves constantly in the concrete and in time and space, but which nevertheless are not something tangible which can be taken and defined as an object alongside of other objects.

Analogously and ultimately for the same reasons, the same formal relationship of tension obtains when we ask whether God appears in his world in a tangible way, whether, for example, he hears prayers or works signs, intervenes in history with his power, and so on. When to the extent that we are religious persons we answer these questions in the affirmative, this does not mean however that what is immediately tangible in this "intervention" does not exist in a functional relationship with the world or that it could not be explained causally....

Let us clarify what is meant by an example which is among the most modest ways in which God intervenes in his world, and so admittedly it cannot and does not intend to represent completely the more specific mode of a higher form of divine "intervention." A "good idea" strikes me which has as its consequence an important decision which proves to be valid and objectively correct. I regard this good idea as an inspiration of God. May I? I might be led to this judgment by its suddenness or by the impossibility of finding a causal or functional explanation for the origin of this good idea. But my judgment is not ultimately justified by such a subjective impression. On the contrary, I have the right, and even the obligation to explain this sudden idea, to trace it back to associations that I am not conscious of or to a physiological and psychological constitution which perhaps cannot be analyzed exactly at the moment, to regard it as a function of myself, of my history, of my world of people and of things, of the world as such. Hence I might explain it, that is, incorporate it along with all the concrete characteristics which it has in particular into the totality of the world which is not God. To this extent, therefore, I cannot see in this "good idea" any special presence of God in the world, any "intervention of God."

But the moment I experience myself as a transcendental subject in my orientation to God and accept it, and the moment I accept this concrete world in all its concreteness and in spite of all the functional interconnectedness of all of its elements, accept it as the concrete world in which my concrete relationship to the absolute ground of my existence unfolds historically for me and I actualize it in freedom, then within this subjective, transcendental relationship to God this "good idea" receives objectively a quite definite and positive significance. Hence I can and must say: it is willed by God in this positive significance as a moment of the one world established in freedom by its ground as the world of my subjective relationship to God, and in this sense it is an "inspiration" of God. Of course it could be objected against this that in this way everything can be regarded as a special providence, as an intervention of God, presupposing only that I accept the concrete constellation of my life and of the world in such a way that it becomes a positive, salvific concretization of my transcendental relationship to God in freedom. But against this objection we can simply ask the counter-question: Why, then, may this not be the case?

If and insofar as something is incorporated positively, not just in theory, but in the concrete exercise of freedom, into one's free relationship to God as the objectification and mediation of this relationship, it is in fact an inspiration, a mighty

deed, however small, of God's providence, as we are accustomed to call it in religious terms. It is a special intervention of God. But this subjective and in fact
correct response of mine in freedom to this or that particular constellation within
the realm of my freedom, a constellation which, though functionally explainable,
concretely mediates my relationship to God, depends, in spite of the subjective
nature of my own decision and response, on factors which can be favorable or
unfavorable, and in this difference are not simply and absolutely subject to my
disposal.

But to this extent we can and must regard, and rightly so, a particular situation
which works out for the good — as distinguished from another situation, which
could have been, but is not — as in fact a special providence of God, as his intervention, as his favorable hearing, as a special grace, even if the opposite situation,
handled by a correct response in human freedom, could have been made such a
special act of God, but in fact was not. Because the subject's response in freedom
is itself really and truly for the subject himself something given to him, without
it losing thereby the character of the subject's own responsible and accountable
action, a good decision along with everything which it presupposes as its mediation correctly has the character of an intervention of God, even though this takes
place in and through human freedom, and hence can be explained functionally to
the degree that the history of freedom can be explained, namely, insofar as it is
based on elements objectified in time and space.

Sallie McFague (b. 1934)

The Body of God (1993), Chapter 5*

Creation: Production, Procreation, or Procreation-Emanation?

The Genesis creation story...does not suggest that the world is God's body;
rather, the world and its creatures are products of God the Maker, the Craftsman,
the Architect, the Sculptor. Whether one looks at Genesis 1 or 2, at the sweeping
narrative of how God called into being the heavens and the earth, the seas and
their teeming creatures, the land and its many animals and plants or at the more
homey, domestic story of the molding of Adam and the other animals from the
earth (and Eve from Adam's rib), the mode of creation is by word or by hand.
In the first story, through the word ("Let there be...") God creates an aesthetic
panorama ("it was very good"); in the second, God sculpts forms from "the dust
of the ground." Creation is production and as such it is external to God; it is
also totally dependent on God for its existence. Many Hebrew Scripture scholars
seem united in the opinion, however, that it is not the externality, the production
aspect of the Genesis account, that is critical, but the dependence of all forms of
existence on God the creator. If dependence, rather than externality, is the critical
feature of the tradition's creation sensibility, then we might consider options other
than the production model, which has several problems.

*Reprinted by permission from *The Body of God* by Sallie McFague, copyright © 1993 Augsburg
Fortress. Pp. 151–56.

The production model emphasizes the beginnings of creation rather than its continuing, ongoing character; it can speak of divine transcendence only in an external way, making it difficult to affirm the immanence of God; and it is intellectual or aesthetic, implying a dualistic hierarchy of mind and body. A procreation model of creation, on the other hand, says simply that the world comes from, is formed from, God rather than out of "nothing" or out of some material other than God. Lest the reader immediately recoil in horror at the thought of the universe as bodying forth from God, let us briefly consider the alternatives. "Out of nothing" (*ex nihilo*) is not in Genesis or even in the Bible (except for a cryptic mention in the book of Maccabees). Rather, it is an invention of the early church fathers to underscore the transcendence of God. But, we might ask, does it also allow for divine immanence, as an adequate model of God and the world should? "Out of some material other than God" suggests that there is another creator, the one who made *this* material, thus undercutting radical dependence of all of reality on God. "Out of God" claims that whatever *is* is in and from God, but it does not say that God is identified with or reduced to what is bodied forth. It claims that we live and move and have our being in God, but not vice versa. A metaphor to express this source of all life is not the Architect who constructs a world, but the Mother who encloses reality in her womb, bodying it forth, generating all life from her being.

Before continuing, let us recall once again that we are dealing with models, not descriptions. Models are to be judged not by whether they correspond with God's being (the face is not available to us), but by whether they are relatively adequate (in other words, more adequate than alternative models) from the perspective of postmodern science, an interpretation of Christian faith, our own embodied experience, and the well-being of our planet and all its life-forms. We *only* have models, and the Genesis story of the external Maker who produces an artifact is not, simply because of its age and status in the tradition, anything other than a model. What we must ask of all models is their relative adequacy on the basis of some agreed-upon criteria. I am suggesting that in light of the criteria operative in this essay, some version of the procreation model of creation is preferable to production models.

To make this suggestion more concrete, let us look at how the procreation model deals with the problems raised by the production model. On the issue of the beginnings of creation versus its continuation, a procreation (organic, growth) model has potential for expressing the ongoing character of creation in ways a production model does not. In the production model, creation is complete, finished, static; what is crafted is seen as an artifact that may be pleasing or beautiful, but it does not change. A procreation model, however, sees creation as emerging from God, as a body (in the case of the evolving universe, billions of bodies) that grows and changes. But our model, we recall, is not only or merely organic; it is also agential. Hence, it combines the procreation model with another in the tradition, the emanationist, in which the life-giving energy of creation emanates from its divine source. The model, therefore, is not a pure procreation one in which the world is seen as God's child (reproduction) rather than as God's construction (production), but is a combination of the procreative and emanationist models: God bodies forth the universe, which is enlivened and empowered by its source. God is not the parent of the child, but the life of the body; our model does not highlight biological generation, but the dependence of all life on God. It borrows from the procreative model its physicality and from the emanationist model its continuing and profound connection with its source of life. Children grow up, move away, and can sever connections with those who gave them life, so the procreation model, while expressing powerfully the bodily base of creation, cannot capture its continuing dependence. An emanationist model not only insists that all life derives from God, but that it continues to do so; thus, the dynamic, changing, evolving body that is all reality does not grow away from God, but in, through, and toward God.

Emanationist models of creation have a dialectical character: creation comes from God, attains partial separation, and returns to its source. Theologies influenced by these models, however, have often been idealistic, that is, centered in the mind, not the body, seeing the second phase, the partial separation, as a "fall" or a lesser state from the first or the third. But if the emanationist model is combined with the procreative or the organic, this tendency is undercut, for the second phase is nothing less than God's *own* embodiment. It is not a lesser stage but, in fact, the only one we can know anything about. It is the back of God and wonderful beyond all imagining: it is the universe.[1] Hence, we suggest that a procreative-emanationist model of divine creation is commensurate with the continuing creation of post-modern science, its story of the evolving history of the universe. It is a model rich in suggestive power for expressing the profound dependence of all things on God, their basic bodily reality, and their changing, growing character.

The model is also helpful when we turn to the issue of divine immanence as well as transcendence in relation to the world. The production model of the tradition has been heavily invested in protecting the transcendence of God, but has often done so by stressing divine control. In other words, transcendence was equated with sovereignty: it meant dominion over. The result is to separate God and the world; God becomes the external Lord over the world. The monarchical and deistic models of God and the world both rely on this view of transcendence, and it has been one of the most problematic legacies of the Hebrew and Christian traditions in innumerable ways. Moreover, it does not help promote an ecological sensibility.

Divine transcendence need not mean God's external sovereignty over the world. A procreative-emanationist model of creation focuses our attention on a transcendent immanence, or an immanental transcendence. That is, it keeps our eyes on what we can see and touch and know: the universe as God's body with God's spirit as its enlivening breath is the place that we turn to learn of *both* divine transcendence and immanence. While transcendence can mean "to exist apart from the material universe," it can also mean "surpassing, excelling or extraordinary." In the model of the universe as God's body, we look for divine transcendence not apart from the material universe, but in those aspects of the material universe that are "surpassing, excelling or extraordinary." This suggests

---

1. This chapter began with a meditation on Exodus 33:23b: "And you shall see my back; but my face shall not be seen."

that the universe could be a way to meditate on divine transcendence in a concrete, embodied way. In the model of the universe as God's body, we are invited to see the extraordinary in the ordinary, to see the surpassing wonder of divine transcendence in the smallest and largest dimensions of the history and present reality of the universe, especially our planet. Whereas in many models of divine transcendence, we must think in either concrete but shallow terms (the domesticated transcendence of the political models — God as king, lord, master over human beings) or radical but abstract terms (God as omnipotent, omniscient, eternal, infinite, and so on), in our model we can think concretely *and* radically. We are asked to contemplate the visible universe, God's body, as the place where the surpassing, extraordinary character of divine presence is to be found. The universe in its age, size, complexity, diversity, history, and beauty is the locus for our imagination to exercise its power in regard to what divine transcendence could, might, mean. It serves as a deep reflecting pool of divine magnificence and grandeur. To contemplate what we know of the universe, from the extraordinary ordinariness of a butterfly's wing to the ordinary extraordinariness of the Milky Way, is beyond all our capacities of imagination: the longer we reflect on either of these phenomena, the more filled with wonder we become. This mode of appreciating divine transcendence, the concrete, radical way, is what I have characterized as the mediating, incarnational way of the Hebrew and Christian traditions. Psalm 104 is an excellent example: "O Lord my God, you are very great. You are clothed with honor and majesty, wrapped in light as with a garment. You stretch out the heavens like a tent, you set the beams of your chambers on the waters, you make the clouds your chariot, you ride on the wings of the wind, you make the winds your messengers, fire and flame your ministers" (1–4). One looks to the *world* to discover the glory of God, for as Gerard Manley Hopkins put it, "The world is charged with the grandeur of God." Only now, the world is the universe: the common creation story has given us a more magnificent, more awesome, way to speak of that grandeur. In this concrete picture we have a more radical metaphor of divine transcendence than either the domesticated or abstract models of transcendence can give us. The universe as God's body gives us a concrete way of meditating on divine transcendence; a meditation that knows no end, for we can never imagine such transcendence to its finish or limits. It will, the longer we contemplate its wonders, whether at the microscopic or the macroscopic levels (as well as the middle level of cows, pine cones, and caterpillars), call forth more and more depths to the meaning of divine transcendence.

To contemplate divine transcendence as radically and concretely embodied means, of course, that it is not one thing: divine transcendence, in this model, would be *in* the differences, in the concrete embodiments, that constitute the universe. It is not the oneness or unity that causes us to marvel at creation, but the age, size, diversity, complexity that the common creation story tells us about. If God in the procreative-emanationist model is not primarily the initiator of creation (the simplicity of the big bang), but the empowering, continuing breath of life throughout its billions of years of history and in each and every entity and life-form on every star and planet, then it is in the *differences* that we see the glory of God. God is many, not one, for the body of God is not one body (except as *a* universe), but the infinite number of bodies, some living and some not, that are the universe. To know God in this model is to contemplate, reflect on, the multitude of bodies in all their diversity that mediate, incarnate, the divine. Once again, there is no way to God except by way of the back. Or to put it in more traditional terms, there is no way to divine transcendence except immanently.

Finally, the procreative-emanationist model does not support a dualistic hierarchy of mind and body as does the production model. The latter depends upon an intellectual/aesthetic context: creation is of the mind, not the body. The production model obviously fits masculine and the procreation model feminine gender construction: " 'higher,' metaphysical or spiritual or *ex nihilo* creation and 'lower' or 'lesser' physical, natural or elemental creation." In the first model, creation derives from a source that is itself disembodied (but presumably mental and agential), while in the second, creation is born of a physical source (but perhaps only physical). The procreative-emanationist model suggests that creation is from a physical source (it is God's body), but also from the life-giving center of the divine body (the spirit of God). This model is not dualistically hierarchical: there is no mind directing the body, but rather a body suffused with the breath and power of life. It also does not privilege the intellect over the body nor reduce creation to physicality alone. The model refuses the stereotypes of masculine versus feminine creation, one from the mind, the other from the body, claiming that neither alone is adequate even to our own human, creative experience, let alone as a metaphor of divine creation. What we see in evolutionary history is neither extreme, but a continuum of matter that gradually over billions of years becomes brain (mind) in varying ways and degrees. We have suggested that spirit is a way of expressing the enormous range of this development, at least from the inchoate gropings of an amoeba to the reflective self-consciousness of a human being (the term, of course, does less well with quarks and with God).

To review and summarize: we began this chapter with a meditation from Exodus 33: "And you shall see my back; but my face shall not be seen." The motifs in this passage have been central to our reflections on a model for expressing the God-world relationship in our time. This organic-agential, procreative-emanationist, body-spirit model underscores creation as the continuing, dynamic, growing embodiment of God, a body given life and power for the evolution of billions of diverse entities and creatures. This body is but the backside of God, not the face; it is the visible, mediated form of God, one that we are invited to contemplate for intimations of divine transcendence. It is a concrete, radical, immanental embodiment of God's glory, magnificence, and power.

James Cone (b. 1938)

A Black Theology of Liberation (1970), Chapter 4*

Black theology...asks not whether love is an essential element of the Christian interpretation of God, but whether the love of God itself can be properly under-

*Reprinted from *A Black Theology of Liberation*, Twentieth Anniversary Edition. Copyright © 1986, 1990 by James H. Cone. Published by Orbis Books. Used by permission of Orbis Books, Maryknoll, N.Y. Pp. 69–70, 80–81.

stood without focusing equally on the biblical view of God's righteousness. Is it possible to understand what God's love means for the oppressed without making *wrath* an essential ingredient of that love? What could love possibly mean in a racist society except the righteous condemnation of everything racist?...A God without wrath does not plan to do too much liberating, for the two concepts belong together. A God minus wrath seems to be a God who is basically not against anything. All we have to do is behave nicely, and everything will work out all right.

Such a view of God leaves us in doubt about God's role in the black-white struggle. Blacks want to know whose side God is on and what kind of decision God is making about the black revolution. We will not accept a God who is on everybody's side — which means that God loves everybody in spite of who they are, and is working (through the acceptable channels of society, of course) to reconcile all persons to the Godhead.

Black theology cannot accept a view of God which does not represent God as being for oppressed blacks and thus against white oppressors. Living in a world of white oppressors, blacks have no time for a neutral God. The brutalities are too great and the pain too severe, and this means we must know where God is and what God is doing in the revolution. There is no use for a God who loves white oppressors *the same as* oppressed blacks. We have had too much of white love, the love that tells blacks to turn the other cheek and go the second mile. What we need is the divine love as expressed in black power, which is the power of blacks to destroy their oppressors, here and now, by any means at their disposal. Unless God is participating in this holy activity, we must reject God's love....

If providence means what Brunner says [i.e., that all that is and all that happens takes place within the knowledge and will of God], it is difficult, if not impossible, to avoid the conclusion that all human suffering is in accordance with the divine plan. This would mean that the death of six million Jews, the genocide of Amerindians, the enslavement and lynching of blacks, and every other inhumanity, happened "within the knowledge and will of God." Only oppressors can make such a claim.

Of course, my opponents could reply that this view of providence does not mean that God *wills* human suffering. It simply means that God permits it in order to protect human freedom. It means further that, although there is oppression in this world, God does not let humankind have the last word about human existence, but translates human evil into the divine purpose. Quoting Paul with approval, Brunner says, "I reckon that the sufferings of this present time are not worthy to be compared with the glory which shall be revealed in us" (Rom. 8:18). The believer looks beyond suffering to the final goal which it must serve; compared with that promised glory, suffering does not count. Suffering becomes the way to eternal life. No human suffering is overlooked by God, and thus providence means that it is redeemable. Thus "the real solution to the problem of theodicy is redemption."

Despite the emphasis on future redemption in present suffering, black theology cannot accept any view of God that even *indirectly* places divine approval on human suffering. The death and resurrection of Jesus does not mean that God promises us a future reality in order that we might tolerate present evil. The suffering that Jesus accepted and which is promised to his disciples is not to be equated with the easy acceptance of human injustice inflicted by white oppressors. God cannot be the God of blacks *and* will their suffering. To be elected by God does not mean freely accepting the evils of oppressors. The suffering which is inseparable from the gospel is that style of existence that arises from a decision to *be* in spite of nonbeing. It is that type of suffering that is inseparable from freedom, the freedom that affirms black liberation despite the white powers of evil. It is suffering in the struggle for liberation.

Providence, then, is not a statement about the future. It does not mean that all things will work out for the best for those who love God. Providence is a statement about present reality — the reality of the liberation of the oppressed. For blacks it is a statement about the reality of blackness and what it means in the liberation struggle against whites. As Tillich says:

> Faith in providence is faith "in spite of" — in spite of the...meaninglessness of existence....[Special providence] gives the individual the certainty that under any circumstances, under any set of conditions, the divine "factor" is active and that therefore the road to his ultimate fulfillment is open.

Black theology interprets this to mean that in spite of whiteness a way is open to blackness, and we do not have to accept white definitions.

It is within this context that divine omnipotence should be interpreted. Omnipotence does not refer to God's absolute power to accomplish what God wants. As John Macquarrie says, omnipotence is "the power to let something stand out from nothing and to be." Translating this idea into the black experience, God's omnipotence is the power to let blacks stand out from whiteness and to be. It is what happens when blacks make ready for the black-white encounter with the full determination that they shall have their freedom or else. In this situation, divine providence is seeing divine reality in the present reality of black liberation — no more, no less.

Leonardo Boff (b. 1938)

Trinity and Society (1986), Chapters 7 and 8*

Consideration of the communion of the three distinct beings of the Trinity produces a critical attitude to personhood, community, society, and the church. On the personal level, our dominant culture stresses the predominance of the individual, of isolated personal development, of the rights of individuals divorced from any consideration of their relation to society. The atrinitarian monotheism of the churches, their ideology of subjectivity, of unity/identity, serve both to reinforce and reflect this distortion. Seeing people as image and likeness of the Trinity implies always setting them in open relationship with others; it is only through being

---

*Reprinted from *Trinity and Society* by Leonardo Boff, trans. Paul Burns. Copyright © 1988 Burns and Oates/Search Press Ltd. Used with permission of Burns and Oates. Pp. 148–51, 157–58, 163.

with others, understanding themselves as others see them, being through others, that they can build their own identities. Personal incommunicability exists only so as to allow communion with other people. In the light of the Trinity, being a person in the image and likeness of the divine Persons means acting as a permanently active web of relationships: relating backwards and upwards to one's origin in the unfathomable mystery of the Father, relating outwards to one's fellow human beings by revealing oneself to them and welcoming the revelation of them in the mystery of the Son, relating inwards to the depths of one's own personality in the mystery of the Spirit.

The Trinity forms an open communion going beyond the existence of the three Persons by including creation. So in the same way human beings cannot concentrate on their own interpersonal relations to the exclusion of a sense of their wider, trans-personal and structural relationships, with society and history. Personalization through communion must not lead to a personalism alienated from the conflicts and processes of social change, but must seek to establish new, more participatory and humanizing relationships....

When set against the ideal of trinitarian communion, modern society in its two principal current embodiments — socialism and capitalism — shows considerable aberrations. Liberal-capitalist society in fact means the dictatorship of the property-owning classes with their individualistic and business interests always shored up by mechanisms of state control. Such regimes have produced the greatest divisions in history between rich and poor, between the races, and between the sexes.... Capitalism, with the profanization it embodies, promotes domination based on the One: one all-embracing capital, one market, one world of consumers, one legitimate view of the world, one way of relating to nature, one way of meeting the Absolute. Differences are regarded as pathological and deviations from the norm; they are either eradicated or at best barely tolerated.

The greatness of trinitarian communion, however, consists precisely in its being a communion of three different beings; in it, mutual acceptance of differences is the vehicle for the plural unity of the three divine Persons. So by their practice and theory, capitalist regimes contradict the challenges and invitations of trinitarian communion. They are not (except through negation) a vehicle for people in general and Christians in particular to experience the Trinity in history.

Societies with a socialist regime are founded on a right principle, that of communion between all and the involvement of all in the means of production; they have grasped the basic relevance of the social element for society. But this social element is understood and put to work collectivistically, that is, without going through the essential process of accepting differences between persons and between communities....

In the light of trinitarian communion, the type of community that emerges from socialist practice seems to annul individuals; it subsumes them into a homogenizing and egalitarian whole; it does not recognize individuals as different-in-relationship, a recognition that would safeguard their differences.

Trinitarian communion is a source of inspiration rather than of criticism in the social sphere. Christians committed to social change based on the needs of majorities, above all, see tri-unity as their permanent utopia. The three "Differents" uphold their difference one from another; by upholding the other and giving themselves totally to the other, they become "Differents" in communion. In the Trinity there is no domination by one side, but convergence of the Three in mutual acceptance and giving. They are different but none is greater or lesser, before or after. Therefore a society that takes its inspiration from trinitarian communion cannot tolerate class differences, dominations based on power (economic, sexual, or ideological) that subjects those who are different to those who exercise that power and marginalizes the former from the latter.

The sort of society that would emerge from inspiration by the trinitarian model would be one of fellowship, equality of opportunity, generosity in the space available for personal and group expression. Only a society of sisters and brothers whose social fabric is woven out of participation and communion of all in everything can justifiably claim to be an image and likeness (albeit pale) of the Trinity, the foundation and final resting-place of the universe....

We need to go beyond the understanding of Trinity as logical mystery and see it as saving mystery. The Trinity has to do with the lives of each of us, our daily experiences, our struggles to follow our conscience, our love and joy, our bearing the sufferings of the world and the tragedies of human existence; it also has to do with the struggle against social injustice, with efforts at building a more human form of society, with the sacrifices and martyrdoms that these endeavors so often bring. If we fail to include the Trinity in our personal and social odyssey, we shall have failed to show the saving mystery, failed in evangelization. If oppressed believers come to appreciate the fact that their struggles for life and liberty are also those of Father, Son, and Holy Spirit, working for the Kingdom of glory and eternal life, then they will have further motives for struggling and resisting; the meaning of their efforts will break out of the restricting framework of history and be inscribed in eternity, in the heart of the absolute Mystery itself. We are not condemned to live alone, cut off from one another; we are called to live together and to enter into the communion of the Trinity. Society is not ultimately set in its unjust and unequal relationships, but summoned to transform itself in the light of the open and egalitarian relationships that obtain in the communion of the Trinity, the goal of social and historical progress. If the Trinity is good news, then it is so particularly for the oppressed and those condemned to solitude...the three Persons want to introduce all of us and the world we live in to their overflowing life of community. This communion is not a promise for the future; it is happening amongst us now, in persons and communities. It is experienced whenever we know true communion of being and having. The Trinity communicates itself whenever communion is established on earth. It is also experienced as hope and anticipated in this hope whenever the oppressed and their allies fight against tyranny and oppression. The communion of the Trinity is then their source of inspiration, plays a part in their protest, is a paradigm of what they are building.

Elizabeth A. Johnson (b. 1941)

She Who Is: The Mystery of God in Feminist Theological Discourse (1992), Chapter 12*

God's Being as Love

Classical theism models its notion of divine being on the root metaphor of motion adapted primarily from the nonpersonal, physical world. If one uses that model it is clearly the case that something already purely in act cannot pass from potency into act, nor can something completely in motion be in any way passive or receptive. Hence, God cannot suffer. But this root metaphor of motion is hardly adequate to God's holy mystery, which is utterly personal, transpersonal, source of all that is personal. A different interpretation becomes possible when the root metaphor is taken from personal reality that is constitutively relational. Then the essence of God can be seen to consist in the motion of personal relations and the act that is love. With this in view it is possible to conceive of suffering as not necessarily a passive state nor a movement from potentiality to act. Rather, suffering can be conceived of ontologically as an expression of divine being insofar as it is an *act* freely engaged as a consequence of care for others. The personal analogy makes it possible to interpret divine suffering as Sophia-God's act of love freely overflowing in compassion.

Feminist theology is rightly wary of overstressing the value of love because of the attention traditionally devoted to agapaic or self-giving love which, without equal regard for self-affirmation and the excellence of mutuality, has operated in the sociological sphere to maintain women's subordination. Set within an inclusive context and continuously regulated by the value of relational autonomy, however, love may yet serve as a crystallization of the relational essence of God's being. We can say that the inconceivable power that gives life to the world, sustains it everywhere and always, joins its crucified history, empowers every event of healing and liberation, and is the deepest mystery toward which the world moves is essentially relational: Holy Wisdom as pure, unbounded love, utterly set against evil, totally on the side of the good.

Love Entails Suffering

Does love entail suffering in God? In the classical tradition with its apathic ideal, the answer is obviously no. Love is purely a matter of the will; to love is to will the good of the one loved. Defending this tradition William Hill reasonably argues that if someone I love is suffering it does them no good if I suffer too; what matters is that I *do* something to relieve the misery. The difficulty with this argument, however, is that the notion of love as simply willing the good of others prescinds from the reciprocity entailed in mature relations. Of course love includes willing the good of the beloved, and the classical idea is right as far as it goes. But as actually lived, and paradigmatically so in the light of women's

---

experience, love includes an openness to the ones loved, a vulnerability to their experience, a solidarity with their well-being, so that one rejoices with their joys and grieves with their sorrows. This is not a dispensable aspect of love but belongs to love's very essence. In fact, a chief source of the energy that generates "willing the good" and relieving misery lies precisely in this experience of compassionate solidarity with the suffering of those we love. In the light of the feminist prizing of mutuality as a moral excellence, love does entail suffering in God.

An Excellence

Speech about the suffering God who loves in solidarity with the conflictual world does not intend to say that God suffers because of some intrinsic deficiency; nor unwillingly through being overtaken by outside forces; nor necessarily under the constraint of nature; nor passively under the dictates of a stronger power. On the contrary, speech about Holy Wisdom's suffering with and for the world point to an act of freedom, the freedom of love deliberately and generously shared in accord with her own integrity. "This is the manner of God's suffering: to suffer as the fruit of love and of the infinite capacity of love for solidarity." As a summation of compassionate love, the symbol of divine suffering appears not as an imperfection but as the highest excellence. . . . But how can a suffering God be of any help? There is an element of truth to one woman's appalled objection to this kind of language with which many would sympathize. If I were at the bottom of a deep pit, aching, cold, and nursing a broken arm, she writes, "what I want and urgently need is a Rescuer with a very bright light and a long ladder, full of strength, joy, and assurance who can get me out of the pit, not a god who sits in the darkness suffering with me." What she rightly rejects is the notion of a suffering God who is powerless, the antithesis of the omnipotent God. However, the human situation of agony and death is more internal to ourselves and more socially complex than this example would allow. Closer to the point is the reflection of another woman who spent endless days and nights on a hospital ward with her tiny, sick daughter, helping the nurses with the other babies when she could. It was a dreadful exposure to the meaningless suffering of the innocent. "On those terrible children's wards," she writes, "I could neither have worshipped nor respected any God who had not himself cried out, 'My God, My God, why hast thou forsaken me?' Because it was so, because the creator loves his creation enough to become helpless with it and suffer in it, totally overwhelmed by the pain of it, I found there was still hope."

This is one way the symbol of a suffering God can help: by signaling that the mystery of God is here in solidarity with those who suffer. In the midst of the isolation of suffering the presence of divine compassion as companion to the pain transforms suffering, not mitigating its evil but bringing an inexplicable consolation and comfort. . . . Communion becomes a profound source of energy for the healing of suffering. Knowing that we are not abandoned makes all the difference.

Speaking about God's suffering can also help by strengthening human responsibility in the face of suffering. The impassible God models a dispassionate, apathic attitude that influences community ideals. Conversely, the suffering God reorders the human ideal toward compassionate solidarity. The logic of the symbol discloses that if God's compassionate love struggles against destructive forces, then being in alliance with God calls for a similar praxis.... Especially in situations of massive suffering due to injustice, such a symbol makes clear that God is to be found on the side of those who are oppressed, as a challenge to oppressors be they individuals or structures. The close correlation between divine pathos and prophetic act in the Bible indicates that responsible action for resistance, correction, and healing are among the truest expressions of living faith.

Comfort and the challenge to responsible praxis do not of themselves resolve everything, especially death which in the end engulfs everyone. Human beings may be consoled, and pour out every effort to heal and liberate, but suffering continues in history. At the very limit of limit situations, the symbol of the suffering God can help by awakening hope that historical failure is not the last evidence of what the future holds. This is a deep mystery, how in the depths of suffering, hope against hope is born....

As the foundation of this hope, Christian faith speaks about the paschal mystery, about Jesus Christ's death and resurrection as the first fruit of an inclusive harvest, about new unimaginable life breaking out through death itself and as a corrective to death. Although for a time there was no glimmer of hope, God was near at hand, nevertheless, and Jesus was not ultimately abandoned. The victory arrives through the living communion of love, overcoming evil from within. To say this is not to rationalize suffering or to find a solution to the problem of evil or to offer cheap consolation. The cross and resurrection scandalize and cannot be reconciled theoretically. Rather, this event deepens the mystery of how God's solidarity with the suffering world brings about a future even for the most godforsaken. It points to the real mystery of the trinitarian God as an ally against suffering and moves the community to the practice of love that corresponds to this mystery. The presence of the living God, even when darkly intuited in the mode of absence, offers new possibilities to the situation from within.

Only a suffering God can help. The compassionate God, spoken about in analogy with women's experience of relationality and care, can help by awakening consolation, responsible human action, and hope against hope in the world marked by radical suffering and evil.

Divine Power

Speaking of the suffering God from a feminist liberation perspective entails reshaping the notion of omnipotence. Both the classical model of power-over and the dialectical view of the absence of power in helpless suffering are riddled with inadequacies. We seek an understanding that does not divide power and compassionate love in a dualistic framework that identifies love with a resignation of power and the exercise of power with a denial of love. Rather, we seek to integrate these two, seeing love as the shape in which divine power appears.

One major resource for this language is the experience of women who know the breakthrough of their own strength, usually under duress: the nurturing power of a mother who enables her children to grow into their own personhood; the dynamic spirit of a preacher who galvanizes her community to take hold of their own dignity; the creative power of an artist who shapes a world with words or material or movement; the justice-making vigor of women who know wrongs, both personal and structural, and stand as strong witnesses to resist and remake; the courage of sick, lonely, or violated women who reach out to establish connectedness, deriving energy that they critically turn toward the well-being of others. All of these and other like women fundamentally detest suffering and mobilize imaginatively and compassionately against it despite the price.

The kind of power they evidence is a vitality, an empowering vigor that reaches out and awakens freedom and strength in oneself and others. It is an energy that brings forth, stirs up, and fosters life, enabling autonomy and friendship. It is a movement of spirit that builds, mends, struggles with and against, celebrates and laments. It transforms people, and bonds them with one another and to the world. Such dynamism is not the antithesis of love but is the shape of love against the forces of nonbeing and death. And it operates in a relational manner.

Feminist theologians are grappling for language to give voice to this understanding of power arising from women's experience. Neither power-over nor powerlessness, it is akin to power-with....

Thinking of Holy Wisdom's "almighty power" along these lines leads to a re-symbolization of divine power not as dominative or controlling power, nor as dialectical power in weakness, nor simply as persuasive power, but as the liberating power of connectedness that is effective in compassionate love. We can say: Sophia-God is in solidarity with those who suffer as a mystery of empowerment. With moral indignation, concern for broken creation, and a sympathy calling for justice, the power of God's compassionate love enters the pain of the world to transform it from within. The victory is not on the model of conquering heroism but of active, nonviolent resistance as those who are afflicted are empowered to take up the cause of resistance, healing, and liberation for themselves and others.

Delores S. Williams (b. 1943)

Sisters in the Wilderness: The Challenge of Womanist God-Talk (1993), Chapters 6 and 8*

While God tells ancient Israelites that "if your brother becomes poor beside you, and sells himself to you, you shall not make him serve as a slave" (Lev. 25:39), God also says, "you may buy male and female slaves from among the nations that are around about you.... You may bequeath them to your sons after you, to inherit as a possession forever; you may make slaves of them, but over your brethren the people of Israel you shall not rule one over the other, with harshness" (Lev. 25:46).... In Jeremiah 34:8–22 God tells the Israelites that "every one should set free his Hebrew slaves, male and female, so that no one should enslave a Jew." There is no mention of freedom for non-Jewish slaves.

The point here is that when non-Jewish people (like many African-American women who now claim themselves to be economically enslaved) read the entire

*Reprinted from *Sisters in the Wilderness: The Challenge of Womanist God-Talk* by Delores S. Williams. Copyright © 1993. Used with permission of Orbis Books, Maryknoll, N.Y. Pp. 146–48, 150–51, 196–99.

Hebrew testament from the point of view of the non-Hebrew slave, there is no clear indication that God is against their perpetual enslavement. Likewise, there is no clear opposition expressed in the Christian testament to the institution of slavery. Whatever may be the reasons why Paul advises slaves to obey their masters and bids Onesimus, the slave, to return to his master and later advises the master to free Onesimus, he does not denounce the institution of slavery. The fact remains: slavery in the Bible is a natural and unprotested institution in the social and economic life of ancient society — except on occasion when the Jews are themselves enslaved. One wonders how biblically derived messages of liberation can be taken seriously by today's masses of poor, homeless African-Americans, female and male, who consider themselves to be experiencing a form of slavery — economic enslavement by the capitalistic American economy. They may consider themselves outside the boundaries of sedentary, "civilized" American culture.

Womanist theologians, especially those who take their slave heritage seriously, are therefore led to question James Cone's assumption that the African-American theologian can today make *paradigmatic* use of the Hebrews' exodus and election experience as recorded in the Bible. Even though Cone sees that for the Hebrews "election is inseparable from the event of the exodus," he does not see that non-Hebrew female slaves, especially those of African descent, are not on equal terms with the Hebrews and are not woven into this biblical story of election and exodus. One might agree with Cone that Jesus had liberation of the oppressed on his mind when he was reported to have said,

> The Spirit of the Lord is upon me, because he has anointed me to preach good news to the poor. He has sent me to proclaim release to the captives and recovering of sight to the blind, to set at liberty those who are oppressed, to proclaim the acceptable year of the Lord. (Luke 4:18–19)

But the non-Jewish person of slave descent may question what Jesus had in mind in Matthew 10:5–6, where he is reported to have charged his disciples, saying, "Go nowhere among the Gentiles, and enter no town of the Samaritans, but go rather to the lost sheep of the house of Israel." This suggests a kind of bias against the non-Jew that accords well with Paul's way of situating Hagar, the female slave, and her progeny outside the promise of freedom he describes in Galatians 5. Biblical scholars may give various interpretations of the Matthew 10 texts derived from their historical critical or literary critical methodology. Nevertheless, the nonliberative strand in the Bible and the tension it apparently places upon black liberation theology's norm for interpreting scripture (i.e., God's liberating action on behalf of all the oppressed) make it difficult to understand how the Bible can function today in the way that James Cone suggests: "It matters little to the oppressed who authored scripture: what is important is whether it can serve as a weapon against oppressors." Equivocal messages and/or silence about God's liberating power on behalf of non-Hebrew, female slaves of African descent do not make effective weapons for African-Americans to use in "wars" against oppressors....

Womanist theologians, in concert with womanist biblical scholars, need to show the African-American denominational churches and black liberation theology the liability of its habit of using the Bible in an uncritical and sometimes too self-serving way. This kind of usage has prohibited the community from seeing that the end result of the biblical exodus event, begun in the book of Exodus, was the violent destruction of a whole nation of people, the Canaanites, described in the book of Joshua. Black liberation theologians today should reconceptualize what it means to lift up uncritically the biblical exodus *event* as a major paradigm for black theological reflection. To respond to the current issues in the black community, theologians should reflect upon exodus from Egypt as *holistic story* rather than *event*. This would allow the community to see the exodus as an extensive reality involving several kinds of events before its completion in the genocide of the Canaanites and the taking of their land. The community would see the violence involved in a liberation struggle supposedly superintended by God.

In the exodus story there are the violent acts of God against Israel's oppressors, the Egyptians. There is the pre-exodus event of the Hebrews obtaining economic resources (reparations?) from the Egyptians before they left Egypt. There is God's violence against the Egyptians as they attempted to subdue the Israelites crossing the Red Sea. There are the violent acts of the Hebrews, sanctioned by God, as they killed every person in the land of Jericho except Rahab and her family. God is supposed to have sanctioned genocide in the land of Makkedah, in Libnah, and in the Promised Land of Canaan. This kind of reflection upon exodus as a holistic story rather than as one event allows black theologians to show the black community the awful models of God projected when the community and theologians use the Bible so that only Israel's or the Hebrews' understanding of God becomes normative for the black community's understanding of how God relates to its life. On the basis of this holistic story, the black community and black theologians must explore the moral status of violence in *scripture* when the violence is mandated and/or supported by God.

What is suggested here is *not* that black theologians in their use of scripture ignore the fact of black people's identification with the exodus of the Israelites from Egypt. This is part of African-American Christian history and should be remembered by the community. Neither do I mean to suggest that black theologians should refrain from referring to the texts in the book of Exodus and to Jesus' words in Luke 4 in ways that are meaningful for the exposition of the gospel in our time. Nor should liberation language and liberation ideas be lost to black theology. However, I suggest that African-American theologians should make it clear to the community that this black way of identifying with God *solely* through the exodus of the Hebrews and Jesus' reported words in Luke belongs to the black historical period of American slavery. Apparently this was the time when God's liberation of the Israelites or the exodus was the subject and "predicate" of the biblical ideas undergirding African-American Christian theology. Such is not the case today. To build contemporary systematic theology only on the exodus and Luke paradigm is to ignore generations of black history subsequent to slavery — that is, to consign the community and the black theological imagination to a kind of historical stalemate that denies the possibility of change with regard to the people's experience of God and with regard to the possibility of God changing in relation to the community....

When womanist theologians engage a survival/quality-of-life hermeneutic in the interpretation of biblical texts, an image of God emerges different from the liberator God championed in some liberation theology. Dialogue is needed here.

Latin American biblical scholar Elsa Tamez rereads the Hagar-Sarah texts from the context of "Christians immersed in the process of liberation" and sees liberative impulses in God's actions in relation to Hagar and Ishmael. But my womanist reading does not see God's action in this text as particularly liberative. I come to the text from a Christian context of concern for poor black women, children and men immersed in a fierce struggle for physical, spiritual and emotional survival and for positive quality of life formation. Thus, while Tamez sees in the text God's word of liberation to the slave woman of African descent, a black American womanist reading from the context of a survival/quality-of-life struggle sees God responding to the African slave Hagar and her child in terms of survival strategies.

The two times that God relates directly to Hagar are in the context of helping her come to see the strategies she must use to save her life and her child's life. The first strategy is to go back to her oppressor and make use of the oppressor's resources. The second survival strategy not only has to do with the woman and child (family) depending upon God to provide when absolutely no other provision is visible, but also includes, upon God's command, the woman Hagar lifting up her child and "holding him fast with your hand" (Gen. 21:18, RSV). According to some biblical scholars this literally means "make your hand firm upon him...which is idiomatic for lending support and encouragement" to the child. The assurance of the survival of mother and child comes from God, who reiterates the promise "for I will make him a great nation" (Gen. 21:18b). In the Hebrew testament world-view, one survived through one's progeny and ancestors.

The feminist "liberation lens" and the womanist "survival lens" can, on occasion, provide a common vision. A case in point is Genesis 16:9, when God tells the runaway slave Hagar to return and submit herself to Sarah, who has physically abused Hagar in a most brutal way. Though the interpretation of this text has been an issue in biblical scholarship, Tamez interprets it in a way consistent with what a womanist survival/quality-of-life hermeneutic would yield:

> What God wants is that she and the child should be saved, and at the moment, the only way to accomplish that is not in the desert, but by returning to the house of Abraham. Ishmael hasn't been born. The first three years of life are crucial. Hagar simply must wait a little longer, because Ishmael must be born in the house of Abraham to prove that he is the first-born (Deut. 21:15–17), and to enter into the household through the rite of circumcision (chap. 17). This will guarantee him participation in the history of salvation, and will give him rights of inheritance in the house of Abraham.

While God is concerned about Ishmael's and Hagar's survival, there are some questions womanists must ask about God's relation to the terms of survival upon which Hagar lives in Abraham and Sarah's household. Does God care more about the oppressor Sarah than about the oppressed Hagar? When Sarah becomes jealous of Ishmael and decides that he — though firstborn — will not inherit along with her son Isaac, she demands that Hagar and Ishmael be thrown out of the house. Abraham opposed this, but God intervened telling him to do as Sarah asks. What are we to say about God's action here? Can we conclude that what looks like God favoring the oppressor female is just the way the story is told in the Bible, that it is not necessarily the way God actually behaves with regard to oppressed-oppressor relationships? If we answer this question affirmatively, do we not discredit all biblical descriptions of God's actions in relation to humankind?

Tamez does not question God's favoring the oppressor Sarah over the oppressed Hagar. Rather, in a liberation mode she concludes: "God let her [Sarah] act that way because he had other plans for Hagar, a better future than in the house of Abraham." But there is nothing in Hagar's story in the Bible to suggest a better future for her. In fact, Hagar's and Ishmael's future seems highly precarious and more threatened than their existence in Abraham's house.

Nevertheless, African-American women as well as African-American people in general have through the years found hope in Hagar's story. I believe the hope oppressed black women get from the Hagar-Sarah texts has more to do with survival and less to do with liberation. When they and their families get into serious social and economic straits, black Christian women have believed that God helps them make a way out of no way. This is precisely what God did for Hagar and Ishmael when they were expelled from Abraham's house and were wandering in the desert without food and water. God opened Hagar's eyes and she saw a well of water that she had not seen before. In the context of the survival struggle of poor African-American women this translates into God providing Hagar [read also African-American women] with *new vision* to see survival resources where she saw none before. God's promise to Hagar throughout her story is one of survival (of her progeny) and not liberation. In Hagar's story liberation is self-initiated and oppressor-initiated. Human initiative "sparks" liberation — not divine initiative. In Genesis 16 Hagar liberates herself; she is a runaway slave. In Genesis 21 Sarah, her oppressor, initiates Hagar's liberation. God merely agrees with Sarah. In both instances Hagar is liberated into precarious circumstances.

On the basis of the Hagar-Sarah texts the feminist and womanist liberationist and the womanist survival/quality-of-life advocates may provide different responses to the question, How does God relate to the oppressed in history? The liberationist may say God relates primarily to liberation efforts. The survivalist may say God relates primarily to survival/quality-of-life efforts. Some feminists and womanists may say God relates to the oppressed both ways at different times or at the same time. Again, the issue is not who is right or wrong. The issue is an understanding of biblical accounts about God that allows various communities of poor, oppressed black women and men to hear and see the *doing* of the good news in a way that is meaningful for their lives.

The truth of the matter may well be that the Bible gives license for us to have it both ways: God liberates and God does not always liberate all the oppressed. God speaks comforting words to the survival and quality-of-life struggle of many families. The biblical stories are told in a way that influences us to believe that God makes choices. And God changes whenever God wills. But African-American Christian women are apt to declare as Hagar did, "Thou are a God of Seeing" (Gen. 16:13). And seeing means acknowledging and ministering to the survival/quality-of-life needs of African-American women and their children.

Part Three

BIOGRAPHICAL AND TEXTUAL INFORMATION

Anselm of Canterbury (ca. 1033–1109)

Anselm was a key figure in the development of medieval Christian theology. He has been called "the major systematic thinker within the early twelfth century Latin Church,"[1] "the highest achievement of ... the medieval Augustinian use of dialectic, the summit of the early scholastic genius and the ripest fruit of the monastic schools,"[2] and simply "the father of scholasticism."[3]

Anselm was born into a noble family in the town of Aosta in northwestern Italy. He received an excellent classical education and became convinced early on of the importance of precision and clarity in writing. The fame of Lanfranc attracted Anselm to the monastery of Bec in Normandy (France), where he arrived about 1060. Shortly thereafter he took his monastic vows. In 1063 Anselm was elected prior of the monastery, and in 1078 abbot. While at Bec, Anselm wrote many major works: *Monologion, Proslogion, On the Grammarian,* and *Epistle on the Incarnation of the Word.* Under Anselm, Bec became a center of monastic learning.

The benefactor of the monastery at Bec was William the Conqueror, who had given Bec lands in both England and Normandy. During one of his visits to England, William's son and successor named Anselm archbishop of Canterbury (1093). But Anselm soon came into conflict there with William II over the matter of investiture (whether a secular ruler had the right to invest a bishop with the symbols of his office). When Anselm went into exile (1097), King William II confiscated his lands in Canterbury. Anselm went to Italy, where he presented his grievances against the king to Pope Urban II (1088–99). From 1097 to 1100 Anselm completed writing his *Why God Became Human* and *On Virginal Conception and Original Sin.* When King William II died in 1100, his brother Henry I seized the English throne. In order to gain church support, he sought the backing of Anselm, who returned to England. Anselm, however, soon broke with the king over the matter of investiture. Anselm again went into exile (1103–6). After the dispute was settled (1107), Anselm was able to return to England and spend the last couple years of his life in peace. During this time, Anselm devoted his theological attention to the problems of grace, free will, and predestination.

Anselm's work is characterized by a tension between faith and its traditional supports (scripture and tradition), on the one hand, and reason and logic, on the other. This tension is clearly exhibited in his *Proslogion,* which is framed in the context of a prayer to God and which simultaneously attempts to furnish one argument, "resting on no other argument for its proof, but sufficient in itself to prove that God truly exists."[4] All the while, Anselm avers that he does not seek to understand in order to believe, but he believes in order to understand (see ch. 1). In fact, the original title of *Proslogion* was *Fides quaerens intellectum* (*Faith Seeking Understanding*).

Anselm's theological work was important for the development of theologi-

---

1. Hopkins, *A Companion to the Study of St. Anselm,* 212.
2. David Knowles, *The Evolution of Medieval Thought* (New York: Vintage Books, 1962), 98.
3. Martin Grabmann, *Die Geschichte der scholastischen Methode* (Basel: Benno Schwabe, 1961), 7.
4. Anselm, Preface to the *Proslogion,* in Eugene R. Fairweather, ed., *A Scholastic Miscellany: Anselm to Ockham* (New York: Macmillan, 1970), 69.

cal method and soteriology in the Middle Ages. In *Why God Became Human,* Anselm attempted to demonstrate the necessity of the incarnation without making direct appeals to scripture or the standard assumptions of Christian faith. The satisfaction theory, which he developed in this treatise, became one of the classic explanations of redemption. Anselm employs a similar methodology in his *Proslogion,* an excerpt from which is included in Part One.

The *Proslogion (Address)* was written in 1078. In the previous year Anselm had written the *Monologion* at the request of fellow monks at Bec. The *Monologion* attempted to establish the being of God solely from the rational consideration of truth and goodness as intellectual concepts. In the *Proslogion* Anselm's reasoning develops into the so-called ontological argument. His argument is perhaps better called an analytical argument because he analyzes the rational implications of the definition of God as "a being than which none greater can be thought" (see ch. 2). A proper analysis of this definition, Anselm argues, leads to the conclusion that God exists not only as an idea in the human mind, but also as a reality outside of the mind. In chapter 3 Anselm offers a second form of his argument, and in chapter 4 he explains how a fool can say that God doesn't exist by distinguishing between the signification of a word ("God") and *understanding* the reality referred to by that word.

The monk Gaunilo of Marmoutier challenged Anselm's argument in his *Book on Behalf of the Fool Who Says in His Heart There Is No God.* Gaunilo argued that one could use Anselm's argument to conclude that a perfect island, for example, must exist if I can conceive of such a perfect island in my mind. In his *Book of Defense against Gaunilo,* Anselm replied that God is a unique case. God is not simply the most perfect member of a genus of finite being; God, rather, transcends every kind of finite being. Every finite reality, even the perfect member of each category of finite thing (such as a perfect island), can be thought of as not existing. This, however, is not the case with God.

Since his day, Anselm's argument on behalf of the reality of God has had its critics as well as its supporters. Although Thomas Aquinas in the thirteenth century and Immanuel Kant in the eighteenth century did not find it cogent, René Descartes formulated his version of the ontological argument in the seventeenth century and Charles Hartshorne defended Anselm in the twentieth century.

Bibliography

Bencivenga, Ermanno. *Logic and Other Nonsense: The Case of Anselm and His God.* Princeton: Princeton University Press, 1993.

Evans, G. R. *Anselm and Talking about God.* New York: Oxford University Press, 1978.

———. *Anselm and a New Generation.* New York: Oxford University Press, 1980.

Hopkins, Jasper. *A Companion to the Study of Saint Anselm.* Minneapolis: University of Minnesota Press, 1972.

Rogers, Katherin A. *The Anselmian Approach to God and Creation.* Lewiston, N.Y.: Edwin Mellen, 1997.

Southern, Richard. *St. Anselm: A Portrait in a Landscape.* New York: Cambridge University Press, 1990.

Van Fleteren, Frederick, and Joseph C. Schnaubelt. *Twenty-five Years (1969–1994) of Anselm Studies: Review and Critique of Recent Scholarly Views.* Lewiston, N.Y.: Edwin Mellen, 1996.

Arius (ca. 250–336)

Arius was born in the middle of the third century in Libya. As a student of Lucian (d. 312) in Antioch, Arius came to share the Antiochene emphasis upon the historicity and humanity of Jesus as well as Lucian's subordinationist understanding of the relationship of the Son to God the Father. By the early fourth century, Arius was a presbyter (priest) in the church of Alexandria (Egypt). There he spread his understanding of God through his major work, *Thalia* (*Banquet*), written about 323. Alexander, bishop of Alexandria, found Arius's teaching about the finite, created nature of the Son objectionable. In the summer of 323, Arius wrote Eusebius of Nicomedia (d. 342) for assistance. In support of Arius's cause, Eusebius appealed to other bishops. When Arius was condemned in a synod called by Alexander at Alexandria later that year, Eusebius sheltered him. He even sponsored a synod at Bithynia, which nullified Arius's excommunication. With the spread of the controversy and with bishops lined up on both sides of the issue, Emperor Constantine was compelled to call a council at Nicea (modern-day Iznik, Turkey) to resolve the dispute. The emperor did not want this theological controversy within the recently legalized religion to split the empire.

In his letter to Eusebius of Nicomedia (sect. 5), Arius is apparently giving his interpretation of Proverbs 8:22–31. This passage had been used previously by Christians in debate with Jewish authors about the possibility of God having a Son. Christian apologists used the text to assert that the Son was present with God from the beginning and had been active in the creation of the world. Now, as Hilary of Poitiers (ca. 315–67) observed in *On the Trinity* (12:36), this weapon, given the church in its struggle against Jewish criticism, had been turned against the Christian faith to suggest that the Son was but a "creature." Arius used this scriptural passage to support his unwavering commitment to a conception of God as utterly one and utterly transcendent. As utterly one, God could not have a Son who was of the same divine essence. As utterly transcendent, God could not be involved with the world of becoming. Consequently, the Son had to be a creature through whom the entire created world was created. Unlike other creatures, the Son or Logos was created directly by God and created "before times." The Son, therefore, is not himself God, but as the highest of the created spiritual beings he is as close as possible to God. Arius's rigid monotheism sought to defend Christianity against the charge of maintaining polytheism, even if in a refined form. Arius's position is clearly articulated in his letter to Alexander (see Part One).

The Council of Nicea (325) declared Arius a heretic after he refused to sign the formula of faith, which stated that Christ was of the same divine nature as God. The emperor exiled Arius to Gaul. But due to the intercession of Bishop Eusebius of Nicomedia, Arius was eventually called back from exile. He was to be readmitted to the church after consenting to a compromise formula about God. Shortly before he was to be reconciled, however, Arius collapsed and died while walking through the streets of Constantinople.

Arius's theological position continued to be held by supporters for four decades after the Council of Nicea. Arianism was again condemned at the Council of Constantinople I (381). Although this condemnation ended the heresy in the empire, Arianism continued among some of the Germanic tribes to the end of the seventh century.

Bibliography

Barnes, Michel R., and Daniel H. Williams, eds. *Arianism after Arius: Essays on the Development of the Fourth Century Trinitarian Conflicts*. Edinburgh: T. & T. Clark, 1993.

Gregg, Robert C., ed. *Arianism: Historical and Theological Reassessments: Papers from the Ninth International Conference on Patristic Studies*. Cambridge, Mass.: Philadelphia Patristic Foundation, 1985.

Gregg, Robert C., and Dennis E. Groh. *Early Arianism — A View of Salvation*. Philadelphia: Fortress Press, 1981.

Hanson, Richard P. C. *The Search for the Christian Doctrine of God: The Arian Controversy 318–81*. Edinburgh: T. & T. Clark, 1988.

Kannengiesser, Charles. *Holy Scripture and Hellenistic Hermeneutics in Alexandrian Christology: The Arian Crisis*. Berkeley: Center for Hermeneutical Studies in Hellenistic and Modern Culture, 1982.

———. *Arius and Athanasius: Two Alexandrian Theologians*. Brookfield, Vt.: Gower Pub. Co., 1991.

Williams, Rowan. *Arius: Heresy and Tradition*. London: Darton, Longman & Todd, 1987.

Athanasius (ca. 296–373)

Athanasius was the chief defender of the Nicene understanding of God in the fourth-century battle against Arianism. He received his philosophical and theological training at Alexandria (Egypt), where he became a deacon. He attended the Council of Nicea in 325 as the secretary of Bishop Alexander. When Alexander died in 328, Athanasius succeeded him in one of the most important ecclesiastical posts in the East. His first years in office were devoted to visiting his extensive patriarchate, which included all of Egypt and Libya. During this time he established important contacts with the Coptic monks of Upper Egypt and their leader Pachomius. By the mid-330s, Athanasius's troubles with Arian supporters began. Whereas some of the eastern emperors endorsed a more tolerant policy toward Arianism in order to keep peace in the East, Athanasius fought Arianism in its different forms in an uncompromising way. As a result, he elicited hostility from other bishops and some of the emperors.

In 335/36 at the Council of Tyre, Athanasius's consecration was deemed uncanonical and he was deposed. Thus began the first of Athanasius's five periods of exile. Upon the death of Emperor Constantine in 337, Athanasius was recalled to his see, but opposition to him had not subsided. At the instigation of Eusebius of Nicomedia, Athanasius was deposed again in 338 by Constantius, emperor in the East. Athanasius took refuge at Rome under the protection of Constantius's brother Constans, emperor in the West. While in Rome, Athanasius appealed to Pope Julius I (337–52), who wrote in vain on his behalf. The council Julius called for 343 at Sardica (modern-day Sofia, Bulgaria) was attended only by western and Egyptian bishops, and their appeal on behalf of Athanasius was not accepted in the East. In 346, however, Constans's influence secured Athanasius's return to

Egypt. Athanasius's "golden decade" of peace (346–56) followed, during which time he wrote *Apology against the Arians* and *On the Decrees of the Nicene Synod*.

Athanasius's continuing defense of the Council of Nicea during decades of debate over the usefulness of the term *homoousios* led to difficulties rooted both in theological and political disputes. He was condemned at the Council of Arles in 353 and again at the Council of Milan in 355. In 356 he went into hiding after a military detachment tried to seize him. This time he withdrew to Upper Egypt, where he was protected in monasteries or friendly houses. While in exile there, he completed his massive *Four Orations against the Arians*, from which there is an excerpt in Part One. He also wrote *The Life of St. Antony* and *The History of the Arians* during this time. In 362, when Julian became emperor and bishops exiled by Emperor Constantius returned to their sees, Athanasius returned to Alexandria and summoned a council which attempted to negotiate differences between supporters of the *homoousios* (of the same essence/nature) and the *homoiousios* (of a similar essence/nature) understandings of the Son's relation to the Father. This regional council prepared the way for the orthodox doctrine of the trinity, which was articulated at the Council of Constantinople I (381). Despite this theological accomplishment, Athanasius was exiled briefly two more times, finally returning to his see by 366. Of his forty-six years as bishop of Alexandria, Athanasius spent seventeen of them in exile.

Athanasius's major contribution as a theologian was to articulate the Nicene view in which God and Christ are one in being. This foundation made possible a number of theological positions influential in Christian theology. For example, Christ being God meant that Christ's revelation was God's revelation. Christ being God meant also that through the incarnation people are brought into the very presence of God and can know God as Christ did. Christ being God meant that salvation was real. For Athanasius the debate with Arianism was not about metaphysical or philosophical points unrelated to life. Athanasius defended the authentic deity of Christ so ardently because only a divine Christ could save humanity, by recreating in it the image of God that had been ruined by the Fall.

In the excerpt from Athanasius in Part One, we find Athanasius's detailed refutation of the various arguments offered by the Arians. Athanasius, for example, appeals to scripture against the Arians. Hebrews 1:3, says Athanasius, supports the belief that the Son is the true image or imprint of the Father's being (*Orations*, sect. 9). According to this text, as well as the testimony of other parts of scripture and tradition, the Word and God's Wisdom were always with God. According to reason, this means that there never was "once" when the Son (God's Word) was not, as the Arians assert. Similarly, the Arian claim that the Son came into existence from nothing lacks validity (*Orations*, sects. 14, 17). Athanasius, moreover, points out the difficulty popular piety poses for the Arian position: Christians worship Christ, yet — according to the Arians — Christ is not really God; therefore, Christians are guilty of idolatry (*Orations*, sect. 17). The excerpt concludes with Athanasius's explanation of what the Bible means when it says that the Word *became* flesh. Here Athanasius distinguishes between the divine substance or essence of the Word, which always is and does not "become," and the love of the Word for humanity, which "becomes" within time and happens in human history.

In the excerpt from Athanasius in Part Two (*Incarnation of the Word*), Athanasius connects redemption with creation. The point of creation was to give life to creatures and to establish communion with God. Both life and communion were dissolving, however, because of the corruption of God's image due to sin. Therefore, God effected the redemption of humanity through the incarnation and ministry of Christ. As this excerpt makes clear, Athanasius emphasizes goodness and love as God's motivation for both incarnation and redemption.

Bibliography

Arnold, Duane. "Athanasian Historiography: A Century of Revision." *Coptic Church Review* 12 (1991):3–14.

Barnes, Timothy David. *Athanasius and Constantius: Theology and Politics in the Constantinian Empire*. Cambridge, Mass.: Harvard University Press, 1993.

Elliott, Thomas. "Constantine and 'the Arian Reaction after Nicaea.'" *Journal of Ecclesiastical History* 43 (1992): 169–94.

Kannengiesser, Charles. *Arius and Athanasius: Two Alexandrian Theologians*. Brookfield, Vt.: Gower Pub. Co., 1991.

Pettersen, Alvyn. *Athanasius*. Harrisburg, Pa.: Morehouse Publishing, 1995.

Widdicombe, Peter. *The Fatherhood of God from Origen to Athanasius*. New York: Oxford University Press, 1994.

Augustine (354–430)

Augustine of Hippo is one of the most influential theologians in the history of the church. He was born in Thagaste (Algeria) of relatively poor but well-patronized parents. Education was his ticket out of a difficult agricultural economy, and his father, Patricius, ensured Augustine's education through the patronage of a local land-owner named Romanianus. In 371 Augustine went to Carthage to study. Soon after he began to live with a woman of unknown name, although their common-law marriage lasted some fifteen years. The two had a son, Adeodatus (Latin for "Given from God"), probably in 373. About this same time Augustine experienced a growing maturity in his studies, what many scholars interpret to be the "first stage" of his conversion journey to Christianity. Through his reading of Cicero's *Hortentius*, described in Book 3 of the *Confessions,* Augustine (at about age nineteen) gave himself over to the pursuit of Wisdom, a quest which was at least as much religious as philosophical. Augustine was particularly drawn to probe the nature of the human soul and the question of good and evil. He joined a Manichean sect, a dualist religion which believed in a primeval conflict between light (identified with spirit) and darkness (identified with matter). From this perspective, the object of religion was to release the particles of light imprisoned in the human being, in which task Jesus and Manes or Mani (the founder of Manicheism) could offer assistance. The Manichees advocated severe asceticism to help in this process of illumination and liberation. Augustine was apparently attracted to this group not only because it accounted for the seemingly uncontrollable urges of his body, but also because it offered a "reasonable" view of religion and avoided the problematic anthropomorphisms of the Hebrew Scriptures. Augustine remained in the group for about nine years (until 383).

The 380s signal a new stage in Augustine's life, demarcated by his arrival in Milan in 384, where he had been appointed professor of rhetoric. There he came under the influence of the bishop, Ambrose, whose extensive background in Greek philosophy certainly overshadowed Augustine's own training. Listening to Ambrose's sermons compelled Augustine to revisit questions of human nature through the lens of a refined, Christianized Platonism. Ambrose's sermons opened Augustine's eyes to "spiritual" (allegorical) interpretations of problematic passages in the scriptures. Augustine's reading of Neoplatonism helped him to grasp more fully the incorporeal nature of God and to conceive of evil not as an independent force in rivalry with God, but as a privation of goodness.

Augustine's intellectual advancements were coupled with a new orientation to social climbing, perhaps facilitated by his mother, Monica, who had accompanied Augustine's family to Milan. A legitimate marriage was arranged, and Augustine's common-law wife was sent back to northern Africa (see *Confessions*, Book 6, 15:25). Augustine's encounter with Ambrose and Neoplatonism in Italy set the stage for Augustine's ultimate conversion to the Christian faith. The final step, however, did not come easily, as Book 8 of the *Confessions* makes clear. His desperation at seeing what he should do, but feeling incapable of making that step has been immortalized in his prayer to God: "Grant me chastity and continence — but not yet." Sitting in his garden in a state of depression, Augustine heard a child call out, "Pick up and read!" Augustine promptly took up the scriptures, which opened to Romans 13:13–14 (" . . . let us live honorably as in the day, not in reveling and drunkenness, not in debauchery and licentiousness, not in quarreling and jealousy. Instead, put on the Lord Jesus Christ, and make no provision for the flesh, to gratify its desires"). These words, Augustine felt, were spoken directly to him from God, and he accepted their direction. This "conversion" in 386 was the final step in his integration of the pursuit of Wisdom with Christian asceticism. Retiring to Cassiciacum, Augustine reflected on providence, the spiritual life and Christian education, writing *Against the Academicians, The Happy Life, Divine Providence and the Problem of Evil,* and his *Soliloquies*. He was baptized in 387.

Before returning to Africa, Augustine's mother and son died. Upon his return to Thagaste in 388, he established a kind of monastery where he and his companions led a simple life of philosophical contemplation. In 391 Augustine arrived in Hippo to found a monastery. He was ordained a priest, and he became increasingly involved in questions of orthodoxy. He wrote several treatises against the Manichees, then turned his attention to the Donatists. The orthodox church in northern Africa was challenged by the immense popularity of Donatism, which refused to recognize the validity of the episcopal consecration of Caecilian, bishop of Carthage, on the ground that one of those who consecrated him had betrayed the church during the persecution of Diocletian (303–5). The Donatists, who venerated the early martyrs, insisted that the members of the church be pure and virtuous. From their perspective, sacraments administered by a sinful person were invalid.

In 395 Augustine was consecrated bishop of Hippo. He then dedicated himself to a thorough campaign against the Donatists, using theological arguments and defending the intervention of the state against them. While his defense of state intervention in matters of heresy would have troublesome implications for the later church, it served to propel Augustine into his public position as bishop. He had evolved from a reader and speculative thinker into an administrator and defender of theological orthodoxy.

In addition to trouble with the Donatists, Augustine addressed another theological controversy which emerged in 411, that of the Pelagians. Pelagius, a native of Britain who had settled in Rome, was troubled by the popularity of Augustine's *Confessions,* a book which seemed to minimize the human contribution to Christian holiness. A monk devoted to the pursuit of Christian perfection, Pelagius found Augustine's notion of original sin problematic. The Pelagians rejected Augustine's idea that after the Fall it was impossible for people not to continue to sin. In contrast, they believed that it was possible to choose good by virtue of one's nature, with guidance from the revealed law and the example of Jesus. Fresh from his problems with the Donatists, Augustine saw in Pelagianism some of the same problems he had been battling for over a decade. The pursuit of Christian perfection, when applied to the community of believers as a whole, might exclude some from the church itself and the healing power of the sacraments. Augustine's response to Pelagianism was an insistence upon the absolute dependence of humanity on God's grace. As the debate grew more intense, Augustine committed more of his rhetorical skills to synthesizing his theological vision. From 414 to 420 Augustine finished *On Nature and Grace* and *On the Trinity,* while he continued to generate books of the *City of God* through 426. Peter Brown describes this period of Augustine's life, during which he was committed wholeheartedly to the case for grace, as "the high-water mark of Augustine's literary career."[1] Augustine's title in the church, doctor of grace, is well deserved.

Augustine was widely influential in his day, both in his capacity as bishop and in his capacity as a writer. In his final years he reviewed his works, compiling a list of them and commenting on his own ideas in his *Retractions.* In a sense, this self-critique pulled Augustine's ideas out of the immediate context of their polemical debates, allowing him to make clear theological statements from his perspective as an older man and to identify issues where he had changed his position. However, on some doctrines he never reached a definitive position.[2] His understanding of original sin continued to trouble him, as he expressed in his letter to Jerome: "Tell me what we are to answer about the children."[3] The changes in Augustine's thought over the course of his life have challenged later commentators to represent accurately the complexity of his thought. Augustine died in 430, as an invading "barbarian" army was about to take the city of Hippo.

The Trinity, written between 399 and 419, is Augustine's greatest dogmatic work. In it he gives a systematic account of the orthodox doctrine of the trinity. He wishes not only to state what the orthodox doctrine is, but also to understand what it means. At the beginning of the excerpt included in Part One, Augus-

---

1. Brown, *Augustine of Hippo,* 354.

2. For some interesting examples of Augustine's changes in position, see Norman L. Geisler, ed., *What Augustine Says* (Grand Rapids: Baker Book House, 1982).

3. See Augustine, Letter 166.16 in *Letters,* vol. 4, trans. Wilfred Parsons (New York: Fathers of the Church, 1955), 21.

tine reviews the course of his reflections about God in the previous portions of *The Trinity*. He observes that, in the process of attempting to contemplate God, human comprehension fails because of human limitations and divine transcendence. An understanding of love, however, provides some insight into the nature of the trinity. Augustine uses the principle of analogy to justify his claim to understand something of the invisible God on the basis of visible creation. Insofar as humanity is made in God's image, it reflects something of God. By looking inward, we discover the "trinity" of mind, knowledge, and will or love (see *The Trinity*, Book 15, sect. 10). But Augustine quickly admits that the human analogy is inadequate to describe God (*The Trinity*, Book 15, sects. 11 and 12). Augustine must ultimately conclude that there "can be no equality between creature and Creator" (*The Trinity*, Book 15, sect. 43). The excerpt concludes by stressing the need for faith (and prayer and right living) before reason. The book closes with a prayer. This approach to theological matters — faith seeking understanding — became an influential paradigm in the Christian tradition, adopted by Anselm of Canterbury and others. Augustine's reflections on the trinity by "psychological" analogy with the human soul (remembering, knowing, and loving) is one of his original contributions to theological discussion of the doctrine of God.

In the excerpts from Augustine in Part Two, Augustine deals with the doctrines of creation, preservation, predestination, and the problem of evil. In the first selection (*Enchiridion*), Augustine lays out his understanding of evil, an understanding dependent upon Neoplatonism and opposed to Manicheism. For Augustine evil is the absence of goodness rather than a force independent of and opposed to God. Creation was made good by God, but as a finite reality creation can become corrupted. The human will, when corrupted by sin, commits evil deeds. God would be justified in permitting all people born after Adam and Eve to go to eternal perdition because of the original sin in which they are born. But the will and love of God mercifully saves some human beings from perdition. In this excerpt, Augustine emphasizes the power of God's will and the gratuity of divine predestination.

In the second excerpt from Augustine in Part Two (*The City of God*), Augustine attempts to demonstrate that the creation of the world occurred in time, without creation implying a change in God's eternal decision to create. In support of his conclusion, Augustine argues that there could be no time before the universe was made because time is the measurement of movement and change. God, as a perfect being, does not change. Without the existence of a creature, whose movement would cause some change, there cannot be time. Moreover, scripture, especially the Genesis account of creation, reveals that the world was not made in time, but was made together with time. Augustine's explication of the difference between time and eternity came to be a standard part of Christian teaching about God and creation.

Bibliography

Brown, Peter. *Augustine of Hippo*. Berkeley: University of California Press, 1967.
Chadwick, Henry. *Augustine*. Past Masters series. New York: Oxford University Press, 1986.

Clark, Mary T. *Augustine*. Outstanding Christian Thinkers series. Washington, D.C.: Georgetown University Press, 1994.

Kristo, J. G. *Looking for God in Time and Memory: Psychology, Theology, and Spirituality
in Augustine's Confessions*. Lanham, Md.: University Press of America, 1991.

Miles, Margaret. *Desire and Delight: A New Reading of Augustine's Confessions*. New York:
Crossroad, 1992.

O'Donnell, James J. *Augustine*. Boston: Twayne Publishers, 1985.

Karl Barth (1886–1968)

Barth is one of the giants of Christian theology in the twentieth century. In the
early part of the century, he declared a decisive "no" to the Protestant liberalism
he had learned from Adolf von Harnack and Wilhelm Herrmann. He charted a
new course for Protestant Reformed theology that became a focal point for others
in the twentieth century.

Barth was born in Basel, Switzerland, on May 10, 1886, to Fritz Barth and
Anna Sartorius. His father was a professor of New Testament and early church
history at the University of Bern, where Barth began his theological studies in
1904. There he was exposed to the theology of Friedrich Schleiermacher, which
initially moved him in the direction of the dominant liberal theology of the day.
He continued theological studies at the universities of Berlin, Tübingen, and Marburg until 1908. At Berlin he encountered Adolf von Harnack, and at Marburg,
Wilhelm Herrmann. From 1909 to 1911, Barth served as assistant minister (cu-
rate) in Geneva. In 1911, he accepted a call to pastor the village church of
Safenwil, Switzerland. He married Nelly Hoffman, a talented violinist, two years
later. Together they had one daughter and four sons.

The ten years Barth spent at Safenwil (1911–21) were the formative period
of his life. His experience in an increasingly industrialized farming community
with all the social problems of the time "made him doubt already before the First
World War the bourgeois optimism over progress and the assimilationist tendencies of culture Protestantism, and indeed made him a Socialist committed to the
cause of the workers."[1] Barth came to believe that religious individualism and
historical relativism had emptied Christianity of its real content. The outbreak of
World War I was for Barth a radical crisis for the modern paradigm. On August 1,
1914, the day the war began, a manifesto was issued by German intellectuals in
support of Kaiser Wilhelm II's war policy. Barth was horrified to learn that almost
all of his theology professors were among the signers of the declaration. Their
support for the war disclosed, in Barth's mind, the ethical failure of theological
liberalism. Barth became very critical of the close link liberalism had established
between modern culture and Christian faith.

Over the course of the next several years, Barth turned to the Bible to discover
a sound basis upon which to build theology. "Barth desired to find a new way
of reading the Bible that might discern the Word of God within the words of the
Bible, a task for which the historical-critical method had shown itself particularly
ill-suited. The literary fruit of this concern is most prominently displayed in his

---

1. Hans Küng, *Great Christian Thinkers* (New York: Continuum, 1994), 199.

first important work, *The Epistle to the Romans.*[2] The book won for Barth an invitation to teach at the University of Göttingen. He took up the post of professor of Reformed theology in 1921. In 1922 he published a revised edition of his commentary on the letter to the Romans. It became the celebrated focus of the new movement called dialectical theology.

From 1921 to 1924 Barth was professor of theology at Göttingen, and then from 1925 to 1929 at Münster. In 1930 he became professor of systematic theology at the University of Bonn. The distinctive patterns of his mature thought began to emerge at this time. Barth's opposition to Hitler's national socialism led to his dismissal from his university position in Bonn. He was invited the following year (1935) to the University of Basel, where he taught for decades. While at Basel he published additional volumes of his *magnum opus, Church Dogmatics.* Even after his retirement in 1962, Barth continued to write.

Barth's *Church Dogmatics* was originally called *Christian Dogmatics* (in 1927). Barth changed the title five years later to oppose any facile use of the term "Christian" and to emphasize that an authentic dogmatics is possible only within the sphere of the church community, not as an individual, intellectual enterprise. The *Church Dogmatics* is a huge, incomplete work, consisting of prolegomena in volumes I.1–2 (1932, 1938); the doctrine of God in volumes II.1–2 (1940, 1942); and the doctrine of creation in volumes III.1–4 (1945–51). Barth left his exposition of the doctrine of reconciliation (IV.1–4) and the doctrine of redemption unfinished. The last completed volume was IV.3 in 1959; the fragmentary IV.4 was broken off in 1967.

As the excerpt in Part One makes clear, Barth declared revelation, not human experience, to be the starting point of theology. Already in 1924 he had insisted on the difference between God's Word and humanity's words (see *Das Wort Gottes und die Theologie; The Word of God and the Word of Man*). God speaks to us through biblical revelation. Therefore, Christianity must return to the message of the Bible and to the theology of the Reformation. Because of his radical insistence upon biblical revelation, Barth was critical of both Protestant liberalism and Roman Catholicism. To him it seemed that Roman Catholic theology believed it had control over God's revelation. If that were the case, then God could not be God. This was the prime concern of Barth's "dialectical" theology. Barth was particularly critical of the principle of analogy. In the preface to the first volume of the *Church Dogmatics* (1932), Barth declared: "I regard the *analogia entis* [analogy of being] as the invention of Antichrist, and I believe that because of it it is impossible ever to become a Roman Catholic, all other reasons for not doing so being to my mind short-sighted and trivial."[3] Barth criticized Roman Catholicism for putting God and human beings on the same level through this analogy of being: God and human persons, although significantly different, are also similar because they share "being."

2. Benjamin C. Leslie, "Karl Barth," in *A New Handbook of Christian Theologians*, ed. Donald W. Musser and Joseph L. Price (Nashville: Abingdon Press, 1996), 50.

3. Karl Barth, *Church Dogmatics,* ed. G. W. Bromiley and T. F. Torrance (Edinburgh: T. & T. Clark, 1932–67), vol. I.1, xiii. See also vol. II.1, 75–84, where Barth declares that there is no analogy on the basis of which the nature and being of God as Lord, Creator, Reconciler, and Redeemer can be accessible to us.

But Barth also criticized liberal Protestantism, which since Schleiermacher had come to focus upon human piety or human religious experience rather than upon God's revelation. Barth believed that the pernicious effect of this orientation toward the person rather than toward God could be seen in the "German Christians" who supported the National Socialism of Adolf Hitler. Because of the equating of God and the human person, many German Christians could see Hitler as offering society something "divine" — order, unity, and discipline. The "Confessing Church," of which Barth was a member, formed in opposition to the nationalistic "German Christians." In 1934 Barth inspired the Barmen Declaration of the "Confessing Church," which repudiated "the false teaching that the church can and must recognize yet other happenings and powers, images and truths as divine revelation alongside this one Word of God."[4] Only by holding fast to God's Word could Christians give effective resistance to the secularizing and paganizing of the church in Nazi Germany. For Barth, God is wholly other and God's Word, Jesus Christ, is the one word Christians are to trust and obey.

In his later writings, Barth did not refer again to the analogy of being, even though he continued to insist on the priority of revelation in theology. He visited Rome after the Second Vatican Council. Catholic theologians such as Hans Urs von Balthasar and Hans Küng evaluated Barth's theology appreciatively. Ecumenical discussions between Protestants and Catholics in the 1970s and 1980s further confirmed that there was considerable common ground. Barth died at the age of eighty-two during his sleep on December 10, 1968.

Bibliography

Barth, Karl. *Church Dogmatics*. Edinburgh: T. & T. Clark, 1957–59.
Bromiley, Geoffrey W. *An Introduction to the Theology of Karl Barth*. Grand Rapids: Eerdmans, 1979.
Busch, Eberhard. *Karl Barth: His Life from Letters and Autobiographical Texts*. Trans. John Bowden. Philadelphia: Fortress Press, 1976.
Hunsinger, George. *How to Read Karl Barth*. New York: Oxford University Press, 1991.
Jüngel, Eberhard. *Karl Barth: A Theological Legacy*. Trans. Garrett E. Paul. Philadelphia: Westminster, 1986.
O'Grady, Colm. *A Survey of the Theology of Karl Barth*. New York: Corpus Books, 1970.

Basil of Caesarea (329–79)

Basil came from a family of material and spiritual substance. His family were landowners in Caesarea, the capital of Cappadocia (a province in Asia Minor; modern-day Turkey). His brothers, like himself, eventually became bishops. These younger brothers, Gregory of Nyssa and Peter of Sebaste, as well as his sister Macrina and he were eventually all venerated as saints. Basil was educated in rhetoric at Constantinople and Athens, where he became friends with Gregory of Nazianzus. Due in part to the influence of his sister, Basil came to endorse an ascetical way of life. He was baptized about 358. Basil visited some of the

---

4. "The Barmen Declaration," in *The German Phoenix*, trans. Franklin H. Littell (Garden City, N.Y.: Doubleday & Co., 1960), 186.

important monastic sites in the East and then set up a small community of his own on his family estates.

In the middle of the fourth century, Arianism held sway among many Christians, including Basil's own bishop, Dianius of Caesarea. Basil opposed Arianism, but he reconciled with Dianius shortly before his death. A few years later (about 365), Basil was ordained a priest. In 370 he became bishop of Caesarea. Basil respected the theology of Origen, and he compiled an anthology of Origen's works, entitled *Philocalia*. Like Origen, Basil was interested in making clear distinctions between God the Father and God the Son. On the other hand, he wanted to defend the full divinity of the Son. Consequently, he sought to unite the so-called semi-Arians and the supporters of Nicea in opposition to Arianism. Basil's preferred formula for speaking of God was three *hypostases* (subsistences or persons) in one *ousia* (substance). For Basil the difference between *ousia* and *hypostasis* was the difference between the universal and the particular. The universal or common element in the Godhead is substance; the common element is distinctively possessed by each of the trinitarian persons. Basil makes this distinction quite clear in his Letter 214. Together with the other Cappadocian Fathers (Gregory of Nyssa and Gregory of Nazianzus), Basil shares credit for showing clearly how it was possible to maintain distinction of person without destroying the unity of the Godhead. In addition, Basil opposed the Pneumatomacheans ("Spirit-fighters"), whose founder has been held to be Macedonius (died ca. 362). The "Spirit-fighters" declared that the Holy Spirit is a creature. In his treatise *On the Spirit,* from which an excerpt is given in Part Two, Basil affirmed the deity of the Spirit and described the Spirit's activities. These two concerns of Basil, opposition to Arianism and to Macedonianism, were represented well by the two Gregories at the Council of Constantinople (381), which condemned Arianism and Macedonianism as heretical.

As bishop, Basil devoted time not only to a defense of Nicene orthodoxy, but also to the establishment of charitable institutions to aid the poor, the ill, and travelers. Among his more important dogmatic works are *Against Eunomius* (364), written against the Anomoean position of Eunomius of Constantinople, and *On the Spirit* (375), addressed to Amphilochius of Iconium. He wrote many letters and he drew up rules for monastic communities. He extolled the virtues of an authentic Christian poverty. He also made significant contributions in the development of the liturgy, especially in the East. Although the extent of his actual contribution to the series of eucharistic prayers known as the Liturgy of St. Basil is uncertain, these prayers do bear some connection to him. For his ascetical, doctrinal, and liturgical contributions, he came to be regarded as a doctor of the church. Basil died on January 1, 379.

Bibliography

Basil, St. *On the Holy Spirit*. Trans. David Anderson. Crestwood, N.Y.: St. Vladimir's Seminary Press, 1980.

Campenhausen, Hans von. *The Fathers of the Greek Church*. New York: Pantheon, 1959.

Fedwick, Paul Jonathan, ed. *Basil of Caesarea, Christian, Humanist, Ascetic: A Sixteen-hundredth Anniversary Symposium*. Toronto: Pontifical Institute of Mediaeval Studies, 1981.

Meredith, Anthony. *The Cappadocians*. London: Geoffrey Chapman, 1995.
Orphanos, Markos. *Creation and Salvation according to St. Basil of Caesarea*. Athens: Gregorios Parisianos, 1975.
Quasten, Johannes. "Basil the Great," in *Patrology*, vol. 3. Westminster, Md.: Christian Classics, 1983.
Rousseau, Philip. *Basil of Caesarea*. Berkeley: University of California Press, 1994.

Leonardo Boff (b. 1938)

Boff was born on December 14, 1938, in Concórdia, Santa Catarina, Brazil to Mansueto and Regina Boff. His hard-working parents had eleven children. Boff's father was a schoolteacher, who helped Boff see the world from the perspective of the poor. After attending primary school in his hometown, Boff attended Franciscan high schools and seminaries in Curitiba and Petrópolis. In 1964, at the age of twenty-six, he was ordained a Franciscan priest. From 1965 to 1970, he pursued advanced studies in Europe, receiving his doctorate in theology from the University of Munich in 1970. There he had written a dissertation on the church as sacrament. Upon completion of his studies in Germany, Boff took a teaching post in systematic theology at the Franciscan seminary in Petrópolis, teaching there from 1970 to 1990. In the early 1970s, he became one of the first Latin American theologians, together with Gustavo Gutiérrez, to advocate a theology of liberation. Boff has served as an adviser to the Brazilian Conference of Catholic Bishops, the Brazilian Conference of Catholic Religious Orders, and the Latin American Conference of Religious. Among the journals which he has edited are *Revista Eclesiástica Brasileira* (1971–86), the Brazilian edition of *Concilium* (since 1971), and *Cadernos Fé e Política* (since 1992).

Boff identifies two experiences that functioned as catalysts in the development of his theology of liberation. The first has been his work as a priest for a number of years in a Petrópolis slum. Despite the miserable conditions of their situation, the poor, Boff discovered, seemed still to be able to find hope and solidarity in the Christian communities they had formed. The second has been Boff's frequent excursions to the diocese of Acre-Purus, which is located in the heart of the Amazon jungle. The Catholic church there is dispersed throughout the jungle. From this experience, Boff came to see that the church for the poor of the jungle is not a hierarchical institution, but a close-knit community, in which faith and daily life are united.

Drawing upon these experiences, Boff became a vocal critic of the hierarchical structure of the Roman Catholic Church. As an alternative conception of the church, he proposed a church of and for the poor. In this understanding of the church, power is not concentrated exclusively in the hierarchical leadership, but is shared by all the people of God who constitute the church. This critique of the church was the principal reason for his summons in May 1984 to appear before the Sacred Congregation for the Doctrine of the Faith (SCDF) to explain and defend his views. Boff took to Rome with him a fifty-page response to the theological questions Cardinal Joseph Ratzinger (prefect of the SCDF) had raised. In April of the following year, Boff was ordered to be "silent under obedience" for a period of one year. During this period, Boff was to make no public appearances, his work as journal editor was curtailed, and the ecclesiastical approval of the Franciscan superior and the local bishop was required for all his writings.

The loss of his teaching and most editorial functions prompted him to make the decision to leave the Franciscan order. He resigned from the priesthood in June 1993. Since that time he has been a professor of ethics at the Federal University of Rio de Janeiro.

Boff has published nearly seventy books and hundreds of articles. Leonardo worked together with his younger brother Clodovis, also a Catholic priest, on a number of publication projects. Leonardo Boff is regarded as one of the most important liberation theologians.

In fidelity to his Franciscan orientation, Boff sees God as the creator and sustainer of all things, but especially as the God of the poor. God is both nurturer and liberator. As Otto Maduro notes, Boff was one of the first male Latin American theologians to retrieve the maternal dimensions of God, expressed in the Bible, and to criticize the patriarchal character of much Christian theology. In his book *Trinity and Society,* from which an excerpt is given in Part Two, Boff speaks of God as both Maternal Father and Paternal Mother. He even suggests the possibility of seeing Mary as an incarnation of the Holy Spirit. As the title of this book and the excerpt below make clear, Boff sees many important consequences of affirming the reality of God as trinitarian. To affirm the trinity means to affirm equality, community, and relationship as the essence of deity and as a model for human living. The trinitarian God shares the divine life with human beings in the world, prompting them to establish egalitarian and cooperative societies in which unity in diversity is upheld.

Bibliography

Boff, Leonardo. *The Lord's Prayer: The Prayer of Integral Liberation.* Maryknoll, N.Y.: Orbis Books, 1983.

————. *Church, Charism and Power: Liberation Theology and the Institutional Church.* New York: Crossroad, 1985.

————. *Introducing Liberation Theology.* With Clodovis Boff. Maryknoll, N.Y.: Orbis Books, 1987.

————. *Trinity and Society.* Maryknoll, N.Y.: Orbis Books, 1988.

Ferm, Deane William. "Leonardo Boff," in *Profiles in Liberation: 36 Portraits of Third World Theologians,* 124–28. Mystic, Conn.: Twenty-Third Publications, 1988.

Maduro, Otto. "Leonardo Boff," in *A New Handbook of Christian Theologians,* ed. Donald W. Musser and Joseph L. Price, 74–84. Nashville: Abingdon Press, 1996.

Bonaventure (ca. 1221–74)

Giovanni di Fidanza was born sometime between 1217 and 1221 in the Tuscany region of Italy. His father, Giovanni, was a physician and his mother was Maria of Ritella. As a young boy, he became seriously ill. But he was saved from death, according to his own testimony, by the intercession of Francis of Assisi, the founder of the Franciscan religious order. Giovanni studied at the University of

Paris, earning his master of arts degree in 1243. At about the same time, he joined the Franciscans, who gave him the name Bonaventure. Bonaventure now pursued the study of theology at Paris until 1248, where one of his teachers was Alexander of Hales, the outstanding Franciscan theologian of the early thirteenth century. With the completion of his theology studies, Bonaventure began to lecture, first on the Bible and then (1251–53) on Lombard's *Sentences*. In 1254 he received his master of theology degree and continued to teach in Paris until 1257. His defense of the right of Franciscans to teach in the university context and his high moral character won such respect from his fellow Franciscans that he was elected minister general of the order in 1257. He assumed leadership of the order at a time when it was troubled by dissension between those (the Spiritual Franciscans) who insisted on strict adherence to a rigorous understanding of apostolic poverty and those who held a more moderate view (the Conventual Franciscans). By personal example and careful diplomacy, Bonaventure was able to steer a middle course and to preserve the unity of the order.

In *The Mind's Road to God* (1259), an excerpt from which is included in Part One, Bonaventure lays out the path by which the mind may ascend to God. The treatise begins as a meditation upon the vision that St. Francis of Assisi had on Mount Alverna. It develops as an interpretation of this vision, and of certain passages in Exodus and Isaiah in which details of the vision find their parallels. The mind's journey begins in the world of the senses, then proceeds higher by looking inward, and finally ascends to the level of apprehending God beyond the human mind. In the tradition of Augustine, Bonaventure finds the impress of the trinity upon creation and upon the human being, who is made in God's image. Like Augustine, he believes that divine illumination can gradually make the vestiges of God in the world clearer. At the highest level of mental contemplation, one comes to see in Christ those things "which exceed all the insight of the human intellect." When the mind is elevated beyond itself through prayerful contemplation and God's grace, "all intellectual operations should be abandoned, and the whole height of our affection should be transferred and transformed into God" (ch. 7). The ultimate goal is mystical wisdom and union with God.

During his lifetime Bonaventure was respected by many. Dante mentions him as a saint in his *Paradiso*. Pope Gregory X named him bishop of Albano (Italy) in 1273 and consecrated him as cardinal in 1274, shortly before his death. Bonaventure died during the course of the Council of Lyons II (1274). Pope Sixtus IV made Bonaventure a saint in 1482, and Pope Sixtus V in the subsequent century declared him to be a doctor of the church. He is often referred to as the Seraphic Doctor. This is probably a reference to his preoccupation with the vision of the Seraph, which is described, for example, in the Prologue to *The Mind's Road to God*.

Bibliography

Bougerol, Jacques Guy. *Introduction to the Works of Bonaventure*. Paterson, N.J.: St. Anthony Guild Press, 1964.

Gilson, Étienne. *The Philosophy of St. Bonaventure*. New York: Sheed & Ward, 1938.

Hayes, Zachary. *The Hidden Center: Spirituality and Speculative Christology in St. Bonaventure.* New York: Paulist Press, 1981.

Rout, Paul. *Francis and Bonaventure.* Liguori, Mo.: Triumph Books, 1997.

Shahan, Robert W., and Francis J. Kovach. *Bonaventure and Aquinas: Enduring Philosophers.* Norman: University of Oklahoma Press, 1976.

Tavard, George H. *Transiency and Permanence: The Nature of Theology according to St. Bonaventure.* St. Bonaventure, N.Y.: Franciscan Institute, 1954.

Tracy, David, ed. *Celebrating the Medieval Heritage: A Colloquy on the Thought of Aquinas and Bonaventure.* Chicago: University of Chicago Press, 1978.

John Calvin (1509–64)

John Calvin's family name was Cauvin. He was born on July 10, 1509, in Noyon, a small town northeast of Paris. John was the youngest of four (possibly five) children, all boys. His mother died four or five years after Calvin's birth. His father, Gérard, was a notary, responsible for the legal affairs of the local cathedral chapter. Shortly after his mother's death, John's father remarried, and John was sent to the Montmors family, a neighboring noble family where he received some of his earliest education. At the age of twelve or fourteen, Calvin was sent by his father to Paris to study for the priesthood at the Collège de la Marche. After preparatory studies in language and logic, Calvin began work on a bachelor's degree in liberal arts in the Collège de Montaigu. After five years of study, Calvin earned his bachelor's and master's degrees. While in Paris he was exposed to the Christian humanism of Erasmus and Jacques Lefèvre d'Etaples. By the end of the 1520s, however, his father had decided that he should become a lawyer rather than a priest. Consequently, Calvin began work on a law degree in 1528, first at Orléans and then at Bourges. In 1531, his father became seriously ill. Calvin returned to Noyon, where he learned that his father was under a sentence of excommunication for having quarreled with the cathedral chapter. Calvin's father died on May 26, 1531.

Although his father's death was a loss, it also meant liberation from the obligation to practice law. Calvin returned to Paris, where he studied Greek and Hebrew at the Collège de France. In 1532 he published, possibly with money inherited from his father, a commentary on Seneca's *On Clemency.* Some historians have regarded this commentary as an indirect appeal to King Francis I to show clemency to his subjects who had embraced Protestant beliefs. Others have regarded it as a work of pure academic scholarship, suggesting that Calvin had not yet been converted to the Protestant cause. It is not clear when Calvin's interest in humanism developed into a commitment to reform the church. Unlike Luther, Calvin did not say much about himself in his treatises and commentaries. Calvin rarely made use of the first person singular. In fact, before his entry into public life, he had been known to remark that his desire was to live in seclusion without being known. Writing near the end of his life, Calvin simply credited God with leading him away from the pursuit of law studies and directing him toward true godliness. Whereas Karl Holl and T. H. L. Parker favor a date between 1527 and 1530 for Calvin's "conversion," John T. McNeill, Heiko Oberman, and Alexandre Ganoczy suggest a later date. They argue that it is inconceivable that

Calvin would have retained benefices after his break with the Roman Church. Since he did not resign his benefices in Noyon until 1534, Calvin's conversion cannot be dated any earlier than 1533. Whether it was early or late, sudden or gradual, Calvin's conversion built upon the evangelical humanism with which he had become familiar at Paris.

In 1534, royal policy became less tolerant of reform-minded humanism. In October of that year, posters attacking the Catholic understanding of the Mass appeared in several French cities, including Paris. King Francis I was alarmed at the strength of the Protestant movement and he sought to arrest those responsible for the posters. Over two hundred people were arrested and twenty-six were executed. Concerned for his own safety, Calvin left Paris and moved to Basel. There he completed the first edition of his *Institutes of the Christian Religion* (1536), which was a relatively short book. The book opens with an address to the French king, indicating that Calvin hoped that he might be able to persuade the king to end the persecution of those with beliefs similar to Calvin's. The word "Institutes" suggests a manual of instruction or a summary, which introduces beginners to the basic principles of a subject. After a brief trip to Italy, Calvin risked a trip to Paris to straighten out his personal affairs. He then headed for Strasbourg, presumably to meet with the reformers of that city and to visit other French refugees. The military situation, however, forced him to make a long detour to the south through Geneva. There he met William Farel, who sought to enlist Calvin's assistance in his attempt to reform the religious and civic life of Geneva. Calvin, however, wanted to live the life of a quiet scholar. Calvin records the encounter with Farel this way: "And when he realized that I was determined to study in privacy in some obscure place, and saw that he gained nothing by entreaty, he descended to cursing, and said that God would surely curse my peace if I held back from giving help at a time of such great need. Terrified by his words, and conscious of my own timidity and cowardice, I gave up my journey and attempted to apply whatever gift I had in defense of my faith."[1] By submitting to Farel's pressure, Calvin's detour became a lasting destination.

Reform of Geneva was not an easy matter. At the time of Calvin's arrival, the city had just aligned itself with Bern and the other Protestant cantons, thereby winning its political independence as a free republic. There was some tension, however, between the native Genevans and the French refugees who had chosen to spend their religious exile in Geneva. Initially it appears that most of the citizens were interested in achieving political independence of Savoy, whose duke controlled the Catholic bishopric of Geneva and through it the town. As Bousma has observed, whereas the French felt that reform would justify the sacrifices they had made as exiles, the native Genevans were wary not to trade the lordship of Savoy for the dictation of foreign ministers.[2] As was the case with other towns that had separated from the Roman Church, the Genevan town council reserved to itself the discipline of excommunication. The power to excommunicate was an important issue for Calvin because he took very seriously his responsibility in administering communion. He believed that the power to excommunicate might

---

1. *Calvin: Commentaries*, trans. Joseph Haroutunian, Library of Christian Classics (Philadelphia: Westminster Press, 1958), 53.
2. Bousma, *John Calvin*, 20.

save at least a few from eternal damnation for having received communion unworthily. The antagonism between Calvin and the city council over this issue intensified during Calvin's first two years in Geneva. The antagonism was further exacerbated by Calvin's reluctance to use nonbiblical language in theological formulations. In May 1538 the city magistrates expelled him and Farel from Geneva. Thus began Calvin's second exile, this time in Strasbourg.

Calvin's time in Strasbourg (1538–41) was happier than it had been in Geneva. Martin Bucer invited Calvin to Strasbourg to serve as pastor to a congregation of French refugees there. During his three years in the city, Calvin achieved a balance between his scholarly inclinations and his pastoral duties. In addition to serving the needs of his congregation, he lectured on the New Testament in the Strasbourg academy. He also published his commentary on Paul's letter to the Romans as well as prepared the second, considerably enlarged edition of the *Institutes* (1539). In August of 1540 Calvin married a member of his Strasbourg congregation, Idelette de Bure, a widow who had two children from a previous marriage. Together Idelette and John had at least one son of their own. Unfortunately, he did not survive infancy, and Idelette died in 1549.

By late 1540 a group in Geneva was actively at work to recall Calvin from his exile. The thought of return to Geneva, however, was unpleasant. In a letter to Farel, Calvin wrote: "Rather would I submit to a hundred other deaths than to that cross on which one must perish daily a thousand times."[3] Bucer, however, encouraged him to return to Geneva. In September 1541 Calvin returned to Geneva, feeling that his authority had been heightened because the town council had invited him back. His first concern was to organize the church of Geneva according to the Word of God and the example of the early church. Calvin drew up his ideas in the *Ecclesiastical Ordinances*. Except for some emendations — for example, the rejection of monthly communion in favor of quarterly — the city council accepted Calvin's ordinances in November 1541. The *Ordinances* established four groups for the administration of the church: pastors, teachers, elders, and deacons. The consistory, made up of pastors and twelve lay elders, was responsible for the enforcement of discipline. They sought to bring every aspect of Genevan life under God's law. This form of church government was one of Calvin's lasting contributions. The inclusion of elders (from the Greek word "presbyters") in the governance of the church eventually led to the label "presbyterian."

Despite the town council's acquiescence in Calvin's blueprint for the structure of the church, there continued to be friction between Calvin and some of the citizens of Geneva. Some chafed at the discipline which the consistory exercised. Others were unhappy about the increasing number of French refugees whom Calvin welcomed to the city. The foreigners threatened to upset the existing power structure and to raise the cost of living. The situation remained tense until about 1555. It is important to note that Calvin was able to effect changes in the life of Genevan society during this time not because of any legal or political office he held, but because of the force of his personality, his determination, and his powers of persuasion. Calvin did not become a citizen of Geneva until 1559,

---

3. Calvin to Farel, March 29, 1540, in *Ioannis Calvini Opera quae supersunt omnia*, ed. G. Baum, E. Cunitz, and E. Reuss (Berlin, 1863–1900), 11:30.

eighteen years after his return to the city. During this period in Geneva, Calvin wrote various theological treatises, prepared the final revisions of the *Institutes* (1559), and preached more than 170 sermons a year. Calvin preached on week-days on the Hebrew scriptures at six in the morning every other week, on the New Testament on Sunday mornings, and on the Psalms on Sunday afternoons. During the last years of his life, he also established the Genevan Academy. Such an institution had been foreshadowed in the *Ecclesiastical Ordinances* of 1541, in which Calvin declared that a college should be established to prepare individuals for the ministry and for civic life through instruction in classical languages, the humanities, and sacred doctrine. Many ministers who were educated in the Academy returned to France and other parts of Europe to attend to the spiritual needs of like-minded Christians, carrying with them a Calvinist understanding of Christian faith. Calvin's influence was spread in this way far beyond the confines of Geneva. In his final years, Calvin suffered from arthritis, kidney stones, and gout. He died on May 27, 1564, and was buried the next day in an unmarked grave in the common cemetery.

In the excerpt from the *Institutes* in Part One, Calvin insists upon the necessity of revelation in scripture as the only guide to sure and authentic knowledge of God. In the excerpt in Part Two, Calvin explicates the teaching of the Bible concerning divine providence and predestination. Here Calvin forcefully underlines the power of God's will and the justice of God's decrees concerning election and reprobation.

Although he was slight in stature and bookish in personality, Calvin left a profound mark on western culture. His influence has been particularly strong in the English-speaking world. Calvin's *Institutes* was translated into English during his lifetime (1561), and it had gone through eleven editions by 1632. Calvin's thought had an important influence on American life from the very beginning. For example, John Robinson, a defender of the strict Calvinism of the Synod of Dort (1618–19), directed the founding of the Plymouth Plantation. The English Calvinist influence in New England was augmented by the Dutch Calvinists of New York and New Jersey, the German Reformed of Pennsylvania and Maryland, and the Scotch-Irish Presbyterians of the mid-Atlantic and southern colonies. "Calvinists founded universities, pioneered the New England town meeting, insisted on the separation of powers in the federal government, played a prominent role in the movement for the abolition of slavery, and even promoted such characteristic institutions of frontier revivalism as 'the anxious bench' and the 'camp-meeting.'"[4] Theologically Calvin left the Christian world a lasting legacy in his *Institutes*, which was the first detailed, comprehensive, and orderly expression of a Protestant understanding of Christian faith.

Bibliography

Bousma, William J. *John Calvin: A Sixteenth-Century Portrait*. New York: Oxford University Press, 1988.
Calvin, John. *Institutes of the Christian Religion*. Ed. J. T. McNeill and trans. F. L. Battles, 2 vols. Philadelphia: Westminster Press, 1960.

---

4. Steinmetz, *Calvin in Context*, 5.

McGrath, Alister E. *A Life of John Calvin: A Study in the Shaping of Western Culture.* Oxford: Basil Blackwell, 1990.

Steinmetz, David. *Calvin in Context.* New York: Oxford University Press, 1995.

Wendel, François. *Calvin: Origins and Development of His Religious Thought.* Durham, N.C.: Labyrinth Press, 1963.

Catherine of Siena (1347–80)

Caterina di Giacomo di Benincasa was born in Siena, Italy, on March 25, 1347, to a family of modest means. Her father was a wool dyer, and she was the twenty-fourth of twenty-five children. She was drawn to the church and cloister of San Domenico, a center of Dominican learning and preaching. Catherine probably learned to read at an early age, but could not write until she was an adult. Even as a child she claimed to have visions and lived austerely. At the age of fifteen, she cut off her hair in defiance of her family's efforts to get her to marry. Shortly thereafter, she joined the Third Order of St. Dominic in Siena, where she became noted for her gift of contemplation and her devotion to the poor. As a "tertiary," Catherine took simple religious vows and was permitted to remain outside of a convent. By the age of twenty-one she was engaged in nursing activities outside her home. Two years later she experienced a sort of "mystical death" and she redoubled the austerities of her life (almost complete fasting and sleep deprivation). She acquired a following and spent time composing letters which offered both spiritual counsel and political observations. By 1374 she was more involved in intercession among political factions in Siena, Pisa, and Florence. She not only wanted to help establish peace within the church and within Italy, Catherine also wanted to encourage a crusade against the Muslims. In 1375 she received the stigmata, visible only to herself. The following year she had an audience with Pope Gregory XI (pope from 1370 to 1378) in Avignon, attempting to convince him to return the papacy back to Rome and reestablish peaceful relations with Florence. She was convinced that the only way to reestablish peace in Italy, promote reform within the church, and to organize a crusade was by returning the papacy to Rome. Pope Gregory XI left Avignon in the fall of 1376.

In 1377 Catherine wrote her major work, *The Dialogue,* a book constructed as a mystical dialogue between God and the soul. In the excerpt given in Part Two, Catherine emphasizes love as the motive behind God's activities, while explaining the compatibility of that love with the reality of human suffering. Catherine remained in Siena at a reformed Dominican convent she had founded until summoned to Rome in 1378 by Pope Urban VI. There she set up her household, met with popes and cardinals, dictated hundreds of letters, and counseled her disciples. She was deeply troubled by the papal schism that occurred shortly after Bartolomeo Prignano, archbishop of Bari, was elected Pope Urban VI. She tried to gain support for Urban, who was being opposed by the antipope Clement VII. Weakened by intense fasting and penitential practices, Catherine died in Rome on April 29, 1380, at the age of thirty-three. She was canonized in 1461 and declared a doctor of the Roman Catholic Church in 1970. She, Teresa of Avila, and

Thérèse de Lisieux are the only three officially recognized female "doctors" (i.e., teachers) of the church. She is the patron saint of Italy.

Bibliography

Catherine of Siena. *The Dialogue*. Trans. Suzanne Noffke. New York: Paulist Press, 1980.
————. *The Letters of St. Catherine of Siena*. Trans. Suzanne Noffke. Binghamton, N.Y.: Center for Medieval and Early Renaissance Studies, 1988.
Raymond of Capua. *The Life of St. Catherine of Siena*. Trans. George Lamb. New York: P. J. Kenedy, 1960.

James Cone (b. 1938)

James Cone is the Charles A. Briggs Professor of Systematic Theology at Union Theological Seminary in New York City. He has been one of the most important figures in black theology for more than twenty-five years.

Cone was born on August 5, 1938, in Fordyce, Arkansas, and raised in the rural town of Bearden. There he experienced racial segregation and discrimination in school and in daily life. But he was also enriched and empowered by his experiences in the religious community that made up the Macedonia African Methodist Episcopal Church. At the age of ten, he presented himself for church membership; at the age of sixteen, he entered the ministry.

As M. Shawn Copeland reports, Cone's experience in the rural South raised for him a troubling theological question. If God is as good and as powerful as black faith insisted, why did blacks suffer so much? This question exercised his mind as a young child and as a student at Philander Smith College in Little Rock, Arkansas. While a student there, Cone read about Martin Luther King, Jr., and the civil rights movement. He also experienced firsthand the 1957 integration crisis at Central High School in Little Rock. After graduating from Philander Smith with a major in religion and philosophy, he entered seminary studies at Garrett Biblical Institute (now Garrett-Evangelical Theological Seminary) in Evanston, Illinois. In the context of the civil rights movement, he began to consider seriously Malcolm X's critique of Christianity. The instances of racism that he encountered at Garrett did not prevent him from passing his comprehensive examinations with distinction and earning the systematic theology prize. He then pursued doctoral studies in systematic theology at Garrett-Northwestern University. In 1965 Cone became the first black American to graduate with a doctorate in theology from Garrett-Northwestern. He wrote his dissertation on Karl Barth's anthropology.

By the late 1960s Cone, like many other African Americans, had come to doubt the wisdom and effectiveness of King's nonviolent approach to social and political change. The call for black power was raised, and black anger against their unjust and oppressive treatment was vented in urban riots. Cone's response to the assassination of Martin Luther King, Jr., and the riots that followed was expressed in *Black Theology and Black Power* (1969), the first of Cone's eight books. There he argued that black power was committed to the liberating service of black men and women oppressed by white racism, just as Jesus had given his life in liberating service of the poor and the outcast. The task of black theology, he wrote, was to analyze the black condition in light of God's revelation in Christ "with the purpose of creating a new understanding of black dignity among black people, and providing the necessary soul in that people, to destroy white racism."[1]

In his second book, *A Black Theology of Liberation* (1970), Cone developed the theme implicit in his first book: the message of the gospel is liberation from racial and social oppression and the corresponding task of theology is passionate participation in reasoned inquiry on behalf of the oppressed. In this book and in his *God of the Oppressed* (1975), Cone argues forcefully that God is revealed in the Bible as Liberator which, in the context of the present experience of the African-American community, means that God is "black." By "black," Cone means that God has made the oppression of the black community God's own. As Cone insists: "Either God is identified with the oppressed to the point that their experience becomes God's experience, or God is a God of racism.... Because God has made the goal of blacks God's own goal, black theology believes that it is not only appropriate but necessary to begin the doctrine of God with an insistence on God's blackness" (see excerpt in Part One).

In one of his more recent works, *Martin & Malcolm & America* (1991), Cone writes a social history of Martin Luther King's and Malcolm X's responses to the condition of black people in America. In addition to social analysis, Cone also proposes in this book models for transformative social praxis. Cone continues today to be a leader in American theology and a provocative public speaker.

Bibliography

Burrow, Rufus. *James H. Cone and Black Liberation Theology.* Jefferson, N.C.: McFarland & Co., 1994.

Cone, James H. *Black Theology and Black Power.* New York: Seabury Press, 1969.

———. *A Black Theology of Liberation.* Philadelphia: Lippincott, 1970.

———. *Martin & Malcolm & America: A Dream or a Nightmare?* Maryknoll, N.Y.: Orbis Books, 1991.

Copeland, M. Shawn. "James Hal Cone," in *A New Handbook of Christian Theologians,* ed. Donald W. Musser and Joseph L. Price, 118–26. Nashville: Abingdon Press, 1996.

Wilmore, Gayraud, and James H. Cone, eds. *Black Theology: A Documentary History,* 2d ed. rev., 2 vols. Maryknoll, N.Y.: Orbis Books, 1993.

Meister Eckhart (ca. 1260–1328)

Johannes Eckhart was the leader of German speculative mysticism in the thirteenth and fourteenth centuries. He was born about 1260 to a noble family in Hochheim (Germany). Sometime between 1275 and 1280, he entered the Dominican order. During his course of studies, he came to know Albert the Great personally. He studied in Paris in 1277. We know little more about his life until he became prior in Erfurt (probably from 1290 to 1300) and vicar of Thuringia (probably in 1293–94). About 1300 Eckhart was sent to Paris to complete his studies. In 1302 Pope Boniface VIII conferred on him the title of *magister* ("master"). Henceforth he was known as Master (Meister in German) Eckhart. At

---

1. Cone, *Black Theology and Black Power,* 117.

about the same time, he engaged in debate with the Franciscan Gonzalvo of Balboa concerning the primacy of the intellect over the will. We can see a reflection of this debate in the first three *Parisian Questions* and in the sermon included in Part One. In 1303 or 1304 he was chosen provincial of the newly founded province of Saxony. In this capacity he supervised forty-seven convents and a number of monasteries. Eckhart remained in this position until 1311, when the general chapter of Naples relieved him of this duty and sent him to Paris, where he was to lecture on Lombard's *Sentences* and/or the Bible. The last two *Parisian Questions* come from this period.

By 1314 Eckhart was a professor of theology at Strasbourg, where he remained until 1322, when he was sent to Cologne. There Eckhart appears to have been the spiritual director and teacher in the Dominican house of studies. His scriptural commentaries and probably most of his sermons come from this period of his life. In this later phase of his life, Eckhart planned a synthesis of all his writings, the *Opus tripartitum* (*Threefold Work*). The first part was to be a book of propositions, from which today we only know the prologue. The second part was to be a book of questions, which was to follow the plan of Aquinas's *Summa Theologiae* and deal with a series of disputed questions. The third part was to be a book of exposition, which would include both his commentaries on the books of the Bible and his sermons. Because he was unable to complete his *Opus tripartitum*, however, Eckhart never gave final form to his teaching.

Some scholars hold that Eckhart developed ideas that were in the air in his day. Marguerite Porete (d. 1310), in *The Mirror of Simple Souls*, had taught, for example, that the soul must recover the image of the trinity by a detachment or "nakedness" that will make it conscious of its nothingness. Although Hadewijch and Mechthild of Magdeburg had an intimation of this idea, Eckhart developed it. Four major themes are discernible in his preaching: (1) detachment, becoming free of oneself and all things, so that the soul can be filled with God; (2) being re-created in God in such a way that we can speak of God giving birth to God in the soul; (3) the nobility of the soul; and (4) the purity and "brilliance" of the divine nature, which is inexpressible.[1] These themes underline the importance of the goal of the spiritual life for Eckhart. According to Eckhart, the soul can be led to recognize not only its similarity and its dissimilarity to God, but ultimately its identity with God. Some of his statements (e.g., the core of the soul and the core of God are one) sounded like blasphemy to other Christians. By such affirmations, Eckhart apparently meant to affirm that God's activity and the activity of the soul in its highest stages are united. He did not necessarily mean to suggest a substantial identity of the human soul and God, but he did mean to suggest that God could be encountered within. Eckhart also suggested that one could "break through" even this stage of intimacy with God to recognize the Godhead beyond God. The "Godhead" is the origin of all things that is beyond God (when God is conceived as Creator). Such talk brought Eckhart into difficulty.

While at Cologne, the archbishop of the city, Henry of Virneburg, began inquisition procedures against Eckhart. Virneburg was a Franciscan, while Eckhart

---

1. Alois Maria Haas, "Schools of Late Medieval Mysticism," in *Christian Spirituality: High Middle Ages and Reformation*, ed. Jill Raitt (New York: Crossroad, 1987), 147–50.

was a Dominican. The time in which Eckhart lived was a time of tension between Franciscans and Dominicans, between secular clergy (i.e., clergy who did not belong to a religious order) and religious clergy, and between the supporters and opponents of Pope John XXII. In the fall of 1326 the episcopal inquisitors appointed by the archbishop published a list of forty-nine charges against Eckhart. The heterodox articles were drawn from his *Liber benedictus,* his sermons, and his scriptural commentaries. Eckhart vigorously defended himself against the charges of heresy. He even challenged the legitimacy of the episcopal commission to pass judgment on him. As a Dominican, he was to be formally judged either by the University of Paris or the pope himself, not by the clergy of Cologne. Eckhart's defense is contained in his statement of defense (*Rechfertigungsschrift*), which is extant. The inquisitors responded with a second list of fifty-nine heterodox propositions, all drawn from his sermons. Eckhart tried to show the orthodoxy of his interpretations. As the trial in Cologne became complicated, Eckhart appealed to the pope, submitting in advance to the decision of the Holy See. He traveled to the court of the Avignon papacy, where his case was heard before the curia. Either while at Avignon or on the return trip home, toward the end of 1327 or early in 1328, Eckhart died.

Pope John XXII published in March 1329 the bull *In agro dominico,* in which he declared that seventeen theses of Eckhart were heretical and eleven others were dangerous (i.e., could lead to heresy) but, with considerable explanation, could be understood in a Catholic sense. Despite this censure, Eckhart was popular with many Christians. He was one of the first medieval Christian theologians to express his ideas in the vernacular.[2] Whereas his Latin works tend to be more academic in nature, his German writings have a more pastoral tone. His thoughts about the birth of God in the soul and his comments upon the spiritual life were influential. Johannes Tauler, Heinrich Suso, and Nicholas of Cusa, in the generations immediately subsequent to Eckhart, drew connections to him. And in the twentieth century there has been a resurgence of interest in Eckhart's writings.

Bibliography

Forman, Robert K. C. *Meister Eckhart: The Mystic as Theologian: An Experiment in Methodology.* Rockport, Mass.: Element, 1991.

Kelley, Carl F. *Meister Eckhart on Divine Knowledge.* New Haven: Yale University Press, 1977.

McGinn, Bernard, ed. *Meister Eckhart and the Beguine Mystics: Hadewijch of Brabant, Mechthild of Magdeburg, and Marguerite Porete.* New York: Continuum, 1994.

McGinn, Bernard, ed. *Meister Eckhart: Teacher and Preacher.* New York: Paulist Press, 1986.

Meister Eckhart: The Essential Sermons, Commentaries, Treatises, and Defense. Trans. and intro. Edmund Colledge and Bernard McGinn. New York: Paulist Press, 1981.

Woods, Richard. *Eckhart's Way.* Collegeville, Minn.: Liturgical Press, 1990.

---

2. See Louis Bouyer et al., *History of Christian Spirituality,* 3 vols. (New York: Seabury Press, 1963), 2:382.

Gregory of Nyssa (ca. 330–94)

Gregory joins his older brother Basil of Caesarea and their friend Gregory of Nazianzus as one of the Cappadocian Fathers. The Cappadocian Fathers contributed significantly to the conceptuality and terminology used to describe the Christian God in the early church. They drew heavily on the tradition of Origen and, during the controversy following the Council of Nicea (325), they were sympathetic to the "homoiousian" position (the Son is of "a similar substance" to the Father), which emphasized the distinctions within the Godhead. By distinguishing between the one substance (Greek: *ousia*) and three subsistences (Greek: *hypostases*) of God, the Cappadocians were able to simultaneously assert the oneness and the threeness of God. In addition, they defended the full divinity of the Holy Spirit. Characteristic of the eastern Christian approach to God, the Cappadocians held that all three subsistences ("persons") have one divine nature, but the Father is the source or principle of the Godhead.

Gregory was born in Caesarea in the Roman province of Cappadocia (modern-day Turkey). His family was well-to-do, devout, and Christian. His father was St. Basil the Elder; his sister was St. Macrina; and his brothers were St. Basil and St. Peter of Sebaste. Not much is known for sure about Gregory's early life. He began a career as a teacher of rhetoric and took up the married life. When his wife died, however, he was persuaded to enter the monastery in Pontus. In 371 his brother persuaded Gregory to be consecrated bishop of Nyssa, an insignificant town under Basil's jurisdiction. Lacking Basil's administrative abilities and incurring opposition from the Arians, Gregory was accused of financial incompetence and was deposed by an Arian-dominated synod in 375 or 376. After leading an itinerant life for a couple of years, he returned to Nyssa. After his brother's death, Gregory become one of the leaders of the church in his area. He was named metropolitan of Caesarea in 380. Gregory opposed both Arianism and Apollinarism, which denied that Christ had a human soul or mind (Greek: *nous*). He took part in the Council of Constantinople I, which formalized definitively the trinitarian understanding of God.

Gregory wrote about biblical exegesis, the moral life, asceticism, and the doctrines of the church. Between 380 and 385, Gregory wrote an extensive refutation against Arianism, entitled *Against Eunomius*. His treatise to Ablabius, "On Not Three Gods," included in Part One, was probably written about 390. Gregory uses the distinction between the universal and the particular to explain how God can be three persons without the oneness of God's nature being destroyed. He uses the analogy of human beings and then later the analogy of gold and gold coins to illustrate his point. There is only one human nature, but this human nature is in all people. The universal — human nature — is one; the particular instantiations of that nature — people — are many. Gregory notes in this regard that we are not always precise in our use of language. We tend, he observes, to bestow the name of nature in the plural on those things which do not differ in nature. This faulty use of language can lead us into theological error when we speak about the trinitarian God. Gregory concludes this treatise by arguing that the basis of distinction in the Godhead is neither nature nor operation (activity), but the mutual relations of the divine persons. In "On Not Three Gods," he speaks of this as "difference in respect of cause." In other words, the difference between the divine persons is difference in their respective mode or manner of existence. Only the Father is "without cause." The Son is "caused" or generated eternally by the Father. And whereas the Son is "directly" from the Father (as first Cause), the Spirit is mediately from the Father. By making such precise distinctions, Gregory was able to uphold the unity of the divine nature and divine activity, while preserving distinction of persons in the Godhead.

Although he believed it is possible to know and speak meaningfully about God, Gregory objected to the univocal application to God of categories and names derived from creatures.[1] God is ultimately mystery. This apophatic aspect (i.e., denying the suitability of human language for describing God) of Gregory's thought may have influenced Pseudo-Dionysius. Gregory was the most philosophically oriented and speculative of the Cappadocian Fathers. Perhaps as a result he is usually not included among the four so-called "ecumenical" doctors of the Greek Church (Basil, Gregory of Nazianzus, John Chrysostom, and Athanasius).

Bibliography

Azkoul, Michael. *St. Gregory of Nyssa and the Tradition of the Fathers*. Lewiston, N.Y.: Edwin Mellen, 1995.

Keith, Graham A. "Our Knowledge of God: The Relevance of the Debate between Eunomius and the Cappadocians." *Tyndale Bulletin* 41 (1990):60–88.

Meredith, Anthony. *The Cappadocians*. London: Geoffrey Chapman, 1995.

Polinska, Wioleta. "Gregory of Nyssa on the Knowability of God." *Koinonia* 7 (1995):125–56.

Venema, Cornelis P. "Gregory of Nyssa on the Trinity." *Mid-America Journal of Theology* 8 (1992):72–94.

Gustavo Gutiérrez (b. 1928)

Born in Lima, Peru, on June 8, 1928, Gustavo Gutiérrez Merino has been at the forefront of liberation theology for decades. His father was a poor urban worker and his mother had no formal schooling. His ethnic background is part Hispanic and part Amerindian (namely, Quechuan). During his teen years, osteomyelitis confined him to bed or wheelchair. After preliminary study of medicine at the University of San Marcos in Lima (1947–50), Gutiérrez switched to theological and philosophical studies at the University of Louvain in Belgium (1951–55). There he earned a master's degree in psychology and philosophy with a thesis on Sigmund Freud. In 1955 he transferred to the Institut Catholique de Lyons in France, where he wrote a master's thesis on religious liberty. While in Lyons, he became familiar with *la nouvelle théologie* ("the new theology") of Yves Congar and Henri de Lubac. Early in 1959 he was ordained a Roman Catholic priest. Shortly thereafter he pursued additional studies at the Gregorian University in Rome (1959–60).

---

1. In this context, univocal application means that the words drawn from human experience and applied to God have exactly the same meaning when applied to God as when they are applied to finite reality. Such univocal application is impossible, according to Gregory, because of the fundamental difference between God as Infinite and created reality as finite.

Gutiérrez then returned home, where he took up a part-time faculty appointment at the Catholic Pontifical University in Lima, while working as a parish priest among the poor in Lima. During the 1960s Gutiérrez reformulated his understanding of theology in light of the tension between his European-oriented education and his experiences with the poor of Peru. His pastoral work among the poor, together with his deeper immersion into Peruvian literature, became the catalyst for his formulation of a theology of liberation.

At a conference in Chimbote, Peru (1968), organized by a group of priests advocating social change, Gutiérrez presented the basic lines of his theology of liberation. Later the same year, he worked as a theological expert at the historic conference of Latin American Bishops (CELAM) in Medellín, Colombia. He played a principal role in drafting several of the Medellín documents, which denounced the institutionalized violence to which the poor were subjected. After developing his ideas further, Gutiérrez published *A Theology of Liberation: History, Politics, and Salvation* in Spanish (1971). It continues to be regarded as a classic statement of Latin American liberation theology. Between the Medellín conference (1968) and the bishops' conference at Puebla, Mexico (1979), Gutiérrez and others had come under some critique from the Vatican. Nonetheless, Puebla did not rescind the "preferential option for the poor" that Gutiérrez had been advocating. The following year the Sacred Congregation for the Doctrine of the Faith (SCDF) initiated an investigation of Gutiérrez's theology. With the support of the Peruvian Catholic bishops, Gutiérrez was able to avoid explicit censure. The SCDF, however, published two "Instructions" (1984, 1986) concerning liberation theology, which criticized the use of Marxist analysis and the idea of class warfare. Yet the Instructions did not repudiate the notion of liberation, properly understood, as part of the church's mission.

Gutiérrez's theology both outlines the methods of liberation theology and articulates its essential principles: rooted in the life experience of the poor, reflection on poverty and suffering reveals God's solidarity with oppressed people and the association of sin with oppression. In the excerpt from Gutiérrez in Part One, we see how he makes authentic knowledge of God contingent upon the performance of justice to the poor and oppressed.

Bibliography

Brown, Robert MacAfee. *Gustavo Gutiérrez*. Maryknoll, N.Y.: Orbis Books, 1990.

Cadorette, Curt. *From the Heart of the People: The Theology of Gustavo Gutiérrez*. Oak Park, Ill.: Meyer-Stone, 1988.

Gutiérrez, Gustavo. *A Theology of Liberation: History, Politics, and Salvation*. Maryknoll, N.Y.: Orbis Books, 1973.

———. *The Power of the Poor in History*. Maryknoll, N.Y.: Orbis Books, 1983.

———. *We Drink from Our Own Wells: The Spiritual Journey of a People*. Maryknoll, N.Y.: Orbis Books, 1984.

———. *On Job: God Talk and the Suffering of the Innocent*. Maryknoll, N.Y.: Orbis Books, 1987.

———. *The Truth Shall Make You Free: Confrontations*. Maryknoll, N.Y.: Orbis Books, 1990.

———. *Las Casas: In Search of the Poor of Jesus Christ*. Maryknoll, N.Y.: Orbis Books, 1993.

McGovern, Arthur F. *Liberation Theology and Its Critics: Toward an Assessment*. Mary-knoll, N.Y.: Orbis Books, 1989.

Nickoloff, James B., ed. *Gustavo Gutiérrez: Essential Writings*. Minneapolis: Fortress Press, 1996.

Taylor, Mark McClain. "Gustavo Gutiérrez" in *A New Handbook of Christian Theologians*, ed. Donald W. Musser and Joseph L. Price, 189–99. Nashville: Abingdon Press, 1996.

Hadewijch of Brabant (mid-thirteenth century)

Biographical information about Hadewijch is almost entirely lacking. Unlike Hildegard of Bingen, Hadewijch had no account written of her life. Although she and her works were known in the fourteenth century, they fell into oblivion by the middle of the sixteenth century. The rediscovery of Hadewijch's works began in the mid-nineteenth century.

Hadewijch probably lived in the middle of the thirteenth century, making her roughly a contemporary of Aquinas and Bonaventure. It is probable that she belonged to the upper class because she is familiar with chivalry and courtly love. Unlike Hildegard in the twelfth century, she was not a nun. Rather, she was a beguine, a devout woman who chose to lead a life of apostolic poverty and contemplation without taking vows as a nun. The beguine movement originated toward the end of the twelfth century, arising largely among noble women. These women rejected both the narrow life of the lady in the castle and the narrow life of the nun in the cloister. Instead they sought a new form of life, in which spiritual contemplation, study, and manual work could be combined in proportions that suited them. The first beguines lived at home individually. Gradually, however, they formed groups, supported themselves by their common work, and submitted to the leadership of a mistress.

Drawing out the clues left in her writings, we can conclude that Hadewijch probably either founded or joined a beguine group and eventually became its mistress. At some point, her authority among the beguines was challenged. Apparently some found her standards too high; perhaps others were jealous of her leadership. The general opinion of scholars at present seems to be that Hadewijch actually was evicted from her beguine community and exiled. In some quarters her teaching may have been suspect.

Hadewijch was familiar with Latin and French, the rules of rhetoric, astronomy, and music. She frequently cites scripture in her writings. She also refers to some of the church fathers, especially Augustine, who is the only nonbiblical saint who ever appeared to her in her recorded visions. Hadewijch greatly respected Augustine's trinitarian thought. But she was also influenced by secular forces. Her poetry is indebted to the tradition of courtly love poems, with which she was familiar in the vernacular.

The central theme of Hadewijch's writings is love. She uses several different terms for love, but *Minne*, drawn from the courtly love tradition, is used most often. A form of Christian love mysticism sprang up during the second half of the twelfth century, in the area roughly corresponding to modern Belgium. This love mysticism emphasized union with God. The deeply personal experience of God as

Love often evoked ecstasy or visions. Hadewijch stands within this context. Writing from a contemporary perspective, John G. Milhaven claims that Hadewijch exemplifies a mutual and embodied way of loving and knowing.[1] Paul Mommaers claims that she is "the most important exponent of love mysticism and one of the loftiest figures in the Western mystical tradition."[2]

There is also a strong trinitarian element in Hadewijch's work. Here too we can see the influence of Augustine, who had written at length about the trinitarian image in the human person (memory, understanding, and love), and the influence of those more recent writers who, like William of Saint Thierry (ca. 1085–1148), utilized this legacy. According to Jean Baptiste Porion, the parallel Hadewijch finds between the structure of our spiritual life and the trinitarian life in God is picked up by a Flemish compatriot in the next century, Jan van Ruysbroeck (1293–1381).[3] Just as God is outwardly active (the "economic" trinity) and inwardly united (the "immanent" trinity), so too our spiritual life should be shaped by outward activity (the life of virtue) and by turning inward again for union with God. Ruysbroeck also adopted and adapted other aspects of Hadewijch's thought, including her theme of living Christ by the virtues and "being God" with God.[4]

A recurring theme in Hadewijch's writings is imitation of Christ in accepting the suffering inherent in life and living the life of virtue. By accepting the pain and suffering of life because Christ did the same, we do not simply become stoic, she says, but rather we participate in the very life of Christ. Similarly, by living the life of virtue because Christ did, we deepen our relationship with Christ and experience God's love for us, decisively manifested in the incarnation.

Most of Hadewijch's letters were probably written for the instruction of beguines. In Letter 6 she declares that "we all wish to be God with God." In Letter 28 (see excerpt in Part One) she addresses the doctrine of the trinity, which she also treats in Letters 17, 18, and 30. In Letter 28 Hadewijch presents a series of statements one after the other concerning the trinity. Her aim is not systematic exposition of God's nature, but expression of the joyful experience of an encounter with God. Insofar as God is trinitarian in nature, so too our experience affects us in a threefold manner. In an authentic experience of God, we experience the power of the Father's presence in us, the enlightenment of the Son in our pursuit of truth, and the holiness of the Spirit in our desire to do God's will. To experience these three things is to experience the totality of God. As she writes in Letter 1:

> O dear child, in proportion as his [i.e., God's] irresistible power is made more clear in you, as his holy will is better perfected in you, and as his radiant truth more fully appears in you, consent to be deprived of sweet repose for the sake of this great totality of God! Illuminate your mind and

1. He cautions: "Hadewijch did not consider her experiential union with Divine Love to be either 'sexual' or 'bodily,' but anyone from the thirteenth or twentieth century reading some of her descriptions of this experience, say, in Vision 7, would find it more similar to sexual experience than to anything else we know." Milhaven's argument is that the love that Hadewijch experienced and valued was a kind of mutuality much like what we call today "embodied" or "sexual." John Giles Milhaven, *Hadewijch and Her Sisters*, x–xi.

2. Paul Mommaers, Preface to *Hadewijch: The Complete Works*, xiii.

3. Jean Baptiste Porion, *Hadewijch: Lettres spirituelles* (Geneva: Martingay, 1972), 24–25.

4. Columba Hart, Introduction to *Hadewijch: The Complete Works*, 15.

adorn yourself with virtues and just works; enlarge your spirit by lofty desires toward God's totality; and dispose your soul for the great fruition of omnipotent Love in the excessive sweetness of our God![5]

In Letter 28, an excerpt from which is included in Part One, Hadewijch describes how our joy and pleasure can be deepened as we grow in our experience and knowledge of God. She speaks of this growth as "walking with God," as progress from walking with God in the divine presence to walking farther with God in divine effusion to walking yet farther in God's totality (see sect. 48). As we grow in our experience and knowledge of God, our soul becomes conformed to God's nature. Hadewijch describes this process of being shaped in accord with the divine nature as "becoming God with God." And the effect of this shaping is the experience of bliss, in which one is no longer able to adequately speak about God (see sect. 121). As we grow in knowledge and experience of God, we experience a "tender friendship" with God.

Bibliography

Dreyer, Elizabeth. *Passionate Women: Two Medieval Mystics.* New York: Paulist Press, 1989.

Hadewijch: The Complete Works. Trans. and intro. Columba Hart, with Preface by Paul Mommaers. New York: Paulist Press, 1980.

McGinn, Bernard, ed. *Meister Eckhart and the Beguine Mystics: Hadewijch of Brabant, Mechthild of Magdeburg, and Marguerite Porete.* New York: Continuum, 1994.

Milhaven, John Giles. *Hadewijch and Her Sisters: Other Ways of Loving and Knowing.* Albany: State University of New York Press, 1993.

Charles Hartshorne (b. 1897)

Together with Alfred North Whitehead, Hartshorne is recognized as the chief influence on the development of process theology. He was born on June 5, 1897, in Kittanning, Pennsylvania. His father was an Episcopalian priest and his mother was the daughter of an Episcopalian priest. According to his own testimony, Hartshorne learned from his parents that God is essentially love and that Christian ethics is summed up in love of God and fellow creatures. He also learned at an early age to regard religion and science as compatible. His father rejected biblical inerrancy and accepted the theory of evolution. The headmaster of his high school held similar views. Hartshorne, however, came to disagree with his parents and some teachers with regard to other matters of religion. In his later teens, he came to reject the resurrection and supernaturalistic understanding of Jesus. Reading Matthew Arnold's *Literature and Dogma* led him to conclude: "Any religious belief I could henceforth accept would have to be a philosophical one, with reasons that I could grasp as convincing."[1] Although he may have left behind Christian orthodox belief, Hartshorne did not lose a religious sensibility. From his teen years on, he developed a religious feeling for nature. In high school he was even inter-

---

5. *Hadewijch: The Complete Works,* 48.
1. Hahn, ed., *The Philosophy of Charles Hartshorne,* 14.

ested in becoming a poet. Eventually, however, his love of philosophy won out over his love of poetry.

Hartshorne spent his first two years of college at Haverford in Pennsylvania, where he was greatly influenced by one of his teachers, Rufus Jones. Jones introduced him to the philosophy of Josiah Royce and to the idea that all people are aware of God to some degree. When the United States entered World War I, Hartshorne volunteered as an orderly in an army medical corps. One day during his service in France, while looking at a beautiful landscape, he suddenly was grasped by a sense of all nature as alive and expressive of feelings. This experience gave him a personal basis for the understanding of nature suggested by Romantic poets. With regard to God, this led Hartshorne to think that God is the "super-mind" of both humanity and nature. As David Ray Griffin has remarked, the rest of his career would involve "developing this twofold idea of God as the soul of a universe constituted by feelings."[2]

After the completion of his service in the medical corps, Hartshorne transferred to Harvard, where he completed his college education. There he encountered professors who reinforced his rejection of materialism and dualism and who supported his desire to bring logical precision to the philosophy of religion. He earned a doctorate at Harvard University in 1923, with a dissertation on the unity of being in the Absolute or Divine Good. He then spent two years in Europe on a fellowship, where he attended lectures by Edmund Husserl and Martin Heidegger. He returned to the United States in 1925 and took up duties as instructor and research fellow at Harvard. At Harvard he edited the papers of Charles Sanders Peirce and served as teaching assistant for Alfred North Whitehead. From the combined influence of Peirce and Whitehead, he came to regard "spontaneity" (Peirce) or "creativity" (Whitehead) as all-pervasive.

Whitehead's doctrine of "prehension" was particularly influential. According to Whitehead's philosophy, individuals are composed of momentary events, each of which "prehends" its predecessor as well as other prior events by sympathetically feeling their "feelings." This idea gave Hartshorne a basis for presenting love as the clue to existence. The idea that the self is actually a society of occasions of experience, each of which is largely constituted by its sympathetic feelings of prior events (including other people), gave him a philosophical basis for regarding his favorite Pauline statement — that we are "members one of another" — as literally true.[3] With such a "social" understanding of the person, Hartshorne thought it was possible to show that we really can, in principle, love other people in the same way that we love ourselves.

In 1928 Hartshorne joined the philosophy department at the University of Chicago, where he taught until 1955. He held a joint appointment in the Divinity School for more than a decade. At Chicago he met and married Dorothy Cooper, who was a musician. He also became good friends with Sewell Wright, an evolutionary biologist. In 1937 he published *Beyond Humanism: Essays in the New Philosophy of Nature,* in which he argued that humanism must give way to the intellectual, aesthetic, and moral love of nature as the body of God. Hartshorne

---

2. Griffin, "Charles Hartshorne," 202.
3. See Hartshorne, *Omnipotence and Other Theological Mistakes,* 106. Griffin, "Charles Hartshorne," 204.

later came to call his understanding of the God-world relation panentheistic (i.e., all is in God and God is in all). Here Hartshorne used the mind-body relationship, understood "panpsychistically,"[4] as a key analogy for understanding the God-world relationship. According to this perspective, God is the mind or the soul of the universe, while the universe is the body of God. Because all creatures have feelings, they can all feel God. With such an understanding, Hartshorne thought that he could clearly explain how God influences all creatures and knows them, thereby sympathizing with them and being "influenced" by them in turn.

In his 1948 book, *The Divine Relativity: A Social Conception of God*, Hartshorne attempted to demonstrate that atheism and classical theism are not the only two possible answers to the question whether a "perfect" being (God) exists. A third answer is dipolar theism, according to which God has both a relative as well as an absolute pole or aspect. Whitehead first formulated such an interpretation, but Hartshorne worked out the idea more fully. The abstract essence of God is necessary, eternal, absolute, and unchanging, whereas the concrete states of God are contingent, temporal, relative, and changing. This distinction between the abstract essence and the concrete states of God is evident in the excerpt given in Part One, where Hartshorne reformulates Anselm of Canterbury's definition of God and where he insists that divine relativity in some respect does not imply a lack of divine absoluteness in all respects. Moreover, Hartshorne strongly emphasizes the point that a relative pole in God is necessary if the biblical claim, God is Love, is really true: "Either God really does love all beings, that is, is related to them by a sympathetic union surpassing any human sympathy, or religion seems a vast fraud" (see Part One).

In 1955 Hartshorne joined the philosophy department at Emory University in Atlanta, which he left in 1962 for the University of Texas at Austin. After teaching in universities for more than fifty years, Hartshorne retired as professor emeritus at Texas in 1978. Since then he has continued to work, publishing several books and many articles, including *Omnipotence and Other Theological Mistakes* (1984). His ideas have influenced other significant theologians of the twentieth century, including Daniel Day Williams, Schubert Ogden, and John Cobb, Jr.

Bibliography

Cobb, John B., and Franklin I. Gamwell, eds. *Existence and Actuality: Conversations with Charles Hartshorne*. Chicago: University of Chicago Press, 1984.

Griffin, David Ray. "Charles Hartshorne," in *A New Handbook of Christian Theologians*, ed. Donald W. Musser and Joseph L. Price, 200–213. Nashville: Abingdon Press, 1996.

Hahn, Lewis Edwin, ed. *The Philosophy of Charles Hartshorne*. Library of Living Philosophers, vol. 20. LaSalle, Ill.: Open Court, 1991.

Hartshorne, Charles. *The Divine Relativity: A Social Conception of God*. New Haven: Yale University Press, 1948.

———. *The Logic of Perfection and Other Essays in Neoclassical Metaphysics*. LaSalle, Ill.: Open Court, 1962.

---

4. The term "panpsychism" literally means everything is or has a "soul." What Hartshorne meant by this term was that everything consists of feelings, in higher or lower forms. Panpsychism, which regards things as sentient (or "psychic"), is opposed to materialism, which regards things as unfeeling matter. Hartshorne's panpsychic understanding of reality holds that to exist is to be in some measure sentient and to sustain social relations with other entities.

————. *A Natural Theology for Our Time.* LaSalle, Ill.: Open Court, 1967.
————. *Omnipotence and Other Theological Mistakes.* Albany: State University of New York Press, 1984.
Sia, Santiago, ed. *Charles Hartshorne's Concept of God: Philosophical and Theological Responses.* Boston: Kluwer, 1990.

Hildegard of Bingen (1098–1179)

Hildegard was the founder and first abbess of the Benedictine community of Rupertsberg at Bingen (Germany). She publicly preached on behalf of monastic and clerical reform. By her contemporaries, she was sought out for advice on everything from health and marital problems to the ultimate destiny of their souls. These activities clearly marked her out from other women of her day. But she was even more remarkable for the extensive body of writings she produced.[1] She wrote a monumental trilogy that combines Christian doctrine and ethics with cosmology. Excerpts from the first book in the trilogy, the *Scivias,* are included in Parts One and Two. The second book in the trilogy, the *Liber vitae meritorum (Book of Life's Merits),* deals with moral psychology and penance. The final volume, *Liber divinorum operum (Book of Divine Works),* describes her most mature understanding of cosmology, history, and eschatology. Later medieval generations remembered Hildegard as an apocalyptic prophet, who had written graphically about the end of the world. In this regard she came to be known as the "Sibyl of the Rhine."[2]

Thanks to her own writings and the biography written by monks Gottfried (Godfrey) of St. Disibod (Disibodenberg) and Dieter (Theodoric) of Echternach in the last quarter of the twelfth century, quite a bit is known about Hildegard's life. The information about the second half of her life is better known than the first part of her life. Hildegard was born into a noble family of Bermersheim or Böckelheim (about twelve miles southwest of Mainz), the youngest of ten children. She enjoyed the advantages of wealth and membership in a large and well-connected family, with easy access to the holders of political and ecclesiastical power. At this time, Benedictine monasticism remained an option for the elite of society. When she was eight years old, her parents, Hildebert and Mechthild, entrusted her to Jutta, the daughter of the Count of Sponheim, who had recently established a hermitage. From Jutta, Hildegard learned to read the Latin Bible and to chant the monastic office. Other women eventually joined Jutta and Hildegard. The expanded community of women ultimately became a Benedictine convent, attached to and dependent upon the monastery at Disibodenberg.

When she was a teenager, Hildegard made her formal profession of virginity (about 1113). We hear nothing more of her until 1136, when Hildegard was

---

1. "At a time when few women wrote as much as the occasional letter, Hildegard's written works not only surpassed those of most of her male contemporaries in the range of their subject matter (from natural history, medicine, and cosmology, to music, poetry, and theology), but also outshone them in visionary beauty and intellectual power" (Flanagan, *Hildegard of Bingen,* xi).

2. See George Tavard, "Apostolic Life and Church Reform," in *Christian Spirituality: High Middle Ages and Reformation,* ed. Jill Raitt (New York: Crossroad, 1987), 3. Bernard McGinn, *The Growth of Mysticism* (New York: Crossroad, 1994), 333.

elected abbess in the place of Jutta, who had died. In 1141 at the age of forty-two, she received the prophetic call that eventually led her to compose the *Scivias* and to begin her public mission of preaching reform. Hildegard experienced her call in the midst of a vision of blinding light, which enabled her to understand the inner meaning of scripture. She heard the command to write down what she saw and heard. At first she was reluctant to do as the voice commanded. She interpreted a subsequent illness as a sign of divine displeasure. Hildegard finally turned to Volmar, a teacher and friend from the monastery at Disibod, for advice. With his help and with the permission of the abbot at Disibod, she was encouraged to begin writing down her visions, which form the basis of the *Scivias*. Hildegard's illness left her as she began to write.

According to her memoirs, Hildegard suffered from poor health and had a propensity for visions from earliest childhood (the first one occurring at about the age of five). At first her visions baffled her. Her visual field was regularly filled with a strange luminosity that she later came to call "the reflection of the living Light." On rare occasions she came into contact with an even greater brightness, which she called "the living Light." She received her visions while fully awake, with her senses functioning normally. She did not seek to induce the visions, nor were the circumstances of her monastic life sufficiently severe to produce such visions. In this regard, Hildegard differs from some later mystics who actively sought out such visions. After many years of consideration, she came to regard her visions as a vehicle for divine revelation. In this regard, Hildegard was like other mystics, for whom visions confirmed their authority to speak on theological and ecclesiastical matters.

Approximately in 1148 Hildegard received a vision in which she was instructed to leave St. Disibod, the male community to which her community of nuns was attached, and to found a new convent on the site of a ruined Carolingian monastery near Bingen. Despite the objections of her abbot and the defection of some of her nuns, she successfully established the new monastery, the Rupertsberg (on the Rhine River near Bingen), to whose physical and financial security she devoted herself throughout the 1150s. During this time she wrote a commentary on the Athanasian Creed for the instruction of her nuns and created liturgical songs for the community (*Symphonia armonie celestium revelationum*). She also wrote two compendia on medicine and natural science (the *Book of Simple Medicine* and the *Book of Composite Medicine*).

By the end of the 1150s, the Rupertsberg was secure enough for Hildegard to leave the monastery to embark on preaching tours. For five years she traveled along the Rhine and Main rivers, preaching at monasteries and giving fiery sermons in Cologne and elsewhere. In the 1160s she spoke out against Emperor Frederick for appointing successive antipopes instead of seeking reconciliation with the legitimate pope, Alexander III (1159–81). She did this despite the fact that Frederick had given her an imperial charter of protection for the Rupertsberg nunnery. In the same decade she wrote against the heretical Cathars. In 1165 she established another convent, at Eibingen on the opposite side of the Rhine River from Rupertsberg. At about the same time, she began work on her final visionary work, *The Book of Divine Works*. This work was interrupted several times, not reaching completion until about 1174. In her final years she suffered from poor health, eventually dying on September 17, 1179, at the age of eighty-one.

Although she is frequently classified as a mystic, scholars such as Caroline Walker Bynum, Bernard McGinn, and Barbara Newman argue that she is more properly identified as a visionary and prophet. Whereas the classic mystic uses ascetical and contemplative discipline in order to attain spiritual union with God, Hildegard did not engage in severe ascetical practices and did not immerse herself in hours of private, contemplative prayer in the pursuit of mystical union.[3] In the tradition of the Hebrew prophets, Hildegard expressed her inadequacy for the task to which God had appointed her, yet she sometimes lapsed from speaking about God in the third person to speaking for God in the first person. So as to highlight her role as an instrument through which God's revelation came, Hildegard denied any education beyond "simple reading," despite the fact that she was well-acquainted with the church fathers and standard biblical commentaries.

As a prophetic reformer, Hildegard placed herself squarely within the camp supporting the reform program begun by Pope Gregory VII (1073–85). In particular, she opposed clerical immorality, simony, and the subordination of the church's prelates to secular powers. From Hildegard's perspective, secular power should be subordinate to the spiritual, princes and prelates should rule with justice, and subjects should offer their superiors prompt obedience.[4] Hildegard perceived no conflict between the spirit of prophecy and the spirit of order.

Hildegard took ten years to complete the writing of the *Scivias* (1141–51), a work of more than five hundred pages. She was assisted in this task by the monk Volmar, her former teacher and current secretary, and by her favorite nun, Richardis von Stade. Seeking confirmation of her visionary and prophetic gifts, Hildegard wrote to Bernard of Clairvaux, who intervened on her behalf with Pope Eugene III (1145–53). The pope read an unfinished copy of the *Scivias* and officially endorsed it, sending Hildegard a letter of apostolic greeting to continue her work. As Barbara Newman has commented, the importance of this papal seal of approval was tremendous. "Not only did it increase Hildegard's confidence and security in the face of continuing self-doubt, but it also authenticated her publicly and protected her from the censure she was bound to attract for violating the deutero-Pauline strictures on female silence and submission."[5]

The title *Scivias* is short for *Scito vias Domini* (*Know the Ways of the Lord*) or *Sci vias lucis* (*Know the Ways of Light*). The text is addressed to a largely clerical and monastic audience, in particular, male theologians who have failed to adequately preach and teach the mysteries of the faith. The work is divided into three books, which deal respectively with creation (and the entry of sin into the world), redemption, and sanctification. Hildegard's work has a structure as complex and uniform as that of the *summae* in the next century, although the specific organization of the work, its tone, and content are quite different.[6] Each unit of her work begins with a simple description of her vision. Occasionally she is addressed

---

3. Newman, *Hildegard of Bingen*, 17. See also McGinn, *The Growth of Mysticism*, 336.
4. Newman, *Hildegard of Bingen*, 21.
5. Ibid., 13.
6. The *Scivias* is permeated with Hildegard's exposition of the fundamental Benedictine virtues of humility, obedience, and discretion. The Benedictine legacy is also evident in her idea of heaven. Rather than conceiving it as the vision of God (as with Aquinas) or as mystical union, she conceives of heaven as

by a divine voice or figure within the vision. At the end of each vision proper, its interpretation is introduced by a formula: "And I heard a voice from heaven, saying. . . . " This formula emphasizes the prophetic nature of her writings. From this point on, the initial vision becomes a text to be interpreted, phrase by phrase, just as traditional monastic commentators would interpret a text from scripture. The interpretation is usually allegorical. It is often followed by teaching that clarifies points of doctrine and morality. Each unit concludes with an admonition, which is repeated at the end of each vision within a particular book.

In the excerpt from Hildegard in Part One, we see how Hildegard uses the image of light and fire to explicate the theological doctrine of the unity of nature and differentiation of persons in the trinity. In section 3, she emphasizes the point that both trinitarian revelation and divine incarnation were motivated by God's love of humanity and intended for eliciting from them a greater love of God. A similar theme is sounded by her older contemporary, Peter Abelard. In section 4, where she elaborates on this theme, Hildegard speaks of the embrace of God's maternal love. Like Augustine, Hildegard finds triads in nature that are reflections of God. But she also uses impersonal images (e.g., stone and flame) in addition to the more traditional images and metaphors drawn from human experience.

In the excerpt from Hildegard in Part Two, we see Hildegard dealing with God's creative and redemptive activities. She uses the metaphor of a forge to describe God's act of creation and she emphasizes a strong connection between human beings and the world. In this vision, Hildegard also offers an interpretation of the Fall that differs somewhat from its portrayal in the book of Genesis.

Hildegard's work is a synthesis of classical Benedictine theology and spirituality in the mid-twelfth century. Hildegard was socially conservative and theologically orthodox, though she was outspoken in the cause of reform and good church order.[7] At the time of the Protestant Reformation, Andreas Osiander claimed Hildegard as a "Protestant" because of her critique of negligent clergy.[8] In the twentieth century, Hildegard's work has been rediscovered and her authorship of her major treatises, once contested, has been authenticated. Although contemporary interpretations of Hildegard have chipped away at the falsified, stereotypical image of the female "mystic" and the presupposition that a medieval woman could not, and therefore did not, write or preach publicly, contemporary interpretations have also included misleading portraits of her. The contemporary portraits of Hildegard as feminist, liberationist, creation-centered mystic, and holistic health practitioner contain a grain of truth, but they also exaggerate. It

---

the unending liturgy of the saints in praise of God. See *Scivias*, Book 3, sect. 13 in Newman, *Hildegard of Bingen*, 525.

7. She condemns simony and pluralism (the holding of multiple benefices by one cleric) and she reiterates the traditional position that priests must be male. She regards women as "an infirm and weak habitation appointed to bear children." And she condemns clerical marriage as the work of the devil. To the objection that priests were married in apostolic times, she replies that God permitted this aberration in the church's infancy because there were so few priests at the time. Now a strict standard of celibacy should be enforced because the church is in its adulthood and the church's ministers are many. See *Scivias*, Book 2, Vision 6, sects. 72 and 76.

8. Bertha Widmer, *Heilsordnung und Zeitgeschehen in der Mystik Hildegards von Bingen* (Basel, 1955), 260. In 1680 Jerome Baptista published a pamphlet with an excerpt from Hildegard's works, in which she allegedly foretold the rise and the fall of the Jesuit order!

is nonetheless true that "Hildegard unites vision with doctrine, religion with science, charismatic jubilation with prophetic indignation, and the longing for social order with the quest for social justice in ways that continue to challenge and inspire."[9]

Bibliography

Dreyer, Elizabeth. *Passionate Women: Two Medieval Mystics.* New York: Paulist Press, 1989.

Flanagan, Sabina. *Hildegard of Bingen, 1098–1179: A Visionary Life.* New York: Routledge, 1989.

Hildegard of Bingen. *Scivias.* Trans. Columba Hart and Jane Bishop. New York: Paulist Press, 1990.

Newman, Barbara. *Sister of Wisdom: St. Hildegard's Theology of the Feminine.* Berkeley: University of California Press, 1987.

———. *Hildegard of Bingen: Scivias.* New York: Paulist Press, 1990.

Sur, Carolyn Worman. *The Feminine Images of God in the Visions of St. Hildegard of Bingen's Scivias.* Lewiston, N.Y.: Edwin Mellen, 1993.

Ulrich, Ingeborg. *Hildegard of Bingen: Mystic, Healer, Companion of the Angels.* Trans. Linda M. Maloney. Collegeville, Minn.: Liturgical Press, 1993.

Irenaeus of Lyons (ca. 130–202)

Irenaeus was one of the leading Christian theologians of the second century. Although his exact birth date is unknown, Irenaeus was born of Greek parents in Asia Minor. According to the testimony of his own writings, he heard and saw Polycarp (ca. 69–155), bishop of Smyrna, the last known living connection with the apostles, before Polycarp's martyrdom in 155. After migrating to Gaul (France), which had close cultural connections with Asia Minor, Irenaeus became a presbyter of the church of Lugdunum (Lyons) during the reign of Marcus Aurelius (161–80). When the bishop of Lyons, Pothinus, was martyred during a period of persecution, Irenaeus was chosen as his successor (about 177). As bishop, Irenaeus vigorously opposed Gnosticism, a rather fashionable intellectual movement in some segments of the second-century church. The Gnostics espoused a sharp dualistic understanding of reality (i.e., spirit vs. matter) and they claimed to possess secret "knowledge" ("gnosis" is the Greek word for knowledge), by means of which redemption from the evil, material world was possible. Irenaeus also acted sometimes as a mediator to resolve disagreements between churches, such as the controversy over the day for celebrating Easter. Pope Victor I (c. 189–99) attempted to bring other churches into line with the Roman practice of celebrating Easter on the Sunday following the fourteenth of the Jewish month Nisan. The churches of Asia Minor, however, celebrated Easter on the same date (the fourteenth of Nisan) as the Jews celebrated Passover, whatever the day of the week on which it fell. Mediating between the parties, Irenaeus stated that differences in external factors, such as dates of festivals, need not be so serious as to de-

---

9. Newman, *Hildegard of Bingen,* 10.

stroy church unity. He reminded Victor that previous popes had been tolerant on this point.

Only two complete works of Irenaeus are still extant, the *Adversus haereses* (*Against Heresies*) and the *Demonstration of the Apostolic Teaching,* excerpts from both of which are given in this volume. *Against Heresies*, originally written in Greek about 180, exists in a Latin translation. Consisting of five books, *Against Heresies* attempts to refute Gnosticism on the basis of arguments drawn from reason, scripture, and the apostolic tradition. Once Gnosticism had been defeated in the church, most Gnostic writings were destroyed. In order to reconstruct Gnostic teaching, scholars relied heavily on Irenaeus, who summarized the Gnostic views in his work (especially Book I of *Against Heresies*). The discovery of the Gnostic library near Nag Hammadi in Egypt in the 1940s disclosed that Irenaeus's exposition of Gnosticism was quite accurate. The *Demonstration* was known only through a reference in Eusebius of Caesarea's fourth-century *History of the Church* until 1904, when a complete Armenian translation was discovered. The *Demonstration*, which was probably intended for the instruction of candidates awaiting baptism, describes and defends fundamental Christian teachings.

Although he did not actually refer to two testaments (the old and the new), Irenaeus did prepare the way for this terminology. He asserted the validity of both testaments at a time when the Gnostics and Marcion were emphasizing the differences between the two parts of the developing Bible. Irenaeus also made important contributions to the development of the creed and the office of bishop. Irenaeus refers to the church's creed as a "rule" of truth, which can be used to combat heresy. Against the Gnostic claim to possess a secret oral tradition from Jesus himself, Irenaeus asserted that the bishops in the different cities of the empire were known as far back as the apostles, and none of these bishops was a Gnostic. The clear teaching of the bishops was a sure guide to the interpretation of scripture. Out of these ideas the notion of "apostolic succession" was gradually developed.

In the first excerpt in Part One, Irenaeus distinguishes the belief of the church from Gnostic teaching. Because God is spiritual and the world is material, the Gnostics held that creation was the work of a demiurge, a being lower and other than God. Irenaeus insists, however, that God is the one and only creator of the world. Irenaeus speaks of the Son and the Spirit as the Word and Wisdom of God. Although he refers to the Son and the Spirit as "the hands" of the Father, Irenaeus also asserts that the Son and the Spirit were always with the Father, even before creation.

In the second excerpt in Part One, Irenaeus briefly describes what the church believes about Father, Son, and Spirit. He emphasizes the interconnections between Father, Son, and Spirit. He also alludes to the principal benefit that derives from knowledge of and communion with the Father, namely, incorruptibility. This knowledge of and communion with the Father is made possible by Christ's "recapitulation," that is, Christ's passing through the various stages of human existence and thereby restoring and renewing them.

In the two excerpts from Irenaeus in Part Two, Irenaeus deals with the doctrine of creation and the problem of evil. In the first excerpt in Part Two, Irenaeus speaks of creation. He states there that God made human beings free. In the second excerpt in Part Two, he explains why God included in human freedom the capacity to do evil. Irenaeus observes that the poor exercise of freedom results from the fact that human beings were not created perfect. This point is also alluded to in the first excerpt in Part Two ("Proof of the Apostolic Preaching"), where Irenaeus speaks of the human person as "a little one" or as a "child," who had to grow and develop in order to attain perfection. Because the first human beings were imperfect "little ones," without a developed sense of discretion and wisdom, they were easily misled by the devil. In the second excerpt in Part Two, Irenaeus states that human beings — as creatures in an infantile state — could not, practically speaking, receive perfection at the very beginning of their development. Nonetheless, God guided them in their growth and development.

Bibliography

Grant, Robert M. *Irenaeus of Lyons*. The Early Church Fathers series. New York: Routledge, 1997.

Lawson, John. *The Biblical Theology of St. Irenaeus*. London: Epworth Press, 1948.

Minns, Denis. *Irenaeus*. Washington, D.C.: Georgetown University Press, 1994.

Norris, Richard A. "Theology and Language in Irenaeus of Lyon." *Anglican Theological Review* 76 (1994): 285–95.

Tiessen, Terrance. "Gnosticism and Heresy: The Response of Irenaeus." In *Hellenization Revisited: Shaping a Christian Response within the Greco-Roman World*, ed. Wendy E. Helleman. Lanham, Md.: University Press of America, 1994.

Timothy, Hamilton B. *The Early Christian Apologists and Greek Philosophy, Exemplified by Irenaeus, Tertullian, and Clement of Alexandria*. Assen: Van Gorcum, 1973.

Elizabeth A. Johnson (b. 1941)

Johnson, the oldest of seven children, was born to Margaret Reed and Walter Johnson on December 6, 1941. She grew up in Brooklyn, New York. At the age of seventeen, she entered the convent of the Congregation of St. Joseph of Brentwood, Long Island (1959). She earned a bachelor's degree in education from Brentwood College (1964), and then began a teaching career, in elementary and high school, on Long Island. While busy teaching, she completed her studies toward a master's degree in theology, which she received from Manhattan College in 1970. In 1977 she began doctoral studies at the Catholic University of America in Washington, D.C., and in 1981 she became the first woman to receive a Ph.D. in its department of theology. After completion of her doctorate, Johnson was appointed assistant professor of theology at Catholic University. Several years later she became the first woman to receive tenure in the university's department of theology. After teaching at Catholic University for ten years (until 1991), she accepted an appointment as professor of theology at Fordham University in the Bronx, New York.

Johnson has been active in major professional organizations, such as the Catholic Theological Society of America (CTSA), the American Academy of Religion, and the College Theology Society. Between 1993 and 1996 she led the

Catholic Theological Society of America, first as vice president and then president. In addition, she has served on the editorial boards of the journals *Theological Studies* and *Concilium*. From 1984 to 1993 she was a member of the Lutheran/ Roman Catholic Dialogue in the United States. Moreover, she has been a consultant to the Leadership Conference of Women Religious, the International Commission on English in the Liturgy, and the National Conference of Catholic Bishops Committee on Women in Church and Society. More recently, she has been a participant in the Common Ground Initiative, organized by the late Cardinal Joseph Bernardin in order to promote dialogue between conservative and progressive Catholics.

A focus of her major publications has been God. Her first book, *Consider Jesus: Waves of Renewal in Christology* (1990), grew out of lectures she gave in South Africa at the invitation of the South African Bishops' Conference. Two years later she published, *She Who Is: The Mystery of God in Feminist Theological Discourse* (1992), from which the excerpt in this volume is taken. The book was hailed by *Library Journal* as "perhaps the best book on feminist theology to date," and it received similar praise from *Choice*. It received several awards for excellence, including the Catholic Press Association Book Award and the prestigious $150,000 Grawemeyer Award for Best Book in Religious Studies. *She Who Is* has been translated into five languages. Since then Johnson has published *Women, Earth, and Creator Spirit* (1993) and numerous articles. Her contributions to church and society were recognized in 1994, when she received honorary doctorates from St. Mary's College (Notre Dame, Ind.) and the Maryknoll School of Theology. In the same year the *U.S. Catholic* magazine gave her its annual award for promoting the cause of women in the church. Most recently she has focused her attention on developing a theology of Mary and the saints in a feminist and ecumenical perspective.

In the excerpt given in Part One, Johnson makes her case for female symbols of God. Simply referring to God as "God" is inadequate, she argues, because it allows the "transpersonal" character of God to recede and it doesn't address the issue of the possibility of women representing God. Although it is not printed in this volume, Johnson then proceeds at this point in her book to explain why ascribing feminine traits to God or identifying a feminine dimension in God (e.g., the Holy Spirit) is also inadequate. Johnson criticizes these attempts at revising patriarchal God language because they still subordinate the feminine to the masculine or stereotype human characteristics as predominantly masculine or feminine. What Johnson wants to retrieve and reformulate are equivalent male and female (not masculine and feminine) images of God. The mystery of God, Johnson states, "is properly understood as neither male nor female but transcends both in an unimaginable way. But insofar as God creates both male and female in the divine image and is the source of the perfections of both, either can equally well be used as metaphor to point to divine mystery" (see excerpt in Part One). In the final part of this first selection, Johnson explores four female metaphors for God — two positive and two "negative." In contrast to much of the classical tradition, her divine metaphors involve a God of suffering. In the excerpt given in Part Two, Johnson develops this theme of divine suffering and reinterprets the classical understanding of divine power.

Bibliography

Johnson, Elizabeth A. *Consider Jesus: Waves of Renewal in Christology*. New York: Crossroad, 1990.

————. *She Who Is: The Mystery of God in Feminist Theological Discourse*. New York: Crossroad, 1992.

————. *Women, Earth, and Creator Spirit*. New York: Paulist Press, 1993.

Julian of Norwich (ca. 1342–1416)

Little is known about Julian's life, not even her given name. She is known to us as "Julian" because it was common practice for an anchoress (i.e., a woman who chooses to renounce the world to live a solitary existence of prayer and contemplation) to be known by the name of the church to which her room was attached. What we do know about her comes from her own writing in *Showings*, from mention of her in wills, and from *The Book of Margery Kempe*.

As a young girl, Julian lived through the entrance of the plague into England, which reached Norwich in January 1349. Subsequent outbreaks in 1359 and 1369 provide some context for Julian's reflections on physical suffering and death. Julian may have been a nun at Carrow Abbey, a Benedictine convent just outside Norwich, before she became an anchoress. The lifestyle of a nun or an anchoress suggests that Julian was from a wealthy family, because by the thirteenth century "the institutional church had pretty well closed off the possibility of convent life for any except the most aristocratic women."[1] If Julian were wealthy, it is not surprising that she was literate in English. The latter half of the fourteenth century, Joan Nuth has observed, saw a gradual growth in vernacular literacy among the laity of the upper and middle classes, including some women.

Edmund Colledge and James Walsh, the editors of the critical edition of *Showings*, have argued that Julian was a woman of substantial learning, having familiarity with Middle English spiritual treatises, such as *The Cloud of Unknowing* and Walter Hinton's *Scale of Perfection*, as well as with some patristic authors, such as Augustine. Colledge and Walsh also believe that Julian could read Latin and was well versed in the rules of classical rhetoric. Other scholars, however, question whether Julian was literate. After all, she describes herself in the Short Text as "a woman, ignorant, weak and frail" (6:135) and in the Long Text as "a simple, unlettered creature" (2:177). By these statements, Julian may have wished to indicate that she was not a scholar in the strict sense because she did not possess a university education. Or Julian may simply have been following the convention of medieval writers. Nuth believes that the evidence is sufficient for recognizing Julian as "the first woman of letters in the English language."[2]

---

1. Elizabeth Petroff, *Consolation of the Blessed* (New York: Alta Gaia Society, 1979), 21. See also Eileen Power, *Medieval English Nunneries c. 1275 to 1535* (Cambridge: Cambridge University Press, 1922), 4–24.

2. Nuth, *Wisdom's Daughter*, 10.

Based upon the evidence of a few wills, in which small sums of money were left to a recluse named Julian of Norwich, it seems safe to conclude that Julian lived at least until 1416. It is not clear whether Julian was enclosed in her room, attached to the church in Norwich, before or after she wrote the Long Text. Margery Kempe consulted an anchoress in Norwich named "Dame Jelyan," probably in 1413. This suggests that Julian must have acquired a reputation for spiritual guidance by then.

Julian's own writing reveals that a week before receiving her first revelation, she had fallen ill and was in danger of dying. She was thirty years old at the time and was given the last rites. Julian was encouraged to gaze upon a crucifix, and in the midst of this activity, she experienced a vision of Christ's passion, accompanied by revelations about the love of God for humankind.[3] The first "revelation" occurred on May 13, 1373. She received the last one on the following night. These revelations were the source of decades of theological reflection, resulting in two versions of *Showings,* or *The Revelations of Divine Love* as it became known. Colledge and Walsh believe that Julian concluded the second version of the text (Long Text) in 1393 and that this second version represents nearly two decades of theological maturation since writing her first version (Short Text). Indeed, in the Long Text of *Showings* Julian admits that she did not completely understand the revelations when she first received them. Although we do not know when she wrote the Short Text of her revelations, it is generally assumed that she did so shortly after the experience. The only extant copy of the Short Text is a fifteenth-century manuscript. Whether it is a faithful copy of the original we do not know.

Our excerpt in Part One is taken from the Long Text, which Julian probably did not begin to write until 1388 or later. In this excerpt, Julian articulates a developed and complex understanding of divine motherhood in the trinity. Although authors before her had used the theme of God's motherhood, Julian develops it significantly. Whereas it was not rare to refer to the motherhood of Jesus (because of the parallel between mothers and Christ who nourish us with their bodies), Julian affirms that motherhood can appropriately be attributed to all three divine persons. Julian lays out her ideas about God in faithfulness to the revelations she had received, but she may have been aware of the suspicion that such ideas could evoke.[4] Although *Showings* is a remarkable text, it did not enjoy wide circulation until relatively recently. Contemporary interest in Julian, particularly focused in her description of the motherhood of God and her belief that "all will be well," reflects the fact that her theological insights continue to provide meaning to Christians today.

---

3. In Julian's day, devotion to the passion of Christ was pervasive. Many believed that personal physical illness was a significant way to share in Christ's suffering. In fact, the *Ancrene Riwle,* which was addressed to women aspiring to be anchoresses, encouraged the cultivation of an awareness of Christ's physical sufferings and the healing effects of illness sent by God. See *The Ancrene Riwle,* trans. Mary B. Salu (London: Burns & Oates, 1955), 46–52, 80.

4. "It is possible that the suspicion of heresy actually attended the early history of Julian's text, for, by contrast to other Middle English spiritual writings, Julian's book had a limited circulation both during and after her lifetime. As a text written in the vernacular by a woman it could have been suspected of heresy during the harsh prosecution of Lollardy after 1414" (Nuth, *Wisdom's Daughter,* 22). See *A Book of Showings,* 25. In this period, Margery Kempe was accused of heresy and brought to trial.

Bibliography

Baker, Denise Nowakowski. *Julian of Norwich's Showings: From Vision to Book*. Princeton: Princeton University Press, 1994.

Bradley, Ritamary. "The Motherhood Theme in Julian of Norwich," *Fourteenth-Century English Mystics Newsletter* 2, no. 4 (1976):25–30.

———. "Patristic Background of the Motherhood Similitude in Julian of Norwich," *Christian Scholar's Review* 8 (1978): 101–13.

Clark, John P. H. "Nature, Grace and the Trinity in Julian of Norwich," *Downside Review* 100 (1982): 203–20.

Jantzen, Grace M. *Julian of Norwich: Mystic and Theologian*. New York: Paulist Press, 1988.

Julian of Norwich. *A Book of Showings to the Anchoress Julian of Norwich*. 2 vols., ed. Edmund Colledge and James Walsh. Critical edition. Toronto: Pontifical Institute of Mediaeval Studies, 1978.

Nuth, Joan M. *Wisdom's Daughter: The Theology of Julian of Norwich*. New York: Crossroad, 1991.

Pelphrey, Brant. *Christ Our Mother: Julian of Norwich*. Wilmington, Del.: Michael Glazier, 1989.

Martin Luther (1483–1546)

Martin Luther was born on November 10, 1483, in Eisleben (Thuringia) to parents of peasant stock, Hans and Margareta. His parents wanted a good education for him; they saw education as the means to social advancement. In 1490, Martin began attending the Latin school at Mansfeld, and in 1501 he matriculated at the University of Erfurt. By the fall of 1502, Luther had completed his bachelor of arts; and by the beginning of 1505 he had earned the master of arts. In the summer of that year, however, he abandoned his study of law and the arts and entered the Augustinian cloister in Erfurt. Legend holds that a summer storm, in which Luther was almost struck by lightning, precipitated his desire to enter the monastery. If he had died at the time of the storm, Luther was not sure that he would have enjoyed eternal life. Leading the life of a good monk was a time-honored way to improve one's chances for a happy destiny.

Luther's years as a monk were not happy. He had been taught that every Christian had to do his or her very best in order to merit salvation. The problem was that, as hard as he prayed, studied, and worked, Luther never thought he had done his best. As a consequence, he felt that God was displeased with him. Luther sorely lacked the sense of tranquility he had expected monastic life to grant. In later life, he wrote: "I was a good monk, and I kept the rule of my order so strictly that I may say that if ever a monk got to heaven by his monkery it was I. All my brothers in the monastery who knew me will bear me out. If I had kept on any longer, I should have killed myself with vigils, prayers, reading, and other work."[1]

Between the years 1505 and 1509 Luther devoted himself to a study of the later scholastic theologians, such as Ockham, D'Ailly, and Biel. From them he learned to distrust the speculative flights of reason that went beyond revelation. At the same time, Luther began preparations for the priesthood, despite his father's objections. He celebrated his first Mass in May of 1507. By 1510, Luther's study

---

1. Bainton, *Here I Stand*, 34.

of Augustine and of the late medieval Augustinians led him to a rapidly growing hostility toward the dominance of Aristotle in theology and toward the nominalist theology of grace as a new form of Pelagianism. In 1512 he completed his doctorate in theology and, in the following year, he began his professorial duties at the University of Wittenberg.

Some time after beginning to lecture at the university on the Psalms and the letters of St. Paul, Luther experienced a new religious insight: God's "righteousness" is not the justice by which God *measures* people and declares them to be sinners, but the righteousness that God *gives* to people *freely* (Rom. 1:17). Scholars disagree about when Luther had this experience. Much recent scholarship prefers a late date, suggesting that it probably occurred in early 1518. Whether Luther's experience of the gracious righteousness of God occurred suddenly in a given moment or over a longer period of time, it is clear that this experience became the key to all his theology. This insight into the nature of "justification" became the starting point of Luther's career as a reformer. To know that the basis of his justification was not his own holiness, but God's mercy and grace transformed Luther's despair about attaining salvation into peace and assurance.

The sale of the St. Peter indulgence in 1517 was the occasion that transformed Luther's personal insight about justification into the driving force behind his steps for reform of the church. Indulgence-sellers such as Johann Tetzel easily won customers with their claim that the purchase of an indulgence entailed the total remission of the temporal punishments for the sins of the purchaser or his or her dead relatives. To believe that the salvation of souls could be bought by indulgence certificates, the profit from which was being used to rebuild St. Peter's Basilica, was to Luther a perversion of the notion of grace as a free gift of God. Moreover, forgiveness of sin and guilt depends upon God's authority, not the pope's. At best the pope could confirm by a subsequent declaration that a sin has already been remitted by God, but he could not make such a declaration about the status of those who had already died. Luther summarized his thoughts about indulgences and the pope's authority to grant them in *Ninety-Five Theses,* which he sent to Archbishop Albrecht of Mainz and which, according to the testimony of Philip Melanchthon, he posted on the door of the Castle Church in Wittenberg on October 31, 1517. Although Luther did not intend at this time to cause a break with the Church of Rome, that date has become in retrospect the "birthday" of the Protestant Reformation. Thanks to the recently invented printing press, Luther's theses were quickly disseminated throughout Germany. Luther even popularized their main ideas in a vernacular "Sermon on Indulgences and Grace" (1517).

In reaction, a heresy investigation against Luther was begun. In 1518 Luther was summoned to the imperial Diet at Augsburg for interrogation by the pope's legate, Cardinal Cajetan. Refusing to recant his position, Luther secretly left Augsburg before he could be arrested. He then made an appeal for the convocation of a general council to determine the legitimacy of his arguments. Instead of a council, Luther was given the opportunity to engage in a public disputation with one of the Roman Church's most skilled apologists, Johann Eck. Prior to his meeting with Eck, Luther held that, although papal decisions might sometimes be mistaken, the decisions of general councils were trustworthy. Eck's clever line of questioning at the Leipzig debate put an end to that conviction. Eck wrested from Luther the admission that John Hus had been right on some matters and that the general council of Constance (1414–18) had been wrong to condemn him. The effect of this admission was dramatic. Luther was publicly branded as a sympathizer of Hus, whom the authorities of the universal church had condemned. Whereas previously Luther had relativized, not rejected, the authority of pope and bishops, he now saw his opponents in the hierarchy as incapable of considering a thorough reform of the church. The "last barrier which restrained his antagonism to Rome" had been cast down.[2]

In the papal bull *Exsurge Domine* of June 1520, forty-one of Luther's statements were identified as heretical and he was threatened with excommunication. Luther did not receive the bull until October. In November he responded by calling once again for a general council. In December of the same year, he publicly burned the papal bull, together with the books of papal church law. On January 3, 1521, Luther was officially excommunicated. In April of the same year, Luther resisted the pressure put upon him at the Diet of Worms to recant. Although he did not literally say "Here I stand, I cannot do otherwise," it is clear that he refused to deviate from his position unless his ideas could be proven to be erroneous according to the testimony of scripture and reason. The Edict of Worms (May 1521) made Luther and his followers outlaws in the Holy Roman Empire.

Due to the intervention of Duke Frederick the Wise, Luther was kept free from imprisonment. While hidden away in the Wartburg castle (1521–22), he completed his translation of the New Testament into German. In the fall of 1524 he abandoned his religious habit. Eight months later (June 1525), Luther married Katharina von Bora. With her and their six children, he continued to live in the monastery he had once inhabited as a cleric. By 1534 Luther had completed his German translation of the entire Bible, which made the scriptures accessible to more Christians. Luther died on February 18, 1546, secure in the knowledge that the work of the Reformation continued.

Although there had been active and vocal reformers prior to Luther, most recently Wycliffe in England and Hus in Bohemia, it was Luther's challenge that set the reforming movement ablaze. Similarly, although Luther was not the only figure in the sixteenth century to contribute decisively to the formation of Protestant Christianity, he was the first to give classic expression to the most important "Protestant principles": First, justification is by grace through faith, not by faith and good works (*Sola gratia, sola fide*). Second, scripture, not scripture and tradition, is the sole authority in the church's life and practice (*Sola scriptura*). Third, all Christians, by virtue of their baptism, have equal access to God; each should be a "priest" to the others (priesthood of all believers). There is no necessary qualitative difference between the spiritual state of the clergy and the spiritual state of the laity. These principles were articulated in the three treatises Luther wrote between August and November of 1520, the *Address to the Christian Nobility of the German Nation, The Babylonian Captivity of the Church,* and *On the Freedom of the Christian.*

Luther's new understanding of the gospel gave theology a new orientation and

---

2. Owen Chadwick, *The Reformation* (Baltimore: Penguin Books, 1964), 51.

the church a new structure. Luther's new understanding represents, in the words of Hans Küng, a paradigm shift par excellence.[3] Luther changed the meaning of some familiar terms of medieval theology, such as grace, faith, and law. Others he simply abandoned, such as the Aristotelian categories of substance/accident and matter/form. Luther replaced the authority of episcopal and papal decrees with the authority of the conscience of the individual believer. And he displaced the scholastic "theology of glory," which claimed to know God on the basis of reason, with his "theology of the cross," which claimed to know God authentically only in Christ crucified, proclaimed in the gospel. The excerpt from the Heidelberg Disputation in Part One makes clear Luther's break with the scholastic tradition, in both its older and newer forms. Luther rejected theology founded upon reason and "philosophy" because it was incapable of knowing God as God really is. He rejected this kind of theology because it sought a "naked" God, not the "hidden" God proclaimed in the scriptures. Instead of speaking abstractly about God "in himself," Luther spoke concretely about God "for us." Instead of speaking about the capacity of human beings to earn merit from God, he spoke of human beings as "simultaneously righteous and sinful" (*simul justus et peccator*). As the excerpt in Part Two from his lectures on Paul's Letter to the Romans makes clear, Luther emphasized very strongly the gratuity of grace and the certainty of predestination. Instead of speaking about the church as a hierarchical and bureaucratic institution, he spoke of the church as the community of believers. Instead of speaking of the sacraments as rituals that caused the transfer of grace almost mechanically, he spoke of the sacraments as promises of Christ and signs of faith. In short, Luther articulated an understanding of Christian faith that, despite its continuities with the previous tradition of the church (e.g., the Augustinian heritage), was both fresh and distinctive. It has left a lasting mark upon the Christian tradition in the West.

Bibliography

Bainton, Roland H. *Here I Stand: A Life of Luther.* New York: Mentor Books, 1950.

Ebeling, Gerhard. *Luther.* London: Collins Books, 1970.

Lull, Timothy F., ed. *Martin Luther's Basic Theological Writings.* Minneapolis: Fortress Press, 1989.

Luther's Works. Ed. Jaroslav Pelikan and Helmut T. Lehmann. 56 vols. Philadelphia: Fortress Press, 1955.

Oberman, Heiko A. *Luther: Man between God and the Devil,* trans. Eileen Walliser-Schwarzbart. New Haven: Yale University Press, 1989.

Todd, John M. *Luther: A Life.* New York: Crossroad, 1982.

Sallie McFague (b. 1934)

Sallie McFague was born to parents of Scottish-Irish descent in Boston. The death of her father, an optometrist, when she was only fourteen was a major loss. McFague was close to her father. and he had encouraged her in academic

---

3. Hans Küng, *Great Christian Thinkers* (New York: Continuum, 1994), 142–44.

pursuits. Her mother, who at the age of ninety-three still works part-time as a bookkeeper, continues to be a role model. As an undergraduate at Smith College in the early 1950s, McFague was taught by first-wave feminists from the 1920s. These familial and educational influences were critical in McFague's decision to enter the field of theology, which had few women at the time. After graduating from Smith College in 1955, she earned a B.D. degree from Yale Divinity School, followed by an M.A. degree from Yale University in 1960. She received her doctorate from Yale in 1964 with a dissertation entitled "Literature and the Christian Life." In 1977 McFague received a Litt.D. degree from Smith College. After brief stints of teaching at Smith College and Yale Divinity School, McFague became editor of *Soundings,* an interdisciplinary journal, in 1967. In 1970 she began her distinguished career at Vanderbilt University (Nashville, Tenn.). From 1975 to 1979, she served as dean of the Divinity School there. McFague is currently the E. Rhodes and Leona B. Carpenter Professor of Theology at the Vanderbilt Divinity School.

In her major published works, McFague has been concerned to identify the metaphorical nature of language about God and to imagine new models for conceiving of God and God's relation to the world. From McFague's perspective, models are extended metaphors with staying power. That is, models are metaphors which have perdured over time because of their explanatory powers. McFague's 1982 book, *Metaphorical Theology: Models of God in Religious Language,* deals with this theme. There she points out that when models are taken literally, they not only lose their metaphorical character, but they also become idolatrous. McFague claims that the monarchical model of God (that is, God imagined as Father and King) has, in fact, become idolatrous and harmful. The monarchical model legitimates the domination of men over women and of the powerful over the powerless. Such hierarchical and patriarchal relationships are in conflict with the kinds of relationships modeled by Jesus and envisioned in his preaching.

In her fourth book, *Models of God: Theology for an Ecological, Nuclear Age* (1987), McFague engages in the thought experiment of constructing new models of God. Here McFague argues that the models of God as Mother, Lover, and Friend are more appropriate and relevant to the current situation of ecological crisis and nuclear threat than the traditional models of God. She uses her three new metaphors, drawn from the experience of human relationships, to reimagine the creative, salvific, and sustaining activities of God. In addition, McFague pairs each form of God's loving activity with a specific dimension of Christian discipleship: justice, healing, and companionship respectively. *Models of God* received the American Academy of Religion's Award for Excellence in 1988.

McFague's next book, *The Body of God: An Ecological Theology* (1993), from which an excerpt is included in Part Two, builds upon her earlier work. Here she takes up the idea, previously proposed, of imaginatively conceiving of the relationship between God and the world in terms of the metaphor of the world as God's body. McFague supports her metaphorical experiment by appealing to the importance of divine embodiment in Christian faith, as the doctrine of the incarnation makes clear, and to the metaphor's appropriateness to the current ecological situation. McFague reminds her readers that she is not talking about a literal description of God's relation to the world, but rather an imaginative construction of that relationship. For this reason, McFague's proposal is to be evaluated — as she states in the excerpt in this volume — by whether it is more relatively adequate than alternatives from the perspective of postmodern science, an interpretation of Christian faith, our own embodied experience, and the well-being of our planet and all its life-forms. *The Body of God* was recognized as the Best Religious Book of 1994 by the Midwest Independent Publishers Association.

McFague's most recent book is *Super, Natural Christians: How We Should Love Nature* (1997).

McFague has made an impact upon contemporary theology by emphasizing the metaphorical nature of language about God and by proposing new ways of conceiving of God's relation to the world that are appropriate to the Christian tradition and the contemporary needs of society.

Bibliography

Armour, Ellen T. "Sallie McFague," in *A New Handbook of Christian Theologians*, ed. Donald W. Musser and Joseph L. Price, 278–86. Nashville: Abingdon Press, 1996.

Bromell, David J. "Sallie McFague's 'Metaphorical Theology,'" in *Journal of the American Academy of Religion* 61 (1993): 485–503.

McFague, Sallie. *Speaking in Parables: A Study in Metaphor and Theology*. Philadelphia: Fortress Press, 1975.

———. *Metaphorical Theology: Models of God in Religious Language*. Philadelphia: Fortress Press, 1982.

———. *Models of God: Theology for an Ecological, Nuclear Age*. Philadelphia: Fortress Press, 1987.

———. *The Body of God: An Ecological Theology*. Minneapolis: Fortress Press, 1993.

Pseudo-Dionysius (ca. 500)

Dionysius the Areopagite is the name assumed by the author of four Greek theological treatises (*Divine Names, The Mystical Theology, The Heavenly Hierarchy,* and *The Ecclesiastical Hierarchy*) that appeared early in the sixth century. The author claims apostolic support for his treatises by publishing them as the work of the Dionysius mentioned in the Acts of the Apostles (17:34), who was baptized after listening to St. Paul preach in the Areopagus of Athens. There is, however, no mention of these treatises before the fifth century, and they are cited for the first time by Severus of Antioch between 518 and 528. Modern scholarship believes the actual author to have been a Syrian theologian or monk, writing about the year 500. Although several figures have been proposed as the author (including Peter the Iberian and Severus of Antioch himself), modern scholars have not come to any agreement in this matter. Partly because the writings were believed to derive from a first-century convert of St. Paul, but also because of their intrinsic value, the Pseudo-Dionysian texts were quite influential, especially in the western church, where John Scotus Erigena provided a Latin translation in the ninth century.

The Pseudo-Dionysian texts attempt to achieve a synthesis of Christian doctrine and Neoplatonic philosophy. In harmony with the Neoplatonism of Proclus (ca. 410–85), Pseudo-Dionysius emphasizes the utter transcendence and oneness of God. God is simply beyond anything that we can understand. God is beyond personality, essence, and even existence. As he observes in his *Divine Names* (1:1): God is "the Universal Cause of existence while Itself not existing, for It is beyond all being." This idea is also clearly expressed in the excerpt from *The Mystical Theology*, reprinted in Part One. Because of the absolute transcendence of God, Pseudo-Dionysius emphasized the need for an apophatic approach to theology (sometimes called the *via negativa, via negationis,* or negative theology) to balance the cataphatic approach (sometimes called the *via affirmativa, via affirmationis,* or positive theology). Whereas the cataphatic approach attempts to say what God is, the apophatic approach says what God is not. Building upon his understanding of God as beyond every assertion and beyond every denial, Pseudo-Dionysius drew out a plan by which people could attain mystical union with God. By leaving behind the perceptions of the intellect and the reasoning of the mind, the human soul can enter a stage of obscurity or "unknowing," in which it can be illuminated by God and brought to "knowledge" of God, who is ineffable.

A triadic structure, derived from the trinity, pervades both *The Heavenly Hierarchy* and *The Ecclesiastical Hierarchy*. In the former text, Pseudo-Dionysius describes the nature of angels, who are divided into three groups of three angelic orders. In the latter text, he writes about the three orders of ministry (bishop, priest, deacon), which have responsibility for initiating the three orders (monk, Christian layperson, and catechumen) into a divine way of life by means of the three-stage process of purification, illumination, and union with God. This depiction of the person's ascent to God (purification, illumination, and union) became the foundation of many subsequent treatises on the mystical life. In Pseudo-Dionysius's conception of things, the ecclesiastical hierarchy is an image of the heavenly hierarchy, and each hierarchy complements the other.

In the excerpt from *The Mystical Theology* in Part One, we see how Pseudo-Dionysius used paradox to make his point that God is beyond being and knowledge. In chapter 1 (sect. 3), he reflects on Moses' ascent of Mt. Sinai, described in Exodus 19 and 20:18–21 and previously commented on by Gregory of Nyssa in his *The Life of Moses*. Pseudo-Dionysius wishes to draw parallels here between Moses' ascent and the ascent of the purified and enlightened Christian to union with God. Pseudo-Dionysius speaks of the role of affirmative (cataphatic) and negative (apophatic) theology in speaking about God (ch. 1, sect. 2; ch. 3). In chapter 3, he makes the point that not all affirmations concerning God are equally inappropriate, just as not all negations concerning God are equally appropriate. The affirmations are arranged in a descending order of decreasing congruity, while the negations are arranged in an ascending order of decreasing incongruity. This pattern of descending affirmations and ascending negations reflects the Neoplatonic procession from the One down into plurality and then the return of all back to the One. From this perspective, when one wishes to make the most appropriate affirmative statement about God, one should begin by speaking of God's oneness and then proceed "downward" to talk of the trinity. Our excerpt concludes in a very strong apophatic mode.

Bibliography

O'Rourke, Fran. *Pseudo-Dionysius and the Metaphysics of Aquinas*. New York: E. J. Brill, 1992.

Pseudo-Dionysius: The Complete Works. Trans. Colm Luibheid, with notes by Paul Rorem, and introductions by Jaroslav Pelikan, Jean Leclercq, and Karlfried Froehlich. New York: Paulist Press, 1987.

Rist, John M. *Man, Soul, and Body: Essays in Ancient Thought from Plato to Dionysius*. Brookfield, Vt.: Variorum, 1996.

Rorem, Paul. *Pseudo-Dionysius: A Commentary on the Texts and an Introduction to Their Influence*. New York: Oxford University Press, 1993.

Karl Rahner (1904–84)

Karl Rahner was born into a middle-class family in Freiburg, Germany, on March 5, 1904. His father was a professor at the local teachers' college and his mother was a homemaker. He attended the local primary and secondary schools, where, according to his own description, he was an average student. Three weeks after finishing school, at the age of eighteen, he entered the Jesuit novitiate in Feldkirch, Austria (1922). His brother Hugo had become a Jesuit three years earlier. After completing his two-year novitiate and taking vows as a Jesuit, Rahner studied philosophy for three years. At this time he was introduced to the scholastic philosophy of the Catholic tradition as well as to modern German philosophy. He engaged in a careful study of Kant and two contemporary Thomists, the Belgian Jesuit Joseph Maréchal (1878–1944) and the French Jesuit Pierre Rousselot (1878–1915), who profoundly influenced his own interpretation of Thomas Aquinas.

Rahner began his theological studies in 1929 at the Jesuit school of theology in Valkenburg, Holland. In addition to learning the strict neo-scholasticism that permeated Catholic seminaries in the wake of the condemnation of Modernism, Rahner became, at this time, thoroughly conversant with patristic theology and Ignatian spirituality. The Ignatian method of prayer and existential decision-making was so significant for his personal development that Rahner could later say: "I think that the spirituality of Ignatius himself, which one learned through the practice of prayer and religious formation, was more significant for me than all learned philosophy and theology inside and outside the Order."[1]

After ordination to the priesthood in 1932 and further theological studies, Rahner returned to his hometown of Freiburg in 1934 in order to pursue a doctorate in philosophy. This period in Freiburg was, in the words of Rahner scholar William V. Dych, to be a time of opportunity and disappointment. The opportunity lay in being able to attend the seminars of philosopher Martin Heidegger. The disappointment occurred in the rejection of Rahner's dissertation on Aquinas by his adviser, Martin Honecker. Influenced by Maréchal's and Rousselot's interpretation of Thomas, Rahner interpreted Aquinas in light of subsequent tran-

---

1. Imhof and Biallowons, *Karl Rahner in Dialogue*, 191.

scendental philosophy. His adviser, however, did not read the text in that light. In 1939 the rejected Freiburg dissertation on Aquinas was published under the title *Geist in Welt*. It was later translated into several languages, appearing in English as *Spirit in the World* (1968).

Rahner's superiors wanted him to teach theology in Innsbruck. In preparation for this post, Rahner began doctoral studies there. He completed his doctorate in 1936 with a dissertation on the typological interpretation of the blood and water that flowed from Jesus' pierced side (John 19:34) by some church fathers. Before beginning his professional duties in the theology faculty at Innsbruck in the fall of 1937, Rahner delivered a series of lectures in Salzburg, in which he applied the philosophy of knowledge he had developed in his philosophical dissertation to the question of knowing God through a historical revelation. These lectures were subsequently published as *Hearers of the Word* (German, 1941). *Spirit in the World* and *Hearers of the Word* were the foundational works upon which Rahner was to develop his philosophical theology.

Rahner's initial appointment at Innsbruck did not last long. In the wake of Germany's annexation of Austria in 1938, the theology faculty was abolished and the Jesuits were banished from Innsbruck. Rahner spent most of the war years in Vienna as a member of the diocesan Pastoral Institute. With the war over, Rahner returned to the reconstituted theology faculty in Innsbruck in 1948 and began a very prolific period of writing and publishing. The first three volumes of collected articles, *Schriften zur Theologie,* appeared in 1954–56. Ultimately, Rahner's articles filled sixteen volumes in German and twenty-two volumes in English, where they were published under the title *Theological Investigations*.

Rahner's attempt to think about the tradition of the church in new and creative ways sometimes led him into conflict with Roman Catholic officials. During the pontificate of Pope Pius XII, Rahner was refused permission to publish an article concerning problems in the contemporary Catholic understanding of Mary, and he was forbidden to discuss the possibility of Mass concelebration. Even after Pius's death, the Holy Office carefully scrutinized Rahner's theological writings. In 1962 Rahner was told that everything he wrote had to be submitted to Rome for prior censorship. Thanks to the intervention of the three German-speaking cardinals and several hundred German professors, the special censorship was dropped the following year.

At the same time preparations were underway for the Second Vatican Council. At the council Rahner was able to exercise significant influence through his role as private adviser to Cardinal König of Vienna and Cardinal Döpfner of Munich as well as through his addresses outside council sessions to the German-speaking bishops and other regional bishops. There is no doubt that by the time the council ended in December 1965 Rahner had exercised enormous influence on the final shape of many of the conciliar documents. Traces of his thought can be found in the council's teaching on the church, papal primacy and the episcopate, the relationship between scripture and tradition, the inspiration of the Bible, the sacraments and the diaconate, and the possibility of salvation outside the church even for atheists. "It is ironic that the ideas of a theologian who only recently had been highly suspect and subject to special censorship had now become part of the Church's official teaching. Not only did the Second Vatican Council end Rahner's official difficulties with Rome, but it also gave him international stature as one of the Church's leading theologians."[2]

From 1964 to 1967 Rahner taught philosophy of religion at the University of Munich. He then accepted a position as professor of dogmatic theology at the University of Münster in 1967. Four years later, with his physical strength declining, Rahner retired from the university and returned to live in Munich. During this so-called retirement he remained busy with writing and lecturing in Germany and abroad. In 1981 he returned to Innsbruck, where he had spent his most productive years, from the mid-1940s to the mid-1960s. He died on March 30, 1984 — a few weeks after his eightieth birthday.

It is quite commonplace to hear the assertion made that Rahner has contributed more to the development of contemporary theology than any other Catholic theologian of the twentieth century. Clearly, he wrote about virtually every area of theology. The bibliography of his books, articles, sermons, and prayers numbers between three and four thousand titles. Rahner influenced Catholic theology, however, not only through his own publications, but also through initiatives such as the series *Quaestiones Disputatae,* which began in 1958 and provided a forum for the scholarly discussion of contemporary theology, and the international journal *Concilium,* which Rahner helped to found and whose first number he edited together with Edward Schillebeeckx in 1965.

Rahner's theological thought is both "transcendental" and "anthropological." That is to say, Rahner sought answers to the question of the possibility of a revelation from God in the transcendental, or given, structures of the human subject. Rahner's theology does not begin with God, scripture, or official church teachings, but with the person who is presupposed by Christianity as the hearer of the gospel. This attention to the meaning of the human person, this "anthropological" focus, is distinctive in Rahner's theology. For Rahner the fundamental experience in which we become conscious of ourselves as selves is that of questioning. In opening ourselves to the unlimited horizon of questioning, we have already transcended ourselves and have moved beyond the limits of any particular explanation. In short, we discover that we are oriented to the Infinite. This orientation, which Rahner called the "supernatural existential," marks the person as a potential hearer of God's word. The radical experience of this unlimited horizon of knowing, this experience of "transcendence," can be ignored or unnoticed. Nonetheless, the basis of all our conscious thinking and activity, Rahner insists, lies in this deeper, prereflective consciousness of infinite reality, toward which we are directed by the very structures of our being as free and knowing subjects. In this sense, even the atheist "knows" God, albeit not consciously as an object of thought, but prereflectively as the source of his or her freedom and the goal of his or her ever striving to know more.

From Rahner's perspective, then, human life and Christian existence presuppose each other. Human life opens out towards the fulfillment of which the gospel speaks. And Christian existence not only presupposes certain human structures, but is their ultimate source: the natural structures of human life as we know them are created by God. "Thus there is an intrinsic point of contact between

2. Dych, *Karl Rahner,* 13.

the human and the Christian dimensions in life, and between philosophy and theology, a unity within their abiding distinction."[3] This approach to theology means that human existence itself is created by and for the Christian message, that human life in its fundamental structures as intelligent and free is, at its core, a personal world intended for response to God's call. In the context of this specific theological anthropology, Rahner can speak of the "anonymous Christianity" of those who are not members of the Christian church. The universal human orientation to God (supernatural existential) is already a share in God's grace or divine self-communication. God communicates God's own being definitively through the Word, who enters into human history, and through the Spirit, who transforms human subjectivity so that it may receive and rejoice in the Word. Through this act of self-communication, God is ultimately revealed to us as a trinitarian God.

Bibliography

Dych, William V. *Karl Rahner*. Outstanding Christian Thinkers series. Collegeville, Minn.: Liturgical Press, 1992.

Imhof, Paul, and Hubert Biallowons, eds. *Karl Rahner in Dialogue: Conversations and Interviews 1965–1982*. New York: Crossroad, 1986.

————. *Faith in a Wintry Season: Conversations and Interviews with Karl Rahner in the Last Years of His Life*. New York: Crossroad, 1990.

Lehmann, Karl, and Albert Raffelt, eds. *The Content of Faith: The Best of Karl Rahner's Theological Writings*. New York: Crossroad, 1993.

Rahner, Karl. *Foundations of Christian Faith: Introduction to the Idea of Christianity*. New York: Seabury Press, 1978.

————. *Theological Investigations*, 22 vols. London: Darton, Longman & Todd, 1961–; New York: Seabury Press, 1974–.

O'Donovan, Leo J., ed. *A World of Grace: An Introduction to the Themes and Foundations of Karl Rahner's Theology*. New York: Seabury Press, 1980.

Vorgrimler, Herbert. *Understanding Karl Rahner: An Introduction to His Life and Thought*. New York: Crossroad, 1986.

Rosemary Radford Ruether (b. 1936)

Rosemary Radford Ruether is one of the leading American Christian feminists of the twentieth century. She was raised in an economically comfortable and pious family. Her father died when she was twelve years old. Her mother, Rebecca Ord Radford, became the most influential person in her early development. A devout Catholic and sincere ecumenist, her mother taught her to appreciate the intellectual and spiritual depths of Catholicism while challenging its clericalism. Ruether's mother communicated to her an understanding of God as the maternal ground of being, which had a profound effect on her developing religious views.

Ruether pursued a fine arts degree at Scripps College in Claremont, California. In the course of her studies, however, she changed her major to religious

---

3. Anne E. Carr, "Starting with the Human" in *A World of Grace: An Introduction to the Themes and Foundations of Karl Rahner's Theology*, ed. Leo J. O'Donovan (New York: Seabury Press, 1980), 18.

studies. One of her classics professors, Robert Palmer, was apparently influential in this decision. From him she learned that, although the deity may be fundamentally one, its manifestations were different and many. Toward the end of her studies at Scripps College, she married Herman Ruether. According to Mary Hembrow Snyder, this creative partnership between Herman and Rosemary yielded "a countercultural commitment to mutuality in male-female relationships, a poignant critique of the clerical domination of Catholic laypeople's lives in the area of reproductive rights, and her social activism, spawned by being married to a political scientist."[1] After completing her undergraduate education, she earned a doctorate in the social and intellectual history of Christian thought at the School of Theology at Claremont. Ruether's theological reflections developed further within the context of the civil rights movement, the women's movement, the Second Vatican Council, and their aftermath.

Ruether's theology consistently emphasizes both critique of patriarchal theology and reconstruction of Christian doctrines and practices, in a way that acknowledges the full personhood of women and of other people who have been dehumanized by patriarchy as well as promotes an ecologically sound relationship between human beings and the earth.

As the excerpt from *Sexism and God-Talk* (1983) in Part One shows, Ruether rejects the dualism of transcendence vs. immanence or spirit vs. matter. She seeks instead to recover elements in the Christian tradition in order to criticize the traditional male concepts of God and to reconstruct an understanding of God that is holistic and liberating. Ruether uses the tradition of analogy to argue for a change in God language: "If all language for God/ess is analogy, if taking a particular human image literally is idolatry, then male language for the divine must lose its privileged place." In addition, Ruether insists that "feminizing" God is insufficient, and she urges caution in the use of parental images of God. Like other liberation theologians, Ruether starts with language for God as Redeemer and Liberator. But unlike some liberationists, she rejects the notion of liberation as "liberation out of or against nature into spirit." For Ruether, God is the God/ess of both creation and redemption; God/ess is the ground of all beings, not just human beings. These ideas are further developed in her more recent book *Gaia and God* (1992).

Bibliography

Ruether, Rosemary Radford. "Beginnings: An Intellectual Autobiography," in *Journeys: The Impact of Personal Experience on Religious Thought,* ed. Gregory Baum. New York: Paulist Press, 1975.

———. *To Change the World: Christology and Cultural Criticism.* New York: Crossroad, 1981.

———. *Sexism and God-Talk: Toward a Feminist Theology.* Boston: Beacon Press, 1983.

———. "The Development of My Theology," in *Religious Studies Review* 15, no. 1 (1989):1–4.

———. *Gaia and God: An Ecofeminist Theology of Earth Healing.* San Francisco: Harper, 1992.

---

1. Snyder, "Rosemary Radford Ruether," 400.

Snyder, Mary Hembrow. "Rosemary Radford Ruether," in *A New Handbook of Christian Theologians*, ed. Donald W. Musser and Joseph L. Price, 399–410. Nashville: Abingdon Press, 1996.

Friedrich Schleiermacher (1768–1834)

Friedrich Ernst Daniel Schleiermacher was born at Breslau on November 21, 1768. His father, Gottlieb, was a Reformed chaplain in the Prussian army. His mother, Katharina-Maria Stubenrauch, came, like his father, from a family of Reformed pastors. Schleiermacher's family was devout. His father experienced a spiritual awakening when Friedrich was nine. Five years later Friedrich himself experienced a spiritual conversion among the Moravian Brethren. In accord with his father's wishes, he was educated in the Moravian school in Niesky, where he was exposed to the pietist religion of the heart. Two years later (1785) Schleiermacher transferred to the Moravian seminary in Barby, a small town on the Elbe River. There Schleiermacher became familiar, through his circle of friends, with the poetry of Goethe and others. He also gained some knowledge of Enlightenment philosophy. The humanism of the poetry and the critical spirit of the philosophy clashed with the pietism of the seminary, which emphasized human sinfulness and seclusion from the wicked world. Schleiermacher came to experience spiritual doubts.

In 1787 Schleiermacher left the Moravian seminary for the University of Halle, which had become a bastion of the Enlightenment. The leading German Enlightenment philosopher Christian Wolff had worked there. And the leading figure in the theology faculty, Johann Salomo Semler (1725–91), gave decisive impetus to the historical-critical analysis of the Bible with his *Treatise on the Free Investigation of the Canon* (1771–75). Although he left the Moravian pietists, Schleiermacher's early education among them left a lasting impression upon him. Schleiermacher credited his experience among the Brethren with the first germination of his "mystical tendency." Fifteen years later he declared that this mystical seed was full grown. In a letter to Georg Reimer (April 30, 1802), Schleiermacher noted that he had "again become a Moravian, only of a higher order." Schleiermacher's spiritual doubts had not culminated in losing faith, but rather in losing his first simple understanding of it.

In 1794 he was ordained. Shortly thereafter he was appointed Reformed preacher at the Charité hospital in Berlin. From a Berlin circle of acquaintances, centered in the home of Henrietta Herz, the wife of a Jewish physician, Schleiermacher became familiar with the Romantic movement in its philosophical and literary forms. Friedrich Schlegel, with whom he shared his rooms, acted as his tutor in the Romantic spirit. His first book, *On Religion: Speeches to Its Cultured Despisers* (1799), reflects that influence, but, as the title itself suggests, the book did not simply adopt the worldview dominant among his circle of friends. Schleiermacher was the only clergyman in his circle. He used his first book to "issue both a critique of his friends' world view and an apology for his own identity and vocation as a preacher by expounding the mood and themes of Romanticism — especially the idea of individuality — in such a way as to argue that the life uninformed by the cultivation of personal religion and religious community is artificially sterile and out of joint with universal being."[1] *On Religion: Speeches* brought Schleiermacher immediate acclaim.

Schleiermacher left Berlin in 1802 in order to assume a provincial pastorate. While in Berlin he had fallen in love with Eleonore Grunow, the wife of another minister. Although unhappily married, Grunow did not leave her husband. So as not to make the situation worse, and to reduce the uneasiness of his church superiors, Schleiermacher resigned his Berlin post. During the two years of his pastorate in Stolp (Pomerania), Schleiermacher kept his sanity amid his unhappiness by translating Plato and writing about ethical theory.

In 1804 Schleiermacher was made professor of theology at Halle, where he lectured on philosophical ethics, hermeneutics, and dogmatic theology. There he also began work on his *Brief Outline of the Study of Theology*, which attempted to describe the nature and proper relationship of the major theological disciplines. Napoleon's invasion of Germany led to the occupation of Halle by the French army and the closing of the university (1806). Without a salary, Schleiermacher was forced to return to Berlin. There King Friedrich Wilhelm III made him a preacher at Trinity Church in 1809. He shared the pulpit with a Lutheran minister. In the same year, at the age of forty-one, he married Henriette von Willich, the twenty-year-old widow of a close friend. As a member of Prussia's department of education, he played a role in the founding of the University of Berlin, where in 1810 he assumed a chair of theology.

At Berlin Schleiermacher lectured on a wide variety of theological topics. He produced in 1821–22 his mature publication on dogmatic theology, entitled *The Christian Faith, Presented in Its Inner Connections according to the Fundamentals of the Evangelical Church*. While a professor at the university, Schleiermacher continued to hold his pulpit. His dual career as preacher and professor discloses a balance between the academic and the pastoral, which Schleiermacher believed to be essential. As he noted in his *Brief Outline for the Study of Theology*, academic theological studies were not intended to make one an academic expert in a specialized subdiscipline of theology, but rather to make one an effective leader in the church. After a distinguished career at Berlin, Schleiermacher died on February 12, 1834.

Friedrich Schleiermacher is regarded by many as the father of modern theology. He exercised a profound effect on later theology by highlighting the experiential component in theological reflection, by insisting on the historical character of theology, and by placing theology in the service of helping the church to continue to develop as it ought. Schleiermacher endorsed the Kantian turn to the subject, but without endorsing Kant's reduction of religion to morality. Theologians today still need to reckon with him above all other nineteenth-century Christian thinkers as "the progenitor of the spirit of modern religious understanding."[2]

As Brian Gerrish has suggested, "liberal evangelical" is perhaps the best label for Schleiermacher's theology.[3] His program was "evangelical" because

---

1. Richard R. Niebuhr, "Friedrich Schleiermacher," in *A Handbook of Christian Theologians*, ed. Dean G. Peerman and Martin E. Marty (Cleveland and New York: World Publishing Co., 1965), 19.
2. Ibid., 18.
3. Gerrish, *A Prince of the Church*, 31–33.

it made evangelical, experiential Protestant consciousness its object of inquiry. For Schleiermacher "feeling" (*Gefühl*) or religious experience is the primary element in religion. From this perspective, the church's doctrines are secondary elements that attempt to adequately describe the primary religious feelings. Schleiermacher's program was also "liberal" because it did not feel bound to the old expressions of Protestant consciousness. Schleiermacher took seriously the scientific and philosophical knowledge of the day.

Schleiermacher's first book, *On Religion: Speeches,* criticizes those educated people who ignore or scorn religion because they have identified it with the external structures of the church and the systems of theological orthodoxy. The core of religion, Schleiermacher insisted, is piety. By this he did not mean an anti-intellectual emotionalism, but — in the words of his second speech — a sense and taste for the infinite, an awareness that the infinite is immediately present in the finite self. Religious feeling involves a sense of harmony with the All. Schleiermacher argued that all human activity — whether artistic, scientific, or moral — was incomplete without such religious feeling.

Schleiermacher's most important mature work is *The Christian Faith,* first published in two parts in 1821–22. In this work, Schleiermacher defines the Christian as the person who is possessed by the feeling of his or her dependence upon God as manifested in Jesus Christ. These two elements are inseparable in the life of the Christian: a general awareness of God and a special relation to Christ. The general awareness of God is, according to Schleiermacher, an "original revelation." Schleiermacher believed that this general awareness of God was part of human nature. All that it takes to recognize it is a little introspection. This was a bold assertion at the beginning of the nineteenth century. Developments in science and rationalist philosophy had made the reality of God less obvious to many educated people. In the wake of such developments, some people had come to endorse deism, while others adopted pantheism. Schleiermacher, however, "knew perfectly well that one no longer has the Christian God either if one says with deism that some events fall outside the divine activity, or if one says with pantheism, as commonly understood, that talk of divine activity adds nothing to talk of natural events."[4]

Schleiermacher's approach to the God question was to speak of God as directing and preserving the entire system of nature and to think of God more as a creative and living impulse than as a person in the human sense. This meant, on the one hand, that Schleiermacher could dispense with the popular notion that God intervenes only occasionally in human affairs. If God intervenes occasionally as a person among other persons, God is drawn into the domain of finite causes and so becomes finite. On the other hand, Schleiermacher held that we must think of ourselves as placed in a closed system of nature, in which the regular course of events is not interrupted. To understand the world scientifically, while remaining religious, meant for Schleiermacher to regard the world not as a machine operating according to immutable laws, but as a law-governed system of nature that has meaning and purpose because it is pervaded by the presence of a living God.

Schleiermacher's social and political orientation, like his new approach to the-

---

4. Ibid., 59–60.

ology, made him a controversial figure. In the 1820s he was cited three times to the Berlin police for his support for a constitutional state and greater freedoms for the people. His desire to awaken a social concern among the upper classes (for example, shortening working hours) made him popular beyond educated circles. According to historian Leopold von Ranke, between twenty and thirty thousand people, drawn from all classes and professions, followed Schleiermacher's coffin to the funeral.

Schleiermacher's *The Christian Faith* influenced in some degree all the theologians of the nineteenth century, even his opponents. His advocacy of the experience of the community of faith as the starting point for theological reflection offered a new model for theology, one whose effects are still seen today. But Schleiermacher has not always been a fashionable theologian. Karl Barth (1886–1968), despite some initial excitement, became a sharp critique of Schleiermacher and his legacy. *The Christian Faith* was not translated into English until 1928, more than a hundred years after its first publication in German. Nonetheless, it is right to regard Schleiermacher as "the paradigmatic theologian of modernity"[5] and to hold his *Christian Faith* as one of the masterpieces of Protestant thought.

Bibliography

Gerrish, B. A. *A Prince of the Church: Schleiermacher and the Beginnings of Modern Theology.* Philadelphia: Fortress Press, 1984.

Niebuhr, Richard R. *Schleiermacher on Christ and Religion.* New York: Scribner's, 1964.

Redeker, Martin. *Schleiermacher: Life and Thought.* Trans. John Wallhausser. Philadelphia: Fortress Press, 1973.

Schleiermacher, Friedrich. *On Religion: Speeches to Its Cultured Despisers.* Trans. John Oman. New York: Harper & Brothers, 1958.

———. *The Christian Faith.* Trans. from the 2d German ed. (1830–31). Ed. H. R. Mackintosh and J. S. Stewart. Philadelphia: Fortress Press, 1976.

Dorothee Soelle (b. 1929)

Dorothee Soelle was born September 30, 1929, in Cologne, Germany, to a middle-class Protestant family. Her father, Hans Nipperdey, was a lawyer, who encouraged her to value education over material comfort. Despite parental indifference to religion, Dorothee became interested in the church (Evangelical Church of the Rhineland) as a high school student. She studied philology, philosophy, theology, and German literature at several universities, receiving her doctorate from the University of Göttingen in 1954. Among her teachers at the University were theologian Friedrich Gogarten and New Testament scholar Ernst Käsemann. In the summer of 1954 she married Dietrich Soelle, with whom she had two daughters and a son. Dietrich and Dorothee were divorced in 1963.

Soelle taught German and theology in high school from 1954 to 1960. She then became a research assistant at the Philosophical Institute of the Techni-

---

5. Hans Küng, *Great Christian Thinkers* (New York: Continuum, 1994), 182–84.

cal University of Aachen. In the early 1960s she returned to Cologne, where she taught German philology at the university. In the fall of 1969, she married Fulbert Steffensky, a professor of religion and education at the University of Hamburg. Together they had a daughter. In the 1970s, Soelle and her husband founded an ecumenical, socially active group called "Political Evening Prayer" (*Politisches Nachtgebet*). Established initially as a protest against the intervention of First World countries in Vietnam, the group eventually addressed itself to problems of economic and social discrimination in Germany. Soelle herself described the group as a movement of "theological-political reflection and action, with aims at an understanding of and feeling for the crucified Christ today, and how Christians need to respond."[1] In 1972 she assumed a position as lecturer on the theological faculty at the University of Mainz, where she remained for three years.

Unable to secure a permanent position in a German university because of her political activities, she accepted in 1975 an invitation from the Union Theological Seminary in New York to become a visiting lecturer in systematic theology. From 1977 to 1987 she was the Harry Emerson Fosdick Visiting Professor at the Seminary. During this time, she spent half of each year in the United States and the other half in Germany, where she was one of the leading spokespersons against nuclear proliferation and political oppression, especially in developing countries and in South Africa. Throughout this period she continued to be a vocal critic of capitalist economics.

Her professional publications span more than thirty years and include more than twenty books and numerous articles. As its German title makes clear, Soelle's first book, *Christ the Representative* (1967, translation of *Stellvertretung: Ein Kapitel nach dem Tode Gottes,* 1965), was her response to the then-current "death of God" theology, represented by Thomas Altizer and Paul van Buren. In this book Soelle attempted to reconcile the reality of World War II, especially the horror of the Holocaust, with the idea of an all-loving God who directs all things to good. She rejected the idea that God is the omnipotent Lord of history, who controls the world's events from above. Instead, she highlighted the suffering Christ as God's representative. As Christ represents God, human beings must represent Christ to each other. "This became the foundation upon which Soelle developed her theology in social and political terms."[2]

After this first book came *The Truth is Concrete* (German, 1967; English, 1969) and *Beyond Mere Obedience* (German, 1968; English, 1970), as well as several other works in German. In 1971 she published *Politische Theologie: Auseinandersetzung mit Rudolf Bultmann,* which was published in English three years later as *Political Theology.* In this book, Soelle approved of Bultmann's existential interpretation of Christian faith, but criticized him for failing to see that human existence is social and not simply individual. From Soelle's perspective, forgiveness is inseparable from social responsibility and resurrection occurs in history, when human beings overcome oppression and transform the social structures that cause it. Among other important books that Soelle

---

1. See *Contemporary Authors,* New Revision series (Detroit: Gale Research, 1984), vol. 11, 484.
2. Trulove, "Soelle," 337–38.

published in the 1970s are *Suffering* (German, 1973; English, 1975), *Revolutionary Patience* (German, 1974; English, 1977), and *Death by Bread Alone* (German, 1975; English, 1976). These works helped to establish Soelle as one of the leaders among European theologians who endorsed political and liberation theology.

In the 1980s and 1990s, Soelle continued to publish theological reflections on social and political issues. From the 1980s come books such as *Of War and Love* (German, 1981; English, 1983) and *The Arms Race Kills Even without a War* (German, 1982; English, 1983). At the same time, Soelle's thought took a feminist direction. In 1984 she published *The Strength of the Weak: Toward a Christian Feminist Identity.* Soelle saw sexism as the "colonialization" of women. From this time she regularly analyzed sexism within the broader context of economic and racial exploitation. Authentic Christianity, Soelle says, entails liberation and the creation of a truly nonexploitative human society. The theme of liberation is strong in Soelle's most recent works, including *The Window of Vulnerability: A Political Spirituality* (1990) and *On Earth as in Heaven: A Liberation Spirituality of Sharing* (1993).

In her writings, Soelle grounds theological reflection in the experiences of ordinary people, particularly in the concrete experiences of people who are marginalized, suffering, and disenfranchised. Soelle also weaves pieces of her own autobiography into her theological reflection. This characteristic is evident in *Death by Bread Alone* as well as in more recent works, such as *Stations of the Cross: A Latin American Pilgrimage* and *Theology for Skeptics: Reflections on God* (1995). In this way, Soelle's theological method can be described as inductive and narrative, rather than deductive and speculative.

Soelle received the Theodore Heuss Medal in 1974 and the Droste Award for Poetry in 1982. Currently she resides in Hamburg, Germany, where she continues to be active in the peace and ecological movements. The focus of her theological work has been the social and political implications of Christian faith. Her theological style blends personal, analytical, and imaginative dimensions, which constitute "an entirely congruent medium for her unification of feminism, mysticism, and socialist pacifism."[3]

Bibliography

Soelle, Dorothee. *Political Theology.* Trans. and with an introduction by John Shelley. Philadelphia: Fortress Press, 1974.

————. *Thinking about God: An Introduction to Theology.* Trans. John Bowden. Philadelphia: Trinity Press International, 1990.

————. *On Earth as in Heaven: A Liberation Spirituality of Sharing.* Trans. Marc Batko. Louisville: Westminster John Knox, 1993.

————. *Theology for Skeptics: Reflections on God.* Trans. Joyce L. Irwin. Minneapolis: Fortress Press, 1995.

Trulove, Sarah Chappell. "Soelle" in *Encyclopedia of World Biography: 20th Century Supplement,* 337–38.

---

3. Trulove, "Soelle," 338.

Elizabeth Cady Stanton (1815–1902)

Elizabeth Cady Stanton was an American social reformer and leader in the struggle for woman suffrage. She was born on November 12, 1815, in Johnstown, New York, the fourth of six children. Her father, Daniel Cady, was a U.S. congressman and later a New York Supreme Court judge. He gave her intellectual curiosity little encouragement, but through him she became aware of the discriminatory treatment of women under the law. The local Presbyterian minister, however, did encourage her to learn Greek and Latin. In 1830 she enrolled in the then-famous "seminary" (i.e., a private school for girls) of Emma Willard in Troy, New York.

At an early age, Cady Stanton became interested in the temperance and abolitionist movements. She spent time at the house of an uncle who opposed slavery. There she met Henry Brewster Stanton, a journalist and abolitionist orator. They were married in 1840, but she insisted that the word "obey" be deleted from her marriage vow. Elizabeth and Henry had seven children.

Following their wedding, the Stantons traveled to London, England, to attend the World Anti-slavery Convention (1840). Women, however, were denied entry to the convention. There she met Lucretia Coffin Mott, to whom admittance had also been denied. Cady Stanton and Mott objected to the injustice of their treatment and strengthened their resolve to combat discrimination against women. In 1847 Cady Stanton and her family moved to Seneca Falls, New York. The following summer, she and Mott organized the first women's rights convention in the United States. The Seneca Falls Convention (1848) was attended by several hundred people, who considered resolutions drawn from the Declaration of Sentiments prepared by Cady Stanton. Modeled after the U.S. Declaration of Independence, the Declaration of Sentiments insisted upon the equality of women and men and better educational and economic opportunities for women. All the resolutions were unanimously adopted with the exception of the suffrage resolution. Conventioneers, including Stanton (for) and Mott (against), "were divided over the suffrage issue, partially because many women feared that a demand for woman suffrage at that moment in history was simply too radical."[1] Nonetheless, a majority vote approved this resolution as well. The public and the press generally ridiculed the women and the convention.

Two or three years later Cady Stanton met Susan B. Anthony. They worked together for the next fifty years, promoting the equal rights of women. From 1868 to 1870, they edited a women's-rights newspaper, entitled the *Revolution*. In 1869 they founded the National Woman Suffrage Association, which after 1890 was called the National-American Woman Suffrage Association. Cady Stanton served as its president until 1892.

Cady Stanton not only wanted women to have the right to vote, she also wanted them to be accorded fair treatment with regard to property ownership, marriage, and divorce. Her views on divorce, reproduction, and religion separated her from more conservative advocates of women's rights. As early as 1889,

---

1. Christine Lunardini, *What Every American Should Know about Women's History* (Holbrook, Mass.: Adams Media, 1997), 65.

she began to recruit women to write a series of biblical interpretations from a woman's point of view. Finally in 1895 *The Woman's Bible* was published. Its publication, however, created a rift between her and the National-American Woman Suffrage Association. Elizabeth Cady Stanton died in New York City on October 26, 1902.

In the excerpt from *The Woman's Bible* in Part One, Cady Stanton makes an explicit connection between the Bible and women's equality. On the basis of Genesis, she speaks of a Heavenly Mother. This terminology, albeit in a different context and with quite different emphases, we have seen before (e.g., Julian of Norwich). Cady Stanton also speaks of the feminine force or feminine element in God. Later Christian feminists, such as Elizabeth Johnson and Sallie McFague, will be wary of "feminine" and "elements" language with reference to God. Nonetheless, Stanton's example of critical biblical interpretation will be emulated and built upon in the next century.

Bibliography

Banner, Lois. *Elizabeth Cady Stanton: A Radical for Women's Rights.* Boston: Little and Brown, 1980.

Griffith, Elisabeth. *In Her Own Right: The Life of Elizabeth Cady Stanton.* New York: Oxford University Press, 1984.

Oakley, Mary Ann B. *Elizabeth Cady Stanton.* Old Westbury, N.Y.: Feminist Press, 1972.

Pellauer, Mary D. *Toward a Tradition of Feminist Theology: The Religious Social Thought of Elizabeth Cady Stanton, Susan B. Anthony, and Anna Howard Shaw.* Brooklyn: Carlson, 1991.

Stanton, Elizabeth Cady. *The Woman's Bible.* New York: European Publishing Co., 1895.

Teresa of Avila (1515–82)

Teresa of Avila (also known as Teresa of Jesus) is one of Christianity's most beloved mystics. Increasingly appreciated as a theologian, she was also an important monastic reformer and continues to be an inspirational figure. Less is known about Teresa's early life than one might like, leading many biographers to rely heavily on the sketchy information Teresa supplies in her *Life,* which she wrote around the age of fifty. As recent scholarship has demonstrated, however, Teresa's works are somewhat encoded; the rhetorical skill which enabled her works to survive severe scrutiny during and after her life hides as much as earlier scholars thought her "clear and candid style" reveals.[1]

Born on March 28, 1515, into a merchant-class family of Jewish origin and educated in an Augustinian convent, Teresa de Cepeda y Ahumada entered the local Carmelite convent of the Incarnation at the age of twenty. There she appears to have been popular both inside and outside the convent. She describes a rather relaxed atmosphere within the convent, including the privilege of visiting her family and entertaining outside visitors in the convent's parlor. Illness and reflection, however, led Teresa to reconsider her religious vocation and decide to

---

1. For a discussion of the hermeneutical issues involved, see Ahlgren, *Teresa of Avila and the Politics of Sanctity,* 77–80, and Weber, *Teresa of Avila and the Rhetoric of Femininity,* 5–16.

work toward founding a smaller, reformed convent. With help from friends and family she founded the Discalced Carmelite convent of San José (St. Joseph) in 1562. The convent was intended to be dedicated to mental prayer and contemplation and strictly cloistered, therefore free of outside influences. Her reforms won the approbation of the head of the order, and in 1567 she was authorized to establish similar religious houses for men. Teresa's foundations continued. Over the course of the next two decades, she founded convents in most of the important cities of sixteenth-century Spain, including Medina del Campo, Toledo, Salamanca, Seville, Segovia, and Burgos. Teresa combined the foundation of these convents with the production of treatises, letters, and other writings which would build a new model for women's religious life.

Teresa's extensive writing career began at the same time as her reforming activities. Partly in response to questions regarding the nature and orthodoxy of her own prayer experiences, but also as an integral part of her reforming agenda, Teresa penned several spiritual relations which became *The Book of Her Life.* This book circulated widely among Carmelite circles and was read by members of the royal court. Concern over the book's ideas, particularly Teresa's descriptions of visions and to some degree her conceptualization of the soul's relationship with God, led to inquisitional inquiries regarding her orthodoxy, the most serious of which involved interviews in the convent she founded in 1575 in Seville. After the interviews, Teresa was ordered into reclusion at the convent of her choice. Retiring to Toledo, Teresa wrote her mystical tour de force, *The Interior Castle,* a chronicling of the seven stages in the soul's mystical journey toward God. One of Teresa's major reasons for writing *The Interior Castle* was her concern that the *Life* might never circulate because it had been confiscated by the Spanish Inquisition for review. Ironically, then, the climate of theological suspicion surrounding mystical and visionary experiences actually encouraged the production of more mystical treatises.

The core of Teresa's theological contributions actually centers around the dilemma presented by the perceived need to define and control religious experience. Teresa wanted to demonstrate clearly the accessibility of Christ to all, the ubiquity of grace available to sinners, and the ability of all humans to achieve deeper union with God in the temple of their souls. Teresa describes this union with God in the excerpt from Book 7 of *The Interior Castle,* reprinted in Part One. Within the context of religious life, a supportive community, spiritual direction, and personal commitment to discernment, Teresa had great confidence in the human potential for intimacy with God. This confidence recalled her own personal experience of a strong calling from God leading her to discover God within herself. The confidence Teresa exhibited in her visions and personal experiences of God was construed as "spiritual arrogance" by some of her contemporaries; others argued that Teresa's visions and holy life exemplified the magnitude of God's grace. Yet Teresa can now be understood as an important defender of the mystical tradition, who presents a distinctive rendering of the mystery of the trinity residing in the individual soul and the possibility of union with this God.[2]

After Teresa was canonized in 1622, her mystical doctrine took on increasing

---

2. See Ahlgren, *Teresa of Avila,* 118–40.

importance within the Roman Catholic tradition. Indeed, the spiritual practices and mystical treatises penned by women of Spain and Latin America in the century after Teresa's death reflect her immense influence and lasting appeal. She was proclaimed a doctor of the Roman Catholic Church in 1970.

Bibliography

Ahlgren, Gillian T. W. *Teresa of Avila and the Politics of Sanctity.* Ithaca, N.Y.: Cornell University Press, 1996.

Billinkoff, Jodi. *The Avila of Saint Teresa: Religious Reforms in a Sixteenth-Century City.* Ithaca, N.Y.: Cornell University Press, 1989.

Teresa of Avila. *The Collected Works of Teresa of Avila.* Trans. Kieran Kavanaugh and Otilio Rodriguez. 3 vols. Washington, D.C.: Institute of Carmelite Studies, 1980.

Weber, Alison. *Teresa of Avila and the Rhetoric of Femininity.* Princeton: Princeton University Press, 1990.

Williams, Rowan. *Teresa of Avila.* Harrisburg, Pa.: Morehouse Publishing, 1991.

Tertullian (ca. 160–225)

Tertullian was a very important third-century theologian who, in his use of ecclesiastical Latin, was instrumental in shaping the vocabulary and thought of western Christianity. What we know about the life of Quintus Septimus Florens Tertullianus is based largely on documents written more than a century after him and from obscure references in his own works. Consequently, scholars regularly dispute the details of his life. He was probably born around 160 in Carthage (in modern-day Tunisia), a cultural center which at the time rivaled Rome. There he received an excellent education in rhetoric, literature, philosophy, and law. His parents were pagan; his father may have been a centurion (i.e., a noncommissioned officer) in the service of the proconsul of Africa. After completing his education in Carthage, he went to Rome, where he may have worked in the law courts.

During his stay in Rome, Tertullian became interested in the Christian movement. From references in some of his early works, it appears that he was impressed by the courage of Christian martyrs as well as by their upright lives and uncompromising belief in one God. When he returned to Carthage, he became a Christian, probably around 195. By the beginning of the third century, the church was a powerful force in Numidia and Proconsularis, the two provinces of Roman Africa. Tertullian prepared catechumens for entry into the church. He also defended Christian beliefs against pagan attack from outside the church and against "heresy" from within the church. It is disputed whether Tertullian was ordained a priest.

During the course of writing for more than two decades, Tertullian touched upon most of the significant issues of theology. More than thirty of his treatises are still extant. In his writings we find an author who is passionate and uncompromising, who enjoys creating a play on words and skewering his opponents (he called Marcion, for example, "a rat from Pontus who gnaws away at the gospels"). His works are filled with memorable phrases, such as "What has Athens to do with Jerusalem?" or "The soul is by nature Christian."

Tertullian's writings can be grouped into three major categories: apologetical, polemical, and moral-ascetical writings. In his *Apology,* written toward the end of the second century, Tertullian defended Christianity against charges of sacrilege and subversion. In one of his most important polemical treatises, *Concerning the Prescription of Heretics* (ca. 200), Tertullian argued that heretics had no right to attempt to use scripture in defense of positions that deviated from the teaching of the apostolic churches. *Against Praxeas,* from which an excerpt is included in Part One, belongs to the category of polemical writings. Tertullian's ascetical writings, especially those written during his Montanist phase, often display an unrestrained harshness and moral rigor. In *Concerning the Dress of Women* (*De cultu feminarum*), Tertullian condemns the use of cosmetics and jewelry, and he declares that the only proper dress for women is that of penitence and mourning, because sin and death entered the world through woman (Eve).

Perhaps as early as 206, Tertullian's ideas began to reflect those of a new prophetic sectarian movement known as Montanism, which had spread from Asia Minor to Africa. Montanus and his followers declared that the end of the world was imminent. In order to prepare for the end, people were enjoined to follow the most stringent moral code. Even the Montanists, however, were not rigorous enough for Tertullian. He eventually broke with them to found his own sect (Tertullianists), a group that existed until the fifth century in Africa.

Although most ancient Christians never forgave him for leaving the church to join the Montanists, modern scholars generally regard Tertullian as one of the formative figures in the development of Christian life and thought in the West. He made his most important theological contributions in the doctrines of God and Christ. Tertullian appears to have been the first Christian to use the Latin word *trinitas* (trinity) with reference to God. Similarly, he was the first to use the term *persona* (person) in a trinitarian context, explaining that the Logos is distinct from the Father as a person, but not as substance (see *Against Praxeas,* ch. 2 in Part One). Although this terminology and this distinction were taken over by the church in the fourth century as a definitive expression of Christian faith, other aspects of his teaching about God were not. Tertullian's exposition of Father, Son, and Spirit discloses subordinationist tendencies, which were rejected definitively at the Councils of Nicea (325) and Constantinople (381).[1] Such an understanding appears when Tertullian speaks of the Son and the Spirit having "the second and third places" assigned to them (*Against Praxeas,* ch. 3), or when he declares that "the Father is the entire substance, but the Son is a derivation and portion of the whole," and that the Father is "greater than the Son" (*Against Praxeas,* ch. 9).

In the excerpt from Tertullian in Part One, Tertullian is engaged in refuting Praxeas, a priest from Asia Minor, who was teaching a form of modalist monarchianism in the early third century. Modalist monarchianism held that the names Father, Son, and Spirit were only different designations of the same subject, the one God. From this point of view, there is no real distinction between Father,

---

1. Subordinationism refers to an understanding or description of the Son and the Holy Spirit that makes either or both of them subordinate to the Father.

Son, and Spirit. Against this point of view, Tertullian attempts to demonstrate the unity of substance, but distinction of persons in God.

In the excerpt from Tertullian in Part Two, Tertullian is engaged in refuting Hermogenes, an artist and Gnostic of Carthage, who had adopted the philosophical position that matter is eternal and the source of evil. In his response, Tertullian rejects Hermogenes' theological explanation of why matter must be regarded as eternal and he explains why Hermogenes' theory fails to absolve God of responsibility for evil in the world. In opposition to Hermogenes, Tertullian defends God's power and goodness by defending the idea of creation out of nothing.

Bibliography

Ayers, Robert H. *Language, Logic, and Reason in the Church Fathers: A Study of Tertullian, Augustine, and Aquinas.* New York: Olms, 1979.

Baney, Margaret Mary. *Some Reflections of Life in North Africa in the Writings of Tertullian.* Washington, D.C.: Catholic University of America Press, 1948.

Barnes, Timothy David. *Tertullian: A Historical and Literary Study.* New York: Oxford University Press, 1985.

Osborn, Eric F. *Tertullian, First Theologian of the West.* New York: Cambridge University Press, 1997.

Timothy, Hamilton B. *The Early Christian Apologists and Greek Philosophy, Exemplified by Irenaeus, Tertullian, and Clement of Alexandria.* Assen: Van Gorcum, 1973.

Thomas Aquinas (1224/25–74)

Thomas Aquinas was born late in 1224 or early 1225 to Landulf and Theodora d'Aquino, members of the lower nobility in the Hohenstaufen kingdom of Sicily. He was born in the family castle at Rocaseca, near the ancient city of Aquino, located about halfway between Rome and Naples. Thomas was taken at the age of five to the abbey of Monte Cassino, the motherhouse of Benedictine monasticism, where his parents planned on his becoming abbot. Due to war between the pope and Emperor Frederick II, Thomas, however, had to be relocated to Naples for his education. There he became familiar with the philosophy of Aristotle and he studied the medieval liberal arts. Thomas felt drawn to the development of his spiritual life. To the displeasure of his family, at the age of nineteen, he joined the Dominican order at Naples in 1244. Like Francis of Assisi, he had to fight against his family's wishes to join a mendicant order. His family kidnapped him and held him for over a year at Rocaseca before they acceded to his desire to become a Dominican.

Life in a mendicant ("begging") order was attractive to Thomas for several reasons. It was a simple life, modeled upon the simplicity or "poverty" of lifestyle practiced in the apostolic age of the church. It was a form of religious communal living that was located not in the rural countryside, but in the cities, where guilds of scholars and students from the different regions of Europe had come together to form universities. Thomas wanted to cultivate a life of the mind in the context of a simple, spiritually oriented life.

The Dominicans sent Thomas to Paris for his novitiate and theological study under Albert the Great (1245–48). In 1248, Thomas accompanied Albert to Cologne for further study and for cursory lecturing on the Bible as a bachelor of theology. Here his fellow friars reputedly dubbed him the "dumb ox" — a reference to his corpulence and his personal reserve.[1] Thomas developed a close relationship with his teacher Albert, who had been working for many years to produce an encyclopedic summary of Aristotelian thought. Previously Aristotle had been known to medieval Christian scholars only as a logician. Now, however, his original thought in the areas of natural science, metaphysics, and anthropology became known to the Christian West. This discovery of Aristotle represented not only an extension of knowledge, but also a potential threat to traditional Christian belief. Aristotle not only offered a coherent conception of reality, devoid of the Christian God, but also held ideas (e.g., the eternity of the world) that were contrary to the teaching of the Christian church. During his four-year stay in Cologne (1248–52), Thomas was ordained a priest.

In 1252 Thomas was sent back to Paris to prepare for the mastership in theology. From 1252 to 1256, he lectured on the *Sentences* of Peter Lombard. In 1256/57 Thomas was appointed to the second Dominican chair of theology at the University of Paris. His job required him to lecture, to preach, and to engage in academic disputations. Two years later he returned to Italy, where he taught at Naples, Orvieto, Rome, and Viterbo (1259–68).

In 1269 Thomas returned to Paris for his second stay as master in theology. Two significant controversies marked this stay (1269–72) in Paris. First, there was debate about the right of mendicant friars to exist in the church. The secular clergy claimed that begging is sinful for anyone who could work. Moreover, they claimed that the chief objectives of the Dominicans — to preach and to provide pastoral care — clashed with the rights of the bishop and his diocesan clergy, to whom those tasks were rightly entrusted. Second, controversy erupted about the proper interpretation of Aristotle and whether it is possible for something to be simultaneously true in philosophy and false in theology. This controversy focused especially upon the work of Siger of Brabant, leader of the "Latin Averroists" among the faculty at the University of Paris.[2] The Latin Averroists presented arguments from Aristotle and Averroës as necessary conclusions of philosophy, even though these conclusions, such as the eternity of the world, the unicity of the human intellect, and the denial of personal immortality, contradicted the truths of Christian faith. In response Stephen Tempier, bishop of Paris, condemned thirteen propositions drawn from the writings of Siger on December 10, 1270. Thomas believed that the principal errors in Siger's work derived not from Aristotle, but from Averroës's interpretation of Aristotle. And, contrary to Siger, Thomas firmly opposed the idea that the conclusions of faith and reason could be opposed.

---

1. Williston Walker et al., *A History of the Christian Church*, 4th ed. (New York: Charles Scribner's Sons, 1985), 340.

2. The term "Latin Averroism" was introduced by Pierre Mandonnet in his book *Siger de Brabant et l'Averroisme latin au XIIIe siècle* (1908/1911). The term refers to a collection of ideas that derived from Averroës's commentary on Aristotle and that were accepted by certain members of the arts faculty at the University of Paris in the second half of the thirteenth century, despite the fact that they contradicted orthodox Christian faith. Averroës is the Latin name for Ibn-Rushd (born 1126), who was the most important medieval Arabic commentator on Aristotle. In medieval texts, he is often simply referred to as "the Commentator."

Thomas returned to Italy in 1272, where he established a Dominican center of studies in Naples. There he followed a daily regimen of early morning confession and Mass, followed by the dictation of his thoughts to his many secretaries until the time for his main meal. After the meal, Thomas went to his cell to pray until siesta time, after which he resumed his writing and dictating until late at night. Then he prayed in the chapel until time for morning prayer, after which he went to bed for a short rest. During his celebration of Mass on December 6, 1273, Thomas was reportedly struck by something — perhaps a mystical experience — that profoundly affected him. After Mass, he did not resume his usual routine. At the time he had been working on Part Three of the *Summa Theologiae.* When asked by his secretary, Reginald of Piperno, why he did not resume work on the *Summa,* Thomas simply replied, "Reginald, I cannot." When pressed by Reginald to return to his routine, but at a slower pace, Thomas reportedly responded, "Reginald, I cannot, because all that I have written seems like straw to me."[3] From this time on, Thomas wrote nothing more. It seems likely that the event of December 6 had a physical dimension as well as a mystical. Perhaps after so many years of driving himself ceaselessly in his philosophical and theological work, Thomas's physical constitution broke down. Although he was approximately only forty-eight years old at the time, Thomas had written about a hundred treatises — approximately two works for each year of his life! After December 6 Thomas's speech and manual dexterity were impaired. At any rate, he no longer taught or wrote, but spent his time in prayer.

Shortly thereafter, Thomas was directed to go to the Second Council of Lyons, which was to begin early in May 1274. Since the main purpose of the council was the reconciliation of Greek Christians with the Latin Church, Thomas was asked to bring along a copy of his *Against the Errors of the Greeks,* which he had written at the request of Pope Urban IV in 1263. Thomas set out for Lyons around the beginning of February. He became ill during the journey, however, and asked to be taken to the Cistercian monastery of Fossanuova, where he died on March 7, 1274.

"Personally, Thomas was a humble and profoundly religious man, as evidenced in the liturgy which he composed for the Feast of Corpus Christi and in his hymns, prayers, and sermons. Intellectually, his work was marked by a clarity, a logical consistency, and a breadth of presentation that places him among the greatest teachers of the church."[4] His combination of intellectual gifts and profound spirituality earned him the title of "Angelic Doctor." Despite the fact that several propositions from his writings were condemned by the bishops of Paris and Canterbury (1277), Thomas's teaching was declared the rule of all teaching and study by Dominicans. In 1323 Pope John XXII canonized him. In 1567, Pope Pius V gave him the title "Universal Doctor of the Church." In 1879, Pope Leo XIII declared his thought the touchstone of Roman Catholic theology. The Code of Canon Law (1917–18) required Catholic educational institutions to treat philosophy and theology according to his method and principles. The *Cat-*

---

3. Weisheipl, *Friar Thomas D'Aquino,* 321.
4. Walker, *A History of the Christian Church,* 341. See also Justo L. González, *A History of Christian Thought,* vol. 2: *From Augustine to the Eve of the Reformation* (Nashville: Abingdon Press, 1971), 2:258–59.

echism of the Catholic Church (1992) frequently cites Thomas as an authority. In sum, Thomas is not only the most important medieval theologian of western Christianity, but also a figure who left a decisive stamp on the development of subsequent Catholic theology. Of course, as with other great figures in the tradition, his heritage has not been entirely positive. Although he modified aspects of the Augustinian approach to theology, he also shared many aspects of Augustine's theology, including its weaknesses. Drawing upon the Aristotelian understanding of biology and the previous tradition of the church, Thomas concluded that women were deficient by nature.[5] And the university context in which he worked gave his theological writing an impersonal quality, characterized often by subtle rational distinctions.

Thomas's three most important theological works are his *Commentary on the Sentences,* the *Summa Contra Gentiles*, and the *Summa Theologiae*. The *Summa Contra Gentiles,* written between 1259 and 1264, was intended for use by Dominican missionaries preaching against Muslims, Jews, and heretical Christians in Spain. Because of its intended apologetic purpose, it tends to make its arguments on the basis of natural reason, rather than by simple appeal to the testimony of the Christian Bible.[6] His other *Summa,* the crown of his genius, was begun in 1265. This encyclopedia of theological knowledge, left unfinished at the time of his death, was intended as a textbook for beginners in theology.

In this work, Thomas argued that theology was necessary for human culture because God destines us for an end that is beyond reason's grasp (*Summa Theologiae,* I, 1, 1.) He did not mean to intimate, however, that reason and revelation were contradictory. Reason, according to Thomas, can apprehend the "preambles of faith" (*praeambula fidei*), i.e., the existence of an omnipotent and omniscient God and the immortality of the soul. It does not, however, know anything of the "articles of faith proper" (*articulos fidei*), i.e., those mysteries of faith necessary for eternal beatitude (e.g., God as trinity, the incarnation of God the Son). Reason, therefore, must be perfected by divine revelation.

Thomas's insistence that the preambles of faith could be attained apart from the divine illumination of the mind, solely through inferential reasoning from the observed character of the world, marked a break with the Augustinian-Franciscan tradition. And Thomas's use of Aristotelian thought to expound Christian faith made him suspect in some circles. On March 7, 1277, the third anniversary of Thomas's death, the bishop of Paris promulgated a list of 219 propositions to be censured. All the Averroist propositions condemned in 1270 appeared in Tempier's list of 1277. But, in addition, a number of non-Averroist propositions, including those of Thomas, were listed.[7]

Consistent with its university context, Thomas's theology is analytical and precise. His theology, however, is also rooted in the teaching of scripture and the church fathers. His attempt to balance the convictions of faith and the conclusions of reason is evident throughout his theological work. Thomas sees nature and grace, reason and revelation, and the natural will and Christian love to be related and complementary. In each pair, the latter term perfects the former, but

---

5. See Hans Küng, *Great Christian Thinkers* (New York: Continuum, 1994), 115–22.
6. See *Summa Contra Gentiles,* I. 2
7. Weisheipl, *Friar Thomas D'Aquino,* 272–77, 331–40.

does not destroy it. As the excerpts from Thomas in Part One make clear, Aquinas was modest, but not skeptical about the human capacity for knowledge and speech about God. We can know that God exists, he wrote, from rational reflection upon the world as an effect of God. We cannot, however, see or comprehend the essence of God in this life. Similarly, we can speak true things about God, but we must remember that appropriate language about God is analogical. In the excerpts from Thomas in Part Two, we see how Aquinas appropriated, in critical fashion, the heritage of both Aristotle and Augustine. In short, Thomas Aquinas formulated an impressive theological system that decisively influenced the subsequent western tradition.

Bibliography

Chenu, M.-D. *Toward Understanding St. Thomas*. Trans. A. M. Landry and D. Hughes. Chicago: Regnery, 1964.

Davies, Brian. *The Thought of Thomas Aquinas*. New York: Oxford University Press, 1993.

Hankey, W. J. *God in Himself: Aquinas' Doctrine of God as Expounded in the Summa Theologiae*. New York: Oxford University Press, 1987.

Ingardia, Richard. *Thomas Aquinas: International Bibliography, 1977–1990*. Bowling Green, Ohio: Philosophy Documentation Center, 1993.

Kretzmann, Norman, and Eleonore Stump, eds. *The Cambridge Companion to Aquinas*. New York: Cambridge University Press, 1993.

Thomas Aquinas. *Summa Theologiae*, with Latin text and English Blackfriars' translation. New York: McGraw-Hill, 1963–.

Weisheipl, James A. *Friar Thomas D'Aquino: His Life, Thought, and Works*. Garden City, N.Y.: Doubleday & Co., 1974.

Paul Tillich (1886–1965)

Paul Tillich was born on August 20, 1886, in Starzeddel, a German town in the province of Brandenburg. He grew up in Schönfliess, a small community east of the Elbe River, where his father was a Lutheran pastor. Life in this medieval town nurtured in Tillich a sense of tradition and a strong attachment to the church as a focal point of meaning in the life of the community. He attended school in Königsberg-Neumark, and then, when his father took up a new position in Berlin, at the Friedrich Wilhelm Gymnasium (an advanced "high school").

After graduation in 1904 from "high school" in Berlin, Tillich attended the universities at Halle and Breslau. There he was challenged to attempt to reconcile the official doctrine of the Lutheran Church with the theological liberalism and scientific spirit that was academically popular at that time. He turned to philosophy in his search for a way to reconcile these two entities. Study of the early nineteenth-century philosopher Schelling proved helpful. From Schelling, Tillich came to see nature as the dynamic manifestation of God's creative spirit, the aim of which is the realization of a freedom that transcends the dichotomy between individual life and universal necessity. Tillich came to work out the relationship between individual and community in terms of theonomy (divine rule) as the resolution of the conflict between heteronomy (adherence to the rule of another) and autonomy (self-rule).

Tillich was also influenced by his teacher Martin Kähler, who in his own writing had distinguished clearly between the historical Jesus (what can be known historically about Jesus) and the Christ of faith (what the church confesses about Jesus as the Christ). Kähler not only influenced Tillich's approach to interpreting the Bible, he also directed Tillich's attention to the importance of the Lutheran doctrine of justification by faith.

With dissertations on Schelling, Tillich received a doctorate in philosophy from the University of Breslau in 1910/11 and a licentiate in theology from the University of Halle in 1912. In the same year he was ordained a pastor in the Evangelical Church of the Prussian Union. With the outbreak of World War I, Tillich enlisted as a military chaplain. As it was for Karl Barth, the war was also a shattering experience for Tillich. The destruction caused by the war made him doubt the adequacy of nineteenth-century humanism. Unlike Barth, however, Tillich still wanted to correlate faith and culture in a positive fashion. In the confused situation after the armistice, Tillich believed that western civilization was entering a new era. He joined the Religious-Socialist movement, whose members believed that the imminent cultural collapse was an opportunity for constructing a new social order.

From 1919 to 1933 Tillich taught at several universities, including the universities of Berlin, Marburg, Dresden, Leipzig, and Frankfurt. As a consequence of his opposition to the Hitler regime and the publication of his book, *The Socialist Decision* (1933), Tillich was removed from his post at the University of Frankfurt. He later commented with pride that he had the honor of being the first non-Jewish professor to be dismissed from a German university. While on a trip to Germany, the American theologian Reinhold Niebuhr learned of Tillich's dismissal. He arranged to have Tillich invited to teach at Union Theological Seminary in New York City. Tillich took up his post at Union in 1933 and he became an American citizen in 1940.

After teaching at Union for twelve years, Tillich moved to Harvard University. While at Harvard, Tillich published two of his most popular books, *The Courage to Be* (1952) and *The Dynamics of Faith* (1957). After seventeen years at Harvard, Tillich assumed a post in the Divinity School of the University of Chicago (1962). He taught at Chicago until his death on October 22, 1965.

Tillich's three-volume *Systematic Theology* (1951–63) offers a substantive statement of his understanding of the correlation between questions raised by human reason in light of human existential experiences and the answers given in revelatory experience and received in faith. Tillich believed that Protestant theology could incorporate the critical attitude and scientific concepts of contemporary thought without endangering its Christian faith. Consequently, he felt comfortable drawing upon the insights of depth psychology and existential philosophy in his attempt to reestablish the relevance of theology for modern secular society. Tillich's work shows that he rejected the anthropomorphic understanding of God in popular Christianity. Instead of speaking of God as a Supreme Being, outside of the world, but intervening in it from time to time, Tillich spoke of God as Being Itself or as the ground of being.

Tillich left a major impression upon theology in the 1950s to the 1970s, particularly in the United States. In the area of theological method, his influence continues. Tillich described the method of theology as the attempt to correlate critically the questions raised by the human situation with the answers given by Christian faith. Another important area of influence has been Tillich's theory of religious symbols. As Warren Kay observes, Tillich was probably the most widely known theologian in the United States while he was alive. Tillich's definition of faith as "ultimate concern" and his description of God as "the ground of being" have worked their way into the vocabulary of theologian and nontheologian alike. Bridging the gap between the faith of Christian tradition and the questioning spirit of modern culture suited Tillich's understanding of his role as a mediator between the old and the new and between the sacred and the secular.

Bibliography

Adams, James Luther. *Paul Tillich's Philosophy of Culture, Science, and Religion*. New York: Schocken Books, 1965.

Adams, James Luther et al., eds. *The Thought of Paul Tillich*. San Francisco: Harper & Row, 1985.

Gilkey, Langdon. *Gilkey on Tillich*. New York: Crossroad, 1990.

Kay, Warren A. "Paul Tillich," in *A New Handbook of Christian Theologians*, ed. Donald W. Musser and Joseph L. Price, 449–59. Nashville: Abingdon Press, 1996.

Kegley, Charles W., ed. *The Theology of Paul Tillich*, 2d ed. New York: Pilgrim Press, 1982.

Pauck, Wilhelm and Marion. *Paul Tillich, His Life and Thought*. New York: Harper & Row, 1976.

Taylor, Mark Kline. *Paul Tillich: Theologian of the Boundaries*. San Francisco: Collins, 1987.

Tillich, Paul. *Systematic Theology*. Chicago: University of Chicago Press, 1951–63.

———. *The Courage to Be*. New Haven: Yale University Press, 1952.

———. *The Dynamics of Faith*. New York: Harper, 1957.

Delores Williams (b. 1943)

Delores Williams is professor of theology and culture at Union Theological Seminary in New York City. She is one of the most important figures in womanist theology in the United States. Womanist theology, which Jacquelyn Grant, Katie Cannon, Kelly Brown Douglas, and Delores Williams began to develop in the 1980s, refers to the theological work of African-American women who have made the experience of black women the primary resource in theological reflection.

Williams was born on November 17, 1943, in Louisville, Kentucky. The religious background of her extended family was diverse. Her mother's relatives were Seventh-Day Adventist and Presbyterian, while her father was Catholic and her stepfather Baptist. The absence of strong denominational ties may have contributed to her nontraditional perspectives on Christianity and her openness to other religious traditions.[1] A very strong influence on Williams was her experience of racial segregation and violence in the South. Childhood memories of the lynching of a black man and the rape of a black woman by a white man powerfully affected Williams. But in addition to white-on-black violence, Williams also became aware of the exploitation black women experienced at the hands of black

---

1. Chapman, *Christianity on Trial*, 152.

men. The fact that so many African-American women resisted exploitation at the hands of both whites and black men, while continuing to hold on to their faith in God, led Williams to a profound respect for the survival qualities and religious experience of African-American women.

Williams did her undergraduate studies at the University of Louisville. During her studies there in the early 1960s, she became involved in the civil rights movement through the NAACP Youth Council. She married Robert Williams, a young minister, while still in college. She had two of her four children before completing her undergraduate education. In 1968 she moved with her family to New York City. While her husband pursued a doctoral degree at Union Seminary, she earned the M.A. degree in comparative religion and literature from Columbia University. Although a mother and spouse, Williams made time to recite and write poetry as well as to take classes from Beverly Harrison and James Cone at Union Seminary. After her own doctoral studies at Union, Williams accepted a teaching position at Harvard Divinity School. She then moved to the school of theology at Drew University, where she taught from 1987 to 1991. In 1991 she returned to her alma mater, Union Theological Seminary, where she continues to work as a professor of theology and culture.

The silence of black male theologians concerning the oppression of black women served as a major catalyst for the development of womanist theology. African-American women who were graduates of Union Theological Seminary, such as Jacquelyn Grant, Katie Cannon, Kelly Brown Douglas, and Delores Williams, took the lead in this development. Influenced by the writings of Alice Walker, who had coined the term in 1983, they began to use the term "womanist" to distinguish themselves from white feminists and black male theologians.[2] Whereas white feminists focused on sexism and black male theologians focused on racism, womanist theologians began to focus on the interrelatedness of sex, race, and class as factors contributing to the oppression of women of color. Williams has been at the forefront of the development of womanist theology.[3] She has identified survival and the building of community as two of the principal concerns of womanist theology.

In *Sisters in the Wilderness*, from which the selection in this book is taken, Williams relates the wilderness experience of Hagar (Gen. 16:1–16; 21:9–21) to the experience of contemporary African-American women. In this book she criticizes other liberation theologians, such as James Cone, for an uncritical use of the liberation threads in the Bible. From Williams's perspective, much of what black theology has affirmed in the Bible as liberating is, in fact, ambivalent. According to the biblical account of the Exodus, for example, God not only liberated the slaves from Egypt, but also sanctioned the genocide of the Canaanites and the taking of their land. In the case of Hagar, God did not stop her exploitation at the hands of Abraham and Sarah, but did contribute to her struggle for survival. In short, although there are liberating threads in the Bible, there are also narra-

---

2. See Williams, "Womanist Theology: Black Women's Voices," 62. Jones, "Womanist Theologians," 513.

3. Ruether, *Women and Redemption*, 229. Chapman observes: "In fact, no womanist scholar has done more to describe the religious experience of African-American women via literature than Delores Williams" (*Christianity on Trial*, 150).

tives filled with sexism and the exploitation of non-Hebrew groups. In Hagar, Williams finds a biblical figure whose experience is most like that of women of color, many of whom have also experienced slavery, poverty, single motherhood, and salvific wilderness encounters with God. Like Hagar, many African-American women have encountered a divine power in their own wilderness that has empowered them to use their own resources in making "a way out of no way." In this wilderness tradition of the Bible, Williams finds the emphasis not on unequivocal liberation, but on survival and the building of community.

Select Bibliography

Chapman, Mark L. *Christianity on Trial: African-American Religious Thought before and after Black Power.* Maryknoll, N.Y.: Orbis Books, 1996.

Chopp, Rebecca S. "Feminist and Womanist Theologies," in *The Modern Theologians: An Introduction to Christian Theology in the Twentieth Century,* ed. David F. Ford, 389–404. Cambridge, Mass.: Blackwell, 1997.

Hennelly, Alfred T. *Liberation Theologies: The Global Pursuit of Justice.* Mystic, Conn.: Twenty-Third Publications, 1995, 115–21.

Jones, Sheilah M. "Womanist Theologians," in *A New Handbook of Christian Theologians,* ed. Donald W. Musser and Joseph L. Price, 513–19. Nashville: Abingdon Press, 1996.

Ruether, Rosemary Radford. *Women and Redemption: A Theological History.* Minneapolis: Fortress Press, 1998, 229–34.

Williams, Delores S. "Womanist Theology: Black Women's Voices," in *Learning to Breathe Free: Liberation Theologies in the United States,* ed. Mar Peter-Raoul, Linda Rennie Forcey, and Robert Frederick Hunters, 62–69. Maryknoll, N.Y.: Orbis Books, 1990.

———. *Sisters in the Wilderness: The Challenge of Womanist God-Talk.* Maryknoll, N.Y.: Orbis Books, 1993.

———. "A Womanist Perspective on Sin," in *A Troubling in My Soul: Womanist Perspectives on Evil,* ed. Emilie Townes, 130–49. Maryknoll, N.Y.: Orbis Books, 1993.

Select Bibliography

General Histories

Ahlstrom, Sydney E. *A Religious History of the American People*. New Haven: Yale University Press, 1972.

Barraclough, Geoffrey, ed. *The Christian World: A Social and Cultural History*. New York: H. N. Abrams, 1981.

Cunliffe-Jones, H., and B. Drewery, eds. *A History of Christian Doctrine*. Philadelphia: Fortress Press, 1980.

Gonzalez, Justo C. *A History of Christian Thought*. 3 vols. Nashville: Abingdon Press, 1970–75.

Green, Vivian. *A New History of Christianity*. New York: Continuum, 1996.

Jedin, Hubert, ed. *History of the Church*. 10 vols. New York: Crossroad, 1980–83.

Kee, Howard Clark. *Christianity: A Social and Cultural History*. Upper Saddle River, N.J.: Prentice-Hall, 1998.

Latourette, Kenneth Scott. *A History of Christianity*. 2 vols. New York: Harper & Row, 1975.

Marty, Martin E. *A Short History of Christianity*. Philadelphia: Fortress Press, 1980.

McManners, John, ed. *The Oxford Illustrated History of Christianity*. New York: Oxford University Press, 1990.

Placher, William C. *A History of Christian Theology: An Introduction*. Philadelphia: Westminster Press, 1983.

Seeberg, Reinhold. *The History of Doctrines*. Grand Rapids: Baker Book House, 1977.

Urban, Linwood. *A Short History of Christian Thought*. Rev. ed. New York: Oxford University Press, 1995.

Walker, Williston, et al. *A History of the Christian Church*. 4th ed. New York: Charles Scribner's Sons, 1985.

Wilken, Robert Louis. *Remembering the Christian Past*. Grand Rapids: Eerdmans, 1995.

Early Church

Bell, David N. *A Cloud of Witnesses: An Introductory History of the Development of Christian Doctrine*. Kalamazoo, Mich.: Cistercian Publications, 1989.

Chadwick, Henry. *The Early Church*. New York: Penguin Books, 1967.

Ferguson, Everett, ed. *Encyclopedia of Early Christianity*. New York: Garland, 1990.

Frend, W. H. C. *Martyrdom and Persecution in the Early Church*. Grand Rapids: Baker Book House, 1981.

———. *The Rise of Christianity*. Philadelphia: Fortress Press, 1984.

Kelly, J. N. D. *Early Christian Doctrines*. Rev. ed. New York: Harper & Row, 1978.

McGinn, Bernard. *The Foundations of Mysticism: Origins to the Fifth Century*. New York: Crossroad, 1994.

McGinn, Bernard, and John Meyendorff, eds. *Christian Spirituality: Origins to the Twelfth Century*. New York: Crossroad, 1985.

Miles, Margaret. *Carnal Knowing: Female Nakedness and Religious Meaning in the Christian West*. New York: Vintage Books, 1989.

Pagels, Elaine. *Adam, Eve, and the Serpent*. New York: Vintage Books, 1989.

Pelikan, Jaroslav. *The Emergence of Catholic Thought*. Chicago: University of Chicago Press, 1971.

Tugwell, Simon. *The Apostolic Fathers*. Harrisburg, Pa.: Morehouse Publishing, 1989.

Von Campenhausen, Hans. *Ecclesiastical Authority and Spiritual Power in the Church of the First Three Centuries*. Stanford: Stanford University Press, 1969.

Wiles, Maurice. *The Making of Christian Doctrine*. Cambridge: Cambridge University Press, 1967.

Medieval/Reformation Church

Brunn, Emilie Zum, and Georgette Epiney-Burgard. *Women Mystics in Medieval Europe*. New York: Paragon House, 1989.

Bynum, Caroline Walker. *Holy Feast, Holy Fast: The Religious Significance of Food to Medieval Women*. Berkeley: University of California Press, 1986.

Cantor, Norman F. *The Civilization of the Middle Ages*. New York: HarperCollins, 1993.

Colish, Marcia L. *An Intellectual History of the Middle Ages*. New Haven: Yale University Press, 1997.

Delumeau, Jean. *Catholicism between Luther and Voltaire: A New View of the Counter Reformation*. Philadelphia: Westminster Press, 1977.

Hillerbrand, Hans J., ed. *The Oxford Encyclopedia of the Reformation*. 4 vols. New York: Oxford University Press, 1996.

Lynch, Joseph H. *The Medieval Church: A Brief History*. New York: Longman, 1992.

McGinn, Bernard. *The Growth of Mysticism*. New York: Crossroad, 1994.

Ozment, Steven. *The Age of Reform, 1250–1550: An Intellectual and Religious History of Late Medieval and Reformation Europe*. New Haven: Yale University Press, 1980.

Pelikan, Jaroslav. *The Growth of Medieval Theology*. Chicago: University of Chicago Press, 1978.

———. *Reformation of Church and Dogma (1300–1700)*. Chicago: University of Chicago Press, 1984.

Raitt, Jill, ed. *Christian Spirituality: High Middle Ages and Reformation*. New York: Crossroad, 1987.

Tierney, Brian, and Sidney Painter. *Western Europe in the Middle Ages, 300–1475*. New York: McGraw-Hill, 1992.

Modern Church

Aston, Nigel, ed. *Religious Change in Europe, 1650–1914*. New York: Oxford University Press, 1997.

Aubert, Roger. *The Church in a Secularized Society*. New York: Paulist Press, 1978.

Baumer, Franklin L. *Modern European Thought: Continuity and Change in Ideas, 1600–1950*. New York: Macmillan, 1977.

Cragg, Gerald R. *The Church and the Age of Reason*. New York: Penguin Viking, 1974.

Dillenberger, John, and Claude Welch. *Protestant Christianity: Interpreted through Its Development*. 2d ed. New York: Macmillan, 1988.

Engel, Mary Potter, and Walter E. Wyman, Jr. *Revisioning the Past: Prospects in Historical Theology*. Minneapolis: Fortress Press, 1992.

Gerrish, B. A. *Continuing the Reformation: Essays on Modern Religious Thought*. Chicago: University of Chicago Press, 1993.

Graf Reventlow, H. *The Authority of the Bible and the Rise of the Modern World*. Philadelphia: Fortress Press, 1985.

Livingston, James. *Modern Christian Thought*. Upper Saddle River, N.J.: Prentice-Hall, 1997.

McCool, Gerald A. *Catholic Theology in the Nineteenth Century: The Quest for a Unitary Method*. New York: Seabury, 1977.

McGrath, Alister E., ed. *The Blackwell Encyclopedia of Modern Christian Thought*. Cambridge: Blackwell, 1993.

Miller, Glenn T. *The Modern Church: From the Dawn of the Reformation to the Eve of the Third Millennium*. Nashville: Abingdon Press, 1997.

O'Meara, Thomas F. *Romantic Idealism and Roman Catholicism: Schelling and the Theologians*. Notre Dame: University of Notre Dame Press, 1982.

———. *Church and Culture: German Catholic Theology 1860–1914*. Notre Dame: University of Notre Dame Press, 1991.

Pelikan, Jaroslav. *Christian Doctrine and Modern Culture (since 1700)*. Chicago: University of Chicago Press, 1989.

Reardon, B. M. G. *Religion in the Age of Romanticism*. Cambridge: Cambridge University Press, 1985.

Schmidt, James, ed. *What Is Enlightenment? Eighteenth Century Questions and Twentieth Century Answers*. Berkeley: University of California Press, 1996.

Schoof, Mark A. *A Survey of Catholic Theology, 1800–1970*. New York: Paulist Press, 1970.

Smart, Ninian, et al. *Nineteenth Century Religious Thought in the West*. 3 vols. Cambridge: Cambridge University Press, 1985.

Thielicke, Helmut. *Modern Faith and Thought*. Grand Rapids: Eerdmans, 1990.

Vidler, Alec. *The Church in an Age of Revolution*. New York: Penguin, 1974.

Welch, Claude. *Protestant Thought in the Nineteenth Century*. 2 vols. New Haven: Yale University Press, 1972, 1985.

God

Ferguson, Everett, ed. *Doctrines of God and Christ in the Early Church*. New York: Garland, 1993.

Grant, Robert M. *The Early Christian Doctrine of God*. Charlottesville: University Press of Virginia, 1966.

Gunton, Colin E., ed. *The Doctrine of Creation: Essays in Dogmatics, History and Philosophy*. Edinburgh: T. & T. Clark, 1997.

Jones, Major J. *The Color of God: The Concept of God in Afro-American Thought*. Macon, Ga.: Mercer University Press, 1987.

Küng, Hans. *Does God Exist? An Answer for Today*. New York: Vintage Books, 1981.

Lonergan, Bernard. *The Way to Nicea: The Dialectical Development of Trinitarian Theology*. Philadelphia: Westminster Press, 1976.

Placher, William C. *The Domestication of Transcendence: How Modern Thinking about God Went Wrong*. Louisville: Westminster John Knox, 1996.

Prestige, George Leonard. *God in Patristic Thought*. London: SPCK, 1959.

Rusch, William G., ed. *The Trinitarian Controversy*. Philadelphia: Fortress Press, 1980.

Swinburne, Richard. *The Christian God*. New York: Oxford University Press, 1994.

Tanner, Kathryn. *God and Creation in Christian Theology: Tyranny or Empowerment?* New York: Blackwell, 1988.

Ward, Graham, ed. *The Postmodern God: A Theological Reader*. Malden, Mass.: Blackwell, 1997.

Wiles, Maurice F. *God's Action in the World*. London: SCM Press, 1986.

Worthing, Mark W. *God, Creation, and Contemporary Physics*. Minneapolis: Fortress Press, 1996.

Part Four

TIMELINE

Chronological Relationships among

Political and Social Events
Intellectual and Cultural Developments
Christian History
Major Christian Writers

Political and Social Events	Intellectual and Cultural Developments	Christian History	Major Christian Writers
37–41 Caligula emperor; unrest in Palestine		c. 30 Crucifixion of Jesus	
41–54 Claudius emperor		48 Council of Jerusalem	54–62 Paul's letters
54–68 Nero emperor	50–65 Writing career of Seneca the younger	60–62 Paul in Rome	
64 Fire in Rome		64 First persecution of Christians	
69–70 Vespasian emperor		c. 67–76 Papacy of Linus	70–85 Synoptic gospels
79–81 Titus emperor	75–79 Flavius Josephus, *History of the Jewish War*	70 Fall of Jerusalem	
81–96 Domitian emperor		74 Capture of Masada	
96–98 Nerva emperor		c. 76–88 Papacy of Anacletus	
98–117 Trajan emperor		c. 88–97 Papacy of Clement I	
		95 Domitian persecution	c. 96 *1 Clement*
			c. 100 *Didache*
		c. 97–105 Papacy of Evaristus	c. 107 Ignatius of Antioch's letters
		c. 105–15 Papacy of Alexander I	c. 108 Polycarp, *Letter to Philippians*
	c. 110 Tacitus, *The Histories*	c. 111 Pliny-Trajan correspondence regarding treatment of Christians	
117–38 Hadrian emperor	c. 120 Tacitus (**b.c. 56**) and Plutarch (**b.c. 46**) die	c. 115–25 Papacy of Sixtus I	c. 120 *Shepherd of Hermas*
122–35 Jewish revolt under Bar Kokhba	c. 125 Pantheon in Rome completed	c. 125–36 Papacy of Telesphorus	
138–61 Antoninus Pius emperor	130–80 Alexandrian gnostic school	c. 136–40 Papacy of Hyginus	
		c. 140–55 Papacy of Pius I	
		144 Marcion expelled from Rome	
161–80 Marcus Aurelius emperor		c. 155–66 Papacy of Anaeletus	c. 155 Justin Martyr, *First Apology*
164–80 Plague in the Roman Empire			c. 160 Justin Martyr, *Second Apology*

Political and Social Events	Intellectual and Cultural Developments	Christian History	Major Christian Writers
	c. 170 Pausanias, *Periegesis*	c. 165 Polycarp martyred in Smyrna	165 Justin Martyr dies (**b.c. 100**)
		c. 166–75 Papacy of Soter	
		172 Rise of Montanism	
180–92 Commodus emperor	180 Catechetical school at Alexandria founded	c. 175–89 Papacy of Eleutherius	c. 185 Irenaeus, *Against Heresies*
		177 Persecution of Christians in Lyons (Blandina martyred)	c. 190 Clement of Alexandria, *Miscellanies*
			197 Tertullian, *Apology*
193–211 Septimius Severus emperor		189–99 Victor I, first Latin-speaking pope	
	c. 199 Galen, a founder of experimental physiology, dies		c. 200 Irenaeus dies (**b.c. 130**)
	c. 200 Neo-Platonism; formation of Neo-Hebrew language	199–217 Papacy of Zephyrinus	c. 200 Tertullian, *On Spectacles*
	203 Origen head of cathechetical school at Alexandria; Plotinus there to **270**	c. 203 Martyrdom of Perpetua	c. 207 Tertullian, *Against Marcion*
			213 Tertullian, *Against Praxeas*
			215 Clement of Alexandria dies (**b.c. 150**)
211–17 Caracalla emperor		217–22 Papacy of Callistus I	c. 222 Tertullian dies (**b.c. 160**)
218–22 Heliogabalus emperor		222–30 Papacy of Urban I	c. 225 Origen, *On First Principles*
222–35 Alexander Severus emperor			
	c. 231 Dionysius becomes head of catechetical school at Alexandria	230–35 Papacy of Pontian	c. 233 Origen, *On Prayer*
235–38 Maximinus emperor		235–36 Papacy of Anterus	c. 236 Origen, *Exhortation to Martyrdom*
		236–50 Papacy of Fabian	
244–49 Philip the Arabian emperor		250 Decian persecution; martyrs revered as saints; Cyprian flees Carthage	c. 248 Origen, *Against Celsus*
248 Rome attacked by Goths			
249–51 Decius emperor			

251–53 Gallus emperor	c. 255 Plotinus, *Enneads*	251 Cyprian asserts authority	c. 251 Cyprian, *On the Unity of the Catholic Church*
253–60 Valerian emperor		251–53 Papacy of Cornelius 253–54 Papacy of Lucius I 254–57 Papacy of Stephen I	254 Origen dies (**b.c. 185**)
260–68 Gallienus emperor	c. 264 Dionysius dies	257–58 Papacy of Sixtus II 257–60 Valerianic persecutions 259–68 Papacy of Dionysius 260–63 Debate over Sabellianism 261–72 Paul of Samosata, bishop of Antioch; Councils against Paul in **264, 265,** and **268**	258 Cyprian of Carthage dies (**b.c. 200**)
268–70 Claudius II emperor		269–74 Papacy of Felix I c. 270 Antony goes to desert 275–83 Papacy of Eutychian	
270–75 Aurelian emperor	c. 276 Manes, founder of Manicheism, dies	280–300 Rise of Manichees 283–96 Papacy of Caius	
284–305 Diocletian emperor 285 Diocletian divides Roman Empire into East and West	c. 300 Earliest religious plays c. 304 Porphyry dies (**b.c. 234**)	296–304 Papacy of Marcellinus 303–5 Diocletian persecution	
307–37 Constantine emperor		308–9 Papacy of Marcellus I 309–10 Papacy of Eusebius 311 Donatist schism 311–14 Papacy of Miltiades	c. 311 Eusebius, first *Ecclesiastical History*
312 Constantine defeats Maxentius at Milvian Bridge 313 Edict of Milan guarantees religious toleration		314 Council of bishops at Arles	

Political and Social Events	Intellectual and Cultural Developments	Christian History	Major Christian Writers
316 Constantine condemns Donatists		314–35 Papacy of Sylvester I	
		323 Arius condemned; Pachomius founds monastery	c. 324 Eusebius, second *Ecclesiastical History*
		325 First Council of Nicea declares Christ *homoousios*, same substance as God	
		328–73 Athanasius, bishop of Alexandria	
330–31 Constantinople made capital of Roman Empire 332 Constantine defeats Goths	c. 330 First basilica of St. Peter's in Rome	335 Athanasius condemned and exiled	c. 335 Athanasius, *Incarnation of the Word*
337 Constantine baptized		336 Papacy of Mark 337–52 Papacy of Julius I 337 Athanasius returns to Alexandria 339–46 Athanasius's second exile	340 Eusebius dies (**b.c. 260**) 346 Pachomius dies (**b.c. 290**)
		352–66 Papacy of Liberius 353 Council of Arles	356 Athanasius, *Orations Against the Arians* 357 Athanasius, *Life of Antony*
		c. 360 Martin of Tours founds first Gallic monastic community 366–84 Papacy of Damasus I	367 Hilary of Poitiers dies (**b.c. 315**) 373 Athanasius dies (**b.c. 300**) 375 Basil of Caesarea, *On the Spirit* 377 Ambrose of Milan, *On Virginity*
378 Visigoths defeat Emperor Valens at Adrianople			379 Basil of Caesarea dies (**b.c. 330**)

Writings	Church	General Events
381 Ambrose, *On the Holy Spirit*	**381** First Council of Constantinople declares divinity of the Spirit and completes Nicene Creed	
383 Jerome, Vulgate translation of Bible		
384 Jerome, *Letter to Eustochium*	**384–99** Papacy of Siricius	
	386 Augustine's conversion to orthodox Christianity	
		391 Emperor Theodosius prohibits pagan sacrifices
c. 390 Gregory of Nyssa, *Life of Moses; On Not Three Gods*	**392–428** Theodore, bishop of Mopsuestia	
c. 395 Gregory of Nyssa dies (**b.c. 335**)	**395–430** Augustine, bishop of Hippo	
396–97 Augustine, *Confessions*		
397 Ambrose of Milan dies (**b.c. 334**)		
399 Evagrius Ponticus dies (**b.c. 345**)	**399–401** Papacy of Anastasius I	
c. 400 Augustine, *On Christian Doctrine*		
401–15 Augustine, *Literal Commentary on Genesis*	**401–17** Papacy of Innocent I	
404–20 Augustine, *On the Trinity*		
407 John Chrysostom dies (**b.c. 347**)		
		410 Sack of Rome by Alaric
411–26 Augustine, *City of God*	**411** Pelagian controversy begins	
413 Augustine, *On the Spirit and the Letter*		
	c. 415 John Cassian founds monasteries in Marseilles	
	417 Pope Innocent I condemns Pelagians	
	417–18 Papacy of Zosimus	
	418–22 Papacy of Boniface I	
420 Jerome dies (**b.c. 347**)		
421 Augustine, *Enchiridion*	**422–32** Papacy of Celestine I	
c. 426 John Cassian, *Conferences*		

Political and Social Events	Intellectual and Cultural Developments	Christian History	Major Christian Writers
429 Vandals establish kingdom in Northern Africa		429–31 Nestorius of Constantinople vs. Cyril of Alexandria (christological controversy)	c. 430 John Cassian, *Institutes*
		431 Council of Ephesus declares Mary Theotokos	430 Augustine dies (b.c. 354)
		432 Patrick's mission to Ireland	
		432–40 Papacy of Sixtus III	c. 435 John Cassian dies (b.c. 360)
		440–61 Papacy of Leo I, "the Great"	
		451 Council of Chalcedon condemns monophysitism and defines two natures of Christ	
452 Huns invade Italy			
455 Sack of Rome by Vandals		461–68 Papacy of Hilary	
		468–83 Papacy of Simplicius	
476 Western Roman Empire collapses	476 Proclus becomes head of the Platonic Academy at Athens		
		483–92 Papacy of Felix II	
		492–96 Papacy of Gelasius I; two powers theory	
		496–98 Papacy of Anastasius II	
c. 496 Clodovis, king of the Franks, converts to Christianity		498–514 Papacy of Symmachus	
	500 *Codex Bezae*, Greek-Latin text of gospels and Acts of the Apostles; Johannes Stobaios, *Anthology of Greek Literature*		after 500 Writing career of Pseudo-Dionysius
507 Franks defeat Visigoths			
		513 Council of Tyre	
		514–23 Papacy of Hormisdas	c. 515 Pseudo-Dionysius, *Mystical Theology*
		523–26 Papacy of John I	
	524 Boethius, *The Consolation of Philosophy*	526–30 Papacy of Felix III	

527–65 Justinian emperor	529 Benedict founds monastery at Monte Cassino; Council of Orange condemns Pelagianism	
	530–32 Papacy of Boniface II	
	533–35 Papacy of John II	
	535–36 Papacy of Agapitus I	
	536–37 Papacy of Silverius	
534 Revised *Code of Justinian* published		
537 Hagia Sophia dedicated under Justinian over an earlier basilica commissioned by Constantine but burned in **532**	537–55 Papacy of Vigilius	
	553 Second Council of Constantinople affirms Chalcedon	
	556–61 Papacy of Pelagius I	
	561–74 Papacy of John III	
568 Lombard invasion of Italy		
	575–79 Papacy of Benedict I	
	579–90 Papacy of Pelagius II	
	590–604 Papacy of Gregory I, "the Great"	c. **591** Gregory the Great, *Moralia on Job*
c. **591** Gregory of Tours, *History of the Franks*	597 Gregory's mission to Anglo-Saxons	
c. **600** Pope Gregory I organizes Schola Cantorum and liturgical music	602 Bishop of London consecrated	c. **600** Gregory the Great, *Dialogues*
	604–6 Papacy of Sabinian	
	607 Papacy of Boniface III	
	608–15 Papacy of Boniface IV	
614 Jerusalem falls to Persians	615–18 Papacy of Adeodatus I	
c. **620** Normans invade Ireland	619–25 Papacy of Boniface V	
	625–38 Papacy of Honorius I	
632 Death of Muhammad		

Political and Social Events	Intellectual and Cultural Developments	Christian History	Major Christian Writers
634 Arab armies take Damascus			636 Isidore of Seville dies (b.c. 570)
638 Arab armies capture Jerusalem			
		640 Papacy of Severinus	
		640–42 Papacy of John IV	
		642–49 Papacy of Theodore I	
		649–53 Papacy of Martin I	
		654–57 Papacy of Eugene I	
		657–72 Papacy of Vitalian	662 Maximus Confessor dies (b.c. 530)
		672–76 Papacy of Adeodatus II	
		676–78 Papacy of Donus	
		678–81 Papacy of Agatho	
		680–81 Third Council of Constantinople rejects monothelitism	
		682–83 Papacy of Leo II	
		684–85 Papacy of Benedict II	
		685–86 Papacy of John V	
		686–87 Papacy of Conon	
		687–701 Papacy of Sergius I	
		701–5 Papacy of John VI	
	c. 700 Lindisfarne gospels copied and illustrated	705–7 Papacy of John VII	
	703–35 Bede helps to establish practice of dating events from the birth of Jesus	708 Papacy of Sisinnius	
		708–15 Papacy of Constantine I	
710 Entry of Moors into Spain; Spain overtaken by 713			
714–41 Career of Charles Martel		715–31 Papacy of Gregory II	
		731–41 Papacy of Gregory III	c. 732 Bede, *Ecclesiastical History of the English Nation*
732 Martel defeats Muslims at Poitiers			735 Bede dies (b. 673)
		738 Boniface organizes church in Germany	

Political/Military Events	Culture & Learning	Papacy & Church	Persons & Works
752 Pepin proclaimed king of Gaul; Carolingian dynasty established		**741–52** Papacy of Zachary	
754–56 Formation of Papal State		**752** Stephen II, dies before consecration	
		752–57 Papacy of Stephen II (III)	**778** Ambrose Autpert dies (b. unknown)
		757–67 Papacy of Paul I	
		768–72 Papacy of Stephen III (IV)	
		772–95 Papacy of Hadrian I	
		787 Second Council of Nicea affirms veneration of icons	
793 Viking raids on England	**790s** Alcuin promotes Carolingian revival of learning		
800 Charlemagne crowned Holy Roman Emperor by Pope Leo III	**c. 800** *Book of Kells*, Irish illuminated text of the gospels	**795–816** Papacy of Leo III	
		816–17 Papacy of Stephen IV (V)	
		817–24 Papacy of Paschal I	
		824–27 Papacy of Eugene II	
		827 Papacy of Valentine	
	829 Basilica of St. Mark in Venice begun	**827–44** Papacy of Gregory IV	
843 Treaty of Verdun divides Carolingian Empire		**844–47** Papacy of Sergius II	
		847–55 Papacy of Leo IV	**851** John the Scot, *On Predestination*
853–57 Normans raid France	**c. 850** Increasing use of the crossbow	**855–58** Papacy of Benedict III	
	c. 860 Cyril and Methodius, apostles to the Slavs, invent Cyrillic alphabet	**858–67** Papacy of Nicholas I	**c. 862–69** John the Scot, *On the Division of Nature*
		867–72 Papacy of Hadrian II	
		869–70 Fourth Council of Constantinople	

Political and Social Events	Intellectual and Cultural Developments	Christian History	Major Christian Writers
c. 875 Vikings settle Iceland		**872–82** Papacy of John VIII **882–84** Papacy of Marinus I **884–85** Papacy of Hadrian III **885–91** Papacy of Stephen V (VI) **891-96** Papacy of Formosus **896** Papacy of Boniface VI **896–97** Papacy of Stephen VI (VII) **897** Papacy of Romanus **897** Papacy of Theodore II **898–900** Papacy of John IX **900–3** Papacy of Benedict IV **903** Papacy of Leo V **904–11** Papacy of Sergius III **910** Foundation of Abbey of Cluny; Cluniac reform of Benedictine order initiated **911-13** Papacy of Anastasius III **913–14** Papacy of Lando **914–28** Papacy of John X **928** Papacy of Leo VI **928-31** Papacy of Stephen VII (VIII) **931-35** Papacy of John XI **936–39** Papacy of Leo VII	**c. 877** John the Scot dies (**b.c. 810**)
936–62 Otto I, king of Germany and later Holy Roman Emperor (**962–73**)		**939–42** Papacy of Stephen VIII (IX) **942–46** Papacy of Marinus II **946–55** Papacy of Agapitus II **955–63** Papacy of John XII **963–65** Papacy of Leo VIII **964** Papacy of Benedict V **965–72** Papacy of John XIII **973–74** Papacy of Benedict VI **974–83** Papacy of Benedict VII	
973–83 Otto II, Holy Roman Emperor			

983 Otto III succeeds Otto II, later becoming emperor (996–1002)
987–1328 Capetian dynasty in France
990–1029 William, duke of Aquitaine

1010 Normans defeat English at Ringmere

1035 Castile becomes a kingdom under Ferdinand I
1042–66 Edward the Confessor, king of England

1053 Normans defeat papal army; Pope Leo IX captured

1059 Lateran Synod issues general prohibition of lay investiture

---

c. 1000 manuscript of *Beowulf*; Leif Eriksson believed to reach North America

1037 Avicenna dies (b. 980)

1050–1125 Romanesque architecture flourishes

1065 Westminster Abbey consecrated

983–84 Papacy of John XIV
985–96 Papacy of John XV

996–99 Papacy of Gregory V
998 Beginning of conversion of Russia
999–1003 Papacy of Sylvester II

1003 Papacy of John XVII
1003–9 Papacy of John XVIII
1009 Norman alliance with papacy
1009–12 Papacy of Sergius IV

1012–24 Papacy of Benedict VIII
1024–32 Papacy of John XIX
1032–45 Papacy of Benedict IX

1045–46 Papacy of Gregory VI
1046–47 Papacy of Clement II
1047–48 Benedict IX pope again
1048 Papacy of Damasus II
1049 Norman alliance collapses
1049–54 Papacy of Leo IX

1054 Schism between Western and Eastern Church
1055–57 Papacy of Victor II
1057 Peter Damian, monk and reformer, becomes cardinal bishop of Ostia
1057–58 Papacy of Stephen IX (X)
1059–61 Papacy of Nicholas II, who establishes rules for papal elections by cardinals
1061–73 Papacy of Alexander II

Political and Social Events	Intellectual and Cultural Developments	Christian History	Major Christian Writers
1066 William, duke of Normandy, becomes king of England after Norman conquest		**1073–85** Papacy of Gregory VII	
1075–85 Conflict between Pope Gregory VII and Henry IV of Germany over lay investiture		**1075** Gregory VII's *Dictatus Papae* insists on papal supremacy in temporal and spiritual matters	
1077 Henry IV does penance at Canossa, is reinstated		**1076** Gregory excommunicates and deposes Henry IV	**1078** John of Fécamp dies (**b.c. 990**)
	c. 1078 Building of Tower of London begins		**1078–79** Anselm, *Proslogion*
1086 William the Conqueror has *Domesday Book* compiled		**1084** Foundation of Carthusian order	
		1086–87 Papacy of Victor III	
	1088 University of Bologna founded	**1088–99** Papacy of Urban II	**1088** Berengar of Tours dies (**b.c. 1000**)
1095 First Crusade declared		**1098** Foundation of Cistercian order; Urban II renews treaty with Normans	**c. 1099** Anselm, *Why God Became Human*
1099 Jerusalem recaptured	**c. 1100** *Song of Roland*	**1099–1118** Papacy of Paschal II	**1102** Anselm, *On the Procession of the Holy Spirit*
			1109 Anselm of Canterbury dies (**b. 1033**)
		1113 Rule of Canons of St. Victor adopted	
		1118–19 Papacy of Gelasius II	
		1119–24 Papacy of Callistus II	
	1120–1200 Early Gothic architecture	**1121** Foundation of Praemonstratensians	

1122 Concordat of Worms declares investment of bishops the right of ecclesiastical authority		1122 Condemnation of Abelard's works on the Trinity	1123–36 Peter Abelard, *Sic et Non*
	c. 1123 Umar Khayyam dies (**b.c. 1038–42**)	1123 First Lateran Council, first ecumenical council held in the West	c. 1125 Bernard of Clairvaux, *The Degrees of Humility and Pride*
		1124–30 Papacy of Honorius II	1128 Bernard, *On Grace and Free Choice*
			1129 Rupert of Deutz dies (**b. 1077**)
	c. 1132 Abbey of St. Denis built	1130–43 Papacy of Innocent II	c. 1130 Bernard, *On Loving God*
			c. 1135 Bernard, *Sermons on the Song of Songs*
1141–44 Geoffrey Plantagenet conquers Normandy	c. 1140 *El Cid* composed; Gratian completes his collection of canon law, *Harmony of Contradictory Laws*	1139 Second Lateran Council	1141 Hugh of St. Victor dies (**b.c. 1090**)
		1141 Council of Sens	c. 1141–51 Hildegard, *Know the Ways*
1143 Christians take over North Africa		1143–44 Papacy of Celestine II	c. 1142 Peter Abelard dies (**b.c. 1079**)
1145 Second Crusade begins	c. 1145 Anna Commena, historian, dies	1144–45 Papacy of Lucius II	
		1145–53 Papacy of Eugene III	1153 Bernard of Clairvaux dies (**b. 1090**)
		1153–54 Papacy of Anastasius IV	
		1154–59 Papacy of Hadrian IV, first English pope	
1155 Frederick Barbarossa crowned emperor	c. 1155 Carmelite order established		1155–58 Peter Lombard, *Sentences*
1158–1214 Alfonso VIII, king of Leon and Castile		1159 Schism between Alexander III and Victor IV	
		1159–81 Papacy of Alexander III	

Political and Social Events	Intellectual and Cultural Developments	Christian History	Major Christian Writers
		1159–64 Victor IV, antipope	1160 Peter Lombard dies (**b.c. 1095**)
1164 Quarrel between King Henry II of England and Thomas Becket begins	c. 1160 University of Paris founded	1164–68 Paschal III, antipope	1165 Elisabeth of Schönau dies (**b. 1128**)
	1163 Building of Notre Dame Cathedral (Paris) begins		
1170 Becket murdered	c. 1170 Chrétien de Troyes, *Lancelot*; Oxford University founded	1168–78 Callistus III, antipope	1173 Richard of St. Victor dies (b. unknown)
	1174 Bell tower, "Leaning Tower," of Pisa begun	1174 Conversion of Peter Valdes; beginning of Waldensian movement	1173/74 Hildegard, *The Book of Divine Works*
1177 Peace of Venice between Frederick Barbarossa and Pope Alexander III		1179 Third Lateran Council	1179 Hildegard of Bingen dies (**b. 1098**)
		c. 1179–80 Innocent III, antipope	
		1181–85 Papacy of Lucius III	
		1184 Council of Verona condemns Cathars, Patarines, and Humiliati	
1185 Norman expedition against Byzantium		1185–87 Papacy of Urban III	
		1187 Papacy of Gregory VIII	
1189 Third Crusade begins		1187–91 Papacy of Clement III	
	1194 Beginning of reconstruction of Chartres Cathedral	1191–98 Papacy of Celestine III	
1198 Philip Augustus of France quarrels with Pope Innocent III	1198 Averroës dies (**b. 1126**)	1198–1216 Papacy of Innocent III	
	c. 1200 *Nibelungenlied*	1200 Innocent interdicts France	
	1200–10 Wolfram von Eschenbach, *Parzifal*		

1202–4 Fourth Crusade	**c. 1200–1350** High Gothic architecture	**1209** Albigensian Crusade
1204 Fourth Crusade enters Constantinople; Latin empire established there	**1204** Moses Maimonides dies **(b. 1135)**	**1210** Innocent III approves Francis of Assisi's first Rule
1215 Magna Carta signed	**1209** Cambridge University founded	**1215** Establishment of Dominican Order; Fourth Lateran Council orders annual confession and communion
1215–50 Reign of Emperor Frederick II		**1216–27** Papacy of Honorius III
		1223 Francis' second Rule approved by papacy
c. 1231 Pope Gregory IX establishes the papal Inquisition	**1230** Walther von der Vogelweide dies **(b. 1172)**	**1227–41** Papacy of Gregory IX
		1241 Papacy of Celestine IV
		1243–54 Papacy of Innocent IV
	1248 Alhambra Palace in Granada begun	**1245** First Council of Lyons
		1254–61 Papacy of Alexander IV
		1257 Bonaventure becomes general of the Franciscan order
	1260 Aristotle's *Politics* translated into Latin	

1202 Joachim of Fiore dies **(b.c. 1135)**

c. 1215 *Ancrene Wisse*, English rule for Anchorites

c. 1240 Hadewijch of Brabant dies (b. unknown)

1259 Bonaventure, *The Mind's Road to God*
1259–64 Thomas Aquinas, *Summa contra Gentiles*

Political and Social Events	Intellectual and Cultural Developments	Christian History	Major Christian Writers
1296–1303 Conflict between Philip IV of France and Boniface VIII 1296 Boniface VIII's *Clericis Laicos* forbids taxation of clergy without papal consent 1302 Boniface asserts papal superiority over kings in *Unam Sanctam*	1271 Marco Polo travels to the Far East c. 1292 Roger Bacon, proponent of experimental science, dies (b.c. 1214) 1296 Arnolfo di Cambio designs Florence cathedral	1261–64 Papacy of Urban IV 1265–68 Papacy of Clement IV 1271–76 Papacy of Gregory X 1274 Second Council of Lyons 1276 Papacy of Innocent V 1276 Papacy of Hadrian V 1276–77 Papacy of John XXI 1277–80 Papacy of Nicholas III 1281–85 Papacy of Martin IV 1285–87 Papacy of Honorius IV 1288–92 Papacy of Nicholas IV 1294 Papacy of Celestine V 1294–1303 Papacy of Boniface VIII 1302 Papal Bull *Unam Sanctam* asserts subjection to pope is necessary for salvation	1265–73 Aquinas, *Summa Theologiae* c. 1270 Mechthild of Magdeburg, *Flowing Light of Godhead* 1274 Bonaventure (b. 1221) and Thomas Aquinas (b.c. 1224) die c. 1282 Mechthild of Magdeburg dies (b.c. 1212) c. 1289 Gertrude of Helfta, *Herald of Divine Love* c. 1291 Mechthild of Hackeborn, *Book of Special Grace* c. 1297 Angela of Foligno, *The Book* c. 1299 Mechthild of Hackeborn dies (b.c. 1241) 1302 Gertrude of Helfta dies (b.c. 1266)

1303 Boniface excommunicates Philip; Philip attacks Boniface, who dies in humiliation at Agnani			1303–4 Papacy of Benedict XI
			1305–14 Papacy of Clement V
			1309 Clement V moves papacy to Avignon, where it remains until 1377
			1308 Duns Scotus dies (**b.c. 1265**)
			1309 Angela of Foligno dies (**b.c. 1248**)
			1310 Marguerite Porete, author of *Mirror for Simple Souls*, executed (b. unknown)
			1311–12 Council of Vienne condemns Beguines and spiritualist Franciscans' interpretation of poverty
1313–17 Widespread famine and epidemics throughout Europe	c. 1314 Dante, *Divine Comedy*		
			1316 Raymond Lull dies (**b. 1236**)
1324 Marsilius of Padua's *Defender of the Peace* advances conciliar thought and denies papal temporal authority			1316–34 Papacy of John XXII
			c. 1327 Meister Eckhart dies (**b.c. 1260**)
	1334 Construction of the papal palace in Avignon begins		1327 John XXII condemns Marsilius of Padua
	1337 Giotto dies		1334–42 Papacy of Benedict XII
1337 Hundred Years' War between England and France begins			
1347 Black Death spreads throughout Italy, France, then England. Anti-semitic violence increases	1348–53 Boccaccio, *Decameron*		1342–52 Papacy of Clement VI
	c. 1360s Clavichord develops		1347 William of Ockham dies (**b.c. 1285**)
			1349 Richard Rolle dies (**b. 1300**)
			1352–62 Papacy of Innocent VI
			1361 Johann Tauler dies (**b. 1300**)
			1362–70 Papacy of Urban V
	1374 Petrarch dies (**b. 1304**)		1366 Henry Suso dies (**b. 1295**)
			1370–78 Papacy of Gregory XI
			1372 Bridget of Sweden dies (**b. 1301**)

Major Christian Writers	Christian History	Intellectual and Cultural Developments	Political and Social Events
		c. 1375 "Robin Hood" ballads appear	
	1377 Gregory XI returns papacy to Rome from Avignon		
c. 1378 Catherine of Siena, *The Dialogue*	1378 Beginning of papal schism		
	April 9 election of Urban VI (Italian), 1378–89		
1378 Julian of Norwich, *Showings* (first version)	Sept. 20 election of Clement VII (French), 1378–94		
	Urban VI remains in Rome; Clement VII returns to Avignon		1381 Peasants' Revolt in England
1380 Catherine of Siena dies (b. 1347)			
1381 Jan van Ruysbroeck dies (b. 1293)			
1384 John Wycliffe dies (b.c. 1338)			
	1389–1404 Boniface IX, Roman pope		
1393 Julian of Norwich, *Showings* (second version)	1394–1417 Benedict XIII, Avignon pope		
		1400 Geoffrey Chaucer dies, leaves *Canterbury Tales* unfinished	
	1404–6 Innocent VII, Roman pope		
	1406–15 Gregory XII, Roman pope		
		c. 1408 Donatello, *David* (statue)	
	1409 Council of Pisa attempts to end papal schism, elects a third pope, Alexander V, 1409–10		
	1410–15 John XXIII, Pisan pope		
c. 1410–40 Thomas à Kempis, *The Imitation of Christ*		c. 1412 Filippo Brunelleschi rediscovers principles of perspective in art	
1413 Jan Hus, *On the Church*	1414–18 Council of Constance condemns Wycliffe and Hus and elects Martin V, 1417–31		

1415 Jan Hus executed (**b.c. 1372**)			1417 End of Great (papal) Schism
c. 1423 Julian of Norwich dies (**b.c. 1342**)	1420 Four Articles of Prague	1425 Louvain University founded	1429 French recapture Orleans 1431 Joan of Arc burned at stake
1429 Jean Gerson dies (**b. 1363**)	1431–37 Council of Basel 1431–47 Papacy of Eugene IV 1437–38 Council of Basel transferred to Ferrara; attempted reunification with Eastern Church		1438 Pragmatic Sanctions of Bourges affirms supremacy of council over pope
	1439 Council of Ferrara moved to Florence	**c. 1440** Lorenzo Valla proves *Donation of Constantine* a forgery 1441 Jan van Eyck dies (**b.c. 1390**)	
	1447–55 Papacy of Nicholas V	**c. 1450** Johannes Gutenberg invents printing press	1449 Anti-semitic violence in Toledo
			1453 Hundred Years' War ends; Eastern Roman Empire ends with conquest of Constantinople 1455 Wars of the Roses begin in England
	1455–58 Papacy of Callistus III	1457 Lorenzo Valla dies	
	1458–64 Papacy of Pius II 1460 Papal bull *Execrabilis* condemns conciliarist theories		
1464 Nicholas of Cusa dies (**b. 1401**)	1464–71 Papacy of Paul II		1469 Marriage of Ferdinand and Isabella
1471 Thomas à Kempis dies (**b. 1380**)	1471–84 Papacy of Sixtus IV		1474 Unification of Castile and Aragon

Political and Social Events	Intellectual and Cultural Developments	Christian History	Major Christian Writers
1478 Spanish Inquisition founded		**1484–92** Papacy of Innocent VIII **1484** Bull *Summis desiderantis affectibus* against witchcraft	
	c. 1485 Sandro Botticelli, *Birth of Venus* **c. 1486** *Malleus maleficarum*		
1492 Reconquest of Granada; expulsion of Jews from Spain; arrival of Columbus to Americas		**1492–1503** Papacy of Alexander VI	
	1494 Humanist Pico della Mirandola dies	**1495–1517** Francisco Jiménez de Cisneros, archbishop of Toledo, promotes humanism	**1495** Gabriel Biel dies (**b.c. 1420**)
	1498 Michelangelo, *Pietà*	**1498** Savonarola (**b. 1452**) burned as heretic	
	1499 Marsilio Ficino dies		
		1500 Papal Jubilee year **1503** Papacy of Pius III **1503–13** Papacy of Julius II	**1500** Erasmus, *Adages* **1503** Erasmus, *Enchiridion*
	1506 New St. Peter's basilica begun in Rome **1508** Foundation of University of Alcalá		
1509–47 Henry VIII, king of England	**1510** Botticelli dies (**b. 1444**)		**1509** Erasmus, *Praise of Folly* **1510** Catherine of Genoa dies (**b. 1447**); her works, *Purgation and Purgatory* and *The Spiritual Dialogue*, are compiled by her disciples **c. 1522**
1511 Pope Julius II founds Holy League of Aragon, England, and Venice to expel French from Italy **1512** Diet of Cologne divides Holy Roman Empire into ten administrative centers		**1512–17** Fifth Lateran Council **1513–21** Papacy of Leo X	

Political / General	Culture & Scholarship	Church Events	Theological & Literary Works
			1515–16 Martin Luther, *Lectures on Romans*
	1516 Niccolo Machiavelli, *The Prince*		**1516** Thomas More, *Utopia*, and Erasmus, *Peraclesis*
		1517 Luther's 95 *Theses* posted	**1518** Martin Luther, *Heidelberg Disputation*
1519 Charles I of Spain elected Holy Roman Emperor Charles V	**1519** Leonardo da Vinci dies (**b. 1452**); Magellan begins trip around the world	**1519** Leipzig Debate between Andreas Carlstadt and Johann Eck	
		1520 Leo X condemns Luther's doctrines and excommunicates him with bull *Exsurge*	**1520** Martin Luther, *Address to the Christian Nobility*, *Babylonian Captivity of the Church*, *Freedom of the Christian*
1521 Diet of Worms declares Luther an outlaw		**1521** Henry VIII, *Defense of the Seven Sacraments against Luther*	
	1522 Publication of Complutensian Bible at University of Alcalá	**1522–23** Papacy of Hadrian VI	
		1523–34 Papacy of Clement VII	**1523** Ulrich Zwingli, *Short Christian Introduction*
			1523–24 Erasmus, *Discourse on Free Will*
1524–25 The Peasants' Revolt in Germany		**1524** Foundation of Theatine order	
			1525 Luther, *Bondage of the Will*
	1526 William Tyndale publishes translation of Bible		**1526** Conrad Grebel dies (**b.c. 1498**)
1527 Henry VIII begins legal proceedings to divorce Catherine of Aragon			**1527** Hans Denck dies (**b.c. 1500**)
		1528 Foundation of Capuchins	**1528** Zwingli, *Commentary on the True and False Religion*
1529 Ottomans lay siege to Vienna		**1529** Marburg Colloquy	
1530 Diet of Augsburg		**1530** Augsburg Confession	
			1531 Ulrich Zwingli dies (**b. 1484**)
		1533 Church of England breaks with Rome	

Major Christian Writers	Christian History	Intellectual and Cultural Developments	Political and Social Events
1535 Thomas More dies (**b. 1477**) **1536** Erasmus dies (**b.c. 1467**) **1536** John Calvin, *Institutes of the Christian Religion* (first edition) **1539** Calvin, *Institutes* (second edition) **1539** Menno Simons, *Book of Fundamentals* **1541** Juan de Valdes dies (**b.c. 1490**) **1542** Sebastian Franck dies (**b.c. 1499**) **1546** Juan Luis Vives (**b.c. 1492**) and Martin Luther (**b. 1483**) die	**1534–49** Papacy of Paul III **1534** Ignatius of Loyola founds Society of Jesus (Jesuits); confirmed by Paul III in **1540** **1535** Ursuline order founded by Angela Merici (**d. 1540**) **1539** Six Articles (England) **1541** Calvin's *Ecclesiastical Ordinances* adopted in Geneva **1542** Establishment of Roman Inquisition (Holy Office) **1545–63** Council of Trent, three major periods: **1545–47, 1551–52, 1562–63** **1549** *Book of Common Prayer* becomes normative in England; Jesuit Francis Xavier (**d. 1552**) starts mission in Japan	**1543** Nicolaus Copernicus, *On the Revolutions of the Celestial Spheres*; Copernicus dies (**b. 1473**); Andreas Vesalius lays foundation of modern anatomy with *On the Structure of the Human Body*	**1535** Catholic and Lutheran forces overthrow Anabaptist rule in Münster **1547–53** Edward VI, king of England

1553–58 Mary I, "Bloody Mary," queen of England			1551 Martin Bucer dies (**b. 1491**)
1555 Peace of Augsburg establishes territorial control of religion within Germany			1556 Ignatius Loyola dies (**b. 1491**)
1558–1603 Elizabeth I, queen of England	1550–55 Papacy of Julius III		1559 Calvin, *Institutes* (third edition)
	1555 Papacy of Marcellus II		1560 Philip Melanchthon dies (**b. 1497**)
	1555–59 Papacy of Paul IV		1561 Menno Simons dies (**b.c. 1496**); John Knox, *Book of Discipline*
	1559 Valdes Index of Prohibited Books		
	1559–65 Papacy of Pius IV		
1562 Wars of religion begin in France	1562 Discalced Carmelite reform begins	1564 Michelangelo dies (**b. 1475**)	1564 John Calvin dies (**b. 1509**)
1563 Thirty-Nine Articles, doctrinal statement of Church of England; given final form in **1571**	1566–72 Papacy of Pius V		c. 1565 Teresa of Avila, *Life*
			1566 Heinrich Bullinger, *Second Helvetic Confession*
	1572–85 Papacy of Gregory XIII		c. 1568 Teresa, *Way of Perfection*
	1575 Oratorians established under Philip Neri		1572 John Knox dies (**b. 1513**)
			1577 Teresa, *The Interior Castle*
			1579–85 John of the Cross, *The Dark Night* and *The Ascent of Mount Carmel*
	1585–90 Papacy of Sixtus V		1582 Teresa of Avila dies (**b. 1515**)
1588 English defeat Spanish Armada			1588 Luis de Molina, *The Harmony of Free Will with the Gifts of Grace*

Political and Social Events	Intellectual and Cultural Developments	Christian History	Major Christian Writers
			1589 Michael Baius dies (**b. 1513**)
		1590 Papacy of Urban VII	
		1590–91 Papacy of Gregory XIV	
		1591 Papacy of Innocent IX	**1591** John of the Cross dies (**b. 1542**)
		1592–1605 Papacy of Clement VIII	
1598 Edict of Nantes grants religious freedom and civil rights to French Huguenots			
	1600 Shakespeare, *Hamlet*		**1600** Luis de Molina dies (**b. 1535**)
	1601 Tycho Brahe dies	**1601** Jesuit Matteo Ricci admitted to Peking	
1603 Scottish and English crowns unite			
1605 Gunpowder Plot in England	**1605** Cervantes, *Don Quixote*, Pt. I	**1605** Papacy of Leo XI	**1605** Theodore Beza dies (**b. 1519**)
	1605–6 Shakespeare, *King Lear* and *Macbeth*	**1605–21** Papacy of Paul V	
1607 England establishes first colony in North America at Jamestown			
	1608 Telescope invented by Hans Lippershey		**1608** Francis de Sales, *Introduction to the Devout Life*
	1609 Telescope refined and used by Galileo Galilei	**1609** Jesuit reductions established in Paraguay	
		1611 King James Bible published	
			1613 Francisco Suarez, *Defense of the Catholic Faith*
	1614 El Greco dies (**b. 1541**)		
	1615 Cervantes, *Don Quixote*, Pt. II	**1615** Jesuits have over 13,000 members in 32 provinces	
	1616 Cervantes (**b. 1547**) and Shakespeare (**b. 1564**) die		**1617** Francisco Suarez dies (**b. 1548**)
1618 Thirty Years' War begins	**1618–19** Johannes Kepler describes planetary motion	**1618–19** Synod of Dort	

1619 Jakob Böhme, *On the Principles of Christianity*	**1620** *Mayflower* lands at Plymouth Rock		**1619** First enslaved Africans arrive in Virginia
1621 Robert Bellarmine dies (**b. 1542**)	**1621–23** Papacy of Gregory XV		**1621** Potatoes planted in Germany for first time
1622 Francis de Sales dies (**b. 1567**)	**1622** Congregation for the Propagation of the Faith established **1623–44** Papacy of Urban VIII		
1624 Jakob Böhme dies (**b. 1575**)	**1624** Foundation of English deism laid with Lord Herbert of Cherbury's *On Truth*		**1624–42** Cardinal Richelieu made first minister of France
		1625 Hugo Grotius, *The Law of War and Peace* **1625** Jan Brueghel the Elder dies (**b. 1568**)	
	1626 Facade of St. Peter's in Rome finished	**1626** Francis Bacon dies (**b. 1561**); Santorio Santorio measures human temperature with thermometer for first time	**1626** Dutch establish New Amsterdam (New York after **1664**)
	1628 Ignatius of Loyola canonized	**1628** William Harvey discovers circulation of blood; John Bunyan (**d. 1688**) and Jacob van Ruisdael (**d. 1682**) born	
	1630–42 Puritan migration to New World	**1630–80** High Baroque period **1630** Johannes Kepler dies (**b. 1571**)	**1630** John Winthrop, first governor of Massachusetts Bay Colony, founds Boston
		1631 John Donne dies (**b. 1572**) **1632** John Locke (**d. 1704**), Baruch Spinoza (**d. 1677**), and Jan Vermeer (**d. 1675**) born	
	1633 Trial of Galileo **1634** Louise de Marillac (**1591–1660**) and Vincent de Paul found the Vincentian Sisters of Charity (formally approved in **1655**)		**1634** *Ark* and *Dove* land at Maryland colony

Political and Social Events	Intellectual and Cultural Developments	Christian History	Major Christian Writers
		1634 Oberammergau Passion Play performed for first time	
	1636 Harvard College founded	**1636** Roger Williams expelled from Massachusetts; founds Providence	
	1637 René Descartes, *Discourse on Method*; Ben Jonson dies (**b. 1572**)	**1637** Anne Hutchinson expelled from Massachusetts; founds Portsmouth; extermination of Christianity in Japan	
	1638 Pieter Brueghel the Younger dies (**b. 1564**)		**1638** Cornelius Jansen dies (**b. 1585**)
1640 Portugal declares independence from Spain	**1640** Peter Paul Rubens dies (**b. 1577**)	**1639** Roger Williams founds first Baptist church in "New World"	**1640** Jansen's *Augustine* published posthumously
	1641 Anthony van Dyck dies (**b. 1599**)		
1642 English Civil War begins	**1642** Galileo dies and (**b. 1564**) Isaac Newton (**d. 1727**) born	**1642–60** Puritans close theaters in England	
1643 Louis XIV of France begins 72-year reign		**1643–47** Westminster Confession	
		1644–55 Papacy of Innocent X	
		1646 Isaac Jogues, S.J., murdered by Iroquois	
1648 Treaty of Westphalia; end of Thirty Years' War		**1649** Maryland Assembly passes Act of Religious Toleration (repealed in **1654**)	
1649–53 English Commonwealth	**1650** Anne Bradstreet publishes first American poem		
	1651 Thomas Hobbes, *Leviathan*		**1652** Gerrard Winstanley, *The Law of Freedom in a Platform*

1656 Pascal, *Provincial Letters* 1660 Gerrard Winstanley dies (**b.c. 1609**) 1666 Bunyan, *Grace Abounding* 1667–74 John Milton, *Paradise Lost*	1655–67 Papacy of Alexander VII 1656 Quakers persecuted in Massachusetts 1661 Bible translated into Algonquin: first American Bible 1664 Trappist Order founded in Normandy 1667–69 Papacy of Clement IX 1670–76 Papacy of Clement X 1671 Rose of Lima (**1586–1617**) is first canonized saint of the New World	1653 Arcangelo Corelli (**d. 1713**) and Johann Pachelbel (**d. 1706**) born 1654 Pascal and Fermat state theory of probability 1656–65 Bernini works on high altar of St. Peter's in Rome 1659 Henry Purcell (**d. 1695**) and Alessandro Scarlatti (**d. 1725**) born 1662 Louis XIV begins to build palace of Versailles; Blaise Pascal dies (**b. 1623**) 1664 Molière, *Le Tartuffe* 1667 Margaret Cavendish becomes member of the Royal Society; no other woman admitted until **1945** 1669 Rembrandt dies (**b. 1606**) 1670 Spinoza, *Tractatus theologico-politicus* 1673 Molière dies (**b. 1622**)	1653–58 Oliver Cromwell as Lord Protector 1660 Stuart line restored to English crown 1665 New Jersey founded; the plague kills more than 100,000 in London 1668 Spain recognizes Portugal's independence 1672 Royal African Company founded; England gains upper hand in slave trade; Czar Peter the Great born (**d. 1725**); France declares war on Dutch 1672–73 Marquette and Joliet expeditions down Mississippi

Political and Social Events	Intellectual and Cultural Developments	Christian History	Major Christian Writers
	1675 Jan Vermeer dies (b. 1632); Leibniz invents differential and integral calculus		1674 John Milton dies (b. 1608)
			1675 Philip Spener, Pia Desideria
	1677 Baruch Spinoza dies (b. 1632)	1676–89 Papacy of Innocent XI	
1678 La Salle explores Great Lakes	1678 John Bunyan, The Pilgrim's Progress, Pt. I		
	1679 Thomas Hobbes dies (b. 1588)		
1681 Royal charter for Pennsylvania	1682 Jacob van Ruisdael (b. 1628) and Murillo (b. 1617) die	1682 Four Gallican Articles	
1682 La Salle claims Louisiana territory for France			
1683 Islamic advance halted as John Sobieski (King John III) of Poland lifts seige of Vienna	1684 John Bunyan, The Pilgrim's Progress, Pt. II		
	1685 J. S. Bach (d. 1750), G. F. Handel (d. 1759), and Domenico Scarlatti (d. 1757) born	1685 Louis XIV revokes Edict of Nantes (1598); Huguenots flee France	
	1687 Isaac Newton introduces new cosmology in Principia Mathematica		
1688 Glorious or Bloodless Revolution; William and Mary take English throne			1688 John Bunyan dies (b. 1628)
1689 Peter the Great becomes Czar of Russia	1690 John Locke, Essay Concerning Human Understanding	1689 Toleration Act in Britain	
		1689–91 Papacy of Alexander VIII	
		1691–1700 Papacy of Innocent XII	1691 George Fox dies (b. 1624)
1692 Salem witch trials		1692 Church of England established in Maryland	
			1694 George Fox, Journal, published posthumously

1695 John Locke, *The Reasonableness of Christianity*	1698 Society for Promoting Christian Knowledge established	1700 Samuel Sewall, *The Selling of Joseph*, first American protest against slavery; John Dryden dies (**b. 1631**)	1700 Approximate population: France 19 million; England and Scotland 7.5 million; Hapsburg dominions 7.5 million; Spain 6 million
	1700–21 Papacy of Clement XI	1701 Yale College founded; Jethro Tull's seed drill improves agricultural productivity	1701–14 War of Spanish Succession
		1704 John Locke dies (**b. 1632**)	1703 Delaware separates from Pennsylvania and becomes colony
1705 Philip Jacob Spener dies (**b. 1635**)		1710 G. W. Leibniz, *Theodicy*	1712 Slave revolts in New York
	1713 Pope Clement XI condemns Jansenism in *Unigenitus*	1714 Gabriel Fahrenheit (**1686–1736**) constructs mercury thermometer	
		1715 Beginning of Rococo period	
	1716 Teaching of Christianity prohibited in China	1716 G. W. Leibniz dies (**b. 1646**)	
		1717 Handel, *Water Music*	
	1719 Jesuits expelled from Russia	1717–18 Lady Mary Wortley Montagu (**1690–1762**) introduces innoculation in England	
	1721–24 Papacy of Innocent XIII	1721 J. S. Bach, *Brandenburg Concertos*	
	1722 Moravian community of Herrnhut founded		
	1724–30 Papacy of Benedict XIII		

Political and Social Events	Intellectual and Cultural Developments	Christian History	Major Christian Writers
	1726 Jonathan Swift, *Gulliver's Travels*; Stephen Hales (**1671–1761**) measures blood pressure		1727 August Hermann Francke dies (**b. 1663**) 1730 Matthew Tindal, *Christianity as Old as Creation*
		1730–40 Papacy of Clement XII 1730–1750s Great Awakening in American colonies	
1732 James Oglethorpe obtains charter to establish Georgia colony		1732 Conrad Beissel founds Ephrata Community in Germantown, Pa.	1733 Matthew Tindal dies (**b.c. 1657**)
	1733–34 Alexander Pope, *Essay on Man*		1736 Joseph Butler, *Analogy of Religion*
	1737 Antonio Stradivari dies (**b. 1644**)	1738 John Wesley's conversion experience	1739 Jonathan Edwards, *Personal Narrative; A History of the Work of Redemption*
1740 Frederick the Great introduces freedom of press and worship in Prussia at beginning of his 46-year reign; Empress Maria Theresa begins her 40-year reign in Austria	1739–40 David Hume, *A Treatise on Human Nature*	1740–58 Papacy of Benedict XIV	1741 Jonathan Edwards's sermon "Sinners in the Hands of an Angry God"
	1741 Antonio Vivaldi dies (**b. 1675**) 1742 Edmund Halley dies (**b. 1656**)	1742 Chinese Rite controversy ended by Pope Benedict XIV	1746 Jonathan Edwards, *A Treatise Concerning Religious Affections* 1748 Alphonsus di Liguori, *Moral Theology*
	1748 Hume, *An Enquiry Concerning Human Understanding*		

1752 Joseph Butler dies (**b. 1692**) 1754 Edwards, *Freedom of the Will* 1758 Jonathan Edwards dies (**b. 1703**); Swedenborg, *On Heaven and Its Wonders and on Hell* 1760 Nikolaus Ludwig von Zinzendorf dies (**b. 1700**) 1771 Swedenborg, *True Christian Religion* 1772 Emmanuel Swedenborg dies (**b. 1688**) 1774–78 *Wolfenbüttel Fragments* published	1758–69 Papacy of Clement XIII 1763 Johann Nikolaus von Hontheim (pseudonym "Justinus Febronius") publishes *On the Condition of the Church and the Rightful Power of the Bishop of Rome* 1769–74 Papacy of Clement XIV 1773 Suppression of the Society of Jesus (Jesuits) 1774 Mother Ann Lee (**1736–84**) leaves England for America, where she founds the American Shakers 1775–99 Papacy of Pius VI	1749 Henry Fielding, *Tom Jones* 1759 Voltaire, *Candide* 1762 Rousseau, *Emile* 1764 Voltaire, *Philosophical Dictionary* 1765 James Watt improves steam engine; paves way for Industrial Revolution 1767 Georg Philipp Telemann dies (**b. 1681**) 1773 Phillis Wheatley, *Poems on Various Subjects*, first book published by black American 1776 David Hume dies (**b. 1711**); Adam Smith (**1723–90**), *Wealth of Nations*	1762 Catherine the Great begins her 34-year reign in Russia 1763 France loses North American possessions in Treaty of Paris; rebellion of Pontiac and Ottawa Indians against British 1772 Russia, Prussia, and Austria partition Poland 1773 Boston Tea Party 1776 Declaration of American Independence

Political and Social Events	Intellectual and Cultural Developments	Christian History	Major Christian Writers
	1777 R. B. Sheridan, *The School for Scandal*		**1777** John Wesley, *A Plain Account of Christian Perfection*
	1778 Carl von Linné (Linnaeus) (**b. 1707**), Jean-Jacques Rousseau (**b. 1712**), and Voltaire (**b. 1694**) die		
1781 End of American Revolutionary War	**1781** Kant, *Critique of Pure Reason*		
1783–1807 Women vote in New Jersey			
	1784 Denis Diderot dies (**b. 1713**)	**1784** Wesley's Deed of Declaration; charter of Methodism	
		1786 Synod of Pistoia	
1787 U.S. Constitution signed			**1787** Alphonsus di Liguori dies (**b. 1696**)
	1788 Kant, *Critique of Practical Reason*		
1789 Louis XVI calls Estates-General in France; storming of the Bastille; Declaration of the Rights of Man	**1789** William Blake, *Songs of Innocence*	**1789** John Carroll of Baltimore named first American bishop	
		1790 Civil Constitution of the Clergy (France)	
1791 France's new constitution	**1791** Wolfgang A. Mozart dies (**b. 1756**); Benjamin Franklin, *Autobiography*		**1791** John Wesley dies (**b. 1703**)
	1792 Mary Wollstonecraft, *A Vindication of the Rights of Women*		
	1793 Eli Whitney invents cotton gin; Kant, *Religion within the Limits of Reason Alone*		
	1795 James Hutton suggests slow geological evolution in *Theory of the Earth*		
	1796 Edward Jenner finds safe vaccine against smallpox		

1799 Napoleon overthrows the Directory; George Washington dies (**b. 1732**)	**1800** Schiller (**1759-1805**), *Maria Stuart*, and Schelling (**1775–1854**), *System of Transcendental Idealism*	**1800–23** Papacy of Pius VII	**1799** Schleiermacher, *On Religion: Speeches to Its Cultured Despisers*
1801 European population: Italy 17.2 million; Spain 10.5 million; Britain 10.4 million; London 864,000; Paris 547,000; Vienna 231,000	**1803** Robert Fulton propels boat by steam power	**1801** Concordat between Napoleon and Pope Pius VII	
1803 Louisiana Purchase	**1804** Immanuel Kant dies (**b. 1724**); Nathaniel Hawthorne (**d. 1864**) and Ludwig Feuerbach (**d. 1872**) born; Beethoven, *Symphony No. 3*, and Schiller, *Wilhelm Tell*		
1804 Toussaint l'Ouverture leads slave revolt; Haiti gains independence; coronation of Napoleon as emperor	**1807** G. W. F. Hegel, *Phenomenology of Spirit*		
1806 Holy Roman Empire dissolved	**1808** Goethe, *Faust*, Pt. I and Beethoven, *Symphonies Nos. 5 and 6*		
1807 Great Britain abolishes slave trade	**1809** Joseph Haydn dies (**b. 1732**); Charles Darwin (**d. 1882**), Felix Mendelssohn (**d. 1847**), Edgar Allan Poe (**d. 1849**) and Alfred Tennyson (**d. 1892**) born		
	1811 Jane Austen, *Sense and Sensibility*		
1812 Napoleon retreats from Russia in defeat; Jews in Prussia are emancipated	**1812** Robert Browning (**d. 1889**) and Charles Dickens (**d. 1870**) are born; Brothers Grimm, *Fairy Tales*	**1812** Daughters of Charity of St. Joseph, established in **1809** by Elizabeth Bayley Seton (**1774–1821**), are formally recognized; Sisters of Loretto in Kentucky are founded by Mary Rhodes, Christina Stuart, and Ann Havern	
1812–15 War between U.S. and Britain			

Political and Social Events	Intellectual and Cultural Developments	Christian History	Major Christian Writers
	1813 Jane Austen, *Pride and Prejudice* **1814** Johann Fichte dies **(b. 1762)**	**1814** Pope Pius VII returns to Rome and restores the Inquisition; also restores the Jesuits	
1815 Congress of Vienna		**1816** American Bible Society founded	
1817 San Martín and Simón Bolívar begin liberation of South America	**1816** Joseph Niepce, French physicist, makes first photographic paper negative; Rossini, *Barber of Seville*	**1817** Lutheran and Reformed Churches in Prussia form Evangelical Union; De Lammenais, *Essay on Indifference in Religion* and Joseph de Maistre, *The Pope*; American Colonization Society proposes to buy slaves' freedom and repatriate them in Liberia	
1819 Children under age of nine are forbidden to work in England's mills; other children are limited to twelve-hour days	**1818** Mary Wollstonecraft Shelley, *Frankenstein*; Karl Marx born **(d. 1883)**	**1819** *Theologische Quartalschrift*, oldest continually published journal for Catholic theology, is established	**1819** J. S. Drey, *Brief Introduction to the Study of Theology*; Georg Hermes, *Philosophical Introduction to Theology*
1820 Missouri Compromise	**1820** Electromagnetism discovered; John Keats, "Ode to a Nightingale" and "Ode on a Grecian Urn"		
1821 Greek War of Independence begins	**1822** Franz Schubert, *Symphony No. 8* (Unfinished)		**1821** Joseph de Maistre dies **(b. 1754)** **1821–22** Schleiermacher, *The Christian Faith* (1st ed.)
1823 Monroe Doctrine	**1824** Beethoven, *Ninth Symphony*	**1823–29** Papacy of Leo XII	**1825** Möhler, *Unity in the Church*

1827 John Keble, *The Christian Year*

1830–31 Schleiermacher, *The Christian Faith* (2d ed.)

1832 Möhler, *Symbolism; Or, Exposition of the Doctrinal Differences between Catholics and Protestants*

1833 John Keble's sermon, "National Apostasy"

1826 Pope Leo XII approves the Society of the Sacred Heart, founded by Madeleine Sophie Barat (**1779–1865**)

1829 Oblate Sisters of Providence founded as first African-American congregation in the U.S.; Catholic Emancipation Act allows Catholics in Great Britain to sit in Parliament and hold public office

1829–30 Papacy of Pius VIII

1830 Joseph Smith founds Church of Jesus Christ of Latter-day Saints (Mormons)

1831–46 Papacy of Gregory XVI

1832 Pope Gregory XVI, *Mirari vos*

1833 Beginning of Oxford Movement

1826 James Fenimore Cooper, *The Last of the Mobicans*

1827 Karl von Baer theorizes about the human ovum; Beethoven dies (**b. 1770**)

1828 Francisco Goya dies (**b. 1746**)

1831 G. W. F. Hegel dies (**b. 1770**)

1832 Charles Lyell publishes theory of geological evolution in *Principles of Geology*

1832 Louisa May Alcott (**d. 1888**), Horatio Alger (**d. 1899**), Lewis Carroll (**d. 1898**), and Eduard Manet (**d. 1883**) are born; Johann von Goethe (**b. 1749**), Jeremy Bentham (**b. 1748**), and Sir Walter Scott (**b. 1771**) die

1833 Oberlin College, first in U.S. to admit women and blacks, is founded

---

1828 Isabella van Wagener (**c. 1797–1883**) escapes slavery and takes the name Sojourner Truth

1829 David Walker, *Appeal to the Coloured Citizens of the World*

1830 July Revolution in France; Belgium wins independence from Netherlands

1831 William Lloyd Garrison (**1805–79**) publishes abolitionist periodical *The Liberator*

1832 First Reform Bill (Britain)

1833 Great Britain abolishes slavery; Philadelphia Female Anti-Slavery Society organized by Lucretia Mott (**1793–1880**) as an auxiliary to the exclusively male Anti-Slavery Society

Political and Social Events	Intellectual and Cultural Developments	Christian History	Major Christian Writers
	1834 Victor Hugo, *The Hunchback of Notre Dame*	**1834** Leopold von Ranke, *The Roman Popes*	**1834** Friedrich Schleiermacher dies (**b. 1768**) **1835** D. F. Strauss, *The Life of Jesus Critically Examined*; Charles Finney, *Lectures on Revivals of Religion*
1836 Mexicans take the Alamo	**1836** Arthur Schopenhauer, *On the Will in Nature*		**1836–42** Joseph von Görres, *Christian Mysticism* **1836** Emerson, *Nature*
1837 Queen Victoria of England (**1819–1901**) begins her 64-year reign; Angelina and Sarah Grimké found the National Female Anti-Slavery Society, one of the few to include women of color from the start	**1837** Samuel Morse invents telegraph; Mary Lyon founds Mount Holyoke Female Seminary; Alexander Pushkin dies (**b. 1799**)	**1837** American Presbyterians split into Old and New School; Sarah Grimké, *Letters on the Equality of the Sexes and the Condition of Woman*	
	1838 Dickens, *Oliver Twist* and *Nicholas Nickleby*	**1838** Emerson, Harvard Divinity School Address **1839** Pope Gregory XVI condemns slave trade	**1838** Johann Adam Möhler dies (**b. 1796**) **1838–47** Drey, *Apologetics*
1840 World Anti-Slavery Conference (London)	**1840** Thomas Hardy (**d. 1928**), Claude Monet (**d. 1928**), Pierre A. Renoir (**d. 1919**), and Auguste Rodin (**d. 1917**) are born **1841** Feuerbach, *The Essence of Christianity* **1843** J. S. Mill, *System of Logic*; Dickens, "A Christmas Carol"	**1841** Catherine McAuley, founder of Sisters of Mercy, dies (**b. 1778**) **1844** YMCA founded in England **1845** J. H. Newman becomes a Roman Catholic; U.S. churches split over slavery: e.g., Southern Baptist Convention **1846–47** Brigham Young leads Mormons from Illinois to Utah	**1843** Kierkegaard, *Either/Or* and *Fear and Trembling* **1845** Newman, *Essay on the Development of Christian Doctrine*; F. C. Baur, *Paul, the Apostle of Jesus Christ* **1846** Kierkegaard, *Concluding Unscientific Postscript*
1845 Potato famine in Ireland; U.S. annexes Texas			

			1847 Bushnell, *Christian Nurture*; Baur, *Critical Investigations of the Canonical Gospels*
		1846–78 Papacy of Pius IX	
	1847 Charlotte Bronte, *Jane Eyre*; Emily Bronte, *Wuthering Heights*; William Thackeray, *Vanity Fair*; Thomas A. Edison and Alexander G. Bell are born; Felix Mendelssohn dies (**b. 1809**)	**1848** Count Rossi, papal premier, assassinated; pope flees Rome	**1853** Baur, *Church History of the First Three Centuries*; Johann Sebastian Drey dies (**b. 1777**); Philip Schaff, *History of the Apostolic Church*
1848 Seneca Falls, N.Y., convention for women's rights; revolutions in Paris, Vienna, Berlin, Venice, Milan, and Rome; end of U.S.-Mexican War	**1848** Karl Marx and Friedrich Engels, *Communist Manifesto*; astronomer Maria Mitchell becomes first woman elected to American Academy of Arts and Sciences		**1854** Kierkegaard, *Attack upon "Christendom"*; Félicité de Lamennais dies (**b. 1782**)
1849 California gold rush	**1850** Nathaniel Hawthorne, *The Scarlet Letter*	**1852** First Plenary Council of Baltimore	**1855** Kierkegaard dies (**b. 1813**)
1850 Harriet Tubman (**ca. 1820–1913**) escapes slavery; slaves led to freedom through the Underground Railroad; U.S. population: 23 million and 3.2 million slaves	**1851** Herman Melville, *Moby Dick*, and Verdi, *Rigoletto*	**1853** Antoinette Brown Blackwell (**1825–1921**) ordained as first American woman minister (South Butler, N.Y., Congregational Church)	
1851 Sojourner Truth addresses Akron women's rights convention	**1852** Harriet Beecher Stowe, *Uncle Tom's Cabin*, and Emily Dickinson's (**1830–86**) first poem published	**1854** Pope Pius IX defines Immaculate Conception	
	1854 Florence Nightingale, *Notes on Nursing*		
	1855 Walt Whitman, *Leaves of Grass*		
	1856 Henry Bessemer invents steel converter		
	1857 Gustave Flaubert, *Madame Bovary*		

Political and Social Events	Intellectual and Cultural Developments	Christian History	Major Christian Writers
1859 John Brown hanged for attack at Harpers Ferry, W. Va.	**1859** Darwin, *Origin of Species*; Henri Bergson (**d. 1941**), John Dewey (**d. 1952**), and Edmund Husserl (**d. 1938**) are born; J. S. Mill, "Essay on Liberty"	**1858** American Isaac Hecker founds the Paulist order; Bernadette Soubirous (**1844–79**) experiences visions of Virgin Mary at Lourdes, France	
1860 U.S. Civil War begins		**1860** Ellen G. H. and James White found the Seventh-Day Adventist Church; *Essays and Reviews* (Britain)	**1860** Ferdinand Christian Baur dies (**b. 1792**)
1861 Unification of Italy	**1861/62** Louis Pasteur (**1822–95**) announces "germ theory" of infection		
	1862 Victor Hugo, *Les Misérables*		
1863 Abraham Lincoln declares Emancipation Proclamation	**1863** Mill, *Utilitarianism*	**1863** Munich Congress of Catholic Scholars	**1863** Ernest Renan, *Life of Jesus*
		1864 Pius IX, *Syllabus of Errors*	**1864** Newman, *Apologia pro Vita Sua*
1865 U.S. Civil War ends; German Social Democratic Labor Party, world's first socialist political party, founded; General German Women's Association also founded; Ku Klux Klan founded in Pulaski, Tenn.	**1865** Lewis Carrol, *Alice in Wonderland*	**1865** William and Catherine Booth found the Salvation Army	**1865–67** Baur, *Lectures on the History of Christian Dogma*
	1866 Alfred Nobel (**1833–96**) invents dynamite and Gregor Mendel (**1822–84**) discovers genetics	**1866** Second Plenary Council of Baltimore	**1866** Bushnell, *The Vicarious Sacrifice*; John Keble dies (**b. 1792**)
1867 Second Reform Bill (Britain)			
1869 Elizabeth Cady Stanton and Susan B. Anthony organize the National Woman Suffrage Association; Suez Canal opened		**1869** First Vatican Council begins	

Political / Social	Culture	Church	Theology
1870–71 Franco-Prussian War	**1870** Peter I. Tchaikovsky, "Romeo and Juliet"; Charles Dickens dies (**b. 1812**)	**1870** End of the Papal States	**1870** Newman, *Essay in Aid of a Grammar of Assent* **1870–74** Albrecht Ritschl, *The Christian Doctrine of Justification and Reconciliation*
1871 Germany united under Emperor Wilhelm I and Chancellor Bismarck	**1871** Darwin, *The Descent of Man*	**1871** First congress of Old Catholics meets in Munich	
	1872 Ludwig Feuerbach dies (**b. 1804**)	**1872** Jesuits expelled from Germany; Charles Russell founds the Jehovah's Witnesses	**1872** Frederick Denison Maurice dies (**b. 1805**); Charles Hodge, *Systematic Theology*; D. F. Strauss, *The Old Faith and the New*
1874 Frances Willard joins the Women's Christian Temperance Union	**1874** First exhibit of Impressionist art in Paris		**1874** Hodge, *What Is Darwinism?*; David Friedrich Strauss dies (**b. 1808**)
		1875 Religious orders abolished in Prussia	**1875** Mary Baker Eddy, *Science and Health*
	1876 Alexander Graham Bell invents telephone		**1876** Horace Bushnell dies (**b. 1802**)
		1878–1903 Papacy of Leo XIII **1879** Pope Leo XIII declares Aquinas as the model for Catholic theology; Mary Baker Eddy founds the First Church of Christ Scientist	**1878** Charles Hodge dies (**b. 1797**)
	1880 Feodor Dostoevsky, *The Brothers Karamazov*; Rodin, *The Thinker*		
1881 Clara Barton founds American Red Cross	**1881** Henrik Ibsen, *Ghosts*; Thomas Carlyle dies (**b. 1795**)	**1881** Vatican archives opened to scholars	
	1882 Ralph Waldo Emerson (**b. 1803**) and Charles Darwin (**b. 1809**) die		**1882** Edward Pusey dies (**b. 1800**)
	1883 Karl Marx dies (**b. 1818**)		
1884 Third Reform Bill (Britain)	**1884** Mark Twain, *Huckleberry Finn*	**1884** Third Plenary Council of Baltimore	
			1885 A. E. Biedermann dies (**b. 1819**)

Political and Social Events	Intellectual and Cultural Developments	Christian History	Major Christian Writers
	1886 Friedrich Nietzsche, *Beyond Good and Evil*		1886–90 Adolf Harnack, *History of Dogma* 1887 Johannes Evangelist Kuhn dies (**b. 1806**) 1889 Albrecht Ritschl dies (**b. 1822**)
	1889 Robert Browning dies (**b. 1812**)	1889 Catholic University of America opens in Washington, D.C.; Daniel Rudd convenes first Black Catholic Congress in Baltimore	1890 John Henry Newman dies (**b. 1801**)
	1892 Toulouse-Lautrec, "At the Moulin Rouge," and Tchaikovsky, "The Nutcracker"	1891 Pope Leo XIII, *Rerum Novarum*; Catherine Drexel founds Sisters of Blessed Sacrament for Indians and Colored People	1892 Kähler, *The So-Called Historical Jesus and the Historic, Biblical Christ*; Joseph Ernest Renan dies (**b. 1823**)
1893 Women get the vote in New Zealand 1894 Alfred Dreyfus affair divides France	1894–95 Invention of movie machine and projector 1895 Karl Benz invents first gas-powered car; Guglielmo Marconi invents wireless telegraph; Wilhelm Röntgen discovers the x-ray 1896 First modern Olympic Games (Athens)		1895 Elizabeth Cady Stanton, *The Woman's Bible* 1897 Charles Hartshorne born
1898 Spanish American War		1899 Dwight L. Moody dies (**b. 1837**); Pope Leo XIII condemns Americanism in *Testem Benevolentiae*	

Theology/Religion	Church	Culture/Science/Politics
1900 Harnack, *The Essence of Christianity*		**1900** Max Planck announces quantum theory; Sigmund Freud, *The Interpretation of Dreams*; John Ruskin (**b. 1819**), Oscar Wilde (**b. 1856**), and Friedrich Nietzsche (**b. 1844**) die
1902 Elizabeth Cady Stanton dies (**b. 1815**); Alfred Loisy, *The Gospel and the Church*; William James, *The Varieties of Religious Experience*; Ernst Troeltsch, *The Absoluteness of Christianity and the History of Religion*	**1903–14** Papacy of Pius X	**1903** National Women's Trade Union League (U.S.) founded
		1903 Wright brothers' first flight
	1904 Max Weber, *The Protestant Ethic and the Birth of Capitalism*	**1904** Giacomo Puccini, "Madame Butterfly"; Anton Chekhov, *The Cherry Orchard*
	1905 Legalized separation of church and state in France	**1905** Albert Einstein formulates Special Theory of Relativity
1906/10 Albert Schweitzer, *The Quest for the Historical Jesus*		**1906** Paul Cézanne dies (**b. 1839**)
	1907 Pope Pius X condemns "modernism" in *Pascendi dominici gregis*	**1907** William James, *Pragmatism*; the first Cubist exhibit in Paris
1910 William James dies (**b. 1842**)	**1910** First World Missionary Conference (Edinburgh)	**1910** Igor Stravinsky, *The Firebird*; Mark Twain dies (**b. 1835**)
		1911 Roald Amundsen reaches South Pole; Marie Curie receives Nobel Prize for chemistry
1912 Martin Kähler dies (**b. 1835**)		**1912** August Strindberg dies (**b. 1849**)
		1913 D. H. Lawrence, *Sons and Lovers*
1914 Johannes Weiss dies (**b. 1863**); Edward Schillebeeckx born	**1914–22** Papacy of Benedict XV	**1914** Panama Canal opens; World War I begins
		1914 Charles Peirce dies (**b. 1839**)

Political and Social Events	Intellectual and Cultural Developments	Christian History	Major Christian Writers
1915 First use of chemical warfare	**1915** Einstein postulates General Theory of Relativity		
1916 Margaret Sanger opens first U.S. birth control clinic	**1916** James Joyce, *Portrait of the Artist as a Young Man*		
1917 Bolsheviks seize power in Russia	**1917** Carl Jung, *Psychology of the Unconscious*; Freud, *Introduction to Psychoanalysis*	**1917** Apparitions of Mary at Fatima, Portugal	**1917** Rauschenbusch, *Theology for the Social Gospel*; Otto, *The Idea of the Holy*
1918 World War I ends		**1918** Billy Graham is born	**1918** Romano Guardini, *The Spirit of Liturgy*; Walter Rauschenbusch dies (**b. 1861**)
1918–20 World-wide influenza epidemic kills more than 20 million	**1919** Bauhaus, founded by Walter Gropius, revolutionizes architecture and industrial arts; T. S. Eliot, "The Wasteland"		**1919** John Macquarrie born; Barth, *The Epistle to the Romans*
1919 League of Nations established			
1920 Nineteenth Amendment gives U.S. women the right to vote			**1920** Nathan Söderblom, *Introduction to the History of Religion*
1922 Mussolini seizes power in Italy	**1922** James Joyce, *Ulysses*	**1922–39** Papacy of Pius XI	**1922** Troeltsch, *Historicism and Its Problems*
	1923 Martin Buber, *I and Thou*; Freud, *The Ego and the Id*		**1923** Ernst Troeltsch dies (**b. 1865**)
	1924 Joseph Conrad (**b. 1857**) and Franz Kafka (**b. 1883**) die		
1925–29 Joseph Stalin eliminates rivals in Communist Party	**1925** F. Scott Fitzgerald, *The Great Gatsby*	**1925** John Scopes trial for violating Tennessee law that prohibits teaching of evolution	**1925** Etienne Gilson, *St. Thomas Aquinas*; Gordon Kaufman born
	1926 Ernest Hemingway, *The Sun Also Rises*; John M. Keynes, *The End of Laissez-Faire*		**1926** Jürgen Moltmann born
	1927 Freud, *The Future of an Illusion*; Martin Heidegger, *Being and Time*; first talking picture	**1927** Mexico confiscates church property	

438

Events	Culture	Church	Theology
1929 New York stock market crash leads to world depression	1928 Margaret Mead, *Coming of Age in Samoa*; Rudolf Carnap, *The Logical Structure of the World*; Maurice Ravel, "Bolero"; Alexander Fleming discovers penicillin	1929 Lateran Treaty between Mussolini and Pope Pius XI	1928 Ludwig Pastor, *History of the Popes* (begun in **1886**); Gustavo Gutiérrez, Hans Küng, Johann Baptist Metz, Schubert Ogden, and Wolfhart Pannenberg are born
1931 Jane Addams becomes first woman to receive Nobel Peace Prize	1929 Vienna Circle formed; William Faulkner, *The Sound and the Fury*	1931 Pope Pius XI, *Quadragesimo anno*	1929 Dorothee Soelle born
1933 Adolf Hitler becomes German chancellor	1932 Aldous Huxley, *Brave New World*	1933 Cardinal von Faulhaber's anti-Nazi treatise "Judaism, Christendom, Germanism"	1930 G. K. Chesterton (**b. 1874**) and Adolf von Harnack (**b. 1851**) die
1935 National Council of Negro Women (U.S.) is organized	1933 Alfred North Whitehead, *Adventures of Ideas*; Leon Trotsky, *History of the Russian Revolution*; Jung, *Psychology and Religion*	1934–39 Evangeline Booth elected General of the Salvation Army	1932 Barth, *Church Dogmatics*, Vol. I.1
1936 Spanish Civil War begins	1936 A. J. Ayer, *Language, Truth and Logic*	1934 Barmen Declaration (against Nazism)	1934 Eberhard Jüngel and Sallie McFague born; Reinhold Niebuhr, *Moral Man and Immoral Society*
1938 Anti-Jewish violence in Germany (Kristallnacht)	1937 Jean Paul Sartre, *Nausea*; John Steinbeck, *Of Mice and Men*; Picasso, "Guernica"	1937 Papal encyclicals against Nazism and Communism; Oxford Conference (Life and Work); Edinburgh Conference (Faith and Order)	1936 Rosemary Radford Ruether born
	1938 Thornton Wilder, "Our Town"; John Dewey, *Experience and Education*		1937 Dietrich Bonhoeffer, *The Cost of Discipleship*; Rudolph Otto dies (**b. 1869**)
			1938 James Cone born

Political and Social Events	Intellectual and Cultural Developments	Christian History	Major Christian Writers
1939–45 World War II	**1939** Karen Horney, *New Ways in Psychoanalysis* (challenged Freudian understanding of women); Sigmund Freud (**b. 1856**) and William B. Yeats (**b. 1865**) die	**1939** U.S. mission to the Vatican **1939–58** Papacy of Pius XII	**1939** David Tracy born; Yves Congar, *Divided Christendom: Principles of a Catholic Ecumenism*
1941 Attack on Pearl Harbor; U.S. enters World War II	**1940** First electron microscope demonstrated; Richard Wright, *Native Son*; Graham Greene, *The Power and the Glory*		**1940** Alfred Loisy dies (**b. 1857**)
1941–45 World War II increases demand for women workers; by 1945 women make up more than half the U.S. labor force			**1941** Reinhold Niebuhr, *The Nature and Destiny of Man;* Rudolf Bultmann, *New Testament and Mythology;* Elizabeth Johnson born
1942 Jewish extermination camps are built	**1942** First computer developed in the U.S.; Enrico Fermi (**1901–54**) splits the atom; Albert Camus, *The Stranger*		
1943 Warsaw Ghetto uprising	**1943** Jean Paul Sartre, *Being and Nothingness*; William Saroyan, *The Human Comedy*	**1943** Pope Pius XII, *Divino Afflante Spiritu*	
	1944 Aaron Copland, "Appalachian Spring"; Tennessee Williams, "The Glass Menagerie"		
1945 Atomic bombs dropped on Hiroshima and Nagasaki; World War II ends; war dead estimated at 35 million plus 10 million in concentration camps	**1945** George Orwell, *Animal Farm*		**1945** Dietrich Bonhoeffer dies (**b. 1906**)
1947 Independence of India declared	**1947** Alfred North Whitehead dies (**b. 1861**)	**1947** Dead Sea scrolls discovered	

1948 State of Israel founded; Gandhi assassinated	**1948** Orwell, *1984*	**1948** World Council of Churches is organized in Amsterdam	**1948** Hartshorne, *The Divine Relativity*; Merton, *The Seven Storey Mountain*
1948–50 Apartheid established in South Africa	**1949** Arthur Miller, "Death of a Salesman"		
1949 U.S.S.R. tests its first atomic bomb		**1950** Pope Pius XII, *Humani Generis*; National Council of the Churches of Christ organized in U.S.: 32 million members; Pope Pius XII proclaims dogma of bodily assumption of Mary	
1950 World population is approx. 2.3 billion; U.N. reports that 480 million out of 800 million children in world are undernourished		**1951** President Truman nominates Gen. Mark Clark as U.S. Ambassador to the Vatican	**1951–63** Paul Tillich, *Systematic Theology*
	1952 Samuel Beckett, "Waiting for Godot"; Ralph Ellison, *The Invisible Man*	**1952** Revised Standard Version of Bible published	**1952** Tillich, *The Courage to Be*
1952 U. S. explodes first hydrogen bomb	**1953** B. F. Skinner, *Science and Human Behavior*; Simone de Beauvoir, *The Second Sex*; Francis Crick and James Watson discover structure of DNA		
1954 *Brown v. Board of Education* outlaws segregation in U.S. schools	**1954** Jonas Salk starts serum innoculation against polio		
1955 Montgomery, Ala., bus boycott begins after arrest of Rosa Parks	**1956** Albert Sabin develops oral vaccine against polio	**1955** Conference of Latin American Bishops (CELAM) founded	**1955** Pierre Teilhard de Chardin dies (**b. 1881**)
	1957 Soviet Union launches Sputnik		**1956** Barth, *The Humanity of God*
		1957 M. L. King forms the Southern Christian Leadership Conference	**1957** Bernard Lonergan, *Insight*
		1958–63 Papacy of John XXIII	
1959 Fidel Castro overthrows Batista in Cuba			**1959** Chardin, *The Phenomenon of Man*

Political and Social Events	Intellectual and Cultural Developments	Christian History	Major Christian Writers
1960 J. F. Kennedy elected U.S. president; U.S. Food and Drug Administration approves "the pill" for contraception	**1960** A.J. Ayer, *Logical Positivism*; laser is developed	**1960** Three women admitted to ministry of Swedish Lutheran Church; Pope John XXIII creates Secretariat for Christian Unity	**1960** Chardin, *The Divine Milieu*
1961 Berlin Wall goes up	**1961** Yuri Gagarin (U.S.S.R.) makes first earth orbit; Ernest Hemingway (**b. 1898**) and Carl Jung (**b. 1875**) die	**1961** Pope John XXIII, *Mater et Magistra*	
1962 Cuban Missile Crisis	**1962** Rachel Carson, *Silent Spring* (concerning effect of pesticides on environment)	**1962–65** Second Vatican Council **1962** Episcopal Church consecrates J. M. Burgess as first black suffragan bishop of Massachusetts	
1963 M. L. King arrested in Birmingham, Ala., demonstration; President Kennedy calls out 3,000 troops; President Kennedy assassinated	**1963** Betty Friedan, *The Feminine Mystique*	**1963** John XXIII, *Pacem in Terris*	
1964 U.S. sends troops to Vietnam; U.S. Civil Rights Act prohibits race and sex discrimination; M. L. King receives Nobel Peace Prize	**1964** *The Autobiography of Malcolm X*	**1963–78** Papacy of Paul VI **1964** Pope Paul VI makes pilgrimage to Holy Land	**1964** Reinhold Niebuhr, *Nature and Destiny of Man*
1965 Malcolm X assassinated in New York; race riots in Watts district of Los Angeles; civil rights violence in Selma, Ala.	**1965** T.S. Eliot dies (**b. 1888**)		**1965** Paul Tillich (**b. 1886**) and Albert Schweitzer (**b. 1875**) die; Moltmann, *Theology of Hope*
1966 National Organization for Women (U.S.) founded		**1966** United Brethren and Methodist Churches vote to merge in 1968 as United Methodist Church; Roman Catholic bishops rule that U.S. Catholics need no longer abstain from eating meat on Fridays (except during Lent)	**1966** Schubert Ogden, *The Reality of God*; Macquarrie, *Principles of Christian Theology*; Hans Urs von Balthasar, *Church and World*

1967 Israel defeats Egypt in Six Day War; President Johnson appoints Thurgood Marshall to Supreme Court; M. L. King leads anti-Vietnam War march in New York; race riots in Cleveland, Newark, Detroit			**1967** Küng, *The Church*; John Courtney Murray dies (**b. 1904**)
1968 M. L. King and Robert F. Kennedy assassinated; 62 nations sign Nuclear Non-Proliferation Treaty		**1967** Land O'Lakes Statement	**1968** Merton, *Faith and Violence; Conjectures of a Guilty Bystander*; Karl Barth (**b.1886**), Martin Luther King (**b. 1929**) and Thomas Merton (**b. 1915**) die
	1969 Neil Armstrong steps on the moon	**1968** Pope Paul VI, *Humanae Vitae* and *Populorum Progressio*; CELAM's Medellín Assembly	**1969** Rahner, *Do You Believe in God?*
			1970 Cone, *A Black Theology of Liberation*
			1971 Küng, *Infallible?: An Inquiry;* Gutiérrez, *A Theology of Liberation*
	1972 Ezra Pound dies (**b. 1885**)		**1972** Lonergan, *Method in Theology*
1973 *Roe v. Wade* decision strikes down antiabortion laws in U.S.; President Allende of Chile, first declared Marxist freely elected as head of state, is ousted by military coup			**1973** Lonergan, *Philosophy of God and Theology*
1973–74 Energy crisis from Arab oil embargo and petroleum shortage		**1974** Four U.S. Episcopal bishops defy church law and ordain eleven women as priests	**1974** Georgia Harkness dies (**b. 1891**)
1974 U.S. President Nixon resigns		**1975** Anglican Church in Canada approves ordination of women; Elizabeth Ann Seton (**1774–1821**) canonized as first American-born saint; previous Episcopal ordination of women is invalidated	**1975** Tracy, *Blessed Rage for Order*

Political and Social Events	Intellectual and Cultural Developments	Christian History	Major Christian Writers
		1976 Episcopal Church approves ordination of women; Archbishop Marcel Lefebvre is suspended by Pope Paul VI for rejecting reforms of Vatican II; convocation of first "Call to Action" Conference	1976 Rudolf Bultmann dies (b. 1884)
1977 U.S. confirms testing of neutron bomb		1977 Tanzanian black activist Bishop Josiah M. Kibira is elected head of Lutheran World Federation	
1978 Israel and Egypt make peace at Camp David	1978 First "test tube baby" born to Lesley Brown in England	1978 CELAM's Puebla Assembly; Pope Paul VI dies; his successor Pope John Paul I dies; Karol Wojtyla becomes Pope John Paul II, first non-Italian pope in 456 years	1978 Küng, *Does God Exist?*; Rahner, *Foundations of Christian Faith*; Leonardo Boff, *Jesus Christ Liberator*
1979 Muslim revolution in Iran; Sandinistas take control in Nicaragua		1979 Pope John Paul II is first pope to visit a Communist country (Poland); Vatican declares that Swiss theologian Hans Küng is no longer to be regarded as Catholic theologian 1979–89 Political activism of Christian conservatives stimulated by Moral Majority	1979 Schillebeeckx, *Jesus: An Experiment in Christology*
1980 Solidarity Trade Union movement begun in Poland; 10-year war between Iran and Iraq begins	1980 Jean Paul Sartre dies (b. 1905)	1980 Oscar Romero, archbishop of San Salvador, is assassinated	1980 Schillebeeckx, *Christ: The Experience of Jesus as Lord*; Metz, *Faith in History and Society*; Dorothy Day dies (b. 1898)
1981 Sandra Day O'Connor becomes first female U.S. Supreme Court justice; Anwar Sadat, president of Egypt, assassinated	1981 AIDS is identified; U.S. space shuttle makes first flight; IBM launches its personal computer	1981 South African Presbyterian Church allows interracial marriage in defiance of apartheid laws; Salvation Army withdraws from World Council of Churches in protest of WCC's political support of "guerrilla" movements	1981 Tracy, *The Analogical Imagination*; Gordon Kaufman, *The Theological Imagination*

1983 Reagan proposes Strategic Defense Initiative; U.S. military invasion of Grenada	**1983** Astronaut Sally Ride is first American woman to travel in space; Rudolf Nureyev becomes director of Paris Opera Ballet; Alice Walker, *The Color Purple*	**1982** Merger of U.S. Presbyterian churches that split in Civil War; World Alliance of Reformed Churches suspends South Africa's two Dutch Reformed churches for heresy of racial segregation	**1982** Congar, *Diversity and Communion* **1982–86** Balthasar, *The Glory of the Lord: A Theological Aesthetics*
		1983 U. S. Catholic bishops publish *The Challenge of Peace*	**1983** Ruether, *Sexism and God-Talk*; Rahner, *God and Revelation*; Jüngel, *God as the Mystery of the World*
		1984 Vatican publishes "Theology of Liberation"	**1984** Macquarrie, *In Search of Deity*; Gutiérrez, *We Drink from Our Own Wells*; Soelle, *The Strength of the Weak*; Karl Rahner (**b. 1904**) and Bernard Lonergan (**b. 1904**) die
		1985 Vatican imposes a year's silence on Leonardo Boff	
	1986 Nuclear reactor at Chernobyl (U.S.S.R.) explodes	**1986** Desmond Tutu becomes first black archbishop of Cape Town, South Africa; Pope John Paul II becomes first pope in recorded history to visit a synagogue; U.S. Catholic bishops publish *Economic Justice for All*	**1986** Elisabeth Schüssler Fiorenza, *In Memory of Her*
1987 Stock market crash; Dow Jones Index falls 23 percent		**1987** Jim Bakker, head of "Praise the Lord" television network, resigns after accusations of adultery	**1987** L. and C. Boff, *Introducing Liberation Theology*; McFague, *Models of God*; Tracy, *Plurality and Ambiguity*
1988 U.S. B-2 "Stealth" bomber unveiled; Reagan and Gorbachev sign Intermediate-Range Nuclear Forces Treaty	**1988** Toni Morrison's *Beloved* wins Pulitzer Prize; Salman Rushdie's *The Satanic Verses* attacked by some Muslims as blasphemous; Stephen Hawking, *A Brief History of Time*	**1988** Eugene A. Marino becomes first black Roman Catholic archbishop in U.S.; Pope John Paul II excommunicates Archbishop Marcel Lefèbvre; Barbara Harris is elected first female Anglican bishop (Massachusetts)	**1988** Boff, *Trinity and Society*; Rita Nakashima Brock, *Journeys by Heart*; Hans Urs von Balthasar dies (**b. 1905**)
1989 Tiananmen democracy protests crushed		**1989** Assassination of six Jesuits and two women at UCA in El Salvador	

Political and Social Events	Intellectual and Cultural Developments	Christian History	Major Christian Writers
1990 Soviet Union collapses; Germany reunited; Nelson Mandela is freed from South African prison; Sandinistas voted out of office	**1990** Hubble Space Telescope launched	**1990** New Revised Standard Version of Bible, incorporating some inclusive language, is published; *Ex Corde Ecclesiae*	**1990** Jon Sobrino, *Spirituality of Liberation*
1991 Persian Gulf War		**1991** Pope John Paul II, *Centesimus Annus*	**1991** Henri de Lubac dies **(b. 1896)**
1992 Rigoberta Menchú, Mayan activist, receives Nobel Peace Prize; Salvadoran Peace Accords end years of civil war; ethnic cleansing begins in Bosnia		**1992** Vatican issues *Catechism of the Catholic Church*, first "major" catechism since the sixteenth century	**1992** Johnson, *She Who Is*
1993 Israel and PLO agree to process for Palestinian self-rule; new initiatives to end violence in Northern Ireland			**1993** McFague, *Body of God*; Delores Williams, *Sisters in the Wilderness*; Kaufman, *In Face of Mystery*; E. Schüssler Fiorenza, *Discipleship of Equals*
1994 Genocide in Rwanda; Nelson Mandela becomes first black president of South Africa		**1994** Pope John Paul II issues *Ordinatio Sacerdotalis*	**1994** Marjorie Hewitt Suchocki, *The Fall to Violence*; Pedro Casaldáliga, *Political Holiness*; Schillebeeckx, *Church: The Human Story of God*
1995 Yitzhak Rabin, prime minister of Israel, assassinated; Oklahoma City federal building bombed; Dayton Peace Agreement prepares prospect of peace in Bosnia			**1995** Soelle, *Theology for Skeptics*; Yves Congar dies **(b. 1904)**
1996 Guatemalan Peace Treaty ends decades of civil war			
1997 123 nations sign anti-landmine treaty; death of Princess Diana	**1997** Ian Wilmut clones first sheep from adult cell	**1997** Mother Teresa dies **(b. 1910)**	
1998 India and Pakistan test nuclear weapons; peace talks in Northern Ireland		**1998** Juan Gerardi, auxiliary bishop of Guatemala, assassinated; John Paul II, *Ad Tuendam Fidem*, papal letter against theological dissent	